Buddhism in Tibet & the Himalayas

Buddhism in Tibet & the Himalayas

Texts & Traditions

Franz-Karl Ehrhard

Vajra Publications

Published by
Vajra Publications
Jyatha, Thamel, Kathmandu, Nepal
Tel.: 977-1-4220562, Fax: 977-1-4246536
e-mail: bidur_la@mos.com.np
www.vajrabooks.com.np

Distributed by
Vajra Books
Kathmandu, Nepal

ISBN No. 978-9937-506-93-9

Typesetting by Nabindra Dongol

Printed in Nepal

Contents

PREFACE 1

I. MADHYAMAKA AND rDZOGS-CHEN

1. Observations on Prāsaṅgika-Madhyamaka in the rNying-ma-pa School 5
2. Some Historical Delineations Concerning Madhyamaka Philosophy in the rNying-ma-pa School 18
3. The "Vision" of rDzogs-chen: A Text and its Histories 35

II. THE SVAYAMBHŪNĀTH STŪPA

4. A Renovation of Svayambhūnāth Stūpa in the 18th Century and its History (According to Tibetan Sources) 55
5. Further Renovations of Svayambhūnāth Stūpa (From the 13th to the 17th Centuries) 63
6. Old and New Tibetan Sources Concerning Svayambhūnāth 71

III. THE BODHNĀTH STŪPA

7. The Stūpa of Bodhnāth: A Preliminary Analysis of the Written Sources 95
8. The Register of the Reliquary of Lord Rang-rig ras-pa 103
9. A Forgotten Incarnation Lineage: The Yol-mo-ba sprul-skus (16th to 18th Centuries) 121

IV. SHERPA BUDDHISM

10. Two Documents on Tibetan Ritual Literature and Spiritual Genealogy 159
11. A Monument of Sherpa Buddhism: The Enlightenment Stūpa in Junbesi 181

V. PILGRIMAGES AND SACRED GEOGRAPHY

12. Tibetan Sources on Muktināth: Individual Reports and Normative Guides 201
13. Concepts of Religious Space in Southern Mustang: The Foundation of the Monastery sKu-tshab gter-lnga 218
14. Religious Geography and Literary Traditions: The Foundation of the Monastery Brag-dkar bSam-gling 229
15. Pilgrims in Search of Sacred Lands 239

VI. Travels and Hidden Lands

16. A "Hidden Land" in the Tibetan-Nepalese Borderlands 259
17. "The Lands are like a Wiped Golden Basin": The Sixth Zhwa-dmar-pa's Journey to Nepal 283
18. "The Story of how Bla-ma Karma Chos-bzang came to Yol-mo": A Family Document from Nepal 294

VII. Buddhist Teachers from Dolpo

19. Two Further Lamas of Dolpo: Ngag-dbang rnam-rgyal (born 1628) and rNam-grol bzang-po (born 1504) 313
20. Sa-'dul dgon-pa: A Temple at the Crossroads of Jumla, Dolpo and Mustang 331

VIII. Himalayan Treasure Discoverers

21. The Role of "Treasure Discoverers" and Their Writings in the Search for Himalayan Sacred Lands 351
22. Political and Ritual Aspects of the Search for Himalayan Sacred Lands 363
23. Kaḥ-thog-pa bSod-nams rgyal-mtshan (1466–1540) and His Activities in Sikkim and Bhutan 379

IX. Manuscript and Block Print Traditions

24. Recently Discovered Manuscripts of the rNying ma rgyud 'bum from Nepal 395
25. The Transmission of the *dMar khrid Tshem bu lugs* and the *Maṇi bka' 'bum* 413
26. The Transmission of the *Thig le bcu drug* and the *Bka' gdams glegs bam* 427

Original publication details 449

Bibliography 453
Western sources 453
Tibetan texts 477

Index 503

Preface

The present volume contains conference presentations and independent articles that I originally wrote, and most of which were published, in the years 1985 to 2007. They are grouped into nine sections corresponding to different areas of interest or project-related research, all related to Buddhism in Tibet and the Himalayas. As they are all based on reading, editing and evaluating the rich historical and literary sources of Buddhist traditions transmitted in this region, I have chosen *Texts and Traditions* as the common theme of the essays. Changes and additions have only been made in order to correct obvious mistakes and update bibliographical references.

Of the three pieces devoted to *Madhyamaka and rDzogs-chen*, one has not been published previously. It is included here in order to document scholarly work undertaken in the field of the philosophical and spiritual traditions of the rNying-ma-pa school, such work having made great strides in recent years. The two sections *The Svayambhūnāth Stūpa* and *The Bodhnāth Stūpa* contain articles written originally for the Department of Archaeology in Kathmandu, together with additional results from the application of 'literary archaeology' when investigating the cultural history of these Buddhist monuments. This approach is also followed in *Sherpa Buddhism*, where a document on the erection of an "enlightenment stūpa" (*byang chub mchod rten*) is presented. Two further documents deal with the spread of the rNying-ma-pa school and its religious traditions in the Solu-Khumbu region of the Nepalese Himalayas.

The four articles in *Pilgrimages and Sacred Geography* all relate to the Mustang region, its different pilgrimage sites and the foundation of monasteries there in the 17th century. Questions regarding religious space and religious geography are confronted mainly with the aid of pilgrimage guidebooks and biographies of Tibetan masters. In *Travels and Hidden Lands*, the Himalayan valleys Langthang and Helambu are considered from a similar perspective, and their status as "hidden lands" (*sbas yul*) is investigated in some detail. One important text in this regard is a rare travelogue written by an influential hierarch of the Karma bKa'-brgyud-pa school. The section on *Buddhist Teachers from Dolpo* centres on another region of the Nepalese Himalayas, and on how Buddhist traditions and temple communities came to flourish in it.

The search for Himalayan sacred lands and the relevance of "treasure discoverers" (*gter ston*) to this endeavour—particularly in the regions of south-eastern Tibet, Sikkim and Bhutan—is the subject of *Himalayan Treasure Discoverers*. Two of these articles have already been republished, bearing witness to the great interest in research on sacred spaces and power places in Tibetan culture. The last section, *Manuscript and Block Print*

Traditions, presents results of research undertaken in connection with my work for the Nepal-German Manuscript Preservation Project (NGMPP) and directs the focus once again to the region of Mang-yul Gung-thang in southwestern Tibet and its literary traditions.

The present compilation of articles was the idea—reinforced over a span of several years—of Bidur Dangol of Vajra Books (Kathmandu). It was also through him that I was introduced to Marceau Reda, who kindly took on the task of assembling the articles and papers and arranging them in an appealing new format. The main editing and correcting was then done by Michael Pahlke with great critical skill. He also produced a comprehensive index of all the articles. His work was financed by the Department of Asian Studies of the University of Munich. The final layout and printing was done by the Dangol Printers. All of these friends and collaborators I wish to thank for their fruitful cooperation.

Particular words of thanks go to Philip Pierce of the Nepal Research Centre (NRC), without whose help in rendering the articles into proper English they would not have been published in the first place. Photographs and maps were made available by Hildegard Diemberger, Niels Gutschow, John Harrison and Robert Kostka. Christoph Cüppers and Burkhard Quessel were of great help with technical matters during different phases of composition. Finally, I am grateful to the original publishers for giving permission to reprint: the Austrian Academy of Sciences (Vienna), the Bavarian Academy of Sciences (Munich), the Naritasan Shinjoji (Tokyo), the Institute for Tibetan and Buddhist Studies (Andiast), the Institute for Geography (Giessen), the Department of Archeology (Kathmandu), the Namgyal Institute of Tibetology (Gangtok), the Amnye Machen Institute (Dharamsala) and the Library of Tibetan Works and Archives (Dharamsala), Brill, Franz Steiner and Indica et Tibetica Publishers, and the Société d'Ethnologie (Nanterre).

Kathmandu, Dasain V.S. 2069 / Autumn A.D. 2012

I.

Madhyamaka and rDzogs-chen

Observations on Prāsaṅgika-Madhyamaka in the rNying-ma-pa School

[1]

The interest devoted to the philosophy of the rNying-ma-pa school has instigated a series of examinations at the beginning of the 1980s concerning the works and speculations of Mi-pham rgya-mtsho (1846–1912). Special attention was paid to his commentaries on the *Madhyamakālaṃkāra* of Śāntarakṣita, the *Jñānasārasamuccaya* of the so-called "tantric Āryadeva", and the scholastic compendium *mKhas pa'i tshul la 'jug pa'i sgo* (abbr. *mKhas 'jug*).[1] All these studies showed ample proof that we have to deal with Mi-pham rgya-mtsho as a distinguished scholar of the "non-partial" (*ris med*) movement, who demonstrates in his works an enormous capability of recreating and structuring the classical texts of Indian Mahāyāna philosophy.

In this paper my focus is not too much on the exegetical achievements of Mi-pham rgya-mtsho, at this point of time I felt rather the need to disclose some of the influences and conditions which shaped Mi-pham rgya-mtsho as a member of the rNying-ma-pa school. Such a perspective is pertinent in two ways: in regard to a study—still to be written—in the polemical controversies between Mi-pham rgya-mtsho and some scholars of the dGe-lugs-pa school,[2] and, on the other hand, to make assessable the philosophical development taking place in the generation of teachers following Mi-pham rgya-mtsho. Notice must be made here of Bod-pa sprul-sku mDo-sngags bstan-pa'i nyi-ma (1900/1907–1959).[3]

1 See Lipman (1981:40–57); Goodman (1981:58–78); Kawamura (1981a:112–126), id. (1981b:956–961), id. (1982:1–19) and (1983:131–145); and Mimaki (1982:353–376). The last-named article contains the most up-to-date bibliography of all the reproductions of Mi-pham rgya-mtsho's works published at the time.

2 An overview of these controversies together with a list of the relevant texts is given by Smith (1969b:5–10). Compare Karma Phuntsho (2005:51–54) for polemics concerning the *gZhan-stong* tradition and Karma Phuntsho (2007:200–203) for the Madhyamaka writings of Mi-pham rgya-mtsho; a study of the debate with dPa'-ris rab-gsal (1840–1912) is available in Viehbeck (2012).

3 Cf. his *lTa grub shan 'byed gnad kyi sgron med yi tshig don rnam bshad 'jam dbyangs dgongs rgyan*, n.p., n.d., an encyclopaedic treatise continuing and developing the ideas of Mi-pham rgya-mtsho into a coherent system. The following works of this author are also accessible to me: *dBu ma bzhi brgya pa'i tshig don rnam par bshad pa klu dbang dgongs rgyan* (= Treasures of the Mi-pham philosophical Tradition, Vol. 1), Junbesi 1978, and *Sher phyin mngon par rtogs pa'i rgyan gyi tshig don rnam par bshad pa mi pham zhal lung* (= Treasures of the Mi-pham philosophical Tradition, Vol. 2), Junbesi 1978. Of special interest in this respect are the collected works of mKhan-po Kun-bzang dpal-ldan, who transmitted Mi-pham rgya-mtsho's teachings to mDo-sngags bstan-pa'i nyi-ma: Vols. 1–5, Paro 1982. The short

In retracing these influences it is important to bear in mind the fact that the most elementary concern in the rNying-ma-pa school pertains to the spiritual discipline of the rDzogs-chen, so that we have to include the very complex subject of the *Mantra-* or *Tantrayāna* in our treatment. Fortunately in the vast corpus of Mi-pham rgya-mtsho's works we find two treatises which relate to both *Sūtra-* and *Mantrayāna*, documented by a short note of mKhan-po Kun-bzang dpal-ldan, co-publisher of Mi-pham rgya-mtsho's literary legacy.[4]

Which two works are here referred to? The first is a relative short text with the title *Don rnam par nges pa shes rab ral gri*, composed in 104 *ślokas* as the colophon states. It is a testimony of Mi-pham rgya-mtsho's endeavour to provide the rNying-ma-pa school with an independent position on the grounds of Buddhist epistemology. Different sets of "dialectical argumentations" (*rigs pa*), "reasonings" (*gtan tshigs*) and categories from the Pramāṇa tradition are interwoven in a very peculiar way, demonstrating Mi-pham rgya-mtsho's own critical standpoint.[5] The second text bears the title *Nges shes rin po che'i sgron me* and is counted among the last works incorporated in the edition of Lhun-grub steng. A supplementary colophon sees the central purpose of this work in the claim that the position of the Mādhyamikas was clearly presented in the "*Tantra*s of the early translation period" (*snga 'gyur rgyud sde*).[6]

The last work, "The Lamp of Precious Certainty", offers thus an appropriate starting-point to keep track of the way the Prāsaṅgika-Madhyamaka was interpreted by Mi-pham

---

description of Mi-pham rgya-mtsho's Madhyamaka approach in *Crystal Mirror*, Vol. V, Emeryville (1977:162–163) stands in that line of transmission.

4 *gSung rab kyi dkar chag snga 'gyur bstan pa'i mdzes rgyan* in *Collected Writings of 'Jam-mgon 'Ju Mi-pham rgya-mtsho,* Vol. 7 (= Ngagyur Nyingmay Sungrab, Vol. 66), p. 683.2 (= fol. 32 a/2): *phyi ma 'di gnyis thun min sngags kyi man ngan khyad 'phags dang 'brel ba yin yang 'dir rang gzhung sde tshan gcig par bkod pa'o*. "Although these last two [works] are connected with the most supreme instructions of the special Mantra[yāna], they are affixed here to the first group of his works (i.e. the texts of the *Sūtrayāna*)."

5 Published together with an interlinear commentary in *Collected Writings of 'Jam-mgon 'Ju Mi-pham rgya-mtsho,* Vol. 3 (= Ngagyur Nyingmay Sungrab, Vol. 62), pp. 787–820 (= fol. 1a–17b). According to *A Catalogue of the United States Library of Congress Collection of Tibetan literature in Microfiche* (= *Bibliographia Philologica Buddhica, Series Maior* III), Tokyo 1983, p. 207, this text was already printed 1964 in Varanasi supplemented by an "abridged version" (*bsdus don*) entitled *Rin chen 'phreng ba*. In addition to a "topical outline" (*sa bcad*), written by Mi-pham rgya-mtsho himself – as stated by *gSung rab kyi dkar chag* (as in note 4), p 683.1 (= fol. 32a/1) – a detailed commentary is also available: *Don rnam par nges pa shes rab ral gri'i 'grel pa thub bstan yongs su rdzogs pa'i snang byed*, Bylakuppe/Delhi 1984. The author, lHag-bsam bstan-pa'i rgyal-mtshan, mKhan-po of dPal-spungs, was the driving force behind the composition of the root text. For a short outline of the root-text, see Kapstein (1988:154).

6 For the different editions, see the appendix. A very first attempt to draw a sketch of Mi-pham rgya-mtsho's philosophy with the help of this text is my unpublished M.A. thesis: *Zur Gnoseologie der rNying-ma-pa-Schule: Mi-phams Nges shes rin po che'i sgron me*, Hamburg 1982. For a complete translation of the text and a detailed investigation into Mi-pham's philosophical position compare Pettit (1999).

rgya-mtsho, the topic I shall restrict myself to in the following. One difficulty in consulting this text, however, lies in the formal arrangement of its content. We are confronted with a narrative frame showing the author as a "Ṛṣī" (*drang srong*) who is forced to answer seven questions put to him by a "mendicant" (*ldom bu pa*). Only by invoking Mañjuśrī the author is able to do so, and out of that reason the main body of the text consists of the answers to the questions posed; the answers are not structured in a strictly logical order, but are written down in loosely connected chains of verses. For convenience sake we can only select relevant passages and complement these with the necessary background material. The richness of argumentation is most obvious in the answer to the last question: "Are there propounded philosophical tenets in the system of the Madhyamaka or not?"[7]

[2]

In an article Seyfort Ruegg has thoroughly investigated this problem which is of utmost importance for the definition of Prāsaṅgika-Madhyamaka in Tibet.[8] In the first part of his study a tension is ascertained between a positive and a negative use of such terms as "philosophical proposition" (*pratijñā / dam bca'*), "philosophical position" (*pakṣa / phyogs*) and "tenet" or "affirmation" (*abhyupagama / khas len*) already germinally present in the works of Nāgārjuna, Āryadeva and Candrakīrti. The suggestions proposed by the Tibetan scholars for the solution of this tension are described *en detail* in the second part, drawing mainly on the works of the dGe-lugs-pa and Sa-skya-pa schools. It is not too far-

---

[7] The seven questions have the following wording:

I.	*lta ba dgag gnyis gang ltar smra*	fols.	3a/1–4b/1
II.	*nyan rang bdag med gnyis rtogs sam*	fols.	4b/1–6b/6
III.	*mnyam bzhag 'dzin stangs yod dam med*	fols.	6b/6–9a/6
IV.	*dpyad nas bsgom mam bzhag nas bsgom*	fols.	9a/6–12b/6
V.	*bden pa gnyis las gang zhig gco*	fols.	12b/6–15b/1
VI.	*mi gcig mthun snang blta bya gang*	fols.	15b/1–19b/3
VII.	*dbu mar khas len yod dam med*	fols.	19b/3–25b/5

The possibility cannot be excluded that these questions have to be seen in connection with the *dKa' gnad brgyad* of Tsong-kha-pa (1357–1419), written as a "memorandum" (*brjed byang*) by his disciple rGyal-tshab Dar-ma rin-chen (1364–1432). A notice of mDo-sngags bstan-pa'i nyi-ma in his most important treatise (as in note 3), pp. 290.6–291.1 (= fols. 80b/6–81a/1) mentions the concrete demarcation of Mi-pham rgya-mtsho's philosophical position from the *khyad chos gtso bo rnam pa brgyad* in the *Madhyamakāvatāra* commentary entitled *Zla ba'i dgongs rgyan*.

[8] See Seyfort Ruegg (1983:205–233). Resuming the initial considerations of Walleser (1917), it was Schayer (1921:39–50) who first took into consideration a general "atheoretische Haltung" in Mahāyāna Buddhism; in this context he speaks of a so-called "*prāsaṅga*-Methode - eine raffinierte Begriffsdialektik" (cf. also Wach (1922:93)). This idea was elaborated by Falk (1943:74), coming to the conclusion that "its (= the Madhyamaka) characteristic *prasaṃga*-method bent on dissolving any conceivable or predicable intellectual notions, on silencing discursive processes (*nāmasamjñavyavahāra*) reveals itself an essentially soteriological method ...".

fetched – I hope – to inject another viewpoint into the discussion of this subject matter, a viewpoint which is based on quite different assumptions.

In introducing his treatment of the problem in the *Nges shes rin po che'i sgron me*, Mi-pham rgya-mtsho states that the "old ones" (*snga rabs pa*) have reached unanimously the conclusion that no tenets are propounded. As is further elaborated, the object of reference of these persons was nevertheless not the Madhyamaka in general, they were analysing if there are tenets or not in the "Great Madhyamaka, free from discursive elaborations" (*spros bral dbu ma chen po*).[9] To this state no concepts are applicable and it is impossible to say "This is our system" or "This is not", so runs their argument. We shall tackle the problem of the identity of these persons and their opinion at the end of this paper.

In the next sequence Mi-pham rgya-mtsho contrasts this statement with another one: all "doctrinal expositions" (*grub mtha'*) like *rten 'brel* or *lam 'bras* have to be expounded on the basis of the scriptural authority of one's own school; in this sense there exists a philosophical system which must be mediated to other persons by way of "language-conventions" (*tha snyad*). As a consequence of these two perspectives there results a contradiction between the words [of the above-mentioned persons] and what they imply (*tshig don gnyis kar 'gal*).

From this introduction we can infer that Mi-pham rgya-mtsho reduced the problem of there being philosophical tenets or not in the system of the [Prāsaṅgika-]Madhyamaka to an opposition between two poles: First, a scope outside the reach of logical discourse, and second, the task of intersubjectively transmitting the Buddhist teachings. Not a single word is wasted on the mention of the concrete situation of "philosophical disputation" (*vivāda / rtsod pa*), the set of circumstances which originally was responsible for raising the whole question. The following remarks in the *Nges shes rin po che'i sgron me* reveal information not only on this point, they lead also directly to one of the suppositions of Mi-pham rgya-mtsho's philosophy. For this reason I shall quote the relevant passage in full (= I):

> Klong-chen rab-'byams-pa spoke thus: whether there are propounded philosophical tenets or not in the Madhyamaka [concerning this problem], the ancient ones adhered to each [of these two] position[s] respectively. Each system was left [thereby] a fault and a quality. So in regard to my own system: for there doesn't exist anything at all in the "Original State" (*gshis*) at the time of the Ultimate Truth, Reality as such, is fathomed, which philosophical tenet could be propounded?

---

9 For the use of this term, cf. note 18. As will become evident in the following, these persons stand for the rNying-ma-pas in general. It must be noticed here that the main motive in Mi-pham rgya-mtsho's works like the *Don rnam par nges pa shes rab ral gri* and the *Nges shes rin po che'i sgron me* is not a polemical, but a didactic one. They were intended first of all to counteract "anti-intellectual" tendencies in the rNying-ma-pa school, providing the members of the tradition with a certain amount of theoretical knowledge in case of eventual debates.

> For that reason and because [lower] doctrinal expositions propound philosophical tenets in regard to Reality as such, there are propounded no tenets whatsoever at the time of disputation and so on, in accordance with the Original State. In the post-meditative phase the doctrinal exposition of Way and Fruit [and so on], the presentation of things as they really are (*yathāvadbhāvikatā*) and their variations (*yāvadbhāvikatā*) are accepted individually without mixing them up. If from now on someone is able to put this theory into words, [this] is the power of [these] my maxims, [so] he said.[10]

The reference to the authority of Klong-chen rab-'byams-pa (1308–1364) in the context of the *khas len* problem merits interest in several ways. Under a general heading we are caused to assess the philosophy of Mi-pham rgya-mtsho against the background of Klong-chen rab-'byams-pa's impressing œuvre;[11] in comparison with it a historical perspective for Mi-pham rgya-mtsho's contribution within the rNying-ma-pa school can be gained. At the same time the achievements of Klong-chen rab-'byams-pa themselves are seen more clearly. Judging by the passage just quoted, the results of his philosophical inquiry were obviously reached in controversy with opinions prevalent at his time and laid bare with the tendency for future application. By this means we get now a glimpse of some of the difficulties surrounding the interpretation of Prāsaṅgika-Madhyamaka in the 14th century. To prove this point we will take a closer look at the beginning and the end of the quotation prior to reconstructing the different aspects connected with the *khas len*.

Two groups of persons were mentioned there who took one-sided positions; those saying there are propounded philosophical tenets in the Prāsaṅgika-Madhyamaka, and

---

[10] This quotation sums up the specific points of the Prāsaṅgika-Madhyamaka presentation in chapter 12 of YID_c: *bshad bya chos kyi rnam grangs rgya cher bshad pa'i le'u*, pp. 643.2–660.2 (= fols. 71a/2–79b/2). According to the *gSung rab kyi dkar chag* Mi-pham rgya-mtsho devoted five explanatory treatises to this work; except for the "commentary to the root-text" (*rtsa mchan*) they were published by Dodrub Chen Rinpoche as appendices to his edition of YID_c. Out of these there is already available in translation the *Yid bzhin mdzod kyi grub mtha' bsdus pa*: H. V. Guenther (1976:137–209), which is a résumé of chapter 12 and 18 of YID_c. At the end of the description of the Prāsaṅgika-Madhyamaka occurs the following note: "The distinction that there are not propounded tenets in conformity with the first state (= *mnyam bzhag*) and that there are propounded tenets in conformity with the second state (= *rjes thob*) should be known according to the clear exposition in the *Rigs mdzod*." (*dang po ltar na khas len med la / gnyis pa ltar na khas len yod pa'i rnam dbye rigs mdzod las gsal bar bstan pa bzhin du shes par bya'o*). If this *Rigs mdzod* stands for *Yid bzhin mdzod*, YID_c, seems to be the definite source for our problem.

[11] In addition to Klong-chen rab-'byams-pa Mi-pham rgya-mtsho mentions several times Rong-zom Chos-kyi bzang-po (11th century) as the second forerunner of his investigations into rNying-ma-pa-philosophy. Only after having consulted the works of these teachers he was able to solve the theoretical difficulties prevalent at his time; cf. especially the remark in his commentary on the *Madhyamakālaṃkāra* in *Collected Writings of 'Jam-mgon 'Ju Mi-pham rgya-mtsho*, Vol. 12 (= Ngagyur Nyingmay Sungrab, Vol. 71), p. 42.3–6 (= fol. 21b/3–6).

those saying there are not. By way of reference to the formulations of Klong-chen rab-'byams-pa we can identify these positions (= II):

> Because the ancient ones made no difference between these two ways (i.e. a time when tenets are propounded and a time when not) it appears that gTsang-[nag-]pa did not propound tenets, while rMa-bya did.[12] As in each [system] a right thing and a fault is found at a same time, it appears that they have not quite hit the correct meaning of the authoritative scriptures. With a mind analysing completely this [subject] and with my eyes opened by the consideration of the whole lot of authoritative theories I clearly differentiated the meaning scattered and hidden in the scriptures. Those who from now on are able to defend this philosophical proposition should be recognized as being the force of this my treatise!

This account closes the treatment of Prāsaṅgika-Madhyamaka in one of Klong-chen rab-'byams-pa's most influential works, the *Yid bzhin mdzod*, and we can see that the problem of whether tenets are propounded or not, was for the rNying-ma-pa school definitely settled in the 14th century. It was achieved in probing the current Madhyamaka literature and Mi-pham rgya-mtsho had just to take it up as was intended by his predecessor. How does this solution look like?

[3]

In Mi-pham rgya-mtsho's brief summary of Klong-chen rab-'byams-pa's position we can recognize three distinctive elements: First, the time Ultimate Truth is fathomed, second, the time of disputation, third, the "post-meditative phase" (*rjes thob*). Without paying attention to the single arguments it can be said in general that in the first two periods no philosophical tenets are propounded, while in the last period the theorems of one's own school are exposed in the form of doctrinal precepts. If the time when Ultimate Truth is fathomed, is equated with the phase of "meditative absorption" (*mnyam bzhag*), we come to the interesting conclusion that the *khas len* problem is solved by Klong-chen rab-'byams-pa with the help of categories drawn from spiritual practice.

---

[12] For gTsang-nag-pa brTson-'grus seng-ge (died 1171) and rMa-bya Byang-chub brtson-'grus (12th century) as disciples of Phya-pa Chos-kyi seng-ge (1109–1169) cf. van der Kuijp (1978:164) and (1983:passim). The difficulties concerning the identification of rMa-bya in the doxographical literature were touched upon by Seyfort Ruegg (1983:230). To evaluate the position of Klong-chen rab-'byams-pa we have to keep in mind that he studied in gSang-phu sNe'u-thog in the first part of the 14th cent. and authored two treaties on Madhyamaka: *Rang rgyud shar gsum gyi don bsdus de kho na nyid la 'jug pa* and *dBu ma thal 'gyur gyi gnas gsal ba rab tu mi gnas pa'i don bsdus*; cf. *Kun mkhyen dri med 'od zer gyi rnam thar mthong ba don ldan* in *Bima sNying thig*, Part 3 (= *sNying thig ya bzhi*, Vol. 9), New-Delhi 1970, p. 70.4–5 (= fol. 35b/4–5).

For the coordination of the pedagogic-didactic aspect with the post-meditative state this conception poses no difficulties, but one question remains: what constitutes the link between the phase of meditative absorption and philosophical debate? The answer is: "The method to remove discursive elaborations" (*spros pa'i 'gog pa'i tshul*).[13] This is for Klong-chen rab-'byams-pa the characteristic feature of the technical procedure if the *prāsaṅga*-method. For this reason, the Prāsaṅgika-Madhyamaka is qualified by him as the "summit of the *lakṣanayāna*" (*mtshan nyid kyi theg pa*). Let's turn now to the situation of debate and see how Klong-chen rab-'byams-pa establishes the fact that no philosophical tenets are propounded (= IIIa):

> As in the Original State, the natural condition, nothing exists by self-nature, and all affirmations involve "attachment to veracity" (*bden zhen*), what is affirmed in the scriptures of "those who speak of a self-nature" (*svabhāvavādin*) is self-contradictory.

The second argument is a common one in the Madhyamaka literature; the Prāsaṅgika-Mādhyamika refrains from any position in distinction to those doctrines which proclaim a "self-nature and are bound by their conceptual commitment to it" (*bhāvābhiniveśa*). However – parallel to Mi-pham rgya-mtsho's quotation – the first claim is marked by an argument which introduces a different terminology: nothing exists [by self-nature] in the Original State, the natural condition. It is exactly at this point that categories of the rDzogs-chen are alluded to and we shall come back to this influence later on. It should be noted, however, that terms like *rang bzhin med pa* and others have undergone some changes due to that influence.[14]

---

13 Cf. the first part of the root-verse for the definition of the Prāsaṅgika-Madhyamaka in *YID*$_c$, Vol. VAM, p. 643.3 (= fol. 71a/3):
/ rgyal ba'i dgongs pa mthar thug snying po'i don /
/ thal 'gyur pas ni spros pa kun 'gog ste /
After quoting *Vigrāhavyavartanī*, v. 29, the first topic concerns the "method how to remove discursive elaborations" (*spros pa'i 'gog pa'i tshul*). In the *Grub mtha' mdzod*, the whole procedure is named *thal 'gyur gyi spros pa gcod pa'i tshul*, ed. Dodrupchen Rinpoche, pp. 131.5–137.5 (= fols. 66a/5–69a/5). These two paragraphs I use in the following.

14 As is stated *in the rDzogs pa chen po bla ma yang tig las gnyis ka'i yang yig nam mkha' klong chen gyi rnam par bshad pa nyi ma snang byed* (= *Three Works on rDzogs-chen Practice*, part 3), New Delhi 1972, p. 309.1 (= fol. 49a/1): *rang bzhin med pa'i go lugs ye med la go ba*. Concerning the Original State we find the following remark: *'dir ni snang srid 'khor 'das kyi chos thams cad rig ngor snang yang gshis ngor ma grub pa ye stong mtha' las 'das pa'i stong par rtogs par bya'o*. Attention must be paid to the use of such terms as *ye med* and *ye stong* in order to retrace the changed application if the Madhyamaka terminology. The author of the just-mentioned work, mKhan-po Ngag-dbang dpal-bzang (1879–1941) of Kaḥ-thog monastery, explicitly refers in the whole passage to the Prāsaṅgika interpretation of Klong-chen rab-'byams-pa: pp. 308.2–309.5 (= fols. 48b/2–49a/5).

A third argument lies again within the boundaries of the Madhyamaka- philosophy, specifically its enlargement by epistemological ideas. Thematically it is devoted to the difference between Prāsaṅgika- and Svātantrika-Madhyamaka (= IIIb):

> Further on the acknowledged theories (?) in the scriptures of those who affirm "objective validation" (*vastubalapravṛtta* / *dngos po stobs zhugs*) are removed by this [*prāsaṅga*-method]; subsequent to having refuted [the opponent] there are no ascertained propositions as in [the system of] the Svātantrika-Mādhyamika.[15]

According to Klong-chen rab-'byams-pa both subgroups of the Madhyamaka employ "five reasonings" (*gtan tshigs lnga*) to prove the emptiness of phenomena. The aim of the Svātantrika is the refutation of the wrong statement of the opponent, supplementing it afterwards with a correct one. The Prāsaṅgika-Mādhyamika in contrast is only motivated by bringing all these of the opponent to an end, stopping with this act the false conceptions of the opponent, his "discursive elaborations" (*spros pa*). He doesn't propound any tenets – if I'm allowed to put it in such a strong way – to effect the spiritual salvation of the opponent. In the works of Klong-chen rab-'byams-pa the opponent bears not only names like *dngos por smra ba* and *rang bzhin smra ba*, he is also styled *spros por smra ba*.[16]

The soteriological implications of the *spros pa'i 'gog tshul* indicated in the situation of the philosophical debate, become fully evident "at the time the Ultimate Truth, Reality as such, is fathomed" (*don dam gnas lugs gzhal ba'i tshe*). As stated by Klong-chen rab-'byams-pa in a further passage, which we don't quote in full length, the minute inspections using the different reasonings are employed on two occasions: First, "the time the [different] doctrines are disputed" (*grub mtha' rtsod dus*), and second, "the time of analyzing by means of *prajñā*, [i.e.] the spiritual way" (*lam shes rab kyi dpyod dus*). The arbitrary equation of meditative absorption and the time Ultimate Truth is fathomed, which prompted the idea that spiritual categories are introduced to solve the philosophical of *khas len*, can be established now with the help of this distinction. Here we can locate the interlacing of the argumentative techniques of the Prāsaṅgika-Madhyamaka with spiritual practice.

---

15 For the distinction between Prāsaṅgika- and Svātantrika-Madhyamaka in the philosophical system of Mi-pham rgya-mtsho – of special importance for the polemics with the dGe-lugs-pa school – cf. Lipman (1981:43ff.) and Sweet (1979:86).

16 For example in the *Grub mtha' mdzod*, p. 132.1 (= fol. 66b/1). The early history of the classical set of reasonings in the Madhyamaka was elucidated by Lindtner (1981, Appendix:205ff.), while the works of T. Tillemans showed the logical implications of one of these arguments; see Tillemans (1983:305–320). In YID_c, Vol. VAM, pp. 645.3–650.2 (= fols. 72a/3–74b/2) Klong-chen rab-'byams-pa extends the set of four or five arguments even up to eight. A teaching on the classical four arguments according to Mi-pham rgya-mtsho's treatment in the *mKhas 'jug* (fol. 131a/5–140b/5) is contained in Thrangu Rinpoche (1978:11ff).

This brings forward a point of view which may not be neglected: the nucleus of the whole question is shifted to the analysis of the experiencer himself. We are told by Klong-chen rab-'byams-pa that at the time of meditative absorption the individual is subjugated to different kinds of experiences or impressions; "at the outside, there are objects visible in various ways" (*phyi sna tshogs snang ba'i yul*), "at the inside, a mind having various conceptions or being free from them" (*nang sna tshogs rtog pa dang mi rtog pa'i sems*), or "the different mental stages of meditation" (*ting nge 'dzin dang sgom pa la sogs pa'i nyams myong*). All these factors are not to be grasped in the sense of a formal account, they are only to be analyzed in order to understand Ultimate Reality, which is *śūnyatā*. In the process no tenets such as "This is my doctrine" (*'di ni rang gi grub mtha'o*), "This is another one" (*'di ni gzhan no*) are propounded; the aim of analyzing is exclusively "the Middle" (*dbu ma*), "free from discursive elaborations" (*spros bral*).[17]

[4]
With this formula, we can resume the beginning of Mi-pham rgya-mtsho's discussion and its mentioning of a "Great Madhyamaka, free from discursive elaborations" (*spros bral dbu ma chen po*), propounding no philosophical tenets. The comparison with Klong-chen rab-'byams-pa[18] showed in which way this kind of Madhyamaka is related to the Prāsaṅgika-Madhyamaka. It is an interpretation of the last one, its special issue being the transfer of the *prāsaṅga* reasoning – as the means of definitely stopping discursive

---

17 The identification of the state of meditating absorption with the viewpoint of the Prāsaṅgika-Madhyamaka of propounding no tenets has far-reaching consequences for the later rNying-ma-pa-philosophy. Mi-pham rgya-mtsho refers for example in his commentary on the *Madhyamakālaṃkāra* (as in note 11) p. 256.3 (= fol. 127b/3) to a "Madhyamaka of Original Knowledge [at the time of] meditative absorption, the profound intention of dPal-ldan zla-ba (= Candrakīrti)" (*mnyam gzhag ye shes kyi dbu ma dpal ldan zla ba'i dgongs pa zab mo*). This happens in his commentary to vv. 67–72 of the *Madhyamakālaṃkāra*, which are – according to the introduction p. 41.1 (= fol. 21a/1) – "one in intention and wording with [the works of] Candrakīrti" (*dpal ldan zla ba dang dgongs pa gcig dang dbyangs gcig tu gyur pa yin no*). The criterion for this attribution lies exactly in the fact that, beginning with v. 68, the topic of the *khas len* is discussed. Furthermore, the theory of *paryāya-* and *aparyāya-paramārthasatya* (for details, cf. the articles in note 15) takes its origins from the commentary on these verses, and v. 68 is quoted by Mi-pham rgya-mtsho in his commentary on the *Jñānasārasamuccaya*, illustrating the Madhyamaka-system in general; cf. Mimaki (1982:363).

18 The term *dbu ma chen po* is used twice in the Prāsaṅgika chapter of *YID*$_c$, Vol. VAM, p. 658.4 (= fol. 78b/4) and p. 660.1 (= fol. 79b/1). At its first occurrence, we hear only what is not the "Great Madhyamaka", the second time *dbu ma chen po* is synonymous with the "*prāsaṅga*-method" (*thal 'gyur tshul*). In rNying-ma-pa scholasticism of the 18th cent. we can observe an assimilation of this epithet for the Prāsaṅgika-Madhyamaka to the *gZhan-stong* teachings, which led to the distinction of a "coarse" (*rags pa*) and a "fine" (*phra ba*) Madhyamaka; cf. dGe-rtse Paṇḍita 'Gyur-med tshe-dbang mchog-grub (1761–1829): *rNying rgyud rtogs brjod,* Vol. 1 (= *rNying ma'i rgyud 'bum*, Vol. 35), Thimbu 1975, pp. 101.4–150.4 (= fols. 51a/4–75b/4) and bDud-'joms Rin-po-che 'Jigs-bral ye-shes rdo-rje (1904–1987): *Bstan pa'i rnam gzhag*, Kalimpong 1967, fols. 72b/3–95b/6. For this, see chapter two of the present publication.

elaborations – to the subjective level of meditative absorption. This at least is the picture we get when approaching it from the philosophical side.

Taking notice of the stress laid on the Original State in both Mi-pham rgya-mtsho's and Klong-chen rab-'byams-pa's argumentation, a state where nothing exists by self-nature and thus every possibility of propounding a tenet fades away, we could also relate this interpretation of Prāsaṅgika-Madhyamaka to the influence of rDzogs-chen thought. A hint in this direction is Mi-pham rgya-mtsho's wording that at time of debate, no tenets are propounded "in accordance with the Original State" (*gshis bzhin*). Yet, for setting up such a hypothesis a better understanding of the rDzogs-chen material is necessary.

In his record of the "difficult points" (*dka' gnad*) in the Prāsaṅgika-chapter of *YID*$_c$, Mi-pham rgya-mtsho singles out, as worthy of discussion, only this linking of the Prāsaṅgika standpoint of propounding no tenets with the Ultimate Truth.[19] Other sources also emphasize Klong-chen rab-'byams-pa's innovative contribution to an interpretation of the Prāsaṅgika-Madhyamaka; and the effects of his explanations were not restricted to scholarly works alone.[20]

Concluding my observations I wish to come back once again to the text which is so revealing for the philosophy of Mi-pham rgya-mtsho and his predecessors, "The Lamp of Precious Certainty". Another passage suitably documents the general attitude of the rNying-ma-pa school towards the Madhyamaka (= IV):

> According to the view of the All-Knowing One (= Klong-chen rab-'byams-pa), our system has to be understood in the following way. If the [teaching of the]

19 *Yid bzhin rin po che'i mdzod kyi dka' gnad* (as in note 10), p. 1060.3–5 (= fol. 30b/3–5). The only further remark states that there are many, up to now unknown statements in the Prāsaṅgika-chapter, but being clearly expressed one has no difficulty in understanding them. In the commentary on the *Madhyamakālaṃkāra* pp. 63.6–64.1 (= fols. 32a/6–b/1) the definition of the Prāsaṅgika-Madhyamaka as the teachings which grasps no extremes like *yod* and *med*, e.g. propounds no tenets, is qualified as the "special view" (*bzhed pa thun mong ma yin pa*) of Klong-chen rab-'byams-pa. mKhan-po Ngag-dbang dpal-bzang talks of *kun mkhyen chos kyi rgyal po'i dgongs pa bla na med pa*; cf. the work mentioned in note 14, p. 309.5 (= fol. 49a/5).

20 Cf. *rDzogs pa chen po klong chen snying tig gi gdod ma'i mgon po'i lam gyi rim pa'i khrid yig ye shes bla ma* (= *Klong chen snying tig*, Vol. 3), Paro 1976, p. 315.1–5 (= fol. 9b/1–5). In this "manual" (*khrid yig*), written by 'Jigs-med gling-pa (1729/30–1798), a spiritual technique is found under the name of "Pondering Reality as such" (*gnas lugs la brtag pa*); with the help of this pondering "one examines from where the mind arises, where it abides, and to which place it evaporates" (*byung gnas 'gro gsum la brtag pa*). In 'Jigs-med gling-pa's words the results of the first part of this exercise is a "state being free from each and every tenet" (*khas len thams cad dang bral ba'i ngang*) and he quotes *Vigrahavyāvartanī*, v. 29b. Applying Klong-chen rab-'byams-pa's Prāsaṅgika interpretation to his specific needs in the context of spiritual instruction, he explains further that this state is not reached by those who boast to be Prāsaṅgikas and analyse by way of the "mind" (*yid*), but only by seeing the "True Nature" (*chos nyid*), the "Great Completion" (*rdzogs pa chen po*).

Madhyamaka should be "the true one" (*lākṣanika*), it has to be the Great Madhyamaka of "Union" (*yuganaddha*), or [with other words] the Madhyamaka free from discursive elaborations. Because, after having been consolidated in harmony with "Original Awareness" (*jñāna*) [at the time of] exalted meditative absorption, its nature [consists in] the total appeasement of all extremes like existence, non-existence, etc.

APPENDIX

NGES *Nges shes rin po che sgron me*

A photostatic reproduction in *Collected Writings of 'Jam-mgon 'Ju Mi-pham rgya-mtsho*, Vol. 8 (= *Ngagyur Nyingmay Sungrab*, Vol. 67), ed. Sonam Tobgay Kazi, Gangtok 1976.

B xylograph edition, published by gSung rab nyams gso rgyun spel spar khang, Tashijong, Palampur (H.P.), n.d.

YID$_c$ *Theg pa chen po'i man ngag gi bstan bcos yid bzhin rin po che'i mdzod kyi 'grel pa padma dkar po*

A photostatic reproduction, ed. Dodrupchen Rinpoche, Gangtok 1966 or 1967 (supposedly reproduced from the A-'dzom Brug-pa Chos-sGar blocks).

B photostatic reproduction in *Mdzod bdun. The famed seven treasuries of Vajrayāna Buddhist philosophy by Kun-mkhyen Klong-chen-pa Dri-med 'od-zer*. Reproduced from prints from the sDe-dge blocks belonging to Lopon Sonam Sangpo, Vol. Ka; eds. Sherab Gyaltsen and Khentse Labrang, Gangtok, 1983.

I *NGES* (A fols. 19b/5–20a/2; B fols. 25a/2–6):

/ klong chen rab 'byams 'di skad du /
/ dbu mar khas len yod med la /
/ snga rabs[1] *pa rnams phyogs rer 'dzin /*
/ lugs rer skyon yon gnyis re gnas /
/ des na rang gi[2] *bzhed pa la /*
/ don dam gnas lugs gzhal ba'i tshe /
/ gshis la cir yang ma grub ltar /
/ khas kyang ci zhig len par byed /
/ de phyir grub mtha' gnas lugs kyi /
/ khas len yin phyir rtsod sogs tshe /
/ gshis bzhin khas len ci yang med /
/ rjes thob lam 'bras grub pa'i mtha' /
/ ji lta[3] *ji snyed rnam bzhag rnams /*
/ ma 'dres sos sor khas len 'dod /
/ phyin chad tshul 'di smra shes na /
/ kho bo'i legs bshad mthu yin gsungs /

1 A: snga sde, 2 A: gis, 3 A: ji ltar

II *YID*$_c$ (A Vol. VAM, fols. 79a/5–b/1; B fols. 232b/7–233a/2):

/ lugs 'di gnyis snga rabs pa dag gis ma phyed pas gtsang pa[1] *ni / khas mi len la / rma bya ni*[2] *len par snang ste gnyis kar*[3] *legs chos re dang skyon re dmigs pa'i phyir*[4] *gzhung ji lta ba bzhin gyi don cung zad ma dgongs par snang ngo / 'di ni rnam par dpyod pa'i blo gros dang gzhung lugs phal po*[5] *che mthong ba las byung*

ba'i mig rgyas pas gzhung na gab cing 'thor ba'i don gsal por phye pa yin no / phyin chad dam bca' 'di 'cha' shes pa rnams ni kho bo'i gzhung 'di'i mthur shes par bya'o /

1 B: brtsad pa po (!), 2 B: smra bya 'di (!), 3 B: gnyis ka, 4 B: phyir ro /, 5 B: phal mo

III *YID_c* (A Vol. VAM, fols. 71b/2–4; B fols. 226b/5–227a/1):
/ gshis ngo bor gang yang rang bzhin ma grub pa dang / khas len pa thams cad bden zhen dang bcas pas na[1] *rang bzhin du smra ba dag gi lugs rang gi gzung khas blangs nang*[2] *'gal ba dang / dngos po stobs zhugs khas len pa po de'i gzhung la grags tshod*[3] *des 'gog pa yin la / bkag pa'i rjes la rang rgyud pa ltar nges pa'i dam bca' med de /*

1 B: pas, 2 B: khas blangs na'ang, 3 B: chod

IV *NGES* (A fols. 20b/5–6; B fols. 26a/4–6):
/ des na kun mkhyen bzhed pa bzhin /
/ rang lugs 'di ltar shes par bya /
/ dbu ma mtshan nyid pa yin na /
/ zung 'jug dbu ma chen po'am /
/ spros bral dbu ma yin dgos te /
/ 'phags pa'i mnyam bzhag ye shes dang /
/ rjes su mthun par gtan phab[1] *nas /*
/ yod med la sogs mtha' rnams kun /
/ nyer zhi'i rang bzhin yin phyir ro /

1 B: phabs

P.S. The different readings in quotations II and III show the necessity of comparing all the editions of Klong-chen rab-'byams-pa's works which are published up to the present. A most interesting account of the edition prepared by the Second rDzogs-chen Rig-'dzin 'Gyur-med Theg-mchog bstan-'dzin (born 1699) is to be found in *rGyal ba gnyis pa kun mkhyen ngag gi dbang po'i gsung rab las mdzod bdun ngal gso gsang ṭīka rnams rmad byung 'phrul gyi phyi chos ji ltar bsgrub pa'i tshul las brtsoms pa'i ngo mtshar gtam gyi gling bu skal bzang rna ba'i dga' ston*, ed. Dodrub Sangyay Lama, Gangtok 1976.
The whole question concerning the editorial history of Klong-chen rab-'byams-pa's works is raised shortly by G. Smith in his introduction to *Rang grol skor gsum* and *Byang chub kyi sems kyun byed rgyal po'i don khrid rin chen gru bo* (= Ngagyur Nyingmay Sungrab, Vol. 4), Gangtok 1969, p. 6. For a relative chronology of Klong-chen rab-'byams-pa works compare Wangchuk (2008:202–221).

Some Historical Delineations Concerning Madhyamaka Philosophy in the rNying-ma-pa School

Using a text by Mi-pham rgya-mtsho (1846–1912), the so-called *Nges shes rin po che'i sgron me* (= *Nges sgron*), I tried to show how the rNying-ma-pa school deals with a subject of utmost importance for the philosophy of the Prāsaṅgika-Madhyamaka: the problem of not propounding one's own "statement" or "position" (*abhyupagama* / *khas len*) in philosophical debate. I mainly wanted to emphasize the background of Mi-pham rgya-mtsho's endeavours to solve this problem, i.e. the work of Klong-chen rab-'byams-pa (1308–1364).[1] Since the source text contains further interesting ideas and in the meantime I have also gained access to a commentary to *Nges sgron*,[2] I would now like to show the changes in Mi-pham rgya-mtsho's argumentation in comparison with Klong-chen rab-'byams-pa. In addition, the findings of that investigation will be contrasted with a concept

---

1 It is quite interesting to compare Klong-chen rab-'byams-pa's treatment of the problem with the few lines Tsong-kha-pa Blo-bzang grags-pa'i-dpal (1357–1419) devotes to the same subject in his *rJe btsun red mda' ba chen po la shu yig* in *Tsong-kha-pa bka'-'bum* (= TTP, Bd. 153) S. 58/5.1–7. At least we find here also the categories of *mnyam bzhag* and *rjes thob* in approaching the Prāsaṅgika-Madhyamaka's specific teaching of not propounding an own position. dGe-'dun chos-'phel (1905–1951) in his *dBu ma'i zab gnad snying por dril ba'i legs bshad klu sgrub dgongs rgyan*, Gangtok: Sherab Gyaltsen 1983, quotes twice the *Red mda' ba'i dris lan* (sic!) in the same context, ibid, S. 40.4 and 68.5. It seems that he's quite indebted to these ideas, as the first part of his work ends with the separation of the state of "meditative absorption" (*mnyam bzhag smra bral gyi ngang*) and the activity of relating the Buddhist teachings to others, and the second part of the text can be regarded as a mere amplification of this idea. For the structure of the *Klu sgrub dgongs rgyan*, see Stoddard (1985:332), and for a complete translation Lopez Jr. (2006:47–116).

2 mKhan-po Kun-bzang dpal-ldan (1872–1943): *Nges shes rin po che'i sgron me'i tshig gi don gsal ba'i 'grel chung blo gros snang ba'i sgo 'byed*, 97 fols., Clement Town, U.P.: Nyingma Lama's College, n.d. The seven questions and answers, which make up the content of *Nges sgron*, are presented by mKhan-po Kun-bzang dpal-ldan as a coherent system; cf. ibid, fol. 91a/4–6 (the number of folios refers to the actual treatment of the questions in the commentary):

I.	*dngos gzhi snang stong zung 'jug gi tshul*	fols.	7a/4–17a/6
II.	*de nyan rang sogs kyi spyod yul min pas zab par bstan pa*	fols.	17a/6–26a/4
III.	*zung 'jug de ji ltar sgom tshul*	fols.	26a/4–35a/1
IV.	*bsgom pa de rgyud ji ltar skyed tshul*	fols.	35a/1–45a/1
V.	*zab mo'i rtogs pa rgyud la skyes pa'i ngor bden gnyis ji ltar 'char shul*	fols.	45a/1–54a/5
VI.	*de'i ngor chos thams cad mnyam pa nyid du 'char tshul gnyis*	fols.	54a/5–67a/4
VII.	*rang gis rtogs pa bzhin gzhan la zab mo'i lta 'doms tshul bstan pa*	fols.	67a/3–87a/4

bearing some terminological similarities to Mi-pham rgya-mtsho's theory, as represented by Kaḥ-thog dGe-rtse Paṇḍita 'Gyur-med Tshe-dbang mchog-grub (1761–1829). The overall question is: what are the implications of the expression "Great Madhyamaka" (*dbu ma chen po*)[3] in the rNying-ma-pa school?

[1]

Klong-chen rab-'byams-pa's contribution to the solution of the *khas len* problem was the introduction of categories drawn from spiritual practice. In the state of meditative absorption (*mnyam bzhag*) – which is free from proliferations (*spros bral*) – no statements are made, while in the phase following absorption (*rjes thob*), a philosophical standpoint is propounded under the perspective of the "Two Truths". That particular aspect of the teaching which is in accordance with the state of meditative absorption is what Mi-pham rgya-mtsho considers as "Real Madhyamaka" (*dbu ma mtshan nyid pa*); he refers to it by the names *zung 'jug dbu ma chen po* and *spros bral dbu ma chen po*. This is exactly the point where Mi-pham rgya-mtsho's terminology appears to differ from that of Klong-chen rab-'byams-pa: "being free from proliferations" (*spros bral*), as a specific mark of the method applied by the Prāsaṅgika-Madhyamaka, was also the reason why Klong-chen rab-'byams-pa spoke of his system as "Great Madhyamaka";[4] but as far as I can see, Klong-chen rab-'byams-pa never uses the term *zung 'jug dbu ma chen po* in this context. As a consequence, the following questions are raised: what are the reference-points of this term and do they perhaps point in a direction other than that of the Prāsaṅgika-Madhyamaka?

To provide the necessary context for these questions, I will again follow the route of Mi-pham rgya-mtsho's argumentation in *Nges sgron*. To the rhetorical question as to whether it is a contradiction to make the above-mentioned separation between *khas len med* and *khas len yod*, while at the same time making doctrinal statements from the perspective of the two truths (this being a mistake in the sense of a view criticised before) Mi-pham rgya-mtsho gives the following answer (I):

> By splitting up [the two levels of *khas len med* and *khas len yod*] as something different, we made a difference between a Madhyamaka of the path, which makes

3 A good overview of the different connotations of the expression *dbu ma chen po* is given by van der Kuijp (1983:35–45). The groundwork in the research in this aspect of the Madhyamaka philosophy in Tibet was done by Seyfort Ruegg; a "Great Madhyamaka" in the rNying-ma-pa school is mentioned by him (1963:77, note 6), and (1969:60). For the person of the Eighth Si-tu-pa Chos-kyi 'byung-gnas, mentioned in both cases, see note 20.

4 See Ehrhard (1988:145, note 18) and chapter one in the present volume. Up to now I could only locate passages where Klong-chen rab-'byams-pa speaks of an *dbu ma chen po* in the sense of *spros bral* (*niṣprapañca*). In *Yid bzhin rin po che'i mdzod kyi 'grel pa padma dkar po*, Gangtok: Dodrub Chen Rinpoche, n.d., p. 840.1–3, this criterion is applied to the set of *phyag rgya chen po / rdzogs pa chen po / dbu ma chen po*.

> distinctions, and a Madhyamaka of meditative absorption, [which is] the main part [of spiritual practice]; between [a Madhyamaka that is] coarse and subtle, cause and result; between the state of cognition (*vijñāna*) and of awareness (*jñāna*), i.e. between a great and a small Madhyamaka. [Thereafter the solution of the *khas len* problem] was explained; how could such mistake occur?

This quotation shows how the term "Great Madhyamaka" – which was only used by Klong-chen rab-'byams-pa as an epithet for the system of the Prāsaṅgika-Madhyamaka – is used by Mi-pham rgya-mtsho in explicit contrast with the notion of a "Small Madhyamaka". This opposition is even reinforced with the help of further definitions. If one takes a closer look at these definitions, the demarcation of *lam gyi dbu ma* and *mnyam bzhag dbu ma* is quite consistent with the concept of Klong-chen rab-'byams-pa, and the difference between "cognition" (*rnam shes*) and "awareness" (*ye shes*) can be interpreted as referring to the Prāsaṅgika-Madhyamaka as well;[5] but the remaining two pairs of opposite terms (*rags pa / phra ba* and *rgyu / 'bras bu*) don't allow such a reconstruction.

This leads us to direct our attention to another aspect of the Madhyamaka philosophy in Tibet: the *gZhan-stong* teaching. This is because, in the rNying-ma-pa school, the distinction between a "coarse" (*rags pa*) and a "subtle" (*phra ba*) Madhyamaka is already associated with the *gZhan-stong*. I shall return to this point later on. For now I would like to complete this survey of Mi-pham rgya-mtsho's ideas and concentrate on the remaining pair of opposite terms in the aforementioned quotation, because the opposition between a Madhyamaka of the "cause" (*rgyu*) and a Madhyamaka of the "result" (*'bras bu*) brings one nearest to the conditions which shaped Mi-pham rgya-mtsho's presentation of a "Great Madhyamaka" in *Nges sgron*. The text itself makes the following points in this regard (II):

---

5 Cf. *Theg pa mtha' dag gi don gsal bar byed pa grub pa'i mtha' rin po che'i mdzod*, Gangtok: Dodrub Chen Rinpoche, n.d., pp. 123.3–125.1; here, in the introductory part of the Prāsaṅgika chapter the well-known distinction is made between an "erring mind" (*blo 'khrul pa*) and a "non-erring mind" (*blo ma 'khrul pa*) – following the position of Candrakīrti in *Madhyamakāvatāra*, VI/23ff. According to Klong-chen rab-'byams-pa the Prāsaṅgika-Madhyamaka understands a "non erring mind" as "awareness, which doesn't exist as something to be talked of, to be thought of, or to be expounded" (*smra bsam brjod du med pa'i ye shes la chos nyid rtogs pa yang dag pa'i blo ma 'khrul pa zhes bya bar btags pa 'dod de*); this is the phase of meditative absorption (*sa thob pa'i mnyam bzhag*). For the "erring mind" there are two types: the one with "pure" (*dag pa*) senses, and the one where the senses are mistaken (*ma dag pa*); the first group makes use of correct knowledge (i.e. *pratyakṣa* and *anumāṇa*) and is associated with the phase following the absorption (*sa thob pa'i rjes thob*). See also the distinction between *ye shes* (= *dmigs med*) and *blo* (= *dmigs bcas*), ibid, S. 130.2–5.

I'm trying here to relate the distinction *rnam shes – ye shes* (resp. *blo – ye shes*) only to the interpretation of the Prāsaṅgika-Madhyamaka as it is represented by Klong-chen rab-'byams-pa. For this distinction in the Jo-nang-pa school, see Seyfort Ruegg (1963:81, note 37).

> Therefore, in all sources of the Madhyamaka [it is stated that] discerning knowledge (*prajñā*), [i.e.] the Madhyamaka of the "cause", analyses [the two truths] by way of logical arguments (*yukti*); and without their being established, the "result", the union [of the two truths], is not established either. Although in the manner of the two truths [Reality-as-it-is] might be fixed by way of logical arguments, [nevertheless] the determination [of Reality-as-it-is] as "Non-differentiation" of the two truths, the [Madhyamaka of the] "result" is the [only] essence of the *Hetu*- and the *Phala-yāna*.
>
> As all [that is practised in conformity with] awareness (*jñāna*) doesn't remain in the two extremes [of existing and non-existing created] by successive arrangement [of the two truths], it is beyond [ordinary] mind. It is therefore the "Middle" and it is "Great". As long as [the two truths are determined] by means of successive arrangement without having [even] touched that awareness, [this Madhyamaka] is not the real intention of all the Jinas, the final [goal], the Great Madhyamaka.

According to this quotation, the main difference between a "Small" and a "Great" Madhyamaka concerns the relations between the "Two Truths" (*satyadvaya*). The *dbu ma chen po* is qualified by "Non-differentiation" (*dbyer med*) of the two truths, their "Union" (*zung 'jug*); in contrast, the "Small Madhyamaka" analyses the two truths with the help of logical arguments, thereby bringing the two levels of evaluating phenomena in the right order.

These two methods of defining the relationship between the two truths are one of the pillars of Mi-pham rgya-mtsho's philosophical system. In a work of mKhan-po mDo-sngags bstan-pa'i nyi-ma (1900/07–1959), who is a representative of this system, they are given the names *snang stong chos kyi bden gnyis dbye tshul* and *gnas snang chos kyi bden gnyis dbye tshul*.[6] Since a full description of these two methods and their respective sources would go beyond the scope of this paper, I will only outline them roughly: the first method defines "relative truth" (*kun rdzob bden pa*) as "that which appears" (*snang ba*) and

6 See *lTa grub shan 'byed gnad kyi sgron me yi tshig don rnam bshad 'jam dbyangs dgongs rgyan*, n.p., n.d., pp. 200.6–215.3. mDo-sngags bstan-pa'i nyi-ma makes the interesting remark that the only philosophical standpoint being able to combine these two methods is the *dbu ma chen po thal 'gyur ba'i lugs*. In relation to the works of Klong-chen rab-'byams-pa the two methods are mentioned by Mi-pham rgya-mtsho in *Le'u bco brgyad pa'i tshig 'grel* (published as an appendix to *Yid bzhin rin po che'i mdzod kyi 'grel pa padma dkar po*, as in note 4) pp. 1080.5–1081.3: *de lta bu'i srol chen po gnyis su gnas pa ni mdo rnams na'ang mang du 'byung ba yin pas phan tshun shan shor bar mi bya la*; compare the root-text pp. 799ff. In his *gZhan stong khas len seng ge nga ro* (as in note 17), pp. 361.3–362.3, Mi-pham rgya-mtsho classifies the *gZhan-stong* way of presenting the two truths as belonging to the *gnas snang chos kyi bden gnyis dbye tshul*, but this presentation must be preceded by the "Highest, the Reality, which is free from proliferations" (*don dam spros pa dang bral ba'i don*); this is guaranteed by the mastery of the scriptures of Nāgārjuna.

"absolute truth" (*don dam bden pa*) as "that which is empty" (*stong pa*), while the second method makes use of the terms "Reality-as-it-is" (*gnas tshul*) and "Reality-as-it-appears" (*snang tshul*); here, relative truth is considered as "incompatibility" (*mi thun pa*) of "Reality-as-it-is" and "Reality-as-it-appears", in contrast with absolute truth, which is the "compatibility" (*thun pa*) of the two realities.[7]

From what I have understood of Mi-pham rgya-mtsho's system so far, the second method mainly has two functions: the first is to introduce some of the *Mantrayāna* concepts – or those of spiritual practice in general – into the discussion of philosophical questions and problems, which in other schools are only dealt with in the context of the *Sūtrayāna*; secondly, there is an attempt of intellectual penetration into certain theories of the *Mantrayāna*. These two tendencies are very important for categorizing more clearly Mi-pham rgya-mtsho's endeavours to elaborate a coherent philosophy of the rNying-ma-pa school.

This short side remark was necessary to show the general implication of a term like *zung 'jug dbu ma chen po*. The phrase "*[bden gnyis] zung 'jug*" can now be interpreted as referring to the simultaneity of the two truths, in the sense of "compatibility of Reality-as-it-is and Reality-as-it-appears" (*gnas snang mthun pa*). It becomes therefore evident that Mi-pham rgya-mtsho extends the application of the term "Great Madhyamaka" to the *Mantrayāna*. Without going into more details here, I think it worthwhile to keep in mind this development in the use of the term *dbu ma chen po*, which for Klong-chen rab-'byams-pa was restricted to the Prāsaṅgika-Madhyamaka only. Nevertheless, this change, or rather extension in the meaning, of the so-called "Great Madhyamaka" can also be seen as the consequence of Klong-chen rab-'byams-pa's thought, as the elaboration of a trait, which

---

7 These two methods were pointed out for the first time by Lipman (1980). They refer also to two distinct "modes of knowledge" (*tshad ma*): the *snang stong chos kyi bden gnyis dbye tshul* is qualified by a "mode of knowledge that evaluates the absolute" (*don dam dpyod byed pa'i tshad ma*) and the *gnas snang chos kyi bden gnyis dbye tshul* by a "mode of knowledge that evaluates the conventional (i.e. the relative)" (*tha snyad dpyod byed pa'i tshad ma*). A good résumé of this theory is given by mKhan-po lHag-bsam rgyal-mtshan (19th/20th century) in his *Don rnam par nges pa shes rab ral gri'i 'grel pa thub bstan yongs su rdzogs pa'i snang byed*, Bylakuppe: Pema Norbu Rinpoche, 1984, pp. 51.5–56.5. At the end of the relevant chapter, the author hints at Mi-pham rgya-mtsho's *Guhyagarbha* commentary as a source for further studies on this subject. The commentary in question is the *gSang 'grel phyogs bcu'i mun sel gyi spyi don 'od gsal snying po*, now available in *rNying ma bka' ma rgyas pa*, vol. 27, Kalimpong: Dupjung Lama and Madhav Nikunj, 1982–1983, pp. 209–467; a general introduction to the function of the two *tshad ma* is given for example on pp. 246.1–248.3. The tradition of the *Guhyagarbhatantra* together with the works of Rong-zom Chos-kyi bzang-po (11th century) were certainly most influential for the development of the second method of defining the two truths. Here we also find the *dag gzigs tha snyad dpyod pa'i tshad ma*, which is for Mi-pham rgya-mtsho the general frame for discussing the teachings of the Tathāgatagarbha. The whole problem of a mode of knowledge, which "appreciates the pure" (*dag gzigs*) is in need of a separate investigation. A good starting point would be the sixth question in *Nges sgron* with its reference to the text *sNang ba lhar sgrub pa* by Rong-zom Chos-kyi bzang-po; this work was published in the "Selected Writings" (*gSung thor bu*) of this author (= Smanrtsis Shesrig Spendzod, Bd. 73, Leh: 'Khor-gdong gTer-sprul 'Chi-med rig-'dzin, 1974, pp. 125–151); see also note 10. Compare Wangchuk (2009:222–225) for a presentation of these materials.

was only hinted at in the works of the earlier author. In *Nges sgron* it is expressed in a more direct way (III):

> The Great Madhyamaka which is free from proliferations and the Great Completion of the Clear Light, [they are] different names for one thing. There can be no other view higher than these.[8]

Here we have that particular teaching of the *Mantrayāna* which is the dominant perspective for both authors in their treatment of the *dbu ma chen po*: the "Great Completion" (*rdzogs pa chen po*). It is first of all Klong-chen rab-'byams-pa's insistence on the state of "meditative absorption" (*mnyam bzhag*), the "being free from proliferations" (*spros bral*), that allows such a rapport of Prāsaṅgika-Madhyamaka and rDzogs-chen. But as in the case of the two methods of defining the two truths, a more theoretical approach also characterises Mi-pham rgya-mtsho's treatment of this subject; he speaks of a "view", a "philosophical theory" (*lta ba*),[9] which is represented by the *dbu ma chen po* and the *rdzogs pa chen po*.

One has the impression that the more implicit identification of Prāsaṅgika-Madhyamaka and rDzogs-chen in the works of Klong-chen rab-'byams-pa as opposed to Mi-pham rgya-mtsho's thorough elaboration of a philosophical basis for both *Sūtra-* and *Mantrayāna* can be explained – at least to some extent – by the fact that "philosophical theory" is not so important for him as it is for Mi-pham rgya-mtsho. The position of the latter is aptly summarized in the following quotation (IV):

---

8 See also Klong-chen rab-'byams-pa in *Chos dbyings rin po che'i mdzod kyi 'grel pa lung gi gter mdzod*, Gangtok: Dodrub Chen Rinpoche, n.d., fol. 70b/1ff.: *rang bzhin rdzogs pa chen po 'di'i lugs kyis mtha' bral la sogs pa'i 'jal tshul phal cher dbu ma thal 'gyur dang mtshungs pa* and in *rDzogs pa chen po sems nyid ngal gso'i 'grel pa shing rta chen po*, Gangtok: Dodrub Chen Rinpoche, 1973, p. 867.1: *mtha' bral dbu mar bslab tshul bstan pa*. In his *lTa grub shan 'byed rnam bshad* (as in note 6) mKhan-po mDo-sngags bstan-pa'i nyi-ma characterizes the position of the "followers of the early translations" (*snga 'gyur pa*) explicitly as *mtha' bral dbu ma*. In this respect I was not able to consult Matsumoto (1982:161-178). The difference between a *mtha' thams cad dang bral ba'i dbu ma* and a *khas len thams cad dang bral ba'i dbu ma* in a not-identified text from the 13th century is mentioned by Sato (1980:216).

9 For the expression *lta ba* in a related context, see Broido (1985:14–18). As a kind of specification I added to the translation "view" in this case the formula "philosophical theory" because the subject is dominated by a theoretical problem (in spite, or just because of the *Mantrayāna*): the relationship of the two truths. In the rNying-ma-pa school one finds also the expression *lta ba* in the texts of the *sNying thig*; here it refers to a spiritual practice consisting in the "vision" of the true nature of the mind. In this case I find the translation of *lta ba* with "vision" quite appropriate. For such a demarcation of a "general view" (*spyi'i lta ba*) and a "direct vision" (*mngon sum gyi lta ba*), see for example *Zhus len bdud rtsi'i gser phreng* in *sNying thig ya bzhi* of Klong-che-pa Dri-med 'od-zer, New-Delhi: Trulku Tsewang Jamyang and L. Tashi, 1971, vol. 3, pp. 9.2ff. On the history of this text, see Ehrhard (1992) and chapter three in the present volume.

> Therefore, that which is called Madhyamaka, [it is] discerning knowledge analysing the two truths individually, [i.e.] the Madhyamaka of the path; and [it is also] that which is effected by [the aforementioned] – the union, where the two truths are of one taste, [i.e.] the Madhyamaka of the result. That is cause [and] result, the view of the *Sūtra-* [and] the *Mantrayāna*. The former is the aspect of discerning knowledge, the latter is exclusively awareness. The latter [Madhyamaka] is therefore praised through the word "Great" as something special.

The definition of the *dbu ma chen po* (i.e. *zung 'jug dbu ma chen po*) as the general view of the *Mantrayāna* must have other sources than Klong-chen rab-'byams-pa.[10] Perhaps the terms of a "coarse" and a "subtle" Madhyamaka may be instrumental in locating them.

[2]

An exhaustive treatment of what the rNying-ma-pa school at the end of the 18th and at the beginning of the 19th century regarded as a "coarse" and a "subtle" Madhyamaka is given by Kaḥ-thog dGe-rtse Paṇḍita 'Gyur-med Tshe-dbang mchog-grub in the first volume of his "catalogue" (*dkar chag*) to the *rNying ma'i rgyud 'bum*.[11] The authority of his findings can still be detected in the *bsTan pa'i rnam gzhag* of the Second bDud-'joms Rin-po-che 'Jigs-bral Ye-shes rdo-rje (1904–1987), where nearly the whole passage is incorporated verbatim.[12]

---

10 A general view of the *Mantrayāna* in the sense of "non-differentiation of the two truths" (*bden pa gnyis dbyer med par lta ba*) is offered by Rong-zom Chos-kyi bzang-po in his *lTa ba'i brjed byang chen mo*; cf. *gSung thor bu* (as in note 7), pp. 231.5–235.1. This text may be one of the other possible sources for this kind of theory. Rong-zom Chos-kyi bzang-po himself compares also this view with the position of the Madhyamaka, but he doesn't use the term *dbu ma chen po* for that purpose; his interest lies primarily in exposing the different aspects under which "relative truth" (*kun rdzob bden pa*) is seen in the *Mantrayāna*. This is achieved by two factors: 1. *yongs su dag pa'i lha'i mtshan nyid du lta ba* and 2. *bden pa gnyis dbyer med par lta ba* (see also the formulations *bden pa gnyis dbyer med pa'i rang bzhin du 'dod pa* and *kun rdzob sgyu ma lha'i dkyil 'khor du 'dod pa* as two of four (!) points, which qualify the *Mantrayāna* in *mDo sngags kyi grub mtha' mthun mi mthun mdor bsdus kyi bsdus byang* (= Rong-zom bka' 'bum, Thimphu: Kunsang Tobgay, 1976), p. 440.3.

The term *dbu ma chen po* is used three times by Rong-zom Chos-kyi bzang-po in his *lTa ba dang grub mtha' sna tshogs pa brjed byang*, ibid, pp. 339.4 and 341.5/6. In all three cases, the "Great Madhyamaka" has no direct association with the *Mantrayāna*, but describes the position of a Madhyamaka, where "mind doesn't exist [as] absolute [truth]" or "doesn't exist at all" (*sems don dam par med / sems kun tu yang med*); the relevant chapter is that on the *rnal 'byor spyod pa'i dbu ma'i lugs*. For the early classifications of the Madhyamaka schools, see Seyfort Ruegg (1980:277–279).

11 Cf. *bDe bar gshegs pa'i bstan pa thams cad kyi snying po rig pa 'dzin pa'i sde snod rdo rje theg pa snga 'gyur rgyud 'bum rin po che'i rtogs pa brjod pa lha'i rnga bo che lta bu'i gtam* in *Tantra*s of the Nyingmapa Tradition, vol. 35, Thimphu: Ngodrub 1975, pp. 111.1–150.4. Short information on 'Gyur-med Tshe-dbang mchog-grub as abbot of Kaḥ-thog monastery are given by H. Eimer and P. Tsering in two articles (1979:485–486) and (1981:13–14).

12 Cf. *gSang sngags snga 'gyur rnying ma pa'i bstan pa'i rnam gzhag mdo tsam brjod pa legs bshad*

The part concerning the "subtle Madhyamaka" is introduced with the words of Slob-dpon sKal-ldan who, in his *dBu ma'i bstan bcos sgron ma*[13] lists the Svātantrika- and the Prāsaṅgika-Madhyamakas as belonging to a "coarse, outer Madhyamaka" (*rags pa phyi'i dbu ma*), which has the task of defeating the opponent and composing authoritative scriptures, while the "subtle, inner Madhyamaka" (*phra ba nang gi dbu ma*) has to be practiced as *rnal 'byor spyod pa'i dbu ma.*[14] Although this distinction seems to be similar to Klong-chen rab-'byams-pa's separation of *rjes thob* and *mnyam bzhag* – and one can even go so far to connect this theory with one of Klong-chen rab-'byams-pa's works[15] – it is quite another doctrine that is presented by 'Gyur-med Tshe-dbang mchog-grub as a "Great Madhyamaka".

It bears the name *nges don dbu ma chen po* and is concerned primarily with the relationship of the Second and Third "Turning of the Wheel of the Dharma" (*dharmacakra-pravartana*), the interpretation of the three "Natures" (*svabhāva*) – *kun btags, gzhan dbang,*

---

snang ba'i dga' ston, Kalimpong: Dudzom Rimpochee, 1967, fols. 77a/4–95b/1 and Dudjom Rinpoche (1991:206ff). An interesting critic of this chapter, recurring to the works of Klong-chen rab-'byams-pa, is to be found in Yontan Gyatso: *Gyi na pa zhig gi blo'i sprin rum las 'ongs pa'i gdong lan lung rigs pa'i thog mda'*, New Delhi, 1979, pp. 118–177.

13 This is the *Madhyamakaratnapradīpa* of Bhāvaviveka / Bhavya (= TTP, vol. 95, no. 5254, p. 326a/6ff.). For a discussion of the authorship of this work, see Seyfort Ruegg (1982:513); the opinion of a Tibetan author on this subject is given in an article published in the same volume by Mimaki (1982:374, note 67). For Klong-chen rab-'byams-pa's quotations from the *Madhyamakaratnapradīpa*, see note 14.

14 *rGyud 'bum rin po che'i rtogs pa brjod pa* (as in note 11), p. 111.2–4 and *bsTan pa'i rnam gzhag* (as in note 12), fol. 77a/4–6: *de la slob dpon skal ldan gyis dbu ma'i bstan bcos rin chen sgron mar / thal rang gi dbu ma ni rags pa phyi'i dbu ma ste / thos bsam las byung ba'i rig[s] par smra bas phyi rol pa dang rtsod pa'i dus dang / bstan bcos chen po byed pa dang / rig[s] pa chen po'i gzhung 'dzugs pa'i tshe smra bar bya ba yin la / phra ba nang gi dbu ma nyams su len pa'i tshe ni rnal 'byor spyod pa'i sbu ma nyid bsgom par bya'o.* The classification of the Svātantrika- and the Prāsaṅgika-Madhyamaka as belonging to the "Coarse Madhyamaka" is not to be found in the original; cf. *Madhyamakaratnapradīpa* (as in note 13), p. 354a/5–7: *de bas de dag dang bdag gis gzhung chen po mang po dag bkod pa ni / phyi rol gyi dbu ma yin no zhes shes par bya'o / pha rol rgol ba bzlog pa dang / bstan bcos chen po'i gzhung dang ni / rtsod pa chen po byung dus su/ rigs pa'i dbu ma'i gzhung smra bya / de nyid don la gtsor byed cing / rnal 'byor nyams su len dus su / phra ba'i rnal bsgom par bya.* For the use of this quotation in the Sa-skya-pa school, see Jackson (1985:28 and notes 44/45.)

15 In his *Grub mtha' rin po che'i mdzod* (as in note 5) Klong-chen rab-'byams-pa quotes at the end of the Prāsaṅgika chapter three times the *Madhyamakaratnapradīpa* as a source for the subject of the *khas len* problem; ibid, pp.135.5–6, 135.6–136.1 and 136.1–2. In the original these are the passages pp. 347a/8–b/2, 344b/1 and 344b/2–3. The quotations are marked by Klong-chen rab-'byams-pa as statements of Nāgārjuna (*dbu ma rin chen sgon mar klu sgrub kyis*); ibid, p. 135.5. Is this a proof for the fact that this text was regarded more as a collection of quotations than as a separate work by a single author?

As 'Gyur-med Tshe-dbang mchog-grub introduces the "Subtle Madhyamaka" immediately after his treatment of the Prāsaṅgika-Madhyamaka with a quotation of the *Madhyamakaratnapradīpa* as well, this might give reason to regard this representation of "Subtle Madhyamaka" as a kind of continuation of the Madhyamaka chapter in the *Grub mtha' rin po che'i mdzod.*

yongs grub – and with the theory of the Tathāgatagarbha. In a word, it deals with the issues which are relevant for the discussion of the *Rang-stong* and *gZhan-stong* position of the Madhyamaka. 'Gyur-med Tshe-dbang mchog-grub's own standpoint can be summed up roughly under the following topics: starting from the superiority of the Third Turning of the Wheel, and thus accepting the position of the *gZhan-stong* concerning the ontological status of the absolute, he is at the same time very keen to keep his position clearly distinct from the philosophy of the Yogācāra (this is mainly done with the help of the distinction between *rnam shes* and *ye shes*). Besides this, the difference between the *Rang-stong* and the *gZhan-stong* view, i.e. the predominance of the Third against the Second Turning of the Wheel, can be reconciled within the perspective of the "meditative absorption" (*mnyam bzhag*), allowing them to become unified.[16]

To some degree one can compare this statements with those of Mi-pham rgya-mtsho, but what is lacking in the latter's works, is the same unrestricted acceptation of a *gZhan-stong* based *nges don dbu ma chen po* as that of 'Gyur-med Tshe-dbang mchog-grub.[17] But

---

16 See *rGyud 'bum rin po che'i rtogs pa brjod pa*, pp. 138.1ff. and *bsTan pa'i rnam gzhag*, fols. 89b/4ff.; see also the good résumé of 'Gyur-med Tshe-dbang mchog-grub's standpoint in his *sLob dpon chen po padmas mdzas pa'i gsang sngags nang gi lam rim pa rgya cher 'grel pa sangs rgyas gnyis pa'i dgongs rgyan* (= Smanrtsis Shesrig Spendzod, vol. 35) Leh: S.W. Tashigangpa, 1972, pp. 347.2–349.3. The difference between the Yogācāra and the gZhan-stong-pa lies in their definition of the "basis of emptiness" (*stong gzhi*); ibid, p. 347.3–4: *stong gzhi gzhan dbang la dgag bya kun btags kyis stong pa yongs grub tu bshad pa dang / stong gzhi chos nyid yongs grub la dgag bya kun btags kyis stong pa don dam pa'i bden par gsungs pa'i snga ma rnam rig smra ba lugs dang / 'phyi ma 'di gnyis rang lugs su dbu ma chen por bzhed cing*; see also note 22.

17 The intermediary position of Mi-pham rgya-mtsho in the discussion of the *Rang-stong* and *gZhan-stong* has already been noted by Lipman (1980:89–91). Compare now Wangchuk (2004:196–201) for the approach of the rNying-ma-pas in general – and Mi-pham rgya-mtsho in particular – to the issue of *Rang-stong* and *gZhan-stong*. This particular position is achieved by Mi-pham rgya-mtsho by means of the categories *ngo bo = stong pa* and *rang bzhin = gsal ba*, drawn from the rDzogs-chen literature. Also in this case he is following Klong-chen rab-'byams-pa, who makes use of these categories in his presentation of the Tathāgatagarbha teaching (cf. *Shing rta chen po* (as in note 8), pp. 310.6ff., *Grub mtha' rin po che'i mdzod* (as in note 5), pp. 170.4ff., and *Padma dkar po* (as in note 4), pp. 792.6ff.; see also note 23.

As a second aid for clearing up one-sided positions, Mi-pham rgya-mtsho recurs also to the above-mentioned method of relating the two truths: the integration of *Sūtra-* and *Mantrayāna*. Already in an early work like the commentary to the *lTa ba'i mgur zab mo* of lCang-skya Rol-pa'i rdo-rje (1820–1892), NNSS, vol. 62, pp. 821–867, he can thus bring his interpretation of a *dbu ma chen po* in harmony with the dGe-lugs-pa school; but at the same time this theoretical frame offers the possibility to turn back attacks launched against the *gZhan-stong* position. See in this context also his *bDe gshegs snying po'i stong thun chen mo seng ge'i nga ro*, NNSS, vol. 62, pp. 563–608; as this work is first of all a commentary to *Ratnagotravibhāga* I/27 – according to the numbering of verses in the Tibetan translation – the respective arguments can also be found in his *Theg pa chen po rgyud bla ma'i bstan bcos kyi mchan 'grel*, NNSS, vol. 62, pp. 359–378 (for the Tathāgatagarbha another early work is of interest too: *gZhi lam 'bras bu'i shan 'byed sangs rgyas padma'i zhal lung*, NNSS, vol. 70, pp. 324–329). The standpoint of Mi-pham rgya-mtsho concerning the *gZhan-stong* in his *gZhan stong khas len seng ge'i nga ro*, NNSS, vol. 70, pp.

without doubt, his works and the importance they gave to the Third Turning of the Wheel and the *gZhan-stong* philosophy were quite influential, as we have already noted. They were also partly responsible for the identification of the gZhan-stong and the rDzogs-chen as one and the same "philosophical view" (*lta ba*); this is documented by a quotation from Tshogs-drug rang-grol (1781–1851):

> If one asks now: that [particular] philosophical view of the rDzogs-chen, with which [position] is it in agreement, [the answer is:] from the two [positions of Madhyamaka, i.e.] the *Rang-stong*, the system of the Prāsaṅgika-Madhyamaka, and the *gZhan-stong*-Madhyamaka, it is in agreement with the *gZhan-stong*-Madhyamaka; from the two, the course, outer Madhyamaka, and the subtle, inner Madhyamaka, it is in agreement with the subtle, inner Madhyamaka; from the three phases of the [Turning of] the Wheel of the Dharma, it is in agreement with the last Wheel – so it is said in the *Dbu ma'i rnam nges bde gshegs snying po'i rgyan.*[18]

What exactly is the reason for the predilection for the *gZhan-stong* philosophy in the rNying-ma-pa school at the beginning of the 19th century, a predilection which doesn't prevail to such en extent one generation later, at the time of Mi-pham rgya-mtsho? A possible answer to this question may be found in the work of another scholar connected with the monastery of Kaḥ-thog, who lived in the first half of the 18th century: Rig-'dzin Tshe-dbang nor-bu (1698–1755). His biography offers several hints pointing to his involvement with the *gZhan-stong* and to his interest in making this doctrine more accessible. The special devotion he developed while studying the *gZhan-stong* philosophy even made him become famous as an incarnation of Sa-bzang Ma-ti Paṇ-chen, one of the two main disciples of Dol-po-pa Shes-rab rgyal-mtshan (1292–1361). His activities in propagating the *gZhan-stong* also included the edition of a set of *Sūtra*s which are

---

359–378 (as in note 6), is instead of the unambiguous title characterized by the same two tendencies just mentioned: apologetic against the adversaries, corrective and critical against the followers.

18 *The Autobiography of Zhabs-dkar sNa-tshogs* (sic!) *rang grol of A-mdo together with his O rgyan sprul pa'i glegs bam*, vol. II, Dolanji 1975, p. 497.1–3: *'o na rdzogs chen gyi lta ba de gang dang mthun snyam na / dbu ma'i thal 'gyur ba'i lugs kyi rang stong dang / gzhan stong dbu ma gnyis kyi gzhan stong dbu ma dang mthun / rags pa phyi yi dbu ma dang phra ba nang gi dbu ma gnyis kyi phra ba nang gi dbu ma dang mthun / chos 'khor rim pa gsum gyi / 'khor lo tha ma dang mthun zhes dbu ma'i rnam nges bde gshegs snying po'i rgyan las gsungs*. It is to be supposed that the quoted work is the *Nges don dbu ma chen po'i tshul rnam par nges pa'i gtam bde gshegs snying po'i rgyan* of 'Gyur-med Tshe-dbang mchog-grub. See *Bod kyi bstan bcos khag cig gi mtshan byang dri med shel dkar phreng ba*, mTsho sngon mi rigs dpe skrun khang, 1985, p. 170. There are listed still more works of 'Gyur-med Tshe-dbang mchog-grub which seem to be of interest for the *gZhan-stong* philosophy. Concerning these works see Makidono (2011: 216, note 5).

authoritative for the Third Turning of the Wheel (*bka' 'khor lo tha ma nges don snying po'i mdo nyi shu*).[19] The influence of Rig-'dzin Tshe-dbang nor-bu was in the same way instrumental in reviving the *gZhan-stong* philosophy in the bKa'-brgyud-pa school, at least this is the impression one has from a very informative passage in the biography of the Eighth Si-tu-pa Chos-kyi 'byung-gnas (1700–1774).[20]

As this demonstration of the rNying-ma-pa school's general interest in the *gZhan-stong* is only substantiated by the example of two scholars from the Kaḥ-thog monastery, it might be worthwhile to make this picture more complete by adding information on other scholars of the 18th and beginning of the 19th century. One who seems promising in this respect is Zhe-chen dBon-sprul 'Gyur-med mThu-stobs rnam-rgyal (born 1787); he studied five years with 'Gyur-med Tshe-dbang mchog-grub and was himself the teacher of rDza dPal-sprul O-rgyan 'Jigs-med Chos-kyi dbang-po (1808–1887), 'Jam-mgon Kong-sprul Blo-gros mtha'-yas (1813–1899) and 'Jam-dbyangs mKhyen-brtse dbang-po (1820–1892).[21]

Finally, mention must be made of the sMin-grol gling tradition and its representative Lo-chen Dharma-śrī (1654–1717). In his voluminous commentary on the *sDom gsum rnam nges* of mNga'-ris Paṇ-chen Padma dbang-rgyal (1487–1542), one can witness a still earlier stage of the assimilation of the *gZhan-stong* philosophy. In the first place, *Rang-stong* and *gZhan-stong* are described in the chapter on "discerning knowledge [resulting

---

19 Cf. mKhas-btsun bzang-po : *Biographical Dictionary of Tibet and Tibetan Buddhism* 4 (= The rNying-ma-pa Tradition 2) Dharamsala 1973, pp. 377–378 and p. 380. The source for this account is the short biography by Brag-dkar rta-so sprul-sku Chos-kyi dbang-phyug (1775–1837): *dPal ldan rig 'dzin kaḥ thog pa chen po tshe dbang nor bu'i zhabs kyi rnam thar mdor bsdus dad pa'i sa bon* in Collected Works of Kaḥ-thog Tshe-dbang nor-bu, vol. I, Dalhousie: Damchoe Sangpo, 1976, pp. 377–391. This edition also contains a "catalogue" of the *Sūtra* collection: *bKa' tha ma don rnam par nges pa nges don snying po'i mdo'i dkar chag bsam 'phel nor bu'i phreng ba.* For the importance of Rig-'dzin Tshe-dbang nor-bu for the *gZhan-stong* in this respect, see Stearns (1999:74–76).

20 Cf. *Tā'i si tur 'bod pa karma bstan pa'i nyin byed kyi rang tshul drangs por brjod pa dri bral shel gyi me long* (= Śata-Piṭaka Series, vol. 77) Delhi: Lokesh Chandra, 1968, pp. 267.1–269.7; compare also the preface by E.G. Smith, p. 8. At the same time the reluctant Si-tu-pa is more or less obliged by Rig-'dzin Tshe-dbang nor-bu to accept the "view" (*lta ba*) of the *gZhan-stong*, he receives from the Kaḥ-thog teacher also a series of initiations in the *sNying thig*. For the investigation of Rig-'dzin Tshe-dbang nor-bu in this tradition, see Prats (1984:197–209).

21 For a short biography of 'Gyur-med mThu-stobs rnam-rgyal, see the *Zhe chen chos 'byung* (= Smanrtsis Shesrig Spendzod, vol. 10) Leh: S.W. Tashigangpa, 1971, pp. 463.3–468.5. Unfortunately the subject of the *gZhan-stong* is not mentioned in a text which is directed to 'Gyur-med mThu-stobs rnam-rgyal and which deals with philosophical problems: *Zhe chen dbon sprul rin po ches dri lan drang pa'i sa bon*; its author is rDzogs-chen rGyal-sras gZhan-phan mtha'-yas (born 1800). Nevertheless, the last-named important teacher of the rDzogs-chen monastery gives a short description of the *gZhan-stong* (as *nges don mthar thug*) – mentioning also Yu-mo grub-chen Mi-bskyod rdo-rje – in another text: *dPal yul dbon sprul rin po che'i dris len zla zhun snang ba*. The two correspondences are contained in *Collected Works of rDzogs-chen rgyal-sras gZhan-phan mtha'-yas*, Thimphu: Ngodrub, 1984, vol. I, pp. 524–543 and vol. II, pp. 271–309.

from] studying" (*thos pa'i shes rab*) on the same level as two distinct "systems of cutting of elaboration" (*spros pa gcod lugs*).[22] This formulation reminds of Klong-chen rab-'byams-pa's definition of Prāsaṅgika-Madhyamaka, and it is exactly his statement on this school as the "peak" (*rtse mo*) of the *Hetuyāna* which we find in the chapter on "discerning knowledge resulting from meditation" (*bsgom gyi byung gi shes rab*). In this chapter the problem in question is the union of the Second and Third Turning of the Wheel of the Dharma and the compatibility of the last one with the *Mantrayāna*. The method of the Prāsaṅgika is now the only and most effective means which stands for "discerning knowledge [resulting from] studying and reflection" (*thos bsam las byung ba'i shes rab*); in contrast to this, the view in "the phase, where it is settled through an experience resulting from meditation" (*sgom byung nyams myong gis gtan la 'bebs pa'i skabs*) is now "this view of the Madhyamaka, which is spoken of in the last [Turning of the] Wheel, being something profound and most excellent" (*'khor lo tha mar gsungs pa'i dbu ma'i lta ba de nyid zab cing ches bzang pa yin te*). Although the name *gZhan-stong* is not used here, it is obvious from the following quotations that this aspect of the Madhyamaka is referred to. It is this "view" that is in total agreement with the *Mantrayāna*, or – verbatim – "with the spiritual experience of the view that is explained in the profound *Tantra*s of the secret *Mantra[yāna]*" (*gsang sngags kyi rgyud sde zab mo rnams nas bshad pa'i lta ba'i nyams len dang yang mthun*).[23]

---

22 Cf. *sDom gsum rnam par nges pa'i 'grel pa legs bshad ngo mtshar dpag bsam gyi snye ma* in *rNying ma bka' ma rgyas pa*, vol. 37 (as in note 7), pp. 377.5–379.5. That a later author like 'Gyur-med Tshe-dbang mchog-grub is indebted to this work can already be seen by comparing the passage in the "basis of emptiness" (see note 16): *rnal 'byor spyod pa'i gzhung du / stong gzhi gzhan dbang dgag bya kun btags kyis stong pa'i yongs grub tu bshad pa dang / rgyud bla ma sogs las chos nyid yongs grub dgag bya kun brtags* (sic!) *kyis stong pas gsungs*; ibid, p. 378.2–4. It is noticeable that Lo-chen Dharma-śrī doesn't identify the last position as his own system, i.e. the "Great Madhyamaka", as does 'Gyur-med Tshe-dbang mchog-grub. Instead, Lo-chen Dharma-śrī also mentions the merits of the *Rang-stong*: "If one asks, what is the intention of dealing with Absolute Truth in terms of being empty of its own essence, [the answer is] when taking the Absolute as object, [this Absolute] doesn't exist in the way that it can be grasped by the mind, [this] is the intention [of the *Rang-stong* position]." (*'o na don dam rang gi ngo bos stong pa ltar gsungs pa'i dgongs pa gang snyam pa / don dam la dmigs nas blos bzung ba ltar ma grub pa la dgongs par yin no*); ibid, p. 379.3. The *dPag bsam snye ma* was completed in the author's fifty-fifth year, a *kun 'dzin gyi lo*, i.e. 1708, in the "main temple" (*gtsug lag khang chen po*) of sMin-grol gling; ibid, pp. 670.5–671.1.

23 *dPag bsam snye ma*, pp. 382.1–4. I summarized here roughly the answer to the relevant problem; the question itself says: *des na kun mkhyen chos gyi rgyal po dri med 'od zer zhabs kyis kyang / grub mtha' mdzo dang yid bzhin mdzod rtsa 'grel la sogs pa'i gsung rab rnams su thos pas gtan la dbab bya ngos 'dzin pa'i skabs su dbu ma thal 'gyur ba rgyu'i theg pa chen po'i rtse mor sgrub pa mdzad cing / sgom pa nyam myong gis gtan la 'bebs pa'i skabs rnams su myong bya gzung 'dzin gnyis dang bral ba'i so so rang rig pa'i ye shes la bzhed pa gnyis mi 'gal lam snyam na / mi 'gal te*; ibid, pp. 381.4–382.1. Here we can clearly see the mechanism, through which the *gZhan-stong* position is "harmonised" with Klong-chen rab-'byams-pa's standpoint of the Prāsaṅgika-Madhyamaka; it is effected by the opposition of the

[3]
These have been some observations on possible sources of a "Great Madhyamaka" in the sense of *nges don dbu ma chen po* as it was taught in the rNying-ma-pa school in the 18th and the 19th century. The different connotations of *spros bral dbu ma chen po* (Klong-chen rab-'byams-pa) and *zung 'jug dbu ma chen po* (Mi-pham rgya-mtsho) being prevalent as well, are a sign of a the different [and intermingling] use of these terms, and we have to proceed with caution if we want to make general statements about them. One has also to take in account the fact, that the material I presented in this paper is not so much of relevance for the period between the 14th and the beginning of the 15th century which is regarded as the climax of the philosophical debate concerning the "Great Madhyamaka" as a synthesis of the Yogācāra- and Madhyamaka doctrines.[24]

But taking Klong-chen rab-'byams-pa as the only representative of this period, raises an important issue: were the rNying-ma-pas at all engaged in this debate – and in the related problem of the formulation of a specific *lta ba* of the *Mantrayāna* against that of the *Sūtrayāna*; or were they rather more occupied with the elaboration of their own doctrinal system? This may give us a clue to the rNying-ma-pa's rather late interest in the philosophy of the *gZhan-stong*, and also in the different approaches of individual teachers in their interpretation of a "Great Madhyamaka".

---

categories *thos pa* (*bsam pa*) – *bsgom pa*.

Although one is not able to find an *dbu ma lta ba* of the Last Wheel in the works of Klong-chen rab-'byams-pa, nevertheless the superiority of the "Third Turning of the Wheel" and the *Mantrayāna* can be noticed as well. But, once again, it is the perspective of the rDzogs-chen which is the dominant force; cf. *Padma dkar po* (see note 4) pp. 812.1–813.3 with the admonition not to develop wrong conceptions concerning the Tathāgatagarbha teaching: *lhun grub gzhi yi gnas lugs 'di zhes bya / sangs rgyas kyi bka' tha ma dang / gsang sngags su lhun grub gzhi'i gnas lugs 'di mchog tu bsngags pas shes byar bya'o*. For Mi-pham rgya-mtsho's recurring to Klong-chen rab-'byams-pa's treatment of the unity of the Second and Third Turning of the Wheel, see his *bDe gshegs snying po'i stong thun chen mo seng ge'i nga ro* (see note 17) pp. 586.2ff.

24 For the chronological dates, see van der Kuijp (1983:35–45) and Seyfort Ruegg (1973:2–6). The only passage I could locate so far in Klong-chen rab-'byams-pa's works pointing to this debate is a polemical remark in the passage in *Padma dkar po* mentioned in note 23; here, some "pretentious meditators" are spoken of, who denigrate the superiority of the Third Turning of the Wheel of the Dharma and the *Mantrayāna* by reducing it to the statement that thus the *Mantrayāna* would advocate the same "view" as the *Yogācāra*, while in reality the *Madhyamaka* is the peak [of all views] (*'dir bod kyi ston sgom gzu lums pa dag na re / gsang sngags 'di sems tsam pa dang lta ba gcig ste / rtse mo dbu ma'o zhes zer ro*). Perhaps it was this nearness and affinity with the gZhan-stong-pas in the conception of the Tathāgatagarbha that motivated Klong-chen rab-'byams-pa to insist so vigorously on the Prāsaṅgika-Madhyamaka as the "peak" of all views himself, thus keeping himself out of the battle. But we still know very little of his exact interpretation of the *Tathāgatagarbha*; see in this respect for example the discussion in *Shing rta chen po* (as in note 8) pp. 212.1–223.5, where *yongs grub* is characterized by three modes of being empty: *rang gis stong pa*, *gzhan gyis stong pa* and *gnyis ka stong pa*. See also the elaborate discussion of Klong-chen rab-'byams-pa's interpretation of Buddhanature in Mathes (2008:98–113).

In the case of Mi-pham rgya-mtsho we can see at least that the rapport with the philosophical theories of Klong-chen rab-'byams-pa made it possible for him to integrate the *nges don dbu ma chen po* in his own system, without having to embrace unequivocally the *gZhan-stong* position. This is clearly some evidence of the rNying-ma-pa's endeavour to define their own philosophical tradition, which was to prove so fruitful again at the end of the 19th and the beginning of the 20th century.[25]

[25] In the biography of mKhan-po Ngag-dbang dpal-bzang (1879–1941), a scholar from Kaḥ-thog, belonging to the generation of Mi-pham rgya-mtsho's disciples, a "subtle Madhyamaka" in the sense of the *nges don dbu ma chen po* is not mentioned anymore. His studies of the Madhyamaka philosophy are done on the basis of Mi-pham rgya-mtsho's system, allowing to include argumentations from the *Mantrayāna* (such as the *rtogs pa bzhi* from the *Guhyagarbhatantra*); cf. *'Od gsal rin chen snying po padma las 'brel rtsal gyi rtogs brjod ngo mtshar sgyu ma'i rol gar* (= NNSS, vol. 1) pp. 151.5–157.5 and 78.3–89.3. This same author wrote also commentaries to the *Catuḥśataka* and the *Madhyamakāvatāra*, published 1984 and 1985 respectively by Patrul Pema Norbu Rinpoche in Bylakuppe. See also the description of *mtha' bral dbu ma'i lam ji ltar 'jug pa'i tshul* and *'od gsal rdzogs pa chen po ji ltar sgom tshul* in *mKhas par bya ba'i gnas drug bstan pa shes bya gsal ba'i me long* of gZhan-phan Chos-kyi snang-ba (1871–1927), Bir/Delhi 1984: Tsondu Senghe, pp. 71.3–75.4.

APPENDIX

The quotations of *Nges sgron* are taken from the edition in *Collected Writings of 'Jam-mgon 'Ju Mi-pham rgya-mtsho*, vol. 8 (= Ngagyur Nyingmay Sungrab, vol. 67) Gangtok: Sonam Tobgay Kazi, 1976, 27 folios (= S. 71–123). For the commentary (= *Nges sgron 'grel chung*), see the reference in note 2.

I *Nges sgron*, fol. 21b/1–3:
/ nged kyis khyad par phyes nas su /
/ shan 'byed lam gyi dbu ma dang /
/ dngos gzhi mnyam bzhag dbu ma gnyis /
/ rags dang phra ba'am rgyu 'bras sam /
/ rnam shes ye shes gnas skabs kyi /
/ dbu ma che chung khyad phyes nas /
/ bshad phyir skyon de ga la 'jug /

Nges sgron 'grel chung, fols. 73a/3–b/1:
/ de la nged kyis 'di ltar skabs kyi khyad par legs par phyes nas su rjes thob shan 'byed lam gyi dbu ma dang dngos gzhi 'phags pa'i mnyam bzhag zung 'jug ye shes kyi dbu ma chen po gnyis rim par rags pa brda'i dbu ma dang / phra ba chos nyid kyi dbu ma'am rgyu dang 'bras bu'i sam rnam shes kyi spyod yul dang ye shes kyi spyod yul gyi gnas skabs kyi dbu ma che chung gi khyad legs par phyes nas phra ba chos nyid kyi dbu ma'am zung 'jug 'bras bu'i dbu ma'am mnyam bzhag ye shes kyi dbu ma'am chen por khas len med par bstan pa dang / rags pa sems kyi spyod yul rjes thob shan 'byed rgyu'am lam gyi dbu mar khas len yod par bshad pa'i phyir na gong du tha snyad bden pa rigs pas dpyad bzod du thal ba la sogs pa'i skyon gsum gzhan la gang brjod pa de dag rang la ga la 'jug ste mi 'jug ces /

II *Nges sgron*, fols. 24a/4–b/1:
/ des na dbu ma'i gzhung kun tu /
/ shes rab rgyu yi dbu ma nyid /
/ rigs pas dpyad cing ma grub par /
/ 'bras bu zung 'jug mi grub phyir /
/ bden pa gnyis kyi tshul du ni /
/ rigs pas gtan la phab na yang /
/ 'bras bu bden pa dbyer med du /
/ grub pa rgyu 'bras theg pa'i bcud /
/ de phyir ye shes de dag ni /
/ res 'jog tshul gyis mtha' gnyis la /

/ mi gnas blo las 'das pa'i phyir /
/ dbu ma yin la chen po'ang yin /
/ ji srid res 'jog tshul gnyis ni /
/ ye shes de la ma reg par /
/ rgyal ba kun gyi dgongs pa'i mthil /
/ mthar thug dbu ma chen po min /

Nges sgron 'grel chung, fols. 82a/4–b/4:
/ des na gnas lugs gtan la dbab pa'i dbu ma'i gzhung bka' dang bstan bcos kun tu snang stong bden pa gnyis la so sor dpyod pa'i tshad mas drangs pa'i shes rab rgyu yi dbu ma nyid rigs pas tshul bzhin du dpyad cing yang dag par ma grub par gyur pa de srid du zung 'jug 'bras bu'i dbu ma'am 'bras bu'i mnyam bzhag gi ye shes bden gnyis zung du 'jug pa nyid mi 'grub pa'i phyir na re zhig dngos po'i chos thams cad kyi gnas lugs snang stong bden pa gnyis kyi tshul du ni bden gnyis dpyod pa'i rigs pa yang dag pas gtan la phab par mdzad na yang 'bras bu gnas lugs bden pa dbyer med dam snang stong zung 'jug spros bral mnyam pa nyid du grub cing rtogs pa ni rgyu dang 'bras bu mdo sngags kyi theg pa'i dgongs bcud zab mo'i gnad dam pa yin par shes par bya'o / de yi phyir na 'phags pa'i mnyam bzhag zung 'jug gi ye shes de dang rjes su mthun par gtan la dbab cing bsgom pa de dag gis ni bden gnyis res 'jog gi bsgom pa'i tshul gyis mtha' gnyis rim gyis spang ba'i tshul gyis mtha' gang la yang mi gnas pas blo las 'das pa'i zung 'jug gi ye shes su la zlo ba'i phyir na dbu ma yin la chen po'ang yin no / de lta na ji srid res 'jog gi bden gnyis bsgom pa'i tshul gyis ni nam zhig res 'jog dang bral ba'i zung 'jug gi ye shes de la dngos su ma reg par de srid du rgyal ba kun gyi dgongs pa'i bcud dam mthil mthar thug pa'i zung 'jug gnyis su med pa'i ye shes dbu ma chen po rang min no /

III *Nges sgron*, fol. 25a/6:
/ spros bral dbu ma chen po dang /
/ 'od gsal rdzogs pa chen po gnyis /
/ don gcig ming gi rnam grangs te /
/ de las lhag pa'i lta ba med /

Nges sgron 'grel chung, fol. 85a/4–6:
/ don rang gi ngo bo snang stong zung du zhugs pa'i spros bral dbu ma chen po dang dbyings ye gnyis su med pa'i 'od gsal rdzogs pa chen po gnyis zung 'jug gnyis su med pa'i ye shes su don gcig la mtshon byed kyi mtshan nam ming gi rnam grangs tsam yin te / de las lhag pa'am mchog tu 'phags pa'i lta ba gzhan med de /

IV *Nges sgron*, fol. 25b/2–3:
/ de phyir dbu ma zhes pa yang /
/ bden gnyis so sor dpyod pa yi /
/ shes rab lam gyi dbu ma dang /
/ des drangs bden gnyis ro gcig pa'i /
/ zung 'jug 'bras bu dbu ma gnyis /
/ rgyu 'bras mdo sngags lta ba ste /
/ snga ma shes rab cha yin la /
/ phyi ma ye shes kho na yin /
/ de phyir phyi ma 'di la ni /
/ chen po'i sgra yis khyad du bsngags /

Nges sgron 'grel chung, fols. 85b/5–86a/4:
/ don de yi phyir na yang snang stong bden gnyis zung du 'jug pa'i dbu ma zhes pa 'di la yang bden gnyis so sor dpyod pa yi tshad ma sems byung shes rab rgyu'am lam gyi dbu ma dang / tshad ma gnyis po des drangs pa yi snang stong bden pa gnyis rnam dbyer med par ro gcig pa'i dngos gzhi 'phags pa'i mnyam bzhag gi ye shes zung 'jug 'bras bu'i dbu ma dang gnyis po yang rim par rgyu dang 'bras bu'am rnam shes dang ye shes kyi gnas skabs yin la / de bzhin du mdo sngags kyi lta ba'i khyad yang rjes dpag dang mngon sum mam rnam shes dang ye shes kyi gnas skabs sam rgyu dang 'bras bu'i tshul gyis snga ma las phyi ma gong nas gong du khyad par 'phags pa ste / snga ma gnyis snang can sems byung shes rab kyi cha yin la phyi ma sems las 'das pa'i zung 'jug gnyis su med pa'i ye shes kho na yin pas so / de yi phyir na phyi ma 'di la ni stong nyid spros bral chen po dang / lhan skyes phyag rgya chen po dang / 'od gsal rdzogs pa chen po sogs chen po'i sgra yis snga ma las khyad par du 'phags par bsngags cing bstan par mdzad pa yin no /

The "Vision" of rDzogs-chen: A Text and its Histories

In the course of being occupied with the person of Zhabs-dkar rDo-rje-'chang or Tshogs-drug rang-grol (1781–1851) and with a song collection composed by him, I attempted to assemble material on a theme that is at once fascinating and inexhaustible: "theory/vision in the system of the Great Perfection" (*rdzogs pa chen po lta ba*). I cannot present here a definitive analysis of this material, as for such a purpose an introduction to the philosophical and spiritual foundations of the multilayered tradition that the "Great Perfection" represents would be necessary.[1] But in this connection a first glance at a particular text is perhaps useful – a text that not only deals with the "vision", but also with several persons whose names are connected with this subject. Though I am still unable to reconstruct completely the history of this text, its composition and its influence completely, a number of strands can at least be brought together that may later result in a complete picture.

Along with the "Wing Strokes of Garuḍa" *(mkha' lding gshogs rlabs)*, the great first work of Tshogs-drug rang-grol, I consulted for my research the so-called *O rgyan sprul pa'i glegs bam*. This latter is a relatively late work, with detailed information on the synthesis of rNying-ma-pa and dGe-lugs-pa teachings, such as was propounded first and foremost by Tshogs-drug rang-grol.[2] In a section of it of somewhat more than two folios a

[1] This kind of introduction is available with the book by Karmay (1988b). On p. 215 there is a short discussion on the relationship between the Madhyamaka doctrine and the teaching of the *sNying thig* which is based on a remark in Roerich's translation of the "Bluc Annals". According to my opinion this remark can be attributed to Roerich's co-worker dGe-'dun Chos-'phel (1905–1951); on the relationship between dGe-'dun Chos-'phel with g.Ya-ma bKra-shis-'khyil, the monastery of Tshogs-drug rang-grol, see Stoddard (1985:135–147).

[2] For Tshogs-drug rang-grol's education as a synthesis of rNying-ma-pa and dGe-lugs-pa teachings, see Ehrhard (1990a:32–43). Reference has already been made to this fact by the editors of the first part of Tshogs-drug rang-grol's autobiography: *The Autobiography of Zhabs-dkar sNa-tshogs* (sic!) *rang-grol of A-mdo together with his O rgyan sprul pa'i glegs bam*, Dolanji: Tsering Wangyal, 1975. Preface: "Zhabs-dkar Rin-po-che is interesting in that he represents a fusion of dGe-lugs-pa and rNying-ma-pa practice." Although in the following only this synthesis and its context will be closely examined, one should not ignore the fact that all schools would have to be taken into consideration in a comprehensive account of Tshogs-drug rang-grol's integrating influence in Amdo during the first half of the 19th century; see above all *O rgyan sprul pa'i glegs bam*, pp. 411.1–416.6. A first contribution to an understanding of the religious and political/social context in Amdo in the 18th century is available in Kapstein (1988/89: 217–244).

topic is introduced which is of not inconsiderable significance for a first treatment of rDzogs-chen in Amdo: the relation of Tsong-kha-pa Blo-bzang grags-pa'i dpal (1357–1419) to his "rNying-ma-pa" teacher lHo-brag grub-chen Nam-mkha' rgyal-mtshan (1326–1401). The section is of extreme interest because, first of all, quotations from the works of lHo-brag grub-chen are cited verbatim and, secondly, because consideration is given to the topic of rDzogs-chen and "vision" (*lta ba*). Thus, for example, it is stated in a fairly long quotation:

> As the doctrinal terms of the Great Perfection exist [in the foregoing quotation from *bDud rtsi'i thigs pa*] as something that has not been mixed up with other tenets, it is by this way that the ultimate goal was obtained [by lHo-brag grub-chen]. But that is not all: Except for the stages where he sets down [or applies] the philosophical tenets of Madhyamaka and Pramāṇa, the master Tsong-kha-pa, too, is in agreement with the [teachings of] Phyag-chen and rDzogs-chen, [namely] in the achievement of spiritual experience..... In fact one is able to understand this once one has looked into the *Zhus lan bdud rtsi sman mchog*, [a work] in which exaggerations concerning the vision were cleared away for [lHo-brag] Grub-chen.[3]

These few particulars made it clear that for an understanding of the wider context affecting those persons who represented the rDzogs-chen teaching in a province dominated by the dGe-lugs-pa school, such as Amdo, the person of lHo-brag grub-chen had to be included in the picture. Moreover, the text "The Best Nectar Medicine [in] Questions and Answers"

A favourite topos by means of which the unity of the new and old schools is illustrated is the "spiritual identity" (*rgyud gcig*) of Padmasambhava, Atiśa and Tsong-kha-pa; cf. Dargyay (1977: 22–24). With regard to the quotation of the Second Dalai Bla-ma, dGe-'dun rgya-mtsho (1475–1542), which is often used in association with it, see *O rgyan sprul pa'i glegs bam*, pp. 466.6–467.1.

3 *O rgyan sprul pa'i glegs bam*, pp. 475.5–476.1: *rdzogs chen gyi chos skad grub mtha' gzhan dang ma 'dres par yod pa'i phyir lam 'di nyid kyis grub par brnyes par ma zad / rje tsong kha pa'ang dbu tshad kyi grub mtha' 'jog skabs ma gtogs nyams bzhes phyag rdzogs dang mthun...don du'ang grub chen la lta ba'i sgro 'dogs bcad pa'i zhus lan bdud rsti sman mchog tu bltas pas shes par nus so*. The attempt made here by Tshogs-drug rang-grol to construe Tsong-kha-pa's relation to the teaching of Phyag-chen and rDzogs-chen from the angle of "spiritual experience" (*nyams len / nyams bzhes*) is worthy of note. The second part of the autobiography offers a parallel to this: *'Gro mgon zhabs dkar ba'i sku tshe smad kyi rnam thar*, Paro: Lama Ngodrub and Sherab Drimey (1983:350,3ff); here Tshogs-drug rang-grol makes a thorough examination of the way in which the spiritual experience is achieved by Tsong-kha-pa (*thugs nyams su bzhes tshul la zhib tu bltas pas...*). Towards this aim he draws on a written work of Tsong-kha-pa, the *rJe btsun red mda' ba chen po la zhu yig* (= *The Tibetan Tripiṭaka,* Tokyo-Kyoto: Suzuki Research Foundation, 1955–1961, No. 6066). This work is also cited by Tshogs-drug rang-grol in his account of Tsong-kha-pa's *dbu ma'i lta ba*; see ibid, pp. 99.4–100.2. For Red-mda'-ba as a main teacher of Tsong-kha-pa, and his role in the Madhyamaka philosophy in Tibet, see Roloff (2008:15–23).

(*zhus lan bdud rtsi sman mchog*) seemed to occupy a central position with regard to the subject of *lta ba*. At that point in time, there was available to me neither the original of this work nor more exact information on the person of lHo-brag grub-chen. Here, however, according to Tshogs-drug rang-grol's remark at least, was one of the sources dealing with the topic of "vision" and Tsong-kha-pa's relation to the rNying-ma-pa school: thus my attention turned towards the 14th century and the teacher of Tsong-kha-pa.[4]

In the spring of 1987, during a period of study in Paris, two editions of the "Collected Works" of lHo-brag grub-chen came into my hands. The older edition of the two has its origins in a manuscript deposited in Thig-phyi in lHo-brag; it numbers close to 500 folios. The second one derives from O-rgyan chos-gling Monastery in Bhutan and, according to the colophon, is based on a single-volume edition of the *bKa' 'bum* of lHo-brag grub-chen. I assumed that this piece of information referred to the manuscript from Thig-phyi.[5]

With these texts in hand, I now had material at my disposal allowing me a closer look at the person of lHo-brag grub-chen, the teachings he imparted and also their influence on Tsong-kha-pa. Without wishing to treat all these sources exhaustively, I shall now make a few observations concerning the encounters between the two teachers. Here the main point

---

4 For a translation of *Zhus len bdud rtsi sman mchog*, see Thurman (1981:213–230). A detailed account of the meeting between Tsong-kha-pa and lHo-brag grub-chen is found in Kaschewsky (1971:125–135). This section also contains, in translation, Tsong-kha-pa's written reply to the text just named: *lHo brag mkhan chen phyag rdor ba la zhus lan sman mchog bdud rtsi'i phreng ba dang phul ba* (= *The Tibetan Tripiṭaka*, No. 6068); ibid, pp. 132–135. According to what I have seen, there are three further documents sent to lHo-brag grub-chen contained in the works of Tsong-kha-pa, all of them *stotras* (cf. *The Tibetan Tripiṭaka*, Nos. 6045–6047).

In order to be able to approach Tsong-kha-pa's philosophy and the history of its development from a more biographically oriented angle, such "petitions" (*zhu yig*) as those sent to lHo-brag grub-chen and Red-mda'-ba (see note 3) must certainly be taken into consideration. Such a document also exists in the case of Bla-ma dBu-ma-pa, Tsong-kha-pa's teacher, who, along with the two persons just named and Chos-rje Don-grub rin-chen (1309–1385), is numbered among "the four incomparable teachers" (*'gran zla dang bral ba'i bla ma bzhi*): *Bla ma dbu ma pa la mdo khams su phul ba* (= *The Tibetan Tripiṭaka*, No. 6067). It is only after an exact analysis of such personal documents that one should think about passing judgement about Tsong-kha-pa's "vision-quest"; see in this connection v.d. Kuijp (1987b:65 and note 31).

5 I. *Collected Writings of lHo-brag Grub-chen Nam-mkha' rgyal-mtshan, Reproduced from a Rare Mansucript Originally Preserved in the Temple of Thig-phyi in Lho-brag*, 2 vols., New Delhi: Tshering Dargye, 1972; II. *The Collected Works (gSung-'bum) of lHo-brag Grub-chen Nam-mkha' rgyal-mtshan, Reproduced from a Rare Mansucript Preserved at O-rgyan Chos-gling Monastery in Bum-thang*, Thimphu/Delhi: Kunsang Togyel, 1985. While the first edition has no separate colophon, one can find detailed information on the history of the Bhutanese edition in *Them yig chos skyong gi bka' rgya can*, ibid, pp. 632.4–684.3. The year *me mo yos*, given as the date of the definitive redaction, is unfortunately without a *rab 'byung*. One of the redactors describes himself as belonging to the Shud-phu family (*shud phu'i rigs can*); lHo-brag grub-chen is also a member of this family, which traces its genealogy from Shud-phu (bu) dPal-gyi seng-ge, one of the twenty-five main disciples of Padmasambhava (see note 12). Regarding a "treasure discoverer" (*gter ston*) from the Shud-phu family in lHo-brag who unearthed works in Bhutan, cf. Aris (1979b:157).

of interest lies in the circumstances leading to the composition of the work *Zhus lan bdud rtsi sman mchog*. I have made use of the following works of lHo-brag grub-chen:

	I.		II.	
– *Phy'i rnam thar bdud rtsi'i phreng ba*	pp.	2–73	pp.	1–50
– *Nang ting nge 'dzin gyi nyams snang rnam thar*	pp.	111–169	pp.	51–92
– *gSang ba'i rnam thar log rtog mun sel*	pp.	171–189	pp.	93–110
– *rJe tsong kha pa mjal tshul*[6]	pp.	190–194	pp.	107–110
– *rJe tsong kha pa'i zhu len*[7]	pp.	195–198	pp.	701–704
– *Zhus lan sman mchog bdud rtsi'i phreng ba*	pp.	899–921	pp.	581–597

6 This text of two folios is an appendix to *gSang ba'i rnam thar log rtog mun sel*. It was disciples of Tsong-kha-pa who urged that it be set down in writing, and this therefore occurred after the actual meeting; see the introduction of the text (I. p. 190.3–6 = II. pp. 107.6–108.1):

> Once, at the time of the [setting in motion of the] Wheel of the Teaching in Thig-phyi, disciples of Blo-bzang grags-pa, the master of the four scriptures (i.e. *Madhyamaka*, *Prajñāpāramitā*, *Vinaya*, *Abhidharma*), such as the Kalyāṇamitra Kun-tu bzang-po, the disciple gSer-ldan-pa from Amdo, Dhvajabhadra [by name], who was prophesied by the personal deity, and numerous other pure Kalyāṇamitras met together with me. They spoke: "When[ever] our noble teacher, the noble Tsong-kha-pa, utters your name, then he sings wonderful praises of the 'incomparable Nam-mkha' rgyal-mtshan' and of the 'great goodness of this Vajrapāṇi, the lord of lHo-brag – his speech and so on'." So tell us of the wonderful visions during the meeting with rJe Tsong-kha-pa and of the manner in which the favourable signs came about. (*yang thig phyir chos 'khor gyi dus cig / rje bka' bzhi pa blo bzang grags pa'i slob ma / bshes gnyen kun tu bzang po dang / yi dam gyis lungs bstan pa'i slob ma mdo smad gser ldan pa dhva dza bha dra sogs dag pa'i bshes gnyen mang po bdag mjal byon byung bas / khong rnams kyi gsung nas / bdag cag rnams kyi bla ma dam pa tsong kha pa chen po / khyod kyi mtshan brjod pa na mtshungs med nam mkha' rgyal mtshan pa zhes dang / lho brag rje btsun phyag rdor pa 'di skad gsung zhes sogs bka' drin che / zhes ngo mtshar ba'i bsngags pa mdzad kyi 'dug pas / rje tsong kha pa dang mjal ba'i dus ngo mtshar ba'i gzigs snang dang / rtags rten 'brel byung tshul rnams gsung 'tshal...*).

Tsong-kha-pa's biographers make thorough use of this work in decribing the meeting between Tsong-kha-pa and lHo-brag grub-chen; thus, for example, the complete text, with transpositions, is cited by Dar-han mKhan-sprul Blo-bzang 'phrin-las (19th century): *'Jam mgon chos kyi rgyal po tsong kha pa chen po'i rnam par thar pa thub bstan mdzes pa'i rgyan gcig ngo mtshar nor bu'i phreng ba*, ed. mTsho sngon mi-rigs dPe-skrun-khang, 1981, pp. 218–227. The reason for this may be that the work *rJe tsong kha pa dang mjal tshul* is to be found in the "Collected Works" of Tsong-kha-pa under the title *lHo brag grub chen dang mjal tshul*; see Yoshimizu (1989, No. 1286 = 1432 (the first text only)).

7 In this brief text are found prophecies of lHo-brag grub-chen concerning the person of Tsong-kha-pa; the greater part of these prophecies, however, are taken from *Zhus lan sman mchog bdud rtsi'i 'phreng ba*. The pertinent passages are:

I. pp. 917.7–917.4	and	pp. 919.7–921.4
II. pp. 593.7–594.3	and	pp. 596.1–597.1

The introductory portion is a listing of the previous births Tsong-kha-pa and lHo-brag grub-chen had in common; they commence with Tsong-kha-pa's incarnation as Paṇḍit Matibhadraśrī of Kashmir. This

What one must bear in mind is first of all the fact that all three biographies mentioned here were composed around the time when Tsong-kha-pa was meeting lHo-brag grub-chen. According to the generally accepted tradition, lHo-brag grub-chen was 70 years old (by Tibetan reckoning) at the time, so that we may take the year 1395 as the date of the meeting. During this period the 38-year-old Tsong-kha-pa was making his way to Tibet's southern border with the intention of going to India to further his studies of the *Sūtra-* and *Mantrayāna.* What statements do the "Outer Biography" (composed in 1395) and the "Inner Biography" (composed in 1396) make concerning the person of Tsong-kha-pa?

Both biographies agree that in the 9th month, the "dog month" (*khyi zla*), four messengers are heralded to lHo-brag grub-chen in a dream; they are to bring him a "document" (*gsung yig*) from "a manifestation of Maitreya" (*bcom ldan 'das mgon po byams pa'i sprul pa zhig*). And the next day these messengers appear with a letter from the hand of the Kalyāṇamitra Blo-bzang grags-pa, at which lHo-brag grub-chen is greatly enjoyed. The "Inner Biography" adds: "From hearing of his accounts, and [in addition] from having had teacher-pupil ties [with him] in earlier [lives], I became very happy at heart." (*khong gi lo rgyus rnams thos pa dang / sngon gyi dpon slob kyi 'grel pas yid rab tu spro ba zhig byung*).

The next reference to the person of Tsong-kha-pa is also the description of a dream: while Tsong-kha-pa is consecrating a temple in 'Ol-kha stag-rtse, lHo-brag grub-chen observes correspondingly miraculous signs. Data on the life span and future activities of Blo-bzang grags-pa follow upon this episode in the "Inner Biography". A third passage in both biographies, finally, mentions the arrival of a disciple of Tsong-kha-pa, 'Jam-dpal rgya-mtsho by name.[8] These are the only bits of information we find in the "Inner" and "Outer Biography" of lHo-brag grub-chen concerning the person of Tsong-kha-pa in the year 1395. In the case of the *phyi'i rnam thar*, the reason for these sparse data probably lies in its being composed before the actual meeting of the two teachers; in the case of the *nang gi rnam thar*, one should recall that this latter genre is concerned more with rendering an account of visionary experiences than with faithfully relating historical events. Thus at the end this work written in the year 1396 the statement is made that lHo-brag grub-chen should write a biography about "the manner in which he beheld the personal deity" (*yi dam lha zhal gzigs tshul*). There follows upon this passage still one more remark concerning Tsong-kha-pa, though for the year 1396:

---

information is confirmed both in *Zhus lan sman mchog bdud rtsi'i phreng ba* and in *rJe tsong kha pa mjal tshul*; such is not case, however, with the other previous births. As further reference is made at the end of this section to the "Collected Works of the Reverend Lord" (*rje btsun pa'i gsung 'bum*), I suggest that *rJe tsong kha pa'i zhu len* be regarded as a later elaboration or compilation.

8 See in this connection *Phy'i rnam thar bdud rtsi'i phreng ba,* II. pp. 41.7–42.2, 42.4–6, 42.6–43.1 and *Nang ting nge 'dzin gyi nyams snang rnam thar*, II. pp. 87.3–5, 87.5–88.1, 88.3–6. The consecration of the temple in 'Ol-kha takes place before the meeting; cf. Dar-han mKhan-sprul: *rNam par thar pa thub bstan mdzes pa'i rgyan* (as in note 6), p. 218.

> On the third day of *ngang pa zla ba*, in the period [between] night and dawn, I heard the words of a prophecy, this sweet-sounding hymn of praise: "Las-kyi rdo-rje, the superb teacher; Blo-bzang grags-pa, the superb disciple; The Best Nectar Medicine, the superb teaching; Sukhāvati, the superb paradise" etc. The next day other prophecies occurred: we would be born together in the paradise of Sukhāvati, and the bond existed that we should meet in this life. After the personal deity Vajrapāṇi had spoken the teaching text with the title The Best Nectar Medicine, I set down this teaching in the form of a letter, that it might delight Blo-bzang grags-pa's heart, with the words: "This medicine – first take it, then experience its taste, and [finally] spit it out only after you have extracted the essence," and presented it to him.[9]

Thus, while in the "Inner Biography", too, there is no information given by lHo-brag grub-chen concerning his meeting with Tsong-kha-pa, we can at least register the fact that the work referred to here, the *bDud rtsi sman mchog*, reached Tsong-kha-pa's hands as a letter. If one takes the date, 1396, into account, this would have occurred after his face-to-face meeting with lHo-brag grub-chen. If one disregards the date, then it might be supposed that this text is the written response that followed upon Tsong-kha-pa's first letter. In my opinion,

---

9 *Nang ting nge 'dzin gyi nyams snang rnam thar*, II. p. 89.5–7: *ngang pa zla ba'i tshes gsum gyi nam thos rangs kyi dus la / lung bstan gyi sgra tshig la snyan pa'i bstod sgra 'di thos so / las kyi rdo rje bla ma'i mchog / blo bzang grags pa slob ma'i mchog / bdud rtsi sman mchog chos kyi mchog / bde ba chen po'i zhing khams mchog / ces pa la sogs tshe phyi ma la bde ba chen po'i zhing khams su lhan cig tu skye ba dang / tshe 'dir yang mjal ba'i 'brel ba yod pa'i lung bstan kyang byung / yi dam phyag na rdo rjes bdud rtsi sman mchog ces bya ba'i chos gsungs nas / sman 'di thog mar 'thung zhing / bar du bro bar myong ba gyis shig / tha ma bcud ma lon par skyugs pa mdzod cig / ces pa'i chos 'dis blo bzang grags pa thugs dgyes pa'i phyir yi ger bris te khong la phul ba yin.* The first three lines of the prophecy have also been cited by Tshogs-drug rang-grol in *O rgyan sprul pa'i glegs bam*, p. 473.1–2; following them is Tsong-kha-pa's reaction (p. 473.3):

> "The nectar-speech of Guhyapati –
> It fulfilled my heart's aspiration,
> Overcame the disease of bad habits.
> It was as if I had reached the Aṭaka paradise."
> (*gsang bdag gsung gi bdud rtsi yis //*
> *yid kyi re ba rdzogs par byas //*
> *nyon mongs nad las rgyal bar gyur //*
> *lcang lo can du phyin par snyam //*)

This verse is taken from *lHo brag mkhan chen phyag rdor ba la zhu lan sman mchog bdud rtsi'i phreng ba dang phul ba* (as in note 4), Ga 72b/4; regarding the translation, see also Kaschewsky (1971:133). According to *Bod rgya tshig mdzod chen mo*, Beijing: Mi-rigs dpe-skrun-khang, 1985, p. 765, Aṭaka / lCang-lo-can is the residence of Guhyapati (i.e. Vajrapāṇi) and Vaiśravana (*gsang bdag dang rnam sras kyi gnas*).

however, this is not the case, as becomes apparent when one has taken into consideration a further work, namely the "Secret Biography". This is likewise a document written by lHo-brag grub-chen and sent to Tsong-kha-pa, and in view of the introduction I would suggest that the "Secret Biography" should be regarded as the first written response.[10]

Although the "Secret Biography" contains a wealth of information on the person of lHo-brag grub-chen and may be regarded as an important testimony concerning the process by which Tsong-kha-pa becomes one of the most influential teachers in Tibet at the end of the 14th century, here again all reference is missing to the direct contact between the two teachers, and to the *bDud rtsi sman mchog*. From this first appraisal of the biographical material I should like to draw two conclusions: first, the text *Zhus lan sman mchog bdud rtsi'i phreng ba* was set down in the form of a letter after the actual meeting between lHo-brag grub-chen and Tsong-kha-pa (in distinction to this latter response the *gSang ba'i rnam thar log rtog mun sel* could then be posited as the first written response); secondly, that only leaves *rJe tshong kha pa mjal tshul* as a source for the description of the two teachers' encounter from the perspective of lHo-brag grub-chen. Let us therefore take a look at what this text has to say:

---

10 See *gSang ba'i rnam thar log rtog mun sel*, I. p. 172.2–6 (= II. p. 94.2–7): "Now to me, the lord Las-kyi rdo-rje, [have come] the official letter of the Dharmarāja Blo-bzang grags-pa, six bales of cloth, six bales of silk, [one] cup mounted with jewels along with a saucer filled with ounces of gold. [Questions were posed] by the dge-bshes from rTse-thang, who holds the four scriptures, 'Jam-dbyangs Kha-che [by name], and Grags-pa blo-gros, who holds the ten scriptures, for the purpose of a meeting; the points asked about [were] numerous, such as: the manner in which I, Las-kyi rdo-rje, first produced *bodhicitta,* how I thereafter (lit. in the middle) demonstrated miracles in great waves for the well-being of living creatures, and how understanding came about. Further, [questions were asked concerning] a number of predictions for the future, concerning means how the Lord Blo-bzang grags-pa himself would be able to let swell the stream of the teaching and the welfare of beings, and whether it was all right that the site for a monastery had [already] been determined. When I heard, [too,] of his deeds, [my] heart was joyed." (*de yang kho bo las kyi rdo rje bdag la / chos rje blo bzang grags pa'i bka' shog / gos chen yug drug / dar chen yug drug dang / rin po che'i phor ba gser srang gis bkang pa'i rten dang bcas pa / rtse thang pa'i dge bshes bka' bzhi 'dzin pa 'jam dbyangs kha che dang / bka' bcu 'dzin pa grags pa blo gros dpon slob rnams kyis 'phrod pa'i don la / bdag las kyi rdo rje'i dang po'i sems bskyed tshul / bar du 'gro ba'i don du rlabs che ba'i rdzu 'phrul ji ltar bstan zhing rtogs pa skye tshul / gzhan yang ma 'ongs pa'i lung bstan pa 'ga' zhig dang/ rje blo bzang grags pa rang gi yang 'gro don dang bstan pa'i rgyun 'phel ba'i thabs dang / dgon gnas gar btab na legs shes sogs kyi zhu ba'i don tshan mang du 'dug cing / khong gi mdzad tshul rnams thos pa sems spro bar gyur*).

The text itself, in its composition, deals more or less with these questions; after an extremely interesting section on the political situation in Central Tibet (I. pp. 183.2–185.6 = II. p. 102.3–104.2), lHo-brag grub-chen comes at the end of the text to talk about the general decline of morals and Buddhist teaching. In the hope of doing his part to ease this situation, he stresses, among other things, that he "esteemed particularly the lineage of the scholars of Shud-phu [and] made [at the same time] glad the Yidams and Dharmapālas of his predecessors" (*dgos shud phu'i mkhan brgyud 'di la gces / ngas bla ma gong ma rnams kyi yi dam chos skyong thams cad mnyes par byas*); I. p. 187.5 = II. p. 105.5. See also notes 4 & 11. *gSang ba'i rnam thar*, I. pp. 172.7–173.1 = II. pp. 94.6–95.2 is cited in *O rgyan sprul pa'i glegs bam*, pp. 566.5–567.2.

After that the one with the four scriptures (i.e. rJe Tsong-kha-pa) spoke first: "I have some doubts about the cycle of vision; in order to remove these I intend to go to India, to where rJe Mitra is staying on the Wood Mountain. [I want to ask you,] Will any obstacles arise or not?" Thus he spoke. When I asked the personal deity about the difficult points of the vision, [the answer came back]: "If you go to India, wonders will occur: for example, your meeting with Mitra; but as your followers are ones who are only on the great *Sambhara-marga* and the *Prayoga-marga*, obstacles will arise for the duration of [your followers'] lives, and you too will not return [to Tibet] after having stayed in India. [But] if by reason of this you apply yourself to means for being of use to the teaching here in Tibet, [this] you will accomplish. Please act accordingly." And so I caused [him] to postpone [his trip].

When afterwards I asked the personal deity about the difficult points of the vision, [the personal deity] proffered the instruction "The Best Nectar Medicine" and said: "Matibhadraśrī's doubts should be removed by this." When I asked [further]: "Who is this Matibhadraśrī?", [the personal deity] said: "Before this birth Blo-bzang grags-pa was active during seven births as a paṇḍit for the welfare of beings; also before these [births] he lived as a paṇḍita with the name of Matibhadraśrī in Kashmir, in mGrin-stan (= *Kaṇṭha-sthāna*).[11]

---

[11] See *rJe tsong kha pa mjal tshul*, I. pp. 192.6–193.3 = II. pp. 109.4–110.1: *de nas re zhig na bka' bzhi pa'i gsung nas / bdag la lta ba'i skor gyi the tshom 'ga' zhig yod pas / 'di sel ba la rgya gar shing gi ri na rje mi tra bzhugs pa'i drung du 'gro 'dod pas / de la bar chad mi 'byung lags sam gsung gin 'dug pa la / lta ba'i gnad rnams bdag gis yi dam la zhu yis / rgya gar la byon na khyed rang mi tra dang mjal ḅa sogs ngo mtshar ba 'ong na'ang / khyed kyi 'khor 'di rnams tshogs lam dang sbyor lam chen po la gnas pa sha stag 'dug pas / 'di rnams kyi tshe'i bar chad du 'gyur ba 'dug cing khyed kyang rgya gar du bzhugs nas tshur mi phebs / de bas bod phyogs 'dir bstan pa la phan pa'i thabs la 'bad na 'grub pas de bzhin mdzod 'tshal zhes zhus shing / bdag gis bshol btab bo / de nas lta ba'i gnad rnams yi dam la zhus pas / bdud rtsi sman mchog ces bya ba'i gdams pa gnang nas 'di ma ti bha dra'i the tshom sel lo gsung / ma ti bha dra shrī de gang lags zhus pas / blo bzang grags pa skye ba 'di'i gong pa paṇ ḍi ta'i skye ba bdun du sems can gyi don byas / 'di ka'i gong du'ang kha che mgrin* (I. *'grin*) *stan du paṇ ḍi ta ma ti bha dra shrī bya bar skyes gsung.*

Cf. also Dar-han mKhan-sprul: *rNam par thar pa thub bstan mdzes pa'i rgyan* (as in note 6), pp. 221–222. By contrast, the biography of Čaqar dGe-bshes Blo-bzang Tshul-khrims (1740–1810): *rJe thams cad mkhyen pa tsong kha pa chen po'i rnam thar go sla bar brjod pa bde legs kun gyi 'byung gnas* assigns two different points in time to the two prophecies. The warning with regard to the trip to India is offered during the personal meeting; the text *Zhus lan sman mchog bdud rtsi'i phreng ba* is the product of a later vision of Vajrapāṇi and is sent in the form of a letter to Tsong-kha-pa; Kaschewsky (1971), vol. 1, pp. 128 and 132 & vol. 2, V. 17r/4–17v/3 and V. 24r/4–6. This sequence of events corresponds to what is found in the *nang gi rnam thar* of lHo-brag grub-chen (as in note 9) and to the observations just made. The discrepancies between *nang gi rnam thar* and *rJe tsong kha pa mjal tshul* may perhaps be explained by the fact that the latter work is intended to provide a brief summary of the contact between the two teachers – a "smoothed-over version" of the true events, so to speak.

In the description of the second vision we find, along with the teaching "The Best Nectar Medicine", references to the person of Tsong-kha-pa in his former births. Two parts may also in fact be distinguished in the composition of the *Zhus lan sman mchog bdud rtsi phreng ba*. The first part, the actual text, is a set of instructions on the "practice of the Clear Light" (*'od gsal bsgom pa*) with detailed descriptions of "sources of error" (*gol sa*) which may arise during the "vision" (*lta ba*), "practice" (*bsgom pa*) and "conduct" (*spyod pa*). It gives the impression of being a self-contained unit defined by the structure of the dialogue between Vajrapāṇi and lHo-brag grub-chen. This structure is retained, too, in a terminating section spanning two folios; standing in the focus of attention, however, is the person of Tsong-kha-pa along with prophecies concerning his past births, future activities, founding of monasteries, the ability to perceive the personal deity, succeeding incarnations, etc. Since the "Great Perfection" (*rdzogs pa chen po*) and the "vision" (*lta ba*) are explicitly addressed in this section, I reproduce the pertinent passage in Appendix I. I shall briefly come back to one point concerning the "vision" in the concluding part of this article.

To this first brief look into the text *Zhus lan sman mchog bdud rtsi 'i phreng ba* and its background I shall not add any more material for the time being. For a more detailed investigation one would certainly have to take into account other works of lHo-brag grub-chen belonging to the genre "answer to/and questions" such as *Zhu len rdo rje 'i phreng ba* (I. pp. 721–745, II. pp. 457–474) and *Zhu len gces phreng* (I. pp. 769–809, II. pp. 491–535), both of which are works originating likewise in visions of Vajrapāṇi passed on to Tsong-kha-pa. It should be noted, however, that these works were received by lHo-brag grub-chen as teachings of the personal deity when he was already forty-nine and sixty-four years old respectively.

Here again, I can only touch briefly on the genealogy of the Shud-phu family, their connections with the rNying-ma-pa school and the bKa'-gdams-pa school, and the *Lam rim* teachings conveyed to Tsong-kha-pa.[12] With regard to the history of the text here under discussion, it is enough for the time being to note that, according to the tradition just adverted to, it was in existence, in all probability, as a letter in the southern Tibetan province of lHo-brag in the year 1396.

Our text appears in a slightly different light when compared with a work from the *mKha' 'gro snying thig*. In this *gter ma* cycle originating from Padma Las-'brel-rtsal (1291–1316) is found in a text, in fact, which upon closer inspection might be taken for a copy of the letter from lHo-brag grub-chen. The only difference is the introductory part and the section with the prophecies at the end; the main section, however, the account of

[12] Here I shall attempt to provide merely a preliminary survey of the genealogy of the "scholars of Shud-phu", according to *Phyi 'i rnam thar bdud rtsi 'i phreng ba*, II. pp. 2.5–14.5. It commences with Shud-phu Mes-tshab in the 10th generation after Shud-phu dPal-gyi seng-ge, Padmasambhava's disciple. Those persons for whom information is available concerning their relationship to the rNying-ma-pa and bKa'-gdams-pa school are identified by a, b and c:

the "sources of error" (*gos sa*), agrees word for word with "The Best Nectar Medicine". The title of this text from the *mKha' 'gro snying thig* is: "The Golden Chain of Nectar [in] Questions and Answers" (*Zhu len bdud rtsi gser phreng*). Once again dialogue is the dominant formal element, though the interlocutors are no longer Vajrapāṇi and lHo-brag grub-chen but Padmasambhava and Ye-shes mtsho-rgyal. The introductory folios show depictions of Padmasambhava's five main partners (Ye-shes mtsho-rgyal, Mandarava, Kala-Siddhi, Śākyadevi and bKra-shis khyi-'dren).[13]

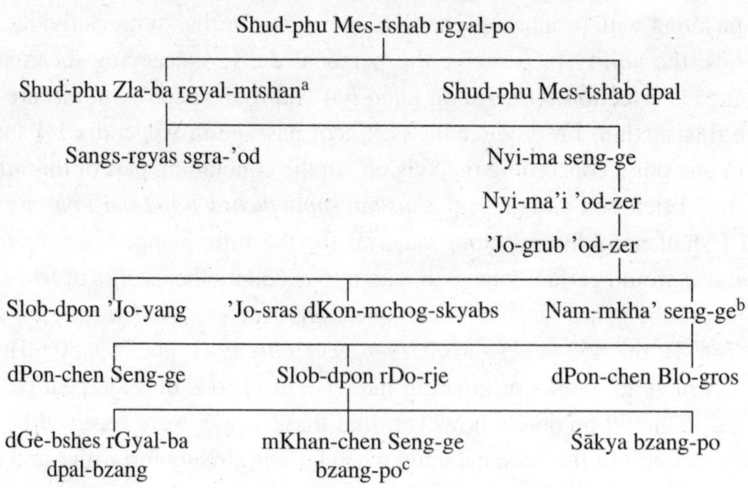

a: "He was very well versed in the teachings of the Old Ones and attained to perfection in the [sādhana of] Yamarāja's black-red executioner" (*rnying ma'i chos shin tu mkhas shing / gshin rje gshed dmar nag gi grub pa thob*). Founder of Thig-phyi Monastery.

b: "From his time onwards the proclamation of the precious bKa'-gdams-pa [teaching] had its beginnning" (*khong gi ring nas bka' gdams rin po che'i bka' srol btsugs pa yin*).

c: "He was versed above all in the teaching of the Old Ones, but he greatly revered and praised the *Vinaya* in accordance with the words: 'Precisely for [a teaching like] that [of the] bKa'-gdams-pa, the least injury is a [great] danger'" (*khyad par rnying ma'i chos la mkhas kyang / bka' gdams pa'i dang tshugs la cung gnod nyen 'dug gsung nas / 'dul ba la bsnyen bsngags cher mdzad pa yin*).

mKhan-chen rGyal-sras bzang-po (1292–1358), the incarnation of dGe-bshes rGyal-ba dpal-bzang, belongs to the next generation; he is the uncle of lHo-brag grub-chen and his first teacher. For his part, mKhan-chen rGyal-sras bzang-po studied under mKhan-chen mTsho-sna-pa and mKhan-chen Mon-gra-pa (see *Phyi 'i rnam thar bdud rtsi phreng ba*, pp. 13.2 and 14.1). The *Lam rim* teachings of mTsho-sna-pa play a great role in Tsong-kha-pa's biography; in this connection, see, for example, Dar-han mKhan-sprul: *rNam par thar pa thub bstan mdzes pa'i rgyan* (as in note 6), pp. 230ff. (*lam sgron gyi 'grel pa mtsho sna pa'i lam rim*). Tsong-kha-pa himself is regarded as the incarnation of mTsho-sna-pa; cf. ibid, pp. 44–48. On mTsho-sna, the administrative capital of Mon-yul, south-east of lHo-brag, see Aris (1979b:135).

13 See *Zhus len bdud rtsi gser phreng* in *mKha' 'gro snying thig*, vol. 2, pp. 1–34 (= *sNying thig ya bzhi*, vol. 5, New Delhi 1971); the part which is identical to the text in *Zhus len bdud rtsi sman mchog* is found on pp. 3.3–30.1. The scene of the dialogue between Padmasambhava and Ye-shes mtsho-rgyal, according

A new history of the text, in other words, this time not with Tsong-kha-pa and the prophecies addressed to him in the middle of things; rather, one's attention is focused on Klong-chen rab-'byams-pa (1308–1364) and on the generations of disciples following him. In order to be able to follow this change of perspective, I shall first refer briefly to possible connections between lHo-brag grub-chen and the tradition deriving from Klong-chen rab-'byams-pa; then, with equal brevity, I shall take up *Zhus len bdud rtsi gser phreng* and the persons mentioned in it.

In a historical work of the 19th century we learn that one of the main three lineages of Klong-chen rab-'byams-pa's teachings passed through his disciple Bya-bral bKra-shis 'byung-gnas. A disciple of the latter, further, is a certain Gu-ru gZhan-phan; concerning him it is said that he is "one of the eight disciples who were prophesied to lHo-brag grub-chen by the personal deity" (*lho brag phyag rdor pa la yi dam gyi lung bstan pa'i slob ma brgyad gyi gcig yin*).[14] Without wishing to overplay this connection, I would nevertheless like to point out that there did exist direct contact between the person of lHo-brag grub-chen and the tradition deriving from Klong-chen rab-'byams-pa. Since the teachings of *mKha' 'gro snying thig* enjoyed great popularity in the 14th century, I regard it as quite possible that they were also taken up by lHo-brag grub-chen and, on the basis of the new visionary form he gave them, were spread abroad still further. Though the reception of the text might also have occurred in the opposite direction (i.e. from lHo-brag grub-chen to the disciples of Klong-chen rab-'byams-pa), a passage of a work referring to the Third Karma-pa Rang-byung rdo-rje (1284–1334) (see note 15) provides adequate reason for believing

to the introduction (p. 31), is gZho-stod Ti-sgro, a side valley west of 'Bri-gung mthil; there the two give themselves over to the practice of *sNying thig*: "During the time we were practicing [the teaching of *sNying thig*] at the rock of gZho-stod Ti-sgro, I became familiar with the reality of *sNying thig*, the Great Perfection [in the form of the] most secret, insurpassble [cycle]. Great wonder arose at my having determined the true state of things directly by the vision, without losing myself in intellectual analysis." (*gzho stod ti sgro brag la sgrub pa mdzad pa'i dus su / yang gsang bla na med pa rdzogs pa chen po snying thig gi don ngo 'phrod / gnas lugs yid dpyod du ma lus par mngon sum du lta bas thag chod nas de la ngo mtshar skyes te*). These are the words of Ye-shes mtsho-rgyal. For another list of the five female partners of Padmasambhava, cf. Aris (1979b:298); Ye-shes mtsho-rgyal is there replaced by a second female from Bhutan.

14 See sTag-sgang mkhas-mchog Ngag-dbang blo-gros, Gu-ru bkra-shis: *bsTan pa'i snying po gsang chen snga 'gyur nges don zab mo'i chos kyi 'byung ba gsal bar byed pa'i legs bshad mkhas pa dga' byed ngo mtshar gtam gyi rol mtsho*, vol. II, Delhi: Lama Ngodrup and Sherab Drimed, 1986, p. 64.4. This lineage continues on further in the son of Gu-ru gZhan-phan, Nam-mkha' rdo-rje (ibid, p. 65.1–6), and in the latter's son 'Od-gsal Klong-yangs (ibid, pp. 65.5–67.2). Both Gu-ru gZhan-phan and Nam-mkha' rdo-rje are at the same time masters of the sādhana of Vajrapāṇi and see the personal deity face to face; when the latter accurs, the special vision of Vajrapāṇi is designated as *gTum po khyung lnga*. One also comes across this form, under the name *Phyag na rdo rje khyung lnga*, in the teachings of lHo-brag grub-chen; see, for example, *Phyi'i rnam thar bdud rtsi'i phreng ba*, I. p. 7.2 and passim. The lineage of the teachings of Klong-chen rab-'byams-pa passing through the persons just mentioned is distinguished by reasons of its fame and excellence (*yongs su grags pa'i brgyud tshul khyad par 'phags pa*); *sNga 'gyur chos 'byung*, vol. II, p. 62.6.

that the writing of *bDud rtsi gser 'phreng* took place before the composition of *bDud rtsi sman mchog*.

Let us now take a look at the persons that *Zhus len bdud rtsi gser 'phreng* mentions directly. For this purpose, we must consult the closing section of the text, which, like the letter addressed to Tsong-kha-pa, contains prophecies. These prophecies likewise feature in the work *Lo rgyus rgyal ba g.yung gis mdzad pa*, a text dealing with the history of *mKha' 'gro snying thig*, ascribed to g.Yung-ston-pa (1284–1365).[15] Let us first let the text speak itself:

> Once he has this birth behind him, he will wander around for a while in the *Saṃbhogakāya* realm. After that he will be born [again] in Bum-thang [in the monastery of] Thar-pa-gling. Once fifteen years have passed, he will work for the welfare of beings. He will open numerous treasure gates; he will display works of wonder unheard of... A son, Sras Zla-ba grags-pa [by name], an incarnation of Hayagrīva, will be born to him. He, too, will work for the welfare of beings [and] for ninety years guard the teaching.

With the aid of the 19th-century historical work mentioned previously we can place this statement in relation to a person from the 14th century:

---

15 See *Lo rgyus rgyal ba g.yung gis mdzad pa* in *mKha' 'gro snying thig*, vol. 3. pp. 409.1–411.3 (= *sNying thig ya bzhi,* vol. 6, New Delhi, 1971). This works contains, furthermore, a comprehensive list of the individual texts of this *gter ma* cycle; among these texts is the work *bDud rtsi gser phreng*. It is characterised in the following words: "Answers to the questions of the Ḍākinī: in order to remove sources of error and doubts, Ye-shes mtsho-rgyal requested [this instruction] from the ācārya [Padmasambhava] and set it down in the form of a written [document]." (*mkha' 'gro zhus len ni gol sa dang the tshom bcad pa'i phyir mtsho rgyal gyis slob dpon la zhus nas yi ger btab pa*); ibid, p. 414.1. This may mean that, also in the tradition of the *mKha' 'gro snying thig*, this text originally existed in the form of a letter. Or must one draw the conclusion from the formulation of the text that lHo-brag grub-chen's letter got into the collection of the *mKha' 'gro snying thig* and only afterwards was promulgated as *gter ma*?

Going against this latter assumption, however, is a further passage from *Lo rgyus rgyal ba g.yung gis mdzad pa* (pp. 415.6–416.1); here the work *mKha' 'gro zhus len* is once again mentioned, in connection with the person of the Third Karma-pa Rang-byung rdo-rje. He is regarded as one of the "master of the teachings" (*chos bdag*) of the *gter ma* of Padma Las-'brel-rtsal, and to all appearences the codification of the *mKha' 'gro zhus len* is due to him or one of his scribes. This story, however, belongs in a future chronicling of the "treasure discoverers" of the *mKha' 'gro snying thig* and cannot be recounted here. Herewith merely the details concerning the original form of the text: "On the three-finger width of the golden written scroll [of the work] "Answers [to] Questions of the Ḍākinī" [was found] a [portion of text] set down in exactly twenty-two lines. On account of the faith of others, it was taken by the Dharmarāja (i.e. Rang-byung rdo-rje), and [thus the treasure work] appeared. If some people blinded by illusion are afraid of the thought that "Tampering with an untouched treasure work will be punished", [we answer:] What Ācārya Padma[sambhava] has set down has been explained [only] in this way. [For] by seeing the golden written scroll, one comes in contact with the body of Ācārya Padma[sambhava]; by meeting up

> rGyal-sras sprul-sku Grags-pa 'od-zer: in *mKha' 'gro snying thig gi zhu lan gser phreng* [it is said of him:] the next [re]birth of Las-'brel-rtsal will wander about in the *Saṃbhogakāya* realm for a while. After that he will be [re]born in Bum-thang [in the monastery of] Thar-pa-gling. Once fifteen years have passed, he will work for the welfare of beings. [A son] will be born to him, an incarnation of Hayagrīva, Sras Zla-ba grags-pa by name. He, too, will work for the welfare of beings.[16]

In Grags-pa 'od-zer (1356–1409), according to the sources used here the incarnation and at the same time son of Klong-chen rab-'byams-pa, we have, therefore, the first linking evidence for the persons mentioned in the prophecies of "The Golden Chain of Nectar." Without great problem, as he his named by name, we can get our hold on a second actor: rGyal-sras Zla-ba grags-pa. He is taken to be the younger of two sons of Grags-pa 'od-zer, and was born like the latter in Bhutan. As the prophecies in the text of *mKha' 'gro snying thig* pertain to both of these persons, father and son, we can probably assume that they were not of inconsiderable significance for the first generation of those who represented

---

with the symbol (i.e. language), one comes in contact with his speech; by meeting up with the purport, one comes in contact with his heart." (*mkha' 'gro zhus len gyi shog ser rtse sor gsum la yig phreng nyi shu rtsa gnyis te byas pa cig gzhan yid ches pa'i phyir chos rjes pas bsnams nas byon no / rmongs pa la la dag gter ma la dbang bka' chad par 'gyur ro snyam du dogs na / slob dpon padma bzhed pa 'di ltar gsungs so / shog ser mthong bas slob dpon padma'i sku dang mjal / brda' 'phrad pas gsung dang mjal / don 'phrad pas thugs dang mjal lo*).

16 See *Zhus len bdud rtsi gser phreng* (as in note 13), p. 32.3–6: *skye ba de 'das nas / longs sku'i zhing khams der gcig nyul / de nas bum thang thar pa gling du skyes / lo bco lnga nas 'gro don byed / gter sgo mang bar 'byed rdzu 'phrul ya ma zung ston / ... / sras zla ba grags pa bya ba rta mgrin gyi sprul pa gcig khrungs / des kyang 'gro don byas / bstan pa mi lo dgu bcu skyong...*; and *sNga 'gyur chos 'byung* (as in note 14), vol. II, p. 79.4–6: *rgyal sras sprul sku grags pa 'od zer ni / mkha' 'gro snying thig gi zhu len gser phreng du / las 'brel rtsal gyi skye ba phyi ma / longs sku'i zhing der gcig nyul / de nas bum thang thar pa gling du skye / lo bco lnga nas 'gro ba'i don byed / sras zla grags pa zhes bya rta mgrin gyi sprul pa zhig 'byung / des kyang 'gro don byed*. It is further stated that the "next rebirth of Padma Las-'brel-rtsal" is Klong-chen rab-'byams-pa; Grags-pa 'od-zer, however, is not only the reincarnation of Klong-chen rab-'byams-pa but also his son: "The Dharmarāja, the great All-knowing One wandered around in the *Saṃbhogakāya* realm ... and then rose forth from out of this [dimension] in the fashion of a son, an incarnation, who schools living beings" (*chos rje kun mkhyen chen po nyid ... longs sku'i zhing nyul ba dang / de las 'gro ba 'dul ba'i sprul pa'i sku sras kyi tshul du shar ba ste*; ibid, pp. 79.6–80.1. According to mKhas-btsun bzang-po (1973, vol. III, pp. 558–559), the dates of Grags-pa 'od-zer are 1356–1409; this information is based on *Zhe chen chos 'byung* by the Second Zhe-chen rgyal-tshab, Padma-rnam-rgyal (1871–1926). It in turn is based on the work just cited, *sNga 'gyur chos 'byung*, by Gu-ru bKra-shis (19th century); see also Tulku Thondub (1984:75–76). Aris (1979b:155) gives 1416 for the year of birth, one *rab 'byung* later, in other words. One should be aware that these prophecies at the end of *Zhus len bdud rtsi gser phreng* are open to different interpretations; the one propounded here is the generally accepted one. An interesting parallel to these prophecies can be found in the 90th chapter of the *Padma bka' thang*: *O rgyan gu ru padma 'byung gnas kyi skye rabs rnam par thar pa rgyas par bkod pa padma bka'i thang yig*, Delhi: Sherab Gyaltsen Lama & Acharya Shedup Tenzin, 1985, pp. 556.1–557.5.

the *sNying thig* teachings in Bhutan; it is through these persons, too, that the second main lineage of Klong-chen rab-'byams-pa's teaching passes. Concerning rGyal-sras Zla-ba grags-pa we know, furthermore, that among his teachers was numbered Tsong-kha-pa Blo-bzang grags-pa'i dpal.[17]

In the text as it is given to us in the collection of the *mKha' 'gro snying thig* we have, in the concluding section, i.e. the prophecies, a document that one could interpret as an attempt to establish the teaching of Klong-chen rab-'byams-pa at the end of the 14th and the beginning of the 15th century along lines of its own. In lHo-brag grub-chen's prophecies to Tsong-kha-pa the same tendency is observable: authoritative statements concerning the founding of a new tradition. In both prophecies the operative element is the principle of incarnation, overlaid or boosted in the "old" school, however, by the stress placed on family tradition, the handling on from father to son.

In this thumbnail sketch that the text "The Best Nectar Medicine"/"The Golden Chain of Nectar" provides us, we thus see in the southern Tibetan province of lHo-brag and in the valley of Bum-thang in Mon at the transition from the 14th to the 15th century the formation of two spiritual movements: the reformation undertaken by Tsong-kha-pa, spreading out over Central Tibet, and the diffusion and further development of the teachings of Klong-chen rab-'byams-pa in Bhutan. The point at which these two movements crossed – in a way that we can retrace – was a set of instructions on the "practice of Clear Light" and the person of lHo-brag grub-chen. The capacity of the teachings associated with him to be integrated and further developed in a fruitful manner was not, however, restricted to this point of time; it is similarly evidenced for the beginning of the 18th century,[18] as well as in the northeastern province of Amdo during the time of Tshogs-drug rang-grol.

---

[17] Regarding the biography of Zla-ba grags-pa, see *sNga 'gyur chos 'byung* (as in note 14), vol. II, pp. 96.5–101.5, and mKhas-btsun bzang-po (as in note 16), pp. 573–575. He hears the teachings of the "Great Perfection" from his father and is ordained as a monk at the age of 12. His name is associated above all with the monastery of bSam-gtan gling. Like Thar-pa-gling, it is held to be one of the eight monasteries founded by Klong-chen rab-'byams-pa in Bhutan. Tulku Thondub (as in note 16), p. 202 draws attention to problems in identifying the son of Klong-chen rab-'byams-pa: "In some texts Grags-pa 'od-zer is the son of Kun-mkhyen and Zla-ba grags-pa is the son of Grags-pa 'od-zer. But other texts say that *Zla-ba*, an incarnation of rTa-mgrin, is the son of Kun-mkhyen." This latter opinion is reported in Aris (1979b:155); and in Aris (1988:30). He refers nevertheless to the first version, without giving an explanation for this contradiction.

[18] I am thinking here of Sle-lung bZhad-pa'i rdo-rje (born 1697), the fifth incarnation of lHo-brag grub-chen; concerning his life, see mKhas-btsun bzang-po (as in note 16), vol. IV, pp. 362–363. His collected works are available in 14 volumes: Leh: Tashigangpa, 1983 ff. Therein are found both commentaries to works of lHo-brag grub-chen, such as *rDo rje gces phreng, gSang ba bsam gyis mi khyab pa*, and *gSang ba bdud rtsi thig pa* (vol. 2, pp. 401–429; vol. 5, pp. 345–369, and ibid, pp. 423–442; vol. 6, pp. 363–366), and to the *mKha' 'gro snying thig* (vol.13, pp. 94–467); the latter text refers to *Rin chen dbang gi phreng ba* in *mKha' 'gro snying thig*, vol. 1, pp. 121–226 (= *sNying thig ya bzhi,* vol. 4, New Delhi 1971).

With that we have come around full circle to the starting point, and in closing I would like to briefly discuss the section of the text that is relevant for the question concerning the *lta ba*. The true vision of "emptiness" (*stong pa nyid*), also called the "direct vision" (*mngon sum lta ba*), is set off from "the vision of the demon Black Bag of Hot Air" (*nag po kha 'byams bdud kyi lta ba*). In Appendix II I reproduce the pertinent passages from both texts; they concern in this case the "sources of error of the vision as such" (*lta ba nyid kyi gol sa*). The pertinent section ends with the relation between "vision" (*lta ba*) and "conduct" (*spyod pa*), i.e. the ethical-social consequence of such a direct experience of emptiness.

As a further facet of the history of our text, a connection may be established between this topic and Padmasambhava's final instruction to his Tibetan disciples. The popular version of this episode doubtless goes back to the account of Padmasambhava's leave-taking in the *sBa bzhed*. Among authors of the 19th and 20th centuries one notes that the expression *nag po kha 'byams bdud kyi lta ba* is used in their recounting of the instructions given on that occasion, a phrase that is not found in the *sBa bzhed*. One reads, for example, in a work of Bod-pa sprul-sku, a disciple of Mi-pham rgya-mtsho (1846–1912):

> When the great O-rgyan[-pa] set out to the country of the *rākṣasa*s, he spoke: "Great king, never let the [category of] conduct fall with respect to the category of vision, and the [category of] vision with respect to that of conduct." And [he spoke further:] "If [once] the [category of] conduct is allowed to fall with respect to the category of vision, there is the danger that the "vision of the demon Black Bag of Hot Air" will occur, in which case no distinction is made [any longer] between good and bad; and if [once] vision is allowed to fall with respect to the category of conduct, in which case one is tied down to an "[individual] characteristic feature in things" (*bhāvalakṣana*), there is no opportunity [any longer] for being set free.[19]

---

[19] See *Kun mkhyen bla ma'i zhal lung sangs rgyas lag 'chang* in "Collected Texts of the rNying-ma-pa rDzogs-chen tradition", Gangtok/Delhi: Pema Thinley, 1985, p. 326.2–4: *o rgyan chen po srin yul du byon khar / rgyal po chen po lta ba'i phyogs su spyod pa mi shor ba dang / spyod pa'i phyogs su lta ba mi shor bar mdzod / ces dang / lta ba'i phyogs su spyod pa shor na dge sdig stong nag po kha 'byams bdud kyi lta ba 'byung nyen dang spyod pa'i phyogs lta ba shor na dngos po dang mtshan mas bcings nas grol ba'i dus med pa gsungs* ... Likewise in mKhan-po Ngag-dbang dpal-bzang (1879–1941): *Khregs chod kyi zin bris chu bo'i bcud 'dus*, Mysore/Delhi: Pema Norbu & Dilgo Chentse, 1985, p. 69.1–2. Concerning the version of the *sBa bzhed*, see the edition of Stein (1961:25.16–26.7); this final instruction of Padmasambhava follows the exposition of *Man ngag lta ba'i phreng ba*. For a translation of this passage, see Karmay (1988b:143–144).

I reproduce the pertinent passage here according to *Sangs rgyas bstan pa'i chos 'byung dris lan nor bu'i phreng ba* of 'Dul-'dzin mKhyen-rab rgya-mtsho (ed. Chentse Labrang), pp. 196.6–197.4: *ji skad du bsam yas su lhos sbad bzhed las / sngags kyi mkhan po padma 'byung gnas kyi brag dmar 'om bu'i tshal du / btsad po rje 'bangs nyi shu rtsa gcig la man ngag lta phreng bshad nas / rgyal po chen po nga'i gsang*

From this last quotation we may infer that the influence of the text "The Best Nectar Medicine" / "The Golden Chain of Nectar" endured without let-up into the 20th century. The details surrounding the "vision of the great perfection" obviously enjoyed such great popularity that they could be identified with Padmasambhava's final instruction with no problem at all. With this observation I will let the retracing of a text and its histories come to rest – a text that was of significance for Tibetans not on account of its history (or histories) but on account of the spiritual practice associated with it.

APPENDIX I

Zhus len sman mchog bdud rtsi 'phreng ba

I. (ed. 1972)	II. (ed. 1985)
lhag mthong rnam dag gi myong ba skye bar byed pa la / bla ma lhag mthong rnam dag skye ba cig la rten dgos / lhag mthong rnam dag mi skye na / nga'i gsang tshig du ltos / gol sa rnams gcod dgos pa lags so / zhi gnas med pa la lta ba'i go yul lhag mthong gi zin pa / 'dod pa rnams ni rgyal ba rnams kyis ma gsungs so / de lta bu mi 'byung gsung / lhag mthong gi myong thon pa'i skabs khyad par can gsang sngags kyi gdams pa thun mong ma yin pa sbyor drug dang rdzogs chen yin gsung / (pp. 918.7–919.2)	*lhag mthong rnam dag gi myong ba skye bar byed pa la / bla ma lhag mthong rnam dag skye ba cig la rten dgos / lhag mthong rnam dag mi skye na / nga'i gsang tshig du ltos / gol sa rnams gcod dgos pa lags so / zhi gnas med pa la lta ba'i go yul lhag mthong gi zin pa 'dod pa rnams ni rgyal ba rnams kyis ma gsungs so / de lta bu mi 'byung gsung / lhag mthong gi myong ba thon pa'i skabs khyad par can gsang sngags kyi gdams pa thun mong ma yin pa sbyor drug dang rdzogs chen yin gsung /* (pp. 595.2–4)
	las kyi rdo rjes zhus pa / rdzogs pa chen po 'di lta ba rnam dag lags sam / zhes gsol pas / gsang bdag gi gsung nas / rdzogs pa chen po yang lta ba mthon po yin mod /
lta ba'i phyogs la klu sgrub dang zla grags kyi bkral ba zhing / 'khrul med yin / de la ma brten pa'i lhag mthong skye ba mi srid gsung / (pp. 919.5–6)	*lta ba'i phyogs la klu sgrub dang zla grags kyi bkral ba 'di / 'khrul med yin / de la ma rten pa'i lhag mthong mtshan nyid pa skye mi srid gsung /* (pp. 595.6–7)

---

sngags 'di lta ba chos kyi sku la bstun las / spyod par byang chub kyi phyogs dang bstun cig / lta ba'i phyogs su spyod pa ma shor bar mdzod / shor na dge sdig med du song / chad lta skyes nas phyis gsor mi rung / spyod pa'i rjes su lta ba 'brangs na dngos po'i mtshan mas bcings nas grol bar mi 'gyur. In my translation I have given precedence to the reading *dngos po'i mtshan ma* over *dngos po dang mtshan ma* (the breaking up of the compound *bhāvalakṣana*).

Appendix II

Zhus len sman mchog bdud rtsi 'phreng ba
(I. pp. 904.5–905.3; II. pp. 585.4–7)

dang po lta ba nyid kyi gol sa ni / chos spyi'i lta ba stong pa mtha' bral du 'dod pa las / gsang sngags 'di'i lugs kyi rnal 'byor pa mngon sum[1] *rjen par 'dod / de gnyis yang don dam pa rtogs na dbye ba med ste / ma rtogs na spyi'i lta ba ni / yid spyod kyi tshig gi lta ba la don rang thog tu mi 'bebs te / gol ba'i lta ba yin / mngon sum gyi lta ba la yid ma ches par yid spyod tshig gi lta ba la gdeng du byas nas /*[2] *thams cad gtad med yin / byar med mtha' bral yin zer nas /*[3] *dge sdig chos la 'jol*[4] *nyog tu spyod cing / las la bzang ngan med / dge ba byas pas phan ma brtags / sdig pa byas pa gnod ma skyal / thams cad mnyam nyid zang thal yin zer nas tha mal nyid du sdod de / de rnams nag po kha 'byams kyi lta ba ces bya ste / lta ba thams cad kyi gol ba'i rtsa ba yin / ma ti bha dra shrīs mngon sum gnyis med rang gsal gyi lta ba dang rgyu 'bras zab mo gzung 'jug du spyod gsung /*

I. 1. *sngon sum*; 2. II. omit; 3. II. add; 4. II. *jol*

Zhus len bdud rtsi gser phreng
(ed. 1971, pp. 9.2–10.2)

dang po lta ba nyid kyi gol sa ni / chos spyi'i lta ba stong pa mtha' bral du 'dod pa las / 'dir snying thig gi rnal 'byor pa mngon sum rjen par 'dod / de gnyis yang dag don dam par rtogs na dbye ma med do / ma rtogs na spyi'i lta ba yid spyod tshig gi lta bas don rang thog tu mi phab ste gol sa'i rtsa ba'i lta ba yin / mngon sum gyi lta ba la yid ma ches par yid spyod tshig gi lta ba don dam du byas nas thams cad gtad med yin byar med yin / mtha' bral yin zer nas dge sdig thams cad 'chol nyog tu spyod cing las la bzang ngan med / dge ba byas pas phan ma btags / sdig pa byas pas gdod ma bskyal thams cad mnyam nyid zang thal yin zer nas tha mal ltar sdod de / de ni nag po kha 'byams bdud kyi lta ba zhes bya lta / lta ba thams cad kyi gol sa'i rtsa ba yin / mtsho rgyal der ma gol bar 'dod na / mngon sum gnyis med rang gsal gyi lta ba dang / rgyu 'bras zab mo zung 'jug du spyod pa gal che gsungs /

II.
The Svayambhūnāth Stūpa

A Renovation of Svayambhūnāth Stūpa in the 18th Century and its History
(According to Tibetan Sources)

If one climbs the steep stone steps situated in the East up to the *stūpa* of Svayambhūnāth and starts walking around the *stūpa* in the prescribed direction, one comes upon the Tibetan monastery known under the name Drugpa Kagyu Gompa. Opposite the stairs leading to the shrine room in the first floor, next to the entrance into the Mūrtisaṃgrālaya Museum, there stands a man-sized stone covered with an inscription in Newari and Tibetan. As early as 1877 a first translation of the Newari text was available, rendered according to the text of a "Buddhist chronicle" (*vaṃśāvalī*),[1] and the Tibetan portion has been translated into Nepali.[2] This inscription describes one renovation of Svayambhūnāth Stūpa extending over a period of eight years, namely from 1751 to 1758.

Rather than going into the details of the actual inscription, such as the list of materials used during the renovation work, or the exact account of the start and end of construction, I should like in the following to restrict myself to taking a closer look at the renovation's background. This is done with the intention of placing the person of Rig-'dzin Tshe-dbang nor-bu (1698–1755), a teacher of the rNying-ma-pa school from Kaḥ-thog in Khams (East Tibet), more in the centre of the account. In my opinion too little attention has been devoted hitherto to him and to his role during the renovation.

That special significance should be attached to Rig-'dzin Tshe-dbang nor-bu in the context of the renovation may be inferred from the inscription's first lines:

> Om svasti! I bow down to all Buddhas and Bodhisattvas. In all times and in all forms I bow down to the spotless lotus feet of the glorious teacher, the excellent rDo-rje Tshe-dbang nor-bu, and take refuge in him.[3]

---

1 See Wright (1877=1966:155–157). The rendering of the "longue inscription bilingue" in Levi (1905=1985/6:5–6) is based on this translation.

2 See Dhungel (1988:4–11).

3 *om svasti / sangs rgyas dang byang / chub sems dpa' thams cad la phyag 'tshal lo / dpal ldan bla ma dam pa rdo rje tshe dbang nor bu'i zhabs kyi padmo dri ma med pa la dus dang rnam pa thams cad du phyag 'tshal zhing skyabs su mchi'o.*

Following a laudation of the *stūpa* the next lines of the inscription speak of the necessity of the planned renovation; in doing so they attach the following honorary titles to Rig-'dzin Tshe-dbang nor-bu:

> Head ornament among all scholars and siddhas, knowledge holder (*vidyādhara*), ruler over all worlds (*cakravartin*), noble rDo-rje Tshe-dbang nor-bu.[4]

Who is then this teacher from the first half of the 18th century and what information do we have about him? In an article from the year 1967 Hugh E. Richardson makes the following remarks concerning the person of Rig-'dzin Tshe-dbang nor-bu:

> Tshe-dbang nor-bu was born in 1698 in the Sa-ngan region of East Tibet and was soon recognized as the reincarnation of one Grub-dbang Padma nor-bu who carried on the spiritual line of gNubs Nam-mkha'i snying-po, a teacher at the time of Khri Srong-lde-btsan .... Tshe-dbang nor-bu studied with the leading rNying-ma-pa teachers and also with those of the Karmapa with whom Kaḥ-thog had a close connection. Among the skills he developed was that of *gter ston*, discoverer of religious texts and objects believed to have been concealed in the remote past. He travelled widely and his activities included the founding or repairing of monasteries in Western Tibet and in Sikkim, and the repair of *mchod rten* (*stūpas*) in Nepal. He was greatly revered by Pho-lha-nas sTobs-rgyas, the ruler of Tibet; and in 1751/52 when trouble arose between the princes of upper and lower Ladakh and there was danger of interference by the Dsungar masters of Kashgaria, Pho-lha and the Seventh Dalai Lama commissioned him to restore peace .... From Ladakh he went to Nepal and not long after, in about 1755, he died at sKyid-grong where is a *mchod rten* containing his relics.[5]

In the meantime the collected writings of the "Tibetan Antiquarian" have become available to us:

1. *Selected Writings of Kaḥ-thog Rig-'dzin Tshe-dbang nor-bu*, 4 vols., Darjeeling, W. B. 1973–1982 and
2. *Collected Works of Kaḥ-thog Rig-'dzin Tshe-dbang nor-bu*, 6 vols., Dalhousie, 1977.

---

4 *mkhas pa dang grub pa thams cad kyi gtsug rgyan du 'gyur pa rig pa 'dzin pa yongs kyi 'khor lo bsgyur ba'i dbang phyug dpal rdo rje tshe dbang nor bu.*

5 See Richardson (1967:8). Biographical material relating to Rig-'dzin Tshe-dbang nor-bu was at the same time drawn upon in Stein (1966:286–287).

For present purposes I shall refer principally to the detailed biography of Rig-'dzin Tshe-dbang nor-bu in vol. 1 of the *Collected Works*,[6] as well as to supplementary material from vol. 1 of the *Selected Writings*. I shall proceed by introducing individual episodes from the biography in order to follow the course of events leading to the renovation of Svayambhūnāth.

Towards the end of the year 1726, Rig-'dzin Tshe-dbang nor-bu for the first time spent some time in the Kathmandu valley; he arrived via Ding-ri and gNya'-nang. But after visiting the two *stūpa*s of Svayambhūnāth and Bodhnāth, as well as other pilgrimage sites such as Yang-le-shod (= Pharphing), he soon left the valley, via the north-western route. Thus we find him in the year 1727 in sKyid-grong, where he visits the famous Avalokiteśvara statue 'Phags-pa Wa-ti[7] and goes about his spiritual practices at the "six forts" *(rdzong drug)* and "three caves" (*phug gsum*) of the yogin Mi-la-ras-pa (1040–1123), (*Biography*, pp. 119–128).

The first reference to activities undertaken by Rig-'dzin Tshe-dbang nor-bu in connection with repairs to a *stūpa* in Nepal can be dated to the beginning of the year 1728. It is at this point in time that he receives from South Tibet, i.e. from the province of gTsang the summons to bring the repair activities at the *stūpa* of Bodhnāth to their conclusion with a "consecration ceremony" (*rab gnas*). This summons comes from bSod-nams stobs-rgyas from Pho-lha (1689–1747), the ruler (or "king") of Tibet, whose reign falls in the years 1728 to 1747. We are lucky to have a detailed study by L. Petech of the political role played by Pho-lha-ba bSod-nams stobs-rgyas and the power struggles in Tibet during the first half of the 18th century and we are therefore in a position to identify the motive for this renovation of Bodhnāth Stūpa: before his battle campaign in Central Tibet, which led to the ending of the Tibetan civil war of 1727–1728 and to his establishing himself as the ruler of Tibet, Pho-lha-ba bSod-nams stobs-rgyas has the *stūpa* of Bodhnāth given a face lifting in order to conjure a happy end to his plans.[8] Thus Rig-'dzin Tshe-dbang nor-bu,

6 *dPal rig 'dzin chen po rdo rje tshe dbang nor bu'i zhabs kyi[s] rnam par thar pa'i cha shas brjod pa ngo mtshar dad pa'i rol mtsho*, 187 fols., in *Collected Works*, vol 1, pp. 1–376. The author of this biography, which was completed in the year 1819, is Brag-dkar rta-so sprul-sku Chos-kyi dbang-phyug (1775–1837), who via his teacher Karma 'Phrin-las bdud-'joms (1726–1789) is in the lineage of Rig-'dzin Tshe-dbang nor-bu (Abbr.: *Biography*).

7 Four such Avalokiteśvara statues are generally distinguished; on the tradition of these statues and their connection with Nepal, see Wylie (1970:14–16, note 20), Dowman (1981:233–235, and Locke (1980:352ff.).

8 See Petech (1972:122): "Pho-lha-nas was marching back to gTsang ...... He encamped at Lu-ma-dgo-dmar, where he decided, as an auspicious deed of propitiation for victory, to restore the decayed *stūpa* of Bya-rung kha-shor in Nepal. He issued orders that the revenue of Khyung-rdzong dkar-po, sKyid-grong and Sa-dga' be set aside for this purpose, and deputed two officials for the task, which was to be finished by the 11th month of the same year."

then only thirty years old, already commanded enough spiritual authority to be entrusted with the concluding act of the renovation (*Biography*, pp. 127–129).

This is not, however, Rig-'dzin Tshe-dbang nor-bu's final contact with Pho-lha-ba bSod-nams stobs-rgyas and the *stūpa* of Bodhnāth. In the year 1747, shortly before the death of Tibet's ruler, we find him, now barely fifty, in Pho-lha-ba's presence in lHa-sa. Also taking part in the rituals that Rig-'dzin Tshe-dbang nor-bu carries out on Pho-lha-ba are the Eighth Si-tu Rin-po-che Chos-kyi 'byung-gnas (1700–1774) and the Seventh dPa'-bo Rin-po-che dPa'-bo gTsug-lag dga'-ba (died 1781). The Seventh 'Brug-chen Rin-po-che bKa'-brgyud 'Phrin-las shing-rta (1718–1766) is also mentioned (*Biography*, pp. 196–198). Shortly thereafter, Rig-'dzin Tshe-dbang nor-bu again sets off towards Nepal, with the purpose of renovating the *stūpa* of Bodhnāth.[9] I would not rule out the possibility that this renovation, too, grew out of a desire on the part of Pho-lha-ba bSod-nams stobs-rgyas, this time to insure success to the continuation of his policies under his youngest son, 'Gyur-med rnam-rgyal.

Be that as it may, when Rig-'dzin Tshe-dbang nor-bu comes to Kathmandu via sKyid-grong in 1748, there to have, without much difficulty, reparations undertaken on Bodhnāth Stūpa and to round them off once again with a consecration ceremony, he meets his friend and colleague, the Eighth Si-tu Rin-po-che, whom he has known since the 1720s, and who likewise is on his second trip to Nepal. Shortly after his arrival in the Valley Rig-'dzin Tshe-dbang looks him up in Kiṃdol Vihāra, a Buddhist Newar monastery located in a hill to the south of the Svayambhūnāth Stūpa (*Biography*, pp. 206–211).[10]

Perhaps it would not be inappropriate to include at this point information provided by E.G. Smith concerning the Eighth Si-tu Rin-po-che:

> In 1748, Si-tu had the opportunity to pay another visit to Nepal. It is possible that he went entrusted with some official commission from the Tibetan Government. He was received warmly by Jayaprakāśamalla of Kathmandu (1736–1768). Raṇajitmalla of Bhatgaon (1722–1769) presented him with a manuscript *Amarakośa* commentary. His account of his meeting with Pṛthvīnārāyaṇa Śāha at the Gorkhā fortress is fascinating yet distressing because of its brevity.

---

9 A letter has been preserved that Rig-'dzin Tshe-dbang nor-bu sent to his native province before departing to Nepal, *Selected Writings*, vol. 1, pp. 732–735: *Me yos mchod rten bya ri kam sho ma'i zhig gso la phebs mdo khams su ltos bcas rnams la ras dgon nas gnang ba* ("Letter written in 1747 to friends in Khams just before his departure for Nepal to undertake restorations at Bodhnāth). Concerning his Ras-dgon monastery, see *Biography*, p. 205.

10 On Kiṃdol Vihāra, see K. Dowman (1981:205–208) and Locke (1985:401–402). A picture of the monastery after a Tibetan block print is found in Kaschewsky (1982:11, illustration 3).

During his stay in Nepal, he was able to complete a translation of a short *Svayambhūpurāṇa*.[11]

Kiṃdol Vihāra is mentioned again when, three years later, in the year 1751, Rig-'dzin Tshe-dbang nor-bu, once more visits Kathmandu, causing great excitement among the population. In between there are two trips to gTsang, where, among others, he meets the Third Paṇ-chen Bla-ma Blo-bzang dpal-ldan ye-shes (1737–1780), and to lHa-sa; there he again meets the Seventh 'Brug-chen Rin-po-che and the Seventh dPa'-bo Rin-po-che. In mTshur-phu, to the northeast of lHa-sa, he gives teachings to the younger generation of the Thirteenth Karma-pa bDud-'dul rdo-rje (1733–1791) and the Tenth Zhwa-dmar-pa Chos-grub rgya-mtsho (1742–1792), and of course the Eighth Si-tu Rin-po-che is not far away either (*Biography*, pp. 217–236).

But contact with Nepal does not break off during this period; a letter has been handed down, for instance, which Rig-'dzin Tshe-dbang nor-bu addressed to the king and ministers of Kathmandu in the year 1749.[12] In it is the first mention of the renovation of the *stūpa* of Svayambhūnāth that Rig-'dzin Tshe-dbang nor-bu considers undertaking. A bit later on there are words to the effect that he desired to bring offering gifts in that year (i.e. 1749) to the *stūpa* of Svayambhūnāth, but that he had to change his plans (*Biography*, p. 225). Finally, we learn in clear terms that at the end of the renovation of the *stūpa* of Bodhnāth in 1748 the rNying-ma-pa Bla-ma from Khams expressed the desire to put Svayambhūnāth Stūpa, too, back into presentable shape; this plan, due to adverse circumstances, however, though approved by the king of Kathmandu Jayaprakāśamalla, and the king of Gorkhā Pṛthvīnārāyaṇa Śāha (1743–1775), could not be carried out for three years (*Biography*, pp. 251–256).

---

11 *The Autobiography and Diaries of Si-tu Paṇ-chen* (= Śata-Piṭaka Series, vol. 77), New Delhi 1968, Introduction, p. 11. The description of the visit in 1748 is found in pp. 263–270 of the text; the first visit of Si-tu Rin-po-che in the year 1723, ibid, pp. 113–130. At that time, too, Si-tu Rin-po-che stayed in the Newar monastery of Kiṃdol; we can therefore assume that up to the middle of the 18th century there was no Tibetan monastery to be found on the hill of Svayambhūnāth Stūpa that might have served as a residence for the lamas. On the activities of Si-tu Rin-po-che in the field of Sanskrit lexicography, see *The Amarakośa in Tibet* (= Śata-Piṭaka Series, vol. 38), New Delhi 1965, Preface, pp. 11–14. His translation of the *Svayambhūpurāṇa* is available under the title *Bal yul rang byung mchod rten chen po'i lo rgyus*, 30 fols., in *Bal yul mchod rten gsum gyi lo rgyus dang gnas bshad can rna ba'i bdud rtsi*: *A Collection of Guide Books to the Three Great Stūpas of the Kathmandu Valley*, place of publ. unmentioned, 1983, pp. 3–61. As the colophon shows (ibid, p. 60), Si-tu Rin-po-che was urged to make the translation by Rig-'dzin Tshe-dbang nor-bu. For the role of this translatiom in the development of Tibetan pilgrimage guides to the Kathmandu Valley, see Decleer (2000:42-51).

12 *Selected Writings*, vol. 1, pp. 737–741: *Bal yul gyi rje bo dang 'dun pa chen po rnams la bsrings pa* ("Verse communication to the notables of Nepal written in 1749"). I assume that this is the written reply mentioned in the *Biography,* p. 217,4-5. For the period between 1749 and 1751 we also have an autobiographical text of Rig-'dzin Tshe-dbang nor-bu in *Collected Works*, vol. 1, pp. 531–559: *Rig pa 'dzin pa tshe dbang nor bu rang nyid kyi spyad rabs las phyung ba lu ma nas snyem pa'i chu ltar sa bon tsam zhig smon pa* ("Autobiographical account covering the years 1749–1751"), 14 fols.

When, in the year 1751, work on the *stūpa* can finally commence, all signs point to its successful completion. The gods Mahādeva-Gaṇeśa and Kumāra-Kārttikeya (both sons of Śiva), who are willing to guarantee the materials for the renovation, manifest themselves, and Viśṇu in the form of a Brahman gives instruction that a "pillar" (skt. *yaṣṭi*) should be chosen for the repair work which is similar to a "sacrificial post for the gods".[13] Not to be outdone by the gods, Jayaprakāśamalla also promises his aid, and Pṛthvīnārāyaṇa Śāha takes upon himself the task of erecting the pillar. This information is contained in the stone inscription and – in the same wording – in Rig-'dzin Tshe-dbang nor-bu's biography (*Biography*, pp. 258–259). It is further recorded that, during this occasion, a stone quarry and a fresh spring came to light on Kiṃdol Hill.[14]

In spite of this promising beginning, however, work did not advance speedily, as Rig-'dzin Tshe-dbang nor-bu was charged by the Seventh Dalai Bla-ma bsKal-bzang rgya-mtsho (1708–1757) with the political mission of laying to rest local feuds in Ladakh and stemming possible attempts by the Dsungars to bring their influence to bear there (*Biography*, pp. 263ff.).[15] Thus the renovation is again delayed for some time, i.e. progresses in fits and starts.

It would go beyond the bounds of this brief account to reproduce all the items in Rig-'dzin Tshe-dbang nor-bu's biography in the years between 1752 and 1755 having to do with the stalled work on the *stūpa*. They are, in any case, numerous and bear witness to the fact that this project occupied the final years of Rig-'dzin Tshe-dbang nor-bu's life. Of particular interest is the information concerning the fashioning of the pillar and the roles

---

13 The Tibetan rendering of Skt. *yaṣṭi* is *srog shing*. Cf. Irwin (1980:16): "The Tibetan term for the axial pillar of a *stūpa* is *srog shing*, literally 'life-wood', corresponding in our language to 'Tree of Life'." For "sacrificial post" (*mchod sdong*) a native dictionary gives the etymology "post for a fire offering" (*mchod me'i sdong bu*). On the problem involved in interpreting the pillar as a sacrificial post, see Irwin, ibid, pp. 13–15. Compare on this point Macdonald & Stahl (1979:63): "The Buddhist *stūpa* too, and there are many *stūpas* which have been erected by Newars in the Kathmandu Valley, derives from the fire-altar. It too represents the universe."

14 See Macdonald & Dvags-po Rin-po-che (1987:105): ".... on the hill of the "Pile of Barley" are found traces of the exhumation of a treasure of stones which was offered by the great and powerful auspicious gods to Rig-'dzin Tshe-dbang nor-bu, at the time of the restoration of the large *stūpa*, and a new spring." Cf. also ibid, p. 117: "In our time, when restoration was carried out at Svayambhū, a stone quarry was discovered and a new spring burst forth", and p. 119: "At the time when the big *stūpa* was being restored, stones appeared where there had been previously none, along with a spring, and everyone was astonished. I have heard it said that there really were many auspicious signs on that occasion." The author of this "description of holy places" (*gnas bshad*) is the Fourth Khams-sprul Rin-po-che Chos-kyi nyi-ma (1743–1779).

15 See the information provided by Richardson (1967); the summons to go on this mission comes only from the Seventh Dalai Bla-ma, not from Pho-lha-ba bSod-nams stobs-rgyas, who by this time is already three years dead. Concerning the attempted exercise of Dsungar influence in Ladakh, which occurred at the end of the brief reign of 'Gyur-med rnam-rgyal, the last king of Tibet (1747–1750), see Petech (1972:232f.).

Jayaprakāśamalla and Pṛthvīnārāyaṇa Śāha play during the prolonged renovation. Finally, in the year 1755, the pillar is erected, and in the context of a description of the end of this first stage an earlier renovation is recalled, that undertaken by gTsang-smyon He-ru-ka (1452–1507) and his disciple lHa-btsun Rin-chen rnam-rgyal (1473–1557) (*Biography*, pp. 313ff.).[16] In this context, too, one finds a "catalogue" (*dkar chag*) of the repair work (*Biography*, pp. 331–334).

Soon after the pillar has been erected and the accompanying ceremonies conducted, Rig-'dzin Tshe-dbang nor-bu retires again to sKyid-grong and dies shortly afterwards. The story of the renovation, however, does not end there. Testifying to this fact is, above all, the second part of the stone inscription, where the year 1758 is given as the date of the final consecration. In order, in conclusion, to take in with a glance this period of time, I shall draw upon a second biography of Rig-'dzin Tshe-dbang nor-bu, which in seven folios documents the most important events.[17]

There we learn that before his departure for sKyid-grong, Rig-'dzin Tshe-dbang nor-bu expressly asks his disciples to see the work still to be done on the Svayambhūnāth Stūpa through to completion. Among them is one "priest" (*mchod dpon*) in particular, bsTan-'dzin rdo-rje, who assumes responsibility for the repair work. With the support of the Seventh 'Brug-chen Rin-po-che, then work is completed in the year 1757. The consecration is finally performed the following year by the Seventh dPa'-bo Rin-po-che. Ten years have thus elapsed from the time in 1748 when, at the conclusion of the renovation of the *stūpa* of Bodhnāth, Rig-'dzin Tshe-dbang nor-bu made the decision to preserve Svayambhūnāth Stūpa, too, from the decay of time.

But as the final lines of the inscription prove, even the stone that recorded this event could not escape decay but had to be restored along with the inscription at a later point in time.

[16] On this renovation under the first king of the Malla dynasty of Kathmandu, Ratnamalla (1484–1520), see Smith (1969a:12). A detailed "catalogue" (*dkar chag*) of the repair work completed in the year 1504 is contained in the text portion, pp. 220–226.

[17] *dPal rig'dzin kaḥ thog pa chen po tshe dbang nor bu'i zhabs kyi rnam thar mdor bsdus dad pa'i sa bon*, 7 fols., in *Collected Works*, vol. 1, pp. 377–391. This text was written 1818, likewise by Brag-dkar rta-so sprul-sku Chos-kyi dbang-phyug. It was inserted by mKhas-btsun bzang-po into his *Biographical Dictionary of Tibet and Tibetan Buddhism* 4, pp. 375–382.

Statue of Kaḥ-thog rig-'dzin Tshe-dbang nor-bu (1698–1755)
in the Mūrtisaṃgrālaya Museum at Svayambhūnāth

Further Renovations of Svayambhūnāth Stūpa (From the 13th to the 17th Centuries)

As I have attempted to show in two earlier articles, it is possible, through the reading and analysis of Tibetan language inscriptions and texts, to obtain information on the architectural and cultural history of Buddhist monuments such as the *stūpa*s of Svayambhūnāth and Bodhnāth.[1] Such an approach has as one of its advantages the uncovering of phases of a monument's history that, for various reasons, are out of the reach of excavation-oriented archaeology; in the second place, an impression is obtained of how these central shrines of the Kathmandu Valley were perceived and described by Tibetan priests and pilgrims. An approach of this type could perhaps be termed 'literary archaeology'.

One document important for the history of Svayambhūnāth Stūpa is the so-called "Inventory of the [Stūpa] Venerable All-Trees" (*'Phags pa shing kun dkar chag*). This work, which comprises ten folios, has been familiar to the interested public since the thirties of the 20th century, and a transliterated version was made as early as 1970. Still, study and evaluation of the catalogue remains to be done; the chief reason for this delay may lie in the text's compilational structure and in the proliferation of misspellings in portions of it.[2]

Happily an older but – with only five folios – less extensive version of *'Phags pa shing kun dkar chag* existed at the time, though unnoticed. A comparison of the two versions now available enables the previously existing difficulties to be cleared away and a fresh look to be taken at the history of the *stūpa* of Svayambhūnāth. As a translation and

---

1 See Ehrhard (1989) and (1990) and chapter four and seven in the present volume.

2 Dowman (1981:189): "An older copy of this important text is needed before it can be edited definitively." To my knowledge the catalogue was mentioned for the first time by Tucci (1931:687), who gives a short overview of the geographical literature of Tibet concerned with India and other foreign countries (during the course of which he classifies our text correctly as a 'guide for pilgrims'). In contrast, Snellgrove (1957:99) states: "One may note the Tibetan version of the founding of Svayambhūnāth merely repeats the account of the *Svayambhūpurāṇa* and no attempt is made to appropriate this *stūpa* also as part of their own history." Snellgrove, unfortunately, is wide off the mark on both counts. As will be shown below, the catalogue describes the *stūpa* and its renovations most definitely as a piece of Tibetan history, and no passage refers to the *Svayambhūpurāṇa*. In Snellgrove's defence it may be said that the translation of the *Svayambhūpurāṇa* available today did not exist at the time. For the bibliographical data, see Ehrhard (1989:5) and chapter four in the present volume. Smith (1969a:7) also had problems dating a renovation by means of our text: "I have no explanation for the date mentioned in the guide to Svayambhūnāth."

study of the older version (= *dKar chag I*) is under preparation, I should like in the following to restrict comparison with the later version (= *dKar chag II*) to the renovations of the *stūpa* described in both texts.[3]

To give in advance the result of a comparison of the two texts under this aspect: *dKar chag I* mentions in two places "the central mast" (*yaṣṭi*) being torn down and set up anew with the financial aid of Tibetan rulers from Central Tibet; these renovations can be dated to the end of the 13th and the beginning of the 15th century. We can even go so far, in characterizing *dKar chag I*, as to take it to be a 'catalogue' that was written down on the occasion of the renovation of 1413. Under this prior state of affairs, *dKar chag II* marks itself out as being an extended version of the older work, likewise describing two renovations, once occurring at the beginning of the 16th century and end of the 17th century. The later work, then, is a catalogue that was fixed in writing on the basis of the older version on the occasion of the renovation of 1680. The mangled and warped syntax of the later text, as well as the problems it poses to dating, thus no longer represents insurmountable difficulties.

In order to be able to offer a first assessment of the information presently available on the history of the renovations of Svayambhūnāth according to the Tibetan sources, I first present the two later periods during which restoration work was carried out (in both cases by yogins of the *bKa'-brgyud-pa* school); and then, as a supplement to this, the early renovations, which lead over to the interesting topic of the cultural exchange between the Newar kings of the Kathmandu Valley and the southern provinces of Tibet.

1. THE RENOVATION OF 1680

The events surrounding the renovation that coincided with the beginning of the reign of Pārthivendramalla (1680–1687) are recounted in greatest detail in *dKar chag II*. This is not surprising, given that the end of the work provided the occasion for the later version of the 'catalogue' being written down. Here is the text particularizing what took place:

> Then, after some time, when the venerable Rang-rig [ras-pa] himself had affixed the great pinnacle (*gañjira*, N. *gajura*) to [Bya-rung] kha-shor [Stūpa], he yielded up what was available in leftover gold, [namely] thirty-two ounces, to King Pārthivendramalla and Tse-kur 'bab-chu (?), saying: "As obviously repair of 'Phags-pa shing-kun Stūpa is necessary in connection with the statues of the four cardinal directions, act [accordingly]".
>
> The king, [however,] did not carry out [the repair] that year; the following year "the central mast" (*yaṣṭi*) broke and tilted to the left. A prophecy having

[3] For a full translation of the older version see chapter six in the present volume; the later version is edited nin Wylie (1970:43–48).

> been communicated to King Pārthivendramalla through *Gaṇapati* (i.e. Gaṇeśa), a treasure of gold was unearthed at Kāśyapa Stūpa. After the craftsmen under the [king's] control had assembled, they erected a sal tree (*spos dkar shing = shing sa la = Shorea robusta*), that is, the central mast six *'dom* thick and forty-seven *'dom* long. Afterwards the 'palace', the discs, the top and the statues of the four cardinal directions were prepared, together with the backside screens, from [a plating of] gold and copper.
>
> The consecration was conducted on the full moon day of the fifth month in the iron-monkey year (1680), and during this time all [the participants] observed rainbows, a rain of flowers and the tones of [sonorous] music.[4]

I shall supplement this information merely with brief biographical data on the person of Rang-rig ras-pa (died 1683). There exists a collection of songs and teachings of this yogin of the 'Brug-pa bKa'-brgyud-pa school, but it contains – to judge by a first perusal of it – no details on the renovation of the Svayambhūnāth Stūpa. Of Rang-rig ras-pa himself we know that he came from Spiti (West Tibet) and, being a tireless wanderer, visited not only the various provinces of Tibet but also the northwest of India, notably the Cakrasaṃvara centre Jalandhara. According to a historical work of the rNying-ma-pa school, he was also the most important "master of the teachings" (*chos bdag*) of the tradition of gTer-ston Nyi-ma grags-pa (1647–1710).[5]

---

4 Ngag-dbang rdo-rje: *dKar chag II*. fols. 7b/6–8b/2: *de nas nam zhig gi tshe / rje btsun rang rig de nyid kha shor gyi ganydzira chen po bkal ba'i dus gser lhag ma srang sum cu so gnyis yod nga* (= pa) *rgyal po pattibhandre ma la dang / tse kur 'bab chu gnyis la gzhag nas / 'phags pa shing kun gyi phyogs bzhi'i sku dang bcas pa zhig gsos dgos pa 'dug pas gyis shig gsungs / rgyal pos de'i lo la ma 'grub / lo rting ma srog shing chag ste g.yon por gyur tshe / rgyal po pattibhandre ma la la tshogs bdag gis lung bstan nas 'od srungs kyi mchod rten mdun nas gser gyi gter bzhes nas / mnga' 'og gi bzo rigs bsdus nas / spos dkar shing la srog shing sbom phra 'dom drug / dkyus 'dom zhe bdun btsug nas khang bzang chos 'khor tog dang phyogs bzhi sku rgyab yol bcas gser zangs las bsgrubs / lcags spre hor zla lnga pa'i tshes bco lnga'i nyin rab tu gnas pa mdzad tshe 'ja' 'od dang me tog gi char rol mo'i sgra sogs kun gyis mthong ba'o.*

Dowman (1981:225) identifies the place where the gold treasure was unearthed as the Kāśyapa Stūpa on the northern slope of Mañjuśrī Hill. If this renovation in the 17th century is compared with the replacement of the mast by Kaḥ-thog rig-'dzin Tshe-dbang nor-bu (1698–1755) in the 18th century, then what invites notice is the fact that in both cases work on Bodhnāth Stūpa preceded the renovation done to Svayambhūnāth; see Ehrhard (1989:5ff) and chapter four of the current publication. According to Riccardi Jr. (1973:337), the wood for a new mast always came from the same sal forest near Bhatgaon. This does not hold true for the renovation, just mentioned, organized by Rig-'dzin Tshe-dbang nor-bu; the lama's biography provides us with the information that the mast was taken from a holy spot in the area of Navakot.

5 See Rang-rig ras-pa: *gSung mgur*, pp. 310ff. regarding songs of Rang-rig ras-pa composed on the occasion of the pinnacle's being set in place on the Bodhnāth Stūpa. The colophon of one of the songs mentions sTag-rtse sku-skye-ba Mi-pham phun-tshogs shes-rab (1654–1715) as a witness to the renovation. This author composed a short text in praise of his teacher (= *sku bstod*); while the myth of Bodhnāth Stūpa is adverted to there, no notice is taken of the renovation of Svayambhūnāth. On the role of Rang-rig ras-pa

2. The Renovation of 1504

This renovation, too, was carried out by a wandering yogin of the bKa'-brgyud-pa school; in contrast to Rang-rig ras-pa, however, there exist two detailed biographies of gTsang-smyon He-ru-ka (1452–1507), so that ascertaining the dates and immediate circumstances of his activities at Svayambhūnāth Stūpa is not a major problem.

Thus we know that he was called upon to undertake the renovation of Svayambhūnāth by King Ratnamalla (1484–1520) and his ministers in the year 1504, and that the work was completed three years later during a first act of consecration attended by miraculous signs. Evaluating the extensive source material relating to this renovation at the beginning of the 16th century would be a worthwhile venture; the foregoing details may satisfy the present purpose of providing a preliminary survey.[6] What should perhaps be specifically noted is that a replacement of the central mast is not explicitly described in this renovation.

The problems in dating this renovation according to *dKar chag II*, which have already been touched by G. E. Smith (see note 2), can be explained from the following circumstance: when *dKar chag II* was written, the information relating to the renovation carried out by gTsang-smyon He-ru-ka was made to apply to the renovation of 1413, the one to be presented next. In the process of excerpting from the old catalogue (*dKar chag I*), the renovation of 1413 was confounded with that of 1504. One result of this was a misdating (the 'serpent year' mentioned in *dKar chag II* refers to the renovation of 1413): a second was a reassignment of personal names.

Thus sNgags-'chang Śākya bzang-po, the 'treasure discoverer' of Bodhnāth-Stūpa in *dKar chag II* is mistakenly associated with the renovation by gTsang-smyon He-ru-ka. If a comparison is made with the corresponding passage in *dKar chag I*, it is clearly seen that the name sNgags-'chang Śākya bzang-po was set down in place of a certain Mahāpaṇḍita Śāriputra, and the entire contents telescoped onto the renovation of 1504. The reason for this mix-up maybe that at another place in *dKar chag I* one dPon-chen Śākya bzang-po is

---

as a disciple of gTer-ston Nyi-ma grags-pa, see *Chos-'byung*, vol. 3, pp. 353.3–355.5. A meeting of the two at Mount Kailāśa is described ibid, vol. 4, p. 374.3–5.

6 gTsang-smyon He-ru-ka stayed in the Kathmandu Valley on three occasions. The account of the first visit, in 1476, is contained in translation in Lewis and Jamspal (1988:192–194); already at that early date Vināyaka (= Gaṇeśa) asked him to renovate the *stūpa* at Svayambhūnāth. Concerning the second visit in the years 1595/96, see Fifth Dalai Lama Ngag-dbang blo-bzang rgya-mtsho: *Byang pa'i rig 'dzin chen po ngag gi dbang po'i rnam par thar pa ngo mtshar bkod pa'i rgya mtsho*, p. 101f. Reference has already been made by Smith (1969a:12) to the third stay (from 1501–1504), the work done on Svayambhūnāth Stūpa and the existence of a detailed catalogue. Among the persons mentioned in this list of donors to the renovation are: three persons bearing the title 'king of Gung-thang', namely Khri rNam-rgyal lde (1422–1502) and his two sons Nor-bu lde (1450–1484) and bSam-grub lde (1459–1505), a king of Gu-ge named 'Phags-pa lha (concerning whom, see Petech (1998:388) and the "ruler of Mustang" (*smon thang sde pa*).

mentioned.[7] The renovations associated with the persons of Mahāpaṇḍita Śāriputra and dPon-chen Śākya bzang-po will concern us in the following.

3. THE RENOVATION OF 1413

The finishing of a restoration of Svayambhūnāth Stūpa was also in the case of *dKar chag I* the occasion for the catalogue's being written. As in the year 1680, a new mast was erected, and we learn that these activities fell during the reign of King Jyotirmalla (1408–1428). Further, we are provided information concerning the donors who helped defray expenses:

> Afterwards the mast broke. The great teacher Śāriputra set it up [again]. Faithful persons such as the great rulers of Central Tibet, "the provincial regents" (*khri dpon*) of lHo and Byang, the Sher (= Shar) mkhan-po of Khams me-nyag [all] offered countless wealth and acted as donors.
>
> The King of Nepal, Śrī Jayajyotirmalladeva, superintended and, after having praised the assembled *bares* in an official writing, called together the craftsmen under his charge. The parasol together with the accompanying discs was completed in a proper manner on the full moon of the fourth month in the serpent year (= 1413).[8]

---

[7] The comments of Dowman (1981:212) are thus no longer applicable: "Then in 1505 in another major restoration, which Yol-mo-ba Śākya bzang-po patronised, the wheel and pinnacle were placed on top by gTsang-smyon, the crazy yogin Sangs-rgyas rgyal-mtshan from West Tibet." Concerning sNgags-'chang Śākya bzang-po and the rediscovery of the *stūpa* of Bodhnāth, see Ehrhard (1990b:7–9) and chapter seven of the current publication. This setting matters straight should not, of course, detract from the fact that the work done by gTsang-smyon He-ru-ka at Svayambhūnāth and by sNgags-'chang Śākya bzang-po at Bodhnāth Stūpa took place at approximately the same time (which may likewise have contributed to the confusion). Cf. *rTogs-brjod,* fol. 16a/2–4: "At this time gTsang-pa (= gTsang-smyon) also came to perform his service at [the *stūpa* of] Shing-kun. On account of a test of their magical prowess he (i.e. gTsang-smyon) spoke *phaṭ* into the cloudless sky, and clouds gathered. At the second *phaṭ*, there was a clap of thunder; at the third [*phaṭ*] hail rained down. The great *Mantradhara* (i.e. sNgags-'chang Śākya bzang-po) spoke three times [the syllable] *huṃ* and made three times the gesture of threat, at which the forests of Nepal and all the mountains bowed their heads [to him]." (*de'i tshe gtsang pa yang shing kun gyi zhabs tog la byon pa dang rdzu 'phrul 'gran pas / kong gi (= gis) nam mkha' sprin med pa la phaṭ ces brjod pas / phrin (= sprin) 'dus / phaṭ gnyis pa la 'brug sgra grag / gsum pa la ser ba phabs so / rigs sngags 'chang ba chen po 'di ni / huṃ gsum brjed cing phyag 'dzub gug pa gsum mdzad pas / bal yul gyi nags tshal ri bo dang bcas pa thams cad mgo gug byed pa byung*).

[8] bSod-nams dpal bzang-po: *dKar chag I*, fols. 4b/6–5a/3: *de nas shing chag pa / paṇḍita chen po sa ri bhu tras btsugs ste / dbus pa gong ma chen po lho byang gi khri dpon / sher mkhan po khams me nyag sogs dad ldan rnams kyis nor dpag tu med pa phul nas sbyin bdag mdzad ste bal po'i rgyal po shri dza ya dzo ma la dhe bos / do dam gyi gtso bo mdzad nas 'khor 'ba' ro rnams gser yig la bsngags nas / mnga' zhabs kyi gzo rigs mkhas pa rnams bdsus te / gdugs chos 'khor rtogs (= gtogs) dang bcas pa sprul lo zla ba bzhi pa'i tshes bco lnga la yang dag par grub.*

Concerning the period of Jayajyotirmalla's reign (1408–1428), cf. Petech (1984:161–168, particularly p. 167f.: "The inscriptions show that the king made substantial offerings to Paśupati on the one side and

We can at least identify the person responsible for setting up the mast, Mahāpaṇḍita Śāriputra, from a historical work. In the process, we obtain at a stroke some insight into the power relationships in the southern Tibetan provinces at the beginning of the 15th century.

During the division of Tibet into three regions (*chol kha,* from Mongolian *colge*) and Central Tibet into thirteen provinces (*khri skor*) undertaken in the 13th century (that is, one hundred and fifty years earlier) under Kubilai Khan and the Sa-skya-pa Bla-ma 'Phags-pa (1235–1280), two spheres of power were established in gTsang: La-stod lHo and La-stod Byang. Provincial regents, or myriarchs (*khri dpon*), exercised control over these territories, having been entrusted with the post in recognition of their political and religious services. Thus we know the first regent of La-stod Byang, for instance, to have been a servant of Bla-ma 'Phags-pa and subsequently to have exercised the office of spiritual teacher to Kubilai Khan.

In spite of the decreasing political influence of the Sa-skya-pa school the post of provincial regent remained in the hands of the previously established families, and so it was, in particular, in the case of the province of La-stod Byang, where at the beginning of the 15th century a pair of brothers shared the task of ruling and administering between themselves: bDag-chen rNam-rgyal grags-bzang (1395–1475) and his younger brother dKon-mchog legs-pa. According to a historical work by the Fifth Dalai Lama (1615–1682), the elder brother studied principally under two spiritual teachers: 'From Upadhyāya Śāriputra of Bodhgayā in India and Bo-dong Phyogs-las rnam-rgyal (1375–1451) he heard many deep and comprehensive teachings.'[9]

I shall forego treatment of other persons mentioned in connection with this renovation and instead merely once again highlight the relation between the Indian teacher Śāriputra and the regent of the province of La-stod Byang. In the future it may be possible to determine whether it was that very bDag-chen rNam-rgyal grags-bzang who acted as donor (in 1413 he was only eighteen years old) or one of his predecessors; however, in my opinion, we can take it as certain that a Buddhist teacher from India was responsible for

---

to Svayambhūnāth on the other." One of the earliest inscriptions at Svayambhūnāth Stūpa was erected on the occasion of the renovation just described; see the information provided by Riccardi Jr. (1973:336).

9 See Ngag-dbang blo-bzang rgya-mtsho: *Gangs can yul gyi sa la dpyod pa'i tho ris kyi rgyal blon gtso bor brjod pa'i deb ther / rdzogs ldan gzhon nu dga' ston dpyid kyi rgyal mo'i glu dbyangs,* fol. 66b/2: *rgya gar rdo rje gdan gyi mkhan po sha ri pu tra dang / bo dong phyogs las rnam rgyal ba la zab rgyas kyi chos mang du gsan.* Concerning the period of the two brothers' rule and that of the other lords of La-stod Byang, see also Tucci (1971:192): "Especially during the time of the two brothers rNam-rgyal grags-pa and dKon-mchog legs-pa ... there was no reason for great disturbances ... Besides the Sa-skya-pas whom they revered as their own Bla-mas, they honoured as their masters the Jo-nang-pas, the Bo-dong-pas ... and impartially they rendered service to the Colleges and to the works of the dGe-ldan-pas being under their authority ... Their great wealth and the wonderful extent of their devotion to the three jewels still lasts." On the significance of bDag-chen rNam-rgyal grags-bzang as a master of *Kālacakratantra* and a founder of one tradition of Tibetan medicine, see Stearns (1980:108). Stress is also laid there on, among other things, his patronship of Vanaratna (1384–1468), concerning whom, see also note 10.

erecting the mast. This is no cause for surprise, in consideration of the fact that Vanaratna (1384–1468), the so-called "last paṇḍita" to reach Tibet, stayed at the beginning of the 15th century at Svayambhūnāth, in the *vihāra* of Śantapuri.[10] The *stūpa* of Svayambhūnāth accordingly continued to be a religious centre during this period, a way station for the transmission of Buddhist teachings from India to the southern provinces of Tibet.

4. THE RENOVATION IN THE SECOND HALF OF THE 13TH CENTURY

The last renovation to be presented in this rough survey of Tibetan activities at the *stūpa* of Svayambhūnāth is the first one specified by *dKar chag I*. From what I have seen up to now, the information provided pertains to the earliest instance of the mast being replaced at the Svayambhūnāth Stūpa:

> After a certain time the mast there broke, dPon-chen Śākya bzang-po donated three large dronas and fifty ounces of gold. The *kalyāṇamitras* from dBus and gTsang, the *bares* from Nepal, [and] the *thakuras* from India having donated much wealth, the [new] mast was set up by the Bla-mas from Central Tibet, father and son. The base of the mast had [a circumference of] seven *'dom*, the length was seventy-two *'dom*.[11]

In order to identify dPon-chen Śākya bzang-po, we must recur to the political situation during the period of Kubilai Khan and Sa-skya-pa Bla-ma 'Phags-pa in the 13th century. The division of Central Tibet into three regions with thirteen provinces led to the appointment of a "chief administrator" (*dpon chen*), who was responsible for governing the whole of the kingdom of Central Tibet, and was answerable to the Mongolian leader. In the dPon-chen

---

10 See Vajracharya (1987:35–36). The *Blue Annals* of 'Gos Lo-tsā-ba gZhon-nu dpal (1392–1481), which he draws on, mention an invitation proffered by prince Rab-brtan kun-bzang 'phags-pa (1389–1442) to Vanaratna to visit rGyal-rtse. In the biography of this prince who built the famous sKu-'bum in rGyal-rtse in 1427, Mahāpaṇḍita Śāriputra is also referred to; Ngag-dbang blo-bzang rgya-mtsho: *Zur thams cad mkhyen pa chos dbyings rang grol gyi rnam thar theg mchog bstan pa'i shing rta*, pp. 49–52. Further, we find mentioned there not only the year 1413 and a renovation of the *stūpa* 'Phags-pa shing-kun but also an invitation offered in the following year to Paṇ-chen Śākya-Srī sa-ri pu-tra to visit the royal court of rGyal-rtse.

11 bSod-nams dpal bzang-po: *dKar chag I*, fol. 3b/2–5: *der te shig nas srog shing chag ste / dpon chen shakya bzang pos gser bre gsum dang gser (= srang) lnga bcu phul / gzhan yang dbus gtsang gis (= gi) dge bshes bal po'i 'ba' ro rgya gar gyi khra kur rnams kyi (= kyis) mang pos phul nas / bla ma dbus pa yab sras kyis srog shing btsug / srog shing gi rtas ba la mdom (= 'dom) bdun srid du mdom (= 'dom) bdun cu rtsa gnyis yod do*. Data such as these on the length of the mast may have caused confusion among later authors with regard to the measurement of particular parts of the *stūpa*. See, for example, Wylie (1970:19): "Bla-ma bTsan-po was obviously misinformed as to the height of the spire of circular discs surmounting the *stūpa*. He says it was seventy *'dom*, or fathoms, but that would make it four-hundred-twenty feet whereas the actual height is about one-hundred-twenty feet." The lama evidently confounded the figure giving the length of the entire mast with the length of the mast containing the thirteen discs.

Śākya bzang-po mentioned as a donor in connection with the renovation of Svayambhūnāth we have, in my opinion, the first chief administrator appointed by Bla-ma 'Phags-pa.

An important piece of evidence supporting this identification is the presence of dPon-chen Śākya bzang-po at the royal court of Gung-thang in the second half of the 13th century. One of the two most important trade routes to Tibet ran through this kingdom, which at the time bordered directly on Nepal, and it is quite sure that, during his stay in Gung-thang, dPon-chen Śākya bzang-po established contact with the royal court at Kathmandu.[12]

In order to arrive at a rounded assessment of the cultural exchanges between the Kathmandu Valley, the chief administrator of Tibet and the Mongolian kingdom we must, in conclusion, refer to a well-known event from the year 1260. In that year, Kubilai Khan put to his spiritual teacher 'Phags-pa the request that a "Golden Pagoda" be built at the monastery of Sa-skya. The Newar king Jayabhimadeva (1258–1271) thereupon sent eighty craftsmen from the Kathmandu Valley to Tibet under the leadership of the promising artist Arniko (1244–1306). The task, involved the building of a *gser thog* (temple with a golden roof) at Sa-skya Monastery, the funds for which were managed by dPon-chen Śākya bzang-po. Work took place in the years 1261–1262.

Without wishing to posit a direct connection between the work of Arniko at Sa-skya and the renovation of the *stūpa* at Svayambhūnāth, I should nevertheless like to point to the figure of dPon-chen Śākya bzang-po, who acted as financial backer in both cases, thus remaining true to his role as chief administrator.[13]

With these remarks concerning the oldest renovation work at Svayambhūnāth according to Tibetan sources.[14] I conclude this first presentation of the so-called *'Phags pa shing kun dkar chag*. This catalogue should be able to provide still further insight for the work of assessing the relation between Tibetan pilgrims and scholars and the *stūpa*.

---

12 See Jackson (1978:211): "The importance of Gung-thang during this period in the eyes of the Sakya rulers of Tibet is indicated by the fact that when the young Gung-thang king 'Bum-lde mgon (1253–1280) returned home from Sakya after visiting his uncle 'Phags-pa, he was accompanied to Ngari by an army headed by the famous official Śākya bzang-po." The source of this information is the genealogy of the Gung-thang kings written by Kaḥ-thog rig-'dzin Tshe-dbang nor-bu (1698–1755). Concerning the rule of king 'Bum-lde mgon it is further stated that the latter in 1270 completed the palace of rDzong-dkar and shortly afterwards also invited Nepalese craftsmen to build a *stūpa* for it. The *stūpa* was later filled with relics deriving from the treasure of Nepalese kings; ibid, p.106.

13 Concerning the invitation made to Newar craftsmen to go to Tibet, see, among other sources, Lo Bue (1985:265). In a work Vitali (1990:103–105) refers at length to the relation between the Sa-skya-pa rulers, the Kathmandu Valley and the rulers of the Yuan dynasty; there too documented evidence is given for the first commissioned work done by Arniko at Sa-skya Monastery.

14 According to Snellgrove (1941:96), the oldest inscription at the *stūpa* of Svayambhūnāth is datable to the year 1372; it documents the *stūpa*'s renovation after it was destroyed in the wake of the Muslim invasions (1346 and 1349); see also Petech (1984:125). An even earlier renovation presumably undertaken in the first half of the 13th century is mentioned in the *Deb ther dmar po* of Tshal-pa Kun-dga' rdo-rje (1309–1364); see chapter 6, note 13.

Old and New
Tibetan Sources Concerning Svayambhūnāth

1. Old and New

The English translation of the chapter dealing with Nepal in the work known as "Detailed Exposition of the Great [Continent] Jambudvīpa" (*'dzam gling chen po'i rgyas bshad*) of Bla-ma bTsan-po (1789–1838) drew attention to the first of many hitherto unknown colourful and rich descriptions of the Kathmandu Valley and its sacred sites in Tibetan literary sources. For all the interest these geographical accounts and pilgrimage guidebooks have generated, however, it is not easy to distinguish what is old and what is new – in other words, to know the period in the long history of cultural and religious contacts between Nepal and Tibet from which a particular text dates.

In order to illustrate this point I direct attention to the two Tibetan works published together with the above-mentioned translation and quoted extensively in the footnotes. The first one is called "Description of the Sacred Sites of Nepal" (*bal po'i gnas yig*) and provides a list of fifty pilgrimage sites in the Valley together with brief statements on each shrine and on the legends associated with them. A translation of this text is available, and the first attempt to date this work – based on its printing colophon – concluded that the text must have been executed as a xylograph in the year 1774. A particular feature of this guidebook is that after the Tibetan name of each sacred site a phrase is added in transliterated Nepali containing the toponym as known to the Hindu population of the Valley. It struck the translator of the text as remarkable that an author of the 18th century should show such respect to the Gorkhāli language. As we know by now, the guidebook was actually printed in the year 1954, and its author, a Newar bhikṣu who had lived in Lhasa and had later settled in the Kiṃdol Vihāra near Svayambhūnāth, was well acquainted with the Hindu names of the individual shrines as current in the 20th century.[1]

A Tibetan block print produced from worn-out blocks on paper which quickly develops a peculiar texture and smell from having been carried around and fingered on numerous

[1] For the translation of the Nepal chapter in Bla-ma bTsan-po's work, see Wylie (1970:11–36). The edition of the *Bal po'i gnas yig* of the Newar bhikṣu Ngag-dbang rdo-rje can be found ibid, pp. 30–41 (= Appendix). The mentioned translation of the text is the one in Dowman (1981:205–284); for the dating of the xylograph to the year 1774, see ibid, p. 187. Concerning additional information on the Newar bhikṣu and the date 1954 for the printing of the guide-book, compare Ehrhard (2004a:64, note 11).

occasions can give easily the impression of being old and rare. It transports the Western reader to a past where pious pilgrims and travellers arrived from the Tibetan plateau in the Nepal Valley. The stories and legends contained in this kind of writings trigger the imagination, causing more recent historical realities to fade away. I still remember this feeling when I obtained such a copy of the second guide-book, to which we shall turn now.

It bears the title "A Register of the Stūpa 'Noble All [Kinds of] Trees' in Nepal and Other Sacred Sites There" (*bal yul mchod rten 'phags pa shing kun dang de'i gnas gzhan rnams kyi dkar chag*) and has been produced as a block print on several occasions, the last one dating at around the same time as the work of the Newar bhikṣu. It looked to me like a genuinely old Tibetan text but only later, after gaining access to different versions of this guidebook, it turned out that the print I had first been presented with had been executed by the so-called "Mongolian Lama" (*sog bla*) Gurudeva (= Gu ru bDe-ba), a religious teacher who in the 1950s founded the monastery dGa'-ldan Chos-'phel gling near the Bodhnāth Stūpa. As I have already traced the rather complicated transmission of this text, it may be merely pointed out here that this guidebook was originally composed in the year 1686 upon the death of a yogin of the 'Brug-pa bKa'-brgyud-pa school known as Rang-rig ras-pa or Rang-rig ras-chen (died 1683). The title suggests that the work is mainly concerned with describing the Mahācaitya Svayambhūnāth or "Noble All [Kinds of] Trees", as it is known to Tibetan pilgrims.[2]

2. NEW

One might regard the two Tibetan guidebooks by the Newar bhikṣu and the disciple of Rang-rig ras-pa as "old" Tibetan sources, since they were already published over thirty years ago. In contrast to these works stands the textual material on Svayambhūnāth discovered in the meantime. Among these "new" Tibetan sources, special mention must be made of a text with the title "Guidebook to the Sacred Sites of the Land of Nepal and a History of its Receptacles: A Clear Speech, Which is a Mirror of Jewels, Eliminating Wrong Conceptions" (*bal yul gyi gnas bshad dang rten gyi lo rgyus nges par brjod pa 'khrul spang nor bu'i me long*). The author of this work, which was filmed by the NGMPP in April 1992, is Brag-dkar rta-so sprul-sku Chos-kyi dbang-phyug (1775–1837), a religious teacher affiliated to the famous hermitage of the great yogin Mi-la-ras-pa in Mang-yul Gung-thang and a representative of the rNying-ma-pa and 'Brug-pa bKa'-brgyud-pa schools of Tibetan Buddhism.

---

[2] For the edition of the register of Svayambhūnāth and the other sacred sites of the Nepal Valley – written by Nas-lung Ngag-dbang rdo-rje, a direct disciple of Rang-rig ras-pa –, see Wylie (1970:33–48 (= Appendix)). Further details on the different printed versions of the text and the dating of the *editio princeps* to the year 1686, can be found in Ehrhard (2002a:146–151) and chapter eight of the present volume.

The text was completed in the year 1816 and is interesting for several reasons. First, the author has travelled on two occasions to the Nepal Valley and investigated on the spot the history and literary traditions of its different sacred sites. The initial journey was undertaken in the year 1792, immediately after the peace treaty between the Qing ruler Qianlong (reign 1736–1796) and the Gorkhas; it took the traveller up to Ṛṣīśvara, a place to the south-west of the Valley known to Tibetan pilgrims as Chu-mig Byang-chub bdud-rtsi. The second journey took place ten years later (in 1802), during which Chos-kyi dbang-phyug stayed in the house of a Newar Buddhist scholar by the name Śrī Harṣa.

Second, the text is marked by a critical approach towards the stories and legends which circulated among Tibetan pilgrims in their attempt to glorify Nepal as a sacred Buddhist land; it can thus provide us, for example, with insights into the transposition of the religious topography of "Khotan" (*li yul*) to "Nepal" (*bal yul*), and the identification of the famous *stūpa* Gomasala-gandha with the Svayambhūcaitya. The author shares this historically oriented view on the oral traditions of Tibetan pilgrims with the Fourth Khams-sprul bsTan-'dzin Chos-kyi nyi-ma (1743–1779), who had visited Nepal in the year 1756 and composed soon afterwards a work with the title "Register of the Sacred Sites of Nepal, The Great Country Upacchandoha: Nectar for the Ears of [the Inhabitants of the] Land of Snows" (*yul chen nye ba'i tshandhoha bal po'i gnas kyi dkar chag gangs can rna ba'i bdud rtsi*).[3]

Third, Chos-kyi dbang-phyug gives an outline of the contents of the *Svayambhūpurāṇa*, the "Mahātmya" or pilgrimage handbook of Newar Buddhists for the Svayambhūcaitya. He mentions therein an earlier translation of the work by lHa-mdong Lo-tsā-ba bShes-gnyen rnam-rgyal (born 1512), while making use personally of the version rendered into the Tibetan language by the Eighth Si-tu-pa Chos-kyi 'byung-gnas (1770–1774). Brag-dkar rta-so sprul-sku pays particular attention to historiographical sources describing Śantapuri, one of the five special "mansions" (*pura*) located in the surroundings of Svayambhūnāth, and he observes that the entrance hall of the temple contains authentic drawings based on the *Svayambhūpurāṇa*.[4]

---

[3] An overview of the life and writings of Brag-dkar rta-so sprul-sku Chos-kyi dbang-phyug can be found in Ehrhard (2004a:89–107). The text dealing with the religious geography of Nepal was filmed by the NGMPP, reel no. L 381/4, and consists of 35 folios (incomplete). For the fact that Ṛṣīśvara and the sacred sites of Mang-yul Gung-thang marked respectively the southern and northern limits of the itinerary of Tibetan pilgrims passing through the Nepal Valley, compare Ehrhard (2003:102–103). A facsimile and a translation of the work of the Fourth Khams-sprul are available in Macdonald (1975:123–144) and Macdonald & Dvags-po Rin-po-che (1981:238–273).

[4] The topography of the pilgrimage places according to the *Svayambhūpurāṇa* has been elucidated by Kölver (1985:136–168). For the different versions of this medieval work of Newar Buddhism, see Brinkhaus (1993:65–70) and Brinkhaus (2001:19–30); the latter article provides details on Śantapuri and the legend of Śāntikara as contained in the *Svayambhūpurāṇa* and depicted on the walls of the entrance hall. Concerning the Tibetan translation of "a concise *Svayambhūpurāṇa*" by the Eighth Si-tu-pa in the

Fourth, the text enumerates the succession of renovations of Svayambhūnāth and Bodhnāth performed by religious authorities from Tibet. In the former case Chos-kyi dbang-phyug begins with the renovation overseen by gTsang-smyon Heruka (1452–1507) at the beginning of the 16th century, followed by the ones of lHa-btsun Rin-chen rnam-rgyal (1473–1557 and gNas Rab-'byams-pa Byams-pa phun-tshogs (1503–1581), both members of the teaching tradition of the famous "Madman of gTsang". The 17th century saw renovations of the Sixth Zhwa-dmar-pa Chos-kyi dbang-phyug (1584–1630) – who covered the shrines of the four Tathāgatas and their consorts on the outer rim of the *stūpa* with sheets made from a gold and copper alloy – and of the above-mentioned 'Brug-pa bKa'-brgyud-pa yogin Rang-rig ras-pa. The final two renovations described in the text of Chos-kyi dbang-phyug, were those of Kaḥ-thog rig-'dzin Tshe-dbang nor-bu (1698–1755) and of a group of religious teachers from Bhutan; these activities took place in the years 1751 to 1758 and 1814 to 1817.[5]

3. OLD

If we look now for the earliest Tibetan source concerning Svayambhūnāth (in particular, as a destination for pilgrims) and further sacred sites in the Nepal Valley, we are led to a work called "A Register of Noble All [Kinds of] Trees: Mind Support of the Buddhas of the Three Times" (*dus gsum sangs rgyas thams cad kyi thugs kyi rten 'phags pa shing kun gyi dkar chag*). It was composed in the year 1413 on the occasion of a further renovation of Svayambhūnāth, and I regard it as "old" because it provides us with information on Tibetan conceptions of the Mahācaitya from the beginning of the 15th century.

This was a most interesting period in the history of cultural and religious relationships between Nepal and Tibet, and it was precisely at that time that Vanaratna (1384–1468), the so-called "last paṇḍita" to reach Tibet during the second diffusion of the Buddhist doctrine, twice took up residence at Svayambhūnāth. This transpired in the years 1426 and 1436, after the yogin from Chittagong (present-day eastern Bengal) returned from his first two journeys to the north. He was afterwards invited to the Govicandra Mahāvihāra in Patan where, among his Tibetan disciples who managed to join him there, we find the "Great Translator" (*lo chen*) bSod-nams rgya-mtsho (1424–1482). This latter stay occurred in the

---

year 1748, see Verhagen (2001:64–65, note 22). Decleer (2000:33–37 & 42–50) details the rediscovery of the text by Chos-kyi 'byung-gnas and the role of the translation as a basic reference for Tibetan pilgrimages to the Nepal Valley.

5 For the renovation of Svayambhūnāth executed by Kaḥ-thog rig-'dzin and a first list of such works based on Tibetan literary sources, see Ehrhard (1989:2–8) and chapter four in the present volume. Compare the overview of the succession of upkeep activity on the Mahācaitya – using the text of Chos-kyi dbang-phyug – in v. Rospatt (2001:200–235). The embellishment of the Tathāgata shrines was accomplished by the Sixth Zhwa-dmar-pa during a journey to Nepal in the years 1629/30; concerning this journey, see Ehrhard (1997a:128–132) and chapter seventeen in the present volume.

year 1466, and the biography of the translator contains details of the shrine of Śantapuri as a meeting place of Buddhist yogins and tantric practitioners.[6]

Although it is not yet possible to identify the persons responsible for the composition of this early register of Svayambhūnāth, we can place them at least in the religious circles of the court of the Fifth Phag-mo-gru sDe-srid Grags-pa rgyal-mtshan (1374–1432), the "sovereign" (*gong ma*) of sNe['u]-gdong and gDan-sa Thel in Central Tibet. The Sixth and Seventh Phag-mo-gru sDe-srid, namely Grags-pa 'byung-gnas (1414–1445) and Kun-dga' legs-pa (1433–1483), were both responsible for invitations to Mahāpaṇḍita Vanaratna to Tibet, and it was from the same circles that Lo-chen bSod-nams rgya-mtsho, the *lo tsā ba* who undertook the arduous journey to the south, came.

As this 15th-century register, which served as the model for the later 17th-century version, is itself based on earlier Tibetan sources concerning Svayambhūnāth, it is hoped that these still older descriptions of the Mahācaitya addressed to Tibetan pilgrims and travellers will be discovered at some time in the future.

[6] The register of the year 1413 was published under the title "A Guide to Svayambhūnāth Stūpa near Kathmandu" in *Rare Tibetan texts from Nepal: A Collection of Guides to Holy Places, lives of Religious Masters, and Khrid yig by the famed Rdza Roṅ-phu Bla-ma*, Dolanji: Tashi Dorji, 1976, pp. 81–90 (see Appendix). For the different journeys of Mahāpaṇḍita Vanaratna to Tibet, see Ehrhard (2004b:246–256). A description of the journey of Lo-chen bSod-nams rgya-mtsho to the Nepal Valley and his sojourn at Śantapuri can be found in Ehrhard (2002b:64–71). A further Tibetan disciple who had visited Vanaratna in Nepal in the year 1464 was Chos-rgyal bsod-nams (1442–1509); see Ehrhard (2004a:71, note 26).

A REGISTER OF "NOBLE ALL [KINDS OF] TREES", MIND SUPPORT OF ALL THE BUDDHAS OF THE THREE TIMES

[1]
Oṃ, may it be auspicious!

Completed from the ocean of compassion
of all the Tathāgatas of the three times,
[this] *Stūpa*, shining brightly forth like a jewel –
may it be victorious for the welfare of [all] beings!

What has been expounded in the *Gośṛṅga-vyākaraṇa-sūtra*
and in the *Mañjuśrī-mūla-tantra*,
and after these words were then condensed by the learned ones [of yore] –
their excellent meaning will be written out [now] as a short register!

[2]
Concerning these things [it is explained] in the following manner: Formerly, at the time of the Buddha Rāṣṭrapāla, this Li-yul existed in the form of a lake. Its name was Goma. At that time were born a thousand sons to Gyam-ring-po, a king who had descended from the Gods of Clear Light and was protecting the doctrine. [While] the other sons took possession of a thousand great countries in Jambudvīpa, the youngest one seized Nepal. His name was King Li. Because the inhabitants of the country exemplified the "ten virtues" (*daśakuśalāni*), the [main] town was called Virtuous One.[7]

At that time there dwelled [there] in samādhi an emanation of Buddha [Śākyamuni], Bhikṣu Jñānasiddhi by name. A king called Viśvadeva received during this period a great number of teachings from Jñānasiddhi [and] erected this Noble All [Kinds of] Trees, a superior receptacle. Jñānasiddhi acted as its custodian. The name of the *stūpa* was Go-ma-sa-la-gan-dha. Afterwards the Dharmarāja [Viśvadeva] passed away, and a statue of the

---

7 For the prophecy of Buddha Śākyamuni concerning a king having a thousand sons, the youngest of which would seize a land called Virtuous One, see *Ārya-gośṛṅga-vyākaraṇa-nāma-mahāyānasūtra* (= TTP, No. 1026), p. 349.1.5–3.6. As the names Li-yul and King Li in the register suggest, the prophecy relates to Khotan (= *li-yul*) as a Buddhist country. For the Tibetan tradition of the so-called "Khotan legend"—the two other literary sources, along with the *Gośṛṅga-vyākaraṇa* being the *Li yul lung bstan pa* and the *Li yul chos kyi lo rgyus*—, see Mayer (1990:48–50). The fact that the adaption of this legend by the register is historically unreliable was criticized soon after the circulation of the text by the Sa-skya-pa scholar Glo-bo mkhan-chen bSod-nams lhun-grub (1456–1532); see his *Mi dbang mgon po rgyal mtshan gyi dris lan rgyal sras bzhad pa'i me tog* in "The Collected Works (Gsuṅ 'bum) of Glo-bo mkhan-chen bSod-nams lhun-grub", Vol. 3, New Delhi: Ngawang Topgay, 1977, p. 10.3–5: "it had [only] been issued to produce faith [in others] by someone who had not much knowledge of the doctrine" (*chos rgyus cher med ba zhig gis gnang dad pa bskyed pa* ...).

Great Mother (= Prajñāpāramitā) manifested itself in his bones; this statue is [still] contained in the [*stūpa* Noble] All [Kinds of] Trees. Afterwards [the Buddhas] Kanakamuni and so forth successively arrived and accomplished an enormous amount of benefit for [all] beings. Also Jñānasiddhi [finally] passed away.[8]

[3]

Then Indra offered the precious jewel of the gods to the noble [*stūpa*]. [The nāga king] Takṣaka offered an ornament of the powerful [nāga called] Kakṣaka. Below the noble [*stūpa*] is a palace of the nāgas. Above [this palace] is a living turtle. Thereupon rests the *yaṣṭi*, seven *'dom* (= forty-two feet) [in circumference] at the base [and a full] forty-two *'dom* (= two-hundred-fifty-two feet) [in length]. There are nineteen "ritual bells" (*ghaṇṭa*) [attached to it]. In the opening [the size] of a [Magadha] *droṇa* on the western side of the *yaṣṭi* are contained forty-eight-thousand self-manifested [images of the] Pañcatathāgata. In all the [openings in the] four directions [of the *yaṣṭi*] are contained a Magadha *droṇa* of relics of the seven Buddhas [of the past and present], [and] eight Magadha bushels (= one-hundred-sixty *droṇa*) of relics of [the Buddha] Śākyamuni are contained in it [as well]. The sixty-two deities of the *Cakrasaṃvara-maṇḍala* which came forth from the skin of King Suvarṇavarman [after he had transformed himself into an ox] are also contained in [an opening the size of] a [Magadha] *droṇa*. It is said that this [*yaṣṭi*] is something in which the auspicious signs in their outer, inner and secret aspects are in agreement.[9]

---

8 According to the quotation of the *Gośṛṅga-vyākaraṇa* (as in note 7), the religious topography of the future Buddhist land of Khotan is centered around a mountain known as "Ox Horn" (*glang ru*) and a river called "Goma". The bank of that river is the location of the *stūpa* "Bestowed on the ground [where the river] Goma [flows]" (*go ma sa la gnang*) or "[Located on] the Bank of the river Goma" (*chu bo go ma'i 'gram*); the designation Go-ma-sa-la-gan-dha is a corrupted form of these two names. According to the work "Prophecy of the Li Country" (*li yul lung bstan pa*) a Khotanese king known as Vijaya Vīrya was responsible for erecting a special *vihāra* and discovering a *stūpa* said to contain relics of Buddha Kāśyapa; see Emmerick (1967:29–33). It is possible that this king served as the model of King Viśvadeva, who according to the register had erected Svayambhū, i.e. Go-ma-sa-la-gan-dha. For a first investigation into the transposition of this legend-cycle from Khotan to Nepal and the identification of the mountain Gośṛṅga with the Svayambhū hill, see Brough (1947:337–339), who comes to the conclusion that "we may therefore imagine that some Tibetan lama who was familiar with the old Tibetan texts dealing with the legends and traditions of Li had attributed them to Nepal." In the 11th century, at the beginning of the second spread of the Buddhist doctrine to Tibet, the religious topography of Li-yul had not yet been transposed to Bal-yul; see Ehrhard (2004a: 393–394, note 144).

9 The presence of the palace of the nāgās and the living turtle below the *stūpa* can be explained by their role as inhabitants of the former lake and obstacle to its outflow; for the alternative role of the turtle in this respect, see Allen (1997:446). In contrast to the tradition of the *Svayambhūpurāṇa,* where the Mahācaitya owes its sacredness to maṇḍalas projected into it and not to being sacred because of relics or other holy objects deposited in it (see v. Rospatt (1999:130)), the description of the *yaṣṭi* as relic container corresponds closely to Tibetan conceptions of the *stūpa* and its most important central part; concerning the function of the Buddhist *stūpa* as both commemorative monument and receptacle of relics—and the general

The Buddha [Śākyamuni himself] has prophesied that this *stūpa* will not be destroyed by the cosmic fire [at the end] of the present kalpa.

[4]
And again from the *[Gośṛṅga-vyākaraṇa-]sūtra*:

> Once when the Buddha [Śākyamuni] was staying in Vaiśālī he spoke to an assembly including Śāriputra and others: "In a region in an easterly direction from here will appear a town by the name of Li-yul or Virtuous One. And on top of the lake [called] Goma will be a mountain [named] "Prophecied Ox-horn" (*glang ru lung bstan*). Out of it will appear the *stūpa* Go-ma-sa-la-gan-dha. In the centre of this lake, which will be like a thousand-petalled lotus, will stand a statue of [the Buddha] Śākyamuni. On the single leaves will rest a thousand Bodhisattvas of the tenth bhūmi."
>
> Then the assembly, including Śāriputra and the others, asked: "What is the reason that such [things] will appear?", and the Buddha [Śākyamuni] replied: "You have to understand that after I have passed into Nirvāṇa, there will appear one-thousand-one of my emanations! And this lake, moreover, it will travel to the southern parts of India!" After these and other prophecies had been made, Śāriputra and Ānanda stood up and cleft the lake with their mendicant staff and club, [and the lake] drained away.[10]

---

classification of relics into four or five categories—, see Ehrhard (2004c:76–79) and chapter eleven of the present volume. The historiographical work of the Second dPa'-bo gTsug-lag phreng-ba (1504–1566) contains the narrative of a Newar king, who joined a *gaṇacakra* in the inner cavern below *shing kun mchod rten* and prayed to be allowed to be present in this sacred realm also in the future. He was transformed into an ox and then killed, and his bones were turned into representations of the sixty-two deities of the *Cakrasaṃvara-maṇḍala*. The gate to this cavern, known as Śantapuri, is impassable owing to a "circle of swords" (*gri'i 'khor lo*). This later attribute is connected to prophecies about King Aṃśuvarman in the *Mañjuśrī-mūla-tantra*; see gTsug-lag phreng-ba: *Dam pa'i chos kyi 'khor lo bsgyur ba rnams kyi byung ba gsal bar byed pa mkhas pa'i dga' ston*, Peking: Mi-rigs dpe-skrun khang, 1986, pp. 173.11–174.1, and *Ārya-mañjuśrī-mūla-tantra* (= TTP, No. 162), p. 260.3.5–6.

[10] For Buddha Śākyamuni residing in Vaiśālī and uttering prophecies about the mountain and the *stūpa* of Khotan and about a multi-pedalled lotus upon the lake covering the country, where a multitude of Buddhas and Bodhisattvas will appear, see *Ārya-gośṛṅga-vyākaraṇa-nāma-mahāyānasūtra* (= TTP, No. 1026), p. 348.1.5–5.8. While the register ascribes the draining of the lake to Śāriputra and Ānanda, the *Sūtra* gives Śāriputra and Vaiśravana as the persons responsible for opening the lake; see ibid, p. 352.55.4–6. Concerning general observations on the myth of the lake drainage in Himalayan regions and the fact that these kinds of legends propose an explanation of the "landscape as it is" and are told in areas where lake drainage has indeed occurred, see Allen (1997:443–445). It should be noted that the travelling of the lake to the southern direction of India – and that implies its relocation to the Nepal Valley – is only to be found in the register's adaption of the prophecies and not in the *Gośṛṅga-vyākaraṇa*.

The remainder of a small [lake] was left behind, and it was poured out by Gaṇapati. [Then] Gaṇapati dissolved into a boulder, and [still today] there exists a self-arisen [statue of what looks like] an elephant [at that place]. Then there appeared four great towns at the empty site of the [former] lake.[11]

[5]
Afterwards, at the time of the Buddha [Śākyamuni], an excellent group of six [bhikṣus] acted as custodians. [King] Aṃśuvarman acted as patron. After the Buddha [Śākyamuni] passed away, [his disciple] Kāśyapa acted as custodian. Then Kāśyapa died; the outer receptacle, [containing as it does his relics,] known as Kāśyapa Stūpa, is to the west [of Noble All [Kinds of] Trees]. Then [Ārya] Nāgārjuna acted as custodian [and King] Suvarṇavarman acted as patron. The sacred site of [the local protector] Śantaputri was [Ārya] Nāgārjuna's chamber for spiritual practice. Opposite its entrance door is a gate to the realms of [Noble] All [Kinds of] Trees, the nāgās [and] of the vighna [demons], [these] three. [The gate is] blocked by a square stone of one *'dom* in length on each of its four sides. When [Ārya] Nāgārjuna discovered the *Phyag na rdo rje u rtsa'i rgyud* from the realm of the nāgās and translated it, it is said that he spoke: "[Come now,] Śantaputri, take a little delight [in it]!"[12]

---

11 A great part text of the early register – including the introductory verses, the "Khotan legend", the description of the *yaṣṭi* and the myth of the lake drainage – has been incorporated into the latter register, composed in the year 1686; see Wylie (1970:43.5–44.26). The text of the disciple of Rang-rig ras-pa provides additional information concerning the self-arisen stone statue of Gaṇeśa, manifested near the remaining small lake. It is stated that "it still exists today in [the temple of Ārya] dBu-khang (= Bhu-kaṃ) in the region of Patan" (*ye rang gi phyogs dbu khang na da lta yang yod*). For the village of Buṃga or Bungamati, located south-east of Patan, housing the temple of Buṃga Lokeśvara or Ārya Bhu-kaṃ, as it is known to Tibetan pilgrims, see Ehrhard (2004a:57–60 et passim).

12 This section of the register, describing the custodians of Svayambhū during the times of Buddha Śākyamuni and his disciple Kāśyapa has also been included in the register of Rang-rig ras-pa's disciple; see Wylie (1970:44.26–45.9). It adds an etiological story of how the *stūpa* received its name Noble All [Kinds of] Trees, namely that [Ārya] Nāgārjuna had cut off his hair and while scattering it around made the wish that all kind of trees should grow at this noble edifice; see ibid, p. 44.29–34. A further addition is the mentioning of a "Vasubandhu Stūpa" next to the one containing the relics of Kāśyapa; see ibid, p. 45.1. The latter text provides greater details relating to the discovery of scriptures by [Ārya] Nāgārjuna, including the famous find of sixteen volumes of Prajñāpāramitā literature written in gold on paper of lapis lazuli and afterwards kept in the Sthaṃ Vihāra in Kathmandu; see ibid, p. 45.5–7. For this temple, known for the stays of Buddhist masters Vibhūticandra (12th/13th century) and Vanaratna, see Ehrhard (2002b:69, note 36). The local protector Śantaputri, whose residence in the entrance of the temple of the same name—which is also associated with [Ārya] Nāgārjuna—derives its designation from the gate leading to the realm of the nāgās; see note 9. Compare the spelling of his name as "Shan-ta-spu-gri" (*spu gri* = razor) in the biography of gTsang-smyon Heruka (1452–1507), who completed a renovation of Svayambhū in the year 1504; rGod-tshang ras-pa sNa-tshogs rang-grol (1482–1559): *gTsang smyon heruka phyogs thams cad las rnam par rgyal ba'i rnam thar rdo rje theg pa'i gsal byed nyi ma'i snying po* (= Śata-Piṭaka Series, 79), New Delhi 1969, p. 226.1–7.

[6]

At that time, after a spell, the *yaṣṭi* broke. dPon-chen Śākya bzang-po offered three large *droṇa* and fifty ounces of gold. Further, after the *kalyāṇamitras* from dBus and gTsang, the "noblemen" (*bhāro*) from Nepal [and] the Thākurīs from India had donated much wealth, a [new] *yaṣṭi* was set up by the religious teachers from dBus, father [and] son. The base of the *yaṣṭi* had [a circumference] of seven *'dom* (= forty-two feet); the length [of it] was seventy-two *'dom* (= four-hundred-twenty feet).[13]

[7]

It has been prophesied that a thousand Buddhas of the past and a thousand Buddhas of the future will appear at this receptacle, [and] that the relics of those who passed into nirvāṇa will be contained in it. The bhikṣu Jñānasiddhi was an emanation of Samantabhadra.

Within the demarcation in the four directions of the inner section of [Noble] All [Kinds of] Trees, where there are stone maṇḍalas and bowls [for offerings], [the *stūpa*] is a palace of the gods; therefore, one should approach it – except for making offerings and rendering services – [only] from its outer zone. On top of the *yaṣṭi* is a crystal, surrounded by ten bars of silver bullion. If one anoints it with the [six kinds of] excellent medicine, one will be liberated from the fate of becoming sick. If one offers armour [and] weapons to it, one will be freed from one's fate of [having to resort to] weapons. If one offers grain or a *gaṇacakra*, one's fortunes will increase and one will be liberated from one's fate of [suffering from] famine. Above [the opening the size of] a *droṇa* on the western side of the *yaṣṭi* there is a cavity: if one offers [there] butter [or one of] the five kinds of precious stones, one will obtain the immeasurable merit of [having performed] an offering to the self-manifested body [of the *stūpa*]. Also, if one performs ritual acts on one's hair, nails and so forth and inserts [these items into the cavity], one will remember one's previous existences. Just by hearing the name [Noble] All [Kinds of] Trees one will be liberated from saṃsāra. [But] if one steals from the riches of this [*stūpa*], in that very lifetime will occur [only more] non-virtuous [deeds], and these will not be matters one will be able to confess; and also in the next life there will be no [single] chance to be born as a human being!

---

[13] Concerning the erection of a new *yaṣṭi* in the second half of the 13th century, commissioned by dPon-chen Śākya bzang-po, the first chief administrator of the Yüan-Sa-skya period in Tibetan history, see Ehrhard (1991:16–18) and chapter five of the present volume.. A still earlier renovation – presumably in the first half of the 13th century – had been undertaken by a member of the Tshal-pa bKa'-brgyud-pa school from the monastery of rTa-sga in Western Tibet; see v. Rospatt (2001:200–201). In this case, too, the *yaṣṭi* was exchanged, and it is interesting to note that the historiographical source describing this event attributed the old *yaṣṭi* to have been set up by [Ārya] Nāgārjuna himself; see Kun-dga' rdo-rje, pp. 146.19–147.9. For reasons that the accounts of these two renovations refer to one and the same event, compare v. Rospatt (2011:163-168).

The religious protector of this [*stūpa*] is Vināyaka, the king of the vighna [demons].[14]

[8]
At the peak of the Vindhya mountain [behind the *stūpa*] is a teaching throne of [the Buddha Śākya]muni. On the side [of the mountain] there are many receptacles, including a chamber for the spiritual practice of [Ārya] Nāgārjuna. To the north of that [mountain] there are two *stūpa*s [containing relics] of King Śuddhodana and [the Buddha Śākyamuni's] mother Māyādevī. To the south of [Noble] All [Kinds of] Trees is a hill which was cut out of [the mountain] Gṛdhakūta [in India] by Hanuman. In the four directions going out from [Noble] All [Kinds of] Trees there are four great treasures; [Ārya] Nāgārjuna put them into [the earth] as requisites for renovations of [Noble] All [Kinds of] Trees in the future. In the east there is a spring that arose from a prayer of [King] Suvarṇavarman; if one drinks from it or performs ablutions, one's obscurations will be cleared away and diseases will not appear [in one's body]. To the south of it, at the empty spot where the corpse of [Ārya] Nāgārjuna melted away, there exists a self-arisen stone statue [of him], a full cubit in height: if one comes across it, one's wrong conceptions will subside. To the south of it there is a self-arisen statue of mGon-po (= Mahākāla); if one brings offerings to it, all obstacles will be cleared away.[15]

---

[14] The first instruction to the pilgrims admonishes them not to step on the socle of the Mahācaitya which encircles the edifice a few feet above the ground. From that structural part onwards the *stūpa* should be regarded as "a palace of the gods". For an early photograph of Svayambhū, where this socle is visible, see Le Bon (1981:57); compare the photograph of Cabahil Stūpa in Gutschow (1997:159). For the observation that the two-storey socle which underlies the whole structure is generally hidden from view, see also Kölver (2000:104). The question of the guardians of the *stūpa* as appointed by the Buddha Śākyamuni is raised by Glo-bo mkhan-chen bSod-nams lhun-grub in his polemic against statements made by the register about the identity of "Go-ma-sa-la-gan-dha" and Svayambhū. He refers in this respect to Vaiśravana, to Saṃjñāya, the general of the *yakṣa*s, and the king of the nāgās. Claiming that Vināyaka, the king of the vighna demons, is the religious protector of the Mahācaitya is another proof that the two *stūpa*s cannot be the same; see his work (as in note 7), pp. 10.7–11.3. The guardians of the Khotanese *stūpa* according to the "Prophecy of the Li Country" can be found in Emmerick (1967:13–15). The biography of gTsang-smyon Heruka lists in contrast to these statements Śantaputri and Viśvakarman as the appointed guardians of the *stūpa*. Svayambhū is in this literary source from the 16th century nevertheless referred to as "Go-ma-sa-la-gan-dha" and the ruler of Nepal as "King of Li-yul" (*li yul rgyal po*); see the work of rGod-tshang ras-pa (as in note 12), pp. 220.7 ff., and pp. 225.7 ff.

[15] The list of instructions to the pilgrims, the identity of the religious protector of the *stūpa* and the list of further sacred sites in the surrounding area are also to be found in the later register; see Wylie (1970:45.14–46.9). The text of Rang-rig ras-pa's disciple adds thrones of Śāriputra and Maudgalyāyana to the one of Buddha Śākyamuni at the top of the Vindhya mountain and a set of five *stūpa*s near the hill of present-day Kiṃdol said to be cut out from the Gṛdhakūta mountain in India. For the transposition of the Vindhya mountain from the south of India to Nepal as reflected in Tibetan sources, see Ehrhard (2004a:329, note 25). This site is known to Newar Buddhists as Jāmāvca, based on the literary tradition of the *Svayambhūpurāṇa*; compare Gutschow (1997:15–16). A further addition of the register from the year 1686 is a self-manifested stone statue, eleven *'dom* (= sixty-six feet) high, said to have appeared

To the south of [the *stūpa*] Bya-rung kha-shor (= Bodhnāth) there are a great number of marvellous receptacles, including Phag-mo'i mngal-chu (= Guhyeśvarī). This [whole] land [of Nepal] is the palace of Śrī Cakrasaṃvara, it is said.[16]

[9]
Then the *yaṣṭi* broke. Mahāpaṇḍita Śāriputra set it up [again]. After faithful persons such as the Great Sovereign [Grags-pa rgyal-mtshan (1374–1432)] from dBus, the myriarchs of [La-stod] lHo and [La-stod] Byang, and the Sher[-pa] mkhan-po of Khams Mi-nyag offered countless wealth and acted as donors, the king of Nepal, Śrī Jayajyotirmalladeva (reign 1408–1428) acted as the main supervisor [of the renovation]. Having praised the assembled "noblemen" (*bhāro*) in an official writing, he called together the craftsmen under his charge. The parasol together with the accompanying discs was completed in a proper manner on the fifteenth day of the fourth [Tibetan] month in the snake year (= 1413). The request letters [for donations] on the occasion of these [activities] and the necessity of acting as supervisors at different times were attended to well by the great hosts, the pair of brothers [called] Yu-gu-li.[17]

---

when King Suvarṇavarman had confessed his sins; see Wylie (1970:46.9–11). A different – and quite early – version of the legend about a water spot associated in this case with King Aṃśuvarman can be found in the biography of Khro-phu Lo-tsā-ba Byams-pa'i dpal (1173–1250), who stayed in Mang-yul Gung-thang and in Nepal between the years 1196 and 1198. According to this work the Newar king had killed the nāga king after performing the spiritual practice of the goddess Māricī. He then put the head jewel of the slain serpent on top of the *yaṣṭi* of the Mahācaitya. Afterwards the former spot where the nāga had resided became a place where offerings to the nāgas could be performed; see *Khro lo chen pos mdzad pa'i dpag bsam 'khri shing* (manuscript), fol. 20a/4–b/1. This literary source from the 13th century gives both the names 'Phags-pa shing-kun and 'Phags-pa rang-byung for Svayambhū, without mentioning the designation "Go-ma-sa-la-gan-dha". For further activities of Khro-phu Lo-tsā-ba in the Nepal Valley, see Ehrhard (2004a:76–77).

[16] See Stein (1988:34–35) for Tibetan conceptions – based on the tradition of the *Saṃvarodayatantra* – of the Nepal Valley as the land Himālaya or Upacchandoha, its two main sacred sites being the *liṅgam* and the *yonī* of Paśupatināth and Guhyeśvarī respectively. This overview is based on the pilgrimage guide book of the Fourth Khams-sprul; the relevant sections are contained in Macdonald (1975:129.3.1–132.1.5) and Macdonald & Dvags-po Rin-po-che (1981:250–252). For this tradition of the *Saṃvarodayatantra* and its application to the Svayambhū sanctuary, see also Kölver (1992:137–141); compare Huntington (2002:22–23) for the projection of the *Cakrasaṃvara-maṇḍala* on the Nepal Valley, with Svayambhū being the centre. From the 10th century onwards the temple known as Śantapuri played a special role for practitioners of the *Cakrasaṃvara* tradition – both Indian and Tibetan; this is reflected in the register under consideration; see note 9. Concerning further material on Śantapuri in this regard, compare Ehrhard (2002b:47–48).

[17] Details on the erection of a new *yaṣṭi* in the year 1413 and on the persons involved in the renovation can be found in Ehrhard (1991:14–16) and chapter five in the present volume. Mahāpaṇḍita Śāriputra was the abbot of Bodhgayā and had been invited in that very year to the court of the Chinese emperor. It is said that the funds for a whitewash of the *stūpa* had been provided by the Ming court; see Ricca and Lo Bue (1993:19). The fact that a religious teacher from the Tangut region (= Mi-nyag) can be found among the donors suggests that he was a member of the imperial delegation responsible for the invitation of

[10]
Salutation [to the *Stūpa*]!

Beginningless noble One in the unconfined Dharmadhātu,
a paradise tree that grants the wishes and needs to [all] beings
[and] shows the great path to complete liberation by way of a chariot –
to you, boundless Omniscient One, arisen by yourself, I bow down [in respect]!

As your deeds are without limit,
one is not able to capture them in a painting.
Yet what has been expounded about you in the *[Gośṛṅga-vyākaraṇa-]sūtra* [and] in the *[Mañjuśrī-mūla-]tantra*, not being learned from [these] tokens –
I, Chos-skyabs dpal[-bzang-po], who has studied much,
relying [only] on [the Buddha Śākyamuni's] doctrine
and on unfailing registers [of yore] – including those [dealing with]
the *Mantradhara* Padmasambhava and
[Ārya] Nāgārjuna, who reached the limit of the right view –
having been requested in a proper way,
[composed] such a sun of a register, which did not exist formerly,
and then the passionless One
[called] Puṇyaśrībhadra (= bSod-nams dpal bzang-po)
compiled it for the benefit of [all] beings
on the full moon day of the first summer month
of the [year of the] water-snake (= 1413),
near "[Noble] All [Kinds of] Trees".[18]

May good fortune increase!

Mahāpaṇḍita Śāriputra. A person called Sher-pa mkhan-po was engaged in inviting Mahāpaṇḍita Vanaratna to undertake a third journey to Tibet in the year 1452; see Ehrhard (2004b:253). For the importance of "hosts" (*gnas po*), i.e. Newar merchants who assisted Tibetan travellers in financial and diplomatic matters, see Ehrhard (2002a:155–156) and Ehrhard (2002b:66–71).

[18] Both the introductory verses and the colophon mention that the authors of the register relied on previous descriptions of the *stūpa*, using Buddhist canonical sources like the *Gośṛṅga-vyākaraṇa-sūtra* and the *Mañjuśrī-mūla-tantra*. It is thus possible that they used registers, probably from the 14th century or earlier, which dealt with accounts concerning the presence of [Ārya] Nāgārjuna and Padmasambhava at the Mahācaitya. These Tibetan literary sources would then, by implication, be responsible for the transposition of the "Khotan legend" to the Nepal Valley. Works of the biographical tradition of Padmasambhava dating from the 16th and 17th centuries include narratives of the great adept's sojourn at Svayambhū, his hiding of treasures at the site, and his taming of a nāga, said to have been the "lord of the territory" (*sa bdag*); see, for example, Blo-gros rgyal-mtshan *Slob dpon sangs rgyas gnyis pa padma 'byung gnas kyi rnam par thar pa yid kyi mun sel*, pp. 79.2–80.1.

APPENDIX

[1a] *// Dus gsum sangs rgyas thams cad kyi thugs kyi rten 'phags pa shing kun gyi dkar chag bzhugs so //*

[1]

[1b] *Oṃ svasti /*

dus gsum bde gshegs thams cad kyi /
thugs rje'i chu gter las grub pa'i /
mchod rten rin chen gzi 'od can /
'gro ba'i dpal du rgyal gyur cig /

mdo sde glang ru lung bstan dang /
'jam dpal rtsa rgyud las bshad pa'i /
tshig rnams mkhas pas bsdus byas nas /
don bzang dkar chags mdor[19] *bsdus bri //*

[2]

de la 'di ltar / sngon sangs rgyas yul 'khor skyong bzhugs pa'i dus / li yul 'di mtshor ru yod cing / de'i ming ni gho ma (= go ma) zhes bya'o / de'i dus 'od gsal lha las babs pa'i chos skyong ba'i rgyal po gyam ring po bya ba la / bu stong rtsa 'byung / bu gzhan rnams kyis 'dzam bu gling du yul chen po stong bzung / chung bas bal yul bzung ste / ming rgyal po li zhes bya'o / yul mi rnams dge ba bcu spyod pas na / grong khyer de yang dge ba zhes bya'o / de dus sangs rgyas kyi sprul pa dge slong dznyānasiddhi (= jñānasiddhi) zhes bya ba ting nge 'dzin la bzhugs so / de dus rgyal po bhi sa dhe ba (= viśvadeva) zhes bya **[2a]** *bas / dznyānasiddhi (= jñānasiddhi) la chos mang po gsan*[20] */ rten khyad par can 'phags pa shing kun 'di bzhengs so / dkon gnyer dznyānasiddhi (= jñānasiddhi) mdzad / mchod rten gyi ming la gho ma saṃ gha tha (= go ma sa la gan dha) zhes bya'o // de nas chos rgyal de mya ngan las 'das shing / gdung la yum chen mo'i sku byon / de yang shing kun gyi nang na bzhugs so // de rjes gser thub la sogs pa rim par byon nas / 'gro don rgya cher po mdzad / dznyānasiddhi (= jñānasiddhi) yang mya ngan las 'das so //*

[3]

de nas brgya byin gyis 'phags pa la lha'i nor bu rin po che phul / 'jog pos ghakṣa (sic) dbang gi rgyan phul lo / 'phags pa'i 'og na klu'i pho brang yod / de'i steng na rus sbal

---

[19] *mdo*

[20] *bsan*

gson po gcig yod / de'i steng na srog shing btsugs yod pa'i rtsa ba la 'dom[21] *bdun / yongs 'dom*[22] *bzhi bcu rtsa gnyis yod / dril bu bcu dgu yod / srog shing gi nub gyi bre mig la / rang byon lha lnga stong bzhi bcu rtsa brgyad bzhugs so // phyogs bzhir sangs rgyas rab bdun gyi ring sel ma gha dha'i bre re re bzhugs / śākya thub pa'i* **[2b]** *ring sel ma gha dha'i khal brgyad bzhugs / rgyal po gser gyi go cha'i pags pa la byon pa'i 'khor lo bde mchog lha drug bcu rtsa gnyis bre la bzhugs // de phyi nang gsum gyi· rten 'brel 'grigs pa yin gsungs / mchod rten 'di bskal pa'i*[23] *me 'jigs par mi nus par sangs rgyas nyid kyis lung bstan no //*

[4]
mdo las kyang /

> *sangs rgyas yangs pa can na bzhugs dus / sha ri bu la sogs pa 'khor rnams la bka' stsal pa / 'di nas shar phyogs kyi logs shig na / dge ba zhes bya'am li yul zhes bya ba'i grong khyer 'byung bar 'gyur bas / mtso gho ma (= go ma) 'di'i steng na / ri glang ru lung bstan yod la / de'i nang nas gho ma la saṃ gha ta'i (= go ma sa la gan dha'i) mchod rten 'byung bar 'gyur ro // mtsho 'di yang pad ma stong dang ldan pa'i lte ba la śākya thub pa'i sku bzhugs / 'dab ma la sa bcu pa'i byang chub sems dpa' stong gnas par 'gyur to // de nas sha ri'i bu la sogs pa 'khor rnams kyis gsol ba / de lta bu 'byung ba'i rgyu mtshan ci lags /* **[3a]** *ces gsol ba dang / bka' stsal pa / nga nyid mya ngan 'das pa'i 'og tu / nga'i sprul pa stong rtsa gcig 'byung bar 'gyur bar rig par bya'o // mtsho 'di yang rgya gar lho phyogs su song shig ces sogs lung bstan nas / de nas sha ri'i bu dang / kun dga' bo langs te / mkhar gsil*[24] *dang dbyug thos mtsho bshags pas deng*[25] */ lhag ma cung zhig lus pa tshogs bdag gis bshos / tshogs bdag pha bong gcig la thim pas*[26] */ rdo rang byon glang po che 'dra ba yod // de nas mtsho'i shul du grong khyer chen po bzhi byung ngo //*

[5]
de nas sangs rgyas bzhugs dus dkon gnyer drug sde bzang pos mdzad / gser gyi go chas sbyin bdag mdzad do / sangs rgyas mya ngan las 'das nas 'od bsrung gis dkon gnyer mdzad do // de nas 'od bsrung grongs / 'od bsrung mchod rten zhes bya phyi rten nub

---

21 *mdom*

22 *mdom*

23 *skal pa'i*

24 *gar bsil*

25 *dengs*

26 *thim pa'i*

phyogs la yod / de rjes klu sgrub kyis dkon gnyer mdzad / 'od zer go chas sbyin bdag mdzad do // shanta putri'i gnas ni klu grub gyi sgrub khang yin / de'i sgo mdun du / shing kun[27] */ klu yul / bgegs yul* **[3b]** *gsum gyi sgo rdo 'dom*[28] *gang gru bzhi pa gcig gis kha bcad yod do // klu sgrub kyis klu yul nas phyag na rdo rje u rtsa'i rgyud ston nas bsgyur bas shanta pu tri cung zhig / mnyes zhes pa'ang zer ro //*

[6]

der re shig nas srog shing chag ste / dpon chen śākya bzang pos gser bre chen gsum dang gser srang lnga bcu phul / gzhan yang dbus gtsang gi dge bshes / bal po'i 'ba' ro / rgya gar gyi khra khur (= tha kur) rnams kyis[29] *nor mang po phul nas / bla ma dbus pa yab sras kyis srog shing btsugs / srog shing gi rtsa ba la 'dom*[30] *bdun srid du 'dom*[31] *bdun cu rtsa gnyis yod do //*

[7]

rten de la 'das pa'i sangs rgyas dang ma 'ongs pa'i sangs rgyas stong 'byung bar 'gyur ro // de dag mya ngan las 'das pa'i ring sel rnams 'dir bzhugs par lung bstan no // dge slong dznyānasiddhi (= jñānasiddhi) ni kun tu bzang po sprul pa'o // shing kun gyi nang mtshams[32] *kyi phyogs bzhi na / rdo'i maṇḍala dang / kong bu*[33] *yod pa'i mtshams phan chad lha'i pho brang yin pas / mchod 'bul dang zhabs tog*[34] *ma gtogs*[35] **[4a]** *de'i phyi rim nas 'gro dgos so // srog shing gi rtse la shel yam bu'i pham bcu yis 'khor ba gcig yod do // de la bzang sman gyis byugs na nad kyi skal pa las thar / go mtshon phul na mtshon gyi skal pa las thar / 'bru dang tshogs 'khor phul bas longs spyod 'phel zhing mu ge'i skal pa las thar ro // srog shin gi nub bre'i steng na khung bu yod / de na mar rin po che sna lnga phul na / rang byung gi sku mchod pa'i bsod nams dpag med thob po // yang skra*[36] *sen sogs la cho ga byas te bcug na skye ba dran par 'gyur ro // shing kun gyi mtshan thos pa tsam gyis 'khor ba las thar bar 'gyur ro // 'di'i dkor la 'bags na tshe 'dir mi dge ba 'byung zhing bshags pa'i gnas med do // tshe phyi ma'ang mir skyes ba'i skabs med do // 'di'i bsrungs ma bgegs kyi rgyal po bhi na ya ga (= vināyaka) yin no //*

---

27 *shin kun*

28 *mdom*

29 *kyi*

30 *mdom*

31 *mdom*

32 *'tshams*

33 *skong bu*

34 *zhabs rtog*

35 *ma rtogs*

36 *spra*

[8]

ri bo 'bigs byed kyi rtse la thub pa'i chos khri yod // 'dabs na klu sgrub kyi sgrub khang sogs rten du ma bzhugs / de'i byang na / rgyal po zas gtsang dang yum sgyu ma lha **[4b]** *mdzes kyi mchod rten gnyis yod / shing kun gyi lho na ha la ba nydzus (sic) bya rgod phung po nas bzhogs pa'i ri yod / shing kun gyi phyogs bzhi na gter chen po bzhi / klu sgrub kyis ma 'ongs pa na shing kun zhig gsos*[37] *kyi chas la bcug yod / shar na gser gyi go cha'i smon lam las byung ba'i chu yod / de las 'thung dang khrus byas na sgrib pa 'dag cing nad mi 'byung ngo // de'i lho na klu sgrub kyi spur zhu*[38] *shul na rdo sku rang byon khru gang pa gcig yod de dang mjal*[39] *na rtog pa zhi 'gro / de'i lho na mgon po'i sku rang byon gcig yod de la mchod na bar chad thams cad sel lo // bya rung kha shor gyi lho na phag mo'i mngal chu sogs ngo mtshar can gyi rten du ma yod do // yul 'di dpal 'khor lo bde mchog gi pho brang yin gsung pa yod do //*

[9]

de nas srog shing chag pa / paṇḍita chen po sha ri bhutras (= shariputras) btsugs ste / dbus pa gong ma chen po lho byang gi khri dpon / sher mkhan po khams mi nyag[40] *sogs dad ldan rnams kyis nor dpag tu med pa phul nas sbyin bdag mdzad ste* **[5a]** *bal po'i rgyal po śrī ja ya dzo ma la dhe bos (sic) / do dam gyi gtso bo mdzad nas 'khor 'ba' ro rnams gser yig la bsngags nas / mnga' zhabs kyi gzo rig mkhas pa rnams bsdus te / gdugs chos 'khor gtogs*[41] *dang bcas pa sbru lo zla bzhi pa'i tshes bco lnga la yang dag par grub / de dag gi skabs su yar mar gyi zhu 'phrin dang / bar skabs kyi do dam byed dgos rnams / gnas po chen po yu gu li sku mched kyis yang dag par mdzad do //*

[10]

// namo /

mtha' bral chos kyi dbyings su thog med 'phags //
dpag[42] *bsam rkang 'thung*[43] *'gro la dgos 'dod ster //*
shing rta'i 'gros ltar rnam grol lam chen ston //
kun mkyhen mtha' yas rang byung khyed la 'dud //

---

37 *zhig bsos*

38 *gzhu*

39 *'jal*

40 *me nyag*

41 *rtogs*

42 *dpa'*

43 *thung*

khyed kyi mdzad 'phrin mtha' yas pas //
ri mor bris bar mi nus mod //
'on kyang mdo rgyud khyod bshad pa'i //
rtags ma mkhas pas bstan pa dang //
sngags 'chang padma 'byung gnas dang //
lta ba mthar phyin klu grub sogs //
'khrul med [5b] *dkar chags la rten nas //*
sngon med dkar chags nyi ma 'di //
mang thos chos skyabs dpal bdag gis //
legs par bskul nas snyoms las can //
pu na śri'i bha tra (= punyaśribhadra) *yis //*
shing kun drung du chu sbrul gyi //
dbyar zla ra ba'i nya chen la //
'gro ba'i don du mdo bzhin sbyar //

dge legs 'phel //

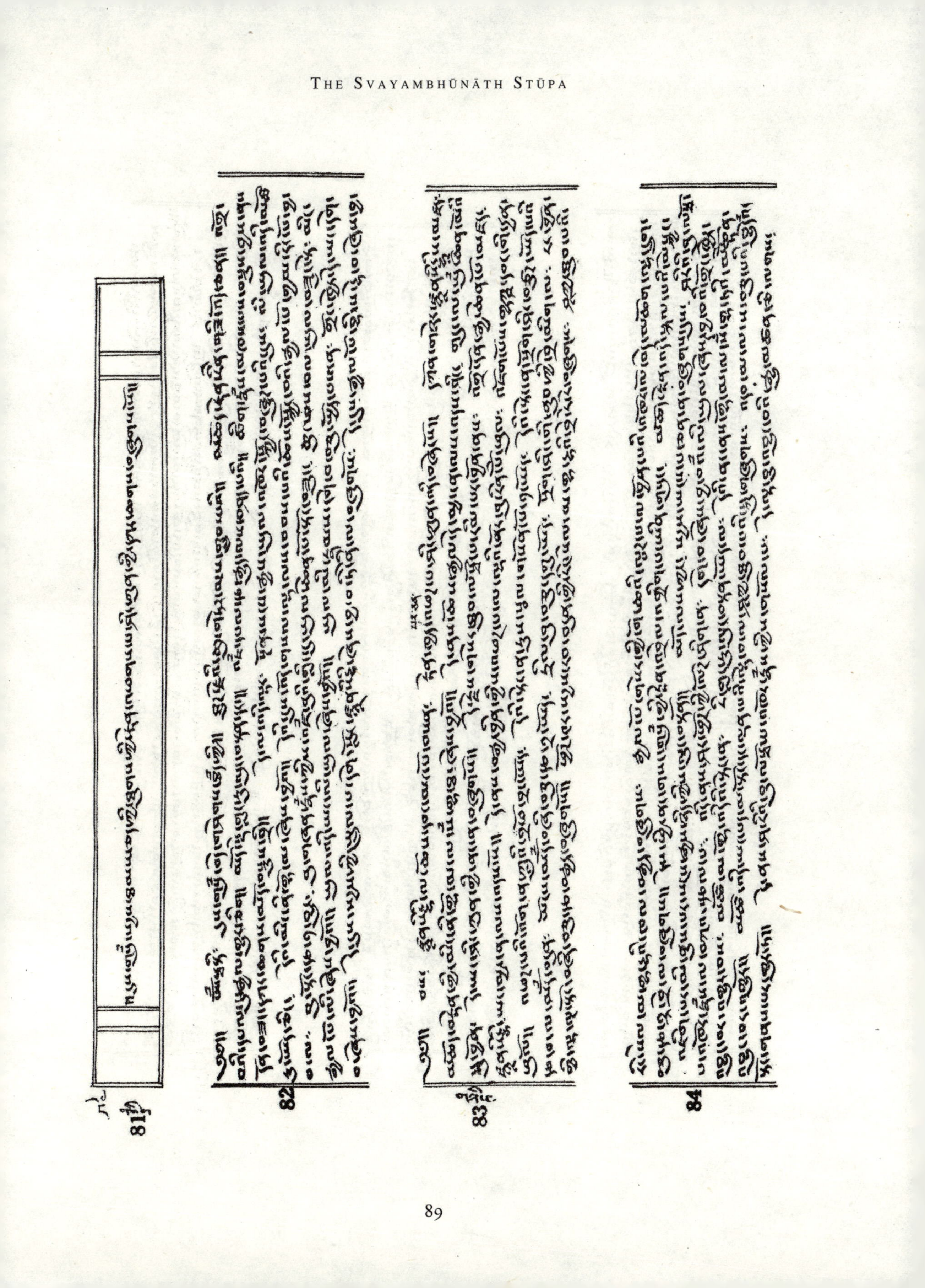

81 [illegible]

82 [illegible]

83 [illegible]

84 [illegible]

85

86

87

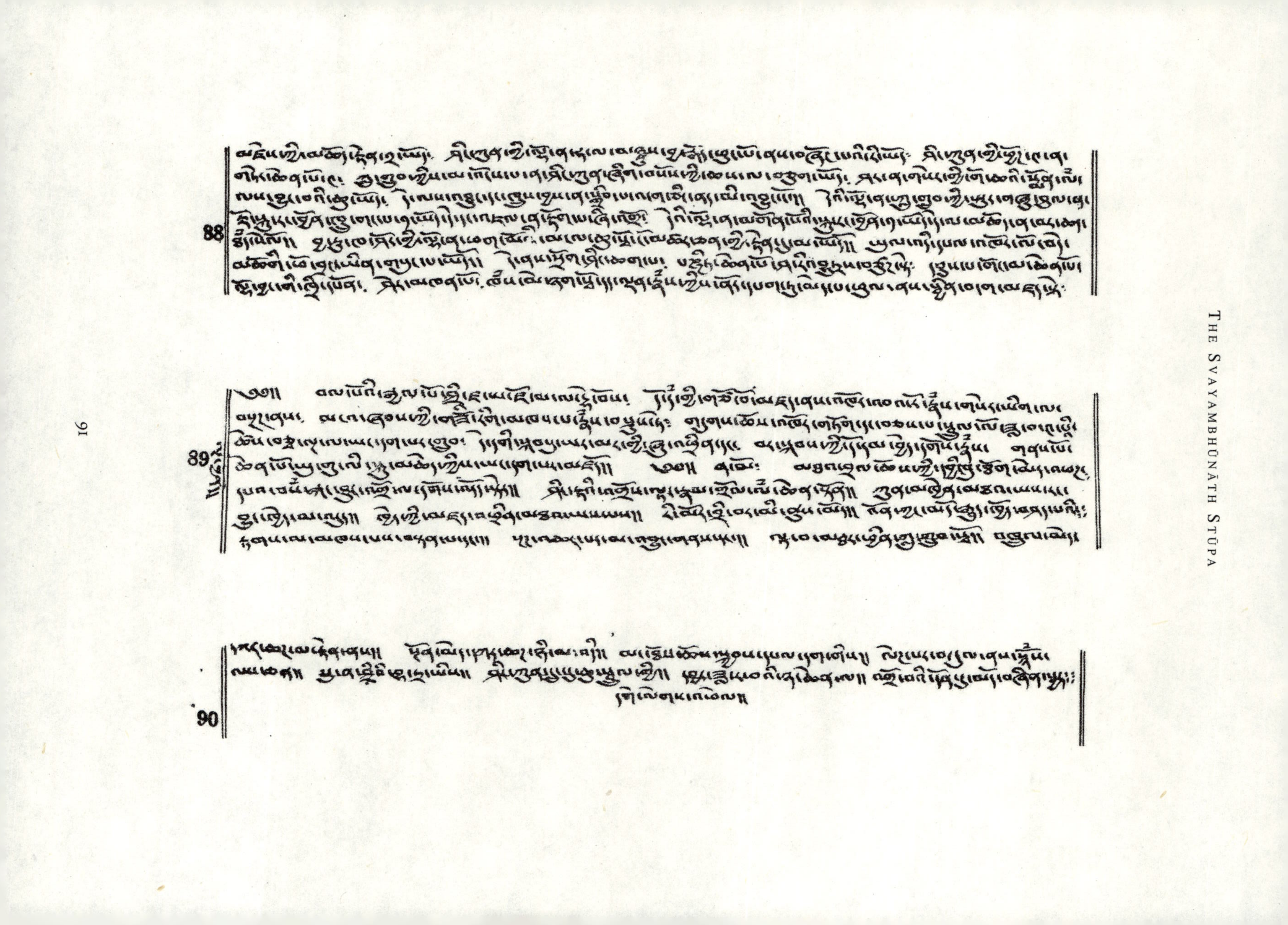

88

89

90

III.

The Bodhnāth Stūpa

The Stūpa of Bodhnāth:
A Preliminary Analysis of the Written Sources

Written sources dealing with the *stūpa* of Bodhnāth are not as numerous as the host of Tibetan pilgrims that daily circle the large complex northeast of Paśupatināth from the early morning hours to late in the evening. L.A. Waddell, who devoted a short article to the *stūpa* over hundred years ago, described it in the following words: "It is the chief place of lamaist pilgrimage in Nepal, attracting far more votaries than the Svayambhūnāth Stūpa, which is not far distant. Its special virtue is reputed to be its power of granting all prayers for worldly wealth, family and everything else asked for." In the same breath, however, he is forced to concede: "But no description or account of the monument seems to be on record."[1]

What is available to Tibetan pilgrims, though, – and Waddell joins their ranks – is a "printed booklet which is sold at the *stūpa*". This booklet is of interest to him, inasmuch as it details how the *stūpa* is brought into direct connection with the most important legendary and historical personalities of "early Lamaism". The particulars Waddell gives concerning the printing of the text at hand are revealing: "The print is a new revision by Puṇya Vajra and another disciple of 'the great Lama Zhabs-dkar'. This latter Lama, I am informed, lived about fifty years ago, and gilded the short spire of the *stūpa* and built the present investing wall."[2]

---

1 See Waddell (1882:186–189). Waddell included this "Note" in his book *Buddhism and Lamaism of Tibet* (1895:314–317). Concerning the name Ma-gu-ta he writes (ibid, p. 189 = p. 317): "The name 'Ma-gu-ta' – pronounced 'Makuta' – is doubtless a contraction for *Makuta badhana*, the pre-Buddhist 'crested chaitya' such as existed at Buddha's death at Kuśinagara." According to Tibetan tradition it is a place name. See *mChod rten chen po bya rung kha shor gyi lo rgyus thos pas grol ba*, fol. 3a/2: *bal yul ma gu ta'i yul gru ru*, and the translation in Dowman (1973:24): "in the country of Nepal in the district of Maguta".

2 The guide for pilgrims to the *stūpa* of Bodhnāth is the text *mChod rten chen po bya rung kha shor gyi lo rgyus thos pas grol ba*, 32 fols.; various editions are available. The edition mentioned by Waddell was made for the occasion of the *stūpa*'s renovation by Zhabs-dkar Tshogs-drug rang-grol (1781–1851); on the biography of this Tibetan yogin from Amdo, see Ehrhard (1990a:32–42) and on his contribution to the decoration of the stūpa of Bodhnāth compare Cüppers (1993:152–155). The first chapter of the text, known as an 'inventory' (*dkar chag*), was translated by Hoffman (1965:42–46), "Der Stūpa der Gänsehirtin"; a complete English rendition is provided by Dowman (1973). The text falls within the literary genre of 'treasure works' (*gter ma*); it owes its final form to the 'treasure discoverer' (*gter ston*) sNgags-'chang Śākya bzang-po (15th/16th century). The name Bya-rung kha-shor or Byar-rung kha-shor (Permission to Do What's Proper) is associated with the person of a woman keeper of geese and an

This text, which bears the title "The History of the Great Stūpa Bya-rung kha-shor, the Hearing of Which Brings Liberation" (*mchod rten chen po bya rung kha shor gyi lo rgyus thos pa grol ba*), is still the most important Tibetan source for speculation on the origin and development of the monumental site of Bodhnāth. All other sources – and particularly the Nepalese documents – are for the most part brief references on the so-called "chronicles" (*vaṃśāvalī*) and occasionally surviving oral traditions, the latter subject to manifold changes over the centuries. A brief description of these sources and their adaptation by Western literature, therefore, would not appear to be inappropriate. Perhaps on this basis a comprehensive history of the *stūpa* can later be formulated.

It was Sylvain Lévi, in his wide-ranging cultural history of Nepal, who first undertook to date the construction of the *stūpa* according to Nepalese tradition, and his result has held its claim to accuracy up to the present: "Popular tradition associates its (= the chaitya of Budha-nāth) construction with expiation of parricide; but the names of the personages vary from one tale to another. If the tradition which connects the name of Mānadeva to this monument is exact the chaitya of Budha-nāth dates from the VIth century of the Christian era."[3] According to this version, Prince Mānadeva obeys the command of his father, King Vikrant, to kill a man lying concealed at a water source. This man is none other than the king himself. The reason for his self-sacrifice is the drying up of the source of "Nārāyaṇa lying on the water" (*jalāśayāna nārāyaṇa*), at the foot of Śivapurī; this state of affairs calls for the sacrifice of a man who possesses the thirty-two traits of a "universal ruler" (*cakravartin*). In order to spare his son, the father thus sacrifices himself. Since following the slaying the head of the victim will not come loose from the hand of the involuntary patricide, the latter seeks counsel from the goddess Maṇi-Yoginī of Sankhu (another name for Vajrayoginī, one of the four yoginīs of the Kathmandu Valley). She directs Mānadeva

---

unnamed king; this king grants the woman, who is without means in appearance only, permission to build a *stūpa*, and does not reverse his decision when the people, envious of her, later protest on account of the building's size. Interesting parallel material relating to this legend and the construction of the *stūpa* of bSam-yas is found in the 58th and 90th chapters of the biography of Padmasambhava; see *O rgyan gu ru padma 'byung gnas kyi skyes rabs rnam par thar pa rgyos par bkod pa padma bka'i thang yig*, Delhi: Sherab Gyaltsen Lama and Acharya Shedup Tenzin, 1984, pp. 362–367 & pp. 552–557. For a translation cf. *The Life and Liberation of Padmasambhava*, part 2: Tibet, Berkeley 1978, pp. 360–363 & pp. 605–609; by an oversight on the part of the publisher, the *stūpa* of Bodhnāth was mistaken for the *stūpa* of Svayambhūnāth. For further references to the Bodhnāth Stūpa in the *gter ma* literature, see Blondeau (1994:34–39).

3 See Lévi (1905:6–8) = *Ancient Nepal: Journal of the Department of Archaeology*, no. 58 (1980:4–5). The tradition to which Lévi here reverts is that of the Buddhist chronicles. Cf. the translation of the corresponding passage of one such chronicle in Wright (1966:66–67); two different versions of the history of the founding are also found there. The enquiry becomes more complicated when, along with the later [Buddhist] chronicles, older ones are drawn upon, such as the *Gopālarājavaṃśāvalī*, see note 7. On the distinction between the earlier *vaṃśāvalīs*, composed around 1400, and the later examples of the genre (compiled in the first decades of the Gorkha rule, i.e. around 1800), cf. Petech (1984:5–9).

to erect a temple in atonement for his act and personally watches over its construction. In gratitude Mānadeva places her likeness at the temple's entrance.

That is not the end, however, of the story of the *stūpa*'s construction according to the Buddhist chronicle. We learn further that Mānadeva composed a prayer, an exaltation of the Buddha, at the installation of the likeness.[4] I do not rule out the possibility that the name of the *stūpa*, the one familiar today to all pilgrims and tourists, may go back to this hymn (Buddha-Nātha→Budh-Nāth→Bodhnāth). One last piece of information from the late *vaṃśāvalī* text has to do, interestingly enough, with a connection Prince Mānadeva had with Tibet, and an additional name of the *stūpa* of Bodhnāth comes up: Khasa Chaitya.[5]

The motif of reincarnation in the case of the founding figure of the *stūpa* of Bodhnāth clearly reflects, in my opinion, the influence of Tibetan traditions in the historical writing of the 19th century; this motif – in the form it takes in *The History of the Great Stūpa Bya-rung kha-shor* – was evidently adopted by the Nepalese Buddhists and projected on the *stūpa*'s Licchavi founder. In none of the Tibetan sources known to me, in any case, does a Tibetan lama with name of Khasa occur. But what is the explanation of the name Khasa, a name Nepalese folk etymology with its explanation of "morning dew" (*khasti*) knew of? Fortunately, we have the record of a Tibetan author of the 18th century who addressed the topic.

---

4 See Lévi (1905:7) = *Ancient Nepal* (1980:4): "The hymn in honour of Buddha, composed by Mānadeva on festivities of inauguration, is still popular with Nepalese Buddhists." Cf. in this connection Wright (1966:67): "The Prince Mānadeva on this occasion composed a special prayer, which is repeated by every Buddhist when performing pūjā in holy places. *The prayer.* Reverence to the Ratna trayaya. I bow to thy lotus-like feet, O Lord! Thou art Buddha-thine asylum I seek. There are countless merits in worshipping Buddha. Thou art the master of religion, etc., (Footnote: The whole of the prayer is given in the original manuscript)."

5 See Wright (1966:67): "According to Bhoṭīya (i.e. Tibetan) tradition, the Lama of Bhoṭ, having died, became incarnate and lived again as the Rāja of Nepal, who built the Buddhist temple; and for this reason the Bhoṭīyas hold it in great veneration." Lévi (1905:8) = *Ancient Nepal* (1980:37) describes this situation in the following words: "Another Tibetan legend current in Nepal considers king Mānadeva as the incarnation of a Tibetan lama named Khasa. Hence the origin of the name Khasa-chaitya often applied to the temple of Budh-nāth." Finally, the details supplied by Oldfield (1880:261): "It is believed to have been built over the tomb, and probably to contain within its garb some of the ashes or other relics of an eminent Tibetan lama named Khasa who, having come to Nipal on a pilgrimage from Lhassa, died, and was either burnt or interred at this spot." Snellgrove (1957:288, note 22) distances himself from this etymology which enjoyed wide-spread favour: "Lévi notes another name for this shrine, viz. *Khasacaitya.* The name in use, however, seems to be *khastichaitya*. This was explained as meaning the shrine of the Dew-Water (from *khasu* = dew; *ti* = water). While building was in progress, the water for mixing became exhausted owing to drought, but by spreading a cloth at night and squeezing the dew from it in the morning, sufficient water was obtained to finish the stūpa." This interpretation, too, the generally accepted one today among the inhabitants of the Kathmandu Valley, is connected with the *stūpa*'s construction by Mānadeva; see Wright (1966): "When Mānadeva began the work of building the temple there was a great drought, so that the workmen making the bricks could only get water by soaking cloths [in the bed of the streams] and wringing out the moisture."

The person in question was the Eighth Si-tu-pa Chos-kyi 'byung-gnas (1700–1774), who visited the Kathmandu Valley during two trips in 1723 and 1748, and who evinced great interest in the cultural traditions of the Late Malla period. In his notes on the second trip we find the following remark:

> What is called by us (i. e. the Tibetans) *Bya-rung kha-shor* the Nepalese designate *Kha-sa cai-tya*. As *kha-sa* appears to be a corrupt form of [the Sanskrit word] kha-ta, it is evidently the case that it means "excavated *stūpa*". Is it not so, given the fact that the Yol-mo-ba Śākya bzang-po unearthed a mound, and consequently this *stūpa* existed as something brought forth from a treasure?
>
> (*nged rang tshos bya rung kha shor zer ba 'di la / bal po rnams kyis / kha sa cai tya zer / kha sa zhes kha ta zur chag pa yin pa 'dra bas / brkos pa'i mchod rten zer rgyu yin 'dra ste / yol mo ba sakya bzang pos de'u 'bur zhig brkos nas mchod rten de gter nas drangs pa yin pas yin nam*).[6]

Abandoning for the time being the thread of enquiry represented by the Tibetan tradition, I should like to recapitulate the material presented thus far: according to the *vaṃśāvalī* text edited and translated by D. Wright and his assistants, and analysed by S. Lévi, the original construction of the *stūpa* of Bodhnāth is ascribed to the Licchavi king Mānadeva I (reigned

---

6 See Chos-kyi 'byung gnas*: Ta'i si tur 'bod pa karma bstan pa'i nyin byed kyi rang tshul dangs por brjod pa dri bral shel gyi me long*, p. 267.5–6; cf. the somewhat misleading translation in Lewis & Jamspal (1988:207): "We then arrived at the place the Nepalese call Khasachaitya and we Tibetans call Jarung Kashor (i.e. Bauddha). The first name is a corrupted 'khata' and so the meaning should be 'dug-out *stūpa*'. When Yornoba bZabo Shakya made a mound, the *stūpa* came out. And so the name came into being." This citation is also reproduced in the biography of sNgags-'chang Śākya bzang-po in sTag-sgang mkhas-mchog Ngag-dbang blo-gros, Gu-ru bkra-shis: *bsTan pa'i snying po gsang chen snga 'gyur nges don zab mo'i chos kyi 'byung ba gsal bar byed pa'i legs bshad mkhas pa dga' byed ngo mtshar gtam gyi rol mtsho*, vol. 3, p. 52.1–3. The etymology espoused by modern Western scholars deviates both from the Nepalese and from the Tibetan interpretation; the name *Khasti* is made to be connected with the relics of the Buddha Kāśyapa. See Wiesner (1977:218): "Eine Tradition besagt, daß der Stūpa Reliquien des Buddha Kāśyapa enthält. Aus dieser Annahme wird auch der Name des Stūpas, Khasti, erklart"; and Slusser (1982:277, note 46): "The name *Khasti* probably relates to the Manuṣi Buddha Kāśyapa, whose relics are said to be enclosed in the stūpa." On the relics of the Buddha Kāśyapa, see *mChod rten chen po bya rung kha shor gyi lo rgyus thos pas grol ba*, fol. 7a/2: *de bzhin gshegs pa 'od bsrungs kyi ring srel ma ga ta'i bre gang srog shing gi nang du bzhugs so gsol*" and the translation in Hoffmann (1965:46); "... und taten unterhalb des hölzernen Pfahles (*yaṣṭi*) ein Drona nach Art von Magadha Reliquien des Buddha Kāśyapa hinein". See also Regmi (1965:571): "By the name Khasti Chaitya one is inclined to believe that this was associated with the Tibetans. Khasti identified with Khasa situated near Kerrong inside Tibetan territory lies on the main thoroughfare between Lhasa and Nepal." This reference to the place named Khasa may at least provide an explanation for the name of the Tibetan lama whom H.A. Oldfield and S. Lévi associate with the *stūpa*. The place itself, however, is not located near Kyirong, but on the second important trade route to Tibet, the one leading via Khasa to Nyalam, and then via Shigatse to Lhasa.

approx. 464–505). The names Bodhnāth and Khasti Chaitya can be connected with this act of founding by Mānadeva; the Tibetan tradition cited in sanction of this founding (through the status of the reincarnated Mānadeva) is more likely to be secondary in nature. Of paramount importance for the Tibetan sources, rather, is the element of rediscovery, the unearthing of a buried edifice; this led to the name Excavated Stūpa. What light do the older *vaṃśāvalī* texts shed on these matters?

In the *Gopālarājavaṃśāvalī* it is said of Mānadeva: "He killed his father unwittingly. As he had committed such a monstrous crime, he wandered crying [in consternation]. On reaching the hillock of Gumvihāra he observed penances. By the merit of these penances, a great chaitya emerged [on the hillock]. He consecrated the chaitya." Gumvihāra (Timber Mountain Monastery), east of Sankhu, is one of the oldest Licchavi monasteries of the Kathmandu Valley, a witness to Buddhism's early presence there. Here again then, as in the later chronicle, there is a connection with the patricide at Sankhu. The *stūpa* that was erected in atonement, however, is now no longer a forerunner of Bodhnāth, in view of the fact that today there still exists a *stūpa* near the Vajrayoginī Temple in Sankhu associated with Mānadeva's act of atonement. Instead, it is written somewhat later in the *Gopālarājavaṃśāvalī*: "King Śri Śivadeva [ruled for] forty-one years and six months. A dome was built in the *vihāra* he founded. He built a big Khasa chaitya."[7]

These, then, are the most important Nepalese sources on the history of Bodhnāth. I shall now supplement them with further material from the Tibetan tradition. A younger contemporary of the previously mentioned Si-tu Paṇ-chen is the Fourth Khams-sprul Rin-po-che Chos-kyi nyi-ma (1743–1779); he bequeathed to posterity a detailed 'description of the sacred abodes' (*gnas bshad*) of the Kathmandu Valley, and in it we find the following details concerning the *stūpa* of Bodhnāth:

---

[7] Vajracarya and Malla (1985:123 & 125). M.S. Slusser (1982:277) has previously looked into the contradictory traditions concerning the founding of the *stūpa* of Bodhnāth: "Nepalese tradition and the chronicles credit its (i.e. Bodhnāth) foundation to Licchavi royalty, the one ascribing it to Mānadeva I as atonement for an unwitting patricide, the other to a successor, Śivadeva I (approx. A.D. 590–604)." She offers the following solution: "It seems probable however that Mānadeva was the builder, because of the persistent tradition that links his name to the Stūpa, and that Śivadeva, the chronicler's choice, was its restorer." Further elucidation will come, according to her, only by way of archaeological investigations, but as Snellgrove (1957:100), has previously noted: "It would be most unwise to start digging into the side of Svayambhūnāth, even with governmental permission. In the case of Bodhnāth, such thoughts scarcely enter the mind, for the whole scene presents itself so firmly in terms of here and now." Cf. also in this connection Malla (1983:127). According to the Tibetan sources, in any case, it must be presumed that there were a number of mounds existing to the northeast of Paśupatināth, and that it would thus not have been so easy for sNgags-'chang Śākya bzang-po to locate the mound housing the *stūpa*. What would prevent us, therefore, from assuming the presence of various constructions of the Licchavi kings in the area? Cf. the description of the 'archaeological work' of sNgags-'chang Śākya bzang-po in bsTan-'dzin nor-bu: *rTogs brjod mkhas pa'i rna rgyan*, pp. 30.4–31.1.

> With regard to the *stūpa* Bya-rung kha-shor, in India and Nepal there are no new accounts when compared to those which are current in Tibet. The name is Kha-shwa chaitya which is pronounced in a mixture of Newari and Tibetan. In several works of the great Vajracharya Mahāvidyādhari, I have seen the spelling Bya-ri kam-shwa-ma. Generally speaking, in ancient times, after demolitions and losses, this *stūpa* was covered with dirt, sand, etc. to the point that it became invisible. When the moment for realizing the prophecies of Guru Rin-po-che arrived, the holy reincarnation, the Yol-mo-ba Rig-'dzin Śākya bzang-po, unearthed it, carried out with exactitude the repairs and restorations, and made known its true worth. The name of the great *stūpa* became once more as famous as that of sun and the moon.[8]

For the Tibetans, therefore, it is with the rediscovery of the *stūpa*, the excavation of a buried site no longer recognized as such, that its reconstructive history commences. Rig-'dzin Śākya bzang-po who bore the agnomen Yol-mo-ba was responsible for the excavation and repair work. Fortunately, biographical material is available on this Tantric master of the rNying-ma-pa school, and we can approximately determine his dates: according to the biography, which I draw on in the following, Rig-'dzin (or sNgags-'chang) Śākya bzang-po met personally with Padma gling-pa (1450–1521) and with 'Bri-gung Kun-dga' rin-chen (1475–1527), so that we may likewise set his dates between the second half of the 15th century and the first half of the 16th. In Nepalese historiography this would correspond to the beginning of the three Malla kingdoms in the Kathmandu Valley, which is assigned to the year 1482 with the death of the king Yakṣamalla.

We shall now, in conclusion, turn to the question of whether, during the excavations by Rig-'dzin Śākya bzang-po, anything is recorded reminiscent of the Licchavi period and the kings Mānadeva and Śivadeva, or of their *stūpa*-building activities. The answer is no. Instead, another Licchavi king enters the picture, who is regarded as the successor of Śivadeva: Aṃśuvarman (ruled approx. 605–621). In a comment on the above citation of Si-tu Paṇ-chen it is written in the biography of Rig-'dzin Śākya bzang-po:

---

8 See Macdonald & Dvags-po Rin-po-che (1987:108). The "great Vajracharya Mahāvidyādhari" referred to here is the rNying-ma-pa teacher Kaḥ-thog rig-'dzin Tshe-dbang nor-bu (1698–1755), an 18th-century Tibetan from East Tibet who left behind valuable documents on the culture of the Late Malla Period; see Ehrhard (1989:1–9) and chapter four in the present volume. On the name Bya-ri kam-sho-ma mentioned here for the *stūpa* of Bodhnāth cf., among other works, Tshe-dbang nor-bu: *Ngo mtshar dad pa'i rol mtsho* p. 209: *mchod rten bya tri kha sho'am / bya tri kam sho / dang bod phyir bya rung kha shor du grags pa'i mchod rten 'dir* ... The forms *Bya-tri kha-sho / Bya-tri ka-sho / Bya-tri kam-sho-ma* are obviously phonetic variations of the Tibetan expression *Bya-rung kha-shor*, in this case, too, the pronunciation approximates what the Fourth Khams-sprul Rin-po-che terms a 'mixture of Newari and Tibetan'.

If that is the case, then evidently something was exposed by this great treasure that was not visible in the case of the earlier *stūpa*. [And it is the case, as] bones of the Nepalese king Aṃśuvarman were brought to light [by Rig-'dzin Śākya bzang-po] from the *stūpa*'s central axis (*yaṣṭi*) and distributed for creatures' well-being.

(*de lta na mchod rten sngar mi mngon pa la gter chen 'dis gsal bar byas pa yin pa 'dra'o / mchod rten gyi srog shing las / bal po'i rgyal po 'od zer go cha'i gdung gter nas bzhengs nas 'gro don la spel*).[9]

The association of the place where the *stūpa* of Bodhnāth stands in its present form with a cemetery was propagated in turn by Rig-'dzin Śākya bzang-po and his successors. In a religious and topographical description of the Kathmandu Valley from the year 1820 it is a matter of certainty for the author Chos-kyi bstan-'dzin 'phrin-las (1789–1838) that the *stūpa* was erected over a cemetery:

---

9 The biography of sNgags-'chang Śākya bzang-po in *sNga 'gyur chos 'byung ngo mtshar gtam gyi rol mtsho* (as in note 6), p. 52.3–5. Cf. also the biography in *Bod du byung ba'i gsang sngags snga 'gyur gyi bstan 'dzin skyes mchog rim byon gyi rnam thar nor bu'i do shal* of Kun-bzang Nges-don klong-yangs (born 1814), included in mKhas-btsun bzang-po : *Biographical Dictionary of Tibet and Tibetan Buddhism* 3, Dharamsala 1973, p. 525: "[Thus] the renovation of the stūpa was carried out to the end; on this occasion bones of the Nepalese king Aṃśuvarman were brought to light" (*mchod rten zhig gsos mthar phyin 'grub / de skabs bal po'i rgyal po 'od zer go cha'i gdung gter nas bzhes*). For a description of the circumstances surrounding the excavation work, cf. the passage mentioned in note 7 from the pen of the Third Yol-mo-ba sprul-sku bsTan-'dzin nor-bu (1598–1644): "When later he (i.e. sNgags-'chang Śākya bzang-po) was making his circumambulations on the top floor [of bSam-yas], he saw a paper scroll fall from above, and thus the command arose to repair the damage [to the *stūpa*] Bya-rung kha-shor. Without the least doubt he [immediately] set off for Nepal. At the time [the *stūpa*] Bya-rung kha-shor was something that couldn't be distinguished from the [other] mounds [of the region]. At first he paid worship to another mound, [thinking to himself] "This must be it". The mound, which thereupon said "Something has to be taken away at the other half [and not here]", is today still standing near the *stūpa*. When [sNgags-'chang Śākya bzang-po] finally discovered the actual [mound] and subjected it to a thorough renovation, he said "In spite of [the fact] that there is no water in the close vicinity, the possibility exists that there is some here." And when he had listened and dug at an empty spot that gave out a rhythmical sound, a water source arose that may be still seen today. In this way [his influence was] great and wonderful. Obviously [the memory] had arisen in his heart of how he earlier, [at the time] of the Jina Kāśyapa, had a birth as a helper [during the construction of the stūpa]" (*de nas dbu [b]rtser zhabs skor mdzad pas thog las shog ril zhig babs pa gzigs pas / bya rung kha shor gyi zhig gso bar lung gi bstan te / tsham tshob med par bal yul la 'phebs / de'i bya rung kha shor kyang ri dang so sor mi phyed pa cig yod de / thog mar 'di yin dgos te / ri gzhan zhig la phyag mdzad pas phyed mar sang ba yin / zer ba'i ri de da lta yang mchod rten dang nye ba na yod do star dngos rnyed de zhig gsos rgyas par mdzad tshe / nye sar chu med pa las / 'di na yod tshod yin gsungs nas der bsan las khrol khrol zer ba'i shul drus pas / chu thon pa yong da lta yod do / 'di lta bu ni che ngo mtshar te / sngon rgyal 'od srungs gyi bsten pa* (= *bstan pa*) *la bran du 'khrungs pa de thigs lo shor 'du go*). For the dynastic history of Aṃśuvarman and its relation to Tibet, see Petech (1988:156–159).

> This (*mchod rten*) is also described as being one of the *mchod rten* erected at each of the eight different cemeteries (*dur khrod*) of the eight *Ma mo* of the retinue of 'Jigs-byed at the time formerly when 'Jigs-byed Nag-po and his retinue were defeated by 'Khor-lo sdom-pa.[10]

Against this background, then, the person of Rig-'dzin Śākya bzang-po and the representatives of the Lamaist priesthood following him who were responsible for the further upkeep of the *stūpa* might be looked into more closely. This would go beyond the bounds of the preliminary survey of the written sources on the *stūpa* of Bodhnāth.[11] Nevertheless, reference may be made to the person of Zil-gnon dbang-rgyal rdo-rje (born 1647), concerning whom we know, on the basis of two edited and translated documents, that he and his successors were appointed to be the Tibetan residents at the *stūpa*.[12]

---

10 See Wylie (1970:21) and also Macdonald & Dvags-po Rin-po-che (1987:108): "Then Śākya bzang-po of Yol-mo and the third titulary of the lineage, the Yol-mo-ba bsTan-'dzin nor-bu, explained that it is one of the group of eight *stūpa*s, eight trees and eight *śmaśāna* as is the case of the Lhun-grub brtsegs pa'i *śmaśāna.* It is thought that the protectress who is in front of the *stūpa*, Puṣka dmar-ser, who takes intestines and eats them, is surely one of the eight Ma mo. Lamas do not accept the tradition concerning their origin. However, if one consults a printed *gter ma*, the *dkar chag* of which is considered as containing the words pronounced by the great teacher [Padmasambhava], this is established; but I'm not going to go into this question here." Cf. also in this connection the details in Dowman (1981:260–262).

11 For further material, see chapter nine in the present volume.

12 See Schuh (1974:423–453) and (1981:309–315). The addressee in both cases is Zil-gnon dbang-rgyal rdo-rje (1647–1716) or his successors. Concerning him we know that he was regarded as the incarnation of the Third Yol-mo-ba sprul-sku bsTan-'dzin nor-bu (1598–1644), and that he likewise undertook a series of renovations of the *stūpa* of Bodhnāth; see Zil-gnon dbang rgyal rdo-rje: *sPrul pa'i rig 'dzin chen po zil gnon dbang rgyal rdo rje'i phyi'i rnam thar*, pp. 9.3–13.5, pp. 43.2–44.4 and pp. 78.2–82.3. The renovation described in the final section took place in 1706/1707.

The Register of the Reliquary of Lord Rang-rig ras-pa

A work quite popular among Tibetan travellers and pilgrims in Nepal was a particular "register" (*dkar chag*) describing the Svayambhūnāth Stūpa and the further sacred sites in the Kathmandu Valley. It has been used as an important document for the study of the history of "Noble All [Kinds of] Trees" (*'phags-pa shing-kun*)[1], as Tibetans call this most sacred edifice in the valley, because it contains descriptions of two renovations, respectively occurring at the beginning of the 16th century and at the end of the 17th century. The hypothesis has been proposed that "A Register of the Stūpa 'Noble All [Kinds of] Trees' in Nepal and Other Sacred Sites There" (*bal yul mchod rten 'phags pa shing kun dang de'i gnas gzhan rnams kyi dkar chag*) was fixed in writing on the occasion of the renovation in the year 1680. This renovation was undertaken at the initiative of Rang-rig ras-pa or Rang-rig ras-chen (died 1683), a yogin of the 'Brug-pa school of Tibetan Buddhism, who also held teaching transmissions of the rNying-ma-pa school. In fact, the furnishing of the Svayambhūnāth Stūpa with a new central mast and further embellishments – which coincided with the beginning of the rulership of King Pārthivendramalla (regnal years 1680–1687) – was preceded by a renovation of the Bodhnāth Stūpa; this magnificent religious building in the Kathmandu Valley is of special importance for the followers of Padmasambhava and his teaching traditions. The latter renovation is mentioned in the collection of "Spiritual Songs" (*mgur*) of Rang-rig ras-pa; by contrast no notice is taken of the renewal of the central part of the Svayambhūnāth Stūpa and other additions to the structure.[2]

---

1 The name "Noble All [Kinds of] Trees" reminds Tibetan pilgrims of the former presence of Nāgārjuna at the *stūpa*. According to the etiological story as contained in the pilgrimage guidebook under investigation, Nāgārjuna had cut off his hair and while scattering it around made the wish that all kinds of trees should grow at this noble *stūpa*; see Wylie, op. cit. (note 4), p. 19, note 35. For a critical attitude towards this etymology according to a Tibetan register of the sacred sites in the Kathmandu valley from the 18th century, see Macdonald & Dvags-po Rin-po-che (1981:245–246).

2 See Ehrhard (1991) and chapter five in the present volume. For Rang-rig ras-pa's position in the lineage of the tradition of the "Northern Treasures" (*byang gter*), the teachings of which he received from rGyal-sras Phyag-rdor nor-bu (died 1658), the younger brother of the Third Yol-mo-ba sprul-sku bsTan-'dzin nor-bu (1598–1644), see *rJe btsun khyab bdag chen po rang rig ras chen gyi gsung mgur dang zhal gdams 'dri med bdud rtsi'i rlabs 'phreng*. (Smanrtsis Shesrig Spendzod 111). Leh: D.W. Tashigang 1982, pp. 343.4–344.5. The compiler of this collection of spiritual songs and instructions was Ngag-dbang rdo-rje from Nas-lung.

The author of the register gives his name as Ngag-dbang rdo-rje from Nas-lung, "who had been nourished by the instructions of the Lord Rang-rig ras-pa" (*rje rang rig ras pa'i man ngag gis 'tsho ba*). Besides the fact that Ngag-dbang rdo-rje had been a close disciple of Rang-rig ras-pa, we do not have much further biographical data on him. At least we know that after the death of his teacher he stayed at lHa-gdong to the east of the mountain rTsib-ri in gTsang province – a famous sacred site of 'Brug-pa *yogins* – where he performed "memorial laudations" (*sku bstod*) on behalf of his guru for a great assemblage of religious practitioners; at that time Ngag-dbang rdo-rje was still remembered as having acted as the "steward" (*gnyer pa*) of Rang-rig ras-pa. These pieces of information we owe to another collection of spiritual songs and instructions, in this case the one of bsTan-'dzin ras-pa (1644/46–1723), another *yogin* of the 'Brug-pa school. Born in the Muktināth valley in Southern Mustang and founder of the famous Shel dgon-pa in the Dol-po region, bsTan-'dzin ras-pa was a member of the spiritual lineage of Rang-rig ras-pa by way of his teacher Rang-grol rdo-rje.[3]

The modern xylograph of the register of Ngag-dbang rdo-rje which circulated among Tibetan travellers and pilgrims was executed by a monk from the sGo-mang college of 'Bras-spungs monastery with the financial help of a person bearing the name Sog-sprul Gu-ru. This designation stands for the so-called "Mongolian Lama" (*sog bla*) Gurudeva (= Gu ru bDe-ba), a dGe-lugs-pa teacher, who in the 1950s founded the monastery of dGa'-ldan Chos-'phel gling near Bodhnāth Stūpa; he is known best among scholars as a publisher of Tibetan books in New Delhi.[4]

---

[3] See *rNal 'byor gyi dbang phyug bstan 'dzin ras pa'i zhal gdams mgur du gsungs pa rnams* (xylograph), NGMPP reel no. L 257/27, fols. 33a/2ff. & 48a/7ff. Both bsTan-'dzin ras-pa and sTag-rtse sku-skye-ba Mi-pham phun-tshogs shes-rab (1654–1715) had been disciples of the Second lCogs-grwa sprul-sku sNyan-grags dpal bzang-po (1617–1680), another important 'Brug-pa bKa'-brgyud-pa master of the 17th century. This Mi-pham phun-tshogs shes-rab was active in the region of Northern Mustang, and the list of his teachers includes Rang-rig ras-pa. He composed two devotional works in honour of him; see *Grub dbang rang rig ras pa'i sku bstod kyi 'grel bshad* (xylograph), 11 fols., NGMPP reel no. L 100/24, and *Grub dbang rang rig zhabs kyi rnam thar la gsol ba 'debs pa* (xylograph), 7 fols., NGMPP reel no. L 100/22 (including further works). All three mentioned block prints were carved in the Mustang region and can be assigned to a particular style of printing of 'Brug-pa materials. To this tradition belongs also the xylograph of the biography of the Second lCogs-grwa sprul-sku, completed by Mi-pham phun-tshogs shes-rab in the year 1688 in Tsa-ri Dag-pa shel-ri and latter carved on wooden blocks in Mustang; see *rJe btsun rdo rje 'chang dngos mi pham ngag dbang snyan grags dpal bzang po'i rnam par thar pa ngo mtshar rgya mtsho'i zlos gar*, 126 fols., in: *The Biography of the Second sDing-po-che Cog-gra Mi-pham-Ngag-dbang-snyan-grags-dpal-bzang and Other Biographical Material Connected with the 'Brug-pa Dkar-brgyud-pa Tradition*. Darjeeling: Chopal Lama 1984, pp. 273–523.

[4] It was this edition of the register which was edited in transliterated form by Turrell Wylie. For the printing colophon of the work, see Wylie (1970:48.9–25). Further information concerning the monastery of dGa'-ldan Chos-'phel gling, particularly its providing refuge for the monks and sacred items of sKyid-grong bSam-gtan gling, and its present role in the annual reconsecration of Bodhnāth Stūpa, is given by Bentor (1996:71–75).

In this edition the text is called a "register-cum-history" (*lo rgyus dkar chag*), and it was obviously produced for the needs of Tibetan refugees pouring into Nepal after the exodus of 1959. In addition to the main body of the work it contains, after the short authorial colophon of Ngag-dbang rdo-rje and the printing colophon of the monk from sGo-mang, a section which could be called a spiritual exhortation for pilgrims. This section was written for people, who actually performed the journey to Svayambhūnāth Stūpa and the other sacred sites in the Kathmandu Valley. In it these pilgrimage places are set in a typological relationship to other places conducive to spiritual practice which the translator lHo-brag Mar-pa (1012–1097) had prophesied to his disciple, the great yogin Mi-la-ras-pa (1028–1111). This is achieved by a literal quotation from the famous *Mi la ras pa'i rnam mgur* of gTsang-smyon Heruka (1452–1507) concerning the location and time when Mi-la-ras-pa and his future disciples would frequent these sites; the list in this quotation includes La-stod rGyal-gyi śrī-ri, Gangs Ti-se, La-phyi gangs-ra, Mang-yul Ri-bo dpal-'bar, Bal-yul Yol-mo gangs-ra, Brin-gyi chu-dbar, gNas-chen Devikoṭi and Tsa-ri, but does not mention any site in the Kathmandu Valley.

Nevertheless, once the later sites have attained the same spiritual status as the former ones, the ordinary pilgrim is admonished to pay respect to the Svayambhūnāth Stūpa and the other places in the Kathmandu Valley, since they are most conducive to spiritual salvation. The section ends thus with the following words:

> If one is already liberated from *saṃsāra* by just hearing the names of these excellent places, what is there to say about visiting them in person and engaging [there] in meditation and practices like prostrations, offerings and circumambulations?[5]

This section seems to have been added to the register of Ngag-dbang rdo-rje at a certain point of time during the circulation of the text, and we only know that it was already part of it when the xylograph was carved in the 1960s. As chance would have it, an older version of the work has survived which may contain a clue about the person responsible for bringing about this transformation from register to pilgrimage guidebook. The title of this version differs from the modern edition first in identifying itself as a "concise register" (*dkar chag mdor bsdus*), a term also used by the author Ngag-dbang rdo-rje in his short colophon. This older version is also a block print, and contains a printing colophon. Its

---

[5] The section called "A Spiritual Exhortation for Pilgrims" is to be found in Wylie, op. cit. (n. 4), pp. 47.25–48.9; for the final statement of this section, see ibid, p. 48.7–9 (... *gnas mchog de rnams kyi mtshan thos pa tsam gyis 'khor ba las grol na / mngon sum du mjal te phyag mchod bskor ba sogs bsgom sgrub la brtson na lta ci smos*). The preceding passage concerning the "prophesied sacred sites" (*lung bstan pa'i gnas*) for Mi-la-ras-pa and his followers is contained in *rJe btsun mi la la ras pa'i rnam thar rgyas par phye ba mgur 'bum*. Hsining: mTsho-sngon mi-rigs dpe-skrun khang 1989, p. 122.5–20. It is also quoted in the pilgrimage guidebook to the region of La-phyi gangs-ra; see Huber (1997:252).

author is a monk named Blo-bzang Chos-'phel. The printing colophon, introduced by two four-line stanzas, follows immediately after the spiritual exhortation to the pilgrims, and I take Blo-bzang Chos-'phel to be the one who added this latter to the original register at the time he carved this version. His own words – after a quite elaborate description of his birthplace – make it clear that he was especially attracted to the sacred sites of the Kathmandu Valley:

> Adjacent of Pulahari in the north, [located] in the middle of a great plain, five and a half miles wide, where saffron grows, and where one can find a cemetery, [a place for] embracing the secret way, [with the name] "Breaking Forth of Great Bliss", and a self-manifested Kaṇika Stūpa. The monk Blo-bzang Chos-'phel, who was born in this place, having more and more generated believing faith in these excellent sites [of the Kathmandu Valley], and thinking of the great benefit for himself and others at the time of performing the pilgrimage, printed [this work] in order that the stream of inexhaustible Dharma gifts might increase. [The blocks] remain at the great *Stūpa* of Bya-rung kha-shor.[6]

We do not have any further information concerning Blo-bzang Chos-'phel or the date his version of the text was carved on wooden blocks, nor at first sight does the description of his birthplace reveal any geographical details useful for its location. But a still earlier version of Ngag-dbang rdo-rje's register which seems to be the original copy has surfaced just recently. It describes not only the *stūpa* of Svayambhūnāth and other sacred sites in the Kathmandu Valley, but also the reliquary of Rang-rig ras-pa. This monument had been erected in the immediate vicinity of the Bodhnāth Stūpa soon after the death of the 'Brug-pa *yogin*. It was on the basis of this original that Blo-bzang Chos-'phel had produced his version.

This original edition, again a xylograph, bears the title "Register of [Sacred Sites] like 'All [Kinds of] Trees' in Nepal and the Reliquary of the Lord Rang-rig [ras-pa]" (*bal yul shing kun sogs dang rje rang rig ras gdung rten gyi dkar chag*).[7] A comparison between

---

6 See *Bal yul mchod rten 'phags pa shing kun dang de'i gnas gzhan rnams kyis (= kyi) dkar chag mdor bsdus* (xylograph), NGMPP reel no. E 816/12, fol. 4b/1–3 (*byang phyogs phu la ha ri'i mdun sa / gur gum skye pa'i thang chen po dpag tshad phyed dang drug gi dbus na / gsang lam bsnol ba'i dur khrod bde chen brdal (= brdol) dang / rang byung mchod rten ka ṇi ka yod pa / de'i sa char skye pa dge slong blo bzang chos 'phel gyis gnas mchog de rnams la yid ches kyi dad pa ches cher skyes (= bskyes) te / gnas bskor la 'gro skabs rang gzhan mang por phan par bsams te / chos sbyin 'dzad med kyi rgyun spel phyir par du bsgrubs te / mchod rten chen po bya rung kha shor du bzhugs*). For the location of the birthplace, see note 12. Compare also Roerich (1979:400) ("... modern Tibetan pilgrims believe that Pullahari was situated in Kāśmīra in the neighbourhood of Śrīnagar.").

7 This xylograph contains six folios and is the second one of a compilation of several works, as can be seen from the letter *Ga* on its margin. Like the work of Blo-bzang Chos-'phel, it is a large-sized xylograph

the original xylograph and Blo-bzang Chos-'phel's makes it clear that the later version – conceivably produced in the 18th century – while endowing the text with the literary quality of a pilgrimage guidebook, left out a substantial portion of Ngag-dbang rdo-rje's register (contained between the section on the renovation of Svayambhūnāth Stūpa and the author's colophon). This portion deals with the history of the reliquary of Rang-rig ras-pa and adds a whole new dimension to the text, which up to now has mainly been used for the study of the renovations of Svayambhūnāth Stūpa.

It is interesting to see how Blo-bzang Chos-'phel brought about this transformation from register to pilgrimage guidebook by two changes of the original text: first, by abandoning the portion concerning the reliquary of Rang-rig ras-pa, and, second, by adding the spiritual exhortations to the pilgrims. However, he did spare one part of the deleted passage, namely the quite elaborate description of his birthplace; thus it turns out that he was a monk from Kashmir, and so born in the same region where Rang-rig ras-pa passed away.

In the following I offer a transliterated edition of that part of the original xylograph of Ngag-dbang rdo-rje which has up to now been lost. In the notes to the translation I merely try to pass on some information which may help to place this important work in its historical and cultural context. Under this new perspective, the register describing Svayambhūnāth Stūpa and other sacred sites in the Kathmandu Valley can now be identified as a literary work composed in the year 1686, immediately after the consecration of the reliquary of the Lord Rang-rig ras-pa on the eastern side of Bodhnāth Stūpa.

TRANSLATION

Praise to the Guru!

With devotion I prostrate myself towards the feet of Rang-rig ras-pa, [no one else but]
Padmasambhava, [the teacher who is] the embodiment of the compassion of all the Jinas,
possessing [the ability of] establishing manifold magical appearances of diligent behaviour,
the protector of gods and men, intimidating the strong and powerful *dregs pa* [demons].

(55x9 cm), but its style of printing is different from that of the 'Brug-pa materials of the 17th/18th centuries from the Mustang region. As a possible production site of this block print, one could point to such dwelling places of 'Brug-pa *yogin*s as lHa-gdong to the east of the mountain rTsib-ri.

[1]
Now, if one asks in which way it is taught that this Lord [Rang-rig ras-pa] has been prophesied as the mind-incarnation of [the One from] Oḍḍiyāna, [it is said] in the treasure scriptures of the Vidyādhara Gar-dbang rdo-rje (1640–1685):

> At the border of Mar[-yul] and Nu in Western Tibet,
> at a place called "Rang-rig",
> a person aware of his own [mind] by himself,
> bearing the name "Rang-rig", will appear!
>
> He is the incarnation of my mind:
> as spiritual support, he wears the dress of a Cotton-Clad One;
> being a *yogin*, whose diligent behaviour has reached completion,
> he will bring happiness to India, Tibet [and] Nepal, [these] three!
>
> In particular, he will renovate the [Bya-rung] kha-shor [*stūpa*],
> [and] by this [act] foreign armies will be kept back for some years![8]

And [it is said] in the ninth chapter of the [*rDo rje*] *phag mo gzhung drug*, [a text] which he had heard from mNga'-bdag Nyang-ral bsTan-'dzin chos-dbang:

> In the Upper Region, there will appear Rang-rig ras-pa!
> He is the incarnation of my mind;
> he will bring happiness to the beings of the six spheres of existence![9]

---

8 There are several texts concerning prophecies in the treasure cycles of Rig-'dzin Gar-dbang rdo-rje. See, for example, *Lung bstan srid gsum gsal byed*, 14 fols., in *rDor sems thugs kyi me long*. Darjeeling: Chopal Lama 1984, pp. 169–196, and *Lung bstan dus gsum kun gsal*, 26 fols. & *Lung bstan gsang ba'i man ngag zab mo*, 4 fols., in *Thugs rje chen po rtsa gsum snying thig*. Dalhousie: Damchoe Sangpo 1985, pp. 259–309 & 311–318. I was not able to identify any prophecy concerning Rang-rig ras-pa in these texts. For the mention of *yul rang rig*, located in Spiti, as the place where Rang-rig ras-pa first gave forth spiritual songs, see the collection of his spiritual songs and instructions (as in note 2), pp. 11.2ff. Soon afterwards he visited Jalandhara and other famous Tantric sites in the Western Himalayas; see ibid, pp. 19.2ff.

9 A short biographical sketch of the life of Rang-rig ras-pa is to be found in mKhas-btsun bzang-po : *Biographical Dictionary of Tibet and Tibetan Buddhism* 8 (= The bKa'-brgyud-pa Tradition 2). Dharamsala: Library of Tibetan Works and Archives 1981, pp. 413.15–419.14. This sketch is taken from the biography of the Sixth 'Brug-chen Mi-pham dbang-po (1641–1717), who is counted among the students of Rang-rig ras-pa. We find there the episode in which it is narrated that the 'Brug-pa *yogin* received a prophecy of Vajravārāhī at the time of his pilgrimage to Tsa-ri in south-eastern Tibet, and thereupon encountered mNga'-bdag Nyang-ral bsTan-'dzin chos-dbang, a descendant of the treasure discoverer mNga'-bdag Nyang-ral Nyi-ma'i 'od-zer (1124–1192), from whom he received the "teaching cycle of the Black Wrathful One" (*khros ma nag mo'i chos skor*); see ibid, p. 417.14–19. This happened

In accordance with those scriptures [it is said] on page sixty of the second volume of [the xylograph of] the [auto]biography of the Great All-knowing Powerful Jina, [the Fifth Dalai Bla-ma] Ngag-gi dbang-phyug Blo-bzang rgya-mtsho (1617–1682):

> I met with the one who is known as the Great Siddha Rang-rig from the Upper Region, a person with great experience and understanding of [the doctrines of] the Great Seal and the Great Perfection, [these] two. While [we sat] in a row for tea, a continuing discussion developed [between us]. Some wonder whether he might be the one of whom it is said in the prophecies of mNga'-bdag [Nyang-ral Nyi-ma'i 'od-zer]: "From the Upper Region there will appear Rang-rig ras-pa!" In any case, it is obvious that he is a person who has identified [the true nature of] the [outer] appearances and his own mind.[10]

[2]
This Rang-rig ras-pa, at the time when he was renovating Bya-rung kha-shor [*stūpa*], went to the eastern side of [Bya-rung] kha-shor [*stūpa*] and performed [there] just a scattering [of offerings] and then made the prophecy: "In the future, if a reliquary of mine is erected [on this spot], great happiness will arise for the beings – and in particular, foreign armies will be kept back – and [thus] joy for Nepal and Tibet!" Then were made ready from [an alloy of] gold and copper the parasol [and] the *gañjira* top of the great [Bya-rung] kha-shor [*stūpa*], together with the pillars [holding it] and the supporting pillars.[11]

Again, by way of Western Tibet, after he had spent a winter in Pulahari in the north, [at the time] when he was proceeding to Oḍḍiyāna in the western direction, he made

in the surroundings of sMra-bo cog in lHo-brag, the family seat of the successors of Nyang-ral Nyi-ma'i 'od-zer. For different ritual texts centring on Vajravārāhī according to this tradition of the rNying-ma-pa school, see Schwieger (1999:3–20).

[10] The reference to the block print edition of the autobiography of the Fifth Dalai Bla-ma is correct. See Ngag-dbang blo-bzang rgya-mtsho: *Za hor gyi ban de ngag dbang blo bzang rgya mtsho'i 'di snang 'khrul pa'i rol rtsed rtogs brjod kyi tshul du bkod pa du kū la'i gos bzang las glegs bam gnyis pa*. Gangtok: Sikkim Research Institute of Tibetology 1992, p. 122.3–4 (= fol. 60b/3–4); compare the type set edition, Lhasa: Bod-ljongs mi-dmangs dpe-skrun khang 1991, p. 115.13–17. The meeting between Rang-rig ras-pa and Ngag-dbang Blo-bzang rgya-mtsho took place in the year 1668. It should be noted that the xylograph of this autobiography circulated among 'Brug-pa *yogin*s in the period when the death of the Great Fifth had been concealed by sDe-srid Sangs-rgyas rgya-mtsho (1653–1705).

[11] The act of selecting the eastern side of the Bodhnāth Stūpa as the place for the reliquary can be seen as establishing this particular spot as a sacred site. This might have contributed to the situation that the eastern side of Bya-rung kha-shor played a role, to some extent, in visions of treasure discoverers of the rNying-ma-pa school. Remarkable in this respect is the description of the events which brought about the revelation of the *Klong chen snying thig* cycle by 'Jigs-med gling-pa (1729/30–1798) in the year 1757; see Gyatso (1998:56–57). 'Jigs-med gling-pa was identified by the *ḍākinī* on that occasion as the person Seng-ge ras-pa.

[another] prophecy: "I myself, a minor meditator, will proceed to O-rgyan gling, [the land of] the beings from Du-va-ri-ka! Then I will make the north of India the place of my death! Erect a relic shrine of mine, at the eastern side of Bya-rung kha-shor [*stūpa*]! In general, [by this act] joy will arise in all [the regions of] Nepal and Tibet, and in particular foreign armies will be kept back for some years!"

[3]

Then, although this great Reverend One had reached the completion of the qualities of renouncing and realization without any remainder, in order to produce the seed of the Rūpakāya he abstained from human food. Then, with diligent behaviour, having taken the outer appearance of a *yogin* – [by smearing] ashes of the dead on his body and so forth – he got with his magic feet to all the sacred sites of Oḍḍiyāna, the island of the Ḍākiṇīs, the land of the Glorious Du-va-ri-ka. And afterwards, in the Mahāvihāra of Nalendra in Kashmir, [located] in the middle of a great plain six and a half miles wide, where saffron grows, adjacent to Pulahari in the north, and where one can find a cemetery, [a place for] embracing the secret way, [with the name] "Breaking Forth of Great Bliss", and a self-manifested Kaṇika Stūpa, there in the middle of [an area of] 3,700,000 cities, he condensed the visible form of the Rūpakāya into the [sphere of] the Dharmadhātu.[12]

For [the purpose of] a receptacle, in the presence of which the believers are able to collect merit, the tongue, the relics [and] the marvellous residues, which had manifested as godly figures, were taken, according to his prophecy, to the great [Bya-rung] kha-shor [*stūpa*].

[4]

A great discussion between the spiritual preceptor and the donor [arose] about requesting the king of Kathmandu for the "earth ritual". 'Bra-mon sgrong-pa spoke: "As there are many ministers and great envy [in] this land of Nepal, I will act as a helper for the request in the presence of the king! Tomorrow the king will go to Co-pa in order to meet the deity in the nine-storied [temple]; you and I, [we] two, should thus proceed [there] taking this

---

[12] The residence of the Indian Siddha Nāḍapāda or Nāropa (956–1040) is known as Pulahari to Tibetan pilgrims, who have paid visits to this site up to the present; for its location in the vicinity of Nālandā in Bihar, see Huber (2000:53). A second Pulahari was located in Kashmir – in the north – and this place served as the starting and returning points for Rang-rig ras-pa's journey to Oḍḍiyāna in the final years of his life. It was also near this place that he passed away and that Blo-bzang Chos-'phel, the redactor and carver of the register-cum-pilgrimage guidebook, had been born. For one mention of the northern Pulahari in the travelogue of sTag-tshang ras-pa (1574–1651), another 'Brug-pa *yogin*, who reached Kashmir and its sacred sites in the period between the years 1613 and 1616, see Tucci (1940:69). The relocation of Pulahari to the north was accompanied by a similar relocation to Kashmir of the prestigious Buddhist monastery of Nālandā (= Nalendra).

horse along [with us]! The voice of the ministers should be silenced [by this present] without anyone noticing it!"

In accordance with these words, the host Chos-dbang and I, [we] two, brought that good horse along with us and arrived at the nine-storied [temple]. Having offered the horse to the king, who was staying near the god Mahādeva, we then made the [following] request: "Whatever there exists of moulds of bones and relics of the teacher Rang-rig [ras-pa], who has passed away [recently], we plan to erect [for them] a reliquary at [Bya-rung] kha-shor [*stūpa*], and therefore it is necessary that you grant your favour for the "earth ritual"! We having extensively offered this request [to him], the king replied: "As the teacher [Rang-rig ras-pa] showed great benevolence to me, perform whatever "earth ritual" is necessary!" Not long after his reply, there were inserted four turquoise ornaments under his feet, [which is a sign of] a great oath according to Nepalese customs.[13]

Afterwards, when King Pārthivendramalla had returned to his palace, the ministers and great elders came together and spread malicious rumours to the king [with the words]: "There is no historical record that Tibetan *stūpas* have been erected in Nepal before. As Tibet is great in agitating means, [there is] every reason not to be happy with permission for the construction of the *stūpa*." The king replied: "In general, the teacher [Rang-rig ras-pa] has been greatly benevolent to me, and the object to which his heart is directed is [Bya-rung] kha-shor [*stūpa*]. Moreover, turquoise ornaments having been inserted under my feet in the presence of Mahādeva, it was said [already] that they can perform whatever "earth ritual" is necessary. As therefore [permission] has already been given, [the matter] is settled." Although the ministers entertained greed, they found no opportunity [to satisfy it] and were freed from their malicious rumours [by this].[14]

---

13 The toponym Co-pa stands for Chobar or Chobāra, a hill to the south-west of the Kathmandu Valley. On the top of this hill is a temple housing a statue of Padmapāṇi Lokeśvara, which goes also by the name Ādinātha. The Sixth Zhwa-dmar-pa Chos-kyi dbang-phyug (1584–1630) saw this statue during his visit to the Valley and identified it as one of the famous self-arisen effigies of the "Brothers Ārya [Avalokiteśvara]" (*'phags pa sku mched*). See *Bal yul du bgrod pa'i lam yig nor bu spel ma'i 'phreng ba*, NGMPP reel no. L 387/3, fol. 24a/2–3; for a description of this interesting travelogue, compare Ehrhard (1997a:126–128) and chapter seventeen in the present volume. The fact that during the rulership of King Pārthivendramalla – one of the sons of Pratāpamalla (regnal years 1641–1674) – the statue was regarded as Mahādeva, i.e. Śiva, points to the change in the political and religious climate in Nepal caused by the Shah dynasty. The year 1685 actually marks the embarkation of the Gorkhalis on the long course dedicated to winning the Malla realms; see Slusser (1982:65).

14 This episode of the king's consent to the construction of the reliquary, its being questioned by his advisers and ministers, and the final reconfirmation, calls to mind the myth of the construction of the Bodhnāth Stūpa and the etymology of its alternative name "Permission To Do What Is Proper" (*bya rung kha shor*). Concerning the literary sources of these events, see Ehrhard (1990b:2, note 2) and chapter seven in the present volume, as well as Blondeau (1994:31–48).

[5]
Then, on the seventeenth day of the eleventh Hor month of the wood-ox [year] (= 1685), when the propitious constellation for the construction [in general] and for [the manufacturing of] the bricks was performed, there was a surprise, for there were brick marks and human footprints clearly visible on each of the bricks. Although rain falls in Nepal without [a distinction between] summer and winter, in this year it was falling everywhere else in Nepal, but it did not rain at [Bya-rung] kha-shor [*stūpa*]: thus [the manufacturing of] the bricks could be completed without any disturbance.

[6]
Afterwards, when the earth had been dug out at the eastern side of [Bya-rung] kha-shor [*stūpa*], at the time of laying the foundation, Padma rdo-rje, the "lord of the site", the master [and] his disciples, uttered manifold harmful words, such as: "I am the 'lord of the site'! [Just] having asked the king [for permission] is not sufficient!" On top of that, even the people from my own quarters showed unsuitable behaviour, and after a Nepalese had carried away what was in the way of tools, they [too] escaped by running away.

When I was sitting the whole night [outside] in the field, thinking: "Someone without water here in Nepal, it seems, has to buy it! Now it is [definitely] decided that the reliquary [of Rang-rig ras-pa] cannot be completed. The teacher, the personal deity and the *ḍākiṇī* will have to give their blessings that the aim of my thoughts can be accomplished! Lacking that, I would rejoice even in dying!"

In a dream at the break of the day, having arrived at the top of a round-shaped mountain to the west of the lake Manosarowar, I saw in the space in front [of that site,] inside a house [which was] a tent of rainbows, the great Reverend One Rang-rig ras-pa himself: his body of greater majesty than even before, having the external appearance of a Heruka, emitting light and being of great dignity. Thinking: "It seems that my teacher has not died [yet]!", in a state of both joy and sorrow, [these] two, [I felt] tears coming forth in great number and was not able to address him from my side. [Thus] the Lord [Rang-rig ras-pa] spoke:

You, showing pride, by saying "I have done [so much already]"
abandon your thoughts completely and listen in a clear way:
the soil of the self-arisen Ālaya[vijñāna] I have identified
with a benevolence which is incomparable;
the full-grown sprout of spiritual experience has developed, [and]
the fruit has ripened [now] – the three Kāyas, [nothing else but] one's own mind!

I, the *yogin* without fixed abode, who has abandoned ordinary deeds
to accomplish the benefit of beings in an impartial way:

although [I] have shown the vanishing of the body [constituted by] causes, outside,
the self-arisen awareness, inside, exists as something unchangeable;
don't you act in a timid fashion –
let your mind be at ease [in the state of] Reality-as-it-is!

You, [who are] someone saying "I", if you are able to listen [to me]:
don't strive for [the world of] conditioned factors –
worry about the mind which is unconditioned!
Thinking: "What is changing has no truth!",
dismiss the ordinary deeds of this life
[and] rely on remote mountain hermitages in an unattached way!

Keep up the original [mind of] recollection [and] knowing as a spiritual practice!
If you have severed the doubts arising from grasping [mind and object] as two,
why should you not be victorious over the demon of obstacles?

At the very moment this was said I awoke from sleep and the night had departed. Although I set it down immediately in writing, some words I obviously forgot – a dream it is indeed something distorted!

[7]
Then, after the mind of Padma rdo-rje, the "lord of the site", had also been freed [from doubts], in accordance with the shape of [Bya-rung] kha-śhor [*stūpa*], there was constructed underground the "mountain", the ten virtues [platform], the stairs [and] the "lion throne" up to the first level. When that was reached, [the *stūpa*] was built above the ground: in the four directions of the central part [of the edifice] were statues manufactured from black stone, [one] of Śākyamuni [Buddha] and three of [Padmasambhava as] Dharmakāya, Saṃbhogakāya and Nirmāṇakāya [i.e. Amitābha, Avalokiteśvara and Padmasambhava], [and] a circle of Yakṣa [deities] in relief from [an alloy of] gold and copper. Above that was the treasury of the central part [of the *stūpa*], nineteen cubits [high], equivalent to the size of the central beam (*yaṣṭi*) [made of] sal wood; from its base up to its summit [were] containers of *dhāraṇī*s with all the proper signs.

In the interior of the bulging [body] of the central part [of the *stūpa*] was a chamber made from copper for the heart, tongue [and] eyes, [all] three, of the Lord [Rang-rig ras-pa]. [Further] contained [in the interior] was a cup full of relics, 5,300 *tsha*[*-tsha* images] from his [fragmented] bones, countless kinds of blessed sacred objects, including fifteen statues and *thang*[*-ka*s], the main ones being statues and *thang*[*-ka*s] of the five classes of [the deity] Khros[-ma] nag[-mo], which were resistant to fire.

[The *stūpa*] was [then] completed in brick, without [any difference between] inside and outside. As for the size, [it was] twenty cubits in each of the [four] directions; from the base to the top [it was] thirty-one cubits [high]. The umbrella [and] the *gañjira*, together with the top fastened to it, were manufactured from [an alloy of] gold and copper.

[8]
In accordance with the prophecy of the teacher [Rang-rig ras-pa] the shape resembled [Bya-rung] kha-shor [*stūpa*] in the same way as a son bears [a resemblance to] his mother. On the thirteenth day of the fourth Hor month of the fire-tiger [year] (= 1686) an assemblage of a crowd of 6,700 persons from Nepal, Tibet and the gorges, and seventy male and female practitioners – headed by Padma rdo-rje, the *upādhyāya* for the consecration [ceremony], and by Chos-grags rgya-mtsho – arranged for a feast in a proper way; and there was a scattering of flowers accompanied by wondrous signs. The consecration [ceremony] was performed one more time by Zil-gnon dbang-rgyal rdo-rje (1647–1716), the holder of the family-lineage of lHa-lung dPal-gyi rdo-rje.[15]

[9]
In such a way, after body, speech and mind of myself and others have been purified and cleaned in the presence of this receptacle, together with the multitude of impurities and sins of the two kinds of obscurations – assembled from beginningless lives up to the present by countless beings, who by [the acts of] seeing and listening have established a connection with material things – may the two kinds of accumulations be completed; and having [finally] reached in this life the state of a Buddha, by benefiting others without [treating them as] particular objects, may the benefit of the teachings and of the beings, [which is] similar to the sky [in its extent], be accomplished without any effort!

---

15 Up to now I have no further information on the persons of Padma rdo-rje and Chos-grags rgya-mtsho. For biographical data concerning Zil-gnon dbang-rgyal rdo-rje – who had received this name from the Fifth Dalai Bla-ma Ngag-dbang Blo-bzang rgya-mtsho –, see Ehrhard (2007) and chapter nine in the present volume. The father of Zil-gnon dbang-rgyal rdo-rje, a disciple of the Third Yol-mo-ba sprul-sku bsTan-'dzin nor-bu, was regarded as an incarnation of lHa-lung dPal-gyi rdo-rje; this incarnation status led family members to appropriate the name. This family acted as caretakers of the Bodhnāth Stūpa, and it is recorded that Zil-gnon dbang-rgyal rdo-rje carried out renovation work at Bya-rung kha-shor in the years 1706/1707.

EDITION

Bal yul shing kun sogs dang rje rang rig gdung rten gyi dkar chag, fols. 4a/3–6a/4

namo guru /

rgyal kun thugs rje'i spyi gzugs padma 'byung /
brtul zhugs rdzu 'phrul sna tshogs bkod pa can /
mthu stobs dregs pa zil gnon lha mi'i mgon /
rang rig ras pa'i zhabs la gus pas 'dud /

[1]
de yang rje de nyid ni o rgyan thugs kyi sprul par lung bstan pa yin te / ji ltar bstan ce na / rig[16] *'dzin gar dbang rdo rje'i gter lung las /*

> *mnga' ris mar nu'i so mtshams su :*
> *yul ni rang rig ces bya ru :*
> *skyes bu rang gis rang rig pa'i :*
> *rang rig ces bya'i ming can 'byung :*
>
> *de nyid nga nyid thugs sprul ste :*
> *rten ni ras pa'i cha byad can :*
> *brtul zhugs mthar phyin rnal 'byor pa :*
> *rgya bod bal gsum bde la 'god :*
>
> *lhag par kha shor nyams gsos byed :*
> *des ni mtha' dmag lo 'ga'*[17] *bzlog :*

ces dang /

mnga' bdag nyang ral bstan 'dzin chos dbang nas gsan pa'i phag mo gzhung drug le'u dgu pa las /

> *stod kyi phyogs su rang rig ras pa 'byung :*
> *de ni kho bo'i thugs kyi sprul pa'o :*
> *des ni 'gro drug sems can bde la 'god :*

---

16 *rigs*
17 *bga'*

ces pa'i lung dang mthun par rgyal dbang thams cad mkhyen gzigs chen po ngag gi dbang phyug blo bzang rgya mtsho'i rnam par thar pa kha pa'i grangs yig drug cu par / la stod phyogs nas rang rig grub chen du grags pa phyag rdzogs gnyis ka la nyams rtogs che ba zhig 'ongs par dang phrad de / ja gral la 'phros glengs mang du byung / la las mnga' bdag gi lung bstan du / stod kyi phyogs nas rang rig ras pa 'byung : zhes pa de yin nam zer / gang ltar **[4b]** *snang sems rang ngo 'phrod pa zhig tu mngon /*

[2]

zhes gsungs pa'i rje rang rig ras pa de nyid kyis bya rung kha shor gyi nyams gsos mdzad dus / kha shor shar 'dabs su phebs nas 'thor tsam zhig mdzad nas ma 'ongs pa nga'i gdung rten zhig bzhengs na sems can la bde rgya che dang lhag par mtha' dmag bzlog pa dang / bal bod la bde skyid 'byung zhes lung bstan / de nas kha shor chen po'i gdugs gaṇdzira tog dang / ka ba ka sten dang bcas pa gser zangs las grub pa mdzad / slar mnga' ris brgyud nas byang pu la ha rir dgun thog gcig bzhugs nas nub phyogs o rgyan la phebs dus / nga sgom chung du va ri ka pa / 'gro ba o rgyan gling du 'gro / shi sa rgya gar byang du byed / bya rung kha shor shar 'dabs su / mi kho bo'i gdung rten de ru bzhengs / spyir bal bod kun la bde skyid 'byung / sgos mtha' dmag lo 'ga' bzlog par 'gyur / ces lung bstan /

[3]

de nas rje btsun chen po de nyid spangs rtogs kyi yon tan ma lus pa mthar son kyang / gzugs sku'i sa bon bskrun phyir mi zas rnams spangs / sku la thal chen sogs dzo ki'i chas bzung / brtul bzhugs kyi spyod pas o rgyan mkha' 'gro gling dpal du va ri ka'i yul gnas thams cad rdzu 'phrul zhabs kyis brtol[18] *nas slar byang phyogs*[19] *phu la ha ri'i mdun sa / gur gum skye pa'i thang chen po dpag tshad phyed dang drug gi dbus na / gsang lam bsnol ba'i dur khrod bde chen brdol*[20] *dang / rang byung mchod rten ka ṇi ka yod pa / grong khyer 'bum phrag so bdun yod pa'i dbus su / kaṣmi na lendra'i gtsug lag khang chen por gzugs sku'i bkod pa chos dbyings su bsdus shing / dad ldan bsod nams bsog rten du ljags ring bsrel*[21] */ ngo mtshar sku tshigs lha skur byon pa rnams lung bstan bzhin kha shor chen po'i drung du spyan drangs te /*

[4]

yam bu rgyal po la sa dpyad zhu ba'i mchod yon bka' bgros che / 'bra mon sgrong pa na re / bal yul 'di blon po mang zhing phrag dog che bas / rgyal por ngas zhu rogs bya'o // sang nyin rgyal po co par dgu thog tu lha mjal du phebs 'ong bas / khyed rang gnyis rta

---

18 *btol*

19 *phyags*

20 *brdal*

21 *srel*

'di khrid las shog / blon po rnams kyi ma tshor bar ngag chod pa bya'o // zer ba bzhin rang gnas po chos dbang gnyis kyis[22] *rta bzang po de khrid dgu thog tu phyin pas / rgyal* **[5a]** *po lha ma hā de va'i drung na bzhugs pa la rta phul nas zhus pa / bla ma rang rig zhing la phebs pa'i gdung rus spar gang yod pa / kha shor du gdung rten bzheng rtsis lags pas sa dpyad bka' drin skyong dgos tshul*[23] *gyi*[24] *zhu ba rgyas par phul bas / rgyal po na re / bla ma khong nged la bka' drin che bas sa dpyad gang du dgos kyang gyis*[25] *shig gsungs byung bas / gsungs ma thag zhabs 'og tu pra men bzhi bcug pa bal lugs kyi mna' chen po yin / de nas rgyal po pa ti phhendra? ma la pho brang du byon pa la / blon po dang rgan chen rnams 'dus nas rgyal por / bal yul du sngar nas bod kyi mchod rten bzhengs pa'i lo rgyus med / bod g.yo thabs che bas mchod rten bzheng du bcug pa mi dga' ba'i rgyu mtshan gyi phra ma zhus tshe / rgyal po'i zhal nas / spyir bla ma kong nga rang la bka' 'drin che ba dang / thugs kyi gtad sa kha shor yin / lhag par ma hā de va'i drung du / rkang 'og tu pra men bcug ste*[26] *sa dpyad gang dgos gyis shig ces sbyin tshar bas kha bsdus gsungs / blon po rnams za 'dod byed rung / glags ma rnyed cing phra ma las grol /*

[5]

de nas shing glang hor zla bcu gcig pa'i tshes bcu bdun gyi nyin / bzo rigs dang / rtsa phag gi skar 'dzin byas pas / rdza phag re re la phag rjes mi'i rkang rjes cam lam mer bsal bas ngo mtshar bar byung / bal yul du dbyar dgun med par char 'bab kyang / de'i lo la bal yul gzhan du babs kyang / kha shor du ma babs pas rdza phag gi mgo thon /

[6]

de nas kha shor shar 'dabs su sa brus nas rmang gting tshe / gnas bdag dpon slob padma rdo rjes / gnas bdag nged yin / rgyal po la zhus pas go mi chod sogs bka' skyon sna tshogs gnang ba'i stengs su / rang phyogs rnams kyis kyang mi 'tshams pa'i spyod 'gros dang / chas yod pa rnams bal po zhig gis[27] *khyer nas bros la shor / bal yul 'dir chu min pa nyo dgos 'dug / da ni gdung rten mi 'grub thag chod / bla ma yi dam mkha' 'gros bdag gi bsam don 'grub par*[28] *byin gyis rlobs shig / de min shi ba rang dga' snyam mtshan gang du zhing sdad pa las / tho rangs*[29] *rmi lam du / ma pham yin zer ba'i mtsho zhig gi nub ri ldum po zhig gi rtser sleb pa'i mdun gyi mkhar 'ja' 'od kyi gur khyim gyi nang na / rje btsun chen*

---

22 *kyi*

23 *chul*

24 *gya*

25 *gyas*

26 *sta*

27 *gi*

28 *'grab par*

29 *tho rang*

po rang rig ras pa de yid sngar ba kyang sku **[5b]** *gzi byin che ba he ru ka'i cha byad 'od zer 'phro zhing zil che ba zhig mthong bas / nga'i bla ma ma grongs pa 'dug snyam dga' ba dang skyo ba gnyis ka'i ngang nas mchi ma mang du shor zhing phar zhu ma nus / rje'i zhal nas /*

khyod nga byas zer ba'i khong yus can /
sems lhug par zhog la lhan ner nyon /
nged kun gzhi rang byung[30] *gi zhing sa la /*
bka' drin mnyam med kyis[31] *rang ngo sprad /*
nyams myong tshad ldan gyi[32] *myu gu rgyas /*
rang sems sku gsum gyi 'bras bu smin /

'gro don phyogs med du 'grub pa yi /
bya btang nges med kyi rnal 'byor nga /
phyi rgyu lus kyi rnam 'gyur bstan mod kyang /
nang rang byung gi rig pa 'pho 'gyur med /
mi khyod rang blo[33] *chung ma byed par /*
blo sems chos nyid du bde bar gyis /

mi nga zer khyod rang nyan srid na /
'dus byas gnyer srid[34] *ma byed par /*
byar med kyi sems la nya ra gyis /
rnam 'gyur la nges pa mi 'dug go /
bsam bzhin du tshe 'di'i bya ba thong /
nges med kyi ri khrod dben pa brten[35] */*

nyams[36] *len du dran shes rnal ma skyongs /*
gnyis 'dzin gyi the tshoms rbad chod na /
bar chad kyi bdud las cis mi rgyal /

ces gsungs pa'i mod la gnyid sad pas nam langs 'dug / de ma thag yi ger bkod kyang tshig 'ga' brjed 'dug / rmi lam 'khrul pa yin mod /

---

30 *byang*
31 *kyi*
32 *gya*
33 *bla*
34 *srad*
35 *brtan*
36 *nyam*

[7]
de[37] *nas gnas bdag gi dgongs pa yang grol nas / kha shor gi bzo dbyibs ji lta ba bzhin / sa 'dzin dge bcu ba dan them skas seng khri bang rim*[38] *dang po*[39] *man chad sa 'og tu mtshon par byas / de phyin sa stengs su brtsigs pa / bum pa'i phyogs bzhir śākya thub pa dang / chos longs sprul gsum gyi sku rdo nag las grub pa / gnod sbyin 'khor lo gser zangs 'bur dod / de steng bum gter spos dkar shing gi srog shing cha tshad dang mtshungs pa khru*[40] *bcu dgu / zhabs mthil nas dbu'i gtsug tor gyi bar gzungs bzhugs mtshan nyid kun ldan / bum ldir nang du rje'i*[41] *thugs ljags spyan gsum bzhugs khang zi*[42] *khyim las grub pa / ring srel ting gang / gdung tsha lnga stong gsum brgya / khros nag sde lnga'i sku thang me thub mas gtsos pa'i sku thang bco lnga sogs byin rlabs rten gyi rigs dpag tu med pa*[43] *bzhugs / phyi nang med pa rdza phag la grub pa / rgyar phyogs re la khru nyi shu / rtsa rtse'i bar la khru sum cu so gcig / gdugs gañdzira*[44] *'phreng tog dang bcas pa gser zangs pa bsgrubs /*

[8]
bla ma'i lung bstan bzhin[45] *bzo dbyibs* **[6a]** *kha shor ji lta ba ma gang du bu blangs pa lta bu / me stag hor zla bzhi pa'i tshes bcu gsum kyi nyin rab tu gnas pa'i mkhan po padma rdo rje / chos grags rgya mtshos gtsos / sgrub pa pho mo bcu phrag bdun dang / bal bod rong gsum gyi khrom drug stong bdun brgya tshogs / dga' ston legs par bshams shing / ngo mtshar ltas dang bcas te me tog 'thor / slar yang lha lung dpal gyi rdo rje'i gdung srol 'dzin pa zil gnon dbang rgyal rdo rjes rab tu gnas par mdzad /*

[9]
de ltar rten[46] *'di nyid la bdag gzhan lus ngag yid gsum dang / zang zing gi 'brel thogs mthong thos kyi 'gro ba ma lus pa'i tshe thog ma med nas da bar du bsags pa'i sdig sgrib gnyis*[47] *ltung dri ma'i tshogs kun byang zhing dag nas / tshogs gnyis rdzogs te sangs rgyas kyi go 'phang tshe 'di nyid la thob nas / dmigs pa med pa'i gzhan don gyis bstan pa dang sems can gyi don nam mkha' dang mnyam par 'bad med du 'grub par gyur cig gu /*

---

37 *da*

38 *bam ram*

39 *dang pa*

40 *'khru*

41 *rjes*

42 *gzi*

43 *mad pa*

44 *ganydzara*

45 *bzhan*

46 *rtan*

47 *nyas*

Note on the illustration:

The book *An Account of the Kingdom of Nepal and of the Territories Annexed to this Dominion by the House of Gorkha* by Francis Hamilton (Edinburgh: A. Constable, 1819) contained two copperplate engravings taken from drawings by Charles Crawford. One showed the Bodhnāth Stūpa together with the reliquary of Raṅ-rig ras-pa: it is the first Western representation of Tibetan monuments in the Kathmandu Valley. Crawford, who later became head of the Cartographic Survey of India, also left several manuscript maps of the Valley and of the route from India to Nepal. For the remarkable precision and aesthetic quality of these maps, see L. Boulnois, Bibliographie du Nepal. Vol. 3 (Sciences Naturelles), Tome 1 (Cartes du Nepal dans les bibliothèques de Paris et de Londres). Paris: Éditions du Centre national de la recherche scientifique 1973, p. 31. Compare also J. Keay, *The Great Arc*. The Dramatic Tale of How India Was Mapped and Everest Was Named. London: Harper Collins 2000, p. 35–38, for Crawford's attempts to measure the Himalayas.

View of the Temple of Bouddhama in Kasacheit.

A Forgotten Incarnation Lineage:
The Yol-mo-ba sprul-skus (16th to 18th Centuries)

One of the most fascinating subjects for someone dealing with Tibetan Buddhism is doubtless the phenomenon of conscious rebirth and the existence of so-called "lines of rebirth" (*skyes rabs*), which may endow a spiritual teacher with a high degree of religious and political power. As studies already exist on this topic,[1] I should like in the following merely to present a further case study of this phenomenon, one that is interesting for several reasons. What I am most concerned about is, first, to demonstrate the process whereby the lineage is constituted as the sequence of its individual representatives and, secondly, to give a summary account of the religious activities of the various members of the lineage in different periods of Tibet's political history. We shall be able in the process to observe not only how an incarnation chain is constituted but also how it later fell into oblivion in the region of its origin.

1. sNGAGS-'CHANG ŚĀKYA BZANG-PO (15th/16th CENTURIES)

The name of the incarnation lineage, "Rebirth from Yol-mo" (*yol mo ba sprul sku*), calls first of all for a more exact definition of the geographical name Yol-mo. The latter denotes a region on the Tibet-Nepal border known presently as Helambu. Tibetan authors regarded this region – lying north-east of Kathmandu along the upper reaches of the Melemchi Khola and the Yangri Khola – as a part of Nepal, as the expression "Yol-mo [which is]

---

1 Some useful remarks on the concepts of hierophany and hierocracy – i.e. the spiritual and temporal aspects of a single line of *sprul sku* type rebirth – are provided by Seyfort Ruegg (1988:1249–1251); they refer mainly to the Karma-pa branch of the bKa'-brgyud-pa school. Compare Everding (1988:182–186) on the historical development of Lamaist lines of birth, as well as pp. 208–209, where some general knowledge concerning the constituting principles of recognized rebirth are presented. See also the remarks by Schwieger (1989:14–15), who stresses the importance of "rebirth-chains" for the social status of Tibetan religious personages. The case examples of the last two studies are lines of rebirth of the 17th and 18th centuries from East Tibet and come from the dGe-lugs-pa school. The text *Bod dang bar khams rgya sog bcas kyi bla sprul rnams kyi 'phreng deb gzhung* in *Bod kyi gal che'i lo rgyus dang yig cha bsdams bsgrigs* (= Gangs can rig mdzod 16), Lhasa: Bod-ljongs bod-yig dpe-skrun khang, 1991, pp. 281–369, contains the hitherto most comprehensive list of lines of rebirth. It was compiled in the years between 1814 and 1820 and documents the practice of the Manchu administration to formalize the recognition of an incarnation by the use of lots; this method became famous under the name "testing in the golden urn" (*gser bum du brtags pa*).

enclosed by glaciers [in] Nepal" (*bal yul gyi yol mo gangs ra*) shows.[2] The attractions of the surroundings, which lent themselves to the practices of Tibetan yogins and hermits, are impressively portrayed in the songs of Mi-la-ras-pa. Yol-mo is a land of blooming mountain flowers where trees dance in the woods, and a playground for monkeys, birds and bees. Rain falls both in the summer and winter; fog banks come together in spring and autumn alike, indistinguishably.

The first founding of a monastery in Yol-mo is made by local historiography to coincide with the arrival of sNgags-'chang Śākya bzang-po, a "treasure discoverer" (*gter ston*) of the rNying-ma-pa school.[3] As written documents concerning this founding, which occurred at the beginning of the 16th century, are available, I here cite from a translation of one of them:

> The man's *rigs* (here "family lineage") is given as Shākya bzang-po, and his *rus* (here "caste") as *drang srong* (Skt. *brahmin*), he being an emanation of Chos-blon Padma Gung-btsan. He is told to build a gompa in a land where the sky looks like the "wheel of worldly existence" (*srid-pa'i 'khor-lo*), and the land like the eight-petalled lotus. After receiving this prophecy, he comes by way of Ribu Pomba (Kyirong) to Kathmandu, where he repairs two *stūpa*s, and then he opens the "outer, inner and secret" doors of Yolmo Gangra.[4]

---

2 For this description, see gTsang-smyon Heruka (1452–1507), *rNal 'byor gyi dbang phyug chen po mi la ras pa'i rnam mgur*, Hsining: mTsho-sngon mi-rigs dpe-skrun khang, 1989, p. 122.11; it is part of a list of sacred places where Mi-la-ras-pa (1028–1111), under the instructions of his teacher Mar-pa (1012–1097), was said to have applied himself to spiritual practices. This list found its way into various "inventories" (*dkar chag[s]*) and "descriptions of sacred sites" (*gnas yig*); see the translation of the relevant passage in Huber (1997:252): "Because Mount dPal-'dar (sic) of Mang-yul and the Snowy Enclave of Yol-mo in Nepal are the places prophesied in the *Avataṃsakasūtra*, meditate there." Concerning Mi-la-ras-pa's stay in Yol-mo, compare the text of gTsang-smyon Heruka, pp. 254.10–264.18; on the circumstances that kept him from going to Mang-yul Ri-bo dpal-'bar, see ibid, pp. 228.6–246.10. In later sources the name "La-stod Yol-mo gangs-ra" is also common; see *sTag-sgang mkhas-mchog Ngag-dbang blo-gros: sNga 'gyur chos 'byung*, p. 673.24. For the term *gangs ra* as a topographical metaphor from the time of the early Tibetan kings, see Hazod (1991:196 and *passim*).

3 Among the finds, the short biography of sNgags-'chang Śākya bzang-po in *Chos 'byung I*, pp. 529.10ff., lays stress on a treasure cycle called *Thugs rje chen po 'khor ba dbyings sgrol*. The uncovering and transmission of a find of this name, however, is generally ascribed to Rig-'dzin Legs-ldan bDud-'joms rdo-rje, the disciple of sNgags-'chang Śākya bzang-po; see, for example, Karmay (1988a:145). This cycle was commented by both the Fifth Dalai Bla-ma Ngag-dbang Blo-bzang rgya-mtsho (1617–1682) and the Second rDo-rje brag Rig-'dzin Padma 'phrin-las (1640–1718).

4 See Clarke (1980:11); in his introduction he says: "The document begins as a future prediction of Padmasambhava in response to a query of his consort as to who will repair Bodhnāth Stūpa if it is destroyed, and as to who will 'open' Yolmo Gangra." A detailed version of this prophecy was filmed by the Nepal-German Manuscript Preservation Project (NGMPP): *Dang po 'jig rten srid pa chags tshul gyis* (= *gyi*) *lo rgyud* (= *rgyus*) *bzur* (= *zur*) *rtsam* (= *tsam*) *cig zhu ba*, 8 fols., reel no. E 2669/5. This text is a

The striking thing in this description of sNgags-'chang Śākya bzang-po's arrival is the fact that Yol-mo gangs-ra is here described as a "hidden land" (*sbas yul*). Both the characterization of an idealized and spiritualized landscape – the sky is like a *bhāvacakra* with eight spokes, the earth like an eight-petalled lotus – and "the gate of the sacred site" (*gnas sgo*) follow the conventional lines of texts dealing with the phenomenon of hidden lands. If the tradition of this genre is drawn on, then Yol-mo gangs-ra is found in a list of seven *sbas yul*; in this context the paradisiacal site bears the name "Lotus Grove" (*padma'i tshal*).[5]

Besides his opening of the hidden land Lotus Grove (and the founding of the first monastery in Yol-mo), sNgags-'chang Śākya bzang-po is credited with the renovation of "two *stūpas*" (*mchod rten rnam gnyis*) in the Kathmandu Valley. Although this appears to refer to the two *stūpa*s of Svayambhūnāth and Bodhnāth (there exists a late, corrupt tradition mentioning a renovation of Svayambhūnāth), sNgags-'chang Śākya bzang-po has remained alive in the memories of Tibetans above all as the "discoverer" and restorer of the Bodhnāth Stūpa. As I have already presented elsewhere material on the activities of sNgags-'chang Śākya bzang-po at the sacred site Bya-rung kha-shor,[6] I should now like to

---

concise Buddhist cosmology that, following treatment of the world's composite structure and the religious activities of sNgags-'chang Śākya bzang-po, gives a genealogy of the latter's family descendants in the region of Helambu.

5 Concerning the theme "'héros fondateurs', qui 'ouvrent la porte d'un lieu'", see Stein (1987:189). For a description of the perfect landscape befitting a holy site, see ibid, p. 196: "En haut, le ciel est une roue à huit raies. Au milieu l'espace médian (*bar-snaṅ*) est orné des huit 'signes fastes' (*bkra-çis rtags-brgyad*, sanskrit *aṣṭamaṅgala*). Et en bas, la Terre est un lotus à huit pétales." For background on the opening of the hidden valley Padma'i-tshal and the transfer of the necessary "introductory lists" (*kha byang*) from Rig-'dzin mChog-ldan mgon-po (1497–1531) to sNgags-'chang Śākya bzang-po, see Ehrhard (1997b:338–340) and chapter sixteen in the present volume. A list of hidden lands according to the Byang-gter tradition is contained in *sBas yul bdun gyi them byang ga'u ma* in *Ma 'ongs lung bstan gsal ba'i sgron me*, 1 (= Smanrtsis Shesrig Spendzod, 33), Leh: S. W. Tashigangpa, 1973, pp. 545.4–548.1. It begins with [bDe-ldan] sKyid-mo lung, which is also located in Nepal (along the upper Buri Gandhaki), while [sBas-pa] Padma'i-tshal is named as the second land.

6 On the rediscovery and renovation of the *stūpa* by sNgags-'chang Śākya bzang-po, see Ehrhard (1990b:7–9) and chapter seven in the present volume. The background to the myth of the *stūpa* has already been dealt with by Blondeau (1982/83:123–126); concerning the date of the text *mChod rten chen po bya rung kha shor gyi lo rgyus thos pas grol ba*, see ibid, p. 126: "A en juger par les élements biographiques rassemblés sur Çākya bzaṅ-po, "redécouvreur" en 1512 de *l'Histoire du grand stūpa Bya-rung kha-çor* (texte qui aurait été découvert une première fois puis recaché par lHa-bcun sngon-mo, contemporain de Rwa locāvā), il semble que ce soit lui qui ait fixé sur le *stūpa* de Bodhnāth, qu'il trouve en ruines et qu'il restaure, la légende de Bya-ruṅ kha-çor." An early block print of this most important of texts on the *stūpa* of Bodhnāth, the printing of which was done in [b]Tsum, was filmed by the NGMPP under reel no. E 2517/4, 18 fols. On sNgags-'chang Śākya bzang-po's association with the renovation carried out on Svayambhūnāth by gTsang-smyon Heruka and how this association came about in a late version of the so-called *'Phags pa shing kun dkar chag*, see Ehrhard (1991:14, note 6) and chapter five in the present volume.

go briefly into the passage of the above cited prophecy, where it is said that the treasure discoverer is an incarnation of Chos-glon Padma Gung-tshan (= Chos-blon Padma Gung-btsan). This ties in with the myth of the *stūpa* of Bodhnāth and leads to the formation of the former birth lineage of the Yol-mo-ba sprul-skus.

The inventory of the *stūpa* "Permission to Do What is Proper" (*bya rung kha shor*), brought to light in the year 1512 by sNgags-'chang Śākya bzang-po during a renovation of bSam-yas, tells the story of the woman keeper of geese who wheedled from the king of Nepal permission to build a big *stūpa*, which she then managed to do with the help of her three sons. During the consecration of the edifice the three brothers swore an oath to get together in their next life in the land of snow, that is, Tibet, in order to introduce the Buddhist teaching there. The three brothers were reborn as Śāntarakṣita, the abbot, Khri Srong-lde'u btsan, the king, and Padmasambhava, the tantric master. Along with the main protagonists, the helper who had a key part in the construction also swore an oath: he wished to be reborn as a "Buddhist minister" (*chos blon*).[7]

In the fifth and final chapter of the inventory, it is prophesied that sNgags-'chang Śākya bzang-po will be a direct reincarnation of this minister, Padma Gung-btsan, and upon him falls anew the task of raising the *stūpa* to majestic proportions. With its claim to run through the man who helped construct the edifice and through the minister Padma Gung-btsan, the lineage of the Yol-mo-ba sprul-skus acquired its self-legitimation; we shall see how this scheme of originally two former births was further expanded upon. First, though, some information will be presented to provide a better understanding of sNgags-'chang Śākya bzang-po and the extent of his influence.

In the citation reproduced above concerning his person according to the local tradition of Helambu, it is stated that his caste is that of a "Brahmin" (*drang srong*). What we can observe here is the process termed by anthropologists Hinduization or Sanskritzation, in which an older – Tibetan – layer of culture is covered over by religio-political concepts of Hinduism. If the Tibetan sources from the 17th to 19th centuries are consulted, what clearly emerges is that *drang srong* is a corruption of the toponym Gram-so/Drang-so, a region in western gTsang where sNgags-'chang Śākya bzang-po was born.[8]

---

7 Concerning the various traditions of the myth of Bodhnāth, see Blondeau (1982/83:125–128); there it is primarily the traditions of the *gter ma* and the *sba bzhed* that are distinguished from one another. Further, there exists a version of the Bon-po school; see Shar-rdza-ba bKra-shis rgyal-mtshan (1859–1933), *Legs bshad rin po che'i gter mdzod dpyod ldan dga' ba'i char*, Beijing: Mi-rigs dpe-skrun khang, 1985, pp. 203.16ff. A more detailed analysis of the myth and its variants has also been undertaken by Blondeau (1994:31–48). Of special interest in this context is the existence of a manuscript of the *Zangs gling ma* biography of Padmasambhava stored in the National Archives, Kathmandu, which has a unique introductory chapter of the myth; it was filmed by the NGMPP under reel no. AT 28/2.

8 See Kun-bzang nges-don klong-yangs: *Bod du byung ba'i gsang sngags snga 'gyur gyi bstan 'dzin skyes mchog rim byon gyi rnam thar nor bu'i do shal*, p. 259.1, where it is said that he was born into a family of "local princes" (*sde dpon*) of Gram-so rdzong in the province of La-stod lHo. In a work of the

Besides in his home province, the treasure discoverer was active at the royal court of Mang-yul Gung-thang as teacher of the prince Kun-bzang Nyi-zla grags-pa (1540–1560); in Mustang (*glo bo*), where he taught the same disciples as Glo-bo mkhan-chen bSod-nams lhun-grub (1456–1532); and finally in Byang Ngam-ring, the political centre of the province of La-stod Byang.[9] What in my opinion offers the best explanation for this presence in the religious and political centres of south-western Tibet and Nepal is sNgags-'chang Śākya bzang-po's role as master and lineage-holder of the Byang-gter tradition. Among other things, he was the teacher of the two brothers mNga'-ris Paṇ-chen Padma dbang-rgyal (1487–1542) and mNga'-ris rig-'dzin Legs-ldan bDud-'joms rdo-rje (born 1512), the latter of whom had an important part to play within the lineage of the Northern Treasures; for this reason I shall deal briefly with one of the localities where the transmission of the teachings occurred.

Episodes involving meetings between sNgags-'chang Śākya bzang-po and Rig-'dzin Legs-ldan bDud-'joms rdo-rje are described in various passages of the latter's biography. Among the teachings Legs-ldan bDud-'joms rdo-rje received during the first meeting with the master we find, interestingly, a treasure work entitled *mChod rten dmar po'i gter ma*, and it is said that he wanted to accompany sNgags-'chang Śākya bzang-po in the role of an attendant during the renovation of Bya-rung kha-shor but then was unable to do so. When finally after some years – in other words, shortly after the renovation of the Bodhnāth

---

Second rDo-rje brag Rig-'dzin (composed in 1680), he is called variously Drang-so gTer-ston Śākya bzang-po, rJe Drang-so ba, Drang-so sprul-sku chen-po, or Drang-so sNgags-'chang Śākya bzang-po; see rDo-rje brag Rig-'dzin Padma 'phrin-las: *'Dus pa'i mdo dbang gi bla ma brgyud pa'i rnam thar ngo mtshar dad pa'i phreng ba*, pp. 316.6, 348.5, 350.4, 321.5 and *passim*. In the biography of the Fourth Yol-mo-ba sprul-sku is found the episode in which the later reincarnation visits the homeland of his predecessor sNgags-'chang Śākya bzang-po; there mention is made of a lake (*drang so'i mtsho mo*) and the activities of his predecessor in the region (see note 35). The region of Gram-so/Drang-so under discussion here can be localized on maps; it lies east of Shel-dkar and contains a fairly large lake that flows into 'Phung-chu. Compare also the biography of Zhabs-dkar Tshogs-drug rang-grol (1781–1851), who, setting out from Shel-dkar in 1822, travelled to Sa-skya monastery by way of the towns of mTsho-sgo and Drang-so; see *sNyigs dus 'gro ba yongs kyi skyabs mgon zhabs dkar rdo rje 'chang chen po'i rnam par thar pa rgyas par bshad pa skal bzang gdul bya thar 'dod rnams kyi re ba skong ba yid bzhin nor bu bsam 'phel dbang gi rgyal po* (*stod cha*), 1982, pp. 890.17–893.11, and Ricard (1994:450–452). This was also the route taken by the Nepalese mission to Peking in the same year; see Hodgson (1880:185).

9 Concerning his role as teacher of the Gung-thang prince, see Tshe-dbang nor-bu: *Bod rje lha btsad po'i gdung rabs mnga' ris smad gung thang du ji ltar byung ba'i tshul deb gter dwangs shel 'phrul gyi me long*, p. 137.15. For his stay in Glo-bo and for his teaching in bDe-grol monastery in Byang Ngam-ring, see rDo-rje brag Rig-'dzin Padma 'phrin-las (as in note 8), pp. 316.6, 321.5 and 358.5ff. bDe-grol monastery was the seat of Thugs-sras Nam-mkha' rgyal-mtshan (1454–1541); it is from him that the First Yol-mo-ba sprul-sku had received the teachings of Rig-'dzin rGod-ldem 'phru-can (1337–1406). For biographical data on Thugs-sras Nam-mkha' rgyal-mtshan, see sTag-sgang mkhas-mchog Ngag-dbang blo-gros (as in note 2), p. 673.7–19.

Stūpa – he undertook a journey to Nepal together with his brother, he returned to Tibet by way of sKyid-grong and met up with sNgags-'chang Śākya bzang-po in Ri-bo dpal-'bar. There, together with the latter, he completed a "one-year retreat" (*lo mtshams*).[10]

The name Ri-bo dpal-'bar turns up again at the final meeting between master and disciple in the year 1527 at bDe-grol monastery in Byang Ngam-ring. On this occasion Legs-ldan bDud-'joms rdo-rje took an oath to maintain in their complete state the treasure teachings of the tradition of Ri-bo bkra-bzang and to follow the spiritual practice of those teachings in Ri-bo dpal-'bar for ten years. Even though shortly thereafter he freed himself from the terms of the vow in order to undertake another journey with his brother – this time to Central Tibet – it is nevertheless clear that the place called Ri-bo dpal-'bar played a pivotal role in the transmission of the Byang-gter teachings from sNgags-'chang Śākya bzang-po to Legs-ldan bDud-'joms rdo-rje. This is not surprising in view of the fact that Rig-'dzin rGod-ldem 'phru-can, the founder of the tradition (he was born on the east side of the mountain Ri-bo bkra-bzang in La-stod Byang), was given possession of the region of Ri-bo dpal-'bar by the Gung-thang king Khri-rgyal bSod-nams lde (1371–1404), and there he rehid a portion of his treasure works for future generations.[11]

sNgags-'chang Śākya bzang-po passed his final years in the hidden valley of Yol-mo gangs-ra, where he died surrounded by his disciples. One of the historiographical works of the rNying-ma-pa school provides detailed information on the prophecies that the First Yol-mo-ba sprul-sku left on this occasion concerning the location of his rebirth. To his disciples he intimated that he would be born in the "lineage of the incarnation of the ruler" (*mnga' bdag pa'i sku brgyud*). As the work further makes clear, the "family line of the ruler" (*mnga' bdag pa'i gdung rigs*) refers to the descendants of treasure discoverer Nyang-

10 For the first meeting, see rDo-rje brag Rig-'dzin Padma 'phrin-las (as in note 8), p. 348.4–6. The pertinent passage reads: *kho rang gi rnam thar lung bstan mchod rten dmar po'i gter ma/ gsol 'debs le'u bdun sogs gsan/ rje drang so ba bal yul du mchod rten bya rung kha shor gyi zhig gsos byon pa'i zhabs phyir 'byon bzhed kyang ma nus par phyir byon*. What is referred to as "his (i.e. sNgags-'chang Śākya bzang-po's) biography [and the] prophecies 'Treasure Work of the Red Stūpa'" is the text *mChod rten chen po bya rung kha shor gyi lo rgyus thos pas grol ba* (as in note 6). It was discovered by sNgags-'chang Śākya bzang-po in the red *stūpa* southwest of the main temple (*dbu rtse gtsug lag khang*) of bSam-yas.

11 Concerning their last meeting, see rDo-rje brag Rig-'dzin Padma 'phrin-las (as in note 8), pp. 358.5–360.1. On the birthplace of Rig-'dzin rGod-ldem 'phru-can, see Schwieger (1988 [1989]:33). The transfer of the property of Ri-bo dpal-'bar monastery to Rig-'dzin rGod-ldem 'phru-can by Khri-rgyal bSod-nams lde is described in Kaḥ-thog rig-'dzin Tshe-dbang nor-bu (as in note 9), p. 119.15–16 (*mang yul ri bo dpal 'bar gyi dgon gnas gzhis bcas phul*); this occurred in 1389. It is stated further that the treasure discoverer opened at this time the gate of the hidden valley of [bDe-ldan] sKyid-mo lung and again concealed there and in Ri-bo dpal-'bar treasure works for future recovery (*rig 'dzin chen pos sbas yul skyid mo lung gi sgo phyes/ dpal 'bar dang skyid mo lung du yang gter mang du sbas*). Concerning the hidden valley [bDe-ldan] sKyid-mo lung, see the text cited in note 5. An inventory of the sacred mountain in the realm of the Gung-thang kings was filmed by the NGMPP under reel no. L 290/14: *Mang yul gyi gnas chen ri bo dpal 'bar gyi dkar chag*, 27 fols.; according to the colophon this text, after being written down, was hidden in rGyang[s] Yon-po lung; concerning this site associated with Padmasambhava, see note 24.

ral Nyi-ma'i 'od-zer (1124–1192), who is regarded for his part as the incarnation of the "ruler" (*mnga' bdag*) Khri Srong-lde'u btsan. The disciples found the reincarnation of sNgags-'chang Śākya bzang-po, Nam-mkha' brgya-byin by name, among the family dGa'-thang nub-ma, one of the three subgroups of the above lineage; these are called *gDan sa smra bo cog po, dGa' thang pa shar ma, dGa' thang pa nub ma*. The family seat lay in the south-eastern province of lHo-brag, and the reincarnation belonged to the fourteenth generation following Nyang-ral Nyi-ma'i 'od-zer.

2. NAM-MKHA' BRGYA-BYIN (16TH CENTURY)

Not much comprehensive information is available on the Second Yol-mo-ba sprul-sku Nam-mkha' brgya-byin, but we can at least track down the names of several of his teachers and contemporaries. Thus it is stated that the ceremony of offering a lock of hair was carried out under one dPal 'Bri-gung-pa chen-po Ratnalakṣmi, who also on the occasion gave the young reincarnation the name Nam-mkha' brgya-byin. We can identify this teacher as the treasure discoverer and master of the 'Bri-gung-pa school Rin-chen phun-tshogs (1509–1557).

We learn further that the young reincarnation studied the method of teaching mantras according to the old school for the most part under Rig-'dzin Legs-ldan bDud-'joms rdo-rje, and another source mentions him as the disciple of the treasure discoverer Zhig-po gling-pa alias Rig-'dzin Gar-gyi dbang-phyug (1524–1583).[12] Like his predecessor, Nam-mkha' brgya-byin undertook a renovation of the Bya-rung kha-shor stūpa in Nepal, and we find that he, too, was a spiritual preceptor at the royal court of Mang-yul Gung-thang. The name of the ruler at the time was Khri-rgyal bSod-nams dbang-phyug lde (1577–1627).[13]

---

12 See mKhas-btsun bzang-po : *Biographical Dictionary of Tibet and Tibetan Buddhism* 4, Dharamsala: Library of Tibetan Works and Archives, 1973, pp. 220–222. The source for this brief biographical sketch of the Second Yol-mo-ba sprul-sku is the text *Rang gi rtogs pa brjod pa* (as in note 16). The mention of Rin-chen phun-tshogs together with Rigs-'dzin Legs-ldan bDud-'joms rdo-rje as the first teachers of the young incarnation points to the contact between the brothers mNga'-ris Paṇ-chen and mNga'-ris rig-'dzin and the treasure discoverer of the 'Bri-gung-pa school. In the work of Rig-'dzin Padma 'phrin-las, which reveals much concerning these connections, it is stated that the latter three persons jointly performed initiatory rituals in bSam-yas, as a result of which happiness and contentment prevailed in Tibet for thirteen years; see rDo-rje brag Rig-'dzin Padma 'phrin-las (as in note 8), p. 330.2–4 (*bsam yas su rje 'bri gung pa rin chen phun tshogs spyan drangs te/ mnga' ris paṇ di ta chen po mched gnyis dang/ chos rgyal 'bri gung pa rin chen phun tshogs te bla ma dam pa gsum gyis rab gnas mnga' gsol sogs rten 'brel mang du mdzas pas/ bod khams su lo bcu gsum gyi bar bde skyid 'byung ba'i rten 'brel 'grig*). On sPrul-sku Nam-mkha' brgya-byin's place in the tradition surrounding Zhig-po gling-pa, see *A Collection of Records of Teachings and Initiations Received by Masters of the Gur-phu or mDo-chen Tradition of the Rnying-ma-pa*, pp. 168–176; this latter treasure discoverer has been known up to now primarily as the teacher of Sog bzlog-pa Blo-gros rgyal-mtshan (1552–1624).

13 For the mention of Nam-mkha' brgya-byin at the court of the Gung-thang king, see Kaḥ-thog rig-'dzin Tshe-dbang nor-bu (as in note 9), p. 143.14–15, where he is called Yol-mo sprul-sku Nam-mkha'

Unfortunately no supplementary data concerning the Second Yol-mo-ba sprul-sku's other activities are obtainable, so that I shall now confine myself to the more exact circumstances surrounding the end of his life and the preparations for the next incarnation. The second main figure in this context is a certain Lo-chen mChog-gi sprul-sku, whom Nam-mkha' brgya-byin healed of a disease by performing on him certain rituals. At a later point in time he sent a message to the east, to Kong-po, written to this sPyan-ras-gzigs dbang Lo-chen along with a rustproof mirror for viewing certain portents of the next incarnation.

This person is in fact the father of the Third Yol-mo-ba sprul-sku; his full name is Rig-'dzin 'Phrin-las dbang-phyug, himself an incarnation of a "great translator" (*lo chen*) with the name Ratnabhadra. As chance would have it, we find the father again in another context, one leading us to the province of gTsang in the religiously and politically eventful period of the waning 16th century. There Rig-'dzin 'Phrin-las dbang-phyug is in the company of the young Jo-nang Tāranātha (1575–1635), who shortly before had met the Ninth Karma-pa dBang-phyug rdo-rje (1556–1603). Some time later Jo-nang Tāranātha mentions meeting the Second Yol-mo-ba sprul-sku in person, at which time he asked him to confer a transmission for the practice of a special Guru Yoga.[14] This must have taken place shortly before the death of sPrul-sku Nam-mkha' brgya-byin, since soon thereafter Jo-nang Tāranātha notes the passing of the Yol-mo-ba sprul-sku along with the arrival of the Sixth Zhwa-dmar-pa Chos-kyi dbang-phyug (1584–1630), from whom he received the teachings of the Karma bKa'-brgyud-pa school. Finally, mention is made of a "testament" (*zhal chems*) that the Yol-mo-ba sprul-sku composed before his death.[15]

The political and religious climate under which we find the next rebirth, the Third Yol-mo-ba sprul-sku, living is thus heralded. The impression that the observations just

---

brgya-byin. This must have been at an quite early age of the ruler, since Khri-rgyal bSod-nams dbang-phyug lde relied in the latter part of his life on the Third Yol-mo-ba sprul-sku bsTan-'dzin nor-bu as his spiritual preceptor; see ibid, p. 143.17–18.

14 For a description of the contacts between the Second Yol-mo-ba sprul-sku and the father of the next incarnation, see mKhas-btsun bzang-po (as in note 12), pp. 221–22; it should be noted that this report was from the perspective of the Third Yol-mo-ba sprul-sku. The source for the meeting between Jo-nang Tāranātha and the two protagonists is the latter's autobiography; see Kun-dga' snying-po: *rGyal khams pa tā ra nā thas bdag nyid kyi rnam thar nges par brjod pa'i deb gter shin tu zhib mo bcos lhug par rtogs brjod*, pp. 53.6–7 & 135.7.

15 See Jo-nang Taranātha Kun-dga' snying-po (as in note 14), pp. 138.5 & 139.7. Concerning the person of Lo-chen Ratnabhadra, it may be noted that he is a teacher of the Jo-nang-pa school; see Ngag-dbang Blo-gros grags-pa, *dPal ldan jo nang pa'i chos 'byung rgyal ba'i chos tshul gsal byed zla ba'i sgron me*, 1992, pp. 40.27–41.5. He founded the monastery Ri-bo gru-'dzin in the valley of gZhad, among others, and Jo-nang Kun-dga' grol-mchog (1507–1566) was one of his disciples. He is named along with Rig-'dzin Legs-ldan bDud-'joms rdo-rje as a teacher of Byang-bdag rigs-'dzin Chos-rgyal dbang-po'i sde (born 1550); see sTag-sgang mKhas-mchog Ngag-dbang blo-gros (as in note 2), p. 557.3. For mention of a biography of Lo-chen mChog-gi sprul-sku written by his son, the Third Yol-mo-ba sprul-sku, see note 55.

made would appear to force on us, namely, that the teachings of the Jo-nang-pa and Karma bKa'-brgyud-pa schools had gained the upper hand in the province of gTsang at the end of the 16th century, should not detract from the fact that the rNying-ma-pa school continued to make its influence felt. The tensions between these various currents were given clear vent to in the life of the next incarnation.

3. BSTAN-'DZIN NOR-BU / STOBS-LDAN SHUGS-'CHANG RTSAL (1598–1644)

Concerning the life and activities of the Third Yol-mo-ba sprul-sku four autobiographical writings are available, of which the "narrative" (*rtogs brjod*), written in 1632, contains the most detailed information on the birth and youth, education and travels as well as the spiritual practices and political activities of the reincarnation. In the following I shall be concerned only with information providing insight into the incarnation status of bsTan-'dzin nor-bu, his teachers and his significance for the Byang-gter tradition. It may be hoped that the complete biography of this interesting figure from the 17th century will one day be published.[16]

Even though the birthplace of the new reincarnation lies in Kong-po, in eastern Tibet, his ties with the province of gTsang, in Central Tibet, are substantial. Thus it is stated that the ruler of the latter province, the sDe-srid gTsang-pa, made the son of Rig-'dzin 'Phrin-las dbang-phyug "partake of excellent provisions" (*mthun rkyen phun gsum tshogs pa gnang 'dug*). The area in and around the birthplace bears the name Klu-lnga, and from a travel report of a later author we know that it is located in the vicinity of the Bu-chu gser-gyi lha-khang; this is one of the four mTha'-'dul temples that go back to the time of Srong-btsan sgam-po.[17]

---

[16] Concerning the autobiographical writings of the Third Yol-mo-ba sprul-sku, see Appendix I. In the following I cite the text *Rang gi rtogs pa brjod pa* according to the second edition. The English introduction for the two-volume edition of the writings of bsTan-'dzin nor-bu mentions the existence of a biography; this datum is confirmed in the Fifth Dalai Bla-ma's biography of his teacher Zur Chos-dbyings rang-grol (1610–1657); see Ngag-dbang blo-bzang rgya-mtsho: *Zur thams cad mkhyen pa chos dbyings rang grol gyi rnam thar theg mchog bstan pa'i shing rta*, fol. 107a/6 (*... rig 'dzin yol mo ba'i rnam thar ...*). For the existence of the *bKa'-'bum*, see note 55.

[17] The ruler of gTsang is mentioned in *Rang gi rtogs pa brjod pa*, p. 104.6; he was probably Karma bsTan-skyong dbang-po (ruled up to 1611). The birthplace, Klu-lnga, is referred to in the biography of Rig-'dzin Tshe-dbang nor-bu, who paid a visit to it; see Chos-kyi dbang-phyug: *dPal rig 'dzin chen po rdo rje tshe dbang nor bu'i zhabs kyis rnam par thar pa'i cha shas brjod pa ngo mtshar dad pa'i rol mtsho*, p. 190.3–4 (*lha ri seng ge'i zhol gu ru chen po'i sgrub phug tu te zhig bzhugs/ de'i mdun klu lnga zhes rig 'dzin yol mo ba bstan 'dzin nor bu sku mched sku bltams pa'i yul du bzhugs ...*). The "brother" (*sku mched*) of bsTan-'dzin nor-bu adverted to here bears the name Phyag-rdor nor-bu (concerning whom, see note 19). The cave of Padmasambhava and the birthplaces of the two brothers is mentioned directly after the account of Rig-'dzin Tshe-dbang nor-bu's sojourn in Bu-chu gser-gyi lha-khang; for the latter temple as a source for treasure works of the rNying-ma-pa school in the 17th century, see Ehrhard (1999:232) and chapter twenty-one in the present volume.

A separate chapter is devoted in the account to the procedure used for determining that the boy was the reincarnation of sPrul-sku Nam-mkha' brgya-byin; this takes us back to the first member and legitimating figure of the Yol-mo-ba sprul-skus: the helper during the construction of the Bodhnāth Stūpa. Thus we find the following statement in connection with the preceding reincarnation, when the problem of determining the incarnation status became acute:

> In the testament of the preceding [incarnation] it is stated: "If the bodily sign [of carrying] loads during the existence as a helper is present, recognize his status, even if [the child] is mute. If it is not present, there is no need [to proceed further], even if he can express himself clearly."[18]

Given the presence of these visible body signs, the status of bsTan-'dzin nor-bu as incarnation of the helper at the construction of the Bodhnāth Stūpa – and by implication also that of the minister Padma Gung-btsan as well as the First and Second Yol-mo-ba sprul-skus – was cleared up. As can be read in two of the four other autobiographical writings, the Third Yol-mo-ba sprul-sku was creatively caught up in the incarnation chain he embodied, not only devoting to it a prose account furnished with pictures – bearing the title *rTogs brjod mkhas pa'i rna rgyan* – but also commemorating each of the individual links of the chain with a poem that stated the birthplace and recapitulated details of the incarnation; this work bears the title "Praise in the Form of a Thread of the Line of Rebirths" (*skyes rabs kyi 'phreng bar bstod pa*).

This latter document, important for the lineage's understanding of itself and for its attempt to gain public recognition, does not, in its presentation of the earlier incarnations, stop with the helper during the building of the *stūpa* and the minister Padma Gung-btsan; other figures are also added, localizing the spiritual activities of the lineage within the real geography and the other worldly realms compatible with the world view of a 17th-century Tibetan Buddhist. As is learned from the colophon of the text in question, bsTan-'dzin nor-bu, when producing the rebirth sequence, let himself be guided by sPrul-sku Nam-mkha'

---

[18] See *Rang gi rtogs pa brjod pa*, p. 106.2–3 (*gong ma'i bka' chems las/ bran du skyes dus kyi sgal pa'i sha rtags pa 'di 'dug na lkug par 'dug kyang bdag rkyen brgyi/ 'di mi 'dug na kha gsal yang byed mi dgos gsungs pa* ...). See the paraphrase in *Chos-'byung I*, p. 563.1–3: "In accordance with the words of the earlier reincarnation: 'If the scar [from carrying] the loads during construction of the Bya-rung kha-shor Stūpa in his existence as helper to the woman goose-keeper is present, recognize his status.' When the articles of clothing were removed and [the body] exposed to eyesight, the scar [from carrying] loads could be seen, and still other [methods of] identifying [the reincarnation] were employed a number of times." (*... sku gong ma'i gsung las/ mchod rten bya rung kha shor bzhengs dus/ bya rdzi'i bran du skyes dus kyi sgal mig 'di yod na bdag rkyen gyis/ gsung pa yod 'dug bzhin/ na bza' phud nas/ ltas pas/ sgal mig kyang gsal bar mthong zhing/ ngos 'dzin gzhang yang mang du mdzad*). For the inspection of bodily signs as confirmation of the incarnation status of the Fourth Yol-mo-ba sprul-sku, see note 40.

brgya-byin's data, so that we can get a good idea, from this example, of how the individual representatives of the incarnation lineage went about establishing and cementing their claim to spiritual powers.

Let us now proceed with the education of the young Yol-mo-ba sprul-sku and his different teachers. Soon after the death of his father we find him in Central Tibet, in Myang, where for the first time he met with the Sixth Zhwa-dmar-pa Chos-kyi dbang-phyug. Under the latter he took the *upāsaka* vows and received the name Karma Thub-bstan snying-po rnam-par rgyal-ba (his full ordination as a bhikṣu would also take place later under the Sixth Zhwa-dmar-pa). In Ngam-ring, in La-stod Byang – a place familiar in connection with the activities of the First Yol-mo-ba sprul-sku – the first person he met was Lo-chen 'Gyur-med bde-chen (1540–1615), a descendant of Thang-stong rgyal-po (1361–1485) and author of the well-known biography of this siddha. According to the illustrations of the life of bsTan-'dzin nor-bu (see Appendix I), it was primarily the teachings of the Ṣaḍaṅga Yoga of the Kālacakra that he studied on a later occasion in gCung Ri-bo-che under Lo-chen 'Gyur-med bde-chen.[19]

Before I take up the next teacher, the young incarnation's visit to the Kathmandu Valley must be mentioned. This occurred sometime in the years between 1614 and 1617 at the invitation of the Malla king Śivasiṃha, who ruled in Kathmandu from 1578 to 1619, and also in Patan from 1598 to 1619. bsTan-'dzin nor-bu performed a "great public consecration" (*khrom dbang chen po*) in front of the king's palace, and a dialogue carried on with the aid of an interpreter has come down to us. He visited, furthermore, the Svayambhūnāth Stūpa and other Buddhist shrines of the Valley. A separate chapter of the autobiography provides information on the activities at the sacred site of Bya-rung kha-shor:

---

[19] See *Rang gi rtogs pa brjod pa*, pp. 112.6–114.1, concerning the *upāsaka* vows under the Sixth Zhwa-dmar-pa, and ibid, pp. 114.1–116.5, concerning the meeting with Lo-chen 'Gyur-med bde-chen; for a meeting with this teacher from the perspective of Jo-nang Tāranātha, see Jo-nang Taranātha Kun-dga' snying-po (as in note 14), p. 152.2–4. Some interesting facts concerning the Ri-bo-che monastery are found in *sTag-sgang mKhas-mchog Ngag-dbang blo-gros* (as in note 2), p. 664.9–12): "gCung Ri-bo-che was first built by the Mahāsiddha Thang-stong rgyal-po; subsequently it was maintained by a series of successors in the family line. Lo-chen 'Gyur-med bde-chen, who was one of them, offered [the monastery] to the Yol-mo gter-ston bsTan-'dzin nor-bu; later sGam-smyon Phyag-rdor nor-bu, the treasure discoverer's younger brother, and the series of the incarnations of sGam-smyon, made it their residence." (*gcung ri bo che ni/ thog mar grub chen thang stong rgyal pos btab/ de nas dbon rgyud kyi rim par bskyangs pa las/ lo chen 'gyur med bde chen gyis yol mo gter ston bstan 'dzin nor bur phul nas/ gter ston gcung sgom smyon phyag rdor nor bu dang/ sgom smyon sprul sku rim byon gyis gdan sa mdzad*). In the autobiography of the Fifth Dalai Bla-ma, this Phyag-rdor nor-bu is mentioned several times (with the spelling sGam-smyon sprul-sku), and the year of his death can be determined to be 1658; see Ngag-dbang blo-bzang rgya-mtsho: *Za hor gyi ban de ngag dbang blo bzang rgya mtsho'i 'di snang 'khrul pa'i rol rtsed rtogs brjod kyi tshul du bkod pa du kū la'i gos bzang las glegs bam gnyis pa*, pp. 698.19–699.4. A text by the younger brother of the Yol-mo-ba sprul-sku was filmed by the NGMPP under reel no. AT 82/12: *rDo rje phur pa'i dbang bshad thos pa don ldan*, 10 fols.

> Afterwards Mahārāja Śivasiṃha acted in that realm as the 'donor' (*dānapāti*), [and] that temple was built for service at [Bya-rung] kha-shor. I arrived [there] for the 'earth ritual'. ... On the very day on which the consecration of this large, self-manifested *stūpa* was renewed, a great shower of flowers occurred.[20]

The young incarnation returned to the province of gTsang via Yol-mo and Mang-yul Gung-thang, where he stayed at the court of Khri-rgyal bSod-nams dbang-phyug lde; soon afterwards he met the gTsang sde-srid Karma Phun-tshogs rnam-rgyal (ruled 1611–1621) in the fortress of bSam-grub rtse. During the following period in Central Tibet bsTan-'dzin nor-bu continued to be busy with his studies, which he also pursued in, among other places, Nyin-byed gling and in the monastery dGa'-ldan Byams-pa gling in Ngam-ring.

At the age of nineteen, that is in 1617, the Yol-mo-ba sprul-sku came into contact with the teacher who reacquainted him with the spiritual practices of the rNying-ma-pa school, and above all with the rituals of the Byang-gter tradition: Rig-'dzin Ngag-gi dbang-po (1580–1639), who, as the incarnation of the above-mentioned mNga'-ris rig-'dzin Legs-ldan bDud-'joms rdo-rje, had been educated by his father, Byang-bdag rigs-'dzin dBang-po'i sde. We know that on a total of four occasions a wealth of treasure teachings was passed on to bsTan-'dzin nor-bu, among which the cycle *Byang gter thugs sgrub rnam gsum* stands out; according to one source, bsTan-'dzin nor-bu was named a spiritual "representative" (*rgyal tshab*) by Rig-'dzin Ngag-gi dbang-po.[21] That this transfer of the

---

20 *Rang gi rtogs pa brjod pa*, p. 136.4–5 (*de nas yul der si hu sing ma hā rā jas sbyin bdag mdzad/ kha shor zhabs drung gi dgon pa 'di thebs pa yin/ de'i sa chog la phyin/ ... rang byung gi mchod rten chen po de nyis* (= *nyid*) *la rab gnas gsos pa'i nyin kyang me tog gi char chen po*). See also the summary of the entire section in sTag-sgang mkhas-mchog Ngag-dbang blo-gros, as in note 9, pp. 563.23–564.1: "The accommodations for the caretaker were newly built next to the great *stūpa* Bya-rung kha-shor; at this point he made a threatening gesture in the direction of an opening in the rock, and since he said, 'If water could come out of it', there later arose a fresh spring. While he was carrying out the consecration at the *stūpa*, a rain of flowers fell; the wishes that were made [on this occasion] were immediately fulfilled, it is said" (*mchod rten chen po bya rung kha shor 'gran gyi dkon gnyer sdod sa gsar du btab/ de'i tshe gad pa gcig la phyag mdzub btsugs te/ 'di nas chu ci byung na gsungs pas slar de nas chu mig dkar mo byung/ mchod rten la rab gnas mdzad pas/ me tog gi char babs/ smon lam 'debs par mdzad pa rnams kyang 'phral du 'grub par byung gsungs*). Some years later the Sixth Zhwa-dmar-pa Chos-kyi dbang-phyug followed the steps of his disciple to the Kathmandu Valley – and to Helambu – and met the next generation of Malla kings; see Ehrhard (1997a:126–132) and chapter seventeen in the present volume.

21 See Kun-bzang nges-don klong-yangs (as in note 8), p. 280.1–2 (*yol mo ba gsum pa bstan 'dzin nor bu snga phyi lan bzhi'i bar du sku drung du phebs par byang gter gtso bor gyur pa'i gter chos zab mo bum pa gang bya'i tshul du rtsal* (= *bstsal*) *te nyid kyi rgyal tshab tu mnga' gsol mdzad*). Concerning the genealogy of Rig-'dzin Ngag-gi dbang-po, it may be noted that his father numbered among the last representatives of the royal house of La-stod Byang, while his mother belonged to the nobility of 'Phyongs-rgyas, the "royal family of Za-hor" (*za hor gyi rgyal rigs*); ibid, p. 277.4. The Fifth Dalai Bla-ma Blo-bzang rgya-mtsho also came from the latter family; the autobiography mentions the presence of Rig-'dzin Ngag-gi dbang-po shortly after the birth of Ngag-dbang Blo-bzang rgya-mtsho in the year 1617; see Ngag-dbang blo-bzang rgya-mtsho (as in note 19), p. 44.5–7.

teachings did not proceed without its problems at the beginning is seen in a revealing description by the Fifth Dalai Bla-ma Blo-bzang rgya-mtsho:

> Only a short period having passed after the return of the precious rebirth (i.e. the Third Yol-mo-ba sprul-sku) from Nyin-byed gling, fear arose over the consumption [of the ingredients] of the *gaṇacakra* because of the [previously obtained spiritual] experience during debating, and manifold erroneous ideas came up, [in particular] the thought that the multitude of ritual acts for subduing worldly gods obviously only harm living beings. At this point the *Mahāvidyādhara* (i.e. Rig-'dzin Ngag-gi dbang-po) focussed his directly staring gaze upon the rebirth, and with the words "Since there are so many cycles here in the old school of hidden mantras [for practising] violent activity – the "rites of submission" (*abhicara*) – are you not ashamed?" envy in the form of a logician's arrogance and dismissal dissolved itself into a subdued object. By virtue of the fact that a trust was born from within that no longer differentiated between teacher and the teaching, a state was reached in which he was purified into a *Mantradhara* of the old school.[22]

Detailing the further activities of bsTan-'dzin nor-bu as a representative of the rNying-ma-pa school would lead us too far afield. He did, in any case, do justice to his role as lineage-holder of the Byang-gter tradition; an exact analysis of the works of the Fifth Dalai Bla-ma, for example, might shed some light on his spiritual and political services during a trying period for the newly established Tibetan government. We know already at least that, long before his trip to the court of the first Manchu emperor, the young Dalai Bla-ma sought out the advice of the Third Yol-mo-ba sprul-sku on that matter, and a personal meeting between Blo-bzang rgya-mtsho and bsTan-'dzin nor-bu is likewise documented for the year 1643.[23]

---

22 See Ngag-dbang blo-bzang rgya-mtsho: *Byang pa'i rig 'dzin chen po ngag gi dbang po'i rnam par thar pa ngo mtshar bkod pa'i rgya mtsho,* p. 516.1–3 (*sprul sku rin po che nyin byed gling nas phyir byon te ring por ma long pas/ rtog ge ba'i nyams kyis tshogs 'khor gsol ba la 'tsher snang dang/ dregs 'dul gyi las tshogs la sems can la gnod pa byed pa 'ba' zhig tu 'dug dgongs pa'i log rtog sna tshogs shar ba na/ rig 'dzin chen pos sprul pa'i sku la spyan gcer gyi gzigs nas/ gsang sngags rnying ma 'di la drag po mngon spyod kyi skor mangs bas thugs khrel yod dam gsung ba na/ mtshan nyid pa'i khyad gsod dang nga rgyal gyi ham thul yul bud de/ bla ma dang chos la mi phyed pa'i mos pa gting nas 'khrungs pas rnying ma ba'i sngags 'chang du gtsang sing gi song go*). The passage was borrowed by sTag-sgang mkhas-mchog Ngag-dbang blo-gros, as in note 9, p. 564.13–19. The composition of the biography of Rig-'dzin Ngag-gi dbang-po by the Fifth Dalai Bla-ma occurred in the year 1654; visionary meetings with Rig-'dzin Legs-ldan bDud-'joms rdo-rje, who urged the thirty-seven-year-old Dalai Bla-ma to disseminate his treasure cycles, are on record as having taken place in that very year; see Karmay (1988a:37).

23 Concerning the Third Yol-mo-ba's reaction to the doubts of the Fifth Dalai Bla-ma as to whether he

The only thing that needs to be focussed on in the following is the importance of the Third Yol-mo-ba sprul-sku as a treasure discoverer, in which capacity he visited the old haunts of the sNgags-'chang Śākya bzang-po. We find him during his first large retreat, which is devoted to the cycles of the *Byang gter thugs sgrub rnam gsum*, in a place frequented a century earlier by the First Yol-mo-ba sprul-sku, namely, Mang-yul Ri-bo dpal-'bar. The name sTobs-ldan shugs-'chang rtsal was given to him by a ḍākinī in a dream, along with a "scroll" (*shog dril*). Finally, several years later, in rGyang[s] Yon-po lung in the province of gTsang, he brought to light "introductory lists" (*kha byang*) and a treasure cycle dedicated to Padmasambhava in his outer form as rDo-rje gro-lod, being assisted in this by his teacher Rig-'dzin Ngag-gi dbang-po. In this cycle were found prophecies that not only concerned the number of rebirths of the minister Padma Gung-btsan but also pertained to the younger brother sPrul-sku Phyag-rdor nor-bu and the person of the Fifth Dalai Bla-ma. These identifications were made by Rig-'dzin Ngag-gi dbang-po.[24]

On this occasion, too, a portion of text was recovered that again refers to Ri-bo dpal-'bar and to a treasure that remained there to be discovered. The find, prophesied for the year 1639, did not occur in spite of preparations that began already in 1638; the Fifth Dalai Bla-ma cites the death of Rig-'dzin Ngag-gi dbang-po as the reason for this, since it caused bsTan-'dzin nor-bu to proceed to Central Tibet and not to the sacred site in Mang-yul Gung-thang.[25] During this time bsTan-'dzin nor-bu, like the First and Second Yol-mo-ba

---

should accept the invitation to the court of the Manchu emperor, see Karmay (1998:518); the written source for this is Fifth Dalai Lama Ngag-dbang blo-bzang rgya-mtsho (as in note 19), p. 242.6–10. A face-to-face meeting with the Third Yol-mo-ba sprul-sku is recorded shortly before this in the autobiography of the Fifth Dalai Bla-ma; see ibid, p. 236.3–18. Also recorded is a vision of Ngag-dbang Blo-bzang rgya-mtsho in which Rig-'dzin Ngag-gi dbang-po was flanked by his two disciples, the Third Yol-mo-ba sprul-sku and Zur Chos-dbyings rang-grol; see Karmay (1988a:217–4) (in the résumé of the text portion – ibid, p. 67 – bsTan-'dzin phrin-las should be emended to bsTan-'dzin nor-bu).

24 This is a brief summary of Fifth Dalai Lama Ngag-dbang blo-bzang rgya-mtsho (as in note 22), pp. 542.6–545.1, reproduced in sTag-sgang mkhas-mchog Ngag-dbang blo-gros, as in note 9, pp. 564.19–565.18. rGyang[s] Yon-po lung is known as a meditation grotto in the vicinity of Grom-pa rGyang[s], one of the four Ru-gnon temples from the time of Srong-btsan sgam-po. Treasure works of the cycle *Le'u bdun ma* had been recovered there as early as 1362 by the hermit bZang-po grags-pa, who passed them on to Rig-'dzin rGod-ldem 'phru-can; concerning this find, which contained texts intended specifically for the kings of Mang-yul Gung-thang, see Schwieger (1988 [1989]:30ff). The sojourn of the Third Yol-mo-ba sprul-sku in rGyang[s] Yon-po lung is described in detail in bsTan-'dzin nor-bu: *Rang gi rtogs pa brjod pa, pp.* 190.1–200.5.

25 See Ngag-dbang blo-bzang rgya-mtsho (as in note 22), p. 545.1–5. In the biography of Zur Chos-dbyings rang-grol, written by the Fifth Dalai Bla-ma, this thwarted treasure discovery is described and interpreted politically; see Fifth Dalai Lama Ngag-dbang blo-bzang rgya-mtsho (as in note 16), p. 125.4-6. There is a late echo of political significance to this affair in prophecies that Kaḥ-thog rig-'dzin Tshe-dbang nor-bu revealed to the ruler Pho-lha bSod-nams stobs-rgyas (1689–1747); see Chos-kyi dbang-phyug (as in note 17), p. 173.2–3: "If the rebirth of [the minister] [Padma] Gung-btsan raises the treasure of [Mang-yul Ri-bo] dpal-'bar, joy [will reign in Tibet] for twenty-five years, it is said." (*gung btsan sprul*

sprul-sku previously, had connections with the royal court of Mang-yul Gung-thang, which was undergoing a decline in the wake of the wars between gTsang and dBus. The following citation shows that these links with the old royal line was very close:

> The chief consort of Khri bSod-nams dbang-phyug lde bore only a daughter but no sons. This daughter, [called] lHa-gcig, later became the companion of the Yol-mo-ba sprul-sku bsTan-'dzin nor-bu. To her [in turn] a daughter was born, with the signs of a ḍākinī, bearing the name Nor-'dzin dbang-mo and known as the reincarnation of Ma-cig Rwa-ma. It is said that, at the age of twenty-five, she entered the City of Heavenly Wanderers to the accompaniment of numerous omens.[26]

bsTan-'dzin nor-bu's daughter will cross our path again in connection with the Fourth Yol-mo-ba sprul-sku. It may be merely pointed out in conclusion that, according to information supplied by Kaḥ-thog rig-'dzin Tshe-dbang nor-bu, the royal family of Mang-yul Gung-thang came to an end with her, an event that is intimately connected with the break-up of another – if rather short-lived – ruling family, the lords of gTsang. As we have seen, bsTan-'dzin nor-bu had contacts with representatives of this family, and the name of the final ruler, Karma bsTan-skyong dbang-po (ruled 1620–1642), likewise occurs in several places in his autobiography.

It would take us too far afield to go into these connections between the Third Yol-mo-ba sprul-sku and the ruling families of Mang-yul Gung-thang and gTsang in detail. He had,

---

pas dpal 'bar gter/ thon na nyer lnga bde bar gsungs). It ought to be recalled that Kaḥ-thog rig-'dzin Tshe-dbang nor-bu also intended to raise the treasure of Mang-yul Ri-bo dpal-'bar but likewise was kept from doing so by unfavourable circumstances; see Schwieger (1990:88–89).

26 See Tshe-dbang nor-bu (as in note 9), p. 144.8–14 (*khri bsod nams dbang phyug lde'i btsun mo dngos la sras mo gcig las sras ma byung zhing/ sras mo lha gcig de phyis yol mo sprul sku bstan 'dzin nor bu'i rigs mar gyur/ de la sras mo ma cig rwa ma'i sprul par grags pa nor 'dzin dbang mo zhes mkha' gro'i* (= *'gro'i*) *mtshan dang ldan pa zhig byung ba ngo mtshar gyi ltas du ma dang bcas dgung lo nyer lnga'i skabs mkha' la spyod pa'i grong khyer du gshegs zhes zer*). This is summarized in Sixth Dog-sprul Rig-'dzin Kun-bzang nges-don klong-yangs (as in note 8), p. 265.1–2 in the following words: "He took as a secret partner the daughter of the king of Gung-thang, [of] the family line of the Mahāsammata [kings], bSod-nams dbang-phyug [by name]; she possessed the signs of a ḍākinī" (*mang bkur gdung rabs gung thang rgyal po bsod nams dbang phyug gi sras mo mkha' 'gro'i mtshan rtags ldan pa gsang yum du bzhes*). Another example from the 15th century shows that it was not uncustomary for a princess of Mang-yul Gung-thang to be given to influential Buddhist yogins; during this time we find the princess Chos-kyi sgron-me, the daughter of Khri lHa-dbang rgyal-mtshan (1404–1464), as the partner of Bo-dong Paṇ-chen Phyogs-las rnam-rgyal (1375–1451); her rebirths attained fame as the Yar-'brog rJe btsun-mas, who presided over bSam-sding monastery in Yar-'brog. See, for example, Tshe-dbang nor-bu (as in note 9), pp. 124.21–125.4. For a detailed description of bsTan-'dzin nor-bu's relation with his consort and daughter, see *Rang gi rtogs pa brjod pa*, pp. 200.5–208.6 & 232.1–245.5.

in any case, a not inappreciable role to play during this period of political upheaval in Tibet, which brought in its wake, by laying the foundations for it, the primacy of the dGa'-ldan Pho-brang government. We know, for instance, that the gTsang-pa Mahārāja, Karma bsTan-skyong dbang-po, sent him to the fortress of Shel-dkar in the province of La-stod lHo, where he carried out "rituals for the repulse of the Mongolian [armies]" (*sog bzlog gi sku rim*). Further, his relations with the Sixth Zhwa-dmar-pa Chos-kyi dbang-phyug continued, and also with the Tenth Karma-pa Chos-dbyings rdo-rje (1604–1674); in the company of the latter, for example, he tarried at La-phyi Chu-dbar on the border of Nepal.[27] Similarly, his contacts with representatives of the rNying-ma-pa school expanded, particularly those residing in the "regions of the gorges" (*rong phyogs*); we find the Third Yol-mo-ba sprul-sku, for example, after a further visit to Shel-dkar – arranged again by the ruler of gTsang – turning up in the valley of [b]Tsum, which today is located on Nepalese territory, this time at the invitation of a certain sNgags-'chang Nam-mkha' seng-ge; in Byams-pa sprin, the old mTha'-'dul temple in the sKyid-grong valley, he was engaged in renovation works financed by, among others, one sNgags-'chang Nam-mkha' kun-bzang.[28]

His greatest act of service to the school of the rNying-ma-pa, however, has to do with the phenomenon of conscious rebirth. Detailed accounts by the Fifth Dalai Bla-ma have been handed down of how, at the instigation of Rig-'dzin Ngag-gi dbang-po, the Third Yol-mo-ba sprul-sku "took upon himself the burden of the residence" (*gdan sa'i khur bzhes*) after the death of his teacher – looking after, in other words, rDo-rje brag monastery in Central Tibet – and at the same time determining the next rebirth of his teacher, the Second rDo-rje brag Rig-'dzin Padma 'phrin-las. He still had time to carry out the investiture of the young rebirth before leaving the mortal plane soon thereafter.[29]

---

27 On his sojourn in Shel-dkar rdzong, see *Rang gi rtogs pa brjod pa*, pp. 232.1ff.; the temple of La-phyi Chu-dbar is first mentioned ibid, p. 204.1, and the common sojourn with the Tenth Karma-pa is found ibid, pp. 227.3 ff. The monastery of Chu-dbar was originally under the control of the Phag-mo gru rulers; later it came into the possession of the Zhwa-dmar-pa incarnations and finally was handed over by the Sixth Zhwa-dmar-pa to the Tenth Karma-pa; see De Rossi Filibeck (1988:159–160).

28 The invitation to visit [b]Tsum is described in *Rang gi rtogs pa brjod pa*, pp. 240.6–241.1. sNgags-'chang Nam-mkha' seng-ge was a member of the family mDo-bo-che which kept up the teachings of the 'Brug-pa bKa'-brgyud-pa school of the same name; he received teachings from, among others, the Second and Third Yol-mo-ba sprul-skus; see *A Collection of Records of Teachings and Initiations Received by Masters of the Gur-phu or mDo-chen Tradition of the Rnying-ma-pa*, pp. 168.1–172.5 & 131.1–138.3 (the cycle *Byang gter thugs sgrub rnam gsum*). Concerning the activities in Byams-pa sprin and the person of sNgags-'chang Nam-mkha' kun-bzang, see *Rang gi rtogs pa brjod pa*, p. 242.4. The latter is a grandson of the treasure discoverer Rig-'dzin bsTan-gnyis gling-pa (1480–1535); see also note 44.

29 See Ngag-dbang blo-bzang rgya-mtsho (as in note 22), pp. 546.5–550.4, and Fifth Dalai Lama Ngag-dbang blo-bzang rgya-mtsho (as in note 16), pp. 124.4ff., where the arrival of the Third Yol-mo-ba sprul-sku at rDo-rje brag monastery and the immediate circumstances surrounding the discovery of the Second rDo-rje brag Rig-'dzin, along with the death of the Third Yol-mo-ba, are described from the perspective of Zur Chos-dbyings rang-grol. Mention is made of a protracted illness that bsTan-'dzin nor-bu fell victim to during his trip to Nepal; see fol. 71a/6 (*rigs 'dzin yol mo ba sngar yam bu rgyal pos gdan drangs dus*

The continuity of the incarnations of the founder of the Byang-gter lineage was thus guaranteed. As for the extension of his own lineage, that of the helper during construction of the Bya-rung kha-shor Stūpa, there were obviously no detailed preparations made for the next incarnation such as could be observed for the first two Yol-mo-ba sprul-skus. In the following we shall see that a new rebirth satisfying the required conditions did, nevertheless, appear. Concerning bsTan-'dzin nor-bu's literary production aimed at consolidating lines of rebirths, it may be said, finally, that they cover in similar fashion the lineage of his teacher and also his own.[30] Did he perhaps slacken his efforts on behalf of the next Yol-mo-ba sprul-sku in order to discover the rebirth of his teacher?

4. ZIL-GNON DBANG-RGYAL RDO-RJE (1647–1716)

A collection of the Fourth Yol-mo-ba sprul-sku's autobiographical writings has been preserved that provides insight into his personality and his activities in the Tibeto-Nepalese border region; the collection comprises an "external biography" (*phyi'i rnam thar*), three "internal biographies" (*nang gi rnam thar*) and one "secret biography" (*gsang ba'i rnam thar*). The availability of quite a great number of manuscript versions of this collection shows the popularity of this representative of the incarnation lineage (see Appendix I and II).

In the English preface to one of the editions, Zil-gnon dbang-rgyal rdo-rje is characterized as "one of the outstanding tantric masters of the rNying-ma-pa tradition during the 17th century. He had strong karmic links with Nepal where he had taken a number of previous embodiments." His relationship to the Third Yol-mo-ba sprul-sku is summarized in the words: "His chief master in his youth was Yol-mo-ba bsTan-'dzin nor-bu, the regent of rDo-rje brag."[31] This statement is based on a rather cursory reading of the

---

bal tshad kyi snyun ro yod pa ...). In sTag-sgang mkhas-mchog Ngag-dbang blo-gros, Gu-ru bkra-shis (as in note 9), p. 566.2–3), his relatively early death is explained in the following words: "As he was not able to uncover the later profound treasure, the fault being that the favourable link broke, it is as if, to all appearances, his term of life, too, was not fulfilled" (*de yang zab gter phyi ma bzhes pa ma grub pas rten 'brel 'chug pa'i skyon gyis sku tshe'ang tshad du 'khyol ba ma byung bar snang ngo*). This refers to the thwarted treasure discovery at Ri-bo dpal-'bar; see note 25.

30 In the colophon of Fifth Dalai Lama Ngag-dbang blo-bzang rgya-mtsho (as in note 22), p. 552.5, the Fifth Dalai Bla-ma mentions a work of Rig-'dzin Yol-mo-ba along with a text of his brother Rig-'dzin Phyag-rdor nor-bu as two of his main literary sources. The biography itself, in structural terms, draws on the verses of the work of bsTan-'dzin nor-bu; in the introduction (p. 429.5) it bears the title *sKyes rabs kyi phreng ba sum cu rtsa gsum gyi gsol 'debs tshigs su bcad pa dri med pad dkar bzhad pa'i 'phreng ba*. See also the text *sKyes rabs kyi 'phreng ba bstod pa pad dkar brgyan 'phreng ba*, translated in Ehrhard, Pierce & Cüppers (1991:18–26).

31 Preface to the first edition; see Appendix I. This preface was incorporated into the second edition, published in the same year; the latter manuscript derives from the library of H.H. the Fourteenth Dalai Lama. In the following I use only the *Phyi'i rnam thar* and cite it according to the first edition, supplementing readings are on the basis of NGMPP reel no. E 2676/4.

introductory folios of the *Phyi'i rnam thar*; in the following I shall look into the passage more carefully and shall attempt to clarify the incarnation status of Zil-gnon dbang-rgyal rdo-rje.

The name Yol-mo-ba bsTan-'dzin nor-bu occurs in the introductory folios in connection with the father of Zil-gnon dbang-rgyal rdo-rje; from the Third Yol-mo-ba sprul-sku the latter had received the name Rigs-'dzin sTobs-ldan dbang-po 'chi-med rgya-mtsho'i sde and was further recognized by him as the incarnation of a series of Buddhist masters. The lineage begins with the Bodhisattva lHa-lung dPal-gyi rdo-rje.[32] It is stated further that the father resided in the monastery rGyal-gling in gTsang during the time when the Third Yol-mo-ba sprul-sku was fulfilling the duties of resident in rDo-rje brag – that is, after the death of Rig-'dzin Ngag-gi dbang-po in 1639. During this period the father addressed a "detailed petition" (*zhu ba'i 'phrin rgyas par*) to his teacher and sent it to the province of dBus, that is, to rDo-rje brag. The reply from the pen of the bsTan-'dzin nor-bu is cited in full in the autobiography, and in comment upon it it is stated:

> In accordance with the permission granted, the father was named to be the representative of the great *stūpa* Bya-rung kha-shor in Nepal; having been appointed, [moreover,] overseer of all monasteries of the nine valleys, he moved to the great *stūpa* [Bya-rung] kha-shor.[33]

---

32 See Zil-gnon dbang-rgyal rdo-rje: *Phyi'i rnam thar*, pp. 5.1–6.1. lHa-lung dPal-gyi rdo-rje likewise plays a role in the myth of the Bodhnāth Stūpa. According to the inventory of sNgags-'chang Śākya bzang-po an elephant that was put to work during the construction of the edifice utters the negative wish to be born as King Glang Dar-ma and to suppress Buddhist teaching; thereupon a raven that happens to have been present expresses the desire to be allowed to kill the anti-Buddhist king in his next rebirth. This is the monk dPal-gyi rdo-rje of lHa-lung; see the block print of *mChod rten chen po bya rung kha shor gyi lo rgyus thos pas grol ba* (as in note 6), fol. 7b/4–6. For a historical interpretation of the attacks of Glang Dar-ma against the first monastery foundings in Tibet and his assassination in 842 by lHa-lung dPal-gyi rdo-rje, the ninth abbot of bSam-yas, see Karmay (1988b:8–9 & 78). Concerning the incarnation status of the father, see *A Collection of Records of Teachings and Initiations Received by Masters of the Gur-phu or mDo-chen Tradition of the Rnying-ma-pa*, p. 539: *lha lung dpal gyi rdo rje nyid/ bsam bzhin sprul pa'i skur byon pa/ rig 'dzin 'chi med rgya mtsho las/ zab gter chos kyi thob yig yod*. These are the formulations of an important member of the mDo-bo-che family, who was a disciple of Rig-'dzin sTobs-ldan dpa'-bo; concerning this person, see note 39.

33 See Zil-gnon dbang-rgyal rdo-rje: *Phyi'i rnam thar*, p. 10.2–3 (*zhes gnang ba stsal pa ltar / pha de nyid la mchod rten chen po bya rung kha shor gyis* (= *gyi*) *gnas 'dzin gtsos* (= *bcol*) *rong khag dgu'i dgon gnas rnams kyi bdag por bdod nas/ kha shor mchod rten chen po'i drung du phebs pa*). The "nine valleys" refer to the region between the Triśūlī Khola and the Bhote Kosi. The administering of the monasteries by an incarnation of lHa-lung dPal-gyi rdo-rje may later have led the local lineage of descent to appropriate the name. See Clarke (1980:7): "... and the priestly lineage of Melemchi was once (it is claimed) Lhalung (*lha-lung*) which connects it to the Nyingmapa lineage." Concerning the dispersion of the lineage along the upper reaches of Melemchi Khola and Balephi Khola, compare also Clarke (1988:108): "Tamang of the Lhalung Lineage." For a parallel presence of a lineage that claims to go back to lHa-lung dPal-gyi rdo-rje, in the upper reaches of the Bemdang Khola, see Jest (1984/85:20).

Faithful to the prophecies of his teacher, Rig-'dzin sTobs-ldan dbang-po took a consort and went about his duties as representative at the Bodhnāth Stūpa; at one point bad omens and dreams occurred – among other things, the whole edifice leaned to the north – and soon thereafter a courier arrived with the news that the Third Yol-mo-ba sprul-sku had passed away; he also bore a letter from sPrul-sku Phyag-rdor nor-bu, the deceased's brother.

There follow descriptions of the dreams that his father and mother had and a trip the parents undertook to La-stod Drang-so, the birthplace of sNgags-'chang Śākya bzang-po. The monastery rGyal-gling in gTsang is again mentioned, where, on the full moon day of the first Tibetan month of 1647, the new rebirth of the Yol-mo-ba sprul-sku came into the world, attended by miraculous signs.[34] The next place named is again La-stod Drang-so, where the boy was required for the first time to put his incarnation status to the test by controlling a natural event: he and his retinue came upon an "overflowing lake" (*mtsho mo lud pa*), and the inhabitants of the region asked him for a "means to counteract" (*bzlog thabs*) the outpour of water. The name of sNgags-'chang Śākya bzang-po was brought up, along with the fact that "the local demons had been put under oath" (*yul 'di'i 'dre srin rnams dam la btags pa yin*) at one time by him. In accordance with a prophecy that the lake should be circumambulated, the child was put on the back of one of his retinue, and after the prescribed circumambulation the lake returned to normal.[35]

In order to succeed to bsTan-'dzin nor-bu's office, he afterwards went to the scene of the latter's activities, namely the site of dNgos-grub mtsho-gling in Mang-yul sKyid-grong. In 1651, when the young reincarnation was now four years old, the political situation in this valley situated on the border between Nepal and Tibet was unfortunately not very peaceful, so that he took up an invitation from the inhabitants of 'Gyes-phug; he was given charge of Sa-sprin monastery and settled down in it with his family.[36]

---

34 See Zil-gnon dbang-rgyal rdo-rje: *Phyi'i rnam thar*, p. 10.3–15.4. I am here attempting to reproduce the flow of narrative in its rough features. A complete and annotated translation of this interesting text would be a rewarding undertaking, particularly in view of the still rather poorly documented background to the reorganization of relations between Kathmandu and Tibet instituted under the Malla king Pratāpamalla (1641–1674); on this subject see, for example, Slusser (1982, vol. 1:70 & 277).

35 See Zil-gnon dbang-rgyal rdo-rje: *Phyi'i rnam thar*, pp. 15.4–16.3. This episode is not based on personal recollection; Zil-gnon dbang-rgyal learned of it later from one of his followers. On the area of Drang-so in La-stod lHo as the homeland of sNgags-'chang Śākya bzang-po, see note 8.

36 *Phyi'i rnam thar*, pp. 16.3–17.1. Concerning the situation in sKyid-grong it is stated: "At the time the eastern bank of the sKyid-grong river was in the possession of the king of Kathmandu, the three [tracts of land] 'Cang, Sher and Dol in the possession of the king of Gorkha, and [the village of] Rag-ma in the possession of the genuine king of Tibet and so forth. Thus people here in Mang-yul devoted themselves totally to strife, [as is customary of] bad times" (*de skabs skyid grong chu shar rgyud rnams yam bu rgyal po'i (= pos) bzung/ 'cang sher dol gsum gor kha rgyal po'i (= pos) bzung/ rag ma bod rgyal po gtsang bas bzung ba sogs/ mang yul 'dir dus zir (= zing) thab (= 'thab) brtsod (= rtsod) kho na byed pa la*). The expression "genuine king of Tibet" must refer to the Fifth Dalai Bla-ma, who in 1642, with the end of the

Next the biography describes the process by which the status of Zil-gnon dbang-rgyal rdo-rje as the rebirth of bsTan-'dzin nor-bu is tested: the "questioning by means of lots" (*brtag pa sgril ba*), carried out in two different places. First, his father met with rGyal-sras Phyag-rdor nor-bu, the brother of the Third Yol-mo-ba sprul-sku, and other priests in Pha-drug Chos-bskor sgang, south of Shel-dkar rdzong. One sGam-po sprul-sku is specifically named as being among them; this sGam-po sprul-sku was in possession of one of the "five treasures that represent the body [of Padmasambhava]" (*sku tshab gter lnga*). The lot was cast in the presence of these sacred objects, which bore the name *sku tshab padma bdud 'dul*, and the answer was positive. The procedure was repeated in front of the statue of the Ārya Wa-ti bzang-po in sKyid-grong, the so-called "Lord of sKyid-grong" (*skyid grong jo bo*), but Phyag-rdor nor-bu and the rebirth's father were not personally present on this occasion. Again the decision fell in favour of the young boy. Although objects from the treasure of rGyang[s] Yon-po lung – including four written scrolls – were thereupon handed over to the father as signs of the incarnation status of his son, certain conditions later failed to be met, so that the recognition extended to the son left something to be desired, with some people harbouring doubts concerning his role as a rebirth.[37]

What was the cause of this doubt surrounding the status of Zil-gnon dbang-rgyal rdo-rje as the Fourth Yol-mo-ba sprul-sku, which repeatedly surfaced in spite of all proof to the contrary? According to my observations, the sources cite two reasons: First, his role as a priest of the rNying-ma-pa school was already legitimated by his status as an offspring of Rig-'dzin sTobs-ldan dbang-po. Thus, in a personal meeting with the Fifth Dalai Bla-ma, he is called merely "the son" (*sras*); the same term is found in an official document from the year 1676, likewise from the Fifth Dalai Bla-ma, confirming Zil-gnon dbang-rgyal rdo-rje as the resident at the Bodhnāth Stūpa.[38] A further piece of evidence for this is a passage

---

gTsang rulers, assumed the reins of power in Tibet. Of interest in this citation is the presence, in the middle of the 17th century, of Gorkha alongside the kingdom of Kathmandu on the trade route to Tibet. Concerning the site called [dKar-ye] dNgos-grub mtsho-gling, see note 51.

37 *Phyi 'i rnam thar*, pp. 17.2–18.3. Obviously the whole affair was reported by sGam-po sprul-sku to the Fifth Dalai Bla-ma; see ibid, pp. 18.2–3 (*slar sgam po sprul skus sne sbyor mdzad nas/ rgyal dbang mchog gi zhabs pad du car* (= *bcar*) *rgyu 'i bka' gros mdzad 'dug kyang/ phyis su rten 'brel ma 'grigs pas/ da lta cung zad grags pa chung zhing 'ga' zhig yid gnyis su 'gyur*). The person in question is sGam-po-pa sprul-sku bZang-po rdo-rje; for a biographical sketch of him, see sTag-sgang mkhas-mchog Ngag-dbang blo-gros, (as in note 9), pp. 731.2–733.11. In the autobiography of the Fifth Dalai Bla-ma, a meeting with the brother of the Third Yol-mo-ba and sGam-po sprul-sku is noted for the year 1651. The latter took novitiate vows under the Fifth Dalai Bla-ma; see Fifth Dalai Lama Ngag-dbang blo-bzang rgya-mtsho (as in note 19), p. 318.13–15. The discussion concerning the young Yol-mo-ba sprul-sku may have taken place on this occasion.

38 See Ngag-dbang blo-bzang rgya-mtsho (as in note 19), p. 680.2–3 (*rigs 'dzin stobs ldan dbang po'i sras zil gnon dbang grags rdo rje*); according to *Phyi 'i rnam thar*, p. 29.1, the name Zil-gnon dbang-grags rdo-rje or Zil-gnon dbang-rgyal rdo-rje was given by the Dalai Bla-ma himself. For the way of addressing him in the official document, see Schuh (1981c:309) (*byang bdag rigs 'dzin yab sras kyi brgyud 'dzin rigs*

in the biography which describes a meeting between Zil-gnon dbang-rgyal rdo-rje and mDo-chen-pa Nor-bu bde-chen (born 1617) in La-ldebs, a high mountain valley south-east of sKyid-grong. This latter teacher, who studied directly under the Third Yol-mo-ba sprul-sku, refused to take part in a consecration that Zil-gnon dbang-rgyal rdo-rje performed for the local populace; the following reason has come down:

> Nor-bu bde-chen spoke: "Now I won't come." The one in attendance [called] 'Jigs[-med] grags[-pa] [spoke up for his part]: "It's all the same whether you are the reincarnation of bsTan-'dzin nor-bu or not. It's enough that you are the son of [Rig-'dzin] sTobs-ldan dbang-po."[39]

A second, related reason was certain remarks by the previous incarnation that probably always stood in the way of official recognition for Zil-gnon dbang-rgyal rdo-rje. This was made clear during a meeting with the Third Yol-mo-ba sprul-sku's daughter, who brought up the following points made by her father concerning a possible rebirth:

> [Some time] after the notion arose to go to the region of La-stod, we, master and disciples, arrived at Drang-so dGa'-ldan. The daughter of the former incarnation was staying there, Chos-'dzin by name, the wife of Drang-so dGa'-ldan-pa. When I offered an invitation as a relative [of hers,] she replied: "This is deceitful and mendacious twaddle; my father, Rig-'dzin Yol-mo-ba, said no further rebirth would come to Tibet." And there were many words besides. On one occasion, [finally,] I went to meet her, no matter what she thought; when I explained to her how the appropriate sign came to be located on my body as well as several of the hidden facts of former times, [i.e., of my past existence,] right then tears came into her eyes and the net of doubt was cut.[40]

'dzin stobs ldan pa'i sras zil gnon dbang grags rdo rje). I supplement the translation given by Schuh as follows: "Zil-gnon dbang-grags rdo-rje, the son of Rig-'dzin sTobs ldan-pa [dbang-po], who maintains the lineage of Byang-bdag Rigs-'dzin, father and son (= Byang-bdag bKra-shis stobs-rgyal and Rig-'dzin Ngag-gi dbang-po)."

39 See Zil-gnon dbang-rgyal rdo-rje: *Phyi'i rnam thar*, p. 39.1–2 (*nor bu bde chen gyis* (= *gyi*) *zhal nas/ nga da len* (= *lan*) *mi yongs/ drung pa 'jigs grags ni/ bstan 'dzin nor bu'i sku skyes yin na'ang 'dra/ min na'ang 'dra/ stobs ldan dbang po'i sras yin pas mchog* (= *chog*). For the studies of Nor-bu bde-chen of the family of mDo-bo-che under the Third Yol-mo-ba sprul-sku, see *A Collection of Records of Teachings and Initiations Received by Masters of the Gur-phu or mDo-chen Tradition of the Rnying-ma-pa*, pp. 75–95; they were undertaken in 1633 at the site of [dKar-ye] dNgos-grub mtsho-gling in Mang-yul sKyid-grong. The father of Nor-bu bde-chen is sNgags-'chang Nam-mkha' seng-ge, who had invited bsTan-'dzin nor-bu to the valley of [b]Tsum; see note 28.

40 See Zil-gnon dbang-rgyal rdo-rje: *Phyi'i rnam thar*, pp. 49.6–50.4 (*yang las* (= *la*) *stod phyogs la 'gro ba'i snang ba shar nas/ nged dpon slob rnams kyi* (= *kyis*) *bram mtsho* (= *grang so*) *dga' ldan du slebs* (=

As in the case of the Third Yol-mo-ba sprul-sku, therefore, it is the visible bodily sign that in the end qualifies Zil-gnon dbang-rgyal rdo-rje as the incarnation of the man who helped construct the Bodhnāth Stūpa, even if the same reputation was not accorded to him as to his predecessor because of it. This is in part obviously due to statements made by bsTan-'dzin nor-bu himself to the effect that there would not be another Yol-mo-ba sprul-sku in Tibet. Against this, we have the activities of Rig-'dzin sTobs-ldan dbang-po, who groomed his son so effectively for the role of resident of Bya-rung kha-shor – and cultivated the memory of his teacher and his teacher's lineage equally effectively – that the myth of the incarnation of the helper during the construction of the magnificent building nevertheless continued to remain alive.

It would be a fruitful endeavour to examine the spiritual and political activities of Zil-gnon dbang-rgyal rdo-rje in detail. For instance, he carried out assignments for the Fifth Dalai Bla-ma in Shel-dkar, maintained close contact with the kings of Gorkha and Kathmandu (his sister was given in marriage to King Pratāpamalla) and on two occasions was appointed overseer of the monasteries of Helambu. Also preserved are thorough accounts of his restoration work at Bya-rung kha-shor.[41] Shortly after this work he founded the monastery bSam-gtan gling in Rag-ma in the valley of Mang-yul sKyid-grong, and in the year 1709 we find him in Mang-yul Ri-bo dpal-'bar busy renovating the temple there. Little is known of the final years of the Fourth Yol-mo-ba sprul-sku's life; it seems that he stayed primarily at bSam-gtan gling. One disciple of him repeatedly mentioned during this period is gTer-dbon Nyi-ma seng-ge; the copying of the "Outer Biography" was done on his initiative.

---

bslebs)/ de na skye bo mngon ma'i (= sngon ma'i) bu mo chos 'dzin zer ba/ drang so dga' ldan pa'i bag gzhes (= bshes) la yod pa/ kho bo'i (= kho bos) gnyen 'phrad la shog byas pas/ nga'i yab rigs 'dzin yol mo ba de nyid/ bod du sku skyes mi 'phebs gsungs pa yod pas/ 'di khos (= ko) rdzun zog lab pa yin zer/ kha stong mang po byas 'dug/ skabs zhig na ci sems kyang/ 'phrad pa la byon byung bas/ nga lus kyi rtags rme ba 'di bzhin yod tshul dang/ mngon (= sngon) gyi gsang ba'i lo rgyus kha cig bshad pas/ de kha rang du mig nas chi ma (= mchi ma) phyung (= byung) shing yid gnyis kyi dra ba mchod (= chod). See the remarks of the Fifth Dalai Bla-ma in Fifth Dalai Lama Ngag-dbang blo-bzang rgya-mtsho (as in note 16), fols. 75b/6ff., where there is mention of a possible rebirth in India. That no further rebirth would come to Tibet is linked with the blocked recovery of the treasure in Ri-bo dpal-'bar; see note 25.

41 See Zil-gnon dbang-rgyal rdo-rje: *Phyi'i rnam thar*, pp. 78.2ff. for the renovation work of the *stūpa* in the years 1706/1707. The statement by Schuh (1974:432): "A charge, primarily religious in motivation, to take up residence at this *stūpa*, which was looked upon as particularly sacred by Tibetans, ought at least to have included certain duties involving maintenance of the *stūpa* ... But the family was evidently not very active in this regard ..." (my translation) must therefore be reconsidered. Concerning the sojourn in Helambu it may be noted that, according to the information supplied by Zil-gnon dbang-rgyal rdo-rje, the first monastery founded by sNgags-'chang Śākya bzang-po, went up in flames in the 16th century, during which "written scrolls" (*gter shog*) and "sacred substances" (*gter rdzas*) from the treasures of Nyang-ral Nyi-ma'i 'od-zer, Guru Chos-dbang and Rig-'dzin rGod-ldem 'phru-can were destroyed; see Zil-gnon dbang-rgyal rdo-rje: *Phyi'i rnam thar*, pp. 75.3–76.1.

5. 'Phrin-las bdud-'joms (1726–1789)

In the process whereby the incarnation of the First Yol-mo-ba sprul-sku was discovered, we saw how the rebirth was born into the family lineage of a treasure discoverer. The Second and Third Yol-mo-ba sprul-skus were each the sons of disciples of the preceding incarnations. This phenomenon will also be witnessed in the case of the Fifth Yol-mo-ba sprul-sku, but since his father simultaneously belonged to a treasure discoverer lineage, this latter needs to be briefly introduced.

gTer-dbon Nyi-ma seng-ge (1687–1738) was a fifth-generation descendant of Rig-'dzin bsTan-gnyis gling-pa (1480–1535). This treasure discoverer of the rNying-ma-pa school had received the transmission of the Byang-gter teachings from sNgags-'chang Śākya bzang-po, and like him had been active at the court of the Gung-thang prince Kun-bzang Nyi-zla grags-pa. Pursuant to the ruler's requests he uncovered treasure works in Mang-yul Ri-bo dpal-'bar – a cycle that had been hidden there by Rig-'dzin rGod-ldem 'phru-can as a "treasure work to be rediscovered" (*yang gter*) – and left behind one offspring, Tshe-dbang bSod-nams rgyal-po by name.[42]

This offspring was the incarnation of sNgags-'chang Che-mchog rdo-rje of the mDo-bo-che family and was made the "representative" (*gnas 'dzin*) of the temple of Mang-yul Byams-pa sprin. Among his teachers we find the Second Yol-mo-ba sprul-sku Nam-mkha' brgya-byin.[43] The lineage was kept alive by the eldest son of Tshe-dbang bSod-nams rgyal-po; his name was sNgags-'chang Nam-mkha' kun-bzang. The Third Yol-mo-ba sprul-sku bsTan-'dzin nor-bu and his brother Phyag-rdor nor-bu are mentioned as his main teachers. What is focussed on above all else in the short sketch of his life is the renovation work done on the temple of Mang-yul Byams-pa sprin, during the course of which bsTan-'dzin nor-bu called Nam-mkha' kun-bzang his "heart's son" (*thugs kyi sras*).[44]

---

42 In providing information on the lineage of Rig-'dzin bsTan-gnyis gling-pa, I shall cite in the following the text by Chos-kyi dbang-phyug: *gTer dbon rig 'dzin brgyud pa'i gdung rabs lo rgyus tshangs pa'i do shal*; for the biography of Rig-'dzin bsTan-gnyis gling-pa, see ibid, pp. 5.4–12.3. This text is based in part on the biography of gTer-dbon Nyi-ma seng-ge, which was written in 1769 by 'Phrin-las bdud-'joms; the latter work was filmed in the autumn of 1991 with the kind assistance of Lama Kunsang of Tarkye-Ghyang; see *Gu ru sūrya seng ge'i rnam thar mdor bsdus nges shes 'dren pa'i shing rta*, 36 fols., NGMPP reel no. E 2691/6.

43 See Chos-kyi dbang-phyug (as in note 42), pp. 12.3–14.1. The lineage of the representatives of the monastery of Byams-pa sprin bears the name *gter dbon rgyud*; for a translation of this term in the case of the family of Rig-'dzin bsTan-gnyis gling-pa, see Schuh (1981c:370): "descendants of treasure discoverers in the [uncle-]nephew [order of succession]" (my translation). The connotations of the often used term *khu dbon* that were read into the term *gter dbon* do not apply; the latter is rather to be understood in the sense of *mes dbon* (ancestor and grandson); for the term *dbon rgyud* in reference to royal descendants, see Uebach (1979:306–307). I would render *gter dbon rgyud* thus as "lineage of the grandsons (i.e. successors) of the treasure discoverers." Therefore the assertions made by Clarke (1983:27) would no longer be valid.

44 See Chos-kyi dbang-phyug (as in note 42), pp. 14.2–15.3. For a description of the meeting from the

The third generation of descendants of Rig-'dzin bsTan-gnyis gling-pa is represented by the son of Nam-mkha' kun-bzang, Guru Śākya rgyal-mtshan; he, too, felt responsible for the temple of Mang-yul Byams-pa sprin, adorning it with statues and the like. Of his sons, the eldest was a certain sNgags-'chang Karma'i mtshan-can, who divided the "convent" (*bla brang*) of Byams-pa sprin into two halves, an "eastern" (*shar ma*) and a "northern" (*byang ma*) one. Further, objects from the treasures of Rig-'dzin bDud-'dul rdo-rje (1615–1672) from Eastern Tibet, came into his hands.[45]

gTer-dbon Nyi-ma seng-ge was the eldest son of sNgags-'chang Karma'i mtshan-can and the father of the Fifth Yol-mo-ba sprul-sku. We learn from his short biography that his "root teacher" (*rtsa ba'i bla ma*) was Zil-gnon dbang-rgyal rdo-rje; under him he studied primarily the treasure cycle *rDzogs chen yang tig ye shes mthong grol,* a finding of Rig-'dzin bsTan-gnyis gling-pa, and became his "heart's son". Singled out, as further teachers, are Kham-lung-pa Padma dbang-rgyal (1657–1731), Kaḥ-thog rig-'dzin Tshe-dbang nor-bu and rDo-dmar-ba Rig-'dzin Padma rdo-rje (died 1738).

The invasion of the Dsungar armies in Tibet in 1717 and the associated persecution of the rNying-ma-pa school led Nyi-ma seng-ge to assume the life of someone holding "the spiritual discipline of being free from worldly obligations" (*bya btang gi brtul zhugs*) and to wander through the hidden lands in the south, as described in the next section of his biographical sketch. With the aid of a teaching from the Byang-gter tradition, the *Byang gter nad bdag stobs 'joms kyi man ngag*, he succeeded in halting an epidemic that was sweeping the Kathmandu Valley during this time; in recognition of this he acquired a piece of land in Yol-mo from the king of Kathmandu, together with an official deed inscribed on a "copperplate" (*zangs yig bka' shog*). Afterwards, in the centre of the hidden land Yol-mo gangs-ra, he built the monastery Padma'i-chos-gling and along with it, according to the "descriptions of the sacred site" (*gnas yig*) and "list of prophecies" (*lung byang*) of

---

perspective of the Third Yol-mo-ba sprul-sku, see note 28. A contemporary of sNgags-'chang Nam-mkha' kun-bzang – and not to be confused with him – was sNgags-'chang Nam-mkha' seng-ge; an offspring of the latter was mDo-bo-che'i sNgags-'chang Nor-bu bde-chen, who refused to accept Zil-gnon dbang-rgyal rdo-rje as the Fourth Yol-mo-ba sprul-sku; see note 39. It may be pointed out that sNgags-'chang Nor-bu bde-chen for his part regarded his own son, bDud-'dul, as the reincarnation of his father; see ibid, p. 15.1–2.

45 See Chos-kyi dbang-phyug (as in note 42), pp. 15.3–17.4. In connection with the treasures of Rig-'dzin bDud-'dul rdo-rje, it may be mentioned that, Guru Śākya rgyal-mtshan studied under gTer-ston Gar-dbang rdo-rje (1640–1685) and also under O-rgyan dpal-bzang (1617–1677); the latter was a disciple of Rig-'dzin bDud-'dul rdo-rje and had brought relics from Khams to the region of present-day Thak Khola in Southern Mustang, which led to the founding of the monastery of sKu-tshab gter-lnga; see Ehrhard (1993b:26) and chapter twelve in the present volume. Guru Śākya rgyal-mtshan also met gTer-ston Nyi-ma grags-pa (1647–1710), another treasure discoverer from Khams, bestowing on him the "complete cycles" (*chos skor yongs rdzogs*) of the teachings of Rig-'dzin bsTan-gnyis gling-pa. Both gTer-ston Gar-dbang rdo-rje and gTer-ston Nyi-ma grags-pa discovered treasure works in the temple of Byams-pa sprin; see Ehrhard (1993a:81, note 5) and chapter ten in the present volume.

Padmasambhava, a temple at the summit of the mountain g.Yang-ri-ma. The temple, however, soon succumbed to natural destruction.[46]

Approximately at the time when gTer-dbon Nyi-ma seng-ge was receiving title to land in Yol-mo from Jaya Jagajjayamalla, there occurred the birth of his son 'Phrin-las bdud-'joms. As we learn from his short biography, the father recognized his son as a reincarnation:

> On the basis of his character, in which, from childhood on, the beneficial effects familiar from his earlier [existence] became increasingly apparent, his father identified him as the reincarnation of the '[spiritual] master of his family' (*rigs bdag*) Zil-gnon dbang-rgyal rdo-rje. An inquiry by lot was also made at the great stūpa Bya-rung kha-shor, and there was a positive response.[47]

Happily, a detailed biography of 'Phrin-las bdud-'joms has been preserved, so that we can hear about the whole affair straight from his mouth, as it was. His father's designation of him as a reincarnation thereby takes on a different accent. The scene of events is a pilgrimage from Helambu to the Kathmandu Valley:

> The way it is said to have happened was that the attendant of my father put a question to me, in foolish talk, as to where the *stūpa* of Bya-rung kha-shor was located, and I [thereupon] raised my finger towards the great *stūpa*, as well as making signs that it was located in that direction; my father's heart was greatly enjoyed. And when afterwards my father, in checking the corresponding omens that occurred in my case, made inquiry by lot at the great *stūpa* in order [to

46 See Tshe-dbang nor-bu (as in note 9), pp. 17.4–19.3. See also the biography of gTer-dbon Nyi-ma seng-ge according to the local tradition of Helambu in Clarke (1980:15–18). There, too, the translation of the two deeds for the land donated by the king of Kathmandu Jaya Jagajjayamalla (ruled 1722–1735) may be found; they date from the years 1723 and 1727. The site where Padma'i-chos-gling monastery was erected is located on the side of the mountain g.Yang-ri-ma, at a "place where the bullock's horn was flung" (*glang ra rgyag sa*). This is the present-day village of Tarkhye-Ghyang. The founding of the temple on top of the mountain g.Yang-ri-ma actually predates the founding of Padma'i-chos-gling; the two foundings correspond to the two land deeds. The details of all these activities in the centre of Helambu in the 1730s are found in the biography of gTer-dbon Nyi-ma seng-ge (as in note 42), fols. 16b–27b. A lengthy discussion follows about the raising of a treasure work in the temple of Mang-yul Byams-pa sprin, an act which is attributed both to gTer-dbon Nyi-ma seng-ge and to gTer-ston Nyi-ma grags-pa. See also sTag-sgang mkhas-mchog Ngag-dbang blo-gros, Gu-ru bkra-shis (as in note 9), pp. 369.25–370.19.

47 See Tshe-dbang nor-bu (as in note 9), p. 22.4–5: *sku na phra mo nas sngon gom (= goms) gyi bag chags bzang po ches cher sad pa'i ngang tshul las yab rje nyid kyi (= kyis) rigs bdag zil gnon dbang rgyal rdo rje'i yang srid du ngos 'dzin par mdzad do/ mchod rten chen po bya rung kha shor gyi drung du brtag sgril mdzad pa'ang bab*. Further variants of the designation "[spiritual] master of the family" can be found in the biography of 'Phrin-las bdud-'joms.

> identify] me as the highest reincarnation of the teacher who is the [spiritual] master of the family, and [although] it came out positive, I nevertheless did not need his [i.e. my father's] offering of all these flatterers and reincarnations.[48]

The incarnation status postulated by his father, gTer-dbon Nyi-ma seng-ge, having been rejected, the fate of the lineage of the Yol-mo-ba sprul-skus in the region of their origin was irremediably sealed by 'Phrin-las bdud-'joms. No concrete reasons are given in the autobiography for this rejection; one may suppose, however, that it had to do with the inheritance of the monastery in Yol-mo founded by his father. On the basis of a passage from the text that has already been dealt with by earlier research, we know that 'Phrin-las bdud-'joms visited the area around the upper reaches of the Yangri Khola after his father's death in 1738 and was so disappointed by the decline of the "monastery's religious morals" (*dgon pa'i chos khrims*) that he avoided returning until 1748, beginning renovation work in Tarkhye-Ghyang only afterwards.[49] Moreover, he was already connected with another spiritual lineage through the family of his mother, so that the social prestige of an incarnation of his father's teacher was no longer of decisive importance. We shall briefly trace these maternal family ties and his education down to the year 1748 in order to obtain at least a rough picture of the last Yol-mo-ba sprul-sku from Helambu.

---

[48] See Tshe-dbang 'Chi-med mgon-po: *Rig 'dzin chen po karma bdud 'joms kyi rnam par thar pa gsal bar byed pa'i nyin byed ngo mtshar snang ba'i gter mdzod*, p. 18.4–6 (*bdag nyid kyi mel tshe ba des bdag la mchod rten bya rung kha shor ga re/ zhes gre mo'i* (= *'bre mo'i*) *tshul gyi dris yod 'dug par/ mchod rten chen po'i thad du mdzub mo sgreng zhing de phyogs su yod pa'i brda' ston byed par yab rje nyid shin tu thugs mnyes te/ de gong rje nyid rang la thugs ltas 'dra'ang byung tshod kyi* (= *kyis*) *gang gi rigs bdag bla ma mchog gi sprul skur dogs pa'i mchod rten chen po'i drung du brtag sgril mdzad pa 'bab 'dug kyang/ bdag la ni go* (= *kho*) *rang gi mchod pa'i spral spral dang sprul sprul gyi dgos pa med do*). It should be noted that in the year 1727 gTer-dbon Nyi-ma seng-ge met Kaḥ-thog rig-'dzin Tshe-dbang nor-bu in Byams-pa sprin and had received teachings from him; before this meeting the guardian deity of Byams-pa sprin had conferred the status of being the rebirth of Yol-mo-ba sprul-sku bsTan-'dzin nor-bu upon the son of a certain gSer-bzang ras-chen; see Chos-kyi dbang-phyug (as in note 17), pp. 125.3–126.2. This event is again testimony to the fact that the claims of Zil-gnon dbang-rgyal rdo-rje were not accepted by official quarters; it may also have been one of the factors contributing to 'Phrin-las bdud-'joms' reaction.

[49] For a treatment of these events, based on the biography of 'Phrin-las bdud-'joms, see Clarke (1983:29–30). But compare Tshe-dbang 'Chi-med mgon-po (as in note 48), pp. 29.6 & 30.3–4, where it is only the rejection of the right of succession and not the activities commencing in his twenty-second year to preserve religious sites that is focussed on. Concerning the biography itself, it may be said that the first part of the text falls under the genre of "narrative" and bears the title *sNang 'phrul pa'i rol rtsed rtogs brjod du gleng ba dpyid kyi nyi ring phul byed* (pp. 16.1–182.5); it was penned by 'Phrin-las bdud-'joms. The concluding part of the biography, covering the years 1786–1789, owes its existence to a disciple named Tshe-dbang 'Chi-med mgon-po (1755–1807) of the mDo-bo-che family (pp. 183.1–266.3). Concerning this disciple, see note 53.

'Phrin-las bdud-'joms's mother, Chos-nyid rang-grol (died 1746), was the daughter of rDo-dmar zhabs-drung Mi-'gyur rdo-rje (born 1675), whose family lineage is known above all as the first Tibetan group that settled in the Glang-'phrang valley north-west of Yol-mo. Like the move of gTer-dbon Nyi-ma seng-ge to the latter hidden land, this settlement process has to be seen in the context of the invasion of the Dsungar armies in Tibet in 1717. It was in Glang-'phrang (present-day Langthang) that 'Phrin-las bdud-'joms was taught by his father and mother how to read and write; the first teachings received from his father are of the Byang-gter tradition.[50] In the same year he travelled with his mother to the region of Mang-yul sKyid-grong, and in [dKar-ye] dNgos-grub mtsho-gling met the "[spiritual] master of our family" (*bdag cag gi rigs kyi bdag po*), an uncle called Rig-'dzin chen-po rDo-dmar-ba Padma rdo-rje, whom we have already met as a teacher of his father gTer-dbon Nyi-ma seng-ge. He took the vows of a novice at the sacred site of Ri-bo dpal-'bar under this member of the rDo-dmar-ba family and received the name Rig-'dzin 'Phrin-las bdud-'joms.[51] A further formulation used to designate his teacher is the "teacher, who is the [spiritual] master of the family" (*rigs kyi bdag po bla ma*); these very same words were also used to characterize Zil-gnon dbang-rgyal rdo-rje as the teacher of the father of 'Phrin-las bdud-'joms, that is, the family of Rig-'dzin bsTan-gnyis gling-pa. Here, perhaps, lies the true reason for the reserve shown towards the incarnation status that 'Phrin-las bdud-'joms's father had wished to see conferred on him: there were stronger ties to his mother's family line (the descendants of rDo-dmar-ba Mi-'gyur rdo-rje) than to his father's (the descendants of Rig-'dzin bsTan-gnyis gling-pa).

---

50 See Tshe-dbang 'Chi-med mgon-po (as in note 48), p. 20.4. Of interest here is the fact that the place where 'Phrin-las bdud-'joms met his father at age eight was the Ca-thang cave at the "Great Sacred Site Heavenly Gate of Half-Moon Form" (*gnas chen zla gam gnam sgo*); this is an alternative name of the Glang-'phrang valley, referring to its status as a hidden land of the rNying-ma-pa school. For a text of rDo-dmar-ba Mi-'gyur rdo-rje dealing with the myth and localisation of the valley "Heavenly Gate of Half-moon Form", see Ehrhard (1997b:341–346) and chapter sixteen in the present volume. A history of the rDo-dmar-ba family – which traces the origin of its members to the region on the border between Gung-thang and La-stod Byang – deals extensively with Rig-'dzin Mi-'gyur rdo-rje and his activities; see Kun-bzang chos-'phel, *rNam grol rtsangs rdo dmar ba'i gdung rabs lo rgyus deb ther padma rāga'i do shal*, pp. 89.1–137.13.

51 See Tshe-dbang 'Chi-med mgon-po (as in note 48), p. 21.2–6. The place called dKar-ye is located in the vicinity of Mang-yul Ri-bo dpal-'bar and was already used as a retreat place by sNgags-'chang Śākya bzang-po; see sTag-sgang mkhas-mchog Ngag-dbang blo-gros, Gu-ru bkra-shis (as in note 9), p. 530.19. This is where Rig-'dzin mChog-ldan mgon-po had been invited by the First Yol-mo-ba sprul-sku; see note 5. The site is also mentioned – under the names *skyid grong gi dgon pa dkar ye* and *skyid grong dkar ye* – by the Second rDo-rje brag Rig-'dzin, in rDo-rje brag Rig-'dzin Padma 'phrin-las (as in note 8), pp. 355.6 & 358.3; it was there that the teachings of sNgags-'chang Śākya bzang-po were transferred to Rig-'dzin Legs-ldan bDud-'joms rdo-rje. It was there, too, that mDo-bo che-ba Nor-bu bde-chen received the teachings of the Third Yol-mo-ba sprul-sku in the year 1633; see note 39. Concerning the visit of Zil-gnon dbang-rgyal rdo-rje to [dKar-ye] dNgos-grub mtsho-gling, see note 36.

Another maternal uncle was likewise one of his teachers (rDo-dmar-ba Mi-'gyur rdo-rje had a total of five sons); his name was rDo-dmar-ba Kun-bzang bsTan-pa'i rgyal-mtshan. His third teacher, whom he met at the age of sixteen, again in [dKar-ye] dNgos-grub mtsho-gling, was Kham-lung-pa gSang-sngags bstan-'dzin, a disciple of the Second rDo-rje brag Rig-'dzin Padma 'phrin-las (1640–1718): and again it were the transmissions of the Byang-gter tradition that were received. In 1744, finally, he came into contact with a representative of the family of mDo-bo-che named O-rgyan gSang-sngags bstan-'dzin, a disciple both of Zil-gnon dbang-rgyal rdo-rje and gTer-bdag gling-pa (1646–1714).

For the year 1747 the biography mentions the sojourn in Mang-yul Byams-pa sprin and the consideration given to renovating this site. It is at this point in time that 'Phrin-las bdud-'joms hears of the arrival of Kaḥ-thog rig-'dzin Tshe-dbang nor-bu in Nepal. Soon thereafter he is in the Kathmandu Valley meeting with this most important of his teachers – in Bya-rgod phung-po-ri, that is, at Kiṃdol Vihāra near Svayambhūnāth. A description follows of a renovation of the Bodhnāth Stūpa, and the teachings that 'Phrin-las bdud-'joms received from Kaḥ-thog rig-'dzin Tshe-dbang nor-bu at Bya-rung kha-shor.[52]

With this visit of 'Phrin-las bdud-'joms to Bodhnāth, we have come to the last contact the local lineage of the Yol-mo-ba sprul-skus had with the Bya-rung kha-shor Stūpa. The myth of the helper to the goose-keeper obviously no longer had the same force as it did a hundred years earlier at the birth of Zil-gnon dbang-rgyal rdo-rje. The Malla dynasty was showing signs of drawing to a close, and the rulers of Gorkha were arming in preparation to seize control of the three kingdoms of the Kathmandu Valley. Concerning 'Phrin-las bdud-'joms, it may be noted that he rebuilt the temple and meditation cells founded in Yol-mo by his father and upheld the tradition – again on the paternal side of his family – of maintaining the temple of Mang-yul Byams-pa sprin. Thus the texts report that in 1765, at the age of thirty-eight, he constructed a new convent, renovated the old temple and had religious objects made. In doing so, he caused the "earlier system of mDo-chen" (*sngar srol mdo chen lugs*) to flourish again.[53]

---

52 See Tshe-dbang 'Chi-med mgon-po (as in note 48), pp. 45.5–50.2. Concerning the Kiṃdol Vihāra and the renovation of the Bodhnāth Stūpa by Rig-'dzin Tshe-dbang nor-bu in 1748, see Ehrhard (1989:4–5) and chapter four in the present volume. Among the teachings that 'Phrin-las bdud-'joms received during his month in Bya-rung kha-shor was one concerning a special transmission of Mahākāruṇika teachings; the text that 'Phrin-las bdud-'joms wrote on this occasion was filmed by NGMPP under reel no. E 1286/26: *'Phags pa thugs rje chen po'i dmar khrid bla ma'i zhal lung zin bris su bkod pa*, 14 fols.

53 SeeTshe-dbang 'Chi-med mgon-po (as in note 48), pp. 128.1ff., and Chos-kyi dbang-phyug (as in note 42), pp. 24.5–25.3. The mDo-bo-che family, to which sNgags-'chang Che-mchog rdo-rje belonged (see note 43), as did sNgags-'chang Nam-mkha' seng-ge (see note 28) and his son Nor-bu bde-chen (see note 39), is obviously one of the oldest and most influential families in Mang-yul Gung-thang. The most important disciple of 'Phrin-las bdud-'joms, Tshe-dbang 'Chi-med mgon-po, wrote, according to his own testimony, a *mDo chen bla brgyud rnam thar*, which up to now has not been recovered; see his autobiography: *Gur gyi sngags ban tshe dbang 'chi med mgon po'i rang tshul chu 'babs su brjod pa lhung*

The name under which 'Phrin-las bdud-'joms was known in the second half of his life shows us, finally, that the last link in the incarnation chain active in the region of its origin – in spite of his own personal choice to disregard the status – repeatedly returned to sacred sites for his spiritual practice that had already been frequented by his predecessors. The name given 'Phrin-las bdud-'joms by his disciples' generation, namely "Dharma Master of mGon-gnang" (*mgon gnang chos rje*), refers to a place in Mang-yul sKyid-grong where the tutelary god Mahākāla had revealed himself directly to the Tangut translator Tsa-mi Sangs-rgyas grags (12th century), conferring on him the rights of ownership to the site; the place is thus called "[the place] conferred by the protector" (*mgon gnang*).[54] bsTan-'dzin nor-bu, the Third Yol-mo-ba sprul-sku, had already stayed in this place; the memory of his visit and its significance remained alive, even if corroborating sources are missing:

> [There] for a long time the reincarnation had stayed, the great Yol-mo-ba [sprul-sku], and the manner in which he met his own father, Lo-chen Chos-rje, in a pure vision, how they posed questions and gave answers to one another, and so on – this is revealed clearly in his [i.e. the Third Yol-mo-ba sprul-sku's] Collected Works. His younger brother, rGyal-sras Phyag-rdor nor-bu, likewise had stayed there.[55]

It is thus these recurring places of sojourn that endow the lineage of the Yol-mo-ba sprul-skus with a certain continuity. They are located primarily in the region of Mang-yul sKyid-grong and were visited from the beginning of the 16th to the end of the 18th centuries. As far as the sites on the territory of Nepal are concerned, that is, the sacred site of Bya-rung kha-shor and the hidden land of Yol-mo gangs-ra, this continuity was lost, and with it the

---

lhung snyan pa'i chu sgra, 1982, p. 15.5. The first part of the text (pp. 12.1–145.5) was completed by its author in 1803; it was expanded by Brag-dkar rta-so sprul-sku Chos-kyi dbang-phyug (pp.146.1–163.4). Along with the biography of 'Phrin-las bdud-'joms, this work contains informative material on the cultural and religious history of Mang-yul sKyid-grong in the 18th century.

54 Besides the name *mgon gnang chos rje* one also finds *rig 'dzin mgon gnang pa chen po*; see Chos-kyi dbang-phyug (as in note 42), p. 22.4. The site and its foundation myth are described, for example, by Zhabs-dkar Tshogs-drug rang-grol, who also pays attention to the natural beauty of this retreat place; see his autobiography (as in note 8), pp. 725.8–765.12, and Ricard (1994:366–385).

55 See Tshe-dbang 'Chi-med mgon-po (as in note 48), p. 183.5–6 (*sprul pa'i sku yol mo ba chen pos yun ring du bzhugs shing dag pa'i gzigs snang su nyid kyi yab lo chen chos rje dang mjal zhing zhu lan mdzad tshul sogs gang gi bka' 'bum du gsal/ cung (= gcung) rgyal ba'i sras po phyag rdor nor bus kyang bzhugs te*). For the father of bsTan-'dzin nor-bu, Lo-chen Ratnabhadra sprul-sku, see note 15. According to *A Collection of Records of Teachings and Initiations Received by Masters of the Gur-phu or mDo-chen Tradition of the Rnying-ma-pa*, p. 84.5, bsTan-'dzin nor-bu wrote a biography of his father. It has no more survived than has the edition of his entire writings. 'Phrin-las bdud-'joms had visionary meetings with the Third Yol-mo-ba sprul-sku at the same site; see Chos-kyi dbang-phyug (as in note 42), p. 25.6.

memory of the incarnation chain which had played such a great role in the upkeep of the *stūpa* (for this sequence of the lineage, see Appendix II).

Another offshoot of this interesting incarnation chain, however, shows that it was not forgotten very long: the memory of the Yol-mo-ba sprul-skus came back again – and were re-continued – in another region in the borderlands of south-western Tibet.[56]

[56] A second line branched off after Zil-gnon dbang-rgyal rdo-rje with a certain mThu-stobs rdo-rje (18th century), whom we can thus also call the Fifth Yol-mo-ba sprul-sku. The next incarnation, a certain Rig-'dzin Padma 'phrin-las (1773–1836) chose dGon-pa byang in the area of gTing-skyes, near the border of Sikkim, as his residence; this lineage exists up to the present, with the Tenth Yol-mo-ba sprul-sku now residing in Gangtok. The history of the "rebirth from Yol-mo" down through this line can be found in mTha'-bral rdo-rje: *mTshungs med dpal mgon bla ma dam pa gting skyes dgon pa byang gi mchog gi sprul gyi 'khrungs rabs bcu'i rnam par thar pa mdo tsam brjod pa.*

APPENDIX I

Editions and Autobiographical Writings of the Third and Fourth Yol-mo-ba sprul-skus

bsTan-'dzin nor-bu

The Autobiography and Collected Writings (gSung thor bu) of the Third Rig-'dzin Yol-mo-ba sPrul-sku bsTan-'dzin nor-bu, Vols. 2, pp. 465 and 376, Dalhousie: Damchoe Sangpo, 1977 [= I].
Collected Writings of Yol-mo sPrul-sku bsTan-'dzin nor-bu, pp. 506, Delhi: Lama Dawa, 1982 [= II].
Autobiographical Writings:

a. *Rig sngags 'chang ba thams cad kyi 'khor los bsgyur ba rgyal ba chen po'i skyes rabs kyi 'phreng ba bstod pa pad dkar brgyan 'phreng* (for a translation, see Ehrhard, Pierce & Cüppers, 1991)
I: 3 fols. (vol. 1, pp. 1–16); II: 3 fols. (pp. 1–6)
b. *rTogs brjod mkhas pa'i rna rgyan*
I: 19 fols. (vol. 1, pp. 6–44); II: 14 fols. (pp. 249–276)
c. *Rang gi rtogs pa brjod pa rdo rje'i sgra ma'i brgyud mangs* (written in 1632)
I: 102 fols. (vol. 1, pp. 63–267); II: 77 fols. (pp. 95–248)
d. No title: "Illustrations to the life of Yol-mo-ba bsTan-'dzin nor-bu" (translation under preparation)
I: 9 fols. (vol. 1, pp. 45–60); II: - - -

Zil-gnon dbang-rgyal rdo-rje

The Autobiographical Reminiscences and Writings of the 17th Century Nyingmapa Visionary, Rig-'dzin Zil-gnon dbang-rgyal rdo-rje, pp. 497, Gangtok-Delhi: Gonpo Tseten, 1977 [= I].
The Collected Autobiographical Writings and Works on rNying-ma-pa Philosophy of Rig-'dzin Zil-gnon dbang-rgyal rdo-rje, pp. 351, Delhi: Tibet House, 1977 [= II].
Collected Writings of Zil-gnon dbang-rgyal rdo-rje. A Collection of Texts by an Exponent of the rNying-ma-pa Tradition from the Sino-Nepalese Borderland, pp. 448, Darjeeling: Konchog Lhadrepa, 1985 (not accessible to me).
Autobiographical Writings:

a. *sPrul pa'i rig 'dzin chen po zil gnon dbang rgyal rdo rje'i phyi'i rnam thar ngo mtshar rmad byung rna ba'i bdud rtsi*
I: 44 fols. (pp. 1–87); II: 25 fols. (pp. 1–51)
b. *sPrul pa'i rig 'dzin chen po zil gnon dbang rgyal rdo rje'i nang gi rnam thar las zhal gdams gsung mgur gyi rim pa nges don rgya mtsho*

I: 64 fols. (pp. 88–215); II: 42 fols. (pp. 53–136)

c. *sPrul pa'i rig 'dzin chen po zil gnon dbang rgyal rdo rje'i nang gi rnam thar las zab lam bla ma'i rnal 'byor gyi rim pa byin rlabs dngos grub kyi bang mdzod*
I: 25 fols. (pp. 216–265); II: 18 fols. (pp. 137–173)

d. *rJe bla ma rig 'dzin grub pa'i dpa' bo zil gnon dbang rgyal rdo rje'i dag snang gsang ba'i rnam thar mkha' 'gro'i 'phrin glu*
I: 16 fols. (pp. 266–296); II: 10 fols. (pp. 175–193)

e. *sPrul pa'i rig 'dzin chen po zil gnon dbang rgyal rdo rje'i nang gi rnam thar las bstan bcos ljags bris kyi rim pa dgos 'dod kun 'byung nor bu'i do shal*
I: 101 fols. (pp. 297–497); II: 78 fols. (pp. 195–351)

APPENDIX II

Two further editions of the collected writings of Zil-gnon dbang-rgyal rdo-rje were filmed by the NGMPP under reel nos. E 2676/4–8 and AT 131/7–132/3. The second edition was part of the Tibetan collection of the Nepalese National Museum (Chauni) and is now preserved in the Nepalese National Archives (Ramshah Path); the illustrations of the sequence of the lineage up to the Fourth Yol-mo-ba sprul-sku are from this latter manuscript.

1. The helper of the woman keeper of geese

2. The Buddhist minister Padma Gung-btsan

3. The treasure-discoverer sNgags-'chang Śākya bzang-po

4. Second Yol-mo-ba sprul-sku Nam-mkha' brgya-byin

5. Third Yol-mo-ba sprul-sku bsTan-'dzin nor-bu

6. Fourth Yol-mo-ba sprul-sku Zil-gnon dbang-rgyal rdo-rje

IV.

Sherpa Buddhism

Two Documents on Tibetan Ritual Literature and Spiritual Genealogy

During an exploratory tour undertaken by the Tibetan Section of the Nepal-German Manuscript Preservation Project (NGMPP) in January 1989 the members came across a small monastery lying at the entrance of the village of Chyangma (Bhandar), a day's walk southeast of Jiri. The monastery is flanked, so as to catch the eye of every trekker, by two rustic replicas of Svayambhūnāth and Bodhnāth Stūpas. Among the texts that the widow of the last head of the monastery turned over to us for filming were two "records [of teachings] received" (*thob yig*)[1] of the teachings of 'Ja'-tshon snying-po (1585–1656) and gTer-bdag gling-pa (1646–1714). The two folded leaves immediately drew attention to themselves as testifying to the spread of certain *gter ma* teachings of the rNying-ma-pa school in Sherpa territory; after they were filmed and given closer scrutiny, I thought it proper to make these documents available to a larger public.

When three months later, in May 1989, the NGMPP team undertook a microfilm expedition to Junbesi, a two days' walk from Chyangma, further material came to light of apparent relevance to the topic of the spread of *gter ma* teachings. In the remarks made during the following initial probe of the texts I shall go into the material briefly. Perhaps these few details concerning the documents filmed in the region of the Likhu Khola and Solu Khola may sharpen interest in the direction of further studies.

---

1 See the definition in *Bod rgya tshig mdzod chen mo*, p. 1197: "A memorandum of what has been received from the stream of teachings, [such as] initiations, readings etc." (*dbang lung sogs chos rgyun thob pa'i brjed tho*). Cf. also Macdonald (1980a:56): "these (i.e. *thob yig*) contain lists of disciplines, precepts and consecrations obtained by an individual and state from whom exactly these were taken." Ibid, p. 58: "Simple lists of transmission of religious teaching constitute by themselves fairly arduous reading for a Tibetan as for a Westerner." To be distinguished from this is the term *tho yig*, which designates a general "list" or "inventory". The opportunity was given to film such an "inventory" of the monastery Phug-mo-che in Junbesi: *Phug mo che ngag dbang sbyin pa'i dpe cha tshang ma thor bkod pa'i tho yig* (18 x 45.5 cm) reel no. L 234/7.

Here, first of all, the titles of two *thob yig* along with supplementaty data:

1. *Yang zab dkon mchog spyi 'dus kyi thob yig*
(42 x 43 cm) reel no. E 2312/19

2. *rDor sems thugs kyi(s) sgrub(s) pa'i dbang lung khrid gsum thob yig*
(35 x 64 cm) reel no. E 2312/20

The putting of the two accession lists to paper goes back to the first half of the 20th century; I arrived at this conclusion by computing forward the dates of known persons mentioned in the documents themselves to the lifetimes of the authors. rDo-rje nor-bu is named as the author of the first document, and bsTan-'dzin rdo-rje as that of the second. The "root teacher" (*rtsa ba'i bla ma*) of both authors is one rDo-rje rgyal-mtshan. The two documents are parallel in composition and segmentation, with the list of the teachings of 'Ja'-tshon snying-po being distinguished merely by a longer introduction; the concluding portions of documents one and two are identical. Orthography is extremely poor, the text being overrun with errors, which I have attempted to correct as far as possible during the editing of the documents.

A closer examination of these folded leaves is justified by two points in particular: they contained a detailed listing of the titles of certain *gter ma* cycles—with information on the sequence of "initiations" (*dbang*) etc.—and they place these teaching in historical perspective by way of a "spiritual genealogy" of their representatives. With these two points we have come to the two central parts of the text into which the documents are divided.

Renewed attention has been paid recently to the aspect of rituals in the Himalayas.[2] As is borne witness to in the two present documents, the actual rituals and initiations – at

2 See Macdonald (1987:5–13) and Karmay (1988a). The latter work contains a useful glossary of technical vocabulary employed in Tibetan rituals. Future research will have the task of showing to what extent the "visions" of the Fifth Dalai Bla-ma were influenced by the tradition of the "northern treasure works" (*byang gter*). The Fifth Dalai Bla-ma's affiliation with this tradition is as follows: Legs-ldan bDud-'joms rdo-rje (born 1512)—bKra-shis stobs-rgyal (1550–1602)—Rig-'dzin Ngag-gi dbang-po (1580–1639)—Third Yol-mo-ba bsTan-'dzin nor-bu (1598–1644)—Zur Chos-dbyings rang-grol (1604–1669)—Fifth Dalai Bla-ma Blo-bzang rgya-mtsho (1617–1682). The statement of Karmay (1988a:14): "Only two manuscript of the work (i.e. the secret biography of the Fifth Dalai Lama, the *gSang ba'i rnam thar rgya can*) are known to exist outside Tibet" must be corrected. Another manuscript was filmed by the NGMPP in the year 1987: *gZigs snang gsang ba rgya can ma*, 578 fols., reel nos. E 2134/2–E 2135/1. See chapter twenty two of the present volume (Appendix).

Macdonald (1987:10–11) points out the difficulties in analysing rituals in territory under Tibetan cultural influence, matters being complicated by the fact that meditation techniques are an integral component of rituals in Tibetan Buddhism ("Dans ce domaine, l'analyse se complique du fait qu'on ne peut exclure du champ des investigations les techniques de méditation; car ces techniques font partie intégrante de la pratique rituelle de tous les ordres religieux tibétains.") In the search for possible solutions

least in the case of *gter ma* teachings – were supplemented by the transmission of the authoritative writings of the respective cycles. Once one knows the ritual literature that a particular area was acquainted with at a particular time, one can automatically draw conclusions concerning the diffusion of the cycle, its topicality and popularity. Problems that have plagued field researchers in their descriptions of modern-day ritual activity may by this means perhaps even be cleared up.

Particularly in the case of the teachings of 'Ja'-tshon snying-po a presentation of the way in which the text cycle *Yang zab dkon mchog spyi 'dus* has been dealt with by the Sherpas in East Nepal during the 19th and 20th centuries may be of not inconsiderable interest, if one bears in mind the diffusion these rituals have had throughout the entire region of Northern Nepal. Both the cycle just mentioned and the *rDor sems thugs kyi sgrub pa* of gTer-bdag gling-pa are "treasure works" (*gter ma*), the composition of which may be placed in the Tibet of the 17th century. That one can still see in the mountain regions of Nepal bordering on Tibet these late-flowering blossoms of a movement which came into full fruition in the 14th century with Klong-chen rab-'byams-pa (1308–1364) and Rig-'dzin rGod-ldem 'phru-can (1337–1406) is of a significance not to be downplayed, particularly at present, for the study of the region's cultural history and geography.[3]

With that we come to the "spiritual genealogy" of the two accession lists. I have chosen this term in order to stress that genealogies in a genre like the *thob yig* (and to certain extent also in the so-called *rus yig*) must be read with an eye to the transmission of spiritual techniques and teachings. A too rationalistic reading of such "lines of descent" easily runs the risk of producing distortions, especially as concerns historical facts.[4] Of

to such problems I would suggest that the works of Tibetan authors be studied who themselves have reflected on the field spanning both meditational techniques and ritual activity. One example would be rTse-le[gs] sNa-tshogs rang-grol (1605–1677); concerning him, see Blondeau (1987:126–127). He studied personally under 'Ja'-tshon snying-po and composed a number of interesting works on the rituals of this teachers; of particular significance, however, are his extensive "Answers to Questions" (*dris lan*). He is also the author of a biography dealing with the closing years of 'Ja'-tshon snying-po's life: *Rig 'dzin chen po 'ja' tshon snying po sku tshe myug gi rnam thar mdor bsdus ngo mtshar snang byed.*

3 In the year 1985 (*shing mo glang*), Bya-bral Rin-po-che Sangs-rgyas rdo-rje compiled an informative "catalogue" (*dkar chag*) to a new edition of the works of 'Ja'-tshon snying-po; see *gSol 'debs le'u bdun dang / 'ja' mtshon dkon spyi / zhi 'khro sogs sgrub thabs snying po rnams dang / gzhan yang chos spyod smon lam skor bcas kyi dkar chag mthong thos thar lam sgo byed*, pp. 4.1ff. At one point in it he talks about the spread of these teachings among the *shar pa, rta mang* and *mon pa*; then he makes the distinction *byang gter = rnying ma / 'ja' tshon = gsar ma*, without forgetting, of course, that both teaching traditions belong to the school of the "Old Ones".

4 I'm thinking particularly of the work done by Clarke (1980), (1983) and (1988) on Helambu and the hypothesis propounded by Oppitz (1968) concerning the migratory history of the Sherpas. In spite of the correcting of the dates of the First Yol-mo-ba sNgags-'chang Śākya bzang-po from the 17th century to the early 16th century – Clarke (1980:14) and ibid, (1988:123) – the role of the following incarnations and the teachings practised by them has yet to be determined. The Third Yol-mo-ba bsTan-'dzin nor-bu (1598–

assistance in the case of the two *thob yig* from Chyangma is the fact that we have access to comparable material, namely the text *Shar pa'i chos 'byung* edited by Sangs-rgays bstan-'dzin and Alexander W. Macdonald in 1971. I therefore reproduce in Appendix I and II the respective lineages of the teachings of 'Ja'-tshon snying-po and gTer-bdag gling-pa.

What can be said, then, on the basis of a comparison of these spiritual genealogies as an initial approach to the topic of the diffusion of particular *gter ma* teachings in Northeast Nepal? What is striking first of all is the conjunction of three teachers Kaḥ-thog rig-'dzin Tshe-dbang nor-bu (1698–1755), Karma 'Phrin-las bdud-'joms (1726–1789) and Brag-dkar rta-so sprul-sku Chos-kyi dbang-phyug (1775–1837). These three, in my opinion, are central figures in the codification and transmission of rNying-ma-pa teachings in the 18th and 19th centuries from South Tibet to Nepal. The further particulars of this transmission, including the number of texts and traditions that had a role to play in it, will have to be reserved for a future study. Reference may be made, though, to the geographical territory in which this process of transmission and diffusion took place: the region generally called Mang-yul with its district town sKyid-[g]rong.[5]

1644) and his incarnation, Zil-gnon dbang-rgyal rdo-rje (1647–1716), deserve particular attention in this regard. Given the fact that Rig-'dzin Nyi-ma seng-ge (1687–1738) views his son Karma 'Phrin-las bdud-'joms (1726–1789) as the incarnation of Zil-gnon dbang-rgyal rdo-rje, there is nothing to keep Karma 'Phrin-las bdud-'joms from being called the Fifth Yol-mo-ba; in this regard, see Chos-kyi dbang-phyug: *gTer dbon rig 'dzin brgyud pa'i gdung rabs*, pp. 22.3–29.3 and chapter nine in the present volume. Only after it becomes clear how the teachings of the *byang gter* and of bsTan-gnyis gling-pa (1480–1535) were passed along in this lineage in the 17th and 18th centuries will one discover the true role of Rig-'dzin Tshe-dbang nor-bu, the great systematizer of *gter ma* teachings in northern Nepal. Statements like "it also seems that Kaḥ-thog rig-'dzin chen-po Tshe-dbang nor-bu (1698–1755) ... may have been of Nyima Senge's spiritual lineage", Clarke (1988:121, note 9) could then be made a bit more concrete.

The contradictions in the migratory history of the Sherpas raised, above all, by a *rus yig* published by Oppitz (1982:287–295) – see Blondeau (1972:406) and Macdonald (1980a:58) – might perhaps also be resolved where one has to devote more attention to the *gter ma* teaching of Ratna gling-pa (1403–1478) and of Thang-stong rgyal-po (1385–1509), or to the generation of disciples who brought these teachings to Solu-Khumbu. A version of the *rus yig* produced by Sangs-rgyas bstan-'dzin was filmed in Junbesi: *Me dpag yod pa'i mi nyag rgyus / mKhan lung lam yig*, 13 fols. (*khyug yig*), reel no. L 233/5. The anthropologist S.B. Ortner, finally, in her books on the history and ritual practices of Sherpa Buddhism, unfortunately only makes limited use of written documents in the Tibetan language. See Ortner (1978:passim) and (1989:207, note 2). For an overview of the history of Sherpa Buddhism, compare Wangmo (2005:22–29) and Berg (2008:27–35).

5 Concerning sKyid-[g]rong and the monastery Byams-sprin lha-khang, see Schuh (1988:13–14, 29, 86 & 91). The handing over of this monastery in the 15th century to one sNgags-'chang Che-mchog rdo-rje and the subsequent administering of it by the family of bsTan-gnyis gling-pa—Karma 'Phrin-las bdud-'joms (1726–1789) being a member of the family in the sixth generation—can be nicely reconstructed with the help of the text *gTer dbon rig 'dzin brgyud pa'i gdung rabs*. Of particular interest is the raising of a "treasure work" in Byams-sprin by Rig-'dzin Nyi-ma grags-pa (1647–1710); cf. sTag-sgang mkhas-mchog Ngag-dbang blo-gros, *sNga 'gyur chos 'byung*, pp. 464.4–467.4.

Concerning the latter "treasure discoverer" (*gter ston*), see also Blondeau (1988:60). According to

Among the inhabitants of Solu-Khumbu who moved to Mang-yul during this period I have been able to identify rDo-rje 'jigs-bral and Karma Nges-don. They both belong to the "Nyang Clan" (*nyang rigs*), and a comparison of the "genealogies" provided here reveals that it was the latter, in particular, who played a large role in transmitting the *gter ma* teachings of 'Ja'-tshon snying-po and gTer-bdag gling-pa. And with this fact we have reached the crucial point where it can be shown that these teaching migrated from Tibet to Nepal through the activities of prominent representatives of a "clan". Only when we have a clearer understanding of such activities in the 18th and 19th centuries will we perhaps be able to get a new perspective on events farther back in time.

---

gTer dbon gdung rab, pp. 19.4ff. (cf. also *sNga 'gyur chos 'byung*, vol. 2, p. 646.4–5), this treasure is also connected with the person of Rig-'dzin Nyi-ma seng-ge (1687–1738). One other *gter ston* who discovered a "treasure" in Byams-sprin is Rig-'dzin Gar-dbang rdo-rje (1640–1685). In his case it was the cycle *Zab tig chos dbyings rang gsal*; cf. *sPrul sku rig 'dzin chen po gar dbang rdo rje snying po'i phyi'i rnam par thar pa nges don rgya mtsho*, fols. 29b–30a. The discovery occurred in the year 1669.

TEXT I

// yang zab dkon mchog spyi 'dus ktu thob (mthob) yig gsal (gsol) byed bzhugs so //
Illuminating record [of teachings] received [of the cycle] "Most Profound Union of the [Three] Jewels"

na mo gu ru ratna siddhi hūṃ /
Namo Guru Ratna Siddhi Hūṃ

gdod ('dod) nas dag pa chos sku 'od mi 'gyur /
From the begining pure Dharmakāya, untransformable light,

ma dang ye shes mkha' 'gro longs spyod rdzogs /
gratified [body of] enjoyment of [all] mothers and wisdom *ḍākiṇīs*,

snang srid kun khyab cir snang sprul pa'i sku /
fully encompassing the world, Nirmāṇakāya, arising by all means,

sku gsum (*sum*) *khyab bdag bla mar* (*mar par*) *'dud* (*'dus*) */*
to the one who pervades the three bodies, to the teacher, I bow down.

rgyal kun sgrub thabs ma lus kun 'dus pa'i /
The innumerable sādhanas of all Jinas, where they are all fulfilled,

snying po dril ba gcig (*cig*) *mchog* (*phyogs*) *rgyal kun tshang /*
concentrated essence, unique and superb, unity of all Jinas,

bla ma dkon mchog spyi 'dus (om.) *sgrubs pa'i gter* (*ter*) */*
treasure that will furnish the all-surpassing pile of Teacher jewels:

gter (*ter*) *tshon bskal* (*skal*) *bzang snying po 'di na shar /*
this treasure's colour – it shone forth in the centre of the Blessed Age (*bhadrakalpa*).

chos tshan gter ma yongs su grags /
The sections of the teaching, the treasure, well known they are.

'di nyid shar gter yin pa bla mas gsungs (*sung*) */*
This very one is the Eastern Treasure[6] – so said the teacher.

[6] The designation "Eastern Treasure" (*shar gter*) for the cycle *Yang zab dkon mchog spyi 'dus* reflects in my view the perspective of the Sherpas; for them Kong-po, the area where the treasure was discovered and where the treasure discoverer was engaged in his activity, lies to the east. In the subdivision of the *gter ma* of the rNying-ma-pa school according to their orientation towards the cardinal points, the "Eastern

de ltar sprul pa'i gter ston chen po 'ja' tshon (chan) snying pos (snying po'i) hom 'phrang (sngo hom grag) lcags (lcag) kyi sgo mo nas spyan drang pa'i yang zab dkon mchog spyi 'dus kyi chos tshan rnams ji ltar thob pa (thobs pa) yin pa la /
Thus, the sections of the teaching [of the cycle] "Most Profound Union of the [Three] Jewels" were brought forth from out of the iron portal [of the place called] "Tripod Gorge"[7] by the great treasure discoverer 'Ja'-tshon snying-po, who is a reincarnation, in which way they [now] have been received [by me]:

thog mar sngon 'gro dngos gzhi nas bzung /
At the beginning, starting with the preparatory exercises [and] the "main part" (*maula*),

skyabs 'gro yig brgya (rgya) mandal
were duly performed the refuge taking, the hundred syllables [of the mantra of Vajrasattva], the maṇḍala [offering],

bla ma'i (bla mis) rnal 'byor smin khrid (khri) legs par (leg par) 'grub ('grubs) nas
after the guru yoga, the instructions leading to fruition was accomplished properly

gu ru'i dgongs (dgong) gsol kyi dbang thob nas /
once the initiation was received, which was asked for from the Teacher, [then]

phyi sgrubs (sgrugs) nang sgrubs (sgrugs) gsang (bsang) sgrubs (sgrugs) tshe sgrubs /
the outer aspect, the inner aspect, the secret aspect, and the long-life aspect [of the *sādhana*]

phrin las (phri las) bzhi 'grubs /
[and] the four activities[8] were performed [by me].

Treasure" is generally associated with the cycle *mKha' 'gro snying thig* and the treasure discoverer Padma-las-'brel-rtsal (1291–1316). See Kun-bzang Nges-don klong-yangs: *sNga 'gyur bstan 'dzin rnam thar*, p. 181.5–6. In an addition to the schema presented in Ehrhard (1990a:84, note 17), I can now assign the "Western Treasure" (*nub gter*) to Rig-'dzin Gar-dbang rdo-rje (1640–1685).

7 See Karmay (1988a:241): "*hom*—triangular iron receptacle used as a fire place." Cf. the information in *sNga 'gyur chos 'byung* (as in note 5), vol. 2. p. 677.5: *brag lung hom 'phrang lcags kyi sgo mo*; the discovery occurred in the year 1620 (*lcags pho spre'u*). Concerning the finding of the treasure it is stated that this cycle, together with a few others, is a "secret treasure" (*gsang gter*), i.e. it was uncovered by the treasure discoverer alone, in contrast to the majority of finds of 'Ja'-tshon snying-po, which are termed "treasure for the multitudes" (*khrom gter*) (*dkon mchog spyi 'dus sogs 'ga' zhig gsang gter las phal cher khrom gter mdzad*); ibid, p. 678.3. Concerning the expression *khrom gter*, see Aris (1989:50).

8 Concerning the four activities cf. Karmay (1988a:239): "*zhi ba*—tranquillity, peace; *rgyas pa*—prosperity, progress, advancement; *dbang*—subjugation; *drag po*—violence, agitation." They are dealt with by Snellgrove (1957:257ff.) in the context of the cycle *Yang zab dkon mchog spyi 'dus.*

rgyab chos (rgyab chog) lung gi (gis) skor la /
[Then concerning] the cycle of readings, [i.e.] the Fortifying Teaching:[9]

oṃ – yang zab lung gi lde mig
Key to the readings of [the cycle of] the Most Profound [Union of the Three Jewels].

āḥ – bka' 'grel (bgrel) ri rgyal lhun grub
Commentary on the promulgated word, [bearing the title] "King of Mountains, Sumeru".

hūṃ – bla ma'i rnam (rnams) thar
Hagiography of the teacher.

ka – gu ru zhi ba'i las byang (las sbyangs)
Sequence of ritual acts[10] for the Guru (i.e. Padmasambhava) in [his] peaceful aspect.

kha – 'phrin las bzhi sgrubs
Performance of the four activities.

ga – 'phrin las bzhi'i sbyin sreg (sbyin sregs)
Fire offerings in accordance with the four activities.[11]

---

[9] In Ehrhard (1990a:56), I have briefly shown how the concept "Fortifying Teaching" (*rgyab chos*) is employed in *gter ma* literature. From what I have observed, the material offered in the "instructions" (*khrid*) is presented in a refined form in the so-called *rgyab yig*. The thing to be determined in the present case is the text on the basis of which the actual instructions were given.

[10] Snellgrove (1957:232) translates *las byang* as "liturgy" (Tucci uses the same expression to render *cho ga*; cf. Macdonald (1987:10–11), basing himself on Blondeau). *Bod rgya tshig mdzod chen mo*, p. 2775 has for *las byang* the definition *bya ba byed pa'i cho ga*: "a [ritual] act (Skt. *vidhi*) whereby some action is performed". See in this respect the translations of Schuh (1973:131) and passim: "*las byang* = Aktivierungsritual" (activation ritual), p. 126: "*gsol byang* = Bittopferritus" (supplication rite), p. 129: "*bzlog byang* = Abwehrritus" (repulsion rite). I have settled on the translation "sequence of ritual acts" in accordance with the etymology of the Sherpa scholar Sangs-rgyas bstan-'dzin: *las ka zhig gi cho ga'i go rim byang bur byas pa yin*: "a sequence of acts for a [particular] activity in the form of a list". Within the framework of the rNying-ma-pa school's *gter ma* literature, this seems to be the generally accepted definition; it is dealt with in detail, for example, in sNa-tshogs rang-grol: *Chos rje mi pham mgon pos dri ba snga phyi tha dad mdzad pa'i dri lan thor bu'i skor rnams phyogs gcig tu bsdebs*, pp. 294.4–295.6. There one finds the etymology *'phrin las kyi gzhung ngam las kyi byang bu*: "a textbook of the [four] activities or a register of the [ritual] acts". The usage of the term *byang bu* in the present context corresponds to the designation of certain text categories of *gter ma* works, such as *lam byang* (itinerary) or *them byang* (table of contents).

[11] According to rTse-le[gs] sNa-tshogs rang-grol (as in note 10), p. 11.2–5, the sequence of the fire offerings corresponds in the school of the Old Ones (rNying-ma-pa) to the individual stages of a "great consecration act" (*dbang sgrub chen mo*):

nga – gu ru drags po'i las byang (las byas)
Sequence of ritual acts for the Guru (i.e. Padmasambhava) in [his] wrathful aspect.

ca – seng gdong ma'i (seng gdong mi) las byang
Sequence of ritual acts for the "Lion-Faced One" (*siṃhamukhā*).

cha – dbang drags 'bar ba'i las thabs (thab)
Ritual technique[12] by which flames up power and wrathfulness.

ja – seng gdong ma'i (seng gdong mi) las thabs
Ritual technique for the "Lion-Faced One" (*siṃhamukhā*).

nya – dbang gi (gis) las thabs (thab)
Ritual technique for the initiation.

ta – lta sgom spyod pa'i rim pa
The stages of vision, meditation [practice] and comportment.

tha – le'u lnga pa pad ma'i (pad me) srog phur
The fifth chapter: "Padmasambhava's Life Dagger".[13]

da – ma hā yo ga'i (yo gi) sgrub thabs (thab)
"Method of realization" (*sādhana*) [according to the teaching] of Mahāyoga.

na – a nu yo ga'i (gi) rdzogs (rdzog) rim
"Stage of perfection" (*nispannakrama*) [according to the teaching] of Atiyoga.

---

sngon 'gro	:	*zhi ba'i sbyin sreg*
sgrub pa'i dngos gzhi	:	*rgyas pa'i sbyin sreg*
dbang skur skabs	:	*dbang gi sbyin sreg*
mthar chos srung	:	*drag po'i sbyin sreg*

Cf. the work *sByin sreg gi las rim don gsal* by Mi-pham rgya-mtsho (1846–1912), as described in Schuh (1973:193–195.

12 Here I base myself on the etymology *las gang zhig 'grub pa'i thabs shes so*: "method by which a [ritual] act is performed". I have avoided the translation "working aid" for *las thabs*, as it has, in my estimation, a somewhat depreciatory undertone.

13 To my question concerning the meaning of this expression I received the following information from Sangs-rgyas bstan-'dzin: *srog shing ltar gnas pa'i gtso phur che mchog*: "Che-mchog, the main phur bu [deity], who abides firm, like the "tree of life" (Skt. *yaṣṭi*)." *Srog shing* designates the central middle axis of a *stūpa* or a statue.

pa – a ti yo ga'i (gi) khrid (khri)
Instructions [according to the teaching] of Atiyoga.[14]

pha – gtum mo (tum mo) bde ('dod) drod 'od 'bar
[The practice of] Inner Heat, the forth-shining of the blissfulness fire.

ba – 'pho ba (pho ba) dkar khung mda' 'phang
[The practice of] Consciousness Transfer, the arrow propelled through the opening.

ma – nyang ban (pan) ting 'dzin (ting ni) zhu lan
Answers to the questions of Nyang (= Myang)-ban Ting[-nge]-'dzin [bzang-po].[15]

tsa – 'dzoms (dzom) yig nam mkha' 'od klong
Letter for the fore-gathering (?)[16], [with the title] Dimension of Sky's Light.

chos tshan 'di yang (yan) gter ston (rton) gyi (kyi) shog (shogs) ser ltar (tar) / 'khrul ('khrul) med glegs bam (kleg bam) lung thob /
[As concerns] this section of the teaching, I have received the readings of the volume, which, like the golden scroll of the treasure discoverer, is without error.

de'i brgyud pa (rgyud pa) ni chos sku snang ba mtha' (tha) yas /
The lineage of this [teaching]: Dharmakāya Amitābha

longs (lung) sku thugs rje (rjes) chen po /
Saṃboghakāya Mahākāruṇika (= Avalokiteśvara)

sprul sku pad ma 'byung gnas (nas) /
Nirmāṇakāya Padmasambhava

mkha' 'gro (gro) ye shes 'tsho (tsho) rgyal /
Ḍākinī Ye-shes 'tsho-rgyal

---

[14] The correlation of the two stages *bskyed rim* (*utpannakrama*), *rdzogs rim* (*niṣpanna- / saṃpanna-krama*) and *rdzogs pa chen po* (*mahā-saṃdhi / -santi*) with the classificatory scheme Mahāyoga, Anuyoga and Atiyoga can be observed in works as early as Padmasambhava's *Man ngag lta ba'i phreng ba*, the *Guhyagarbhatantra* and the corresponding commentarial literature. See Karmay (1988b:138) and Ehrhard (1990a:8–10).

[15] Concerning this work, see Tucci (1958:52–54); it was filmed by the NGMPP under reel no. E 787/29. 'Ja'-tshon snying-po is regarded as an incarnation of Myang-ban Ting-nge-'dzin bzang-po. On the role of this minister of King Khri-lDe srong-btsan (776–815) in the codification of the *sNying thig* teachings, see Karmay (1988b:209–210).

[16] The meaning of *'dzom(s) yig* is unclear to me. The reading *'jom(s) yig* is also possible.

myang ban (pan) ting 'dzin bzang po /
Myang-ban Ting[-nge]-'dzin bzang-po

rig 'dzin 'ja' tshon snying po /
Rig-'dzin 'Ja'-tshon snying-po (1585–1656)

rig 'dzin bdud ('du) 'dul rdo rje /
Rig-'dzin bDud-'dul rdo-rje (1615–1672)

rig 'dzin klong gsal snying po /
Rig-'dzin Klong-gsal snying-po (1625–1692)

pad ma (pad me) bde ('des) chen gling pa (kling po) /
Padma bDe-chen gling-pa (1663–1713)[17]

rdo rje (rdo rjes) tshe dbang nor bu (nor bu'i) /
rDo-rje Tshe-dbang nor-bu (1698–1755)

'dren mchog pad ma rgyal po /
'Dren-mchog Padma rgyal-po

rdo rje (rdo rjes) 'jigs bral (brag) /
rDo-rje 'jigs-bral[18]

kar ma nges don (ngos stan) /
Karma Nges-don[19]

---

17 A short biographical account of Padma bDe-chen gling-pa is found in *sNga 'gyur chos 'byung* (as in note 5), vol. 3, pp. 186.3–187.1. He unearthed the *gter ma* cycle *Klong gsal ḍā ki snying thig*. For Kaḥ-thog rig-'dzin Tshe-dbang nor-bu's connection with Padma bDe-chen gling-pa, see *Tshe dbang nor bu'i rnam thar*, pp. 65ff. and chapter twenty in the present volume.

18 Concerning rDo-rje 'jigs-bral, cf. the data in Sangs-rgyas bstan-'dzin: *Shar pa'i chos 'byung*, pp. 56.3–58.6; his name here is given as Nyang-rigs rDo-rje 'jigs-bral. He is the founder of the village temple of bKra-shis mthong-smon, the oldest monastery in Junbesi. In *Shar pa'i chos 'byung*, p. 54.4, rDo-rje 'jigs-bral is mentioned as the teacher of 'Dren-mchog Chos-kyi dbang-phyug = Brag-dkar rta-so sprul-sku Chos-kyi dbang-phyug (1775–1837), cf. Appendix II. Two texts from the hand of rDo-rje 'jigs-bral were filmed: reel nos. L 236/3 and L250/3. Accordingly the monastery's foundation may be dated to the middle or the second half of the 18th century. Ortner (1989:62) has, in contrast to this, the dates 1695/1720; the signboard of the temple itself gives a still earlier date (1636) (this date obviously refers to the activities of Bla-ma rDo-rje bzang-po; see Macdonald (1980b:70–73).

19 Data concerning Karma Nges-don, too, are found in the *Shar pa'i chos 'byung*, pp. 80.3–81.3. Like rDo-rje 'jigs-bral, he belongs to the clan of the Nyang; for further information, see note 33.

kar ma don grub ('grubs) /
Karma Don-grub[20]

bstan (rten) 'dzin rdo rje (rdo rjes) /
bsTan-'dzin rdo-rje

bstan (ston) 'dzin chos (chod) dar /
bsTan-'dzin Chos-dar

rtsa ba'i bla ma (bla mas) rdo rje (rdo rjes) rgyal mtshan ('tshan) gyi zhabs (bzhabs) drung (drungs) du / bdag rdo rje (rdo rjes) nor bus (nor bu'i) legs par (leg par) thob pa (mthobs pa) yin pa la /
The root teacher rDo-rje rgyal-mtshan. In his presence I, rDo-rje nor-bu, have duly received [this section of the teaching].

brgyud pa (rgyud pa) de rnams kyi (kyis) mi bar la khyi ma shor /
With no dog having slipped in between those men who keep the lineage,[21]

steng (stengs) du rig 'dzin gyi gral (bral) ma zhig /
with the line of Vidyādharas not having dissolved above,

'og du sman (smed) rak gi (rag gi) mtsho ma skams /
with the ocean of medicine and blood not having dried up below,[22]

bar du gsang (bsang) sngags rnying ma'i (snying ma'i) bstan pa (sten pa) mi nub cing sgra di ri ri ('di'i)
may the teaching of the Old Ones not decline in the middle (i.e. in the world of men), and may its voice sound [evermore]!

---

20 Bla-ma Karma Don-grub is mentioned in the *Shar pa'i chos 'byung* (as in note 18), pp. 73.4ff. as a model of a "free-giving lord" (Skt. *dānapati*); he sponsored the founding of sTeng-po-che monastery in Khumbu and founded in Solu the family monastery bDe-skyid bsam-gling above the village temple of bKra-shis mthong-smon. See the information provided by Ortner (1989:101, 108, 129–130 and 145). According to these pieces of information his dates are 1850–1931. As stated in *Pha mes kyi byung rabs rin chen gser gyi nyag thag* (filmed in Junbesi under reel no. L 250/3), he was a great-grandson of rDo-rje 'jigs-bral.

21 The meaning of the phrase *mi bar la khyi ma shor* refers to the fact that no persons should be part of the lineage who have broken their samaya vows. I have rendered it here in accordance with a parallel passage in the *Shar pa'i chos 'byung* (as in note 18), p. 55.4–5: *brgyud pa mi bar la khyi ma shor ba / steng du rig 'dzin gyi gral ma zhigs / 'og tu bu slob kyi dad ma log / bar du sman rak gi mtsho ma skams / gsang sngags rnying ma'i snyan grags ma nub par 'ur dir re.*

22 See Karmay (1988a:240): "*sman rak gtor gsum*—the three kinds of oblation: *sman*, medicine; *rak* = rakta, blood; *gtor* = gtor ma, sacrificial cake."

dkyil 'khor thams (rda) cad kyi (kyis) mdangs ma yal bar khra lam me /
May the radiance of all maṇḍalas, not fading, shine forth [evermore]!

rig (rigs) 'dzin brgud pa'i bum chu ma skam par 'od si li li /
The water in the flask of those who keep the Vidyādhara lineage, not drying up,—may its light pour down!

dam can srung ma'i (srungs mi) mthu (thugs) rtsal ma 'gags par tsha khyug ge (gis) /
The might of the guardians, who have taken the vow, not being stemmed,—may its heat flare!

yi dam (yid dam) lha'i byin rlabs (rlobs) ma nyams par (nyam bar) rtsal thib thib (thibs) /
The blessing of the yidams and the gods, not decreasing,—may its power increase!

rdo rje (rdo rjes) spun kyi yi dam tshig (tshigs) ma nyams par gtsang (rtsang) lhang nge /
May the vows of the Vajra brothers, not flagging, become ever purer!

yid ches (chad) khungs (khung) btsun pa'i (rtson pa'i) phyir du /
That [this] source of confidence might be trustworthy [for others],

drin can rtsa ba'i bla ma (bla mas) rdo rje (rdo rjes) rgyal mtshan gyis (kyi) phyag (phyags) rtags (ta) /
from the kind root teacher rDo-rje rgyal-mtshan [it received] the hand sign (i.e. thumb print).

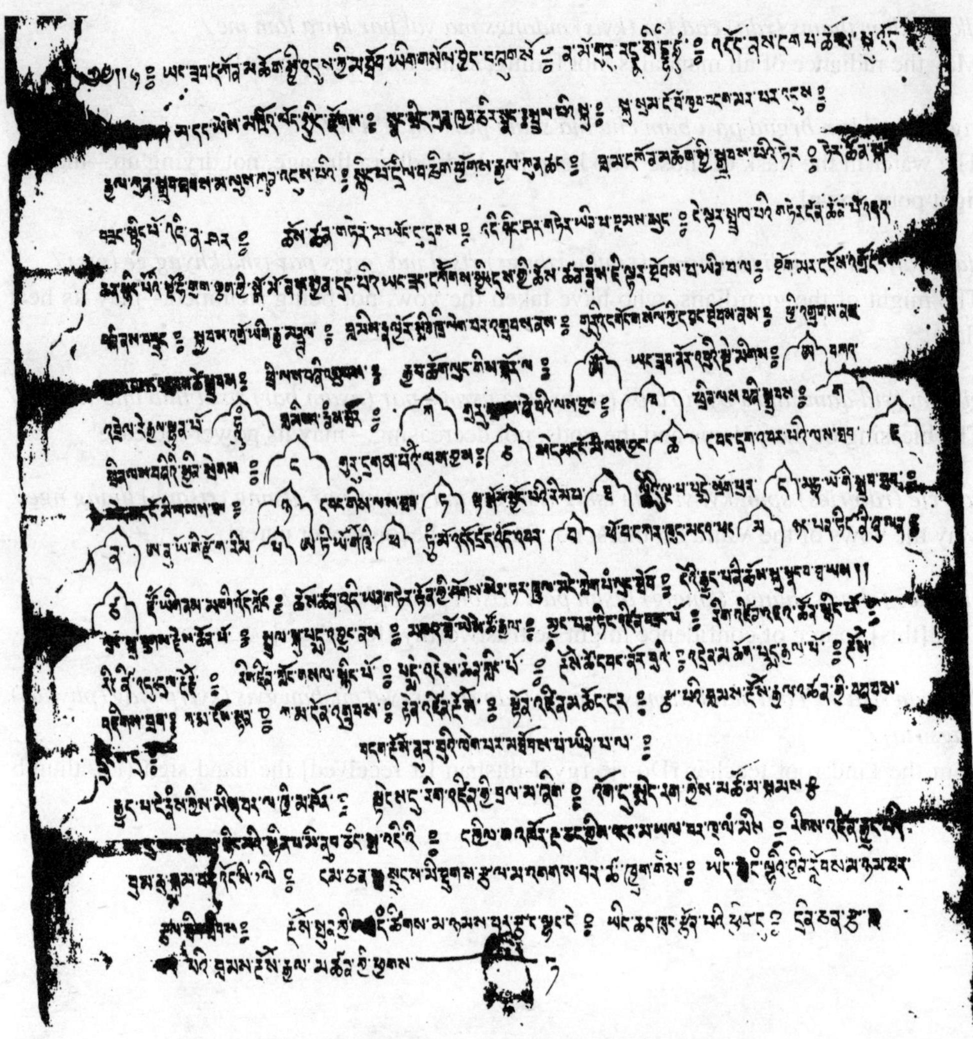

Yang zab dkon mchog spyi 'dus of 'Ja'-tshon snying-po (1585–1656) – discovered 1620

Text 2

// gter chen chos kyi (kyis) rgyal pos ngam (rgyal dam) shod gnam (gnams) lcags brag (brags) nas spyan drangs pa'i rdor sems thugs kyi (kyis) sgrub pa'i (sgrubs pa'i) dbang lung khrid gsum thob pa la /
Now as to how initiation, reading and instruction of [the cycle] "Realization of Vajrasattva's Heart" were received, being unearthed from [the mountain] Heaven-iron-Rock in Ngam-shod by the great treasure [discoverer], the Dharmarāja:[23]

*thog mar ras bris (dri) tshom bu'i dkyil 'khor du thod pa bdud rtsi me long sin dhura shel rdo dang bcas pa (*add. *la) ston nas dbang bzhi smin byed thob (mthob) /*
At the beginning the four initiations leading to fruition were received, after the skull bowl [and] nectar, [as well as] the mirror [and] cinnabar,[24] together with the crystal were [first] shown on a maṇḍala of pieces of painted cloth.

mtha' rten yig brgya'i (rgya'i) bzlas (zlas) lung dang bcas pa thob (mthob) /
[Then] the last, sustaining [ceremony][25] was received together with the reading for the recitation of the Hundred Syllables [of Vajrasattva].

rgyab rten (ston) lung gi (gis) skor (bskor) la /
[Then] in the cycle of readings of the "Fortifying support"[26] [the following] was received:

ka – rdor sems thugs kyi (kyis) sgrub pa'i (sgrubs pa'i) khrid yig /
Instructional text on [the cycle] "Realization of Vajrasattva's Heart".

kha – rdor sems rab gnas kyi (kyis) cho ga (chog ga)
Consecration ritual of Vajrasattva.

ga – rdor sems thugs kyi (kyis) sgrub pa'i (sgrubs pa'i) dbang mchog
Highest initiation according to [the cycle] "Realization of Vajrasattva's Heart".

---

23 On the discovery of the treasure *rDor sems thugs kyi sgrub pa* by gTer-bdag gling-pa in the year 1674, see Schwieger (1985:lvi–lvii, note 138). The Fifth Dalai Bla-ma and his scribe 'Jam-dbyangs grags-pa had a hand in recording it; concerning the latter, see Karmay (1988a:16 & 65).

24 See Karmay (1988a:241): "*sindhu ra*—Skt., red lead; cinnabar or sacred ash." Cf. also *Bod rgya tshig mdzod chen mo*, pp. 2922–2923.

25 Cf. *Bod rgya tshig mdzod chen mo*, p. 1203: *mtha' rten gyi dbang*. See also the text mentioned in the introduction to the appendices (reel no. L 235/6): *mtha' brten dang bcas pa'i dbang bskur*. For a detailed treatment of the term *mtha' rten gyi rim pa* as the final ceremonial act of an initiation, see Schuh (1976:90, 96 and passim).

26 I take *rgyab rten* in the sense of *rgyab chos*; see note 9.

nga – rdor sems thugs kyi (kyis) sgrub pa'i (sgrubs pa'i) dngos grub (grubs) bzhi sbyor
Application of the four siddhis according to [the cycle] "Realization of Vajrasattva's Heart".

ca – rdor sems thugs kyi (kyis) sgrub pa'i (sgrubs pa'i) rmi lam kyi (kyis) man ngag
Teaching concerning dreams according to [the cycle] "Realization of Vajrasattva's Heart".

cha – rdor sems thugs kyi (kyis) sgrub pa'i (sgrubs pa'i) gdams pa (rdam pa)
Precepts [concerning the cycle] "Realization of Vajrasattva's Heart".

ja – gnyis 'dzin 'khrul rtsad gcod (brtsad) kyi (kyis) man ngag
Teaching on totally uprooting the aberrations of dualistic grasping.

nya – rdor sems thugs kyi (kyis) sgrub pa'i (sgrubs pa'i) rdzogs rim snang bzhi kyi (kyis) man ngag
"Stage of perfection" (*nispannakrama*) [according to the cycle] "Realization of Vajrasattva's Heart", teaching of the four types of manifestation.[27]

ta – dge sbyor gsang 'dus bzhugs pa'i man ngag
Teaching concerning the resting in the secret gathering, where goodness is practiced.

tha – mgron lam gsum kyi (kyis) man ngag
Teaching concerning the three paths of the wanderer.

da – gsum pa tsha tsha (tsa tsha) 'debs pa'i (deb pa'i) man ngag
Teaching concerning the forming of three sided (?) offering figures.

na – bsnyen (snyen) yig sdig (sdigs) sgrib (sgribs) kun sbyong (sbyongs)
Text on the approaching [the deity], the complete purification of offences and obscurations.

pa – rgyud kyis (= kyi) gser skyems
Libation offering to the lineage [protectors].

pha – dag yig
Orthography.

27 "Four types of manifestation" (*snang ba bzhi*) is a term from the *sNying thig* teachings; see in this respect Namkhai Norbu (1986:101–105).

ba – sbyin sreg (sregs)
Burnt Offerings.

ma – bsnyen (snyan) bsgrub (sgrubs) 'phrin las rnam (rnams) grol lam bzang
Approaching and realizing [the deity], the excellent way to become fully liberated in [all four] activities.

tsa – gnas lung gshin po (shin po) rjes 'dzin dang gson po'i (son po'i) sgrib (sgribs) sbyong (sbyongs)
Showing the place [of rebirth]:[28] Taking care of the dead and purifying the obscurations of the living.

tsha – ro sreg (bsregs) cho ga
Cremation Ritual.

dza – gter ston kyi (kyis) bskang gso
Atonement ritual[29] of the treasure discoverer.

bcas thob (mthob) /
Was received.

de'i brgyud pa ni /
The lineage of this [teaching]:

chos sku kun tu bzang po /
Dharmakāya Samantabhadra

longs sku rdo rje sems dpa' (pa) /
Saṃbhogakāya Vajrasattva

sprul sku dga' rab rdo rje (rdo rjes) /
Nirmāṇakāya dGa'-rab rdo-rje

---

28 I was provided by Sangs-rgyas bstan-'dzin with the following etymology for the expression *gnas lung*: "prediction concerning the next place [of rebirth] of the consciousness in its in-between state" (*bar do'i rnam shes gnas gong mar lung ston pa'o*). Cf. Schuh (1981a:253): "*gnas lung gi cho ga* = Totenzeremonie" (death ceremony), and Schwieger (1985:160): "*gnas lung gi cho ga*: Ritual zur Wegweisung in die [nächste] Existenz" (ritual for pointing the way to the [next] existence).

29 See Karmay (1988a:238): "*bskang gso*—atonement ritual", and Schuh (1973:passim): "*bskang ba* = Zufriedenstellungsritus" (reconciliation rite).

shrī sing ha /
Śrīsiṃha

hūṃ ka ra /
Hūṃkāra

bi ma la /
Vimalamitra

o rgyan pa /
[Padmasambhava,] the one [from] Oḍḍiyāna

ye shes 'tsho (tshogs) rgyal /
Ye-shes 'tsho-rgyal

bai ro tsa na /
Vairocana

gter bdag gling pa /
gTer-bdag gling-pa (1646–1714)

gsang sngags bstan (bsten) 'dzin /
Sangs-sngags bstan-'dzin[30]

kar ma bdud 'joms /
Karma bDud-'joms (1726–1789)[31]

---

30 The man named here is mDo-chen-pa O-rgyan gSang-sngags bstan-'dzin, a direct disciple of gTer-bdag gling-pa and the Fourth Yol-mo-ba Zil-gnon dbang-rgyal rdo-rje; see Tshe-dbang 'Chi-med mgon-po: *Karma bdud 'joms rnam thar*, pp. 40.6–41-41.4. Under gTer-bdag gling-pa he studied, besides the *rDor sems thugs kyi sgrub pa*, the cycles *Thugs rje chen po bde gshegs kun 'dus, A ti zab don snying po* and *Gu ru drag po.*

31 Beside the name Karma bDud-'joms one also finds 'Phrin-las bdud-'joms or Rig-'dzin 'Phrin-las bdud-'joms. He and his father, Rig-'dzin Nyi-ma seng-ge (1687–1738), were both disciples of Kaḥ-thog rig-'dzin Tshe-dbang nor-bu (1698–1755). *Karma bdud 'joms rnam thar* offers a detailed biography; excerpts from the biography are found in Clarke (1983:28–31). But this work, compiled and finalized in the year 1791 (*lcags mo phag*) by mDo-chen-pa Tshe-dbang 'Chi-med mgon-po (1755–1807), provides still further, hitherto untapped details concerning the various *gter ma* lineages in the Nepalese-Tibetan border region. The mother of Karma bDud-'joms, for example, was the daughter of rDo-dmar-ba Mi-'gyur rdo-rje (on this master of the 17th century, whose favourite residence was the Glang-'phrang valley, see *The Collected Works of rDo-dmar Zhabs-drung Mi-'gyur rdo-rje*, Delhi 1981). On the status of Karma bDud-'joms as the Fifth Yol-mo-ba, see note 4 and chapter nine in the present volume.

chos kyi dbang phyug /
Chos-kyi dbang-phyug (1775–1837)[32]

kar ma nges don /
Karma Nges-don[33]

kar ma don 'grub /
Karma Don-grub

bstan (bsten) 'dzin rdo rje (rdo rjes) /
bsTan-'dzin rdo-rje

gsang (bsangs) sngags chos dar /
gSang-sngags chos-dar

rtsa ba'i bla ma rdo rje (rdo rjes) rgyal mtshan zhabs drung du bdag bstan (bsten) 'dzin rdo rje (rdo rjes) legs par thob (mthobs) /
the root teacher rDo-rje rgyal-mtshan. In his presence I, bsTan-'dzin rdo-rje, have duly received [this teaching].

brgyud pa de rnams mi'i (ma'i) bar la khyi ma shor /
With no dog having slipped in between those men who keep the lineage,[34]

steng du rig (rigs) 'dzin gyi (gyis) gral (bral) ma zhig /
with the line of the Vidyādharas not having dissolved above,

---

[32] Here we have Brag-dkar rta-so sprul-sku Chos-kyi dbang-phyug. He is known principally as the author of the comprehensive and very clearly structured biography of Kah-thog rig-'dzin Tshe-dbang nor-bu: *Tshe dbang nor bu'i rnam thar*; he composed, in addition, an extremely informative genealogy of the family of his teacher Karma bDud-'joms: *gTer dbon gdung rabs*. He is the reincarnation of Brag-dkar rdo-rje 'dzin pa Ye-shes chos-grags (1705–1772), who likewise studied under Rig-'dzin Tshe-dbang nor-bu. The founding of the monastery Brag-dkar rta-so in sKyid-grong dates back to lHa-btsun Rin-chen rnam-rgyal (1473–1557), the best- known disciple of gTsang-smyon He-ru-ka (1452–1507).

[33] Cf. *Shar pa'i chos 'byung* (as in note 18), pp. 80.3–81.3, where Karma Nges-don and his disciples are treated. He himself is described in the following words: "The most important of the actual disciples of Brag-dkar Chos-kyi dbang-phyug , Karma Nges-don bstan-spel of the Nyang clan" (*brag dkar chos kyi dbang phyug gi dngos slob gtso bo nyang rigs karma nges don bstan spel*). According to Tshe-dbang 'Chi-med mgon-po: *Karma bdud 'joms rnam thar*, p. 254.4–5, he is also a disciple of Karma bDud-'joms: "the assembly, like that of the teachers from the east—the teacher Karma Nges-don of the Nyang clan etc. ...." (*nyang rigs bla ma karma nges don sogs shar phyogs kyi bla ma dag sogs phyogs 'dus pa ....*). Cf. ibid, p. 205.5: *shar pa'i bla ma nges don pa ....*, and p. 206.3: *bla ma nges don ....* (the transmission of the cycle *Yang tig gi khrid mun* in the years 1788 and 1789).

[34] See note 21.

'og du sman rak (rag) gi (kyis) mtsho ma skams (skam) /
with the ocean of medicine and blood not having dried up below,[35]

bar du gsang (gsangs) sngags rnying ma'i (snying ma'i) bstan pa (bston pa) mi nub cing sgra 'di ri ri ('dir ri) /
may the teaching of the Old Ones not decline in the middle (i.e. in the world of men), and may its voice sound [evermore]!

dkyil 'khor thams (bda') cad kyi (kyis) mdangs ma yal bar khra lam me /
May the radiance of all maṇḍalas, not fading, shine forth [evermore]!

rig (rigs) 'dzin brgyud pa'i bum chu ma skam par 'od si li li (si la li) /
The water in the flask of those who keep the Vidyādhara lineage, not drying up,—may its light pour down!

dam can srung ma'i (bsrungs ma'i) mthu (thugs) rtsal ma 'gags par tsha khyug ge /
The might of the guardians, who have taken the vow, not being stemmed,—may its heat flare!

rdo rje (rdo rjes) theg pa'i byin rlabs (brlabs) ma nyams (nyam) par rtsal thib thib /
The blessing of the Vajrayāna, not decreasing,—may its power increase!

rdo rje (rdo rjes) spun kyi dam tshig ma nyams (nyam) par gtsang lhang nge /
May the vows of the Vajra brothers, not flagging, become ever purer!

yid ches (mchod) khungs (khung) btsun pa'i (rtson pa'i) phyir du /
That [this] source of confidence might be trustworthy [for others],

drin can rtsa ba'i bla ma rdo rje (rdo rjes) rgyal mtshan phyag rtags (ta) khrul med /
from the kind root-teacher rDo-rje rgyal-mtshan [it received] the true hand sign (i.e. thumb print).

nyi ma de ring (din ri) rdo rje (rdo rjes) sems dpa'i (pa'i) dbang legs par thob (thobs) /
(Confirmation:) Duly received on this day the initiation of Vajrasattva.

---

35 See note 22.

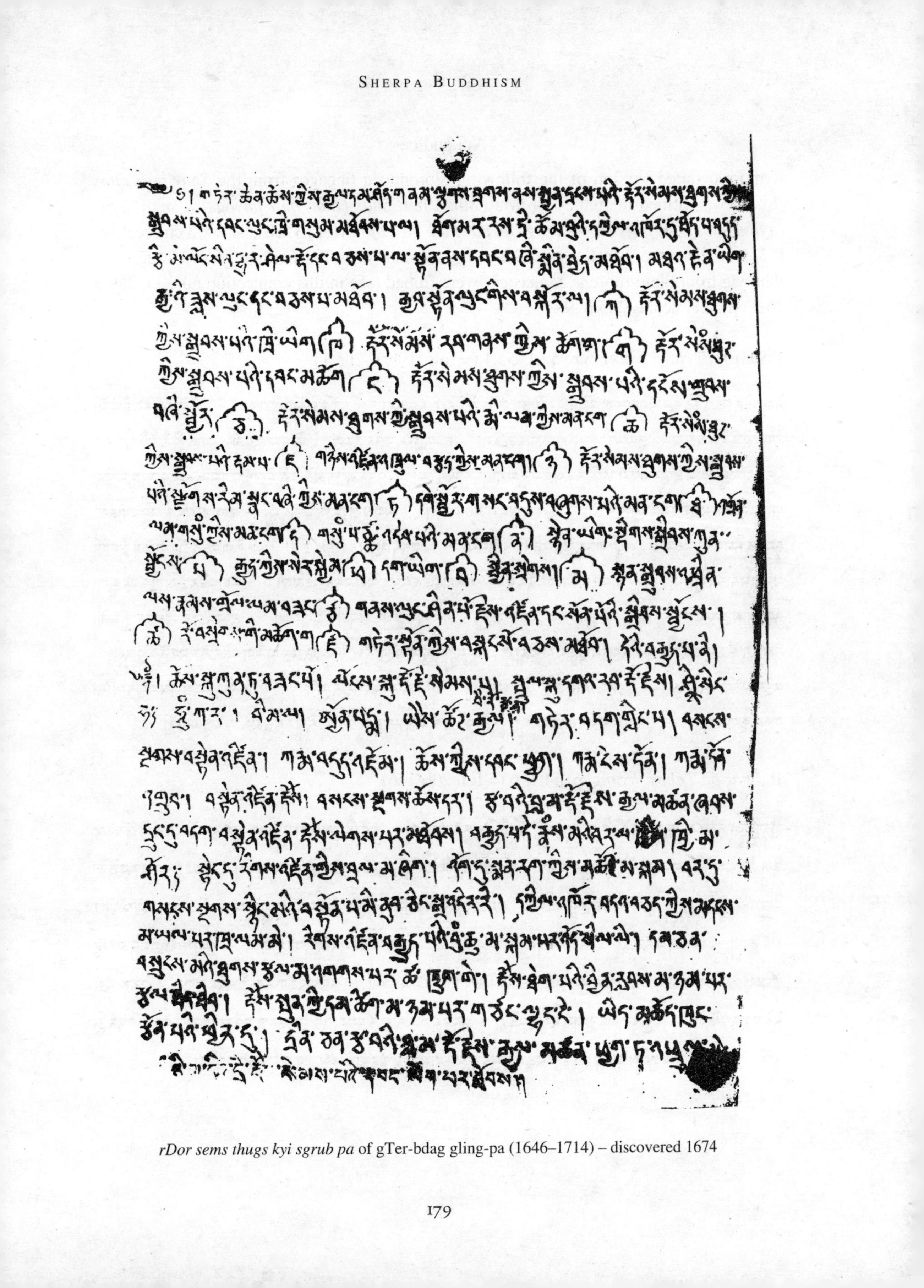

rDor sems thugs kyi sgrub pa of gTer-bdag gling-pa (1646–1714) – discovered 1674

Appendices

A more detailed version of the following reproduced lineages from the *Shar pa'i chos 'byung* was filmed in Junbesi on May 8th, 1989: *Shar khum bu'i phyogs su snga 'gyur rnying ma'i chos brgyud bye brag rim par thob pa'i thob yig*, 13 fols., 41 x 8.5 cm, reel no. L 235/6. The author is mKhan-po Sangs-rgyas bstan-'dzin. Furthermore, seven large-scale *thob yig* from Phug-mo-che Monastery were filmed (see in this connection note 1): 280 x 46.5 cm, reel nos. L 235/8–9.

I. *Shar pa'i chos 'byung*, pp. 52.1–53.1 (= fols. 19b/1–20a/1):

རིག་འཛིན་འཇའ་ཚོན་སྙིང་པོའམ་ལས་འཕྲོ་གླིང་པའི་ཟབ་གཏེར་གྱི་ཆོས་སྐོར་ལའང་། དཀོན་མཆོག་སྤྱི་འདུས། ཞི་ཁྲོ་ངེས་དོན་སྙིང་པོ། ཐུགས་རྗེ་ཆེན་པོ་ནམ་མཁའི་རྒྱལ་པོ། དཔལ་མགོན་མ་ནིང་། རྟ་ཕག་ཡིད་བཞིན་ནོར་བུ། ཚེ་སྒྲུབ་འཆི་མེད་ལྕགས་ཀྱི་རི་བོའི་སྐོར་དང་པོད་དྲུག་བཞུགས་པ་རྗེ་ལྷར་ཐོབ་པའང་རེ་རེ་ནས་ཐོབ་ཚུལ་གཞན་དུ་ཡོད་ཅིང་། འདིར་དཀོན་མཆོག་སྤྱི་ངེས་སྙིང་སྒྲུབ་མའི་དབང་ལུང་ཁྲིད་གསུམ་ལེགས་པར་ཐོབ་པའི་བརྒྱུད་པ་ནི། ཆོས་སྐུ་སྣང་བ་མཐའ་ཡས། ལོངས་སྐུ་ཐུགས་རྗེ་ཆེན་པོ། སྤྲུལ་སྐུ་པད་མ་འབྱུང་གནས། ཉང་བན་ཏིང་འཛིན་བཟང་པོ། གཏེར་སྟོན་འཇའ་ཚོན་སྙིང་པོ། བདུད་འདུལ་ནུས་ལྡན་རྡོ་རྗེ། རིག་འཛིན་ཀློང་གསལ་སྙིང་པོ། པད་མ་བདེ་ཆེན་གླིང་པ། རིག་འཛིན་ཚེ་དབང་ནོར་བུ། རིག་འཛིན་འཕྲིན་ལས་བདུད་འཇོམས། རིག་འཛིན་ཆོས་ཀྱི་དབང་ཕྱུག ཉང་རིགས་ཀར་མ་ངེས་དོན། ཨོ་རྒྱན་གསང་བསྟན་འཛིན། གསང་སྔགས་པད་མ་མཐུ་སྟོབས། རྩ་བའི་བླ་མ་ཡོན་ཏན་རྒྱ་མཚོ། དེས་བདག་ཚོ་རྣམས་ལ་ལེགས་པར་གནང་སྟེ་ཐོབ་པ་ཡིན། ཡང་བརྒྱུད་ཚུལ་གཅིག་ནི། གཞན་འདྲ་ལ་རིག་འཛིན་ཚེ་དབང་ནོར་བུ་ནས། འདྲེན་མཆོག་པད་མ་རྒྱལ་པོ། ཉང་རིགས་རྡོ་རྗེ་འཇིགས་བྲལ། ཀར་མ་ངེས་དོན་བསྟན་འཕེལ། ཨོ་རྒྱན་གསང་སྔགས་བསྟན་འཛིན། གསང་སྔགས་པད་མ་མཐུ་སྟོབས་སམ་པད་མ་ཚེ་དབང་། རྩ་བའི་བླ་མ་ཡོན་ཏན་རྒྱ་མཚོ། དེས་བདག་རྣམས་ལ་བསྒྱུལ་པའོ།

II. *Shar pa'i chos 'byung*, p. 54.1–6 (= fol. 20b/1–6):

སྨིན་གླིང་གཏེར་ཆེན་འགྱུར་མེད་རྡོ་རྗེའི་ཟབ་གཏེར་གྱི་སྐོར་ནི་ཤིན་ཏུ་མང་ནའང་། འདི་ཡི་ཕྱོགས་ལ་བྲ་སྐབས་སུ་དར་བ་རྡོ་སེམས་ཀྱི་སྐོར་ཙམ་ཞིག་ཡིན་པས་དེའི་དབང་ལུང་ཁྲིད་ཀྱི་བརྒྱུད་པ་ནི། ཆོས་སྐུ་ཀུན་ཏུ་བཟང་པོ། ལོངས་སྐུ་རྡོ་རྗེ་སེམས་དཔའ། སྤྲུལ་སྐུ་དགའ་རབ་རྡོ་རྗེ། རིག་འཛིན་ཤྲཱི་སིང་ཧ། སློབ་དཔོན་རྡོ་རྗེ་ཧཱུྃ་མཛད། པཎ་ཆེན་བི་མ་ལ་མི་ཏྲ། སློབ་དཔོན་པད་མ་འབྱུང་གནས། མཁའ་འགྲོ་ཡེ་ཤེས་མཚོ་རྒྱལ། ལོ་ཆེན་བཻ་རོ་ཙ་ན། རིག་འཛིན་གཏེར་བདག་གླིང་པ། རིག་འཛིན་པད་མ་དབང་གྲགས། སྔགས་འཆང་པད་མ་མཐུ་སྟོབས། སྔགས་འཆང་བསྟན་འཛིན་དབང་པོ། ཉང་རིགས་རྡོ་རྗེ་འཇིགས་བྲལ། འདྲེན་མཆོག་ཆོས་ཀྱི་དབང་ཕྱུག ཀར་མ་ངེས་དོན་བསྟན་འཕེལ། ཨོ་རྒྱན་གསང་སྔགས་བསྟན་འཛིན། ཉང་རིགས་པད་མ་ཚེ་དབང་། དྲིན་ཅན་རྩ་བའི་བླ་མ་ངག་དབང་ཡོན་ཏན་རྒྱ་མཚོ། དེས་བདག་ཚོ་ལ་ཐུགས་བརྩེ་བ་ཆེན་པོས་བཟུང་སྟེ་ཕུན་སུམ་ཚོགས་པ་ལྔ་ལྡན་གྱི་སྒོ་ནས་ལེགས་པར་སྩལ་པ་ཡིན།

A Monument of Sherpa Buddhism: The Enlightenment Stūpa in Junbesi

All travellers who have visited the village of Junbesi in Solu-Khumbu in eastern Nepal and have afterwards directed their steps to the monastery of Thub-bstan chos-gling, the residence of 'Khrul-zhig Rin-po-che Ngag-dbang Chos-kyi blo-gros (1924–2011), have passed a *stūpa* at the outskirts of the village, remarkable because of its impressive size. This religious edifice can be identified as one of the set of the eight *caitya*s, or *mchod rten*, commemorating central events in the life of the Buddha Śākyamuni, in this case the enlightenment in Bodhgayā (Fig. 1).

In May 1989, during a microfilm expedition of the Nepal-German Manuscript Preservation Project (NGMPP) to the family temple of bDe-skyid bsam-gling, located in the vicinity of the *stūpa*, a document was filmed which sheds some light on this Tibetan monument and the circumstances surrounding its construction. The document was made accessible by Phur-ba rdo-rje alias Ang rdo-rje, one of the four sons of [Rig-'dzin] 'Gyur-med rdo-rje, the main sponsor of this undertaking. It is written in *dbu can* script on a roll of Nepalese paper 52 x 63.5 cm; it was catalogued under NGMPP reel no. L 251/4 (= running-no. L 2978) (Fig. 2).

A translation of this register is worthwhile for several reasons, the most obvious one being its description of the presence of the teaching tradition of sMin-grol gling in Solu at a time when sTeng-po-che monastery in Khumbu and its mother cloister, rDza-rong phu in Tibet, has just lost their founders. It provides at the same time evidence of the role of different members of the Nyang family as important figures in the history of Sherpa Buddhism—whether as religious teachers or donors—and it gives, of course, a detailed report of the contents of the Enlightenment Stūpa, including how the different relics were inserted into the shrine and which ritual texts were used in the different stages of preparing the building site, the actual construction and the final consecration.

I have added a few notes to the translated text which should help the reader to a fuller understanding of the document. A fresh look at the Enlightnement Stūpa in Junbesi can thus bring home the fact that such religious edifices served the function of both commemorative monument and receptacle of relics: it reminded the Sherpas of the enlightenment of the Buddha Śākyamuni in Bodhgaya, and was considered at the same time as a reliquary of the founders of the monasteries of rDza-rong phu and sTeng-po-che.

Certificate of the Contents of the Enlightenment Stūpa of g.Yu-lding-ma, the Main Monastery of the Glorious Sho-rong [Valley]

May the precious doctrine increase!

[I]
śrī śrī śrī vijayantu!

Having deeply thought of [all] the beings equal to the sky with knowledge and love,
[he finally obtained] in the ocean of countless kalpas the fruit of the two collections [of wisdom and merit]—
to the son of Śuddhodana, to the instantly complete [Buddha Śākyamuni],
I pray with great devotion from the bottom of my heart!

When you [my] protector, being free of fear and [any] faults, in Magadha
obtained the Highest Enlightenment in a single cross-legged position —
a *stūpa* corresponding to this excellent marvellous deed [was erected],
being especially noble and fine [by reason of] its Dharmakāya relics.

Accordingly, at the sacred site of Padma[sambhava] belonging to the royal domain of Li-yul (= Nepal),
in the hidden land of Sho-rong, near [the monastery of] Don-grub chos-gling,
in the valley of medicinal herbs called g.Yu-lding-ma,
a wonderful and incomparable [*stūpa*] was erected: Ala la!

[II]
After this prelude string of verses, spoken by way of an offering, there will [now] be written down a short introduction. The residence where many qualified Kalyānamitras have arrived, including [Bla ma] 'Phags-rtse and [sNgags-'chang] rDo-rje bzang-po [alias] gSer-ba Ye-shes rgyal-mtshan, [all] from the undeceived family of the Upper Great Treasure-Discoverer Nyi-ma'i 'od-zer (1124–1192)[1]—

[1] The "gold" (*gser ba*) lineage of the "Nyang family" (*nyang rigs*) of the Sherpas of eastern Nepal traces its origins back to mNga'-bdag Nyang-ral Nyi-ma'i 'od-zer, the famous treasure-discoverer of the rNying-ma-pa school of Tibetan Buddhism. For the differences in the genealogy of the successors of Nyi-ma'i 'od-zer who kept the family seat in lHo-brag sMra-bo-lcog and those among the descendants who moved to the south of the Everest region, see Childs (1997:24f.). A genealogical record of the members of the Nyang family residing in bDe-skyid chos-gling in Junbesi was filmed by the NGMPP; see *Pha mes kyi byung rabs rin chen gser gyi nyag thag* (24 x 70 cm), reel no. L 251/3 (= running-no. L 2977). This document is used on the following for identifying the different representatives of the family.

which is these days known everywhere as g.Yu-lding-ma, namely [the temple of] bDe-skyid bsam-gling, the main monastery within the hidden land Sho-rong—in this sphere of visible prosperity, [which is] an alpine pasture in a valley of medicinal herbs, the one who is called Nyang-rigs bla-ma Karma Nges-don, formerly erected the perfect form of a monastery.[2]

Both Bla-ma 'Phags-rtse and gSer-ba Ye-shes rgyal-mtshan are remembered as the first members of the Nyang family who settled in present-day Solu. The arrival of Bla-ma 'Phags-rtse is described, for example, in the narrative of how the Nāga goddess Klu-mo dkar-mo became the protective deity of the new area of residence; see Berg (1998:25f.). This story is based on the so-called "History of the Sherpas" (*shar pa'i chos 'byung*) written by mKhan-po Sangs-rgyas bstan-'dzin (1924–1990); see *Shar pa'i chos 'byung sngon med tshang pa'i dbyu gu*, pp 29.1ff. Biographical details on gSer-ba Ye-shes rgyal-mtshan can be found in the so-called "Book of the Bones" (*rus yig*), an important historiographical source for the reconstruction of the arrival of the Sherpas from Khams to the present-day Nepal. This text was located in Me-tog dpag-yas, where the author of the document under investigation hailed from; see Oppitz (1982:292f.). gSer-ba Ye-shes rgyal-mtshan is especially known as the founder of Don-grub chos-gling, the "main monastery" (*dgon gzhung*) of Junbesi. According to the text from Me-tog dpag-yas, he received the name "*Mantradhara*" (*sngags 'chang*) rDo-rje bzang-po from a certain Bla-ma Lo-paṇ ras-chen. This teacher can now be identified as a disciple of gTsang-smyon Heruka (1452–1507), the famous author and editor of bKa'-brgyud-pa hagiographical literature; for the role of Lo-paṇ ras-chen [or Śrī Lo-paṇ-pa] 'Jam-dpal chos-lha, who acted as gTsang-smyon's scribe and secretary and stayed mainly in rGyal-gyi Śrī in La-stod lHo, see Ehrhard (2000a:18, note 16). According to the *Pha mes kyi byung rabs*, line 19, [sNgags-'chang] rDo-rje bzang-po is the son of Bla-ma 'Phags-rtse, and thus the activities of both father and son can be dated to the 16th century; this corresponds quite well to the generally accepted arrival of the first Tibetan settlers in the Everest area.

2 The status of Solu as a "hidden land" (*sbas yul*) has to be seen in the context of prophecies, ascribed to the treasure-discoverer Ratna gling-pa (1403–1478), which were the motivating force behind the Sherpas' migration to the region of Khumbu; see Buffetrille (2000:276–281). This information is based on a pilgrimage guidebook for Solu, written by mKhan-po Sangs-rgyas bstan-'dzin and his disciple Padma thar-phyin (born 1963). It bears the title *sBas yul khum bu shod lung gi gnas bshad du babs lung bstan mdor bsdus*; see (ibid:254f.). The region of Solu is described in this text as being topographically situated in "the lower valley of the hidden land Khum-bu", modern-day Solu obviously deriving its name from the toponym "lower valley" (*shod lung*). The name "Gorge of the White Willow" (*sho rong*) used in the document under investigation is not attested elsewhere; most Tibetan sources available to me speak normally of Solu as the "Gorge of the Mountain Ridges" (*[g]shong[s] rong*).

The temple Don-grub chos-gling was re-established by rDo-rje 'jigs-bral, another member of the Nyang family. According to the *Pha mes kyi byung rabs*, lines 19–25, rDo-rje 'jigs-bral alias Rig-'dzin dbang-po, followed six generations after [sNgags-'chang] rDo-rje bzang-po. This new foundation can be dated to the middle or second half of the 18th century; see Ehrhard (1993a:87, note 18) and chapter ten in the present volume. The foundation of bDe-skyid bsam-gling or g.Yu-lding-ma, a temple located above Don-grub chos-gling, is in general ascribed to Karma Don-grub (1850–1931), the great-grandson of rDo-rje 'jigs-bral; the designation main monastery seems to have been appropriated for this new edifice. For information on Karma Don-grub, see Ehrhard (1993a:88, note 20) and chapter ten in the present volume. The fact that the document under investigation mentions a certain Karma Nges-don as the person responsible for the foundation of the new temple might be explained by his role as teacher of Karma Don-grub. It is further known that Karma Nges-don was one of those members of the Nyang family, who travelled in the 18th/19th centuries to Mang-yul Gung-thang and followed the teaching tradition of Karma

Although [this site] generated a great wave [of deeds] for the benefit of the doctrine and beings, by the force of time a great earthquake occurred, and thus the conditions for destruction emerged. Because of that, rDza-sprul Ngag-dbang bsTan-'dzin nor-bu (1867–1940), the embodiment of the Great Translator g.Yu-sgra snying-po, the one whose name is hard to pronounce (i.e. who just passed away), and the music of whose fame pervades the three grounds (= the earth, below the earth and above the earth), requested on behalf of Nyang-gdung bla-ma Rig-'dzin 'Gyur-med rdo-rje [the abbot] Ācārya Ngag-dbang rgyal-mtshan of sTeng[-po-che] dgon[-pa] Theg-mchog gling to come [to that site with the words:] "It should be erected in that way!" and by setting down the golden spot of the disciple on his forehead.[3]

On the fifth day of the second month of the fire-snake year of the 16th *rab byung* (= 1941), [at the time of] a good constellation of the planets and stars, extensive smoke and libation offerings were made, and then the earth was pacified by means of the [rituals of the cycle] *Tshogs las rin chen phreng ba*. According to the words of dByangs-can grub-pa'i rdo-rje, the master from dNgul-chu (1809–1887), the measurement [of the *stūpa*] was set down devoid of faults and

---

'Phrin-las bdud-'joms (1726–1789) and Brag-dkar rta-so sprul-sku Chos-kyi dbang-phyug (1775–1837). For theses relationships and the names of further members of the Nyang family associated with the tradition of Brag-dkar rta-so, the famous retreat site of the great yogi Mi-la-ras-pa, see Ehrhard (1993a:93, note 33) and chapter ten in the present volume, as well as Ehrhard (1997c:262, note 21) and chapter twenty-four in the present volume.

[3] The monastery of sTeng-po-che in the Khumbu region was founded in the year 1915, and the final consecration took place in the year 1919; these are the dates given in the *Shar pa'i chos 'byung* (as in note 1), pp. 60.6–62.6. The person responsible for its construction was sTeng-po-che bla-ma Ngag-dbang Nor-bu bzang-po (1848–1934), who had acted upon the advice of his teacher rDza-sprul Ngag-dbang bsTan-'dzin nor-bu, the head of rDza-rong phu monastery on the northern side of the Everest range and spiritual authority of the Sherpas at the beginning of the 20th century. For the founding and building of sTeng-po-che, see Ortner (1989:129–138); refer to Nimri Aziz ((1978:209–215) for the religious career of rDza-sprul Ngag-dbang bsTan-'dzin nor-bu (and that of 'Khrul-zhig Kun-bzang mthong-grol rdo-rje), the construction of the rDza-rong phu monastery in Dingri in 1902, and the spiritual influence of these teachers.

The sTeng-po-che monastery in Khumbu was heavily damaged by the great earthquake on 15 January 1934, and the same earthquake had caused the destruction of the temple of bDe-skyid bsam-gling in Solu. For this Himalayan earthquake of great intensity, the area of greatest devastation having been North Bihar and Nepal, see Chaudhary (1995:56f.); this reference I owe to David P. Jackson. Shortly before his death the rDza-rong phu bla-ma obviously sent Ngag-dbang rgyal-mtshan, the successor of Ngag-dbang Nor-bu bzang-po in sTeng-po-che, to Solu in order to complete the reconstruction of bDe-skyid bsam-gling with the erection of the Enlightenment Stūpa. The connection between the Nyang family from Solu and the monastery in Khumbu had been quite close, the previously mentioned Karma Don-grub having been one of the three main donors for the construction of sTeng-po-che; see Ortner (1989:101, 108, 129f. and 145). According to the *Pha mes kyi byung rabs,* line 30, [Rig-'dzin] 'Gyur-med rdo-rje, the main sponsor for the Enlightenment Stūpa in Junbesi, was the only son of Karma Don-grub.

errors and stone masons, including Zla-ba nor-bu from Gangs-ri khang-sa, were invited. The side of the foundation was fifteen cubits, and [the height of the *stūpa*] from the foundation up to the tip was thirty cubits. The sun and the moon of the umbrella top was manufactured from [an alloy of] gold and copper, [and] the offering pole for the goddesses (i.e. the *yaṣṭī*], which was full of heaps of the four kinds of relics, was prepared in a perfect way with the help of virtue collected before (i.e. in an earlier life).[4]

[III]

[Now] a short explanation of the way in which were offered the series of the insertions of the *dhāraṇī*s into that [*stūpa*]. Into the "lion throne" were meticulously deposited meritorious implements which possess the quality for [promoting] happiness in the worldly realm, headed up by a [depiction of] a circle [encompassing] Gaṇapati and male and female *yakṣa*s, together with a treasure vase for the fertility of the soil, impregnated with the blessings of the spiritual realization of the Mahāvajradhara rDza-sprul [Ngag-dbang bsTan-'dzin nor-bu], a great copper vessel replete with a streaming variety of earth and stones from pilgrimage places all over India and Tibet, a variety of pills and grains, different jewels, the sweet smell of painted and carved [representations of] the eight auspicious symbols and objects and the seven precious stones—[all this] filled [to the brim] and enclosed with a lid—and so forth.

In the first "step" were properly contained, in a standard-size copper vessel, [first] the Dharmakāya or Dharma relics, [namely] the print of the *dhāraṇī* [collection] in the sMin[-grol] gling [tradition], [which is] a sealed pronouncement [consisting of] section *na,* the Mantras of the Dharmapālas, [and] section *dza,* the cycle of the Sūtrapiṭaka.

---

4 The text by means of which the *sa 'dul* was performed seems to be the cycle *Tshogs las rin chen phreng ba* of the Third Karma-pa Rang-byung rdo-rje (1284–1339). This collection of works is devoted to the spiritual practice of the "demon as the object to be cut off" (*bdud kyi gcod yul*). The Third Karma-pa is known to have been the main link by which this tradition entered the Karma bKa'-brgyud-pa school of Tibetan Buddhism. The codification of these *gCod* teachings was later developed by Karma chag-med alias Rāga-asya (1603–1671), who was another major contributor to the Karma bKa'-brgyud *gCod* and the editor of Rang-byung rdo-rje's *Tshogs las rin chen phreng ba*; on this transmission of *gCod* teachings, see Gyatso (1985:335f.).

The work used as a proportional manual for the construction of an enlightenment *stūpa* is from the pen of the dGe-lugs-pa master dByangs-can grub-pa'i rdo-rje. His collected writings contain such a work with the title *mChod rten gyi thig rtsa bklag pa'i sgrub pa* (9 fols.); see the catalogue *Zhwa ser bstan pa'i sgron me rje tsong kha pa chen pos gtsos skyes chen dam pa rim byung gi gsung 'bum dkar chag phyogs gcig tu bsgrigs pa'i dri med zla shel gtsang ma'i me long*, Hsinhua: Bod ljongs mi dmangs dpe skrun khang, 1990, p. 693.26. For the translation of the proportional manual of an enlightenment *stūpa* written by Bu-ston Rin-chen grub (1290–1364), see Pema Dorjee (1996:143–150).

In the fourth "step" were properly contained the *yaṣṭī* [of] Deodar, the wood of the gods, with unreversed signs of the cardinal directions [and] richly incised with mantras and the five classes of the great *dhāraṇīs*. At the [lower] end [of it were placed]: five complete [sets of] the extensive version of the *dhāraṇī* [collection] in the sMin[-grol gling tradition], whatever amount [was possible] of the medium version of the *dhāraṇī* [collection in the sMin-grol gling tradition], forty-eight paper ribbons of the print from sTeng[-po]-che [dgon-pa] of the Samantabhadra *dhāraṇī*, twenty-three paper ribbons of the Mahāvidyā [*dhāraṇī*], five hundred [paper ribbons] of the Hundred Syllable [*dhāraṇī* of Vajrasattva], two hundred fifteen paper ribbons of the *dMigs brtse ma* [prayer], eighteen paper ribbons of the Arapatsa [*dhāraṇī* of Mañjuśrī], forty-eight sheets of the [*Ārya-*] *dhvaja-agrakeyūra* [*-nāma-dhāraṇī*], sixty-three [sheets of the *dhāraṇī*] *mChod rten* [*gcig btab na*] *bye ba* [*btab par*] *'gyur* [*ba*, thirty-eight sheets of the *Uṣṇīṣavijayā-dhāraṇī*, sixteen sheets of [the *dhāraṇī* of] Seng[-ge] gdong[-ma], the Vajraguru [dhāraṇī of Padmasambhava], the Ṣaḍakṣarī [*dhāraṇī* of Avalokiteśvara] and so forth—whatever amount [was possible], beyond any imagination.

[Furthermore] thirty-eight paintings of the thirty-five Buddhas [of confession], each a receptacle of the Buddha's body, one print each of [the cycle *Thugs rje chen po*] *bde* [*gshegs*] *kun* [*'dus*] of sMin-gling [gTer-bdag gling-pa] (1646–1714) and [the depiction of] the succession of the [individual members of the] incarnation chain of the Great Treasure-Discoverer; one [print of the] teacher [Buddha Śākyamuni] surrounded by the "Eight Great Sons" (*aṣṭamahāputra*), thirty images of the three roots (i.e. bla ma, yi dam, mkha' 'gro ma) of the *Bla* [*ma thugs*] *sgrub* [cycle] of 'Ja'-tshon snying-po (1585–1656), thirty-four paintings of the well-established Dharmakāya, including the one of the valley of [Jo-mo] Tshe-ring-ma, [the one] where the receptacles of [Buddha's] body, speech [and] mind are united, and the one of the *stūpa* with the wheel [of the Kalyānamitras who are] energetic about their vows. [There were contained] as well twenty-two "All-good-Wheels" [of visual poetry], together with ten ["All-good-]Wheels" of [the goddess] Tārā.[5]

---

5 The Tibeto-Buddhist *stūpa* in all its styles comprises the "lion throne" (*seng khri*), the intermediate section (the six symbolic structures from the "base of the virtues" (*rmang dge ba bcu*) up to the *harmikā*), and the upper section (all the structures from the "lotus that supports an umbrella" (*gdugs 'degs pad*) up to the spherical pinnacle); see Pema Dorjee (1996:61–65). The first up to the fourth steps are immediately above the "base of ten virtues". The different kinds of relics were placed into the lower section of the *stūpa* and that part of the intermediate section consisting of the four steps. For the literary genre dealing with the actual process of consecration, the so-called "texts on inserting dhāraṇīs" (*gzungs 'bul*), see Martin (1994:304f.); a selective bibliography of this type of literature can be found in Bentor (1996:367–

[IV]
Second, the corporal relics: the salted remains of the noble guide [rDza-sprul] Ngag-dbang bsTan-'dzin nor-bu, sātstsha [relics] manufactured from clay [amounting to roughly four thousand eight hundred items and] the receptacle of the Dharmakāya, mixed with the [crushed] bones of sTeng[-po]-che bla-ma Ngag-dbang Nor-bu bzang-po.

Third, the clothing relics: hair of the noble guide 'Khrul-zhig Kun-bzang mthong-grol rdo-rje (born 1862), [Mahā]vajradhara rDza-sprul [Ngag-dbang bsTan-'dzin nor-bu], [and] sTeng[-po-che] dgon[-pa] bla-ma [Ngag-dbang Nor-bu bzang-po].

Fourth, the mustard seed-like relics: "increasing bone" of [Buddha] Kāśyapa, the flesh of a seven-times reborn [Brahmin], whose taste is the basis of liberation, the flesh of the treasure-discoverer Ratna gling-pa (1403–1478), pellets from Tsa-ri [brought by] the precious rDza-sprul [Ngag-dbang bsTan-'dzin nor-bu]; "maṇi pellets" [which are] a nectareous Dharma medicine, a selection of medicine, including that of Ācārya [Padmasambhava], the mighty [Buddha Śākya]muni [and the goddess] Tārā; pellets of sacred substances in which the support is condensed; Dharma medicine of the sMin[-grol] gling [tradition]; nectareous pellets [and] sacred substances of the Sa-skya [tradition]; "maṇi pellets" mixed with the starter which had come forth from the treasure [discovery of the cycle] *Byang gter thugs rje chen po* [of rGod-ldem 'phru-can (1337–1406)]. [All this] was placed there, together with leaves of the Tree of Enlightenment in Vajrāsana (= Bodhgayā).[6]

---

369). These texts provide a general classification of relics into four or five categories: 1. "Dharmakāya relics" (*chos sku ring bsrel*), 2. "Dharma relics" (*chos kyi ring bsrel*), 3. "corporeal relics" (*sku gdung ring bsrel*), 4. "clothing relics" (*sku bal ring bsrel*), 5. "mustard seed-like relics" (*yungs 'bru lta bu'i ring bsrel*). As the wording of the document under investigation suggests, the first two categories can collapse into one and then one arrives at the number of four kinds of relics. For a description of the historical process by which Buddhist formulas like the *dhāraṇīs* came to serve as relics, involving the association of organic and spiritual *śarīra*, see Fontein (1995:26–28).

As both rDza-rong phu monastery in Tibet and sTeng-po-che monastery in Nepal followed the teaching tradition of sMin-grol gling in dBus, it is not surprising to find specific *dhāraṇī* from that tradition inserted into the Enlightenment Stūpa in Junbesi. For the spread of the treasure-cycles of 'Ja'-tshon snying-po and gTer-bdag gling-pa in the region of Solu, see Ehrhard (1993a:81-96) and chapter ten in the present volume. For the little-known form of Avalokiteśvara called "Lord of the Dance" (*gar dbang*), which has as its textual source the treasure-cycle *Thugs rje chen po bde gshegs kun 'dus* of gTer-bdag gling-pa, refer to Kohn (1997:368); the *maṇi ril grub* festival, which originated in the rDza-rong phu monastery and was practised in public rituals in the Khumbu region is based on this particular form of Mahākāruṇika.

6 The last category in the above-mentioned relic classification, including "increasing bones" (*'phel gdung*) or "pearls" which manifest from the physical bodies of Buddhist saints, occupies a unique place

In a carved-out opening in the *yaṣṭī* there were [also] contained and spread out some [more items, namely part of the above-mentioned] mustard seed-like relics and [copies of the] pure *Uṣṇīṣavijayā-dhāraṇī* and so forth.

Also [in the *stūpa*] were a small box sealed with *la la* ink and set out [there]—so that [even] a destructive man would insert it in a vase of crystal—with two statues, a big and a small one, of the Eleven-faced Avalokiteśvara, released from the hands of Smyung-gnas bla-ma Shes-rab rdo-rje (1884–1945); an old statue if the mighty [Buddha Śākya]muni, one cubit high, [and a statue of] Vajrapāṇi, just six inches high. In front of [these icons were] painted and carved [items] as described above, including [depictions of] two rivers, [all kinds of] necessities, the eight auspicious symbols and so forth, together with vajra [and] ghaṇṭā, a stream of earth [and] stones [from pilgrimage sites], pellets, nāga medicine and so forth.

Inside the sun and moon [on top of the *stūpa*] were contained [amulets] liberating when worn [on one's own body], [in accordance with] the *mKha' 'gro snying thig* [cycle] of Klong-chen [rab-'byams-pa] (1308–1364); [and] as much as [possible] of the [*sNying thig tantra*] *Sangs rgyas sras gcig*.[7]

---

in the Tibetan cult of relics. Especially appreciated among treasure-discoverers of the rNying-ma-pa school are the so-called "pellets of Brahmin flesh". Such sacred substances were found, for example, by Ratna gling-pa at a treasure site called dGe-ri in the year 1438; for an assessment of this finding and the observation that "increasing bones" are among those items which bridge the divide between relics and miraculous events, see Martin (1994:280 & 295). Another famous rNying-ma-pa treasure-discoverer who unearthed relics and sacred substances [which like a Tibetan beer starter could be used for the production of maṇi pellets] is rGod-ldem 'phru-can. The cycle of the Mahākāruṇika teachings of the "Northern Treasures" (*byang gter*), discovered by him, is generally known as *Phyi sgrub 'gro ba kun grol* and forms together with the *Nang sgrub rig 'dzin gdung sgrub* and the *gSangs sgrub guru sngon po* respectively the "outer, inner and secret" *sādhana*s of the Byang-gter tradition; see Ehrhard (1996a:59, note 9) and chapter nineteen in the present volume.

[7] The Bhutanese master Shes-rab rdo-rje, who is called "teacher of the fasting ritual" (*smyung gnas bla ma*), arrived in Nepal with orders to carry out a renovation of the Svayambhūcaitya on behalf of the king of Bhutan. He stayed afterwards in sKyid-grong in the region of Mang-yul Gung-thang and constructed a first monastery in sPang-zhing in the year 1922. There followed more such foundations in various Himalayan valleys, including [b]Tsum and Yol-mo [gangs-rwa]; this teacher of the 'Brug-pa bKa'-brgyud-pa school is also known to have been active in the "eastern gorges" (*rong shar*), namely the area populated by the Sherpas. For a sketch of his life, see Dobremez & Jest (1976:120f.).

Klong-chen rab-'byams-pa, the great codifier and commentator of the rDzogs-chen tradition of the rNying-ma-pa school, is especially famous for the way he systematized the traditions of both the *mKha' 'gro snying thig* and the *Bi ma snying thig*; for his role in the transmission in the "Seminal Heart Teachings of the Ḍakiṇīs", see, for example, Germano & Gyatso (2000:251–265). The title of the *sNying thig Tantra* called "The only son of the Buddha" (*sangs rgyas sras gcig*) could refer to the work *bsTan pa bu gcig gi rgyud gser gyi snying po nyi ma rab tu snang byed*, which is part of the "Seminal Heart Teachings of Vima[lamitra]"; this short text, in either calligraphic or printed form, can be worn on the body as an amulet.

All the above-mentioned *dhāraṇī*s, moreover, were packed in fine silk, which was applied with faultless signs, and the method of wherever inserting them [was] the practice of sMin[-grol] gling; like a beautiful stream, a [river] Gaṅgā of healing medicine, they were inserted above [and] below (i.e. in the first and the fourth "steps"], and afterwards wrapped properly in Chinese *a shed* [and] *sman rtse* silk. In order that no damage by water occurs, it was [all] properly overlaid with wax and covered thickly with birch bark.

It may be added just how much was used for expenditures [and] the different ways of offering the various kinds of precious stones, [such as] turquoise [and] *byu ru*, has not surfaced in written form. And if I wrote it down, this would [only] turn into the fault of showing off one's virtue.

[V]
Additional ritual observances which followed, including the empowerment of the *dhāraṇī*s, were also performed in the right way. This receptacle now: earlier we imagined the service for the doctrine and the beings [only] as an object for the weariness of others, [but] after the wish had been approved to erect a noble receptacle where one and all are able to collect merit, we consider it now mainly as the reliquary of the noble guides bearing the name Ngag-dbang, father [and] son, [these] two (= rDza-sprul Ngag-dbang bsTan-'dzin nor-bu and sTeng-po-che bla-ma Ngag-dbang Nor-bu bzang-po), and indeed the erection of it [has resulted in] exceedingly great merit. As the [Third Karma-pa] Rang-byung rdo-rje has said:

The relics if the Jinas [are] most excellent jewels:
they make all one's wishes come true.
The bones of the Śrāvakas, Pratyekabuddhas [and] Bodhisattvas,
and likewise those of ones [who were] possessed of yogic [powers] —
when one makes offerings [to them] and wears them on one's body,
no evil spirits are able to cause calamity there.

Therefore, if one holds [to that receptacle] and sees, hears and remembers [it], one is able to clear away all the sins [and] obscurations, collected over a thousand kalpas, and successively attains [all] the qualities of the Buddhist "path" (*mārga*) and "[the ten] levels [of a Bodhisattva]" (*daśabhūmi*).

Not only [that]; the most sublime benefit above everything else [is] the [one derived from] making offerings to the teacher and praying to him. If those possessed of knowledge wish to see [this benefit] now to some extent, in the way explained in all the *Sūtra*s [and] [*Tantra*s], they will understand it if they see it there. There is no need for people like me to report succinctly by [mere] repetition.

Given that there should be contained as many of sātstsha [relics in the reliquary as possible], it was fitting to prepare an extensive [number of them]. Fearing that they could disappear into a cleft or that damage might occur to the receptacle, just [the right amount] was inserted [into the *stūpa*]. In order that all these [sātstsha relics] would not be consumed until future times, [still more] were properly put in tin cans or the like, and the correct practices having been performed, covering [them] securely with a lid and so forth, and the sealing with in *la la* ink and [wrapping up in birch] bark, [the items] were inserted into an opening properly hollowed out of a wall. In continuation [thereof] prayers were offered to the end that not too long [in the future] these [remaining] sātstsha [relics] would be inserted in a *stūpa* to be erected as an additional son (i.e. replica) equivalent to the [original] *stūpa* in the main monastery or the lower one [by] whoever would rejoice in doing so.

[VI]
After this amazing great receptacle had been properly completed with the period of two months, on Wednesday, the second day of what is known as the month of Vaiśakhā, [the day of] the coming together of the three superior festivals [of Buddha Śākyamuni], including the memorial of the Fearless Jina's Complete Enlightenment in Vajrāsana, [the texts] *Thugs* [*rje*] *chen* [*po bde gshegs kun 'dus*] of the sMin[-grol] gling [tradition] and the *Rab gnas dge legs 'dod 'jo'i* [*yon bdag bsgo ba'i stong thun nyer kho* of gTer-bdag gling-pa were recited according to] the main and lower [monasteries]. And when from the lower [monastery] the consecration ritual was properly performed, the Ācārya and all the craftsmen together with their friends had to be made glad with presents, and clear and ringing songs of good luck had to be intoned [in the main monastery]![8]

---

[8] The literary source for the quotation of the Third Karma-pa concerning the beneficial effect of the Buddhist relics has not yet been identified. It is not contained in the above-mentioned cycle *Tshogs las rin chen phreng ba* (see note 4).

Concerning the texts used for the consecration of the Enlightenment Stūpa in Junbesi, it should be noted that there exist actually two works of gTer-bdag gling-pa on the consecration ritual, each bearing the title "Wish-fulfilling Cow of [All] Auspicious Things"; see Bentor (1996:358): *Rab gnas dge legs 'dod 'jo'i yon bdag bsgo ba'i stong thun nyer mkho* and *rTen gsum rab tu gnas pa'i cho ga gde legs 'dod 'jo*. I have opted for the first text, since it highlights the role of the donor in the title—an important consideration in the context of a public consecration ritual.

[VII]
Saying [it] once more:

According to the instructions on how to build [it] from the completely pure *Tantra*s and authoritative scriptures,
a *stūpa* has been produced in a perfect way, [and so] become the field of complete liberation and merit:
the complete number of materials and offerings having been put together by [Nyang-gdung bla-ma] Rig-'dzin 'Gyur-med [rdo-rje], the permanent sponsor of completely white [motivation].

By performing the service of erecting a receptacle in such a way,
needless to say, one will attain enlightenment.
By seeing, hearing, remembering [and] touching [it], one plants the seed for a "higher rebirth" (*abhyudaya*) and for [the state of] "true happiness" (*niśreyasa*).
[Knowing this], who would not become full of faith?

Thus, by making prostrations [and] circumambulations with one's body,
by making distinct [and] well-sounding prayers with one's voice,
[and] with a completely pure [motivation of] "special insight" (*adhyāya*) [and a feeling of] gladness in one's mind —
one should eagerly offer food, fragrant water and silken shawls [to the *stūpa*]!

E ma [ho]! By the power of having achieved these marvellous virtues,
may the doctrine of the Jina be spread, and the community of those who hold it,
may the span of their lives and the labour of their deeds increase like the waxing moon,
and may all living beings travel to the paradise of "Great Bliss" (*sukhāvatī*)!

[VIII]
When this great noble receptacle, a marvellous and elegant [structure,] had been erected at the main monastery of g.Yu-lding-ma, the order came from Ācārya Ngag[-dbang] rgyal[-mtshan] of sTeng-po-che dgon-pa: "A small certificate of the contents [of the *stūpa* accompanied by] words of praise must be written down!" and as accordingly the disciple of the noble man, Nyang-rigs O-rgyan bstan-'dzin [alias A-yu] from Me-tog dpag-yas wrote it down in the way it came to his mind, may the appearance of good virtue be the cause that in all directions the doctrine of the Jina will remain for a long time to come !

May it be virtuous! Sarva mangalaṃ!

Transliteration of the Tibetan Document

// dPal gyi sho rong dgon gzhung g.yu lding ma'i byang chub mchod rten bzhugs byang nyung gsal lhag bsam rnam dkar sgron me zhes bya ba bzhugs so // dge legs 'phel // [2]

// pra ham sta de śa na ha ri ṇyum? // // bstan pa rin po che rgyas par gyur cig // [3]

[I]
// śrī śrī śrī bhī dzayantu /
mkha' mnyam 'gro la mkhyen brtses rab dgongs nas /
grangs med bskal pa rgya mtsor tshogs gnyis 'bras /
lhun por rdzogs pa'i zas gtsang sras po la /
snying nas gus pa chen po'i (= *pos*) *gsol ba 'debs /* [4]

mgon khyod mi 'jigs skyon bral mā gha dhar (= *ma ga dhar*) */*
skyil krung gcig la byang chub mchog brnyes tshe /
ngo mtshar mdzad bzang dang mthun mchod pa'i rten /
chos sku'i ring bsrel khyad 'phags legs bskrun ltar /

li yul rgyal khams char gtogs padma'i gnas / [5]
sbas yul sho rong don grub chos gling gi /
nye 'dabs g.yu lding ma zhes sman ljongs su /
rmad byung 'gran bral bzhengs so a la la /

[II]
zhes mchod par brjod pa'i tshig phreng sngon du song nas gleng gzhi mdo tsam bris pa la / gter ston chen po gong ma nyi [6] *ma 'od zer gdung brgyud 'khrul bral 'phags rtse dang rdo rje bzang po gser ba ye shes rgyal mtshan sogs tshad ldan dge ba'i bshes gnyen du ma byon pa'i gdan sa / sbas yul sho rong nang mtshan* (= *tshan*) *dgon gzhung don grub chos gling nye 'dab* (= *'dabs*) *bde skyid bsam gling ngam* [7] *dengs skabs yongs grags g.yu lding ma zhes sman ljongs ne'u bsing mngon par bkra pa'i khams su / sngar nyang rigs bla ma karma nges don zhes bya bas dgon pa'i bkod pa phun tshogs bzhengs nas bstan 'gro'i don rlabs po che mdzad kyang dus dbang gis sa g.yo chen* [8] *po zhig byung nas 'jig rkyen byung bar rten* (= *brten*) */ nyang gdung bla ma rig 'dzin 'gyur med rdo rje la / lo tsā chen po g.yu sgra snying po'i yang srid mtshan brjod par dka' ba rdza sprul ngag dbang bstan 'dzin nor bu zhes snyan pa'i rol mo sa gsum khyab pa nyid nas / 'di ltar bzhengs* [9] *dgos pa'i bka' slob gser thig spyi bor lhung bas*

steng dgon theg mchog gling gi slob dpon ngag dbang rgyal mtshan phebs zhus te / rab byung bcu drug pa'i lcags sprul zla ba gnyis pa'i tshes lnga gza' skar 'phrod sbyor bzang bar bsang brngan gser skyems rgyas [10] *par mchod gnas / tshogs las rin chen phreng ba'i sgo nas sa btul / dngul chu rje dbyangs can grub pa'i rdo rje'i gsung ltar tha chad skyon bral tshad la phab cing rdo bzo sgang ri khang sa zla ba nor bu sogs bsus te sa 'dzin rgyar khru bco lnga / sa 'dzin nas tog gi bar* [11] *khru sum cu / gdugs tog nyi zla gser zangs las sgrub pa ring bsrel rnam bzhi'i phyur bur gtams pa'i lha mo'i mchod sdong sngon bsags dge ba'i dpung pas phul phyin grub shing /*

[III]

de nang gzungs 'bul rim pa ji ltar phul tshul mdo tsam zhus pa [12] *la / seng khri'i nang du gnod sbyin pho mo tshogs bdag 'khor lo sa bcud bum gter bcas rdza sprul rdo rje 'chang chen po'i sgrub pa'i byin ldan gtsos 'jig rten khams su bde skyid ldan pa'i bsod nams lag cha / rgya bod yongs kyi gnas chen rnams kyi sa sna* [13] *rdo sna chu rgyun ril bu 'bru sna rin po sna tshogs bkra shis rtags rdzas brgyad rin chen sna bdun bris 'bur dri bzang gis khengs par zangs bum che ba zhig bkang la kha gcod bkag pa sogs nan tan bgyis la bzhugs su gsol / bang rim dang por chos* [14] *sku'am chos kyi ring bsrel smin gling gzungs par bka' rgya ma na pa chos skyong sngags dang dza pa mdo sde'i skor zangs bum tshad ldan zhig du legs par bzhugs / bang rim bzhi bar (= par) lha shing de ba dā ru phyogs rtags ma log par srog shing sngags* [15] *dang gzungs chen sde lnga bcas rgyas par bris mthar / smin gling gzungs rgyas pa cha tshang lnga / gzungs 'bring gang mang / steng che'i spar kun bzang gzungs shog ldebs gras kha* 48 (/) *rig pa chen po shog gras* 23 (/) *yig brgya* 500 (/) *dmigs* [16] *brtse ma* 215 (/) *a ra pa tsa shog gras* 18 (/) *rgyal mtshan rtse mo'i dpung rgyan ldeb* 48 (/) *mchod rten bye 'gyur* 63 (/) *uṣṇiṣa ldeb* 38 (/) *seng gdong ldeb* 16 (/) *ba dzra gu ru yig drug sogs gang mang bsam las 'das pa dang / sku rten sangs rgyas so lnga'i* [17] *zhal thang* 38 (/) *smin gling bde kun dang gter chen sku 'phreng rim byon sku par re re / ston par nye sras brgyad kyis bskor ba gcig / 'ja' tshon bla sgrub rtsa gsum snang brnyan* 30 (/) *sku gsung thugs rten gsum 'dzom tshe ring ljongs dang sdom* [18] *brtson 'khor lo mchod rten sogs bkod legs chos sku'i zhal thang* 34 (/) *gzhan yang kun bzang 'khor lo* 22 (/) *sgrol ma'i 'khor lo bcu bcas kyang bzhugs /*

[IV]

gnyis pa sku gdung ring bsrel 'dren mchog ngag dbang bstan 'dzin nor [19] *bu'i gdung tshwa dang steng che bla ma ngag dbang nor bu bzang po'i sku rus bsres pa'i chos sku'i rten 'jim pa las grub pa'i sātstsha bzhi stong brgyad brgya brdal tsam dang / gsum pa sku bal ring bsrel 'dren mchog 'khrul zhig kun bzang mthong* [20] *grol rdo rje / rdza sprul rdo rje 'chang / steng dgon bla ma'i dbu lo sogs dang / bzhi pa yungs 'bru lta bu'i ring bsrel 'od srung 'phel gdung / myong grol rten skye bdun sku sha gter ston ratna gling sku sha / rdza sprul rin po che'i rtsa ri ril bu / bdud rtsi chos sman* [21] *ma ṇi ril bu sman 'dam slob dpon / thub dbang / sgrol ma bcas dang / rten bsdus dam rdzas ril bu / smin gling chos sman / sa skya'i dam rdzas bdud rtsi ril bu / byang gter thugs chen gter byon phab gta'* (= *phabs rta*) *bsres pa'i ma ṇi ril bu / rdo rje gdan* [22] *kyi byang chub shing lo bcas bzhugs / gong gi yungs 'bru lta bu'i ring bsrel char gtogs 'ga' dang gtsug gtor rnam rgyal dri med gzungs sogs srog shing la khung bu brus te spros par bzhugs / gzhan yang smyung gnas bla* [23] *ma shes rab rdo rje phyag nas 'thor ba'i bcu gcig zhal che chung gnyis / thub dbang rnying sku khru tshad gcig phyag rdor sor drug tsam de mdun chu gnyis nyer spyod bkra shis rtags sogs gong gsal ltar bris 'bur / rdor dril / sa rdo chu* [24] *rgyun ril bu klu sman bcas shel bum bcug 'byung ba'i mi gnod ched sgam chung la la snag gis bkag cing spros par bzhugs so / nyi zla'i nang klong chen mkha' 'gro snying thig btags grol / sangs rgyas sras gcig gang mang bzhugs / gong* [25] *gi gzungs de dag kyang mi nor ba'i mtshan ma btab la bzang gos kyi klubs te gang dang gang la 'bul tshul smin gling phyag bzhes gsos sman ganga'i* (= *gangā'i*) *rgyun bzang ltar gong 'og ma ma 'khrul bar* (= *par*) *phul la de phyin rgya dar a shed sman rtse dar* [26] *gos legs par btum / de phyir chu skyon mi 'byung ched spra tshil gyis legs par g.yog la gro gas zab par bsgril ba'o // de yang 'gro song ji tsam song tshul g.yu byu ru rin po che'i rigs dang bzang sman phyul tshul tha dag yi ger 'drir* [27] *ma langs la / 'dri* (= *bri*) *yang dge ba ngoms pa'i skyon du 'gyur ro //*

[V]

gzungs sgrub sogs zhar byung yan lag gi cho ga rnams kyang tshul bzhin bgyis la / rten 'di yang sngar bdag med 'o brgyal ba'i gnas la bstan 'gro'i zhabs tog [28] *dmigs te rang gzhan bsod rnams gsog pa'i rten mchog bzhengs 'dun gnang khar da ni khyad par 'dren mchog dam pa ngag dbang mtshan can yab sras rnam gnyis kyi gdung rten gtsor dmigs te bzhengs pa ni bsod nams* [29] *lhag par che la / rje rang byung rdo rjes / rgyal ba'i ring bsrel nor bu mchog / dgos 'dod thams cad 'byung bar byed / nyan thos rang rgyal byang chub sems / de bzhin rnal 'byor ldan pa'i gdung / mchod cing lus la bcangs pa yis /* [30] *gdon kun phyogs su nye mi nus / zhes gsungs pas de ni 'chang ba dang mthong thos dran pas bskal pa stong du bsags pa'i sdig sgrib 'dag cing sa lam gyi yon tan rim pas rdzogs par nus so // ma zad bla ma mchod cing gsol ba btab* [31] *pa'i phan yon gzhan las khyad par 'phags la 'dir re zhig de tsam la blo ldan rnams kyis gzigs par spro na mdo rgyud kun nas gsungs pas der gzigs na rtogs la / bdag 'dras bskyar gsal zhus dgos pa med do // sku gdung bsres* [32] *pa'i sātstsha mang tsam bzhugs rgyu'i 'dug pas rgya che tsam grub rung / rong kha song zhing rten la gnod pa byung dog de tsam bzhugs su gsol la / de dag kyang ma 'ongs pa'i bar du chud mi 'dza' ba'i ched lcags krin sogs su legs par bcug la* [33] *kha gcod sogs dam par bkab la la snag dang gro gas btum pa sogs lag len rnam dag bgyis la brtsigs pa'i legs par bcar ba'i mtshams bcad la bzhugs su gsol / de phro (= 'phro) gdung bsres sātstsha rnams 'di dang dgon* [34] *gzhung dgon bshams gang dga' zhig la ring min mchod rten lang bu brtsegs pa zhig bzhengs la bzhugs su gsol rgyu smon lam 'debs par mdzad pa'o //*

[VI]

de ltar ngo mtshar rten mchog zla gnyis ring la legs par grub nas [35] *rgyal ba nyid mi 'jig rdo rje gdan du mngon par byang chub dus sogs khyad 'phags dus chen gsum 'dzom sa ga zla bar grags pa'i tshes gnyis res gza' lhag par smin gling thugs chen dang rab gnas dge legs 'dod 'jo'i bcas* [36] *bsham gzhung ltar bshams nas rab tu gnas pa'i cho ga legs par bgyi ste slob dpon dang bzo bo grogs byed kun yon gyis mnyes par byas te bkra shis pa'i snyan glu di ri ri sgrogs par bya'o //*

[VII]

slar smras pa /

rnam dag rgyud gzhung grub pa'i [37] *man ngag bzhin /*
rnam grol bsod nams zhing 'gyur mchod pa'i rten /
rnam dkar gtan sbyin rig 'dzin 'gyur med kyis /
rnam mang rgyu yon sbyar te phul phyin bskrun /

'di ltar rten bzhengs bskur bsti bgyis pa yis /
byang [38] *chub thob par 'gyur ba smos cig dgos /*
mthong thos dran reg mngon mtho nges legs kyi /
sa bon 'jog la mi dad su zhig mchis /

de phyir lus kyi phyag 'tshal bskor ba dang /
ngag nas lhang lhang snyan pa'i gsol ba 'debs /
yid [39] *ni yi rang lhag bsam rnam dag gis /*
lha bshos dri chab snyan dar 'bul la brtson /

e ma rmad byung dge ba sgrub pa'i mthus /
thub bstan dar zhing de 'dzin skyes bu'i tshogs /
sku tshe mdzad phrin yar zla ltar 'phel nas /
'gro [40] *kun bde chen zhing du bsgrod par shog //*

[VIII]

ces dgon gzhung g.yu lding mar ngo mtshar bkod legs rten mchog dam pa 'di nyid bzhengs skabs / bzhugs byang smon tshig nyung ngu zhig 'dri (= 'bri) dgos zhes slob dpon ngag rgyal lags nas bka' phebs pas / dam pa nyid kyis (= kyi)** [41] **bka' slob ltar me tog dpag yas nyang rigs o rgyan bstan 'dzin nam a yu'i ming can pas shar ma bris pas dge legs snang ba phyogs kun thub bstan yun ring du gnas pa'i rgyu gyur cig // // dge'o // sarba mangalaṃ //

Fig. 1

Fig. 2

V.

Pilgrimages and Sacred Geography

Tibetan Sources on Muktināth: Individual Reports and Normative Guides

In the year 1729 Kaḥ-thog rig-'dzin Tshe-dbang nor-bu (1698–1755) left the territory of Nub-ris and made his way across the Tibetan high plateau (*byang thang*) towards Mustang (*mnga' ris glo bo*). Before and after spending several months at the court there and prior to heading on further to Dol-po, he stayed some days in a "sacred site" (*gnas*), which he describes in the following words:

> I went to "Hundred-and-some springs", the renowned holy spot revered by both Hindus and Buddhists, which is called Mu-mu-ni-se-ṭa or Mu-khun-kse-ṭa in the *Hevajramūlatantra*, and is called Mu-ṭa-ṣata in border dialects. It is a place where a natural fire burns on rock and water, and where ḍākinīs mass together like clouds.[1]

In the following I shall take a brief look at this locale against the background of several individual biographical sketches and related genres, such as have been preserved in Tibetan texts of the 16th to 19th centuries; this will be supplemented by the presentation of corresponding texts from the genre "description of sacred sites" (*gnas yig*) and "inventories" (*dkar chag*). These observations may perhaps enhance somewhat our understanding of the conception of religious space in northern Nepal and that of the history of the pilgrimage site Muktināth.

1. Muktināth and the Buddhist *Tantras*

In the travel report of Kaḥ-thog rig-'dzin Tshe-dbang nor-bu, reference is made, in clarification of the names *Mu-mu-ni-se-ṭa* and *Mu-khun-kṣe-ṭa* to the *Hevajratantra*; we must therefore deal briefly with the Indian *pītha* tradition, such as it is preserved in the Buddhist *Tantras*.

---

[1] Jackson (1978:212) and id. (1984:5–8 & 11–12, note 11). The source of this quotation is Chos-kyi dbang-phyug: *dPal rig 'dzin chen po rdo rje tshe dbang nor bu'i zhabs kyis rnam par thar pa'i cha shas brjod pa ngo mtshar dad pa'i rol* pp. 144.6–145.2. Before the two visits to Muktināth, Kaḥ-thog rig-'dzin Tshe-dbang nor-bu stayed with "high ranking officers" (*dpon drung che gras*) who went by the title of *khri thog pa* (enthroned ruler); see ibid, p. 146. The seat of this family is the fortress of rDzar (*rdzar rdzong*); see also note 14.

Since the works of Tucci, one has become familiar with the notion that the schemata of twenty-four, thirty-two (as in the case of the *Hevajratantra*) or thirty-six sites for tantric practice (Skt. *pīṭha* / Tib. *gnas*) may refer both to the yogin's body and to geographically real places. These sites were the destination of small, exclusive groups of yogins and yoginīs who followed the spiritual practice of certain cycles of *Tantra*. Further research has addressed with greater interest the question of how these schemata of the *Vajrakāya* became transplanted from the Indian context to the Himalayan regions and how this transposition entailed the formation of pilgrimage centres in the Tibet of the 12th and 13th centuries.[2]

This process, however, was critically reflected upon by members of the Tibetan priesthood, and Sa-skya Paṇḍita Kun-dga' rgyal-mtshan (1182–1251), for example, offers convincing testimony in his works that he was fully aware of the true location of certain pilgrimage centres in the Indian subcontinent; his polemics gave rise to a plethora of writings concerning questions of religious geography, particularly among the bKa'-brgyud-pa school.

It is thus not surprising that the location of the Munmuni of the *Hevajratantra* was also debated, it being one of the four "fields" (Skt. *kṣetra* / Tib. *zhing*).[3] Interestingly, the discussion of the question at the beginning of the 16th century was carried out by members of the royal court of Mustang, where at the time the school of the Sa-skya-pas had gained a foothold. Of pertinence was the position taken by Glo-bo mkhan-chen bSod-nams lhun-grub (1456–1532), as conveyed to his nephew, "Prince" mGon-po rgyal-mtshan. Having drawn on various sources, Glo-bo mkhan-chen comes to the conclusion that Munmuni is located in the south-eastern part of India.[4]

Before summoning up a further teacher from Mustang of the 16th century, I should like to mention briefly that the designation Mu-khun-kṣe-ṭa, ascribed by Kaḥ-thog rig-'dzin Tshe-dbang nor-bu to the *Hevajratantra*, is not found in it. As has been remarked by

---

2 Macdonald (1990) and Huber (1990). These two works provide information particularly on La-phyi, Tsa-ri and Ti-se, the three most important spiritual practice sites in the *Cakrasaṃvaratantra* tradition. Concerning Tsa-ri and the connection between psycho-physiological processes in the body of a yogin and the treading of a geographical locality, see Stein (1988:37–43).

3 Snellgrove (1959:68, vol. 1): "These are the different kinds of places of pilgrimage, some of which are known as 'seats' (*pīṭha*), some as 'fields' (*kṣetra*), some as 'meeting-places' (*melāpaka*) and some as 'cemeteries' (*śmaśāna*)," and ibid, p. 70: "The *kṣetra*s are Munmuni, Kāruṇyapāṭaka, Devīkoṭa, and Karmārapāṭaka."

4 See bSod-nams lhun-grub: *Mi'i dbang po mgon po rgyal mtshan gyi dri lan padma'i snying po* p. 18.2–4; Jackson (1978:212–213) has already referred to this passage. Cf. also Jackson (1984:125): "The name mGon-po rgyal-mtshan is prominent among the names of those to whom Glo-bo mkhan-chen wrote letters and instructions." These writings contain further material on the geographical location of places denoted by spiritual toponyms. For a descriptive catalogue of the writings of Glo-bo mkhan-chen, see Kramer (2008:171–298).

David Jackson, the toponym Mu-khun can be located in the "Gung-thang Chronicle" (likewise compiled by Kaḥ-thog rig-'dzin Tshe-dbang nor-bu on the basis of an analysis of old sources); there it refers to the place where one of the thirteen "ruler fortresses" (*btsan rdzong*) of the Gung-thang king Khri-rgyal 'Bum-lde mgon (1253–1280) was erected in the 13th century. I may add the observation of Charles Ramble that, for the *se skad* speakers in northern Baragaun, Mukha refers to rDzar-rdzong on the valley Muktināth.[5]

2. INDIAN AND TIBETAN YOGIS IN MUKTINĀTH

Two hundred years before Kaḥ-thog rig-'dzin Tshe-dbang nor-bu, a young Tibetan priest visited the holy site of Muktināth and remained there for more than three years. The description of this sojourn, which began in 1528, as documented in the autobiography of Jo-nang Kun-dga' grol-mchog (1507–1566), provides first of all insight into the early period of Mustang as a region dominated by Buddhism (the formal conversion of this part of Nepal to Buddhism may be dated to the 15th century), and secondly, shows Muktināth to be a place of pilgrimage for Nepalese and Indian kings.

Jo-nang Kun-dga' grol-mchog,[6] interestingly, begins his description with exactly the same formula from the *Hevajratantra* that we discussed with Kaḥ-thog rig-'dzin Tshe-dbang nor-bu; in my opinion, the source for the later citation by the teacher from Kaḥ-thog lies in the autobiography of Kun-dga' grol-mchog. The latter, in contrast to the former, quotes the passage from the *Hevajratantra* true to the original, adding to it only the paraphrase sGrol-ba'i zhing (= Muktikṣetra); in the dialect of Indian Prakrit that was common along the yogins of his period, Muktikṣetra is pronounced as Mukuṭakṣetra. The sacred site itself is characterized as "one hundred and eight trees together with one hundred and eight spouts" (*shing sdong brgya rtsa brgyad / chu mig brgya rtsa brgyad dang bcas pa*).[7]

5 Jackson (1978:212–213) and Ramble (1987:21), compare Ramble (1984:161) concerning the state of the ruins. For the Tibetan Text of the "Gung-thang Chronicle", see Tshe-dbang nor-bu: *Bod rje lha btsad po'i gdung rabs mnga' ris smad gung thang du ji ltar byung ba'i tshul deb gter dwangs shel 'phrul gyi me long*, p. 108: *ta mang se mon kha gnon du / glo smad mu khun srin rdzong brtsigs.* Macdonald (1989:170) notes the difficulties in identifying the group of the Se-mon Tamang and calls this citation "the oldest historical mention of Tamang in Nepal." Cf. also Vinding (1988:172): "The Tamang se mon is probably a reference to the Tamang Thakalis."

6 Jackson (1984:60) calls him "a noble monk from Lo Monthang who went on to become one of the foremost Buddhist masters of 16th century Tibet"; see also ibid, p. 71: "Kun-dga' grol-mchog eventually became the head of Jo-nang monastery; the famous Tāranātha is considered to have been his immediate rebirth" (ibid, p. 175 and passim). He is also the author of an extensive biography of Glo-bo mkhan-chen; see his *Glo bo mkhan chen bsod nams lhun grub kyi rtogs brjod dpal ldan bla ma 'jam pa'i dbyangs kyi rnam thar legs bshad gsum ldan*. Descendants of Kun-dga' grol-mchog were still living in the 17th century in sNye-shang; cf. Kun-bzang klong-yangs: *rTogs brjod mu tig gi mchun bu zhes pa'i gtam*, fol. 52a.

7 Kun-dga' grol-mchog: *Zhen pa rang grol lhug par brjod pa'i gtam skal bzang dad pa'i shing rta 'dren byed*, p. 386.1–2; concerning the alternative name of Muktināth, i.e. Muktikṣetra (salvation field), see

The following citation provides an idea of the extent to which pilgrimages were made to this place and which groups were involved:

> They came together like a gathering of birds striking [the ground] on that ford where the yearly washing-ceremony of the Indian king, his queen, his sons, ministers etc. [took place]. And after they had thronged together for the great delivery of alms, I came to the resting place where countless yogins of various [spiritual] lineages had assembled.
> As in this year [also] King De-bum rā-dza had arrived in full splendour with his retinue, very many groups of yogins had shown up. It was during this occasion that I met up with them. I was able to understand the majority of what the yogins said.[8]

There follow examples of various Buddhist terms and concepts that Kun-dga' grol-mchog used in common with Indian yogins. Of note is the listing of individual groups of yogins, which are subdivided somewhat in the manner of the eighteen groups of Śrāvakas in Buddhism. Kun-dga' grol-mchog mentions the intervals of one and a half and one year and eight to nine months that he spent in the company of the Indian yogins, receiving numerous "instructions" (*man ngag*). He celebrated in their midst a *gaṇacakrapūja* and later received the name Mahātapasitraguru; the remark is made that "he had the body of a Tibetan but the mind of an Indian" (*khyod lus bod sems rgya gar ba*). On the basis of comparative material, we may identify the Indian ascetics among whom Kun-dga' grol-mchog principally studied as Naṭeśvarī yogins.[9]

Messerschmidt (1989:90). There may likewise be found a description of the spot with the one hundred and eight spouts and an explanation of the meaning of the water for Hindu pilgrims; ibid, p. 97.

8 Kun-dga' grol-mchog: *Zhen pa rang grol lhug par brjod pa'i gtam skal bzang dad pa'i shing rta 'dren byed*, p. 386.3–6: *... rgya gar gyi rgyal po / btsun mo / sras blon po sogs lo dus la khrus kyi 'jug ngogs der bya dus* (= *'dus*) *btab pa ltar 'tshog* (= *tshogs*) *cing / sbyin gtong rgya chen po la bsnyegs nas / ... / rigs tha dad pa'i rnal 'byor pa dpag tu med pa 'du ba'i bsti gnas ga la ba der phyin pas / de lo de bum rā dza 'khor bcas gzabs sprod byas byon pa la bsten* (= *brten*) */ dzo ki tshogs shin tu mang ba 'dus 'dug pa'i skabs de dang 'dzom / kho bos dzo ki'i skad phal cher go ...* King De-bum rā-dza can be identified as Dibum or Dimma, one of the Malla kings of Parbat (the alternative name of Parbat being Malebum). On this king, the third ruler of Parbat who expanded the domains of the kingdom in 1488, see Shrestha (1984/85:6); Pandey (1971/72) presents a critique of the early western references to king "Dimba". Concerning the four-day journey from Beni, the old capital of Parbat, to Muktināth and the first descriptions of the pilgrimage site from western sources, see Kirkpatrick (1811:287) and Hamilton (1816:272–273).

9 Kun-dga' grol-mchog: *Zhen pa rang grol lhug par brjod pa'i gtam skal bzang dad pa'i shing rta 'dren byed*, pp. 387.2–390.6. Cf. the list of yogins (ibid, p. 387.2–3) with that in Kun-dga' snying-po: *Grub chen bhuddhagupta'i rnam thar rje btsun nyid kyi zhal lung las gzhan du rang rtog gi dri mas ma sbags pa'i yi ge yang dag pa'o*, pp. 535.5–6. The latter passage was dealt with by Tucci (1931:686–687). There he writes of "Nāthapanthins, though of a specific Buddhist branch." In the same text, the group of Naṭeśvarī

During the same time, then, when the authenticity of spiritual toponyms from the *Tantra*s was being judged at the court of Mustang from theoretical and polemical points of view, a young priest who came from the social environs of the court was practising tantric teachings in Muktināth, the place sacred to Indian yogins, and the identification of this place as one of the four *kṣetra*s of the *Hevajratantra* had already been made. What we may observe here is the process by which the site of the one hundred and eight spouts, previously frequented primarily by Nepalese and Indian pilgrims, was so to speak "canonized" in Mustang of the 16th century by an important representative of Tibetan religiosity.

If we turn now to a great Tibetan yogin of the 17th century who was born in the vicinity of Muktināth and enjoyed a great reputation as a yogin of the 'Brug-pa bKa'-brgyud-pa school, we can see how the geography of the shrine was tied into a second tantric system, thereby undergoing a high degree of idealization or spiritualization. In the palace of Rab-rgyal rtse-mo we have the old fortress of rDzong, the birthplace of bsTan-'dzin ras-pa (1644/46–1723):

On a pile of jewels, the mountain before me,
the palace Rab-rgyal rtse-mo.
Having arranged the precious stones of many lands [around it],
in the manner of Mt. Sumeru and the four continents:
[to the sacred site] I present this offering of a country [that is like] a maṇḍala.

Where *gtse shing* (?) and also all [kinds of] herbs grow; where the melodious sound of diverse bird calls rings out,
The place where all gods and all humans make offerings, [that is,] in the palace of Vajravārāhī:
It was prophesied under the name Mu-ku by the Jina, [and] the siddha Dza-vi opened the gate of the sacred site;
[This place] is one of the thirty-two *mahāpīṭha*s.
There offerings are made by all the *dharmarāja*s from India;
the stream of yogin pilgrims is uninterrupted.
[This place] is the fire hole of the Brahmins;
uninterrupted are the offerings of substances to be burned.

yogins is mentioned along with their exponent Tīrthanātha; Kun-dga' grol-mchog studied under disciples of this Tīrthanātha in Muktināth.

[The place] whose glory encompasses the whole world – with folded hands, I bring it this brief "praise of the sacred site".[10]

3. THE NOBLE FAMILIES OF rDZONG AND rDZAR

It is known that the noble family of sKyar-skya gang-pa constructed the fortresses of rDzong, rDzar and sKag in the 15th century, and that the representatives of this family are also designated in the sources as *khri thog pa*.[11] Up to now, it has primarily been the biography of bsTan-'dzin ras-pa that one has turned to for the history of this family; it is clear from it that Khro-bo skyabs-pa was the builder of the fortresses and the first "lord of the fortress" (*rdzong dpon*) of Rab-rgyal rtse-mo.

The biography of bsTan-'dzin ras-pa, however, offers only little information on the successors of Khro-bo skyabs-pa, and the description of the events in the 17th century is moulded by personal experiences during the conflicts between Mustang and the rulers of the Muktināth valley (*rgyal blon 'khrugs pa*). As these conflicts led to the intervention of the rulers of Jumla, the relation between Jumla and Mustang and the history of the lords of rDzong and rDzar have primarily been described against the background of these conflicts.[12]

---

[10] bsTan-'dzin ras-pa: *rNal 'byor gyi dbang phyug bstan 'dzin ras pa'i zhal gdams mgur du gsungs pa rnams*, fol. 50b/4–6: *mdun ri rin chen spungs pa'i steng / pho brang rab rgyal rtse mo la / yul phran mang po'i khra* (= *phra*) *bkod nas / ri rab gling bzhi'i tshul du ni / mandal yul gyi mchod pa 'bul / gtse shing sman sna kun kyang skye / bya skad sna tshogs skad snyan sgrog / lha mi kun gyis mchod pa'i gnas / rdo rje phag mo'i pho brang du / rgyal ba'i lung bstan mu ku zhes / grub thob dza vis gnas sgo phye / gsum cu so gnyis gnas chen yin / rgya gar rgyal kun gyi* (= *gyis*) *mchod / dzo ki'i gan* (= *gnas*) *bskor rgyun mi chad / bram ze rnams kyis* (= *kyi*) *hūṃ* (= *hom*) *khung yin / bsreg rdzas mchod pa rgyun mi 'chad* (= *chad*) */ grags pas 'dzam gling kun la khyab / thal sbyar gnas bstod bsdus tsam 'bul*. This designation of Muktināth as a palace of Vajravārāhī suggests that bsTan-'dzin ras-pa localized the site within the system of the *Cakrasaṃvaratantra*; this is expected, given that he himself spent many years at the most important sacred places associated with this tantric cycle: in Tsa-ri, at Kailāśa and in La-phyi. Contradicting this is the mention of the list of thirty-two *pīṭhas*, which comes from the *Hevajratantra*. Concerning the concept of "gate of a sacred site" (*gnas sgo*) and its being opened by a "héro fondateur", see Stein (1987:189). Might the siddha Dza-vi-ba Grub-chen Dzā-ha-bhi, whose teachings reached 'Bri-gung Rin-chen phun-tshogs (1509–1557) by way of Vajranātha?

[11] Schuh (1990:6) and Schuh (1992:102); cf. also ibid, p. 37: "at a later point in time the *dpon po* of rDzong resettled in rDzar." Concerning *khro-bo skyabs-pa*, see ibid, p. 108. Ramble (1984:106–107) provides a brief survey of the settlement of the Muktināth valley by the noble family and the sequence of fortress constructions: sKag → rDzong → rDzar; concerning the name of the fortress of rDzar he writes: "The name is said to signify the superiority of its location over that of rDzong ..." Cf. Ramble (1987:226).

[12] See Jackson (1978:220–221) and the synopsis in Ramble/Vinding (1987:9) and Vinding (1988:173); for a more detailed view of the political dependency between Mustang and Jumla in the 17th and 18th centuries, cf. Schuh (1992:59–78). For the description of bsTan-'dzin ras-pa, see bsTan-'dzin ras-pa: *rNal 'byor gyi dbang phyug bstan 'dzin ras pa'i rnam thar mdzad pa nyung ngu gcig*, fols. 1a–3b and bsTan-

In the following I shall briefly present two further biographies of the 17th century that may shed some light on the second half of that century and the ruling families of the fortresses beneath the shrine of Muktināth; after the school of the Sa-skya-pa/Jo-nang-pa and that of the bKa'-brgyud-pa, they are texts from the school of the rNying-ma-pa. The first biography is that of O-rgyan dpal-bzang (1617–1677), and the second text deals with the life of Kun-bzang klong-yangs (1644–1696), the main disciple and "successor" (*rgyal tshab*) of O-rgyan dpal-bzang.

O-rgyan dpal-bzang was a disciple of gTer-ston bDud-'dul rdo-rje (1615–1672) and has been known up to now principally as the founder of the monastery sKu-tshab gter-lnga southwest of Jomsom.[13] The founding of a monastery community in the vicinity of Muktināth only a few years before his death shows us the local rulers, the fortress lords, in the role of "donor" (*yon bdag*) typical of the Buddhist society of Tibet, whereas O-rgyan dpal-bzang himself fulfilled the function of a "priest" (*mchod gnas*). The following citation is pertinent:

> After having delivered an invitation, the dPon-drung khri-pa Tshe-gnas rgyal-po from the fortress Rab-rgyal rtse[-mo] requested [the performance of] a consecration for long life; he then donated as gift for the consecration thirteen [presents] of good quality, such as eighteen rupees [etc.] His younger brother, the officer bDe-skyid bsam-grub, donated a horse and a total of twenty silver ingots.
>
> And in order that the [Buddhist] teaching might spread on the Hill of Clear Light, [the master] cut the hair of each of the daughters of the dPon-drung Khro-bo tshe-dbang and the dPon-drung bDe-skyid bsam-grub with the words <illegible>; later in Chu-mig brgya-rtsa it happened that Ngag-dbang bu-khrid, the wife of the khri-pa, donated the sum of one hundred rupees.[14]

'dzin ras-pa (as in note 10), fols. 46a–47a. Compare Schaeffer (2004:26–30) for a sketch of the life of bsTan-'dzin ras-pa and his trials.

13 For a description of sKu-tshab gter-lnga, see Snellgrove (1961a=1989:186–187) and id. (1979:79–81 and passim). For the text and the translation of *sKu tshab gter lnga dkar chag*, see ibid, pp. 84–101 and 133–143; the text was filmed by the NGMPP: reel no. L 257/24 (26 fols.). Snellgrove dates the founding of the monastery to the middle of the 17th century; the biography of O-rgyan dpal-bzang (fol. 317a) mentions the year 1668 (*sa pho spre lo*) as the date for the construction of the "monastery site" (*dgon gnas*), by name Hill of Clear Light (*'od gsal sgang*). The place is also called "the site of the Guru's (i.e. Padmasambhava's) practices" (*gu ru'i sgrub gnas 'od gsal sgang*): ibid, fol. 323a. For an overview of the life and travels of O-rgyan dpal-bzang and the foundation of sKu-tshab gter-lnga, see chapter thirteen in the present volume.

14 O-rgyan dpal-bzang: *Rigs brgya dbang po 'dren mchog slob dpon dpal bzang po'i rnam par thar pa dad pa'i spu long g.yo byed mthong bas yid 'phrog ngo mtshar 'phreng ba'i gtam rmad du byung ba*, fols. 323b/3–6: *rdzong rab rgyal rtse nas dpon drung khri pa tshe gnas rgyal po'i* (= *pos*) *spyan 'dren zhus nas*

Let us keep in mind, then, first of all that, at the time of the founding of the monastery of sKu-tshab gter-lnga by O-rgyan dpal-bzang, the fortress of rDzong was in the hands of a certain Tshe-gnas rgyal-po, who had a younger brother called bDe-skyid bsam-grub. Of further note is the fact that the sacred site of Muktināth was the place where the ruling family of rDzar and rDzong assembled with the priests of the rNying-ma-pa school. This link was by no means severed, however, at the death of O-rgyan dpal-bzang in 1677; Kun-bzang klong-yangs, the successor of O-rgyan dpal-bzang, was likewise in Muktināth one year later, fulfilling the same functions as his teacher:

> The dPon-drung khri-pa Tshe-gnas rgyal-po went with me together to Chu-mig brgya-rtsa; with the aid [of the sādhana] of the wrathful deity, I offered the sprinkling of the water, the skull plate and the ritual noose to the retinue of those in charge etc. To their sons I granted the consecration of long life etc., and to the dPon-drung eight tola of *khro-chen* (a kind of copper) etc. in order to reinforce the consolation [upon the death of their teacher].[15]

A short time later Kun-bzang klong-yangs travelled to Central Tibet where, among others, he met gTer-bdag gling-pa (1646–1714) in sMin-grol gling and Rig-'dzin Padma 'phrin-las (1640–1718) in rDo-rje brag; this journey was financed in part by Tshe-gnas rgyal-po, and also by the latter's younger brother bDe-skyid bsam-grub. Whereas the donations of the elder brother came from rDzong rab-rgyal rtse, the seat of bDe-skyid bsam-grub is given as rDzar.

---

tshe dbang zhus pas dbang yon du a (= a las) bco brgyad kyi mtshan pa bcu gsum mtshan bzang po zhig phul cing / khong gi cung po (= gcung po) dpon drung bde skyid bsam grub kyis rta gcig dngul nyi shu'i gnam brangs (= rnam grangs) phu (= phul) zhing 'od gsal gang (= sgang) der bstan pa rgyas phyir bra ba (= grwa pa) ... zer dpon drung khro bo tshe dbang dang dpon drung bde skyid bsam grub gnyis pa'i sras mo re re skra cad (= bcad) / slar chu mig brgya rtsar khri pa'i btsun mo ngag dbang bu khrid kyis a las brgya drang (= grangs) zhig phu (= phul) 'byung ngo. The custom of having the daughters of a princely family ordained by a teacher of the rNying-ma-pa school was kept up for over another fifty years, as the biography of Kaḥ-thog rig-'dzin Tshe-dbang nor-bu documents: "They (= the higher officers; see note 1) asked for a link with the teaching that they paid respect to, and inasmuch as each of the daughters of the individual [officers] had faith and entered into the gate of the teaching etc., there arose a great number of noviciates of the [Buddhist] teaching"; Chos-kyi dbang-phyug: *dPal rig 'dzin chen po rdo rje tshe dbang nor bu'i zhabs kyis rnam par thar pa'i cha shas brjod pa ngo mtshar dad pa'i rol mtsho* in *The Collected Works of Kaḥ-thog Rig-'dzin chen-po Tshe-dbang nor-bu*, vol 1, p. 146.2–3: ... *dpon drung che gras rnams kyi (= kyis) zhabs gus chos 'brel zhus shing so so'i sras mo re yang chos sgor bcug pa sogs dad chos btsun gsar ma mang zhig byung.*

15 Kun-bzang klong-yangs (as in note 6), fols. 32b/6–34a/2: *dpon drung khri ba tshe gnas rgyal po dang nge (= nged) rang lhan du chu mig brgya rtsar phebs / sme rtsegs (= brtsegs) sgo nas khrus gsol dbu thod kha rtags (= btags) do dam 'khor la sogs phul / sras rnams la tshe dbang sogs dang dpon drung du khro chen dngul brgyad sogs thugs gsos (= gso) spangs (= dpangs) mthor phul.*

Having returned from Central Tibet, Kun-bzang klong-yangs in 1680 again met up with the "officer brothers" (*dpon drung sku mched*), and the next thing we learn is that dPon-drung Tshe-gnas rgyal-po left this world. His death is immediately followed by the enthronement of the younger brother, and this can only be interpreted, in my opinion, as meaning that bDe-skyid bsam-grub became his brother's successor as the ruler of rDzong.

Before entering further into these particulars, we may briefly refer to events in Muktināth that followed in the wake of the death of Tshe-gnas rgyal-po (another member of the ruling family, a certain Ong bKra-shis rtse-mo, died around the same time):

> The next day in Chu-mig brgya-rtsa, without any idea of how to determine the cardinal directions etc., I (i.e. Kun-bzang klong-yangs), having brought the piles of the maṇḍala as gifts to the three sources of the Ye-shes me-lha, produced clay imprints from earth, on a spot where many brightly white reliquaries could be found that had collapsed by themselves ... Afterwards maṇi [walls] were constructed in combination with *stūpa*s by this same officer (i.e. dPon-drung bDe-skyid bsam-grub), and the extremely fine maṇi [walls] that [still] exist in Chu-mig brgya-rtsa are the very same ones.[16]

For the succeeding years, the autobiography of Kun-bzang klong-yangs mentions the ruler bDe-skyid bsam-grub – also referred to with the title *dharmarāja* (*chos rgyal*) – as the ruler of rDzar, rDzong and sKag; he also bore the main costs for the extension of the monastery buildings in sKu-tshab gter-lnga, which commenced in 1684. The situation changed only in the year 1687, for it was then that Kun-bzang klong-yangs received a further invitation from bDe-skyid bsam-grub, sent from rDzar, whereas an invitation to visit rDzong was communicated by dPon-drung Khro-bo dar-po and his wife.[17]

From these observations I draw the conclusion, within the framework of this article, that in the seventh to ninth decades of the 17th century the fortresses of Muktināth valley were dominated by the ruling family of rDzar.[18]

---

16 Kun-bzang klong-yangs (as in note 6), fols. 45a/5–46b/1: *sang nyin phyogs rtsis sogs kyi rnam rtog med par chu mig brgya rtsar ye shes me lha rtsa gsum gyi dkyil 'khor phung po yon du phul pas sku gdung shin tu dkar ba rang log mang du 'dug par sa tsha tsha btab*; and fol. 46a/1–2: *de phyin dpon drung de nyid gyi (= gyis) maṇi mchod rten spel mar bzhengs pas da lta'i chu mig brgya rtsar gyi maṇi shin tu mtshan kyis che ba 'di yin no.*

17 Kun-bzang klong-yangs (as in note 6), fols. 53b/6–54a/3. The family of dPon-drug Khro[-bo] dar[-po] also received teachings from bsTan-'dzin ras-pa; the latter conferred on them a consecration when he returned to the Muktināth valley, which probably occurred around this time. See bsTan-'dzin ras-pa (as in note 10), fol. 51a/5–6: *de'i dus dpon drung khro dar yab yum khu dbon kyi khrom dbang gi dbang gzhi gting zhing sna len bzang po mdzad.*

18 See also *Gu ru pad ma'i rnam thar las thang yig ga'u ma'i dkar chags* in *Padma'i bka'i thang yig*

This ascendance coincided with the construction of the monastery complex of sKu-tshab gter-lnga and the officiating of rNying-ma-pa teachers as priests of the ruling families. The sacred site of Muktināth thereby takes on an added dimension: it is the place where rituals were performed for the officers and members of these families, and in whose physical surroundings the donors left behind signs of their generosity.

4. The Idealized Landscape of Muktināth

One hundred years later the family of rDzar was still active in the spread of rNying-ma-pa teachings. We know, for instance, on the basis of the just mentioned catalogue, that they financed at this time the copying of a biography of Padmasambhava familiar under the title *sKyes rabs rnam thar ga'u bdun ma*. The catalogue also contains an encomium, rich in detail, of the sacred site of Muktināth, concerning which I should here merely like to highlight the mention in it of the "Maṇḍala of Sixty-two Deities of the Mother *Tantra*" (*ma rgyud re gnyis lha'i dkyil 'khor*); this formulation reconfirms the previous observation that Muktināth was imported into the system of the *Cakrasaṃvaratantra*.

It being stated in conclusion that the sacred site is a "unique jewel adorning the world" (*gnas 'di 'dzam gling mdzes pa'i rgyan gcig yin*), a subdivision of geographical space is undertaken, leading to the question of how Muktināth and its wider surroundings are represented in the pilgrimage guides for Tibetan Buddhists. The subdivision begins with the upper part (*phu*) of the Muktināth valley, which is described as a mountain paradise where flowers glisten in the pastures: a "place of meditative trance" (*bsam gtan gnas*). There then follows a description of the lower lying region of the valley:

> In the lower part: the Secret Cave of the Guru, Dhaulāgiri [and] the self-arisen stone statue of the sNa-ri Jo-bo; as well as the five treasures representing the body (i.e. the teaching) of rGyal-dbang Padma[sambhava], etc.: whether having arisen [by themselves] or being constructed [by men], innumerable supports [of body, speech and mind], these three, are found [there].[19]

---

ga'u ma, p. 9.1, where Tshe-gnas rgyal-po is listed under the lineage of the rulers of rDzar. His son is mentioned there under the name Ngag-dbang rnam-rgyal. In my opinion, this is the dPon-drung khri-sde Ngag-dbang rnam-rgyal listed by Kun-bzang klong-yangs; cf. Kun-bzang klong-yangs (as in note 6), fols. 83b/2–3 and 84b/1–6. Whereas the first passage tells of an invitation from rDzar, we find the prince shortly thereafter in sKag-rdzong rtse, where he is placed on the throne by 'Dzum-lang rgyal-po Bir-ba-dhur (the ceremony it refers to took place in Bārbung in 1695). For further information on the identity of this ruler of Jumla, also known as Bhi-ri-sras, see chapter twenty in the present volume.

19 *Gu ru pad ma'i rnam thar las thang yig ga'u ma'i dkar chags* in *Padma'i bka'i thang yig ga'u ma*, p. 10.2–3: *mdo na gu ru'i gsang phug mu le gangs / rang byon rdo sku sna ri jo bo dang / rgyal dbang padma'i sku tshab gter lnga sogs / 'khrungs dang bzhengs sogs grangs med rten gsum bzhugs*. Between the upper and lower parts, in the "middle" (*bar*), lies rDzar and the "six governed regions" (*rgyal khab drug*); these latter probably coincide only partially with the six villages of the Muktināth valley, as one of the territories is called by the up to now unidentified toponym *gnyan yod*.

With the Dhaulāgiri Himāl (*mu-le / mu-li gangs* or *gangs-chen*) and the Padmasambhava Cave on its north-eastern flank (west of Larjung), we have reached the southern periphery of the region visited by Tibetan pilgrims and described in the corresponding handbooks. The standard compilation of pilgrimage guides for southern Mustang, already published several times, begins with a text devoted to Muktināth and ends with a description of Dhaulāgiri, the Sacred Cave and the Avalokiteśvara statue of sNa-ri.[20]

Before I go into the description of Muktināth offered by the genre of pilgrimage guides, a brief look should be taken at the compilation of the text as a whole – this in order to establish criteria for dating the collection. The main part of the text is devoted to the Dhaulāgiri Himāl, that is, to an enumeration of the spiritual qualities of the snow-covered mountain; particular significance falls to it by reason of the cave in which Padmasambhava is said to have stayed. This part of the collection bears the title "Description of the Two Sacred Sites 'Great Glacier' and 'Secret Cave'" (*gangs chen gsang phug gnyis kyi gnas yig*).

As is learned from the introduction to this section, the description of the two sites is based on a prophecy of a Ḍākinī (*gnas bshad lung bstan*); these prophecies were channelled through a certain sNgags-'chang Tshe-ring, who was staying in the Padmasambhava cave in a male iron-monkey year (*lcags pho sprel lo*). These descriptions are followed by a further dream, in which the local mountain deity (*lha btsan gzhi bdag*) manifests itself, again, apparently to sNgags-'chang Tshe-ring. The next item mentioned is the self-arisen Avalokiteśvara statue, the Lord of sNa-ri (*sna ri jo bo*); this statue was unearthed from the mountain and cave (*gangs chen dang gu ru gsang phug gnyis nas gdan drangs pa*). The list of pilgrimage sites of the Dhaulāgiri Himāl is rounded out with this status, it being stated that "in these three, the Great Glacier, the Secret Cave and the Lord [of sNa-ri], all pilgrimage sites of the world were complete."[21]

---

20 See Snellgrove (1979:106–128 & 151–170) for the text and translation of the compilation, which can be subdivided into four sections. The collection was also edited by Macdonald (1979:246–253). The *gNas chen chu mig brgya rtsa'i dang cong zhi sku tshab gter lnga mu li rin chen gangs gu ru gsang phug sna ris jo bo sogs kyi dkar chags dngul dkar me long* edition is incomplete (fols. 10 and 11 are missing). The first mention of this pilgrimage guide is found in Tucci (1956:10ff.), where also the mountain name of Mu-le is connected with the region of the Bārbung Khola: "Mu luṅ (rMu luṅ), the valley of Mu, rMu." On the location of the cave complex, see Gebauer (1983:76).

21 Snellgrove (1979:168); *gangs chen gsang phug jo bo 'di gsum la / 'jam bu gling gnas kun 'di la tshangs* (Macdonald (1979:253) reads *changs*). Concerning the white stone statue of Avalokiteśvara in Narshang, above Larjung, see Snellgrove (1961a=1989:181). Before the text in conclusion once more urges pilgrims, on the basis of cautionary examples, not to fail to visit these three sites before going on further to India, a text bearing the title *'Byung ba bzhi lha'i gnas yig* is interposed. The remark by Macdonald (1979:244) about the prophecy concerning the land of Thags must be viewed in connection with these deities: *'o na shar phyogs thags zhes bya bar 'gro na 'byung ba bzhi'i lha rnams 'dren bya dgos gsungs so.*

The site of sKu-tshab gter-lnga is mentioned only briefly in the collection of pilgrimage guides. Even though it is a fine shrine of Padmasambhava, the same significance is not attached to it as to the Dhaulāgiri Himāl and the Secret Cave; this may be taken as an indication that at the time when Dhaulāgiri was spiritualized, so to speak, as the goal of Tibetan pilgrims heading south, the fame of the site of Padmasambhava's practices south-west of Jomsom had already paled. This is reflected in the toponyms which are listed under sKu-tshab gter-lnga in the third section of the text:

> The place reached by a one-day walk south of the sacred site of Chu-mig brgya-rtsa was called in former times Hill of Clear Light and nowadays is also called 'Grum-pa lha-khang. There clearly visible imprints of the foot and knee together with the hand of the Guru [Padmasambhava] are found.[22]

The second part of the text collection describes a place that likewise lies one day from Muktināth, but in a northern direction. This site, too, was believed to be trod upon by the feet of Padmasambhava and furthermore is associated with the eighty-four mahāsiddhas. The destination for pilgrims is once again a cave, and in my opinion the place acquired its name from a certain kind of white rock, i.e. limestone:

> As for the meaning of [g]Cong-[g]zhi, it is a sacred site on which Ācārya Padma[sambhava] set foot and likewise was blessed by the eighty mahāsiddhas. In the pure vision of bKa'-brgyud Bla-ma Rin-po-che Mi-pham yongs-'dus and sGrub-pa chen-po sTag-rtse-ba, that which [once] came forth as protuberances of *gcong-gzhi* [stone] was perceived as [being the deity] bDe-mchog lhan-skyes in union.[23]

---

22 Text as in note 20, pp. 67.6–68.2: *gnas chen chu mig brgya rtsa nas lho phyogs su nyin lam gcig phyin pa ni / sngon kyis (= gyi) 'dus (= dus) 'od gsal gangs (= sgang) zhes su grags / da lta 'grum pa lha khang yang zer / zhes pa gu ru'i zhabs rjes dang / zhabs pus kyis (= kyi) rjes / phyag gnyis ka'i rjes bcas gsal bar bzhugs shing*. Both names, 'Od-gsal gangs (= sgang) and 'Grum-pa lha-khang, are also found in the text of Macdonald (1979:248). In Snellgrove (1979:158=112), the distinction between two chronological phases is missing along with the name 'Grum-pa lha-khang. The etymology of the latter toponym may be the name sGrom-bu lha-khang; see Pad-ma dbang-'dus: *mKha' mnyam 'gro ba'i rtsug (= gtsug) brgyan (= rgyan) pad ma dbang 'dus kyi rnam par thar pa gsal bar bkod pa la rmongs mun thib po sal (= sel) ba'i sgron me* p. 437.2–3: 'When I arrived at the Temple of the [Stored] Chest, the seat of Kun-bzang klong-yangs, in order to encounter the five treasures that represent the body (i.e. the teaching of Padmasambhava) ...' (*... kun bzang klong yangs kyi gdan sa sgrom bu lha khang la sku tshab gter lnga mjal du phyin dus*). This information furnished by Padma dBang-'dus (born 1697), dates to the decades of the 1730's or 1740's, i.e. to approximately the same time as the visit of Kaḥ-thog rig-'dzin Tshe-dbang nor-bu to southern Mustang (cf. notes 1 & 29).

23 Text as in note 20, pp. 66.6–67.2: *gcong gzhi zhes bya ba / slob dpon padmas kyang zhabs kyis bcags shing / grub chen brgyad bcus kyang byin gyis brlabs pa'i gnas chen / skabs brgyad (= bka' brgyud?) bla ma rin po che mi pham yongs 'dus dang / grub thob chen po rtag rtse ba'i gzigs shang la / gcong bzhi (=*

I base my argument that the name [g]Cong-[g]zhi refers to a limestone or calcite concretion primarily on the Tibetan medical tradition, according to which there are of several kinds, which are variously able to alleviate disorder of air, bile, phlegm and their combinations. Snellgrove's translation, "self produced place of promenade" (*gcong gzhi rang byung*) does not occur in the description of the site of [g]Cong-[g]zhi for Tibetan pilgrims but is taken from passage describing the Dhaulāgiri Himāl.[24] What else can we glean from this citation?

Although the wording of the passage is not unambiguous and I have up to now not succeeded in identifying a bKa'-brgyud Bla-ma named Mi-pham yongs-'dus, I should like to mention the person known under the name of sTag-rtse-ba. The latter is sTag-rtse sku-skye-ba Mi-pham phun-tshogs shes-rab, a teacher of the 'Brug-pa school active at the court of the Mustang king bSam-grub dpal-'bar (fl. ca. 1675); he is known further as the author of a biography of the Second sDing-po-che Cog-gra Mi-pham Ngag-dbang snyan-grags dpal-bzang (1617–1680).[25]

In summary, it may be stated that the dates of persons associated with the founding of monasteries or retreat sites in southern and northern Mustang may be determined first and foremost for the 17th century (the founding of sKu-tshab gter-lnga: 1668). In the succeeding period, following the establishment of these sites by priests of the rNying-ma-pa school, such as O-rgyan dpal-bzang, or ones of the bKa'-brgyud-pa school, such as sTag-rtse sku-skye-ba, an expanding idealization and spiritualization of the landscape occurred, which in the end took in the territory of the Dhaulāgiri Himāl and northern Mustang. Under these

---

gzhi) 'bur du thon pa'i 'di nyid ni / bde mchog lhan skyes yab yum du gzigs shing. The first description of this cave by a visitor from the West is in Tucci (1953=1977:56), under the name "Self-Arisen Stūpa" (*rang byung mchod rten*): "The cavern owes its name to a big round natural pillar which stands in the middle of it, almost as if it supported the weight of the vault." In Tucci (1956:11), interestingly, this cave is equated with the secret cave on the northeast flank of Dhaulāgiri. Tucci's identification of one of the figures formed from stone as mNga'-ris Jo-bo, i.e. Atiśa, is thus not valid; it is rather the previously mentioned Avalokiteśvara statue sNa-ri Jo-bo.

24 See Snellgrove (1961a=1989:189) for a description of the cave and the expression *gcong gzhi rang byung*. Cf. also Snellgrove (1979:117): "Like a wish granting gem is the Self-Produced Place of Promenade" (= p. 162: *yid bzhin nor bu gcong gzhi rang byon 'khrung*s), and note 40 concerning the problems this passage poses. If, on the contrary, one translates as 'here has appeared the self-arisen [formation of] *gcong gzhi* [stone], the wish-granting gem', then the problems dissolve. For the different kinds of limestone (proper spelling *cong zhi*) in Tibetan materia medica, see Parfionovitch, Y. et al. (1992:17, 61, 173 and 217).

25 Concerning King bSam-grub dpal-'bar, see Jackson (1984:150): "He revered the venerable sTag-rtse-ba Mi-pham-shes-rab-phun-tshogs as his chief preceptor." A block print edition of his "Collected Works" was filmed in 1986 by the NGMPP (L 100/1 – L 100/27); the biography of the Second sDing-po-che Cog-gra is located in the National Archives/Kathmandu, 242 fols. (= AT 33/1). A "praise to the sacred site" (*gnas bstod*) of [g]Cong-[g]zhi from the pen of sTag-rtse sku-skye-ba was used by pilgrims when visiting the place; see chapter fifteen in the present volume.

circumstances, I would venture to place the date of the vision of the above-mentioned sNgags-'chang Tshe-ring (*lcags pho sprel lo*) in the year 1740.[26] This expansion has been described in the following words: "Here we see the southward thrust of frontier Bon-pos and Lamas ..., and the transformation of local mountain, earth and water spirits into keepers of the Buddhist law."[27]

The first part of pilgrimage guides whose compilation we can now date to the 18th century describes in detail the old shrine of Muktināth and the merit that accrues to the pilgrim in making offerings at the site. I shall not go into these descriptions in detail but merely sketch briefly the structural composition of the text: Following a set praise for Padmasambhava (missing in the edition of Snellgrove), the visit of this master is placed in "the first world period" *(skal pa dang po)*, as distinguished from the visit of the eighty-four mahāsiddhas (*skal pa bar ma*); the feats of the latter are marked by sacral acts involving water: First they block the outflow of a poisonous lake in La-stod rGyal-gyi śrī[-ri] (this place name is missing in the edition of Macdonald), and later undertake a pilgrimage to Gangs Ti-se and mTsho Ma-pham; following a ritual bathing in the latter lake, they take one hundred and eight buckets of water from it and settle down in Muktināth (Snellgrove translates "eighty-four ladle-fulls of water", the text reading *chu ku ba brgya dang brgyad*; no figures given in the edition of Macdonald).

There follows an idealized description of the site. Interestingly, it begins with the identification of it as the maṇḍala of Cakrasaṃvara. Of the places listed next, one may single out, among with the one hundred and eight spouts, the serpent deity dGa'-bo 'Jogs-pa and the fire burning atop the water source (*chu mig me 'bar*). Before extolling the merits that come from making offerings at the site[28] and listing the sources of the mentioned accounts, the text deals with the nearby surroundings of Muktināth. Here the name of the

---

26 As Snellgrove (1979:113, note 37) has already remarked, several manuscripts read the name as *yon bdag mtshan can sngags 'chang tshe ring* (one of them being the text as in note 20, p. 68.6: *bdag yon bdag gis* (= *gi*) *mtshan can* ...). Might he not be a member of the princely family of rDzar, which figured in the 17th and 18th centuries as "donors" (*yon bdag*) of the rNying-ma-pa school? Cf. also the passage cited in note 19 from *Gu ru pad ma'i rnam thar las thang yig ga'u ma'i dkar chags* in *Padma'i bka'i thang yig ga'u ma*, where the list of the sacred sites of the south commences with the Secret Cave.

27 Macdonald (1979:245). On Muktināth (*chu mig brgya rtsa*) in the works of Bon-po scholars of the 20th century, however, see bsTan-'dzin rnam-dag: *Bod yul gnas kyi lam yig gsal ba'i dmig bu*, p. 28 and dPal-ldan tshul-khrims: *Sangs rgyas g.yung drung bon kyi bstan pa'i byung ba brjod pa'i legs bshad skal pa bzang po'i mgrin brgyan rab gsal chu shel nor bu do shel*, p. 494. Cf. also the map in Cech (1992:392 (opp.)): *Chu mig brgyad* (sic) *cu rtsa gnyis*. Concerning the circumambulation of the sacred site by adherents of the Bon-po school during the Yartung festival, see Ramble (1984:157–158)=(1987:230–231).

28 For a description of the summer festival in Muktināth and the ritual circumambulation of the sacred place by the Buddhist monks of rDzar and Purang that takes place on the occasion, see Ramble (1984:157) = id. (1987:230). On the collection of earth and water from Muktināth as sacred elements and their insertion into *stūpas*, see also Mumford (1989:97).

valley of sTed in the north-east occurs, which was also frequented by Padmasambhava, and where an inexhaustible salt mine is said to be located.

I should like to close this compilation of Tibetan sources on Muktināth with a "spiritual song" (*mgur*) of Kaḥ-thog rig-'dzin Tshe-dbang nor-bu; it was composed in 1727, when the teacher from East Tibet first visited the pilgrimage site. The starting point of his journey was Mang-yul and the sacred sites there:

> E ma ho!
> Wonderful sacred site, on the border of Nepal and Tibet,
> the white glacier mount, like a hoisted victory banner.
> He called it Land of the Great God of Existence (i.e. Śiva).
> He who is the Lord, the Kalyānamitra O-rgyan chen-po!
>
> On the front-side, the rocky mount [with] the vajra peaks,
> Hundred-and-some spouts of ambrosial water it is called.
> Supreme practice site, where shines forth the wonderful light –
> that which is the place for the profound treasures' numerous teachings.[29]

[29] Tshe-dbang nor-bu: *dPal rig pa 'dzin pa chen po tshe dbang nor bu'i gsung mgur zhal gdams kyi tshogs ji snyed pa* pp. 25.6–26.1: *e ma ho / gnas ya la mtshan pa bal bod mtshams / ri gangs dkar rgyal mtshan 'phyar 'dra ba / khong srid pa'i lha chen gling du zhes / rje o rgyan chen po'i dge bsnyen lags / de mdun ngos brag ri rdo rje spo / chab bdud rtsi chu mig brgya rtsa zhes / sgrub gnas mchog ngo mtshar gzi byin 'bar / gter zab chos mang po'i bzhugs gnas lags*. In the colophon to the song (ibid, p. 28.3–4), Rig-'dzin Tshe-dbang nor-bu calls the place "a border community of Mang-yul sKyid-grong" (*mang yul skyid grong gi sde mthar thug pa bal bod mtshams chu mig brgya rtsa*). The connection with the region has been maintained up to the 20th century; see, e.g., the ornamental furnishings of dGon-pa gsar-ba in Muktināth; Jest (1981:67): "Two chörten represent the Jowo of Kyirong." Snellgrove (1961a=1989:200) describes a nun who looked after the needs of pilgrims in Muktināth; she was a disciple of Brag-dkar Rin-po-che, i.e. Brag-dkar-ba bsTan-'dzin nor-bu (1899–1959) from Brag-dkar rta-so in Mang-yul Gung-thang.

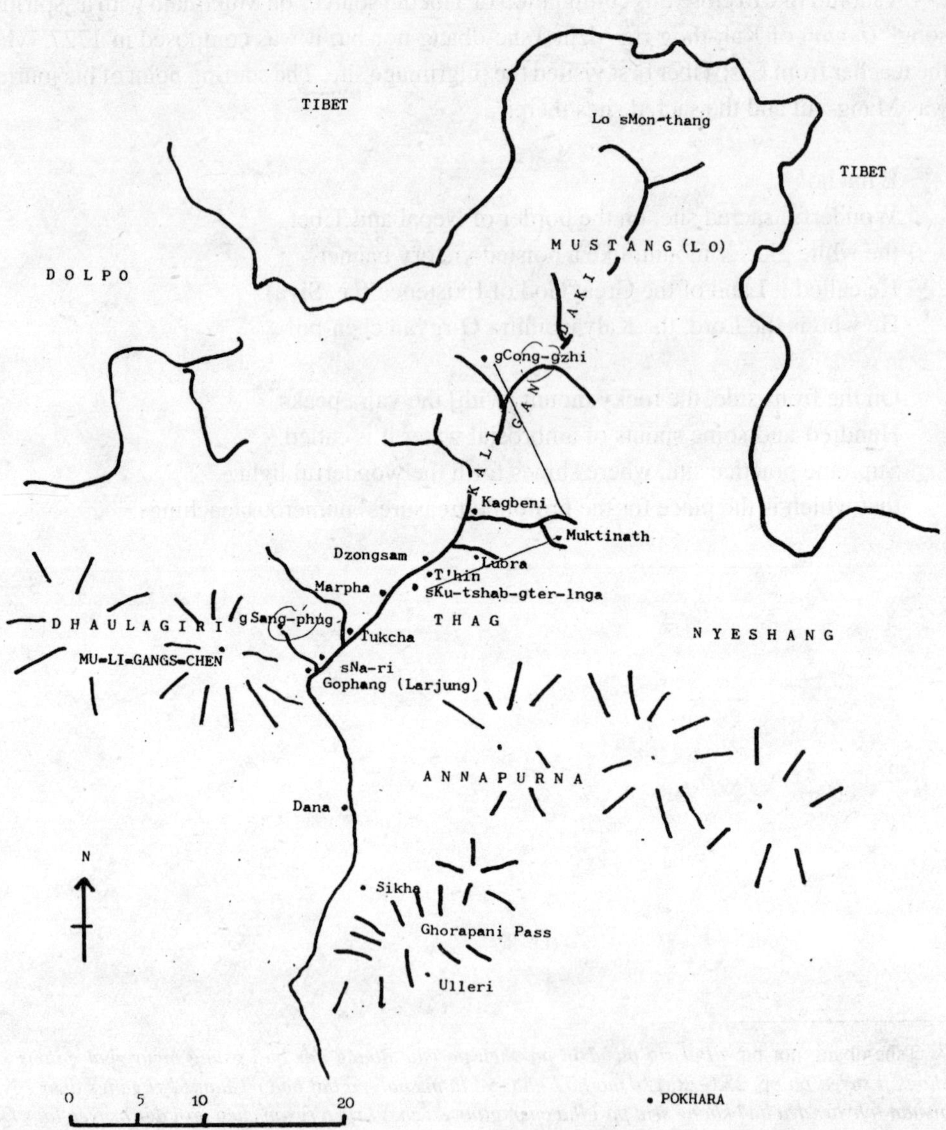

Maps taken from Snellgrove (1979)

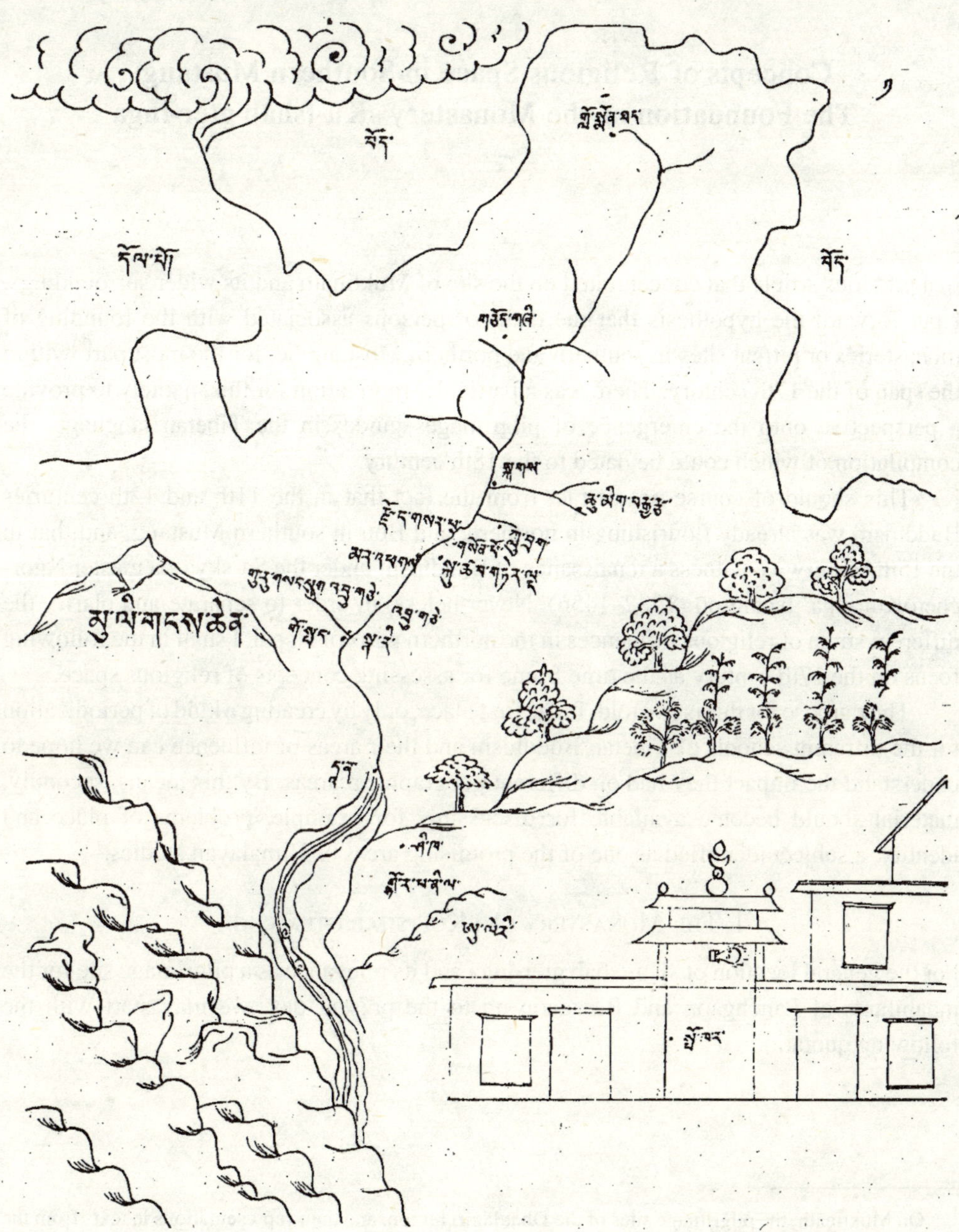

Drawn by mTshams-pa Ngag-dbang

Concepts of Religious Space in Southern Mustang: The Foundation of the Monastery sKu-tshab gter-lnga

In a previous article that concentrated on the site of Muktināth and its wider surroundings, I put forward the hypothesis that the dates of persons associated with the founding of monasteries or retreat sites in southern and northern Mustang lie, for the most part, within the span of the 17th century. There was a particular motivation for this, namely to provide a perspective onto the emergence of pilgrimages guides in the Tibetan language, the compilation of which could be dated to the 18th century.

This should of course not detract from the fact that in the 11th and 12th centuries Buddhism was already flourishing in northern, and Bon in southern Mustang, and that in the 15th century we witness a renaissance of Buddhism under the Sa-skya-pa master Ngor-chen Kun-dga' bzang-po (1382–1456). Nevertheless, in order to separate and clarify the different strata of religious influences in the northern parts of Nepal, I shall in the following focus on the 17th century as the time frame for assessing concepts of religious space.

The purpose for this is twofold: In the first place, only by creating a kind of periodization for the different schools of Tibetan Buddhism and their areas of influence can we hope to understand the impact they had on different geographical areas. By this means, secondly, material should become available for discussing, for example, problems of place and identity, a subject identified as one of the promising areas of Himalayan studies.[1]

1. The Monastery of sKu-tshab gter-lnga

For the general location of sKu-tshab gter-lnga and its relevance as a pilgrimage site for the inhabitants of Panchgaon and Baragaon up to the present day, we may start with the following quotation:

---

[1] On Muktināth, the pilgrimage sites of the Dhaulāgiri region, and their representations in texts from the genre "descriptions of sacred sites" (*gnas yig*) and "inventories" (*dkar chag*), see Ehrhard (1993b) and chapter twelve in the present volume. In addition, it should be noted that there also exists an inventory for the Dhaulāgiri Himāl and the Padmasambhava cave from the pen of the Bon-po master bsTan-'dzin Nyi-ma (19th century): *gNas chen mu le gangs dang gu ru gsang phug gi dkar chag kun snang gsal sgron*, 16 fols., NGMPP reel no. L 407/5. Its wording follows the Buddhist tradition. Concerning research trends in studies of place and identity, see Ellingson (1992).

> The monastery of Kutsapternga (sKu-tshab gter-lnga): "Five Treasures of Bodily Representation" is located on a level site at an altitude of 3000 m on a spur dominating the valley to the north-east of Mārphā with a beautiful view of the Kāli Gaṇḍakī Valley. Until 1973, the temple with its courtyard and dwellings opened to the north-east.
>
> The normal approach is from the east by the route from Ṭhini. On the way up, the faithful worship a sacred lake and the imprints left by Guru Rinpoche. Many pilgrims come to the temple for the annual ceremonies (seventh lunar month) to worship the five treasures brought from the monastery of Samye (bSam-yas) in Central Tibet. (Fig. 1)

We shall take a closer look at the five treasures and their place of origin in the next section. Concerning the renovations of the monastery, it is known that the assembly hall was repainted in 1956 and the monastery extended in 1973 by adding a gallery of two storeys on the southern side of the main building. An earlier enlargement took place in 1938. This occurred under the supervision of a lama from eastern Tibet by the name of Sangs-rgyas bzang-po (born 1894).[2]

At the time of the first construction of buildings, the place was called "Monastery Site, Hill of Clear Light" (*dgon gnas 'od gsal sgang*) or "Site of the Guru's (i.e. Padmasambhava's) practices" (*gu ru'i sgrub gnas*). These first building activities were started by O-rgyan dpal-bzang (1617–1677) in the year 1668, and the place was selected precisely because of the former presence of Padmasambhava, the great adept and propagator of Vajrayāna Buddhism in Tibet. This fact and the date of the first construction can be found in the biography of O-rgyan dpal-bzang. In the following I shall sketch the life and the travels of O-rgyan dpal-bzang on the basis of this text. The background to the foundation of the monastery sKu-tshab gter-lnga should thereby become clear, and we shall see which concepts of religious space were relevant at that time.

---

2 For the quotation, see Jest (1981:71). There are also mentioned the renovations of 1956 and 1973. The enlargement carried out by Sangs-rgyas bzang-po in 1938 is described in Sangs-rgyas bzang-po: *Sangs rgyas bzang po'i rnam thar zhes bya ba'i me long*, fols. 63b–64b. A short résumé of this priest's activities in northern and southern Mustang was provided by Tucci (1956:13f.). Uncertain of his dates at the time, Jackson (1978:196) tentatively placed him in the 18th century. Sangs-rgyas bzang-po was a disciple of the rNying-ma-pa teacher mKhan-chen gZhan-dga' (1871–1927). For more details on the life of Sangs-rgyas bzang-po and his religious influence in southern Mustang, see Ehrhard (2003) and chapter fifteen in the present volume.

2. THE LIFE AND TRAVELS OF O-RGYAN DPAL-BZANG

The birthplace of O-rgyan dpal-bzang is given in the biography as "a protrusion of what is known as Glo-bo, the land of the gods Som-po," and more exactly, "a meeting ground of all the people of India and Tibet, where all sorts of substances of the south and the north appeared spontaneously, dGa'-rab rdzong". This means that O-rgyan dpal-bzang was born into the family of the rulers of dGa'-rab rdzong near present-day Ṭhini.[3]

The line goes back to an "officer" (*zhal ngo*) of 'Ug-po gling from western Tibet (sTod) and the first ancestor in this line mentioned by name is rGyal gNam-phur. His mother's family is known as "King with the Wrathful Eye" (*rgyal sdang mig can*), or "King with Three Eyes" (*rgyal po spyan gsum pa*). The first ancestor in the mother's side is called dPal Ti-pha-phad.[4]

After first studies under a maternal uncle and an official of the noble family sKyar-skya sgang-pa in the Muktināth valley, O-rgyan dpal-bzang proceeded to the Sa-skya-pa monastery rTa-nag Thub-bstan rnam-rgyal, which was founded in Central Tibet by Go-rams-pa bSod-nams seng-ge (1425–1489). His teacher there was Ngag-dbang chos-grags (1572–1641), and by this time O-rgyan dpal-bzang had reached the age of twenty.[5] He subsequently returned to his homeland and remained there for one year, but his wish to master the teachings of the "true meaning" (*nges don*) drove him back to Tibet again, this

---

3 O-rgyan dpal-bzang: *Rigs brgya dbang po 'dren mchog slob dpon dpal bzang po'i rnam par thar pa dad pa'i spu long g.yo byed mthong bas yid 'phrog ngo mtshar 'phreng ba'i gtam rmad du byung ba*, fols. 7a/6–b/2: *glo bo zhes grags pa'i 'bur du dod pa lha yul som po zhes pa ... rgya bod kyi mi thams cad kyi 'du gnas lho byang gi rdzas sna thams cad rang bzhin du byung ba dga' rab rdzong*. As early as the 13th century Mustang was divided into "upper Lo" (*glo bo stod*) and "lower Lo" (*glo bo smad*); lower Lo included the Muktināth valley and Kāgbeni. For references, see Jackson (1984:5). The term "land of the gods" (*lha yul*) is used in the Bon-po literature for describing Mang-yul Gung-thang; see dPal-ldan tshul-khrims: *Sangs rgyas g.yung drung bon gyi bstan pa'i byung ba brjod pa'i legs bshad skal pa bzang po'i mgrin rgyan rab gsal chu shel nor bu do shel*, p. 492. The latter is one of the thirty-seven meeting grounds of the Bon religion (*bon gyi 'du gnas*) see Uebach: (1999:270).

4 O-rgyan dpal-bzang (as in note 3), fols. 7b/2–8a/1. For the difficulties in interpreting the name 'Ug-po gling in the translation of the Cimang *bem-chag,* see Ramble & Vinding (1987:24, note 42). According to the passage just mentioned we can at least exclude now the possibility that 'Ug-po/pa gling refers to the "great residence of the rNying-ma-pa" in gTsang. The "king with the wrathful eye" (*rgyal sdang mig can*) is also mentioned in the Cimang *bem-chag*; ibid, pp. 16f. He is treated there as a historical person. According to rDo-rje brag Rig-'dzin Padma 'phrin-las: *'Dus pa mdo dbang gi bla ma brgyud pa'i rnam thar ngo mtshar dad pa'i phreng ba,* p. 272, the lineage *ldang mig gi spyan gsum ldan pa'i rgyud* is a royal lineage equivalent to that of the rulers of Mang-yul Gung-thang; so here the name is used generically. For the term *bem-chag* and the classification of this kind of literature as 'basic law texts' or 'constitutions', see Schuh (1995:6).

5 Jackson (1978:221) mentioned that the traditional connection of the Kāgbeni monastic community with rTa-nag Thub-bstan rnam-rgyal is indicated in the index of a manuscript obtained by Giuseppe Tucci in Kāgbeni; compare Tucci (1956:15). For the works of Ngag-dbang chos-grags, see *dKar chag mthong bas yid 'phrog chos mdzod bye ba'i lde mig* (A Bibliography of Sa-skya-pa Literature), pp. 107–111.

time to bSam-yas and the Yar-klungs valley. In 'Phyongs-rgyas he came upon the "treasure discoverer" (*gter ston*) lHa-btsun Nam-mkha' 'jigs-med (1597–1653), but an auspicious connection was not created between the two.

In the year 1642 O-rgyan dpal-bzang reached lHo sPa-gro, that is the western part of Bhutan. This area is called "What is hidden, the Place of the Ḍākiṇīs" (*sbas pa mkha' 'gro'i gnas*). There he stayed for three years and studied a great number of treasure teachings under a member of the family of Padma gling-pa (1450–1521) and other teachers. During this period he heard for the first time the name of the treasure discoverer Rig-'dzin bDud-'dul rdo-rje (1615–1672) of mDo-khams.

O-rgyan dpal-bzang followed a long and difficult route to reach Dar-rtse-mdo, present-day Tachienlu or Kangding in Sichuan. Soon after his arrival he met Rig-'dzin bDud-'dul rdo-rje in person, from whom he received treasure teachings during the following three years. At his farewell he was presented with various sacred objects and substances, and obviously also those relics which provided the name for the monastery site in the Kāli Gaṇḍakī valley[6] (Fig. 2). Though he asked for a "prophecy of the place" (*gnas kyi lung bstan*), i.e. an indication of which spot he should continue his religious practices at, O-rgyan dpal-bzang was not sent to the region of southern Mustang. His teacher advised him instead to go the site of Ri-bo dpal-'bar, a holy mountain some 6500 m in height which dominates the south of the valley of sKyid-grong. It is one of the most important sacred sites of the old kingdom of Mang-yul Gung-thang.

Difficulties on his way back made it impossible for O-rgyan dpal-bzang to visit his old teachers in Bhutan. The alternative route led him on the other hand to the "hidden valley" (*sbas yul*) 'Bras-mo gshongs, present-day Sikkim. In the centre of this territory, in Brag-dkar bKra-shis lding, he met Phun-tshogs rnam-rgyal (1604–1670), a member of the influential mNga'-bdag family and preceptor to the first local Buddhist king who had been enthroned not long before, in 1642. There he continued receiving treasure teachings.[7] Phun-tshogs rnam-rgyal wanted to station him in Legs-rtse, located in Sikkim, but O-rgyan dpal-bzang refused this offer, and in fulfilling the prophecy of Rig-'dzin bDud-'dul rdo-rje continued his journey to Mang-yul Gung-thang.

---

6 For references to Rig-'dzin bDud-'dul rdo-rje and his opening of the "hidden valley" gNas Padma-bkod, south-east of Kong-po, see Ehrhard (1994:9–10) and chapter twenty-one in the present volume. The five treasures that represent the body or teachings [of Padmasambhava] (*sku tshab gter lnga*) are: three statues (one of Padmasambhava, one of rDo-rje gro-lod, one of Ye-shes mtsho-rgyal), together with half the Master's overcoat and one of his boots. The autobiography explicitly states that O-rgyan dpal-bzang also received written materials from Rig-'dzin bDud-'dul rdo-rje; O-rgyan dpal-bzang (as in note 3), fol. 209b: *mnga' ris la byon skabs su / lung bstan bka' shog kyi glegs bu gnyis / gu ru mtho rgyal gyi dbu lo shog gser dam rdzas bcas ... gnang yang.*

7 I should like to point out that, under Phun-tshogs rnam-rgyal, O-rgyan dpal-bzang studied the cycle *Chos rgyal srong btsan sgam po'i bka' 'bum* and the teachings of the treasure discoverer Zhig-po gling-pa (1524–1583); O-rgyan dpal-bzang (as in note 3), fols. 219bff. & 225bff.

The first master O-rgyan dpal-bzang met in Ri-bo dpal-'bar was Nor-bu bde-chen (born 1617), a member of the Gur family and the lineage holder of the mDo-chen bKa'-brgyud-pa. Before finally settling down for a three-year retreat in Ri-bo dpal-'bar, O-rgyan dpal-bzang went to visit a number of remote places. Having taken up one invitation from Ku-thang rTsum, which is today located on Nepalese territory, he followed another one to visit Kathmandu and sKye-ba lung, a "hidden valley" near the newly opened trade route between Nepal and Tibet via Kuti / gNya'-lam.[8]

In 1666, after his retreat, Nor-bu bde-chen invited O-rgyan dpal-bzang to La-'debs (south of sKyid-grong), where he gave initiations and teachings for a period of three months. It was only then that a message reached him from his home country. The biography recounts in the following words:

> From Glo-bo, the country of his birth, [from] four laymen and monks, including the bhikṣu Phun-tshogs chos-'phel from the monastic settlement of sKag, the monastery community and commoners of Som-po, an invitation [in the form of] a supplication letter together with presents arrived by way of Nepal, stating that he should come to Glo-bo.[9]

After a stay in Brag-dkar rta-so (north-west of sKyid-grong), where he met a teacher by the name of Karma Chos-'phel, O-rgyan dpal-bzang went on the next year to sNye-shang Brag-dkar. Due to an intense spiritual experience with a certain Karma Blo-bzang, he was finally able to arrive without hindrance in Som-po, as stated in his biography.[10] More than thirty years after his departure he was given a proper welcome. Along with the inhabitants

---

8 sKye-ba lung is also mentioned by the Sixth Zhwa-dmar-pa (1584–1630) in connection with his trip to the Kathmandu Valley: "A holy site that was blessed by Ācārya Padma[sambhava]"; for further references, see Ehrhard (1997a:129) and chapter seventeen in the present volume. O-rgyan dpal-bzang was invited there by Rig-'dzin sTobs-ldan dbang-po, a disciple of the Third Yol-mo-ba sprul-sku bsTan-'dzin nor-bu (1598–1644).

9 O-rgyan dpal-bzang (as in note 3), fol. 313b/2–3: *'khrungs yul glo bo'i* (= *bo*) *nas dge slong phun tshogs chos 'phel sogs skya btsun bzhi skag chos sde som po lha sde ma* (= *mi*) *sde nas glo bor phebs dgos tshul zhu yig rten dang bcas spyan 'dren bal yul nas byung bas*. It should be noted here that the Hill of Clear Light was also sponsored by the monastery community and the commoners of rDzar, sKag, rDzong and Sum-po in later years; see Kun-bzang klong-yangs: *rTogs brjod mu tig gi mchun bu zhes pa'i gtam*, fol. 49a/3–4: *rim par rdzar skag rdzong / sum po dga' rab rdzong rnams nas lha sde mi sde rnams kyis gser phreng phebs bsus grangs las 'das pa 'byung*. This statement refers to events of 1686, exactly twenty years after the invitation to O-rgyan dpal-bzang.

10 Karma Blo-bzang has already been mentioned by Snellgrove (1961a=1989:216) as the founding lama of the monastery of Brag-dkar in sNye-shang. He was also responsible for the foundation of the monastery of gNam-gung in Dol-po. Ordained by the Sixth Zhwa-dmar-pa, he was nominated "representative" (*gnas 'dzin pa*) of Brag-dkar rta-so. This post he was later to hand over to the above-mentioned Karma Chos-'phel. For more details on the life of Karma Blo-bzang and his activities, see Ehrhard (2001:101–106) and chapter fourteen in the present volume.

of Som-po, the people of Tshug and sKag are also mentioned as having joined in the celebrations.

The journey continued. O-rgyan dpal-bzang was invited by a priest from Dol-po to the valley of Bar-bung or Bar-rong, the "middle gorge", a "hidden valley" to the north of the Dhaulāgiri Himāl. This led him via Charka to Punga, Terang and Pingring and from there to sKag (Fig. 3).[11] Having given several public initiations, he returned to the Kāli Gaṇḍakī valley where, at the urging of the inhabitants of Som-po, he founded a monastic settlement at the site "Hill of Clear Light" on the eighth Tibetan month of the year 1668. The disciples from Dol-po are specifically mentioned as being involved in the festivities.

The further activities of O-rgyan dpal-bzang included travels back to the region of sKyid-grong, during one of which he passed again through the "hidden valley" Ku-thang rTsum. He also stayed one more time in Brag-dkar rta-so, and a journey to northern Mustang is also mentioned in the biography, on which occasion he exchanged presents with the "ruler" (*sde bdag*). From 1673 onwards O-rgyan dpal-bzang was busy furnishing the temple near Som-po with statues and installing proper containers for the relics. This was interrupted by a retreat performed by eight monks, which was supervised by O-rgyan dpal-bzang himself. It was the treasure teachings of Padmasambhava that occasioned one final journey, the treasure discoverer Gar-dbang rdo-rje (1640–1685) having asked him to inspect some findings he had recovered. Soon after returning from Shel-phug north of the Manaslu region, O-rgyan dpal-bzang died in the fourth Tibetan month of the year 1677.

3. THE "HIDDEN VALLEY" AS A CONCEPT OF RELIGIOUS SPACE

In retracing the steps of O-rgyan dpal-bzang, we have encountered a number of areas ranging from small spots to full-sized kingdoms, each designated as "hidden" (*sbas pa*) or a "hidden valley" (*sbas yul*). On the trans-regional level there were sPa-gro (in Bhutan), Sikkim and Padma-bkod on the far south-eastern border of Tibet. The regional level, i.e. the areas within several days' travel from southern Mustang, was highlighted by two examples: Ku-thang rTsum and Bar-rong.[12] On the local level, I would even go as far as to

[11] Two of the disciples of O-rgyan dpal-bzang, both of whose biographies have survived, were active around Dol-po sKag: Kun-bzang klong-yangs (1644–1696) and O-rgyan bstan-'dzin (1657–1737); see Kun-bzang klong-yangs (as in note 9), fol. 7aff. and O-rgyan bstan-'dzin: *rNal 'byor gyi dbang phyug o rgyan bstan 'dzin zhes bya ba'i ri khrod kyi nyams dbyangs*, pp. 7ff. Each of the texts mentions the presence of Karma Blo-bzang in the region in the years 1659/60. For the role of O-rgyan bstan-'dzin in creating a "hidden valley" in southern Dol-po, see Ehrhard (1998:5–9) and chapter twenty in the present volume.

[12] For local beliefs surrounding the concept of *sbas yul* in Tichurong and Barbung, see Jest (1971:71): "La tradition rapporte que les premiers habitants résidant sur la rive droite de la Bheri, pay caché, *sbas yul* t., ouvert aux hommes par Padmasambhava, sont venus du Tibet." And Jest (1975:62): "vallée encaisée, la Barbung était un 'pays caché', *sbas yul*." Ku-thang rTsum needs to be seen in connection with the "hidden valley" Ku-thang sKyid-mo lung; see note 14.

see the foundation of sKu-tshab gter-lnga in the context of erecting a temple in a "hidden valley".

Let me give two arguments for this: First, the biography praises O-rgyan dpal-bzang by saying that "he is a special great being who opens doors etc. to sites that are hidden." This ability is there described as referring specially to sKye-ba lung, the "hidden valley" in the vicinity of the trade route between Nepal and Tibet, which had recently been established in the 17th century. Secondly, the pilgrimage guide of the 18th century describing the arrival of O-rgyan dpal-bzang at the "Hill of Clear Light" uses the same stereotypes that can be found in texts on the opening of "hidden valleys": the natural features of the landscape take in the shape of natural and supernatural beings, signs of the former presence of Padmasambhava are recognized and so forth.[13]

Another case may be adduced to exemplify the prevalence of this concept in the geographical area under discussion, showing that in the 17th and 18th centuries "hidden valleys" attracted not only members of the rNying-ma-pa school but also ones of the 'Brug-pa bKa'-brgyud-pa school. Towards the end of his life, bsTan-'dzin ras-pa (1644/46–1723), the founder of Shel dgon-pa in Dol-po (and a native of the area around Muktināth), had a vision of Padmasambhava. The Master admonished him to go to Ku-thang sKyid-mo lung. The priest describes in great detail his activities in this valley north-east of Manaslu, and makes special mention of the treasure discoveries of gTer-ston Gar-dbang rdo-rje in that sacred spot. Although he had problems with the local communities, he stayed around three years, and also visited Ku-thang rTsum.[14]

What can we say, after this final observation, about the status of "hidden valleys" as a concept of religious space? Foremost is the palpable and visible presence of the body or teachings of Padmasambhava, the landscape being impregnated with his body marks, and relics or statues representing the master being widely on display. After the signs are recognized or the holy objects installed by a person with the necessary traits the place comes to possess a new spiritual quality, often visualized as a maṇḍala with four entry points. The geographical dimensions of the place can vary to a great extent, as already mentioned, and it can offer refuge to the followers of Padmasambhava in troublesome

---

13 See O-rgyan dpal-bzang (as in note 3), fol. 308b/1ff.: *sbas pa'i gnas sgo sogs 'byed pa'i skyes chen dam pa yin pa ... sbas yul skye ba lung pa'i gnas sgo 'byed thub tshul dang gnas de nas gter thon pa'i lung bstan sogs zhal lung mang du rig 'dzin chen pos gsungs pa yod.* For a description of O-rgyan dpal-bzang's arrival at 'Od-gsal sgang according to the pilgrimage guide, see Snellgrove (1979:90–92).

14 For bsTan-'dzin ras-pa's opening of the "hidden valley" Ku-thang sKyid-mo lung, see bsTan-'dzin ras-pa: *rJe btsun bstan 'dzin ras pa de nyid kyi gsang ba'i rnam thar sa khyis phan gyis / mgur ma'i kha 'gros gnas ngo bzung tshul mya ngan 'das tshul dkar chag dang bcas chos tshan lnga*, fols. 17b/2–23a/2 (*lung bstan bzhin gnas sgo phye*) and fols. 23a/2–34a/4 (*gnas sgo phye nas ngos bzung tshul*). Compare Aris (1979a:2ff.). The printing of this work, known also as *bsTan 'dzin ras pa'i gsang ba'i rnam thar*, was partly financed by sponsors from rDzong, rDzar and sKag.

times. Having once been opened, it normally becomes the destination of pilgrims, who circumambulate either the place as a whole or the different objects in it, thereby coming into direct contact with the holy artifacts. More detailed studies will be necessary to provide an exact idea of the different locations of the "hidden valleys", but it has at least become clear by now that they always lie in the southern border regions of Tibet.

For the present I should merely like to stress the fact the sacred sites are often in the vicinity of a trade route, thus implying that the emergence of a "hidden valley" in a specific geographical area has also a strong impact on patterns of economic and cultural exchange. O-rgyan dpal-bzang was active on both the two main routes of the Nepal-Tibet trade (via sKyid-grong and via Kuti / gNya'-lam), and setting up a monastery along the trade route between Beni in Nepal and the Tibetan highlands was surely a proper act in a time of deepening relations between the two countries. It is also interesting to note that before the foundation of sKu-tshab gter-lnga, he visited Dol-po sKag, the first of two customs stations on the way to Jumla.

As geographical research is engaged in reconstructing the settlement history of a region like Kāgbeni, the crossing point of the north-south and east-west routes[15], the existence of "hidden valleys" on the regional and local levels may give some clue as to the influence of Tibetan Buddhism in that area. It most certainly was a motivating force in the travels of many traders and pilgrims that passed through the region. And it most certainly moulded places and identities.

[15] See Pohle (1993:58–59) and Seeber (1994:84f.). The latter offers observations on the geo-strategic location of the fortress of Kāgbeni (and of dGa'-rab rdzong). Kāgbeni as the meeting point of all the routes is also described by Snellgrove (1961a=1989:166): "To the east goes the track to Muktināth and on to Nye-shang and Nar; to the south goes another to Tukchā and beyond to the faint limits of the Tibetan Buddhist world; to the west goes the track to Dol-po whence we had come and to the north there is another to Lo (Mustang) and Tibet."

Fig. 1: The monastery of sKu-tshab gter-lnga (Photo: Ehrhard 1988)

Fig. 2: The five treasures that represent the body of teaching [of Padmasambhava] (*sKu tshab gter lnga*). Painting by mTshams-pa Ngag-dbang

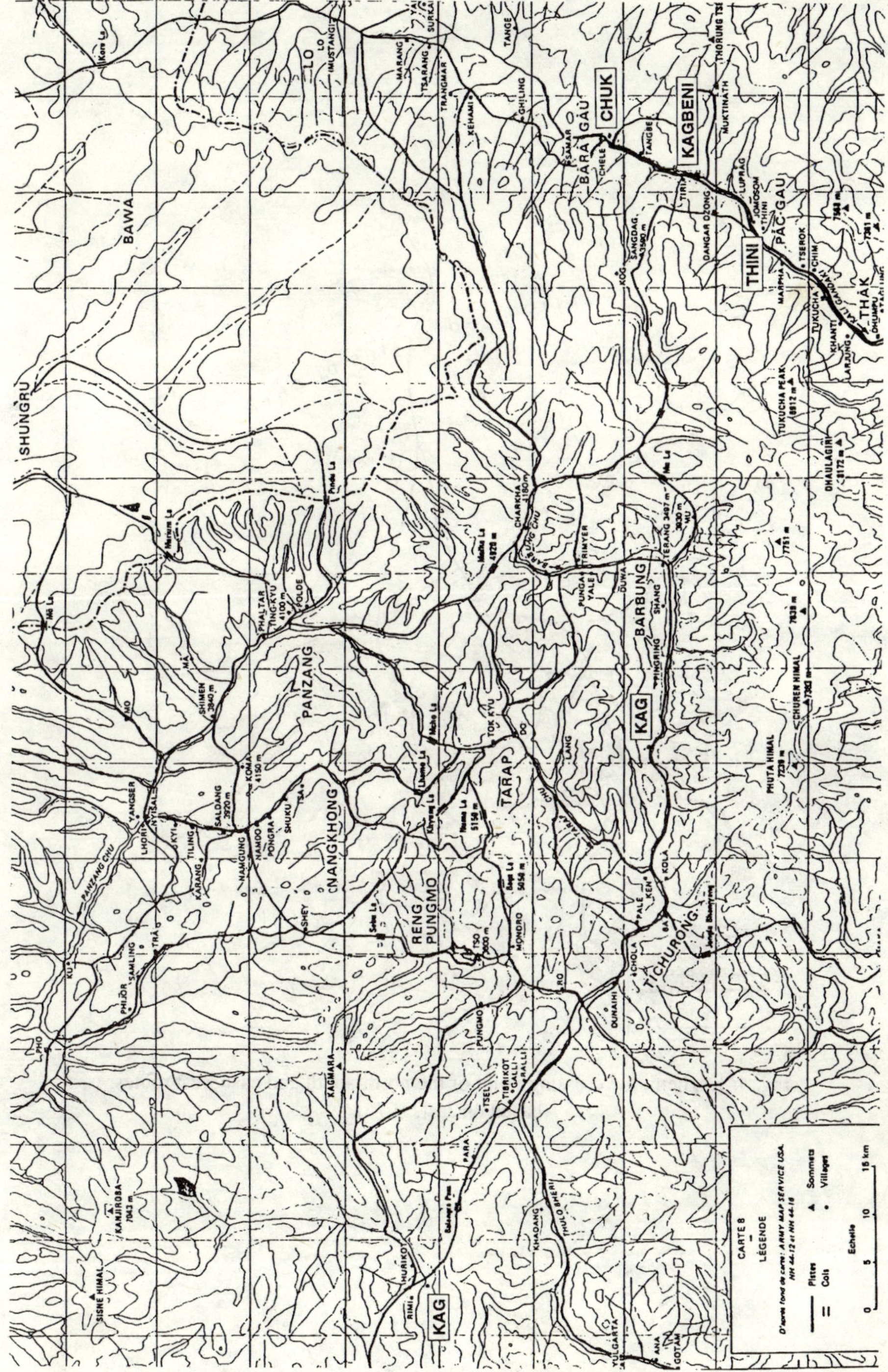

Fig. 3: Kāgbeni and the eastern route to Jumlā (based on Jest, 1975)

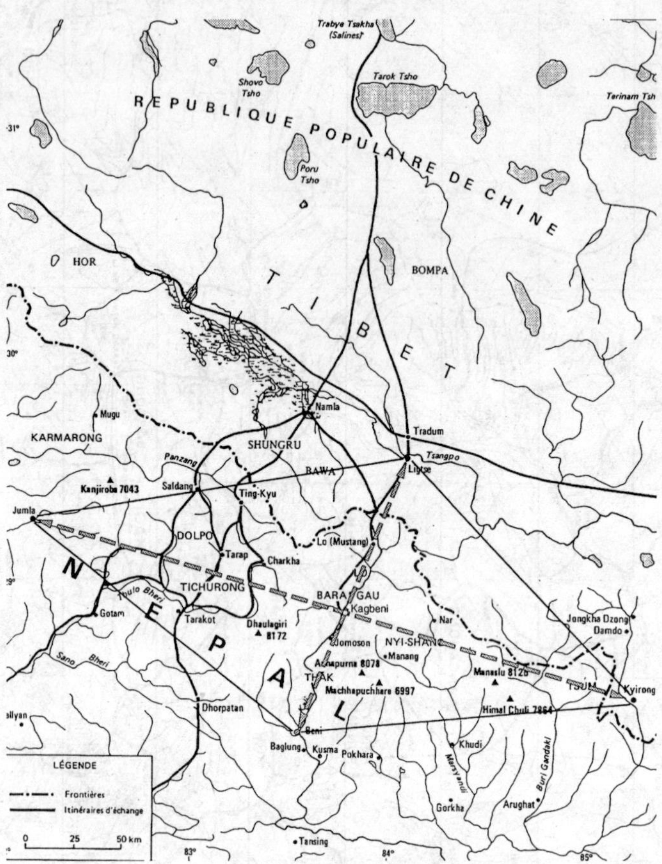

Fig. 4: Kāgbeni, the crossing point of the north-south and east-west routes (based on Jest, 1975)

Religious Geography and Literary Traditions: The Foundation of the Monastery Brag-dkar bSam-gling

Introduction

Recent years have seen a considerable increase of knowledge about the history of settlements and cultural landscapes in the Tibetan-speaking regions of the Himalayas. Especially in the case of Mustang—and neighbouring valleys of northern Nepal—an interdisciplinary project of the German Research Council was able to produce results based both on observational research and textual studies over a period of several years.

Within this project I had the chance to work on the topic of the religious geography of the region. I dealt mainly with questions about the history and spatial distribution of specific religious cults in areas like southern and northern Mustang, with the aim of providing a framework for helping to identify concepts of religious space. Using for the most part literary sources in the Tibetan language, I came to the conclusion that one must first understand the textual traditions of Mang-yul Gung-thang in order to be able to fully comprehend the cultural history of areas like Dolpo, Mustang and Manang.

The following observations constitute a case study. They deal with the monastery of Brag-dkar bSam-gling in Manang and with the life and travels of Karma Blo-bzang, who is known as the founder of this monastery. By following the steps of this teacher of the Karma or Kaṃ-tshang bKa'-brgyud-pa school, we can gain a sense of the historical importance and geographical extension of the religious traditions of Mang-yul Gung-thang, and can see at the same time to what extent the borderlands between Nepal and Tibet attracted Tibetan priests and yogins to reside there throughout the 17th century.

Resident of Brag-dkar rta-so

The autobiography of Karma Blo-bzang provides no information concerning the year of birth of this master. As his two main teachers were Grub-mchog dbang-po (1563–1618) and the Sixth Zhwa-dmar-pa Chos-kyi dbang-phyug (1584–1630), we can at least place his birth in the final years of the 16th century.

The first of these two teachers was mainly responsible for the upkeep of the site Ras-chung phug in the valley of Yar-[k]lung[s] in Central Tibet; it was there that the young boy studied with Grub-mchog dbang-po for a period of seven years (see Pl. 1). The teachings he received were from a transmission which came through a certain Byams-pa phun-tshogs (1503–1581), and indeed Karma Blo-bzang was later recognized as the "reincarnation" (*sprul sku*) of this master.[1] Studies continued with the Sixth Zhwa-dmar-pa up till the age of twenty; it was then that Karma Blo-bzang was requested by this important hierarch of the Kaṃ-tshang bKa'-brgyud-pa school to move to "western Tibet" (*stod*) and to become the resident priest of the monastery Brag-dkar rta-so, a site that is closely connected with the name of the great yogin Mi-la-ras-pa (1028–1111) (see Pl. 2). According to a later chronicle, the trip of Karma Blo-bzang to western Tibet was generously sponsored by Karma bsTan-skyong dbang-po (regnal years 1620–1642), the ruler of Central Tibet at that time.[2]

After spending nine years—mainly in retreat—in Brag-dkar rta-so, Karma Blo-bzang left the region of Mang-yul Gung-thang and travelled still further west, to the sacred mountain Gangs Rin-po-che (Kailāśa). On this pilgrimage tour he also travelled through the region of Limi (= Sli-mi) and through the nomad lands of Gro-shod. Via Mustang (= Glo-bo) he then reached for the first time the high mountain valley of sNye-shang, and there became acquainted with an old *vihāra* of modest size. Testing the ground at the spot where this building was located, he found it appropriate for the construction of a larger *vihāra* and nominated an overseer for that purpose. He also gave instructions to the quite extensive religious community of sNye-shang.[3]

Soon afterwards we see Karma Blo-bzang again in the company of the Sixth Zhwa-dmar-pa, and also in that of the Tenth Karma-pa Chos-dbyings rdo-rje (1604–1674), visiting the different sacred sites of south-western Tibet. While the Sixth Zhwa-dmar-pa travelled to Nepal and spent fruitful time at the courts of the Malla kings of Kathmandu,

---

1 For a short biography of Grub-mchog dbang-po, see Chos-kyi 'byung-gnas & Tshe-dbang Kun-khyab: *sGrub brgyud karma kaṃ tshang brgyud pa rin po che'i rnam par thar pa rab 'byams nor bu zla ba chu shel gyi phreng ba*, vol. 2, pp. 343.6–344.7; Byams-pa phun-tshogs was a disciple of lHa-btsun Rin-chen rnam-rgyal (1473–1557), the founder of Brag-dkar rta-so. A complete autobiography is also available: *mKhas grub chen po byams pa phun tshogs kyi rnam thar*, NGMPP reel no. L 783/3. For a physical representation of Byams-pa phun-tshogs, see the statue in Pal (1991:121); the statement that he flourished in the second half of the 13th century should be corrected.

2 The chronicle of the monastery of Brag-dkar rta-so by Chos-kyi dbang-phyug gives details of the nomination of Karma Blo-bzang as "resident" (*gdan 'dzin pa*) of the Mi-la-ras-pa site; see *Drang srong dga' ba'i dal gtam*, fol. 30b/4–5.

3 See Karma Blo-bzang: *mKhas grub chen po karma blo bzang ba rnam thar mchod sprin rgya mtsho*, fol. 14a/1–3: *de nas glo bo rgyud (= brgyud) nas snye shang gi brag dkar bsam gling du phebs / gtsug lag khang rnying pa chung / ri zur 'dir gtsug lag khang che tsam zhig gis (= gi) sa dpyad gzigs nas zhal bkod bzhag / de 'dus (= dus) snye shang gis (= gi) grwa rgyun mang po khrid)*. For the observation that the monastery of Braga (= Brag-dkar) was founded in the 15th century, see van Spengen (1987:139f.). The presence of members of the Tshal-pa bKa'-brgyud-pa school in sNye-shang is already documented in the 13th century; see, for example, the biography of bTsun-pa Chos-legs (1437–1521) by 'Jigs-med bzang-po & dBang-phyug dpal-ldan: *dPal ldan bla ma dam pa chos legs mtshan can gyi rnam thar*, fol. 10b/5ff. For the establishment of the Tshal-pa tradition in areas like Nub-ris, Glo-bo and Dol-po at that time, cf. Vitali (1996:397ff.). See notes 7 & 10 for references to the presence of an important teacher of the Jo-nang-pa school in sNye-shang (and Bar-bong).

Patan and Bhaktapur, the Tenth Karma-pa left for a pilgrimage to the sacred mountain Gangs Rin-po-che. On his way back he stopped in the town of rDzong-dkar, the capital of Gung-thang, and from there Karma Blo-bzang guided this patriarch of the Kaṃ-tshang bKa'-brgyud-pa school to the monastery Brag-dkar rta-so. As soon afterwards the demise of the Sixth Zhwa-dmar-pa was lamented, we can place this excursion in the years 1629/30.[4]

The visit of the Tenth Karma-pa to the site which was under the supervision of Karma Blo-bzang prompted the latter to undertake major building activities and change the actual site by connecting, for example, two different caves of Mi-la-ras-pa. Also at other sacred sites of the yogin, Karma Blo-bzang threw himself into renovating old structures and erecting new buildings: in Grod-phug, in the region of gNya'-nang, he constructed ten new *vihāras*; and in Yol-mo, present-day Helambu, the temple of rGod-tshang gling was renovated thanks to his efforts. Detailed information is also available on his service to the statue and the temple of the Ārya Wa-ti bzang-po in sKyid-grong, the centre of Mang-yul. Craftsmen from Nepal were engaged in all these undertakings.

After his stay in sKyid-grong and his offerings to the miraculously manifested statue of Avalokiteśvara, Karma Blo-bzang received an invitation from Mustang. By way of the valley of Nepal and Gorkha he thus entered a second time the high mountain valley of sNye-shang. There he laid the foundation for the *vihāra* of Brag-dkar bSam-gling, and also inaugurated a teaching seminary. Afterwards he spent half a year at Muktināth (= Chu-mig brgya-rtsa); among his audience, the name of dPon-drung rin-po-che bSod-nams rgyal-po is accorded special mention: he was a member of the noble sKyar-skya [s]gang-pa family, the rulers of the Muktināth Valley.[5]

TRAVELS IN MUSTANG AND DOLPO

The invitation for the next visit of Karma Blo-bzang to the region of Mustang came from dPon-drung Khro-bo rnam-rgyal, the ruling prince of the Muktināth Valley in the first half

---

4 For biographical data concerning the Sixth Zhwa-dmar-pa and the Tenth Karma-pa, see Chos-kyi 'byung-gnas & Tshe-dbang Kun-khyab (as in note 1), pp. 255.2–299.2 and pp. 324.1–336.4. The activities of the Tenth Karma-pa as an artist are sketched by Jackson (1996:247–258); for the journey of the Sixth Zhwa-dmar-pa to the valley of Nepal, see Ehrhard (1997a:128–132) and chapter seventeen in the present volume.

5 The activities of Karma Blo-bzang in gNya'-nang are documented in pilgrimage guides to the area; see Huber (1997:272). For the second stay in sNye-shang, see Karma Blo-bzang (as in note 3), fol. 39a/4–b/2: *yang glo bo nas gnyer pa rab bzang gdan 'dren du byung nas / skyid grong bol po (= bal po) rgyud (= brgyud) gor kha dang tsu ra'i rong nas snye shang du sleb (= bslebs) / brag dkar bsam gling gis (= gi) gtsug lag khang gsar pa'i gzhi legs par gting / chos grwa yang btsugs*). Different members of the sKyar-skya [s]gang-pa noble family, who were donors to Tibetan priests, as well as the idealized landscape of Muktināth are described in Ehrhard (1993b:26–28) and chapter twelve in the present volume. For Muktināth as a Hindu pilgrimage place, see Kaschewsky (1994:139–146).

of the 17th century. In sNye-shang Karma Blo-bzang was welcomed by the monastic community and the laity of Brag-dkar bSam-gling, where he gave extensive teachings based on the cycle *Yang zab dkon mchog spyi 'dus*, a "treasure-work" (*gter ma*) recovered by Rig-'dzin 'Ja'-tshon snying-po (1585–1656).

While he was in rDzar, his host was the above-mentioned bSod-nams rgyal-po. There invitations came to him from sKag and rDzong, issued by dPon-drung Khro-bo rgyal-mtshan and Khro-bo bsam-grub respectively. Karma Blo-bzang was thus greatly honoured at the three fortresses of the Muktināth Valley by each of the dukes and received a large number of offerings.[6]

After his return from a trip to northern Mustang, the next step in establishing the monastery of Brag-dkar bSam-gling was furnishing the new building with statues and *stūpa*s, and applying paintings to the inner walls of the *vihāra*. For this purpose four craftsmen from the Nepal Valley came to sNye-shang and stayed there for a period of nine months. The supervision of the work was entrusted to Karma dBang-rgyal, a disciple of Karma Blo-bzang, and the one who sculpted the great statue of the future Buddha Maitreya; the autobiography devotes special attention to a pair of *stūpa*s in the new monastery that contained many sacred articles and relics (see Pls. 4).

Another invitation to Karma Blo-bzang arrived from the region of Dol-po, and thus the master travelled to the valley of Bar-bong, to the former residence of Jo-nang Kun-dga' grol-mchog (1507–1566). After one month in the valley he moved on to rTa-rab, where he encountered the temples of dGon-pa Me-'byems and Byams-pa lha-khang. Back in Bar-bong Karma Blo-bzang founded a monastery under the name gSang-sngags chos-gling and gave extensive teachings according to the traditions of the *Ras chung snyan brgyud* and the treasure-works of Rig-'dzin 'Ja'-tshon snying-po.[7]

Still other regions of Dol-po were visited by Karma Blo-bzang. Thus we find him at the monastery of dMar-sgom—founded by bSod-nams blo-gros (1516–1581)—where he stayed in the company of a certain Zhabs-drung dPal-ldan don-grub. Among his disciples

---

6 For the genealogy of the sKyar-skya [s]gang-pa family, and especially the person of Khro-bo rnam-rgyal, see Schuh (1995:49f.); cf. also Vitali (1997:1032ff.). This third visit to sNye-shang is described in Karma Blo-bzang (as in note 3), fol. 46b/2–4: *de rjes glo bo nas dpon drung khro bo rnam rgyal dang / bla ma bu chen / bde gshegs bsod nams rgyal po'i btsun mo / brag dkar bsam gling lha sde mi sde thams cad kyis gdan 'dren la rten gsum ba'i bkod pa rim pa du ma dang bcas bsam gling chos sder slebs* (= *bslebs*). Shortly before this journey Karma Blo-bzang had travelled to gCung Ri-bo-che in Byang, where he had studied the cycle *Yang zab dkon mchog spyi 'dus* under a direct disciple of Rig-'dzin 'Ja'-tshon snying-po; for the contents of this cycle, see Ehrhard (1993a:81–89) and chapter ten in the present volume.

7 The details of the furnishing of Brag-dkar bSam-gling can be found in Karma Blo-bzang (as in note 3), fols. 52a/3–57b/2. For the area of sTeng-[b]shod lung in Bar-bong, to which Karma Blo-bzang was invited, see Ehrhard (1998:10f., note 8) and chapter twenty in the present volume. The stay of Kun-dga' grol-mchog in the region is described in his work *Zhen pa rang grol lhug par brjod pa'i gtam skal bzang dad pa'i shing rta 'dren byed*, pp. 453.3ff.

are mentioned members of the family of rNam-grol bzang-po (born 1504), an important teacher of Dol-po's easternmost valley. Soon afterwards a teaching seminary was inaugurated at the pilgrimage site "Crystal-Mountain Dragon-Roar" (*shel gyi ri bo 'brug sgra*) for a period of five months; a group of fifty-eight people were willing to enter a three-year retreat at this most important "holy place" (*gnas*) of Dol-po. Karma Blo-bzang took great interest in the legends about Grub-thob Seng-ge ye-shes, a contemporary of 'Bri-gung 'Jig-rten mgon-po (1143–1212), who had opened the place as a pilgrimage site and whose "relics" (*gdung rten*) were an object of veneration. After declining the offer to take up duties as resident of the monastery of dMar-sgom, Karma Blo-bzang returned via rTa-rab to the southern part of Dol-po.[8]

Following his arrival at gSang-sngags chos-gling, the autobiography relates an episode which deserves to be attended to carefully:

> Again, when I came to gSang-sngags chos-gling and stayed there, the two brother kings of Jumla happened to arrive on their way to Mustang. Both had the behaviour of the sons of gods. An interpreter was appointed [and I spoke]: "Mahāraja[s], isn't it cold for some [of you]?" [They replied:] "Lama, because of your kindness we haven't frozen."
>
> [Then I spoke again:] "For what reason did you come here?" [One of them replied:] "As a king of the border and we—[these] two [parties]—don't suit [each other], a time of quarrels has descended upon us; [thus] I have to go to Thags [and] Glo[-bo]. Which of the two [parties] will win, [and] which will be defeated—we have come [here] to ask [you such] a prophecy. It is a great kindness that you, a great lama of Tibet, have arrived as our subject. If you stay [here] forever, happiness will come to us; therefore you must stay!" Offering whatever service was possible, they thus spoke [to me].
>
> For an answer [to their question] I investigated the mind of the Maharāja[s] [and spoke:] "I myself am actually not a good lama, [but] my teacher is the Omniscient One (= Buddha Śākyamuni). I myself, I don't know very much, but you kings of Jumla—you are [among] the greatest kings on earth; this is told in our Dharma [scriptures]. No king will take the risk of waging war against you. If one appears, he will have [only] the wish to be defeated."

---

[8] The teacher dPal-ldan don-grub and the tradition of the monastery dMar-sgom are dealt with in Ehrhard (1996a:57ff.) and chapter nineteen in the present volume; this information is based on a *thob yig* ('record of teachings received') by Ngag-dbang rnam-rgyal (born 1628), a disciple of Karma Blo-bzang. For references to the site Crystal-Mountain Dragon-Roar, see ibid: p. 63, note 14, and Schicklgruber (1996:118, note 4). The opening of this site by Grub-thob Seng-ge ye-shes is described in 'Phrin-las chos-'phel: *gNas chen shel gyi rib bo 'brug sgra'i dkar chag mthong ba don ldan dad pa'i skya rengs*, fol. 9a/5ff.; for further relevant material on this sacred mountain in Dolpo, see Mathes (1999:65–74).

With a "Hā! Hā!" [the kings] went away glad at heart. Later I heard the news that the king of the Indian border was defeated, having been deceived from inside [his court], and that all his territory was lost to Jumla.[9]

Later Years and Disciples

As an invitation had arrived from the "ruling prince" (*khri thog pa*) of the Muktināth Valley, Karma Blo-bzang made his way again to sNye-shang, and from there he went on to the valley of Nepal, where he undertook a pilgrimage to holy places, including the *stūpa*s of Svayambhūnāth and Bodhnāth. In Yol-mo he revisited the monastery of rGod-tshang gling and met there his disciple Karma Gu-ru.

When Karma Blo-bzang had nearly reached the age of seventy years he retired to the region of sNar, to the north of sNye-shang. There he stayed mainly in a cave called bSam-grub phug, a site that had been blessed in earlier times by the presence of Jo-nang Kun-dga' grol-mchog; the cave itself had had its name given to it by a fellow yogin who had met Karma Blo-bzang there. This was O-rgyan dpal-bzang (1617–1677), a native of southern Mustang, who is still remembered as the founder of the monastery sKu-tshab gter-lnga near the fortress of dGa'-rab rdzong.[10]

---

9 For this episode, see Karma Blo-bzang (as in note 3), fols. 70a/3–71a/5: *slar gsang sngags chos gling du phyin sdad yod skabs / rgyal po 'dzum lang sku mchad (= mched) gnyis glo bor phebs pa'i zhor la 'phebs byung / lha'i bu 'dra ba rnams (= rnam) spyod can gnyis 'dug / lo tstsha bcug / mahāradza / la la grang mo ma byung ngam byas bas / bla ma khyed kyis (= kyi) bka' drin las 'khyags po ma byung lo / 'dir ci la byon byas pas / mtha'i rgyal po gcig dang nged gnyis ma 'tshams par 'khrug dus btab zin / nga thab lo (= thag glo) la 'gro rgyu yin / nged gnyis su rgyal su pham gyi lung bstan zhu ru 'ongs pa yin / khyed bod kyi bla ma chen po nga'i mnga' 'bangs su phebs pa bka' drin che / rgyun du bzhugs pa na nged la skyid yongs pas bzhugs dgos / zhabs rtogs (= togs) gang drag 'bul gsungs byung / de la lan rgyal po chen po thugs la brtags / nga bla ma bzang po rang min / nga'i bla mas (= bla ma) ni thams cad mkhyen pa yin / ngas ni cher mi shes / 'on khyang khyed 'dzum lang rgyal po ni sa'i steng na che ba'i rgyal po yin par nged kyi chos nas bshad / khyed la 'dren bsdo ba'i rgyal po ni mi yongs / gal te byung na kho pham 'dod pa yin mod byas pas / hā hā zer dga' nas songs bas / de nas rgya gar mtha'i rgyal po de nang bslus byung nas 'pham / mnga' zhabs thams cad 'dzum lang la shor 'dug zer ba thos byung.*

The role of Jumla in the western regions of Nepal and the sovereignty it had established over Mustang by at least the 1630s is dealt with by Schuh (1994:68ff.). The rulers of Jumla were in later years also active in financing renovations of Tibetan temples in southern Dol-po; see Ehrhard (1998:5–7) and chapter twenty in the present volume. The king of the Indian border referred to is the king of Parbat.

10 The stay of Jo-nang Kun-dga' grol-mchog in sNar is also reported by him in his autobiography (as in note 7), pp. 406.3ff. & 453.1–3. An account of the foundation of the monastery sKu-tshab gter-lnga, in the year 1668, and basic biographical data on O-rgyan dpal-bzang are given in Ehrhard (1993c) and chapter thirteen in the present volume. Before the actual foundation, O-rgyan dpal-bzang had travelled to the valley of Bar-bong as well, having been invited there by the same family that brought Karma Blo-bzang to southern Dol-po. For an investigation into the history of this family the life story of Kun-bzang klong-yangs (1644–1696) would be a good starting point.

Among the activities of Karma Blo-bzang in sNar that should be mentioned is the construction of a *stūpa*, which was finalized by a proper "act of consecration" (*rab gnas*). A similar act of consecration was also finally conducted for the monastery Brag-dkar bSam-gling in sNye-shang; this event, said to have been accompanied by many auspicious signs, is dated in the autobiography to the year 1664 (see Pl. 3).

Let me close this account of the life of Karma Blo-bzang with a list of his most important disciples. The chronicle of Brag-dkar rta-so calls them the "four great sons, who fulfilled [his] commission" (*bka' babs kyi bu chen bzhi*). These are the "treasure-discoverer" (*gter ston*) Gar-dbang rdo-rje snying-po (1640–1685), rGyal-dbang seng-ge (born 1628), Śākya bDud-'dul – from the family of Rig-'dzin bsTan-gnyis gling-pa (1480–1535) – and the previously mentioned Bla-ma Karma Gu-ru.[11]

CONCLUSION

There is one final point I want to emphasize at the end of this paper. It concerns the geographical extension of the religious influence of the Karma or Kaṃ-tshang bKa'-brgyud-pa school as exemplified in the activities of Karma Blo-bzang. The geographical range of his religious influence can be seen as a structure that brings, first, the monasteries of Ras-chung phug (in the valley of Yar-[k]lung[s]) and Brag-dkar rta-so (in Mang-yul Gung-thang) into a spatial relationship. This I would like to call a transregional structure of "spatial efficacy" (*Raumwirksamkeit*) manifested by this specific monastic tradition. On a regional level, secondly, this spatial efficacy extends from Brag-dkar rta-so to the monastery of Brag-dkar bSam-gling in sNye-shang. If we focus on the spiritual and political career of Karma Blo-bzang in southern Mustang and Dol-po we could, thirdly, speak of a local level of spatial efficacy.

These observations concerning the person who was behind the foundation of the best-known religious building in Manang (and who followed up this project throughout his whole life) are based mainly on one literary tradition; they definitely need to be supplemented

---

[11] The date of the consecration of Brag-dkar bSam-gling is the only year noted by name in the whole autobiography; see Karma Blo-bzang (as in note 3), fols. 81b/5–82a/2: *glo bo rgyud (= brgyud) snye shang brag dkar gyi lha khang gi rab gnas la spyan 'dren bzhus / shing 'brug zla ba drug pa'i tshes bcos (= bco) lnga'i nyin rab gnas mdzad / bkra shis pa'i dge mtshan dpag med byung.*

For the list of the disciples, see Brag-dkar rta-so sprul-sku Chos-kyi dbang-phyug: *Grub pa'i gnas chen brag dkar rta so'i gnas dang gdan rabs bla ma brgyud pa'i lo rgyus mdo tsam brjod pa mos ldan dad pa'i gdung sel drang srong dga' ba'i dal gtam*, fol. 33a/5–b/1: *zab mo gter gyi bka' bab pa gter ston gar dbang rdo rje / snyan brgyud yid bzhin nor bu'i bka' bab pa zwa phug pa rgyal dbang seng ge / shes bya rig gnas kyi bka' bab pa byams sprin gter dbon gu ru śākya bdud 'dul / mngon spyod drag po mthu'i bka' bab pa gu ru phug pa karma gu ru sde 'di bzhi la bka' bab kyi bu chen bzhir grags.* It should be mentioned that the last-named disciple was the father of the Eighth Zhwa-dmar-pa Chos-kyi don-grub (1695–1732); see Chos-kyi 'byung-gnas & Tshe-dbang Kun-khyab (as in note 1), p. 351.1. Further disciples of Karma Blo-bzang are listed in Mathes (2001:167–194).

by a wider range of sources.[12] But it should have become clear that literary traditions can be used to guide us in identifying certain concepts of religious geography and thus to widen our knowledge still more about the history of settlements and cultural landscapes.

12 For the relationship between Ras-chung phug and Brag-dkar rta-so, see Brag-dkar rta-so sprul-sku Chos-kyi dbang-phyug: *Bya bral chos kyi dbang phyug gi rang 'tshang lhug par brjod pa 'khrul snang sgyu ma'i rol rtsed*, fol. 153b/5–6: ... *ras chung phug nas skyong srol* ...; Brag-dkar bSam-gling is called a "son monastery" (*bu dgon*) of Brag-dkar rta-so by the same author; see ibid, fol. 202b/3ff. An interesting view on the competition that existed between Karma Blo-bzang and dPag-bsam ye-shes (1598–1667), a member of the 'Brug-pa bKa'-brgyud-pa school also active in the Nepal-Tibet borderlands, can be found in Bod mkhas-pa Mi-pham dGe-legs rnam-par rgyal-ba: *rJe btsun grub pa'i dbang phyug dam pa dpag bsam ye shes zhabs kyi rnam par thar pa mchog gi spyod tshul rgya msho'i snying po*, fol. 48a/4–b/4. In using the term "spatial efficacy" (Raumwirksamkeit), I follow Hoheisel & Rinschede (1989:9).

Fig. 1: Ras-chung phug. Taken from Richardson (1998)

Fig. 2: Brag-dkar rta-so (Ehrhard 1997)

Fig. 3: Brag-dkar bSam-gling (Ehrhard 1996)

Fig. 4: Two stūpas erected at Brag-dkar bSam-gling by a disciple of Karma Blo-bzang (Ehrhard 1996)

Pilgrims in Search of Sacred Lands

> Sacred landscape is a constellation of natural phenomena constituted as a meaningful system by means of artificial and religious signs, by telling names or etiological stories fixed to certain places, and by rituals which actualize the space.
>
> (Cancik, 1985–1986:260)

INTRODUCTION

Tibetan pilgrimage practices have attracted a lot of scholarly interest in recent years, and it seems that some Tibetologists have become pilgrims themselves, engaged in search for sacred lands in the Himalayan valleys and in Tibet proper. Concerning the motivation of the individual Tibetan pilgrim who descends from the harsh climate of the Trans-Himalaya to the heat and humidity of the regions in the south, I quote two statements that can be found in the relevant literature. They were produced by Tibetan pilgrims – a layman and an educated lama –when asked for the "basic reason" or "main cause" (*rtsa don*) for their spiritual travels:

> Why did I go on pilgrimage you ask? All of pilgrimage comes from the utterance of the Buddha. Without the utterance of the Buddha nothing of pilgrimage would exist. Because of the utterance of the Buddha I made the round of the *gNas*. The utterance of the Buddha was the *rTsa don.*
>
> *gNas skor* comes out of the utterance of the Buddha just as all of religion has so come into being ... It is not like the rules which are set down in the *Sūtra*s and which one must obey, yet it is the utterance of the Buddha, nevertheless, which is the root of pilgrimage.[1]

Concerning the motivation of Tibetologists in their search for understanding sacred lands we will not find the same unanimity; but we can detect at least one common feature with

---

1 Ekvall & Downs (1987:129); "utterance of the Buddha" is the translation of *sangs rgyas kyi bka'*. For further religious motivations of Tibetan pilgrims compared to secular ones, see ibid, pp. 131–140. The Tibetan terms *gnas* and *gnas skor* can be translated respectively as "sacred site" and "to move round [a] sacred site[s]", i.e. to go on pilgrimage.

the Tibetan pilgrims. The "utterance of the Buddha" again functions as the mainspring of their endeavours: this is the case if we take this expression in the sense of religious books or texts of Buddhism, especially those which describe the spiritual qualities of a landscape considered sacred by the Tibetan tradition. Obtaining a copy of the so-called "guidebook" (*lam yig*) or "inventory" (*dkar chag[s]*) of a specific site means for the Tibetologist to gain access to the "utterance of the Buddha" describing that specific site.

Since the inventory to the region of Mustang as a sacred land has already been dealt with on several occasions – and since the subject of this article is the "search" of pilgrims – I propose to follow another track: I will consult the "biographies" (*rnam thar*) of two Tibetan lamas who have visited the pilgrimage sites in Northern and Southern Mustang at different times (Pls. 1 & 2).[2] We thus get a glimpse into the sacred landscape as it was conceived by individual pilgrims. Like the guide-books and the inventories, the biographies survive as manuscripts in village temples and in households or in modern day library collections.

O-RGYAN CHOS-'PHEL AND HIS TRAVELS TO [G]CONG-[G]ZHI AND MUKTINĀTH

This lama was born in the year 1755 in the region of the sacred mountain Gangs Ti-se (Kailāśa) in Western Tibet. He received the name O-rgyan chos-'phel ("The one who increases the teaching of O-rgyan [Rin-po-che]") because he was born on the tenth day of the Tibetan month, which is dedicated to the memory of Guru Padmasambhava. The most important teacher of O-rgyan chos-'phel was a Sa-skya-pa master from the Ngor-pa tradition called Ngag-dbang Kun-dga' lhun-grub (died 1773); this master had founded a monastery at the site of sPos-ri near the sacred lake Ma-pham mtsho (Manosarowar), and it was there that the young boy received his spiritual training.[3] A special feature of this training was that he mainly obtained transmissions of "treasure teachings" (*gter chos*) of the rNying-ma-pa school from the discoveries of Rig-'dzin Gar-dbang rdo-rje (1640–1685)

---

[2] For the *dkar chag[s]* genre as the primary "literary aspect" of Tibetan pilgrimage, see [Large-] Blondeau (1960:213–15). A résumé of the relevant text dealing with Southern and Northern Mustang with Muktināth at the centre is given in Ehrhard (1993b:28–30) and chapter twelve in the present volume. A critical stance against this genre as "only superficially helpful" and as "obliterat[ing] landscape" is taken by Huber (1994:34) and by Ramble (1995:115f.); compare the view in Ehrhard (1997b:336–346) and chapter sixteen in the present volume, that the existence of corresponding texts, i.e. inventories and guide-books, generates perception of sacred landscape in the Tibetan cultural sphere.

[3] For the early education see O-rgyan chos-'phel: *O rgyan chos 'phel gyi nyi tshe skye ba 'di'i rtogs brjod phyi yi rnam thar*, fols. 27b/2–36b/2 (*chos sgor zhugs pa'i gros byas tshul*); the complete text covers events up to the year 1811. sPos-ri is an old sacred site in the Ma-pham mtsho region known to followers of the Bon-po school; see bsTan-'dzin rnam-bdag: *sNga rabs bod kyi byung ba brjod pa'i 'bel gtam lung gi snying po*, pp. 40.17–18. For the term "The great sacred sites, the mountains and the lake, [these] three" (*gnas chen ri mtsho gsum*) – comprising the two mountains Gangs Ti-se and sPos-ri, together with the sacred lake Ma-pham mtsho –, see also Bellezza (1997:16).

and Rig-'dzin 'Ja'-tshon snying-po (1585–1656); this is not surprising given that his teacher, Ngag-dbang Kun-dga' lhun-grub, was regarded as an incarnation of the last-named treasure discoverer.

Until his thirty-fifth year, i.e. up to 1790, O-rgyan chos-'phel stayed mainly at the monastery of sPos-ri, and he interrupted his spiritual practices only occasionally to visit important temples in the Gangs Ti-se region. The autobiography mentions especially the temple of 'Khor-chags (Khojarnāth) as the main goal of these "regional pilgrimages" of O-rgyan chos-'phel; on this spot he circumambulated and paid his respects to the three statues of Mañjuśrī, Avalokiteśvara and Vajrapāṇi, known to Tibetan pilgrims under the name "Lords [who are the] protectors of the three [tantric] families" (*jo bo rigs gsum mgon po*).

The first of his travels which can be understood in the sense of a "trans-regional pilgrimage" started in 1791 and brought O-rgyan chos-'phel to the region of Mang-yul and its district town sKyid-grong. After visiting the temple of Byams[-pa] sprin he came into the presence of the famous Jo-bo Wa-ti bzang-po, a statue of Padmapāṇi Lokeśvara which is believed to have manifested itself miraculously from a sandalwood tree. He then met the "incarnation" (*sprul sku*) of his teacher Ngag-dbang Kun-dga' lhun-grub in the monastery of Grwa-phu chos-gling. Afterwards the journey continued on to Nepal, where he brought offerings to the *stūpa*s of Svayambhūnāth and Bodhnāth, but was not able to visit the minor shrines in the valley. Here we have to keep in mind that in 1791 the Nepal-Tibet war was in its final stage and that – according to the words of O-rgyan chos-'phel – the danger of attracting diseases was very high. The return trip led through the valley of La-[l]de[bs] and after paying another visit to the incarnation of his teacher in Grwa-phu chos-gling, the pilgrim came to the end of his wanderings in the temple of [s]Pra-[b]dun in the area of Byang, like Byams[-pa] sprin a religious building which was said to have been erected by Srong-btsan sgam-po, considered to be the first Buddhist king of Tibet.[4]

The temple of [s]Pra-[b]dun in Byang served now as the starting point for the second "trans-regional pilgrimage" of O-rgyan chos-'phel; it began exactly ten years after the journey to Mang-yul and Nepal, i.e. in 1801. This journey brought him to the sacred sites of Northern and Southern Mustang and also in close – and not so close – contact with the rulers of these regions. After reaching sMon-thang, the capital of Northern Mustang, the rNying-ma-pa teacher from Western Tibet soon obtained an audience with dBang-rgyal rdo-rje, the "Dharmarāja" (*chos rgyal*) of Mustang. The reason for this swift contact was a

---

4 The description of the pilgrimage to Mang-yul and the Nepal Valley can be found in O-rgyan chos-'phel (as in note 3), fols. 101b/3–106b/6. The most accessible pilgrimage guide to the temple of Khojarnāth is by another member of the Ngor-pa tradition, Ngag-dbang bSod-nams rgyal-mtshan: *Lhar bcas 'gro ba'i mchod sdong jo bo sku mched gsum sngon byung gi gtam rabs brjod pa rin chen baiḍūrya sngon po'i pi waṃ*. For the significance of temples dating to the early royal period in the search for Himalayan sacred lands, see Ehrhard (1994:10f.) and chapter twenty-one in the present volume.

renovation project in the Gangs Ti-se area which had received financial assistance from the king of Mustang in recent times.

The conversation between the king and the lama touched mainly upon this renovation and the spiritual affiliations of dBang-rgyal rdo-rje and O-rgyan chos-'phel; the king himself stated that he belonged to "the teaching tradition of the great Vidyādhara" *(rig 'dzin chen po'i chos brgyud)* i.e. the lineage of Kaḥ-thog rig-'dzin Tshe-dbang nor-bu (1698–1755). For the lama it was the proper moment to reflect upon the motivation for his journey to Mustang:

> [If you ask:] "What is the reason that I have come now to this country?" it is to circumambulate and offer prayers to the sacred places [here], the principal ones [being] the "Hundred-and-some Springs" – the pilgrimage site that was prophesied in the *brTag gnyis*, [i.e.] the *Hevajratantra* – and the *vihāra* of dGe-dkar with the nine roofs: the earliest [case of] taming the ground in the realm of Tibet which the Guru [Padmasambhava undertook].[5]

This statement by O-rgyan chos-'phel to the king of Mustang gives us a first impression of the strategy governing how sacred landscape was created in a Himalayan context, and of the way individual sites became places which kept up the memory of Buddhist saints like Padmasambhava. In the case of Muktināth – or "Hundred-and-some Springs" as it was known to Tibetan pilgrims – the toponym Munmuni, one of the four "fields" (*kṣetra*) according to the Indian *pīṭha* tradition of the *Hevajratantra*, was transplanted from an Indian setting to the Himalayan region of Southern Mustang. Generally this transposition entailed the formation of pilgrimage centres in the Tibet of the 12th and 13th centuries.

The act of "taming the ground" (*sa 'dul*) has particular relevance to the introduction of Buddhism into Tibet and to the Himalayan experience of it. The temples said to have been built during the reign of King Srong-btsan sgam-po were erected "to tame the borders and the areas beyond the borders", and the legends of how Padmasambhava subdued the local spirits and converted wild and uncultivated regions to the Buddhist faith are uncountable. The case of the *vihāra* of dGe-dkar in Northern Mustang was seen as the prototype of this act of taming the earth by erecting religious edifices, and we will have a

---

5 See O-rgyan chos-'phel (as in note 3), fol. 144a/6–b/1: *da lam sa phyogs 'dir yong ba don ga lags / kye rdo rje rtsa brgyud (= rgyud) rtag (= brtag) gnyis las / lung zin gnas chen chu mig brgya rtsa dang / gu ru'i bod khams sa 'dul snga ba dge sgar gtsug lag dgu thog gi (= gis) tsos (= gtsos) gnas skor smon lam 'debs pa* ... Although the site is known in most of the sources under the name "[Temple of] White Virtue" (*dge dkar*), the meaning is here "Encampment of Virtue" (*dge sgar*). This spelling is also preserved in "dGon-pa sGar" as contained in a modern pilgrimage guide; see sMan-lha Phun-tshogs: *Nepāl nang pa'i gnas yig dngul dkar me long*, p. 88.5–6.

closer look at this temple later on.[6] Let us follow now again the steps of O-rgyan chos-'phel and see if there are further memorial sites that he encountered during his pilgrimage in Mustang.

Having paid his respects at the different monasteries and temples of sMon-thang and having received a "passport, [i.e.] an official document" (*lam yig bka' shog*) from King dBang-rgyal rdo-rje, the lama left the capital of Northern Mustang and reached the town of Tsang-rang soon afterwards. There he learned of a pilgrimage site known for its many sacred items that had formed naturally; this place was known by the name [g]Cong-[g]zhi, a term referring to a limestone or calcite concretion which – according to the Tibetan medical tradition – is able to alleviate bodily disorders. O-rgyan chos-'phel followed the route to this cave and could identify the different sacred items according to a "praise of the sacred site" (*gnas bstod*) by a certain Mi-pham phun-tshogs shes-rab or sTag-rtse sku-skye-ba (1654–1715); this teacher of the 'Brug-pa bKa'-brgyud-pa school had been active at the court of the Mustang king bSam-grub dpal-'bar and was a disciple of the famous yogin Rang-rig ras-pa (died 1683). There exist several versions of the "guide to the sacred site" and they all refer to the visions of this sTag-rtse sku-skye-ba, namely the different forms of tantric gods and goddesses in the limestone concretion of the cave; these texts also mention that Padmasambhava had set foot there (Pls. 3 & 4).[7]

The description of Muktināth contained in the autobiography of O-rgyan chos-'phel is of some historical interest since it is stated, for example, that the pagoda-style temple near the water-spouts had been erected by a king of Jumla; another temple in the "sacred field" (*muktikṣetra*) is associated with a Tibetan master called rGyal-dbang seng-ge (born 1628). Among the further details of O-rgyan chos-'phel's stay in the Muktināth Valley one should also highlight the fact that he failed to accept the invitation of Khro-bo dpal-mgon, the ruler of rDzar. True to his bond with the "king of upper Mustang" (*glo stod rgyal po*), he only gave religious instructions to an uncle of Khro-bo dpal-mgon. The ruler himself is referred to by the name "king of lower Mustang" (*glo smad rgyal po*). The lama stated why he kept his distance from him: "[it was] a time when the kings of Mustang, the upper and the lower [one], were not in agreement [with each other]" (*glo rgyal stod smad mi 'grig pa'i dus*).

---

6 For the process of the transposition of the *Vajrakāya* as set down in the Buddhist *Tantra*s in the case of Muktināth, see Ehrhard (1993b:23f.) and chapter twelve in the present volume. The term *sa 'dul* and its implications for the Himalayan experience was dealt with by Aris (1990:94–96). A temple in the Barbong Valley, between Jumla and Muktināth, bears the name "Temple, where the ground was tamed" (*sa 'dul dgon pa*); see Ehrhard (1998:5–7) and chapter twenty in the present volume.

7 A part of the *gnas yig* of [g]Cong-[g]zhi was also incorporated into the inventory of the pilgrimage places of the Muktināth area; see Ehrhard (1993b:29f.) and chapter twelve in the present volume. A more complete text with the title *Cong zhi rang byon gyi gnas yig* can be found in sMan-lha Phun-tshogs (as in note 5), pp. 89f.

On his return trip to the north O-rgyan chos-'phel did not stop in the village of Sa-dmar but took up quarters on the road above [g]Cong-[g]zhi. After passing the so-called "Hundred-and-some *stūpa*s" (*mchod rten brgya rtsa*) he finally reached the *vihāra* of dGe-dkar. Offerings were presented there in the shrines of the upper and lower floors.[8] Without paying further attention to O-rgyan chos-'phel's second stay at the court of sMon-thang and the exchange of religious teachings between himself and King dBang-rgyal rdo-rje, we shall now turn to another pilgrim and teacher of the rNying-ma-pa school; he was also attracted to the sacred sites of Mustang, and especially to the temple of dGe-dkar.

SANGS-RGYAS BZANG-PO AND HIS ACTIVITIES AT DGE-DKAR AND MGAR-PHUG

This lama originated in the region of Khams in Eastern Tibet, where he was born in the year 1894. He received the name Sangs-rgyas bzang-po ("Good Buddha") from O-rgyan che-mchog, a teacher who was regarded as an incarnation of Klong-chen rab-'byams-pa (1308–1364); the list of his early teachers also includes the treasure discoverer bSod-rgyal Rin-po-che (1856–1926). The most important influence on the spiritual career of Sangs-rgyas bzang-po was exercised by the Khams-pa master gZhan-phan Chos-kyi snang-ba (1871–1927), generally known by his nickname gZhan-dga'. In the period from his twenty-third to his thirty-fourth year – i.e. from 1916 up to 1927 – Sangs-rgyas bzang-po attended mainly upon this teacher, who gave a new orientation to the non-dGe-lugs-pa traditions of Buddhist learning in Eastern Tibet; the chief places where he studied under gZhan-dga' and other masters of the rNying-ma-pa tradition were the monasteries of rDzogs-chen, Zhe-chen and Zur-mang.[9]

After the death of his main teacher, Sangs-rgyas bzang-po embarked on a journey which we can call an "international pilgrimage". Leaving Eastern Tibet in 1928, he reached the monastery of bSam-yas and the sacred sites located nearby in the year 1929; up to 1931 he stayed in Central Tibet, visiting such monasteries as rDo-rje brag and sMin-grol gling, paying homage to statues like the Jo-bo 'Jam-dpal rdo-rje in Rwa-sgreng, and seeing places

---

8 The pilgrimage to [g]Cong-[g]zhi, Muktināth and dGe-dkar is contained in O-rgyan chos-'phel (as in note 3), fols. 152b/6–156b/2; for further information on the teacher rGyal-dbang seng-ge, see Ehrhard (1998:4 & note 5) and chapter twenty in the present volume. The rise of the Tibetan enclave in the Muktināth Valley and the lineage of its rulers up to the middle of the 18th century is dealt with by Schuh (1995:42–54); for the political situation in the Muktināth Valley in the 19th century and the position of Northern Mustang during the transition of power from Jumla to the king of Gorkha, see also Schuh (1994:42–53 & 54–68). Compare the description of the role of dBang-rgyal rdo-rje during the Nepal-Tibet war in Jackson (1984:151); this king of Mustang also renovated the temple of dGe-dkar.

9 The first and second chapters of the autobiography of Sangs-rgyas bzang-po (written in 1945) are devoted to the region of his birth and its religious traditions, and to his own spiritual training; see Sangs-rgyas bzang-po: *Sangs rgyas bzang po'i rnam thar zhes bya ba'i me long*, fols. 3a–9a (*skyes pa'i yul gyi rnam grangs bshad pa*), and fols. 9a–30a (*dam pa'i lha chos la zhugs nas dka' ba spyad tshul*).

like Gangs-ri thod-dkar, the favourite hermitage of Klong-chen rab-'byams-pa. It should be noted that he exchanged teachings along the way with other religious dignitaries, one being the gZims-'og Rin-po-che (born 1884) of 'Phan-yul Nā-len-dra; this institution was at that time one of the few large Sa-skya-pa monasteries within a day or two's journey from lHa sa. During this very period, a "seminary for textual exposition" (*bshad grwa*) at 'Phan-yul Nā-len-dra was headed by another Khams-pa disciple of gZhan-dga'.

For Sangs-rgyas bzang-po the time had not yet come for a fixed abode and regular sessions of teachings. In 1932 – a "monkey year" (*sprel lo*), the year in which pilgrimages to Tsa-ri are traditionally undertaken – he had the idea of joining the great pilgrimage to that sacred land in the south-eastern border region of Tibet. Having attended religious ceremonies conducted by 'Bri-gung sKyabs-mgon Zhi-ba'i blo-gros (1886–1943), he left for the monastery of Dwags-la sgam-po and afterwards arrived at the holy mountain Dag-pa shel-ri and other pilgrimage places in Tsa-ri; the autobiography makes special mention of the auspicious signs that occurred when Sangs-rgyas bzang-po paid his respects to the statue of the Byar-smad Jo-bo.[10] Crossing over to "Bhutan" (*'brug yul*), the pilgrim continued on to India, where he visited Bodhgaya, the historic site of Buddha Śākyamuni's enlightenment. The next country he saw was Nepal and the objects of his veneration there were the shrines of Svayambhūnāth, Bodhnāth and Namo Buddha, recognized by Tibetan pilgrims as the "three kinds of *stūpa*s" (*mchod rten rnam gsum*). At a memorial site of Padmasambhava to the south-west of the Kathmandu valley, which is called by Tibetans "Spring Enlightenment Nectar" (*chu mig byang chub bdud rtsi*) and by Nepalese "Ṛṣīśvara", he met a fellow pilgrim who reported to him about the numerous sacred items that are located in the region of Mang-yul, the foremost one being the statue of Jo-bo Wa-ti bzang-po in sKyid-grong. The lama from Khams followed up this hint in his search for sacred lands, and was soon circumambulating the building which housed the self-manifested Avalokiteśvara and the temple of Byams[-pa] sprin.

Passing his thirty-ninth year in 1933, he finally arrived at a small monastery where he found some rest from his tireless travelling and which served as a kind of base camp for his activities during the next twelve years. This monastery was located at Brag-dkar rta-so, the famous site of Tibet's great yogin Mi-la-ras-pa; the teacher from Khams was given a warm welcome there by the resident lama bsTan-'dzin nor-bu (1899–1959) and his father 'Phrin-las chos-dbang (1879–1940). In the company of father and son he made excursions to other sacred sites in the region and undertook a retreat for several months. Sangs-rgyas bzang-po

---

[10] The third and final chapter of the autobiography contains the travels of Sangs-rgyas bzang-po which I have labelled "international pilgrimage"; see Sangs-rgyas bzang-po (as in note 9), fols. 30a–73b (*rgyal khams nges med du don gnyis gzugs brnyan gyi rang bzhin bya ba byed pa'i tshul*). The description of the journey to Tsa-ri can be found ibid, fols. 40a/4–43b/4. For the lama from Khams who taught the tradition of gZhan-dga' at 'Phan-yul Nā-len-dra, see Jackson (1998:144–151).

also conducted teaching-sessions at Brag-dkar rta-so, and among his audience we find two persons who hailed from the region of Northern Mustang. They were sKu-zhabs Klu-sgrub and his son, who was called mGar-phug sprul-sku; we can thus identify them as the lamas in charge of the monastery mGar-phug. In 1934 sKu-zhabs Klu-sgrub issued an official invitation to the Khams-pa teacher to visit their monastery, which is located to the northeast of sMon-thang.[11]

It took another year before Sangs-rgyas bzang-po followed up this invitation. The reason was another pilgrimage to India and Nepal, where he was able to visit further historical sites associated with the life of Buddha Śākyamuni, i.e. Rajgir, Sarnath, Kushinagara and Lumbini. Passing the sacred lake of mTsho padma or Rewalsar, north of Mandir, and after a prolonged stay in Delhi he took the route through Kinnaur to the Gangs Ti-se region. Before circumambulating the sacred mountain several times – performing the so-called "circle of the snow [mountain]" (*gangs skor*) – he met there the Bon-po master Khyung-sprul 'Jigs-med Nam-mkha' rdo-rje (1897–1955), himself a disciple of Padma bDe-ba'i rgyal-po (1873-1933) from Khams.

As in the case of O-rgyan chos-'phel, the temple of [s]Pra-[b]dun in Byang served Sangs-rgyas bzang-po as the starting point for another section of his "international pilgrimage": the sacred sites of Mustang. In 1935 he reached the monastery of mGar-phug, characterizing the site with the words: "it is known to have received the blessings of [Kaḥ-thog] rig-'dzin Tshe-dbang nor-bu" (*rig 'dzin tshe dbang nor bu'i byin rlabs par grags pa*) (Pl. 5). Staying there for the rest of the year, he composed several works, including a "guidebook to the pilgrimage places in India" (*rgya gar gnas yig*).

The next year he journeyed to the south in the company of mGar-phug sprul-sku. The description of the sacred landscape contained in the autobiography of Sangs-rgyas bzang-po differs from the earlier one of O-rgyan chos-'phel in one particular aspect: it includes memorial sites of Padmasambhava to the south of Muktināth and in the region of Thags. The first place he visited was the village of Thini (= *som bhi*) and a temple, containing the relics of Padmasambhava which had come forth from a treasure of Rig-'dzin bDud-'dul rdo-rje (1615–1672) from Khams. In Thags it was a cave that reminded the Tibetan pilgrim of the former presence of Padmasambhava; it was called the "Secret Cave of the Guru" (*gu ru gsang phug*). Having stopped in the monasteries of Mar-phag and Tshe-rog, he then directed his steps to the site of "Hundred-and-some Springs", i.e. Muktināth. Sangs-rgyas bzang-po thus visited the sacred sites that make up the main part of the inventory of the

---

[11] A description of the pilgrimage to Bhutan, India and Nepal is contained in Sangs-rgyas bzang-po (as in note 9), fols. 43b/4–45a/3; for the travels in the region of Mang-yul in the years 1933 and 1934, see ibid, fols. 45a/3–50b/1. For the succession of the resident lamas of Brag-dkar rta-so after the period of Chos-kyi dbang-phyug (1775–1837), see sKyabs-rje Brag-dkar-ba bsTan 'dzin nor-bu: *gDan rabs lo rgyus drang srong dga' ba'i dal gtam gyi kha skong* in *sKyabs rje brag dkar pa dkar brgyud bstan 'dzin nor bu'i gsung 'bum skor*, pp. 5.1ff. This text was written at the behest of Sangs-rgyas bzang-po.

pilgrimage places in Mustang. The text itself starts with Muktināth and ends with a description of the Dhaulāgiri Himāl and the "Secret Cave of the Guru".[12]

After this first pilgrimage to Southern Mustang and the region of Thags the lama from Khams proceeded to the temple of dGe-dkar in the year 1937; his stay at this most important pilgrimage site of Northern Mustang lasted for nearly five years, i.e. up to 1942. Among his first activities there the autobiography mentions a "minor renovation" (*zhig gso phran*) of the *vihāra* and the composition of a guidebook to that place.

Although this text has not surfaced up to now, we have at least a reference to the etiological myth of the sacred site as it was written down in this text. Sangs-rgyas bzang-po refers to that myth on the occasion of building a new "house for spiritual practices" (*sgrub khang*) there:

> Now, what is called Glo-bo dGe-dkar: when Guru Rin-po-che (= Padmasambhava) erected [the monastery of] bSam-yas, because the gods and spirits headed by the *nāga*s (snakes) and *rākṣasī*s (female demons) created obstacles, [he had] to suppress [them and thus] erected on the heart of the supine *rākṣasī* of Mustang a nine-storied *vihāra,* and on her [outstretched] limbs hundred-and-some *stūpa*s and so on. [This has been written down] more extensively in the description of the sacred site. Accordingly I gave the name "Island of All embracing Light" to that site of spiritual practice, which is said to have been that [same] hermitage that was in earlier times called the "treasure place" [of Sangs-rgyas bla-ma].

As this quotation shows, the mythical foundation of the temple of dGe-dkar is closely connected with the erection of Tibet's oldest monastery by the Buddhist saint Padmasambhava. The act of pinning down the female demon – or taming the ground – which we generally know from the legends concerning King Srong-btsan sgam-po, is thereby applied to the local context of Mustang. Another hint of the antiquity of the site is its status as a place, where Sangs-rgyas bla-ma (born ca. 1000), the first treasure discoverer of the rNying-ma-pa school, had unearthed some of his findings. The aura of the sacred landscape also inspired Sangs-rgyas bzang-po: he wrote down a general introduction to the

---

12 The second journey to Nepal and India, the arrival in Northern Mustang and the journey to the sacred sites of Southern Mustang can be found in Sangs-rgyas bzang-po (as in note 9), fols. 50b/1–55a/3. For the travels of the fellow pilgrim Khyung-sprul 'Jigs-med Nam-mkha' rdo-rje (1897–1955) in India, Kinnaur and the Gangs Ti-se region – in the years 1933–1935 –, see Kvaerne (1988:77–80). The main part of the inventory of the sacred sites of the Mustang area concerns the Dhaulāgiri Himāl; see Ehrhard (1993b:28f.) and chapter twelve in the present volume. A guidebook of the Bon-po school that idealizes and spiritualizes the Dhaulāgiri Himāl – written in 1863 – is mentioned by Ramble (1995:105–107).

philosophical and spiritual doctrine of that school, and in 1938 also erected a *stūpa* near the temple, filling it with precious relics (Pls. 6 & 7).[13]

At the end of this year a second pilgrimage was conducted to Southern Mustang; on that occasion he followed an invitation of the "sponsors of the region of Thags" (*thags phyogs sbyin bdag rnams*). Having made offerings at the so-called secret cave, he again put up at the monastery of Mar-phag and conducted rituals for the local population; in the process the custom of "sacrificing animals" (*dmar mchod*) was changed into one of using "substitute offering substances" (*dkar mchod).* He then visited again dGon-pa sGang, i.e. the monastery near Thini, where relics from the findings of Rig-'dzin bDud-'dul rdo-rje were kept, and paid special attention to the religious buildings, which were in a state of decay at that time. Concerning teachers who had earlier stayed there, the name of Kaḥ-thog rig-'dzin was still remembered together with that of Kun-bzang klong-yangs (1644–1699) from "the region of the gorge of Jumla" (*rong 'dzum lang phyogs*), a direct disciple of O-rgyan dpal-bzang (1617–1677), who had founded the monastery. The former presence of Kaḥ-thog rig-'dzin was still felt and sensed by the pilgrim, the syllable *hūṃ* having manifested miraculously on a resting place during the visit of this master from Khams in 1750.

Returning to dGe-dkar, Sangs-rgyas bzang-po settled down to stay there for most of the time until the year 1942; either there or at mGar-phug he instructed a growing number of disciples. He also followed up on an invitation to sMon-thang and gave teachings to a group of Sa-skya-pa monks headed by a certain bKra-shis chos-'phel. Eventually he left Mustang and, using his base camp in Brag-dkar rta-so for another journey – this time to the sacred sites of Mi-la-ras-pa in La-phyi – he finally settled in the region of Mang-yul for longer sessions of teachings; among the persons who sent their disciples to him we find the Bhutanese lama Shes-rab rdo-rje (1884–1945). In that region Sangs-rgyas bzang-po had a residence of his own which he called "Palace of Great Bliss" (*bde chen pho brang*); it was there that his work on the rDzogs-chen doctrine, written in dGe-dkar, was carved on wooden blocks, sponsored by the local population.[14]

---

[13] For the quotation, see Sangs-rgyas bzang-po (as in note 9), fol. 55b/3–5 (*de yang glo bo dge dkar zhes gu ru rin po che'i bsam yas bzhengs pa la klu srin gtsos lha 'dre'i bar chad byas bas kha gnon du glo bo srin mo rgan (= gan) skyal (= kyal) gyi snying gar lha khang dgu thog dang yan lag rnams la mchod rten brgya rtsa bzhengs pa sogs rgyas par gnas yig bzhin du bdag gi (= gis) ri khrod de nyid sngon gter gnas yin zer ba'i bsgrub (= sgrub) gnas la 'od gsal kun khyab gling zhes ming btags pa'o*). The text on the rDzogs-chen doctrine was purchased by Giuseppe Tucci in 1954 and is part of the collection of the IsIAO; see Tucci (1956:14) and Sangs rgyas bzang-po: *mTsho skyes gsang gsum chos 'byung padma'i rgyal tshab*. Concerning Sangs-rgyas bla-ma and his findings see – among others – Vitali (1997:1026).

[14] The description of the second journey to Southern Mustang and Thags can be found in Sangs-rgyas bzang-po (as in note 9), fols. 57b/4–59a/2. For the teachers connected with dGon-pa sGang – or sKu-tshab gter-lnga, as the place is known to pilgrims –, see Ehrhard (1993c) and chapter thirteen in the present volume. The visit of Kaḥ-thog rig-'dzin to the site can be found in Brag-dkar rta-so sprul-sku Chos-kyi dbang-phyug: *dPal rig 'dzin chen po rdo rje tshe dbang nor bu'i zhabs kyi rnam par thar pa'i cha shas*

CONCLUSION

The pilgrimages of O-rgyan chos-'phel and Sangs-rgyas bzang-po and their search for sacred lands in Northern and Southern Mustang have led us to several sites and corresponding legends. It should now be possible – by reviewing the individual sites once again – to sketch the different cultural contexts which framed the sacred landscape in this particular Himalayan region. First we have to consider the following three possibilities through which a particular piece of territory was perceived in an idealized and spiritualized way:

1. In the case of Muktināth we could see how a sacred realm was created by transplanting the spiritual geography of the Buddhist *Tantra*s from India to the Himalayan region. The pilgrimage site came into being through an act of transposition or transcription.
2. The legendary topography of the foundation myth of dGe-dkar is a good example of how sacred landscape was created by etiological stories. Religious buildings – and statues – kept alive the memory of an important event in the mythical past (a statue of Padmasambhava in his likeness is kept to the present day in the *vihāra* of dGe-dkar).
3. Memorial sites are also based on historical narratives as documented by the site of dGon-pa sGang or sKu-tshab gter-lnga. The narratives in this case refer to the foundation of the monastery by O-rgyan dpal-bzang (in 1668) or to later visits by great religious teachers like Kaḥ-thog rig-'dzin from Khams (in 1750).

The two caves that we encountered in Northern and Southern Mustang – i.e. [g]Cong-[g]zhi and the "Secret Cave of the Guru" – show that this is not a clear-cut scheme and that two possibilities can also apply to a specific site at the same time. First, it is stated, by both the inventory and the autobiographies considered here, that Padmasambhava set foot on these two spots on the left bank of the Kāli Gaṇḍakī River; the caves are thus included in the legendary topography of the saint's activities in Mustang. Secondly, the two caves can also be considered as memorial sites; this becomes more clear when we look at the corresponding historical narratives associated with them.

---

brjod pa ngo mtshar dad pa'i rol mtsho in *Collected Works of Kaḥ-thog Tshe-dbang nor-bu*, pp. 220.3–4 & 221.2–4. The syllable *hūṃ* had manifested when Kaḥ-thog rig-'dzin had a vision of his teacher O-rgyan bstan-'dzin (1657–1737), whom he had earlier met at Sa-'dul dgon-pa in 1730; for this rNying-ma-pa master, who also hailed from the "region of the gorge of Jumla", and his stay in dGon-pa sGang in 1699, see Ehrhard (1998:4–9 & note 15) and chapter twenty in the present volume. A first notice of Sangs-rgyas bzang-po's influence on the changing customs of sacrifice in Thags was given by Tucci (1956:14); compare also the observations by Ramble (1997:399 & 410).

Through texts like the above-mentioned praise of the sacred site a visitor to [g]Cong-[g]zhi in Northern Mustang is reminded of the former presence of a 'Brug-pa bKa'-brgyud master who was active at the court of the king of Mustang in the 17th century. It is thus plausible to argue that the site gained prominence as a goal for pilgrims at about this time. If the thesis holds that the initial vision which was responsible for the idealization and spiritualization of the Dhaulāgiri Himāl – and the region of Thags – can be traced back to a member of the princely family of rDzar (in the Muktināth Valley) in the year 1740, on the other hand, the time frame for the popularization of the cave in Southern Mustang would be the 18th century. We could thus speak of a process of sacralizing the natural environment in a movement from north to south.[15] There is still little knowledge about the founding dates of monasteries in the region of Thags. But at least in the case of Tshe-rog, which was visited by Sangs-rgyas bzang-po, the fact is now available that its founder was a certain Kun-bzang Rig-grol rdo-rje (1731–1792) from Mang-yul.[16] This is another piece of evidence that the 18th century can be taken as the particular period when the influence of Buddhist teachers made itself felt in that territory, where Southern Mustang was bordering on the kingdom of Parbat.

Reconsidering finally the regional, the trans-regional and the international pilgrimages of O-rgyan chos-'phel and Sangs-rgyas bzang-po and this time paying special attention to the objects of worship mentioned in their autobiographies, we can allow the different statues of the transcendent Bodhisattvas which they encountered during their searches for sacred lands to come into focus. In Western Tibet the Lords [who are] the protectors of the three [tantric] families obviously enjoyed obviously great popularity, in Central Tibet it was the Mañjuśrī statue in Rwa-sgreng that attracted pilgrims, and in South-eastern Tibet prayers were directed towards the Jo-bo of Byar-smad. As attested in both autobiographies, on the route through Mang-yul – which connected Nepal and Tibet – the self-manifested statue of the Jo-bo Wa-ti bzang-po, the "Lord of sKyid-grong", counted as the most important goal for Tibetan travellers.

A naturally formed icon of the Bodhisattva Avalokiteśvara was also located in the region of Thags, and according to the exhortations contained in the inventory of the sacred

---

15 The statue of Padmasambhava in his likeness is the "inner sacred item" (*nang rten*) of the *vihāra* of dGe-dkar; see sMan-lha Phun-tshogs (as in note 5), p. 88.3–4 (*de'i nang rten tsan dan las grub pa'i gu ru nga 'dra bzhengs pa*), and p. 88.6 (*de'i nang rten gtso bo gu ru nga 'dra*). For arguments concerning the dating of the inventory of the sacred sites of the Muktināth area, see Ehrhard (1993b:30) and chapter twelve in the present volume.

16 A description of the monastery of Tshe-rog is given by Rai (1994:73–76); for data on the founding lama of this monastery, see Brag-dkar rta-so sprul-sku Chos-kyi dbang-phyug: *gTer dbon rig 'dzin brgyud pa'i gdung rabs lo rgyus tshangs pa'i do shal*, fol. 17a/1–5. O-rgyan chos-'phel met Kun-bzang Rig-grol rdo-rje during his pilgrimage to Mang-yul in the year 1791; see O-rgyan chos-'phel (as in note 3), fol. 106a/7–b/1.

sites of Mustang the Tibetan pilgrims on their way to India were supposed to visit the "Great Snow Mountain (= Dhaulāgiri Himāl), the Secret Cave, [and] the Lord [Avalokiteśvara], these three" (*gangs chen gsang phug jo bo 'di gsum*). The legends surrounding this sNa-ri Jo-bo should definitely be seen in connection with those concerning the Jo-bo Wa-ti bzang-po; it is known, for example, that the custodians of the statue in Thags had contact in the 19th century with the religious teacher in Mang-yul who had been responsible for the upkeep of the "Lord of sKyid-grong".[17] As an important component of the sacred landscape as perceived by Buddhist pilgrims, such statues of the Bodhisattva Avalokiteśvara were able to confer special blessings, because they were not created artificially by human hands, but had arisen by themselves from the natural environment.

[17] More details on the stone statue of the "Lord of Nari" (*sna ri / gnya' ri jo bo*) above Larjung and on its description in the inventory are given by Ehrhard (1993b:29 & 34, note 21) and chapter twelve in this volume; compare the information on the so-called "Ārya [Avalokiteśvara] who liberates from the six forms of existence" (*'phags pa 'gro ba drug sgrol*) in Lahul (West Tibet) in Schubert (1935:127–136). The iconographical details of this statue apply also to the one above Larjung; thus the doubts of Vinding (1998:290, note 19) concerning a form of Avalokiteśvara with six arms should be cleared away. For the visits of the custodians responsible for the statue in Thags to the region of Mang-yul, see Brag-dkar rta-so sprul-sku Chos-kyi dbang-phyug: *Bya bral ba chos kyi dbang phyug gi rang 'tshang lhug pa brjod pa 'khrul snang sgyu ma'i rol rtsed*, fols. 225b/5ff., 229b/5ff. & 257/6ff.; these journeys took place during the year 1831.

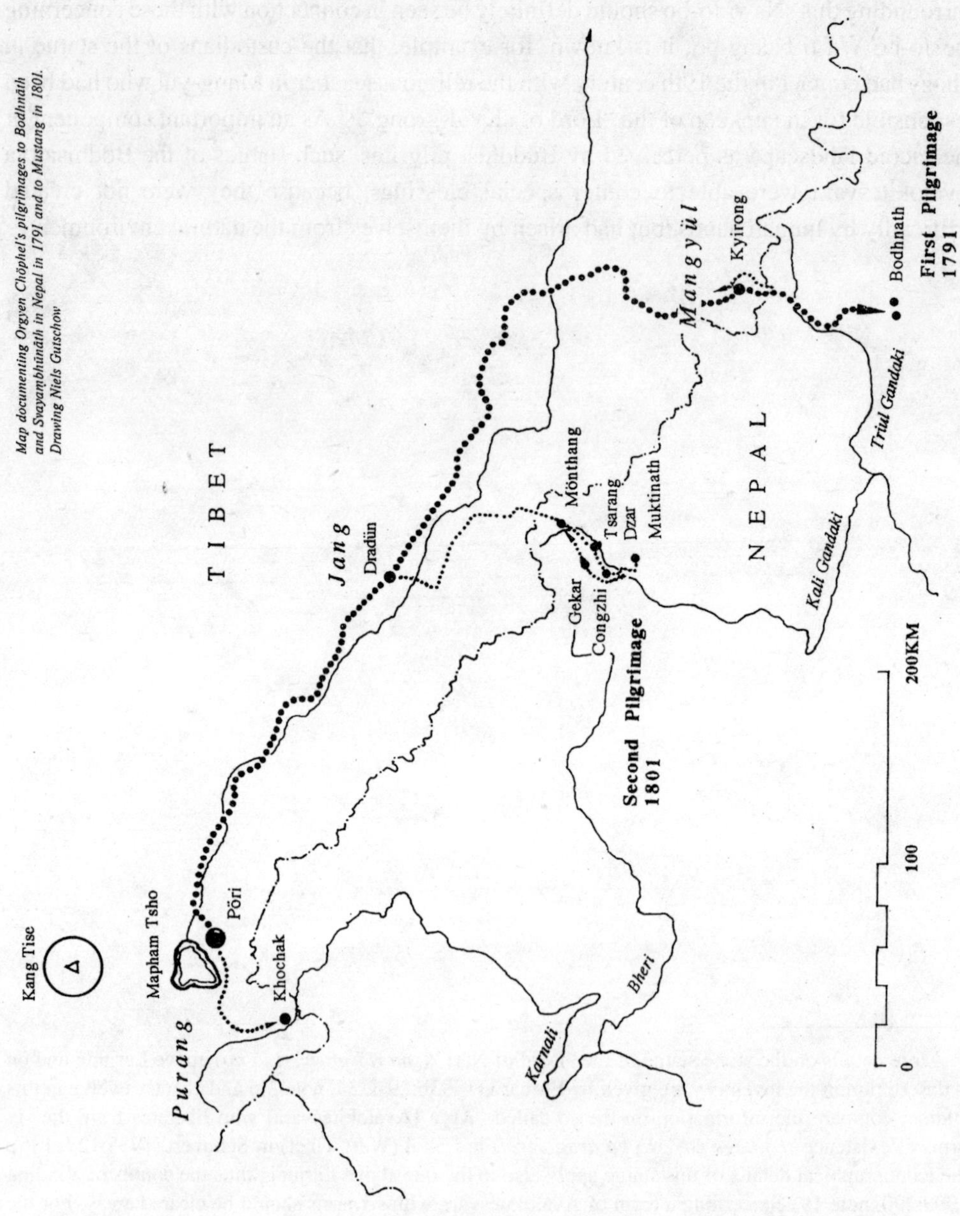

Map documenting Orgyen Chöphel's pilgrimages to Bodhnāth and Svayaṃbhūnāth in Nepal in 1791 and to Mustang in 1801. Drawing Niels Gutschow

Plate 1

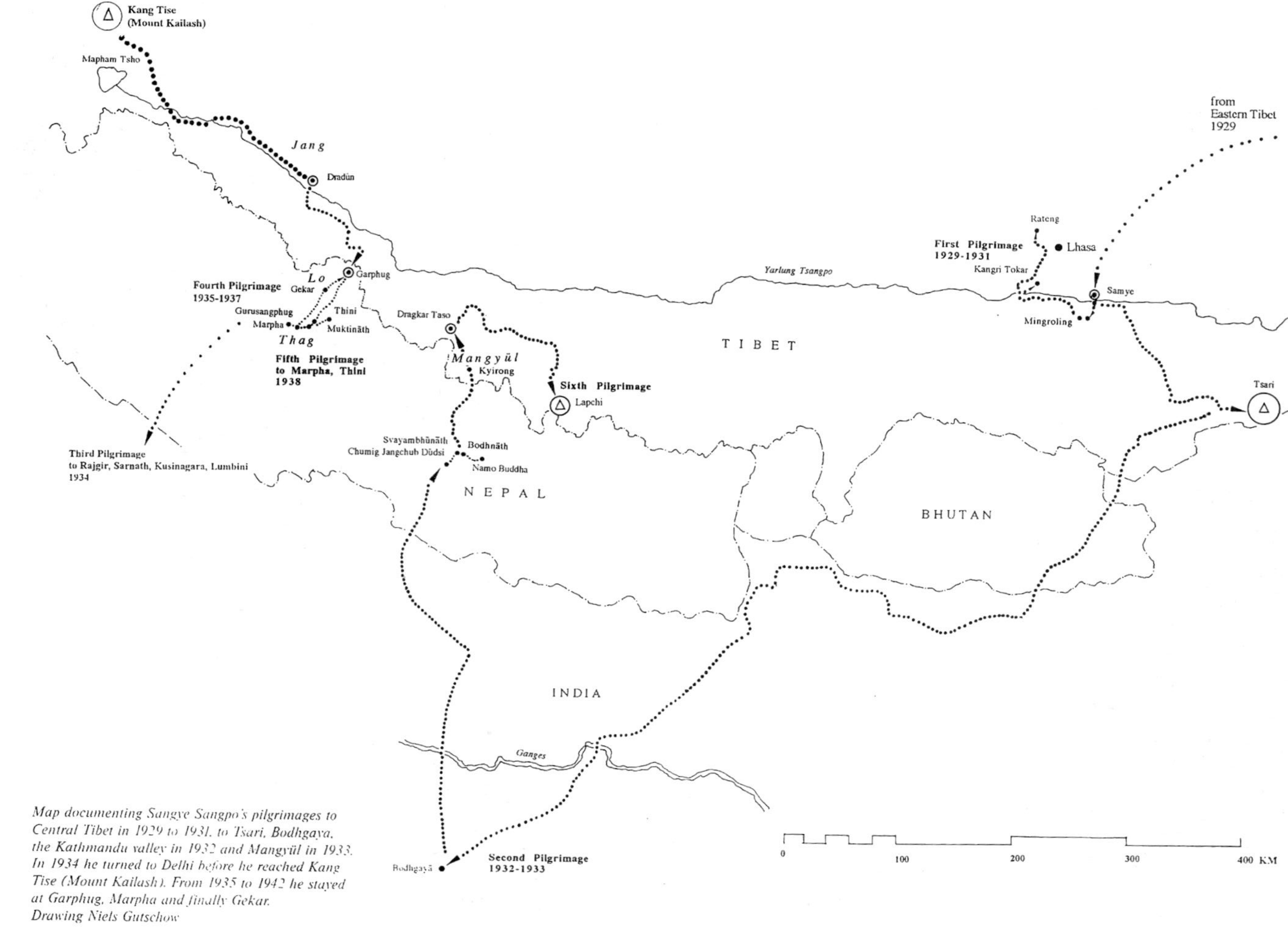

Map documenting Sangye Sangpo's pilgrimages to Central Tibet in 1929 to 1931, to Tsari, Bodhgaya, the Kathmandu valley in 1932 and Mangyül in 1933. In 1934 he turned to Delhi before he reached Kang Tise (Mount Kailash). From 1935 to 1942 he stayed at Garphug, Marpha and finally Gekar. Drawing Niels Gutschow

Plate 2

Plate 3: Chörten in the cave of Congzhi near Samar in northern Mustang (Ehrhard 1995)

Plate 4: Access path leading up the cliff towards the cave of Congzhi (Ehrhard 1995)

Plate 5: Garphug: the monastery in northern Mustang where Sangye Sangpo stayed in 1935 (Ehrhard 1995)

Plate 6: Gekar, the valley and the monastery with the stūpa erected by Sangye Sangpo in the southwestern corner (Ehrhard 1995)

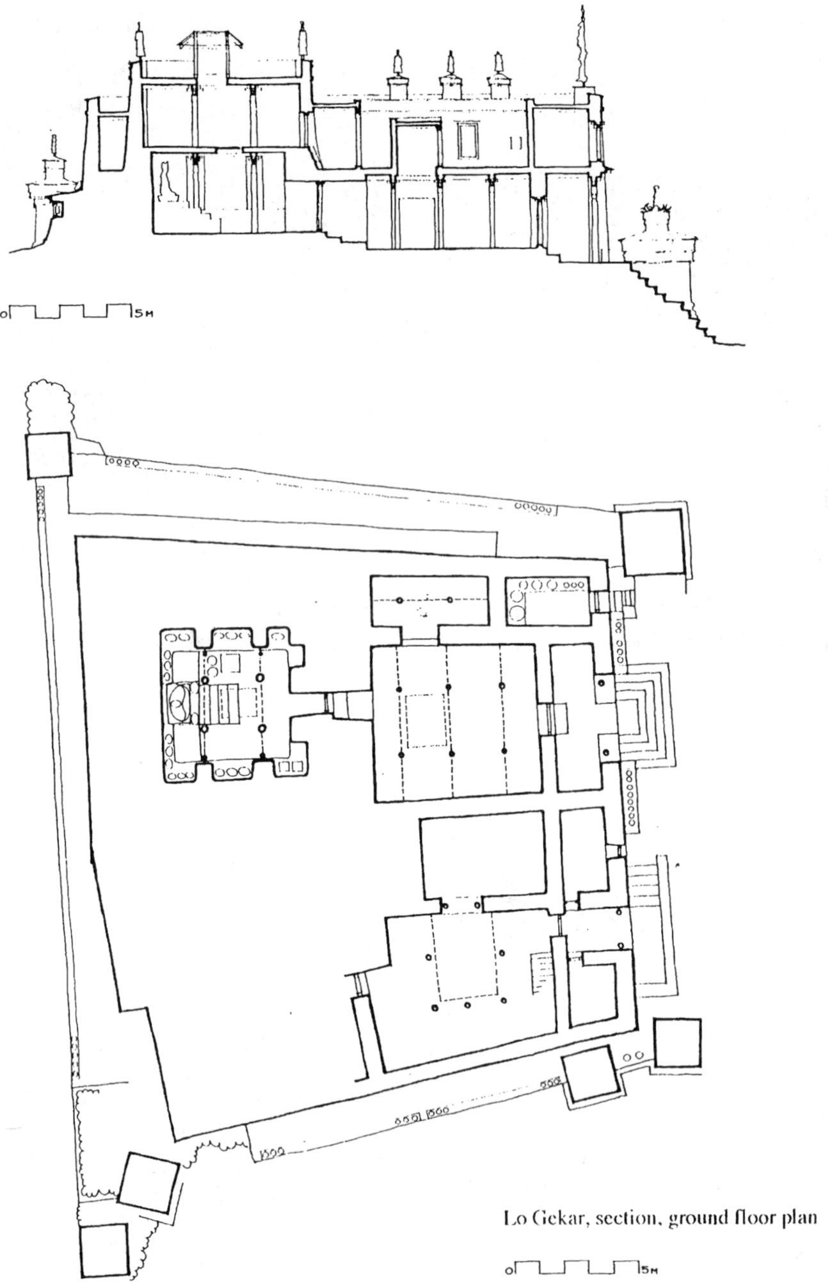

Plate 7:
Gekar: ground plan and section of the monastery, where Sangye Sangpo stayed from 1937 to 1942.
Survey and drawing John Harrison

VI.

Travels and Hidden Lands

A "Hidden Land" in the Tibetan-Nepalese Borderlands

Hidden firmament, great bliss – a gate to heaven
With the half-moon's form – this, the highest sphere
of the lotus' middle:
all beings who, by seeing, hearing or remembrance,
have made connection [with this spot],
may they attain the highest level of a king of the Vidyāḍharas.
rDo-dmar-ba Mi-'gyur rdo-rje (born 1675)

Introduction

Scholarly interest in "hidden lands" (*sbas yul*) as objects of study in their own right was sparked, to all appearances, first in the case of mKhan-pa lung, Artemisia Valley. Difficulties immediately arose, however, in determining the valley's exact location, as there existed a mKhan-pa lung in Shar Khum-bu (East Nepal) and one in Bhutan.[1] Within a few years these difficulties were cleared up, inasmuch as it was possible to identify the locations of mKhan-pa lung both in Shar Khum-bu and in Bhutan, and as the corresponding written sources were available in translation: one Artemisia Valley is located above the confluence of the Arun and Choyang rivers in the north-eastern part of Nepal, and a mountain valley in Bhutan just south of the Tibetan border likewise bears this name. The "guides to sacred places" (*gnas yig*) as they bear upon both of these traditions of the mythology of mKhan-pa lung refer to the persons of Rig-'dzin rGod-ldem 'phru-can

---

1 Cf. Aris (1979b:80): "In 1969, the late Professor Franz Bernhard of Hamburg University paid a brief visit to Bhutan. One of his aims was to try to locate the position of mKhan-pa lung and enquire into its mythology. While pursuing his researches in Nepal he had come across a guidebook to a hidden valley bearing the same name in the Shar Khum-bu area and had been told that another mKhan-pa lung existed somewhere in Bhutan." The guidebook in question is likely to have been the *Rong phu rdza yi gangs kyi gnas yig dad pa'i gdong ldan dga' skyed dbyar gyi rnga sgra* of Ngag-dbang bsTan-'dzin nor-bu (1867–1940), as this text was cited and perused for its relevance to the etymology of the Artemisia Valley by Geshe Gendun Lodro (1974:164–67). Geshe Gendun Lodro was a lecturer and then professor of Tibetology at Hamburg University from 1967 to 1979. The *Rong phu rdza yi gangs kyi gnas yig dad pa'i gdong ldan dga' skyed dbyar gyi rnga sgra* is also mentioned in Macdonald (1973b:225 = 1987:1); cf. ibid (233 = 9f.).

(1337–1406) and Rig-'dzin Padma gling-pa (1450–1521) both "treasure discoverers" *(gter ston)* of the teachings of Padmasambhava.[2]

The question arose as to how the two traditions are related to one another: in other words, how is the spread of the myth from Bhutan to Nepal or from Nepal to Bhutan to be explained. The preliminary hypothesis reached by Aris was that the mythology of the Bhutanese mKhan-pa lung was reset in a Nepalese context, though with the added restriction that the key is found in the person of Rig-'dzin rGod-ldem 'phru-can and the "treasure works" (*gter ma*) ascribed to him. Could it be proved that writings of this treasure discoverer contain authentic material on the hidden valley of mKhan-pa lung, then another explanation for the myth's displacement would have to be sought.

In the meantime it has been established as certain that the treasure works of Rig-'dzin rGod-ldem 'phru-can contain probably the most abundant material relating to the topic of "hidden lands". There is the added fact that in recent years field research has been carried out in the Arun valley, the results of which enable a closer look to be taken at the local traditions concerning the Nepalese mKhan-pa lung.[3] Taking up this strand, I should like in the following pages to pursue the stories in the Tibetan sources relating to the Artemisia Valley only as far as they shed light on a neighbouring hidden land. In a second step, the text material relating to the latter will be presented. This is done primarily with a view towards explaining the existence of hidden lands and their mythologies by way of the

---

2 Concerning the mKhan-pa lung located in Nepal, cf. Reinhard (1978), which contains a first translation of the texts *sBas yul mkhan pa lung gi gnas yig mthong ba don ldan* and *sBas yul mkhan pa lung gi lde mig mthong thos reg pa*; ibid, pp. 16–35. Concerning the Bhutanese mKhan-pa lung, see Aris (1979b:60–82). These two texts are likewise mentioned: *sBas yul 'bras mo gshong dang mkhan pa lung gi gnas yig* and *sBas yul mkhan pa ljongs kyi gnas yig padma gling pa'i gter ma*; the latter is translated in part, ibid, pp. 63–70. Concerning Padma gling-pa's discovery of the "guide to the sacred place" and the detailed circumstances surrounding the transfer of the land ownership to the treasure discoverer, see Aris (1989:67).

3 For Rig-'dzin rGod-ldem 'phru-can and his treasure works, see Schwieger (1985:XXX–XXXVIII); a first analysis of the discovery of the hidden lands by the treasure discoverer and various lists of "regions located to the south" are found ibid, p. xxxvii. Diemberger (1992:421–22) describes the mKhan-pa lung of the Upper Arun valley as a pilgrimage site and as place where treasure works of Padmasambhava were still coming to light in the twentieth century. She draws upon two works of Ngag-dbang bsTan-'dzin nor-bu, *gCod yul nyon mongs zhi byed kyi bka' gter bla ma brgyud pa'i rnam mthar sbyin rlabs gter mtsho* and *Dus mthar chos smra ba'i ngag dbang bstan 'dzin nor bu'i rnam thar 'chi med bdud rtsi'i rol mtsho,* as source material for a description of the discovery of the hidden land by Rig-'dzin rGod-ldem 'phru-can and its rediscovery by Rig-'dzin Nyi-zla klong-gsal. Cf. Aris (1990:97): "To my knowledge, all of them (i.e. the *sbas yul*) can be satisfactorily identified with known valleys in Nepal, Sikkim, Bhutan and south-eastern Tibet. The earthly paradises awaiting the faithful in these valleys are described in terms which sublimate the real Himalayan landscape. Their identification as "hidden lands" was accepted just as much by the groups living in their close vicinity as by the Tibetans who were mainly responsible for developing their cult."

existence of corresponding texts. Perhaps it is the text that, in the Tibetan cultural sphere, brings forth the *maṇḍala* and sacred *landscape*.

TREASURE DISCOVERERS OF THE 16TH AND 17TH CENTURIES

To go by the sources relating to mKhan-pa lung as contained in the works of Ngag-dbang bsTan-'dzin nor-bu, the hidden land in north-eastern Nepal was discovered for the first time by Rig-'dzin rGod-ldem 'phru-can, when in technical terms, he "opened the gate" (*sgo 'byed pa*) to the Artemisia Valley. At a later point, it was opened anew by Rig-'dzin Nyi-zla klong-gsal. In order to illumine the relation between these two persons an additional treasure discoverer must be introduced, the so-called mNga'-ris gter-ston Gar-dbang rdo-rje (1640–1685).[4]

Rig-'dzin Nyi-zla klong-gsal (died 1695) opened the valley of mKhan-pa lung few years after his meeting with the gTer-ston Gar-dbang rdo-rje (the text as in note 5, fol. 88b/3 mentions a "dragon year" (*'brug lo*), corresponding in my opinion to 1688). But even before this meeting we witness Rig-'dzin Nyi-zla klong-gsal already entering into a hidden valley; concerning the year 1680 it is written:

Finally he set off on the third day of the eighth month of the year of the monkey,

---

4 For biographical material relating to mNga'-ris gter-ston Gar-dbang rdo-rje, see, for example, sTag-sgang mkhas-mchog Ngag-dbang blo-gros, *bsTan pa'i snying po gsang chen snga 'gyur nges don zab mo'i chos kyi 'byung ba gsal bar byed pa'i legs bshad mkhas pa dga' byed ngo mtshar gtam gyi rol mtsho*, vol. 2, pp. 204.4–209.2 and Ngag-dbang bstan-'dzin nor-bu: *gCod yul nyon mongs zhi byed kyi bka' gter bla ma brgyud pa'i rnam mthar sbyin rlabs gter mtsho*, fols. 53a/3–60b/4. He uncovered various "treasure works" in the region of Mang-yul, such as *Zab thig chos dbyings rang gsal* in Byams-sprin and *Thugs rje chen po rtsa gsum snying thig* in sKyid-grong. In 1671 he travelled to the hidden land of sKyid-mo lung and there found the cycle *rDo rje sems dpa' thugs kyi me long*. It is said of the individual texts of the cycle that they were first discovered by Rig-'dzin rGod-ldem 'phru-can in Zang-zang lha-brag (north of the gTsang-po) but then hidden again. In the end they were brought to light a second time by Gar-dbang rdo-rje. Cf. *bKa' rdzogs pa chen po rdor sems thugs kyi me long las lo rgyus gsal byed sgron me*, p. 27: *byang zang zang lha brag gi sked pa dbus snying mdzod sbug par sbas pa'o / …… / rig 'dzin rgod kyi ldem khru can gyis spyan drangs pa'o / slar yang skyid lung bkra shis dpal bzang gis (= gi) ri la sbas / brag seng ge'i gdong pa 'dra ba nas bya bral gar dbang rdo rjes rnyed pa'o.* The hidden land of sKyid-mo lung and Gar-dbang rdo-rje were mentioned for the first time by Aris (1975:56ff. & 76). The dates of the treasure discoverer, uncertain at the time, were later assigned by Aris (1979a:3), in the case of his birth, to the year 1580; this date was placed one sixty-year cycle (*rab byung*) too early.

The lineage and spiritual practice of the *gCod* tradition that Ngag-dbang bsTan-'dzin nor-bu presents in the two works, *gCod yul nyon mongs zhi byed kyi bka' gter bla ma brgyud pa'i rnam mthar sbyin rlabs gter mtsho* and *sPyod yul nyon mongs zhi byed log 'dren zil gnon ltas ngan g.yang 'gug gi khrid gzhung ma rig mun sel* are part of the cycle *rDo rje sems dpa' thugs kyi me long* and were passed by Gar-dbang rdo-rje to Rig-'dzin Nyi-zla klong-gsal in his capacity as "master of the teaching" (*chos bdag*); the latter then formulated it into a system in its own right. See in this connection *sPyod yul nyon mongs zhi byed log 'dren zil gnon ltas ngan g.yang 'gug gi khrid gzhung ma rig mun sel*, p. 380.1–6; for the treasure discovery in sKyid-mo lung, cf. also note 21.

> offering prayers of supplications to the master Guru U-rgyan (= Padmasambhava). Even though numerous illusions cropped up along the way, he strode on further without giving way to doubt, and [so] he came to the centre of the "sacred place". How he saw the upper and lower caves where Padmasambhava had practised, [as well as] the small [cave] of his practice, the foot impressions, the impressions of bodily parts etc., together with many miraculous signs – [this all] becomes clear in a separate history.[5]

We learn of the site in question only that the entry point had been barred for many years, but that it was originally opened by Ma-gcig Lab-sgron (1031–1129); the geographical particulars concerning this entry point state "in the direction of gNya'-nang rtsa-sgo, the eastern gate of the hidden land Glang-'phreng" (*sbas yul glang 'phreng gi shar sgo gnya' nang rtsa sgo la gtad pa*; ibid, fol. 73a/3). In consequence of this piece of information I conclude that Rig-'dzin Nyi-zla klong-gsal entered the hidden land of Glang-'phreng. The biography makes it furthermore clear that the "Bird Cave" (*bya phug*) was the starting point of the journey, and that shortly prior to it a meeting with "the teacher rDo-dmar-ba father and son" (*bla ma do (= rdo) dmar ba yab sras*) came about.[6]

---

5 bsTan-'dzin nor-bu: *gCod yul nyon mongs zhi byed kyi bka' gter bla ma brgyud pa'i rnam mthar sbyin rlabs gter mtsho*, fol. 73a/5–b/1: *slar sprel lo zla ba brgyad pa'i tshes gsum nyin gu ru o rgyan rje la gsol ba 'debs bzhin phebs pas / phebs lam la cho 'phrul sna tshogs byung yang / the tshom ma mdzad pa phebs te nas mthil du phyag phebs / padma'i sgrub phug gong 'og sgrub chung / zhabs rjes / sku rjes sogs ngo mtshar ba'i rtags mang po dang bcas gzigs pa'i lo rgyus zur du gsal.* In a song that Rig-'dzin Nyi-zla klong-gsal intones on this occasion, the hidden land is addressed by the name of Padma'i-tshal; ibid, fol. 74a/4 (concerning this region, see note 10). It might therefore be supposed that he had entered into the region of Yol-mo. In line with the passage referred to below, however, I assume that it was the hidden land of Glang-'phrang. The text's sparse geographical details make an exact identification of localities at times difficult.

6 Text as in note 5, fol. 73a/1–2; the text also contains a biography of Kun-mkhyen Chos-kyi dbang-phyug (born 1679), the son of Rig-'dzin Nyi-zla klong-gsal. There, concerning the father's arrival at the Bird Cave, it is written: "Following that, upon his arrival in the lower part of the valley sNgo-ri, he met Bla-ma rDo-dmar-ba there, on account of the great friendship with him that existed from former times; in the course of the conversation they had, the express request was made that he take up quarters first in the Bird Cave. So, on the eighth day, he came to the spot known as Bird Cave, the practice site where Mi-la-ras-pa's female disciple Sa-le-'od had attained release [in the form] of the rainbow body, [i.e.] the western gate of gNam-sgo zla-gam (*de nas sngo ri'i mdar phebs pa na bla ma do (= rdo) dmar ba sgar nas thugs 'dris che bar brten der mjal 'phrad mdzad pa'i bka' mol du / re zhig bya phug tu bzhugs dgos nan cher gsungs par brten / gnam sgo zla gam nub sgo mi la ras ma sa le 'od 'ja' lus grol ba brnyed pa'i grub gnas bya phug tu grags pa der tshes brgyad la phebs*), ibid, fol. 96b/4–6.

Cf. Huber (1989:63): "And in upper gNya'-nang there is the birth place of Ra rDo-rje-grags and the ḍākiṇī of wisdom Sa-le-'od", the citation of the place name gNya'-nang stod in the original is confirmed by the text as in note 5, fol. 72b/5: *gnya'stod kyi bya phug*.

But that is not the last that is heard of the hidden valleys; in the biography of Rig-'dzin Nyi-zla klong-gsal it is written further:

> Finally, after having returned to the Bird Cave and living in strict seclusion, the prophecy [came to him,] "You should look for the way to the hidden valley of Zla-gam gnam-sgo"; trusting [in the prophecy], he set out to look for the way, and in all the valleys and all the passes (i.e. at the "gates of the sacred place" (*gnas sgo*), which are hard to traverse) he brought offerings in the form of smoke and libation ceremonies. By this means the mist, wind and clouds were driven away, and on the top of a pass he caught sight of a Yeti with the face of a rat. Recognizing that it was the "tutelary god of the treasures" (*gter srung*), he recited [the text] *mChod sprin nor bu do shal*.
>
> Thereupon the disciple [named] Rab-rgyas immediately lost his senses and could no longer be found; [but in the end,] through prayers to Guru [Padmasambhava] and the conducting of smoke and libation ceremonies, he was found, and his disturbed mind set at peace. This and other things [happened thus], as is written in a separate "guide book" (*lam yig*).[7]

The hidden valleys of Glang-'phreng / Glang-'phrang and Zla-gam gnam-sgo will keep us fully occupied in the pages to come. For the present I should merely like to note that, even before the opening of mKhan-pa lung, Rig-'dzin Nyi-zla klong-gsal was intensively involved in the search for such secluded spots and in the corresponding rituals at the "gates of the sacred place" (*gnas sgo*). The geographical area in which this search was carried on is the region of gNya'-nang, apparently also the region where a certain rDo-dmar-ba was active.

Rig-'dzin Nyi-zla klong-gsal, however, was not the only person at the end of the seventeenth century to suspect the existence of hidden valleys in the area. Similar accounts exist also in the case of Rig-'dzin Nyi-ma grags-pa (1647–1710), a treasure discoverer from Khams (East Tibet) and disciple of the First rDzogs-chen Padma Rig-'dzin (1625–1697). He, too, met gTer-ston Gar-dbang rdo-rje in the year 1676, and (like Rig-'dzin Nyi-zla klong-gsal) was chosen by the latter to become a "master of the teaching" (*chos bdag*)

---

7 Text as in note 5, fol. 74b/1–5: *slar bya phug tu phebs nas sku tshams dam por bzhugs skabs nyin cig mtshan lam du sbas yul zla gam gnas (= gnam) sgo'i lam tshol zhig bya ba'i lung bstan la brten / lam 'tshol bar phebs pas la rong kun tu bgrod dka'i gnas sgor bsangs mchod / gser skyems kyis brngan pas rmugs rlungs sprin sogs dwangs pa dang / la rtser mi rgod byi gdong can gzigs / gter bsrung yin par mkhyen nas mchod sprin nor bu'i do shal gsungs / zhal slob rab rgyas de ma thag tu smyo nas gar song ma byung bar / gu rur gsol 'debs dang / bsangs gser skyems mdzad pas rnyed / sems smyo ba bsangs pa sogs lam yig zur du bzhugs pa ltar ro.* Up to now I have been unable to identify the work *mChod sprin nor bu do shal.* On the role of animals in the context of entry in a hidden land and the finding of a treasure work, see also note 21.

of a particular cycle of treasure writings. And before meeting Rig-'dzin Nyi-zla klong-gsal personally, he passed through the territory just mentioned:

> From visiting, by way of La-kha-gangs etc., the places lHa-mtsho srin-mtsho [in] dPal-mo dpal-thang, gNya'-nang, La-phyi, Ding-ri etc., he noticed that a hidden land was evidently located in La-phyi gangs-ra.[8]

So much for one generation of treasure discoverers and their disciples who were active in south-western Tibet in the seventeenth century. Before entering more closely upon the topic Glang-'phreng / Glang-'phrang and Zla-gam gnam-sgo, I shall cast a brief glance at events of the sixteenth century and another generation of treasure discoverers. This is intended, firstly, to make it possible to place the sources on mKhan-pa lung in a wider context and, secondly, to introduce the names of some people that will prove useful for the second part of these preliminary remarks.

We find the Artemisia Valley mentioned in the biography of Rig-'dzin mChog-ldan mgon-po (1497–1531), a treasure discoverer whose activities in Bhutan are already known. As we know that mChog-ldan mgon-po personally met Rig-'dzin Padma gling-pa, and numbered among the latter's disciples, I take it as fact that, in the following citation, the mKhan-pa lung being spoken of refers to the highland plain of Bhutan:

> Even though he was of the firm determination to construct at the "gate of the sacred place" sBas-yul mKhan-pa lung a temple together with a monastery compound that would exert great influence, because of different circumstances, which were caused by some with a mistaken attitude, such as the nun Khyung Tshang-ba, he died.[9]

---

8 sTag-sgang mkhas-mchog Ngag-dbang blo-gros, (as in note 4), vol. 4, p. 381.1–2: *de nas la kha gangs la sogs brgyud nas lha mtsho srin mtsho dpal mo dpal thang / snya nam / la phyi / ding ri sogs gnas gzigs pas la phyi gangs rar sbas yul zhig 'dug pa gzigs*. Rig-'dzin Nyi-ma grags-pa is adverted to briefly in Blondeau (1988:69, note 24); as far as I know, the most detailed biography is contained in sTag-sgang mkhas-mchog Ngag-dbang blo-gros, (as in note 4), vol. 4, p. 338.3–vol. 5, p. 57.6. Like mNga'-ris gter-ston Gar-dbang rdo-rje, he raised a treasure work in Byams-sprin; ibid, vol. 4, p. 337.4 (the find took place in 1676). Cf. also the continuation of the above citation: "Although at this time one prophecy, among others, [came to him] that a small treasure hidden by rGa Lo[-tsā-ba] was located in dPal-mo dpal-thang, and a corresponding companion piece in Khams-bu lung in gTsang-rong, he attached no significance to it and did not make disclosure [of the treasure work]" (*'di skabs dpal mo dpal thang du rga los sbas pa'i gter phran zhig yod pa dang / gtsang rong khams bu lung du gter phran zung zhig yod pa sogs lung bstan gsal yang / do gal ma mdzad pas bzhes ma grub*); ibid, p. 381.3–4. For the activities of Padmasambhava in the region of dPal-mo dpal-thang, see *O rgyan gu ru padma 'byung gnas kyi skye rabs rnam par thar pa rgyas par bkod pa padma bka'i thang yig*, pp. 374.6–375.4, p. 566.3–4 and p. 717.4–6. Concerning the plain of dPal-thang in general, cf. Aufschnaiter (1976:181f.).

9 sTag-sgang mkhas-mchog Ngag-dbang blo-gros, (as in note 4), vol. 2, p. 620.2–4: *sbas yul mkhan pa*

But Rig-'dzin mChog-ldan mgon-po's efforts were not confined to Bhutan and Dwags-po; we find him also in south-western Tibet, in sKyid-grong, there too in a lively exchange of views and experiences with other treasure discoverers. This time it is sNgags-'chang Śākya bzang-po, another master of the rNying-ma-pa school from the sixteenth century, who uncovered the treasures. His connection with the Bodhnāth Stūpa in Nepal – it owes its present form to him – is a matter of common knowledge. In the meeting of the two treasure discoverers a role is also played by texts:

> During this time Rig-'dzin mChog-ldan mgon-po set off to pay a visit to the Jo-bo of sKyid-grong... That treasure discoverer, [who is] an incarnation, having given to this master (i.e. sNgags-'chang Śākya bzang-po) many "introduction lists" (*kha byang*) of commonly known valleys, and one valley in particular, spoke to him: "Since now you possess the prophecies for opening and maintaining the "gates of the hidden lands", do that by all possible means." Uttering prayers for proper guidance and "truth-speaking" prayers, [sNgags-'chang Śākya bzang-po] came into the hidden land Padma'i-tshal or Yol-mo gangs-ra, and founded the monastery Tsu-ti.[10]

---

lung gi gnas sgor / gtsug lag khang / dgon gnas dang bcas pa stobs che ba zhig bzhengs pa'i dgongs pa gtad kyang / ban ma khyung tshang ba sogs log pa'i blo can 'ga' zhig gis byed pas (= *pa'i*) *gzhan rkyen gyis sku gshegs*. Aris (1979b:158) presents Rig-'dzin mChog-ldan mgon-po as being the incarnation of rDo-rje gling-pa (1346–1405); this status is defended by Padma gling-pa against doubts from certain quarters; see Aris (1989:92f.). It was probably mChog-ldan mgon-po's efforts in rTse-le[gs] dgon-pa in Dwags-po that led to rTse-le[gs] sNa-tshogs rang-grol (1605–1677) being regarded for his part as the incarnation of mChog-ldan mgon-po; cf. Blondeau (1987:126). It looks as though this relatively unknown treasure discoverer of the sixteenth century enjoyed the thorough confidence of Padma gling-pa and was also counselled by the latter in questions relating to the disclosure of treasure works; Gu-ru bsTan-gnyis gling-pa (1480–1535) is also mentioned in a related prophecy; see sTag-sgang mkhas-mchog Ngag-dbang blo-gros, (as in note 4), vol. 2, p. 618.2–4.

A somewhat expanded version of Rig-'dzin mChog-ldan mgon-po's attempted founding of a monastery at the border of mKhan-pa lung may be found in mKhas-btsun bzang-po (1973:713): *sbas yul mkhan pa lung gi gnas sgo bar mar gtsug lag khang dgon gnas rgya cher bskrun pa'i dgongs bzhed dang / ban par o rgyan rin po che'i sku chen po gser zangs las grub pa 'gran zla bral ba bzhengs / de dus bdud sprul skyes bo log pa'i blo can dag gis bar du gcod pas gtsug lag khang bzhengs 'phror lus so*. For the complete biography, cf. sTag-sgang mkhas-mchog Ngag-dbang blo-gros, (as in note 4), vol. 2, pp. 612.1–621.5.

10 sTag-sgang mkhas-mchog Ngag-dbang blo-gros, (as in note 4), vol. 3, p. 54.1–4: *de skabs rig 'dzin mchog ldan mgon po skyid grong jo bo mjal bar phebs pa / ... / gter ston sprul sku des sbas yul spyi sger gyi kha byang mang po rje 'di par gnang nas / sbas yul sgo 'byed pa dang / 'dzin pa'i bka' khyod la yod pas cis kyang lag tu longs par mdzod gsungs / zhal ta dang bden brjod smon lam mdzad pa bzhin / bas yul padma'i tshal lam / yol mo gangs rar phebs tsu ṭi mgon pa btab*. The complete biography of sNgags-'chang Śākya bzang-po is found ibid, pp. 49.6–56.6. The hidden land called Lotus Grove or Snow Chain of Yol-mo is Helambu, which lies to the north-east of Kathmandu. Concerning the monastery Churi-Ghyang, see Clarke (1980:11–15).

The example of the opening of the hidden land Lotus Grove and the activities of Rig-'dzin mChog-ldan mgon-po demonstrates very nicely how the next material of the treasure works was passed on from one treasure discoverer to the next, and how great the circulation of such lists obviously was in the sixteenth century. The geographical dimension of the territory in which the hidden lands were located is also revealing: it extends from Bhutan to the regions south of sKyid-grong. Communication between these tracts, which were separated by many a day's walk over overgrown valleys and mountain chains, appears to have functioned without too much difficulty. What, then, might have been the reasons for the exchange of text material at certain fixed locations, such as we have been able to observe in the case of Rig-'dzin mChog-ldan mgon-po and sNgags-'chang Śākya bzang-po?

One of the explanations, in my opinion, lies in the existence of the royal court of Gung-thang. The rulers of this family, who had made their influence felt in western Tibet in the eleventh and beginning of the twelfth centuries, by the thirteenth century had large regions of that territory under their control, thanks to their connections with the Sa-skya-pa school (and so with the Mongols). Although in the fifteenth and sixteenth centuries they were no longer at the came of their power, they nevertheless distinguished themselves by reason of their great spiritual authority. Thus we find, for example, the treasure discoverers just mentioned among a group of spiritual dignitaries of the rNying-ma-pa school, whom the king of Gung-thang, Nyi-zla grags-pa (1514–1560) designated to be "the field of his offerings" (*mchod gnas*):

> By putting his trust in such "imperial preceptors" (*ti shri*) as the supremely excellent tutor, occupant of Padma[sambhava]'s throne [and] great Vidyādhara mChog-ldan mgon-po and the great treasure discoverer bsTan-gnyis gling-pa, and further, by honouring as teachers who were the field of his offering many powerful persons, such as the lord of the *Mantradhara*s bSam-yas dkar-chen Kun-dga' grags-pa, Yol-mo-ba Śākya bzang-po and the *Mantradhara* gSang-sngags rdo-rje, [Kun-bzang Nyi-zla grags-pa] magnified the status of the teachings, [which is] the joy of the Tibetan people.[11]

---

[11] Tshe-dbang nor-bu: *Bod rje lha btsad po'i gdung rabs mnga' ris smad gung thang du ji ltar byung ba'i tshul deb gter dwangs shel 'phrul gyi me long*, p. 661.5–7: *yongs 'dzin dam pa yang gu ru'i padma'i rgyal tshab rig 'dzin chen po mchog ldan mgon po dang gter ston chen po bstan gnyis gling pa sogs ti shri bsten shing / gzhan yang sngags 'chang ba'i dbang po bsam yas dkar chen kun dga' grags pa dang / yol mo ba Śākya bzang po / sngags 'chang gsang sngags rdo rje sogs nus par ldan pa mang po yang bla ma'i mchod gnas bkur nas / bod yul bde ba'i bstan rim yang rgya cher mdzad cing*. On the expression "field of offering" (*mchod gnas*) and the traditional relation between the worldly patron and the spiritual teacher, see, among many other works, Buffetrille (1989:370f.). The history of the kingdom of Gung-thang is sketched by Jackson (1976 and 1978), who in the process became the first Western scholar to advert to the royal genealogy of Rig-'dzin Tshe-dbang nor-bu. From this work, too, the dates of King Nyi-zla grags-pa (1514–1560) can be easily deduced. That the term *ti shri* (*ti shih*) is used for labeling the highest

As we have already seen, Rig-'dzin mChog-ldan mgon-po and sNgags-'chang Śākya bzang-po exchanged texts, which led to the opening of the valley Padma'i-tshal. But bsTan-gnyis gling-pa (1480–1535), who is named alongside Rig-'dzin mChog-ldan mgon-po as an "imperial preceptor", also turned over material deriving from the treasure works of Padmasambhava, in this case to King Kun-bzang Nyi-zla grags-pa himself. What is interesting thereby is the fact that they were objects originally concealed in Bhutan:

> The treasures of Gu-ru Tshe-brtan rgyal-mtshan, [i.e.] the golden treasure scrolls that were hidden in the cave [called] Seng-ge bsam-'grub in sPa-gro sTag-tshang, I have brought them forth again from my own treasure itself and handed them over in their entirety [to King Nyi-zla grags-pa]. Joy and a favourable association arose thereby.[12]

With this detour to the treasures of Gu-ru Tshe-brtan rgyal-mtshan and their presence in Gung-thang in the sixteenth century we come now to the hidden land that will occupy us in the following pages. For our point of departure, the hidden land mKhan-pa lung, I shall venture the conclusion, from these few observations, that the text material on which the myth is based is part of a literature that passed in various versions through the hands of various authors and commentators. In the process it was easy for overlapping traditions and differing ways of defining geographical reality to arise.

---

religious authorities at the king's court is not so surprising if one remembers the close connection of Gung-thang with the Sa-skya-pa school.

Of the three persons mentioned in the citation, I have been able to identify bSam-yas dkar-chen Kun-dga' grags-pa in three different biographies, those of sNgags-'chang Śākya bzang-po, mChog-ldan mgon-po and 'Bri-gung Rin-chen phun-tshogs (1509/10–1557). See mKhas-btsun bzang-po (1973:525, 711 & 723).

12 bsTan-gnyis gling-pa: *Rigs* (sic) *'dzin bstan gnyis gling pa'i rnam thar las / rnal lam lung bstan gyi skor*, p. 115.5–6: *gu ru tshe brtan rgyal mtshan gyi gter ma / spa gro stag tshang seng ge bsam 'grub kyi phug tu sbas pa'i gter shog ser slar kho bo rang gi gter gnas bton nas tshang ma yang phul bas bkra shis shing rten 'brel bzang bar byung*, cf. the description of the original find, ibid, p. 94.4–5: *stag tshang seng ge bsam 'grub kyi phug na sngar gu ru tshe brtan rgyal mtshan gyis gter snying shog ser mang po la la shog ril / la la ni dpe gras su 'dug pa yang khur nas / kun gyi gter tshab tu 'bras sa lu phul re bcug*. This is paraphrased in sTag-sgang mkhas-mchog Ngag-dbang blo-gros, (as in note 4), vol. 2, p. 625.4–5 in the following words: "The golden scrolls that had been formerly been [recovered] from sPa-gro sTag-tshang [and then] hidden by the treasure discoverer Tshe-brtan rgyal-mtshan as a treasure [to be] re-[discovered]—a few I brought fourth, some in the form of paper scrolls and some in the form of bound volumes" (*spa gro stag tshang nas sngon gter ston tshe brtan rgyal mtshan gyis yang gter du sbas pa'i shog ser la la shog dril dang / la la pustir yod pa 'ga' yang dgan drangs*).

For the complete biography of Gu-ru bsTan-gnyis gling-pa, see ibid, pp. 621.5–628.4. Like mNga'-ris gter-ston Gar-dbang rdo-rje (cf. note 4), he recovered treasure works of Rig-'dzin rGod-ldem 'phru-can; see Schuh (1981b:325) and *Rigs* (sic) *'dzin bstan gnyis gling pa'i rnam thar las / rNal lam lung bstan gyi skor*, pp. 116.6ff. The details in mKhas-btsun bzang-po (1973:447–55) are taken from the latter text; in this biography the king of Gung-thang bears the name Khri bDud-'dul mgon-po lde.

We need also to consider that the greater part of this literature was "prophecy" (*lung bstan*), which is subject to various interpretations from the outset. Only when we have analysed in greater detail the history and influence of such genres as "guides to sacred places" (*gnas yig*) and "travel guides" (*lam yig*), as well as those of "route lists" (*lam byang*) and "introduction lists" (*kha byang*), and have compared with one another the *gter ma* cycles from which they derive, can we hope to come to an understanding of the phenomenon of hidden lands in its functionality and complexity.

THE HIDDEN LAND HEAVENLY GATE OF HALF-MOON FORM

In the spring of 1990 I undertook, in my capacity as head of the Tibetan section of the Nepal-German Manuscript Preservation Project (NGMPP), a microfilm expedition to the southern part of Helambu. At two different places we were able to film a text that referred to the hidden land gNam-sgo zla-gam.[13] In order to make the text available to interested readers, I reproduce text B in a newly transliterated *dbu can* version.

Shortly before the expedition, two works of rDo-dmar Zhabs-drung Mi-'gyur rdo-rje (born 1675) likewise dealing with the hidden land Heavenly Gate of Half-Moon Form came into my hands. Whereas the text *gNam sgo zla gam gyi nges pa brjod pa sum rtse na dga' ma'i glu dbyangs* comprises spiritual songs extolling the valley's virtues, the text *gNam sgo zla gam gyi ngos 'dzin phan bde snying po* contains a fairly long piece of polemic

---

13 Text A: Gu-ru Tshe-brtan rgyal-mtshan: *gNam sgo zla gam lam yig*, 16 fols. (incomplete); Text B: Gu-ru Tshe-brtan rgyal-mtshan: *sBas yul gnam sgo zla gam gyis (= gyi) gnas yig lam byang gsal ba'i me long*, 9 fols. (complete). The two texts are indentical except for two insertions in Text A, buy these do not affect the formal composition of the text. Only Text B contains a colophon, which reads: "After [this work] had been brought fourth from the extreme end of the Chu-mo cave in Mon by Tshe-brtan rgyal-mtshan, the treasure discoverer, who is a reincarnation, it was [also] passed on by Rig-'dzin rGod-ldem 'phru-can – in what corresponds to this separate record – as a part of [his] treasures." (*sprul pa'i gter ston tshe ldan (= brtan) rgyal mtshan gyi (= gyis) mon chu mo phrug (= phug) gi mtha' nas spyan drangs nas khol don (= 'don) du bris pa 'dri (= 'di) dang 'dra bar rig 'dzin rgod kyi ldem 'phru can gyis gter las cha shas gcig gnang ba'o*). Concerning Gu-ru Tshe-brtan rgyal-mtshan and his finds in the Chu-mo cave in sPa-gro, see Aris (1979b:43 & 157); the prophecies relating to him are found in the *O rgyan gu ru padma 'byung gnas kyi skye rabs rnam par thar pa rgyas par bkod pa padma bka'i thang yig* of O-rgyan gling-pa, p. 580.3–5, and the corresponding biographical data in sTag-sgang mkhas-mchog Ngag-dbang blo-gros, (as in note 4), vol. 2, pp. 558.4–561.3. There he is called one of the "five treasure discoverer kings" (*gter ston kyi rgyal po lnga*). Another *gnas yig* recovered by Tshe-brtan rgyal-mtshan from the Chu-mo cave was published in Dharamsala in 1985: *sBas yul skar po ljongs kyi gnas yig*. The work *sBas yul padma'i tshal gyi gnas yig kun tu gsal ba'i me long* (Gangtok 1983) by the same treasure discoverer is actually not concerned with the hidden land Lotus Grove but is identical, with minor deviations, to our text A of the guide-book to gNam-sgo zla-gam. Displacement of the myth of the Heavenly Gate of Half-Moon Form continues up to the twentieth century. Two parts may be distinguished in text B, which is reproduced hereunder. I would call the first part (fols. 1b–5b), in accordance with the title, a "guide to the sacred place" (*gnas yig*), and the second part (fols. 6a–16b) a "route list" (*lam byang*). This material has also been studied in an unpublished M.A. thesis; see Childs (1993).

on the exact location of the hidden land, and it not only offers geographical arguments but also cites various authoritative writings.[14]

In consideration of the topic *Maṇḍala and Landscape* it is the second text of rDo-dmar-ba Mi-'gyur rdo-rje I shall be treating, particularly with regard to the identification of the hidden land according to the "gates of the sacred place" (*gnas sgo*). These gates define on the one hand the position of the *sbas yul* as the centre of the *maṇḍala*, and on the other are themselves the concrete entry points to the area in the centre. I shall proceed by tracing the arguments presented for the purpose of legitimating the status of a hidden land, that is, of conferring such a status upon a geographically bounded region.

Following the introductory verses the actual text begins with a citation of Padmasambhava referring to the "extremely secret hidden land" (*gsang ba chen po sbas pa'i yul*) Heavenly Gate of Half-Moon Form. This citation is found at the beginning of Gu-ru Tshe-brtan rgyal-mtshan's "guide to the sacred place":

> It is even more excellent than all the other secure hidden lands that have been described previously. It is easily reached and lies near Tibet. In other treasure mines, [however], it is not dealt with in detail. [If it is asked] why, [the answer is] because it is a secret and protected place.[15]

The superiority of this particular hidden land is further proved by the quality of the *yogin*s who live there as well as by its extraordinary natural features, such as the "caves where [the spiritual practice] is carried out" (*sgrub gnas*), the footprints of Padmasambhava, etc.

The "location of the sacred place" (*gnas kyi chags tshul*) leads to rDo-dmar-ba Mi-'gyur rdo-rje's distancing himself from certain unspecified persons and to his emphasizing his own opinion in the matter:

> It is [asserted] in this regard by persons like us who possess no supernatural knowledge that Glang-'phrang and gNam-sgo zla-gam are identical, [and that] Padma'i-tshal and Yol-mo are identical. This crucial point has not been understood

[14] Two editions of the complete works of rDo-dmar Zhabs-drung Mi-'gyur rdo-rje exist to date: Delhi 1979 and Delhi 1981. In the foreword of the first edition it is mentioned that parts of the works of the author had already been published, namely, *Songs of Two 17th Century Lamas of Gnya'-nang,* Dolanji 1977, and *Instructions on Nyingmapa Contemplative Practice*, Delhi 1977. I have access to neither volume. The text rDo-dmar Zhabs-drung Mi-'gyur rdo-rje: *gNam sgo zla gam gyi ngos 'dzin phan bde snying po* (Identification of the [abode] Heavenly Gate of Half-Moon Form, [bearing the title] "Essence of Usefulness and Bliss") I cite in the following according to the Delhi edition of 1981.

[15] rDo-dmar Zhabs-drung Mi-'gyur rdo-rje (as in note 14), fol. 2a/5–6: *gong du bshad pa'i sbas yul bstan pa de dag las kyang khyad par du 'phags shing / bgrod sla la bod du thag nye ba / gter kha gzhang na rgyas par bshad pa med de / ci'i phyir na gsang zhing gab pa'i gnas yin pa'i phyir ro.* Cf. *gSal ba'i me long,* fol. 1b/2–4.

up to now, [for] after the notion was put forward that while Glang-'phrang was Glang-'phrang, gNam-sgo zla-gam was something totally superior to it, [some people] sought [the hidden land], bearing the hardship of putting at risk the life of friends who placed trust in the possibility of passages over the glacier chains [dividing] dPal-khud and gNya'-nang khur-bu. As it is futile to speak one's mind on this way of going about things, I have no further dilated [upon it].[16]

At this point I should like to recall the person of Rig-'dzin Nyi-zla klong-gsal and his previously described entry into the hidden land Heavenly Gate of Half-Moon Form. We saw there that the search for Zla-gam gnam-sgo was accompanied by the performance of rituals at nigh impassable "gates to the sacred place", and that the life of a disciple was endangered. In consideration of the further fact that Rig-'dzin Nyi-zla klong-gsal met a certain Do/rDo-dmar-ba at the outset of his undertaking, I shall tentatively assume that rDo-dmar-ba Mi-'gyur rdo-rje is taking exception in his polemic to Rig-'dzin Nyi-zla klong-gsal's identification of gNam-sgo zla-gam. To judge by their dates, rDo-dmar-ba Mi-'gyur rdo-rje (born 1675) was the son of the rDo-dmar-ba that Rig-'dzin Nyi-zla klong-gsal (died 1695) met.

Our author, after extending his polemic to cover rituals and divinations employed when searching for hidden lands, proceeds in the next section to discuss two further opinions concerning the identification of gNam-sgo zla-gam, whose accuracy he likewise challenges, on the basis of geographical details. On this occasion he cites a text:

> In the "route list" (*lam byang*) for Yol-mo it is said: "It is entered from the inside of gNam-sgo zla-gam, the gate at the north."[17]

---

16 rDo-dmar Zhabs-drung Mi-'gyur rdo-rje (as in note 14), fol. 3a/1–4: *de la mngon shes kyi 'phongs pa'i skye bo bdag dang 'dra ba rnams kyis ni glang 'phrang dang gnam sgo zla gam don gcig pa / padma tshal dang yol mo don gcig pa'i gnad ka chen po 'di ngon chad ma go ste / glang 'phrang ni glang 'phrang rang yin gyi / gnam sgo zla gam ni de bas ches lhag pa zhig yod par bsam nas dpal khud dang / gnya' nang khur bu'i gangs rgyud kyis* (= *kyi*) *'gro sa gar 'dug rnams la blo thub kyi zla bo dag gi lus srog rgyab* (b) *skyur gyi dka' spyad ngang du blangs te btsal ba / de'i tshul rnams rgyas par yi ge'i ngal bas ma spros shing*. According to Aufschnaiter (1976:181f.), the name dPal-khud, or dPal-khung, is used for the lake lHa-mtsho srin-mtsho in the plain of dPal-thang, see note 8.

17 rDo-dmar Zhabs-drung Mi-'gyur rdo-rje (as in note 14), fol. 4a/2: *yol mo'i lam byang las byang sgo zla gam gnam sgo'i nang nas 'jug*; cf. also ibid, fol. 4b/1: *yol mo'i lam byang las byang zla gam gnam sgo'i nang nas 'jug*. See also the text gTer-ston sprul-pa lha-btsun: *sBas yul padma'i tshal gyi lam byang*, fol. 2b/2–3: *shar yang ri rdzi che la yangs pa'i mtshams nas 'jug / lho rgya gar siddhi'i chu rkang nas 'jug / nub mkha' 'gro bde mchog tshal nas 'jug / byang zla gam gnam sgo'i nang nas 'jug'o*. The title of this text contains the phrase "copied from the written text of lHa-btsun, the treasure discoverer, who is a reincarnation" (*gter ston sprul pa lha btsun kyi phyag ris las bshus pa*). Is this the lHa-btsun Nam-mkha' 'jigs-med (1597–1653) who reopened the hidden land 'Bras-mo ljongs? See in this connection note 19.

In view of the north-south orientation of gNam-sgo zla-gam and Yol-mo it is then argued that the position of the hidden land Heavenly Gate of Half-Moon Form can apply only to Glang-'phrang. As the next step, Glang-'phrang is placed in the centre of a geographical co-ordinate system with gNya'-nang in the east, Yol-mo in the south, Mang-yul in the west, and dPal-thang in the north. The main argument continues to be the citation from the *Yol mo'i lam byang* and the description based on the prophecy of Padmasambhava stating that the hidden land is easy to reach, lies near to Tibet and is an extremely secure location. With that the identification of gNam-sgo zla-gam is complete: according to rDo-dmar-ba Mi-'gyur rdo-rje, only Glang-'phrang fulfils the geographical conditions as given in the authoritative writings (see Plate 1).

Of aid in answering the question as to which texts were available to our author are the sources listed in the next section:

1. The "route list" (*lam byang*) for gNam-sgo zla-gam, which was uncovered by Gu-ru Tshe-brtan rgyal-mtshan.
2. A short summary of the same, which came out of the treasure of Rig-'dzin rGod-ldem 'phru-can (*de las cung bsdus pa rig 'dzin rgod ldem gyi gter byon de*).
3. A text called *Them byang ga'u bdun ma.*
4. The many chapters and sections of a category of texts called *bsKul byang chen mo.*
5. Small fragments of the other route lists.[18]

The "four large gates" (*sgo chen po bzhi*) providing entry to the hidden land of gNam-sgo zla-gam are mentioned twice in surviving writings of Gu-ru Tshe-brtan rgyal-mtshan /

[18] rDo-dmar Zhabs-drung Mi-'gyur rdo-rje (as in note 14), fol. 4b/4–5. Concerning the text of Gu-ru Tshe-brtan rgyal-mtshan and the connection with Rig-'dzin rGod-ldem 'phru-can, see the translation of the colophon in note 13. As it is only the *lam byang* that is cited by rDo-dmar-ba Mi-'gyur rdo-rje as the treasure of Gu-ru Tshe-brtan rgyal-mtshan, one could perhaps regard the first part of the text reproduced in the appendix, the *gnas yig*, as Rig-'dzin rGod-ldem 'phru-can's summary. Concerning the term *bskul byang chen mo*, the following details are found in the text *dNgul dkar me long*, p. 8.2–4: "Further the prophecies [entitled] 'Seven Large Catalogues of Exhortations' came forth among the prophecies [of Padmasambhava] that cannot be grasped by the mind, among the twenty-five sections of teaching of the *Thugs sgrub* cycle. As they were prophesied in association with the blossoming and decline of the lineage of the *dharmarājas* of Tibet, and with their end, these prophecies are extremely widespread, as well as clear and easily understood" (*de yang lung bstan bsam gyis mi khyab pa rnams kyi nang nas / thugs sgrub chos tsan nyer lnga'i nang nas lung bstan bkul byang chen mo bdun 'byung ba 'di rnams / bod chos rgyal gyis (= gyi) gdung rabs dar rgud dang mthar chad pa dang sbyar nas gsung pas / lung bstan 'di rnams shin tu rgyas shing gsal la go bdo ba yin la*). As for the *Thugs sgrub* cycle, it is part of the treasures of Rig-'dzin rGod-ldem 'phru-can, see chapter nineteen of the present volume. Finally, in the case of the route lists mentioned above under 5, I refer to the section of the *Yol mo'i lam byang* cited in note 17.

Rig-'dzin rGod-ldem 'phru-can (fol. 3b/1–3 and fols. 6b/5–7a/1 of the text reproduced here:

I.	*shar sgo*	*gnya' nang phyogs la gtad pa*
	nub sgo	*mang yul skyid grong phyogs la gtad pa*
	lho sgo	*bal po'i yul gyi yol mo gangs ra la gtad pa*
	byang sgo	*gung thang phyogs kyi dpal mo dpal thang gyi mtsho chen la gtad pa*
II.	*shar sgo*	*gnya' nang rtsa sgo la gtad yod*
	lho sgo	*bal yul gyi yol mo gangs ra la gtad yod*
	nub sgo	*mang yul skyid grong gi gangs rgyal mtshan la gtad yod*
	byang sgo	*dpal mo thang gi dpal thang gi mtsho chen la gtad yod*

These four gates lead to the centre of the *maṇḍala*, and in the text itself we find a detailed description of entry through the northern gate (ibid, fol. 7b/6ff.). The hidden land for its part has the form of an eight-petaled lotus; here we have the *maṇḍala* as such in front of us (ibid, fols. 14a/6–15a/5):

	byang kyi 'dab ma	
nub byang mtshams		*byang shar mtshams*
nub kyi 'dab ma		*shar gyi 'dab ma*
lho nub mtshams		*shar lho mtshams*
	lho kyi 'dab ma	

In the next passage of text rDo-dmar-ba Mi-'gyur rdo-rje goes into the question of the extent to which the geographical reality that goes by the name of Glang-'phrang meets the standards of a hidden land. First he cites three examples to prove that it is the act of "identification of a sacred place" (*gnas kyi ngos 'dzin*) – by the right person at the right time – that allows a particular piece of territory to become a sacred place. Ri-bo dpal-'bar in Mang-yul is cited as the first example; of this place where Padmasambhava left behind treasure works, it was prophesied that it would be "seized" (*'dzin pa*) by men when the time for them to do so had come. Examples two and three refer to two concrete cases of identification, the first by Mi-la-ras-pa (1040–1123), and the second by lHa-btsun Nam-mkha' 'jigs-med (1597–1653): it was only the visit of Mi-la-ras-pa to 'Dre-lung skyo-mo that made a sacred place out of it, and the hidden land of 'Bras-mo ljongs existed before its opening by lHa-btsun Nam-mkha' 'jigs-med only as a normal bounded territory with name Mon-pa.[19]

---

[19] For the first example a citation is given from the *Ri bo dpal 'bar gyi gnas yig*: "What is called Ri-bo dpal-'bar—visit this place during the era of decline. Those with [suitable] karma, having found this place,

A legend follows giving an etymology of Glang-'phrang and leading to the topic of the "opening of the gate to the sacred place" (*gnas sgo 'byed pa*).

> Now for the origin of what is called Glang-'phrang a bull is said to have to be killed once in 'Bri-bstim during the consecration feast for the erection of a *stūpa* of gold and silver by one patron. In the evening the bull fled to that sacred land by reason of his supernatural knowledge. The valley was discovered by virtue of the fact that the owner followed its trail; for this reason [the valley] is known under the name Bull Passage – so it is said in the tales of the people of old.[20]

The legends provokes the rhetorical objection that whoever opens the gate to a sacred place has to be "an outstanding personality of great fame" (*yongs grags kyi skyes chen dam pa zhig*); a bull hardly meets this criterion. rDo-dmar-ba Mi-'gyur rdo-rje counters this objection by referring to the concept – intricately developed in Tibetan Buddhism – of the "Buddha body" (*sku*). In response to the newly raised question of whether the manifoldly supple Dharmakāya can manifest as an animal he says:

> In the story of the treasure discoverer Gar-dbang rdo-rje [it is told of how] the "master of the treasures" (*gter bdag*) transformed himself into a wild animal, and [the treasure discoverer], following the tracks pointing out the way, was able to uncover the treasure. As there are many other [such] stories, such as [the statue] 'Phags-pa Wa-ti in sKyid-grong being found by a white cow, the Jo-bo [statue]

realize the 'heart treasure' of Padmasambhava" (*ri bo dpal 'bar zhes bya ba / gnas de snyigs ma'i dus su btsal / las can gnas de rnyed pa'i tshe / padma 'byung gnas thugs gter 'grub*). This citation I was able to trace to the text collection *Byang gter lugs kyi rnam thar dang ma 'ongs lung bstan*, Delhi 1983, p. 498.3–4; a text entitled *Mang yul gyi gnas chen ri bo dpal 'bar gyi dkar chag*, 6 fols., was likewise filmed in Helambu, in the spring of 1990 (reel no. L 290/14).

For the place called 'Dre-lung skyo-mo, see Huber (1989:10 & 13), where also Mi-la-ras-pa and La-phyi are taken up in details. The opening of 'Bras-mo ljongs by lHa-btsun Nam-mkha' 'jigs-med occurred in the year 1646 after supplication was made by 'Ja'-tshon snying-po (1585–1656) and bDud-'dul rdo-rje (1615–1672); see mKhas-btsun bzang-po (1973:780) and sTag-sgang mkhas-mchog Ngag-dbang blo-gros, (as in note 4), vol. 3, p. 309. According to the latter source, Kong-po rGod-tshang sprul-sku mKhas-mchog Padma legs-grub, i.e. rTse-le[gs] sNa-tshogs rang-grol (1605–1677), was also one of the supplicants.

20 rDo-dmar Zhabs-drung Mi-'gyur rdo-rje (as in note 14), fol. 5b/3–5: *glang 'phrang zer ba'i khungs kyang sngon 'bri bstim du yon bdag gcig gi gser dngul gyi mchod rten bzhengs pa'i rab ston la glang zhig bsad gyur / do nub glang des rang gi mngon par shes pa'i stobs kyi (= kyis) gsang ba'i yul 'dir bros / de'i rjes su bdag po des bsnyegs pa las lung pa rnyed / rgyu mtshan de la brten nas glang 'phrang du grags / zhes rgan rabs dag gi rgyun las byung ngo*. For the place called 'Bri-bstim, see the map in Macdonald (1973a:7): Birdim (northeast of Syabrubesi). Serviceable maps indicate a mountain and a place named Langsisa at the extreme eastern end of the mountain valley of Langthang. If these place names are connected with the legend just cited, then the etymology "place where the bull died" (*glang shi sa*) results.

> in Byar-smad by a white goat, and the Jo-bo [statue] of Kong-po lha-chu by a piebald goat, so too in this case things were such that the "master of the sacred place" (*gnas bdag*), the upāsaka Vajrasādhu, assumed the form of a bull and, making appeal to the consciousness of those persons with [suitable] karma, opened the "gate to the sacred place" (*gnas sgo*).[21]

Even though the status of Glang-'phrang as the hidden land Heavenly Gate of Half-Moon Form now appears to be definitely established, rDo-dmar-ba Mi-'gyur rdo-rje directs his criticism in a concluding passage of text against two other false opinions concerning the geographical size of gNam-sgo zla-gam and the application of the term "hidden land". The first opinion concerning its size, requiring correction, states that gNam-sgo zla-gam extends from Mang-yul to gNya'-nang: this our author turns aside with the argument that there is nothing to this effect in any of the "entry lists" (*them byang*), and every experienced traveller knows that between Mang-yul and gNya'-nang there is only Glang-'phrang, and no other region of the required size.

Those who champion the second opinion make a distinction between a "hidden land" (*sbas yul*) and a "hidden boundary region" (*sbas 'debs*), asserting that Glang-'phrang is counted among the "hidden boundary regions". Thereupon rDo-dmar-ba Mi-'gyur rdo-rje brings to bear the argument that the term "hidden boundary region" is not clearly taught in the "treasure writings" (*gter lung*), although it might be understood, in accordance with one particular citation, in the sense of "border" (*so mtshams*). The citation reads:

---

21 rDo-dmar Zhabs-drung Mi-'gyur rdo-rje (as in note 14), fol. 6a/5–b/2: *gter ston gar dbang rdo rje'i gter byung du / gter bdag ri dwags su sprul nas lam drangs pa'i rjes su 'brengs pas gter 'thon tshul dang / skyid grong 'phags pa wa ti ba dkar mo gcig gi rnyed pa dang / byar smad kyi jo bo ra dkar mo gcig gi rnyed pa dang / kong po lha chu jo bo ra rgya mo gcig gi rnyed pa sogs lo rgyus mang bas tshul 'di ni gnas bdag dge bsnyen chen po rdo rje legs pa nyid glang gi gzugs su sprul nas las can gyi gang zag de rgyud bskul te gnas sgo phye ba yin no*. Cf. the description of mNga'-ris gter-ston Gar-dbang rdo-rje's treasure discovery in sTag-sgang mkhas-mchog Ngag-dbang blo-gros, (as in note 4), vol. 3, p. 207.3–6: "Setting off to raise the treasure, he caught sight of a red animal running in front of him; he followed its tracks, and out of a deep rocky abyss, from which no man can escape, the "introduction lists of the treasures" (*gter kyi kha byang*) came into his hands. Thus were the cycles of *rDor sems thugs kyi me long* brought forth from the treasure in the hidden land of sKyid-mo lung" (*gter bzhes par byon pas ri dwags dmar po zhig sngon la 'gro bar gzigs nas / de'i rje su byon pas mi mi thar ba'i brag g.yang chen po zhig nas gter kyi kha byang rnams phyag tu son pa bzhin sbas yul skyid mo lung nas rdor sems thugs kyi me long skor rnams gter nas gdan drangs shing*). See the text as in note 5, fol. 57b/4ff.

In the winter of 1989 I filmed a work on the 'Phags-pa Wa-ti statue by Brag-dkar rta-so sprul-sku Chos-kyi dbang-phyug (1775–1837): *'Phags mchog thugs rje chen po rang byung wa ti bzang po'i rnam par thar pa*, 100 fols.; this text contains the legend that the four generally accepted Avalokiteśvara statues have been found by an Arhat after following a red (!) cow; see Ehrhard (2004a:237f.).

> When the time has come, wish for a secluded abode, the entrance to a valley.
> For this there are entry lists containing the borders.[22]

A further passage, which I shall not go into in detail, contains a list of various regions and marks out the relations between "hidden lands" and "hidden boundary regions". rDo-dmar-ba Mi-'gyur rdo-rje draws the conclusion that a *sbas 'debs* is in every case placed at the threshold to a *sbas yul*; as regards the status of the Bull Passage Valley, it follows that Mang-yul is a "hidden boundary region", and Glang-'phrang the actual "hidden land".

The "old *yogin* who places trust in the highest vehicle" (*theg pa mchog la mos pa'i rtogs ldan rgan po*) brings his discussion to an end with the definition of a *sbas yul*; I shall join with him:

> In short, a "hidden land" is a place where a person flees in the face of terrifying enemy troops. Its characteristic is that is that of a fully secure place. If, therefore, Yol-mo and La-phyi for example, are termed "hidden lands", what is to be said [of a land] that surpasses even them in matters of security?[23]

---

22 rDo-dmar Zhabs-drung Mi-'gyur rdo-rje (as in note 14), fol. 7b/3: *dus la bab na sa rong sgo snyogs / de la so mtshams bzung ba'i them byang yod*. This citation could be traced to the work *dNgul dkar me long*, p. 31.2. The entry lists under discussion are there connnected with the "seven catalogues of exhortations", see note 18. The citation itself is taken from one of these catalogues, the *bsKul byang lus kyi gzhung shing*. The work *dNgul dkar me long* as a whole is a compilation of various prophecies and exhortations directed principally at the lineage of the kings of Gung-thang. Concerning the hidden lands, i.e. the time of flight to the regions and the persons upon whom the task of opening them up devolves, reference is made in eight different places to a text called *sBas yul spyi'i them byang*. This text has happily been published in the volume of collected works *Byang gter lugs kyi rnam thar dang ma 'ongs lung bstan,* Gangtok 1983, and it doubtless represents one of the most highly authentic documents on the literature of hidden lands; Rig-'dzin rGod-ldem 'phru-can is cited as the "treasure discoverer", and thus we meet up with him again as a key figure in this field of enquiry.

23 rDo-dmar Zhabs-drung Mi-'gyur rdo-rje (as in note 14), fols. 7b/5–8a/1: *mdor na sbas yul ni mtha' dmag gdug pa can la 'brogs pa'i yul yin la / de'i mtshan nyid ni sa btsan pa kho na yin pas / yol mo dang la phyi sogs kyang sbas yul du gsungs na / de bas ches bstan pa 'di smos ci dgos*. One piece of evidence from the sixteenth century that the entire region of Gung-thang was regarded as a hidden land is a passage from the *rNam 'byor dbang phyug lha btsun chos kyi rgyal po'i rnam thar smad cha* of lHa-btsun Rin-chen rnam-rgyal (1473–1557): "here in the hidden land of Gung-thang, which is reckoned among the three parts of mNga'-ris" (*mnga' ris skor gsum char gtogs sbas yul gung thang 'dir*); ibid, fol. 5b/3.

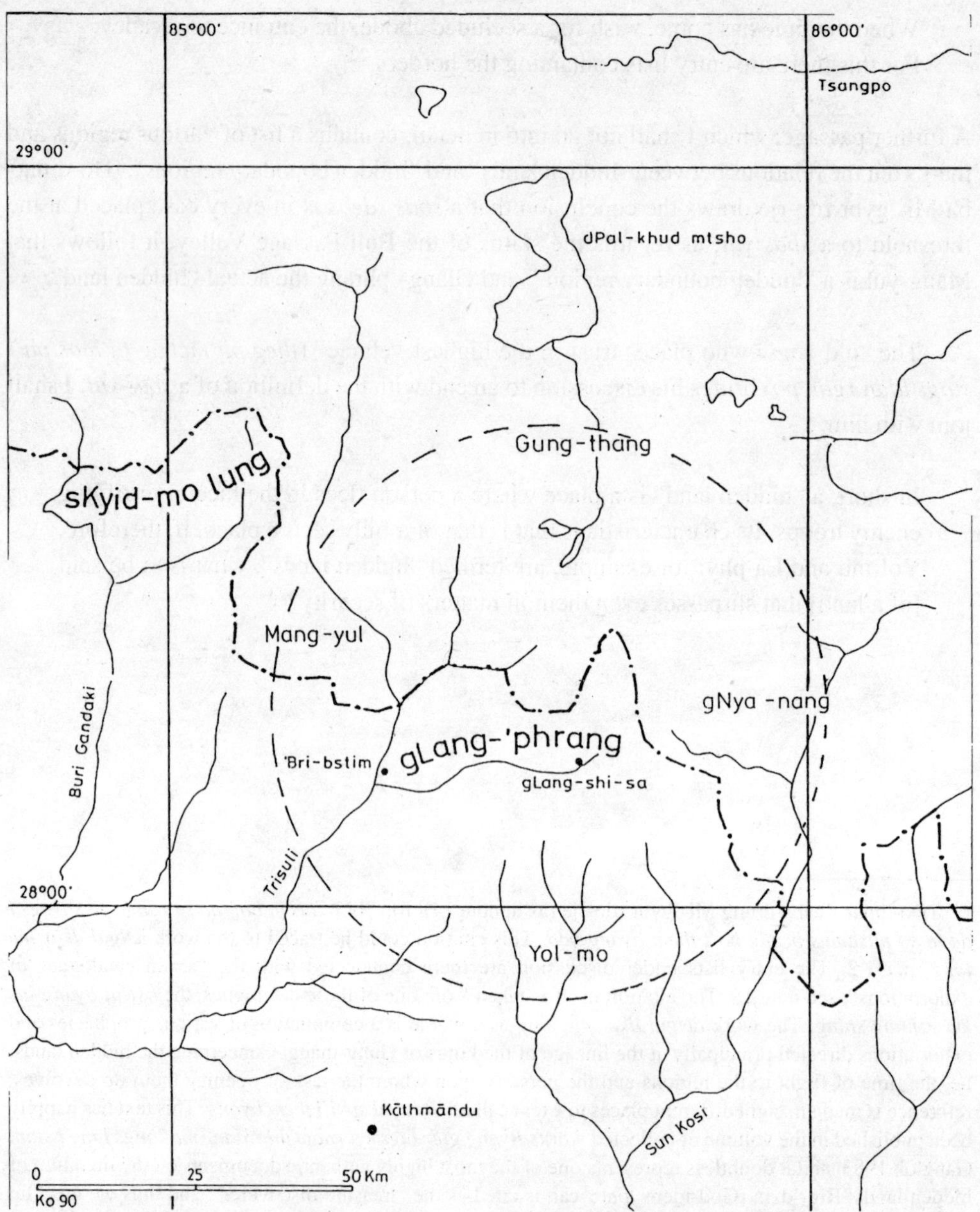

Plate 1: Map: North of Kathmandu, Nepal

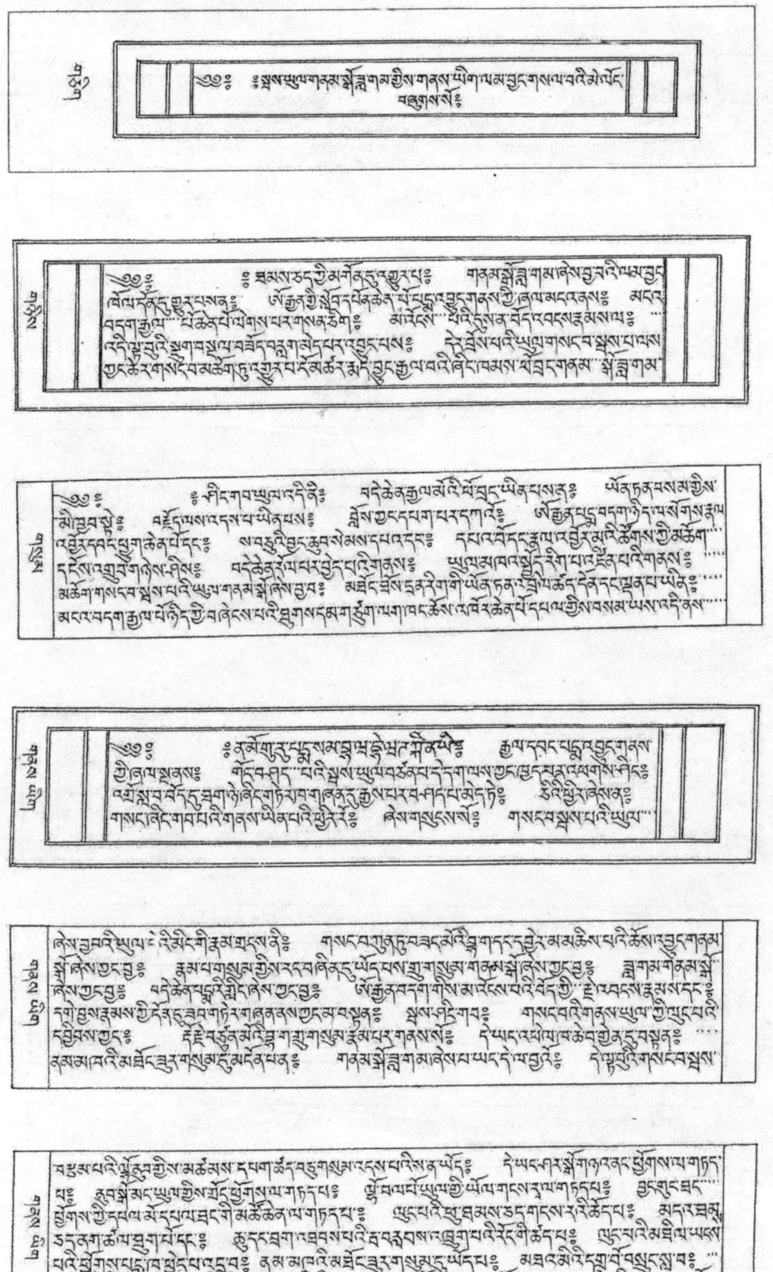

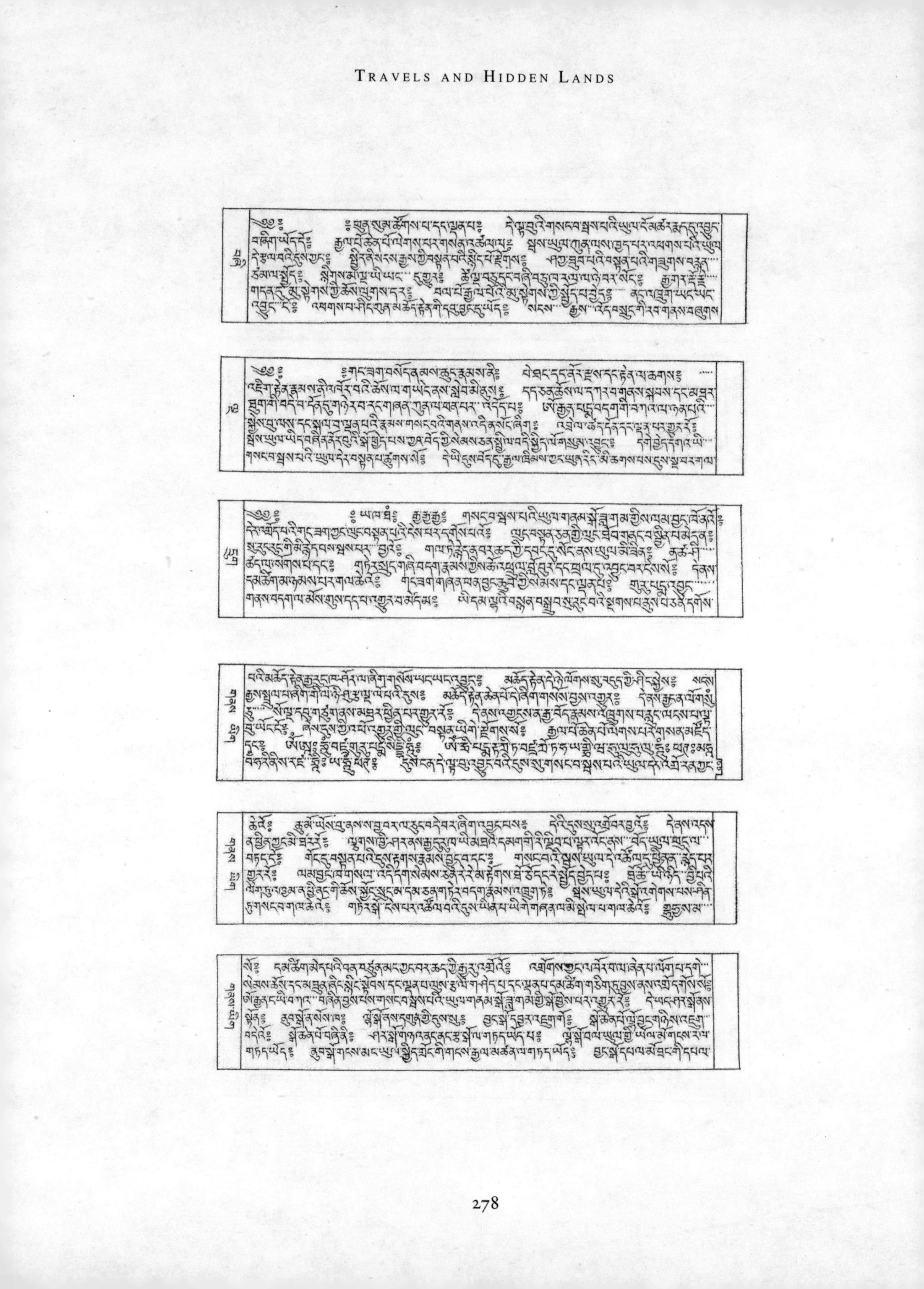

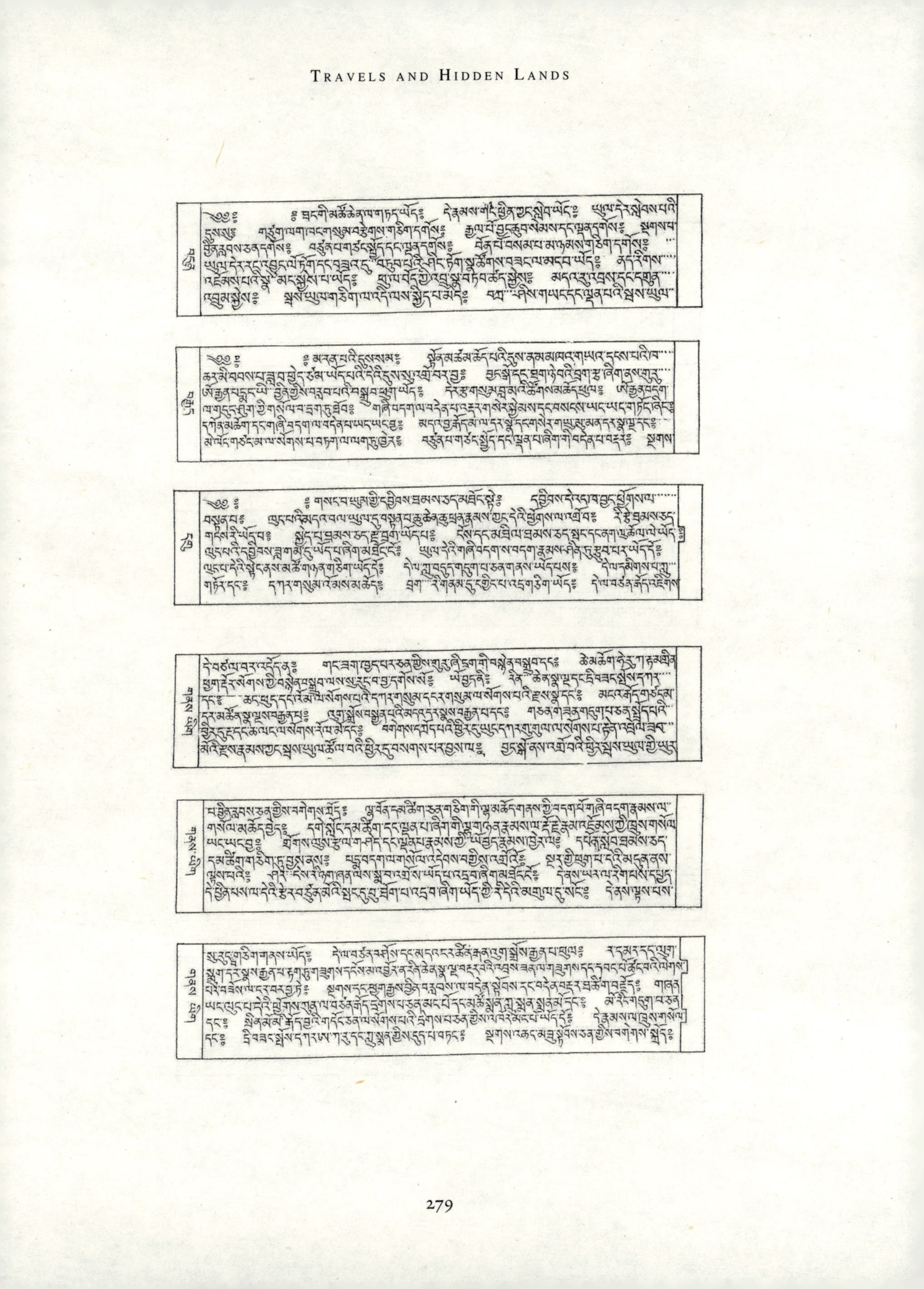

༄༅༔ ༔ རང་གྲོགས་རྣམས་ལ་བསྲུང་འཁོར་བསྒོམ༔ ལྷ་འདྲེ་ཟིལ་གྱིས་གནོན༔ དཀོན
མཆོག་ལ་མཆོད་པ་འབུལ༔ ཡིད་ཀྱི་སྤྲུལ་ནས་ཀྱང་འབུལ༔ མཎྜལ་ལ་སོགས་རྣམ་དག་བྱ༔ མཆོད་སྐྱོན
ལ་གླུ་གཏོར་གླུ་མཆོད་གཏོང་༔ ཡུལ་དེའི་ལྷ་རྣ་དགུ་གཉན་རྡོ་རྗེ་ལེགས་པ་ཡོད་པས༔ གསོལ་མཆོད་བྱ༔
བཙན་ཆོད་རྡེག་པ་ཅན་ལ་གསོལ་མཆོད་འབུལ༔ ལྷ་བོན་གྱིས་ལྷ་གསོལ་བྱ་ཧྲ་འགྲོ༔ དེ་ལྟ་བུའི་གནས་ཚོལ་དུས
བྱའོ༔ ནང་དུ་སྒྲིབ་ནས་ཀྱང་བྱའོ༔ ཕྱི་ལ་བོད་ཀྱི་འབྲུ་སྣ་བཏབ་ཚོད་སྦྱོང་༔ མདའ་འདུར་ཞབས་དང་དགུན་འབུམ
སྦྱོང་༔ ཐོས་ཡུལ་གཅིག་ལ་འདི་ལས་སྐྱིད་པ་མེད༔ དེ་ནས་ལམ་ཁ་དེ་ནས་འཕྱི་ལ་རིག་པས་དཔྱད་ལ་སོང་༔

༄༅༔ ༔ ཨོ་རྒྱན་པདྨའི་གསོལ་འདེབས་ལ་འབད༔ ཉོན་མོངས་དང་མཐའ་མལ་བའི
སྐད་ཆ་མི་བྱེད༔ རི་གཉན་གནས་བདག་ཡུལ་གཉན་པོ་དེ་པ་རྣམས་ལ་ཁྲེ་མི་འདེབས༔ གཙན་གཟན་གདུག་པ
ཅན་སྲོད་དགོས་བྱུང་ནམ་གཏོགས་རོལ་མོའི་སྒྲ་དྲག་པོ་ཡང་ནམ་མི་བྱ༔ གསང་བའི་སྦས་པའི་ཡུལ་དེར་བཀའ་ཤིན་ཏུ་གཅན
པ་ཡིན་པས༔ དང་པོ་ནས་རིམ་བཞིན་གྱིས་གཞི་བདག་རྣམས་ལ་འབྲེལ་སུ་བཙུག༔ དྲག་འདུལ་གྱི་ལས་མི་བྱེད༔
ཞི་དུལ་བྱང་སེམས་ཀྱི་སྤྱོད་ནས་བྱ༔ སྒྲོགས་མཚན་ཀུན་གྱིས་བཤོན་འགྲོན་མི་བྱ༔ དམ་ཚིག་ལ་གནས་པར་བྱ༔ ཀུན
གཙང་སྤྱོད་དང་ལྡན་པར་གལ་ཆེའོ༔ དེ་ལྟ་བུ་སྦས་ཡུལ་ཚོལ་བའི་དུས་སུ་བྱ༔ དེ་ལྟར་མ་བྱས་ན་བྱུན་དང་ཁ་ཆར

༄༅༔ ༔ ཡུལ་དེ་ཟིན་ནས་གནས་ཀྱང་བཀྲ་ཤིས་ཤིང་༔ བདེ་སྐྱིད་ལྡན་ལུས་ཚོགས་པ་འབྱུང་ངོ་༔
དགེ་སྦྱོང་སངས་རྒྱས་ཀྱི་བསྟན་པ་དར་རྒྱས་སོ༔ ཁྱད་པར་དུ་གསང་སྔགས་ཟབ་མོ་སྒྲུབ་པ་རྒྱུན་མི་ཆད་པ་བྱེད་བདུན
དང་མཐུ་རྩལ་ཡོད་པས་གསང་བ་སྦས་པའི་ཡུལ་དེ་ཟིན་པས་ཀྱང་ས་དང་པོ་མ་ཐོབ་ལམ་ཀྱི་བདེ་ན་པ་མཐོང་པར་འགྱུར་རོ༔
བདུད་འབྱུང་བདག་ལ་མོས་གུས་དང་༔ གསོལ་འདེབས་དང་རྩ་གསུམ་བླ་མའི་བསྒྲུབ་པ་གལ་ཆེའོ༔ ཡུལ་དེ་སྔོན
ལྷ་ཡི་དབང་པོ་ཆེ་ལ་སོགས་ལྷ་རྣམས་ཀྱི་ལོངས་སྤྱོད་པའི་ཡུལ་ཡིན་པའོ༔ གཏེར་ན་གཙང་སྤྱོད་དང་ལྡན་པར་བྱ༔
ཡུལ་དེ་མི་འགྲོ་སླ་དེ་སྲུགས་མི་ཐར་པས༔ སྔོན་དུ་དུད་འགྲོ་དང་གནག་ཤི་སྐོར་བྱེད་པ་ཡང་༔ ཡུལ་དེ་རུ

མིག་མཐོང་རི་ལ་ཐོ་རེ་བརྩེགས་ལ་བཞག༔ དེ་ལྟར་མ་བྱས་ན་ཡུལ་གྱིས་སྒོ་འདི་བྱ་ཆོད་གདོང་པ་ཅན་གྱི་ལམ་བྲུམ་དུ་བཅུག
ཡོད་དོ༔ དེ་ནས་ལམ་རྟགས་ཀྱིན་བྱིན་པས༔ གནས་ཀྱི་མཐིལ་དུ་སླེབ་ཡོད་དེ༔ སྤར་བཤད་པའི་མཆོད་པ་དང་༔
ཡན་ལག་བདུན་པ་དང་༔ གཞི་བདག་གནས་བདག་རྣམས་ལ་གསོལ་མཆོད་རྒྱས་པ་རེ་བགྱིས༔ ཁྱད་པར་དུ་སྐྱིག
མ་ཐག་ལམ་མོའི་མདོས་བཏོང་བ་གལ་ཆེ༔ ལྷ་བོན་གྱི་སྐྱང་རྒྱས་དང་གཡག་ལུག་ར་གསུམ་དཀར་སེར་གཟུགས
བརྙན་བཅོས་ལ་དར་སྣས་བརྒྱན་པ་བརྟེན་དུ་འཛུགས༔ ཁྲེལ་གསོལ་བསངས་གསེར་སྐྱེམས་འབུལ་ལོ༔ ཉི
བཟང་དང་ཙན་དན་དཀར་དམར་སོགས་ཀྱི་བསངས་རྫས་གང་འཛོམས་དུད་པ་བཏང་༔ ཐབ་གཞོབ་ནམ་ཡང་མི་བྱ༔

བུ་ཡུག་ཚུབ་མ་དྲག་ཏུ་ཡོང་༔ སྲུ་སྐད་མི་གཅིག་པ་དང་འུར་སྒྲ་བྲག་ཆེམ་ཆེམ་པོ་ཡོང་༔ ཡུལ་གྱི་སྒོ་འདེ་བྱ་གདོང་གྱི
ཆེའ་སྤྲུལ་ལྟ་ཚོགས་སྟོན༔ གནས་བདག་གཞི་བདག་རྣམས་ཁྲེལ་ནས༔ རྣལ་འབྱོར་པ་ལ་གཙན་གཟན་གྱི་གནོད་པ
འབྱུང་ངོ་༔ ཡུལ་དེའི་གཞི་བདག་ཙང་ནས་གླུ་སྨན་གྱི་གནས་ས་ཡིན་པས་ཁྲེལ་གསོལ་གསོལ་མཆོད་གླུ་གཏོར་ཆབ
སྒྲི་རིང་དང་མདའ་དར་ལ་སོགས་པའི་གོང་དུ་བཤད་པ་ལྟར་བགྱིས༔ ཡུལ་དེའི་གཞི་བདག་རྣམས་རང་རང་གི་མཐུན
པའི་གཟུང་པོ་བསྟན་ཏུ་གཙུག༔ ཨོ་རྒྱན་པདྨ་བདག་གི་བཀའ་ཡི་ཡུལ་བདག་རྣམས་ལ་བདེན་པ་ཡང་ཡང་བརྗོད༔
དེ་ལྟར་བྱས་ན་ཆེ་འཕྲུལ་དང་གདུག་བརྩུབ་སྤྲུལ་དུ་ཞི་ནས༔ ཞི་བདག་གནས་བདག་རྣམས་ཀྱི་གྲུབ་རྒྱ་ཆེན་བསམ་དོན་སྒྲུབ༔

ལྷ་དགེ་བསྙེན་རྡོ་རྗེ་ལེགས་པ་ཡོད་པས་བཀྲ་ཤིས་གཙང་དང་ཕུན་རྫས་ཀྱི་མཆོད༔ གསོག་དབྱུགས་དང་ཤ་ཁྲག་མ
གཏོར༔ མཆོད་པ་འོས་པ་མཆོད༔ ལྷོ་ན་གྱི་དུས་ཚང་སྨྲ་པ་དང་གུར་ལྟང་དབང་ཕྱུག་ཆེན་པོ་གནས་ཡིན་པས༔
དེ་གཉིས་མཆོད་ན་འཁོར་དང་བཅས༔ སྤྱོད་འདོལ་ཞིང་བཀྲ་ཤིས་པར་འགྱུར་རོ༔ ཚེས་ཁྲིམས་གནས་དགོས་པས་དེ
གཉིས་ལ་འབྲུ་དང་རིན་པོ་ཆེ་ཡི་མཆོད༔ ལུང་པའི་རྩེ་ཐམས་ཅད་ཟླ་མོ་དུ་ཡོད་པ༔ ཐི་ལ་ཐམས་ཅད་པདྨ་འདབ
བརྒྱད་དུ་འཁྱིལ་པ་འདྲ་བ་ཡོད༔ འདབ་མ་རེ་ལ་གྲོང་ཁྱེར་བརྒྱ་རེ་འཆེ༔ ཕུ་ལ་གཡག་རྫོང་ལ་སོགས་རི་དྭགས་སྣ
ཚོགས་ཡོད༔ མདའ་ལ་གཙན་གཟན་ཡོད༔ རྒྱ་དང་བྲག་གི་མཆོད་པས་མཐའ་མི་དཀྲ་བ་ཐམས་ཅད་བསྐྱུར་སྣ

བཅུ་བཞི་པ

༄༅། །པས། གནས་སྐབས་དང་མཐར་ཐུག་གི་ཐབས་མ་དོན་འགྲུབ་པོ། ཡུལ་དེ་བ་ལ་ཕྱུག
ཆགས་ས་ཡང་ཡོད་པས་རིག་པས་དཔྱད་ནས། གནས་བདག་གཞི་བདག་རྣམས་ལ་གསོལ་མཆོད་བདེན་བརྗོད་དང་ཙྪ
ལམ་བཅོལ་བས་ཕྱུག་གི་ཐར་བར་འགྱུར་རོ། གང་གི་དུས་རྟག་དེའི་དུས་སུ་རྟ་ཡང་ཆགས་སོ། བོད་དུ་རྟ་ཀ་ཡི་དམག
གི་ཉེན་པ་ན་གང་ནས་བལྟས་ཀྱང་སྐྱོབ་བསྐྱལ་གྱི་ཡོད། སྐྱོ་བ་ལས་མེད། རི་མགོ་ཐམས་ཅད་ཆགས་སྤང་གི་འཛིགས་པ
ཞིག་འབྱུང་བས་དེའི་དུས་སུ། བོད་ཀྱི་དགེ་བྱེད་ཐམས་ཅད་གསང་བའི་ཡུལ་དེར་སོང་ཞིག། གཞན་སྐྱབས་ཡུལ
ཆེན་པོ་རྣམས་ནི་འཚོལ་ཐབ་རིང་ལ། ཐག་ཉེ་བའི་གསང་བ་སྦས་པའི་ཡུལ་ནི། གནམ་སྒོ་ཟླ་གམ་ཞེས་བྱ་བ

བཅོ་ལྔ

༄༅། །ཕྱུང་པོ་འཛིང་ལུས་འགྲོ་བ་བརྒྱ་ཅིག་ཡོད་དོ། རྒྱལ་རབས་བདུན་བརྒྱུད་ཡི་བར་ལ
ཤིན་ཏུ་བདེ་བས་སོ། གསང་བའི་ཡུལ་དེ་ནི་བྱང་ཆུབ་སེམས་དཔའ་ས་བཅུ་ཐོབ་པའི་སྐྱིད་ཡུལ་ཡིན་པས།
ས་བཅུ་ཐོབ་པ་དང་ཁྱད་པར་མེད་དོ། ཡུལ་དེར་གྲོང་ཁྱེར་དགུ་བརྒྱ་ལྔ་བཅུ་ཡོད་པས་སོ། ཡུལ་དེའི་དབུས་སུ་རྡོ་ཕ
པོ་ང་སྐྱོ་ཁྲུས་བལ་ཡུ་བྱ་ཞིག་ཡོད། དེའི་འོག་ན་ཤེལ་གྱི་བྲག་པ་འདིན་དུ་ལྡ་ཡོད་བཞིན་གྱི་ནོར་བུ་རིན་པོ་ཆེ
བསམ་འཕེལ་འཆོང་དུ་གི་པ་ལྔ་ང་ཡ། ཐོ་གང་བ་གཅིག་ཡོད། དེའི་ཡུལ་དེའི་ནང་དུ་བྱང་དུ་ལྷུན་པ་ཡིན་པས།
དེའི་སྟེང་དུ་ལྷ་ཁང་བཞེངས། ཤར་གྱི་འདབ་མ་ལ་རྒྱལ་ཁྲིམས་ཅན་གྱི་གླིང་ཤར་ཀྱི་ མཆོད་ཡི་ལྷ་ཁང་བཞེངས།

བཅུ་དྲུག

༄༅། །གང་བ་ཡོད། དེ་ན་དྲག་པོ་མི་རིང་ནི་རི་ས་དམར་པོ་ལ། གཏེར་ཁ་མང་པོའི་གཏེར
ཀ་དྲ་ཡོད་དོ། ནུབ་བྱང་མཚམས་ན་ལུང་པ་ཉམས་དགའ་བ་གཅིག་ཡོད། དེའི་ནང་ནས་པདྨ་འབྱུང་གནས་བདག
གི་སྐུ་ཕྱག་དབྱེན་མགོན་ཕྱིན་ལྡན་ཅན་མཐོང་བ་ཙམ། ཉེ་དེར་ཛོང་ཕུག་ལ་སྒྲུབ་པ་ཡོད། དེའི་ནང་ན་ལྷ་ཡི
དབང་པོ་རྒྱ་བྱིན་གྱི་ཕྱུག་པའི་ཐབས་མཁའ་འཕེལ་ནོར་བུ་དང་། ལྷོ་བརྒྱད་དགྲ་བ་པར་རྗེམས་པའི་ཕྱུར་པ་པདྨ་བདག་གི་སོར
རྒྱུད་པ་གཅིག ལྷོགས་དང་ཕྱོགས་མཚམས་ཀུན་ཏུ་དབྱེན་གནས་དང་ཡང་རྫོང་ཐུབ་དུ་མ་ཡོད། ལྷོད་པའི་མདུན་
ཙཱ་ཤིང་དང་ནགས་སྣ་ཚོགས་ཡོད། མ་འོངས་པ་ན་ཨོ་རྒྱན་བདག་གི་ཐུགས་ཀྱི་སྐྱུ་པ་མོན་པའི་རྒྱལ་ཅན་གཅིག་གི་ཚོད

བཅུ་བདུན་ ཕྱི

འདི་ནི་ཤིན་ཏུ་ཉེ་ཞིང་འཚོལ་སླ་བ་ཡིན་ཏེ། དུས་ལ་བབས་པའི་ཚེ་ལྷག་པ་དམ་ཚིག་ཅན་བྱིན་རླབས་བསམ་པ
དཀར་བའི་རྒྱུད་ལ་དགེ་བསྙེན་རྡོ་རྗེ་ལེགས་པ་ཐེབས། ཡུལ་དེ་ལྟ་བུ་ཞིག་དེ་ན་ཡོད་ཟེར་གནས་ལུང་བྱུང་བར་འགྱུར་རོ། དེ
བས་ན་ལྷག་སེམས་བྱིན་རླབས་ཅན་གཡུལ་ཆེའོ། སླ་མ་ཨོ་རྒྱན་བདག་དང་མི་གཉིས་གཅིག་དུས་པར་ཡོད་དོ། ཡུལ་དེ་འཛིན
པ་ལ་མངའ་བདག་རྒྱལ་པོ་ཉིད་ཀྱི་རིང་ལ་ཕེབ་འདི་ལྷག་པ་བྱིན་རླབས་ཅན་གྱིས་འཛིན་དགོས་སོ། དོ་སོག་དུ་བུ་བའི
དམག་ལས་ཐར་བར་འདོད་ན་དེར་འབྲོས་ཤིག གནས་སྐབས་མཐར་ཐུག་དོན་དུ་གཉེར་བ་རྣམས་དེར་འབྲོས་ཤིག སྙིང
རྗེ་ལྡན་སེམས་རྣམས་དེར་སོང་ཞིག ཡུལ་དེ་ཆགས་ནས་ཀྱང་ལྷག་གི་བསྒྲུབ་པ་བདུན་བརྒྱུ་ཡོང་བར་འགྱུར་རོ།

བཅོ་བརྒྱད་ ཕྱི

ལྷོའི་འདབ་མ་ལ་ཐུགས་པའི་གླིང་བདེ་ཀ་ཤེ་ཀ་ཞི་ཁྲོའི་ལྷ་ཁང་བཞེངས། ནུབ་ཀྱི་འདབ་མ་ལ་སྨན་གླིང་དུ་ཀུན་བཟང
སྣང་བ་མཐའ་ཡས་ཀྱི་ལྷ་ཁང་བཞེངས། བྱང་གི་འདབ་མ་ལ་ཀུན་གྱི་ཐུབ་མིང་གླིང་དུ་སྒྲུབ་པ་ཐུགས་རྗེའི་ལྷ
ཁང་བཞེངས། ལྷོ་ནུབ་ཀྱི་མཚམས་ན་ཐང་མོ་ལོང་འདྲ་བ་ཡོད། དེར་དམངས་ཀྱི་ཁྲིམ་བརྒྱ་གྲོང་འཆོ་བར
ཡོད། དེར་བཀྲ་ཤིས་སྒོ་མང་གྱིས་མཆོད་རྟེན་བཞེངས། ཤར་ལྷོ་མཚམས་ན་ལུང་སྟོང་ཞིག་ཡོད། དེར་ལྷགས
རྗེ་ཡོད་པས། མཁར་བའི་གླིང་དུ་འདུག བདུད་འདུལ་མཆོད་རྟེན་བཞེངས་པར་བྱེད། བྱང་ཤར་ནས
ལུང་སྟོང་ཆེན་པོ་རྒྱ་བོ་གྲང་ལྡན་གྱི་ཕྱོགས་ནས་འབབས་པ་ཡོད། དེ་ནས་ཆུ་དང་རྒྱལ ཐོག་ལ་སོགས་པའི

བཅུ་དགུ་ ཕྱི

དུས་གཙུག་ནས། ཡུལ་དེ་ལྷ་ཡུལ་དང་མཉམ་པར་བྱེད་དོ། ལུང་པའི་དེའི་ཕྱུ་མ་དང་ཡི་བར་ལ་མི་སྲུང་ནོ་ཞིག
བདུན་གྱིས་ཡོད་དོ། ཡུལ་དེར་མི་སྡེ་པ་རྣམས་སྐད་ཀྱི་རྡོང་མཚམས་སུ་ཡུལ་བཏབ་པས། གྲོང་ཁྱེར་ལྔ
བརྒྱ་འཚོ་བའི་ལུང་པ་ཡོད་པས། རྒྱ་ཕྲན་གཅིག་ཆགས་སོ། དེ་ཡང་གསུང་བའི་སྦས་པའི་ཡུལ་དེར་དགེ་བྱེད
རྣམས་ཀྱི་འདུལ་ཞིང་འགྱུར་རོ། ཁྱད་པར་བར་པ་བཞུགས་རྗེའི་ཆེན་པོའི་ཡུལ་དེའི་སྙིང་བྱང་རྣམས་ཀྱང་། སྦས་པའི
ཡུལ་དེ་ལ་ཡོད་པས། ཨོ་རྒྱན་བདག་ལ་མོས་གུས་ཀྱི་གསོལ་བ་བཏབ་པས། རིམ་གྱིས་རྙེད་པར་འགྱུར་རོ།
གཞན་ཡང་ལུང་པ་འདི་རིས་གནས་ཐམས་ཅད་ལ་ཨོ་རྒྱན་བདག་གི་བྱིན་གྱིས་རླབས་པའི་རྟག་དང་ཕྱག་རྒྱ་གཏེར་ཁ་ནི་མང་པོ

[illegible]

༄༅། ། ༔ ཡོད༔ རྒྱབ་སྦྱད་མཚམས་དེར་ལྷུང་པ་ཤྲཱི་ཧུ་དོ་མཚོ་ར་པ་དེར་པདྨ་འབྱུང་གནས
རིག་འཛིན་གྱི་ཡུལ་ལྷ་ཁང་དང་ཆེ་མཆོག་ཧེ་རུ་ཀའི་པོ་བྲང་བཞེངས་ལ་སྒྲུབ་པའི་སྒོ་ཆེན་པོ་ཅིག་ཕྱེ་བཞིན༔ པདྨ་བདག
གི་ཞལ་དངོས་སུ་མཇལ་ནས་དབང་བསྐུར་རོ༔ གདམས་སྐོར་པར་གྱུར་ཏོ༔ ཡི་དམ་ལྷའི་ཞལ་མཐོང་ངོ༔
དཔའ་བོ་མཁའ་འགྲོ་མ་རྣམས་ཀྱི་ དངོས་འགྲུབ་ ཐོབ་རོ༔ ཆོས་ སྐྱོང་དམ་ཅན་སྲུང་མ་རྣམས་ཀྱི་འབག་ལ་ཆེན་བསྐུར་ཆད
ཞེ་ལ་ལོ༔ ཡུལ་ལྷ་གཞི་བདག་རྣམས་ཀྱི་སྲུན་ ཆེན་བསམ་དོན་ སྒྲུབ༔ ཀཻ་ཆོད་ལྷ་བཙུན་པ་བཞི་བཙུན་དུས
སུ་གསང་བ་སྒྲུབ་པའི་ཡུལ་དེ་ཉིད་པར་གསུང་ ལོ༔ ཨོ་རྒྱན་གྱི་སློབ་ དཔོན་ཆེན་པོ་པདྨ་འབྱུང་གནས་ཐུགས་ རྗེ་ཆེན

[illegible]

པོ་དང་ལྷན་དེ༔ ཆོས་རྒྱལ་ཁྲི་སྲོང་ལྡེའུ་བཙན་དང་༔ མཁའ་འགྲོ་ཡེ་ཤེས་མཚོ་རྒྱལ་དང་༔ པ་གོར་བཻ་རོ་ཙ
ན་ལ་སོགས་ རྗེ་འབངས་རྣམས་ལ་ཞལ་གདམས་སུ་གནང་བའོ༔ སམ་ཡཱ་ རྒྱ་རྒྱ་རྒྱ༔ ཅེས་པའང་སྤྲུལ་པའི
གཏེར་སྟོན་ཆེ་ལྡན་རྒྱལ་མཚན་གྱི་མེན་ཆུ་མོ་ཕྱུག་ གི་མཐའ་ནས་སྤྱན་དྲངས་ནས་ ཞལ་དོན་དུ་བྲིས་པ་ འདི་དང
འདྲ་བར་རིག་འཛིན་ ཚོད་ཀྱི་ལྷེམ་སྤྲུ་ཅན་ ཀྱིས་གཏེར་ལས་ཆ་ཤས་ གཅིག་གནང་བའོ༔ དགེའོ༔ ལས
ཅན་སྐྱེས་བུ་ ཐམས་ཅད་པདྨ་ཆོལ་དུ་འདུས་པར་ཤོག་ཅིག༔ དགེའོ༔

"The Lands are like a Wiped Golden Basin": The Sixth Zhwa-dmar-pa's Journey to Nepal

During my first extended stay in Nepal in 1979 two works by Sandy Macdonald served in particular to engage my fantasy – works that I have constantly come back to at more or less regular intervals: the edition of the Tibetan text of the *Bal po gnas kyi dkar chag* of the Fourth Khams-sprul Rin-po-che (1743–1779) and the *Shar pa'i chos 'byung* of Sangs-rgyas bstan-'dzin (1924–1990).[1] In the case of the former, I obtained information on the sacred sites of the Kathmandu Valley and the various legends associated with them, and in that of the latter, a dialogue was set going with a teacher of the rNying-ma-pa school in the mountains of Nepal.

After I began working at the Nepal Research Centre and for the Nepal-German Manuscript Preservation Project in 1988, my attention has continued to be drawn to such topics as the history of the Buddhist monuments of the Kathmandu Valley, the cultural exchange between Tibet and Nepal, and the spread of the rNying-ma-pa teachings in the north of the kingdom. By way of thanks for all of his stimulating inputs and the lively exchange of ideas we have had over the past years, I should like to offer the recipient of our felicitation a few remarks on a Tibetan text which came into my hands and which has hitherto not been published.

1. The Text

It is a work of the Sixth Zhwa-dmar-pa Chos-kyi dbang-phyug (1584–1630) entitled *Bal yul du bgrod pa'i lam yig nor bu spel ma'i 'phreng ba* ("Route Description for Travelling to Nepal [with the title] 'Rosary of Well-arranged Jewels'"); the forty-eight-folio manuscript in *dbu med* script was filmed in April 1992 in Samagaon, at the foot of the Manaslu. The

---

1 For the *Bal po gnas kyi dkar chag*, see Macdonald (1975:89–144). A French translation is available in Macdonald & Dvags-po Rin-po-che (1981:237–273), an English translation in Macdonald & Dvags-po Rin-po-che (1987:100–134).

The *Shar pa'i chos 'byung* may be found in mKhan-po Sangs-rgyas bstan-'dzin: *Documents pour l'étude de la religion et l'organisation sociale des Sherpa*. I had the opportunity to bring out the supplementary volume *Ne shar lo rgyus jo glang gangs 'od* together with Sandy under the title *Snowlight of Everest*. For further work done in collaboration with Sangs-rgyas bstan-'dzin, see Ehrhard (1993a:77–100) and chapter ten in the present volume, as well as Buffetrille (1997).

work describes a journey undertaken in 1629/30, the starting and end point of which was the sacred site of La-phyi in the south-west of Tibet on the border with Nepal, and which took the Sixth Zhwa-dmar-pa to Kathmandu, Patan and Bhaktapur. Up to now the text has been referred to only in connection with La-phyi, the Thirty-fourth 'Bri-gung hierarch, bsTan-'dzin Chos-kyi blo-gros (1869–1906), having used it as a source for his description of that place.[2]

What makes the text of further interest is its detailed description of the daily stages on the route between Kodari and Sankhu, the contacts between the Sixth Zhwa-dmar-pa and the kings Lakṣminarasiṃha (reign: 1619–1641, in Kathmandu), Siddhinarasiṃha (reign: 1619–1661, in Patan) and Jagajjyotirmalla (reign: 1614–1637, in Bhaktapur), the information on the Buddhist shrines (such as Svayambhūnāth), and especially the account of the stopover in Helambu on the way back to La-phyi. The final folios offer a kind of area orientation of Nepal, including an ethnographic breakdown of the people who had settled on the edge of the Valley.

This brings me to the question of the historical conditions under which the present text was produced and the function that such a travel account served. Shortly before his arrival in the border town of 'Gram (present-day Khasa), the Sixth Zhwa-dmar-pa received through a messenger a personal letter from Karma bsTan-skyong dbang-po, who reigned over Central Tibet from 1620 to 1642; in it was written, "This time defer your wish to go to India and return from Nepal as quickly as possible."[3] We may thus conclude that the trip of the religious dignitary had been sanctioned by the ruler of gTsang and involved some diplomatic tasks. It is known, further, that the minting of silver coins began in Nepal during the first years of the 17th century. The silver was acquired from profits that the trade between Tibet and India brought, and Nepalese trading houses were established in Lhasa

---

2 See Huber (1989:21): "A *lam yig* for La-phyi by the Sixth Zhwa-dmar-pa Chos-kyi dbang-phyug (1584–1635) written shortly before his death." For the text of the *lam yig*, see ibid, pp. 32f. and its translation pp. 52f. In his survey of the history of La-phyi, Huber describes the pilgrimage to La-phyi undertaken in common by the Sixth Zhwa-dmar-pa and the Tenth Karma-pa Chos-dbyings rdo-rje (1604–1674); at this time the site, which had been under the Zhwa-dmar-pa lineage since the middle of the 15th century, was once turned over by Chos-kyi dbang-phyug to the Tenth Karma-pa. Huber notes rightly that this occurred in 1630, and this is also the year in which the *lam-yig* was written; the altering of the death year from 1630 to 1635, however is a hypercorrection (ibid, pp. 95f.). De Rossi Filibeck (1988:162) fails to associate the name Gar-dbang Chos-kyi dbang-phyug with the Sixth Zhwa-dmar-pa.

Parallel material on La-phyi during this period may be found in bsTan-'dzin nor-bu: *La phyi gnya' nang skor gyi lam yig*. Concerning the Third Yol-mo-ba sprul-sku, see also note 17.

3 *Bal yul du bgrod pa'i lam yig*, fol. 12a/4: *da res rgya gar du bgrod pa'i mdun ma shol zhig / bal yul nas kyang myur du 'doc cig*. During his stay at Svayambhūnāth the Sixth Zhwa-dmar-pa took part in a "memorial service" (*tshogs kyi mchod pa*) that was financed by Karma bsTan-skyong dbang-po; shortly before this he had met the Jumla king Vikrama Śāha (reign: 1602–1631), who was returning from a pilgrimage to India (ibid, fols. 22a/3–23a/2).

during the same period; these developments signified a great change in relations between Tibet and Nepal.[4]

At the same time, Nepal was the destination of scholars and artists from India, who settled down in the Kathmandu Valley under the protection of the Malla kings. Siddhinarasiṃha, the step-brother of Lakṣminarasiṃha, played a major role in consolidating and spreading Kṛṣṇaism in Nepal and was likewise greatly influenced by Vaiṣṇava belief. Further, he erected temples for the god Śiva and founded new *vihāra*s for the Buddhists. Is it surprising, then, in an atmosphere so receptive to both secular and spiritual impulses, that the first European to travel to Nepal, the Jesuit missionary João Cabral (1599–1669), should have chosen this time to do so? His route led via Bhutan to Central Tibet, where he met the ruler Karma bsTan-skyong dbang-po, and from there, in the year 1628, he went on via Nepal to India. In his letters Cabral tells of "this new way through the Kingdom of Nepal ... was so dangerous and hazardous."[5]

This was the very same route taken one year later by the Sixth Zhwa-dmar-pa, also at the instigation of the ruler of gTsang. From these few superficially assembled observations we may conclude that the period in which the text of the Sixth Zhwa-dmar-pa was put together was one of revitalized economic and cultural exchange between India, Nepal and Tibet. Its value for the ruler of gTsang and the dignitaries of the bKa'-brgyud-pa school doubtless consisted in its detailed account of the shorter but more perilous route that led from gZhis-ka-rtse via Shel-dkar and gNya'-lam to the Kathmandu Valley, not to mention its summary description of the local morals and customs that follows upon the actual itinerary (fols. 42b/3–45b/4). The concluding section, a compressed ethnography (fols. 45b/4–48b/4), may even lend support to the assumption that the function of the *Bal yul du bgrod pa'i lam yig* was to document the need and practicability of mission work among those ethnic groups through whose territories the recently established trade route passed.

2. THE JOURNEY

In this section I shall briefly retrace the Sixth Zhwa-dmar-pa's stops along the way, whenever they provide insight into the cultural geography and cultural history of the region that in the modern administrative nomenclature of Nepal is called Sindhu Palchok. Having left La-phyi, the Sixth Zhwa-dmar-pa went by way of Mi-la-ras-pa's cave Grod-pa phug to Ku-ti (this is the name used, not gNya'-nang); the place is described as a "large bazaar of

---

4 For a historical survey of the coins minted in Nepal and sent to Tibet, see Rhodes & Gabrisch (1989:72–76). Concerning the establishment of the Nepalese trading houses under King Lakṣminarasiṃha, see ibid, p. 69; there reference is made to Wright (1877:211). Cf. also Rhodes (1989:113–117).

5 For the religious atmosphere in Nepal at the beginning of the 17th century and the role of Siddhinarasiṃha, see Lienhard (1992:227–234). On the brief letter passages that document the journey of João Cabral, see Gettelman (1982:97–110), and (1990:269–277).

Nepal and Tibet" (*bal bod kyi tshong 'dus chen po*). On the way to 'Gram is a place called Tshogs-bsham; there the Sixth Zhwa-dmar-pa visited the sacred site bDe-chen steng and was entertained by "descendants" (*rigs kyi dbon po*) of O-rgyan-pa Rin-chen dpal (1230–1309).[6] Nearby there is a cave that had been visited by Padmasambhava.

After the arrival of the courier sent by the ruler Karma bsTan-skyong dbang-po and a short stay in 'Gram, the Sixth Zhwa-dmar-pa continued his journey, "crossing a bridge suspended on iron chains that was the cause of great astonishment" (*lcags thigs sding la brten pa'i zam pa mchog tu ngo mtshar ba yang brgal te*); shortly afterwards he met six traders who came from the land of the Mang-kar.[7] The way continued through a forested region, and a pass was crossed without any problem. Later, however, the path turned into a "narrow trail" (*'phrang*), the very sight of it aroused fear. It bore the name "Hairless Wolf" (*spyang ki spu med*), and legend has it that a deer, the manifestation of a Bodhisattva, had disclosed it in an earlier period.[8]

The next places that the Sixth Zhwa-dmar-pa passed through are called Dum-kham and rTag-pa gnas-sa; lying not far from the latter is sKye-ba lung, a "holy site that was blessed by Ācārya Padma[sambhava]" (*slob dpon padmas sbyin gyis brlabs pa'i gnas*).[9] The next stops along the way are Shing-skam, 'Dar-thil and sPang-sgang, in each of which places the holy man from Tibet was invited to stay and served with food and drink. In return he conferred the "authorization for the recitation of the Avalokiteśvara [mantra]"

---

6 bDe-chen steng is one of the sites where rGod-tshang-pa mGon-po rdo-rje (1189–1258) engaged in his religious practices. He was the teacher of O-rgyan-pa Rin-chen dpal, who met the master there at the age of twenty-two; see bSod-nams 'od-zer: *dPal ldan bla ma dam pa grub chen u rgyan pa'i rnam par thar pa byin rlabs kyi chu rgyun*, pp. 18.3ff. I was able to film a description of the sacred site in December 1992 in Kodari: *Grub pa'i sti gnas chen po dpal bde chen steng gi gnas bshad nor bu'i 'phreng ba*, 23 fols. According to Lama Lhundrub of Kodari, the Sherpas who have settled in and around the border village still make pilgrimage to bDe-chen steng; this group of Sherpas migrated to Kodari from the region centred on Bigu Gompa.

7 The place where the bridge suspended on iron chains was located is today marked by the Friendship Bridge constructed by the Chinese government. As for the toponyms 'Gram means "height" or "slope", whereas the Tibetan name for Kodari is bCa'-sne sgang; this I would translate as "hill at the end/edge of the precipice". Compare the name Chyenegang noted by Aufschnaiter on the Lapchi Kang map.

8 On the significance of animals in creating paths and opening up "gates to sacred sites" (*gnas sgo*), see Ehrhard (1997b:335–364) and chapter sixteen in the present volume. The name sPyang-kyi spu med and the following toponyms are found also in the diaries of the Eighth Si-tu Paṇ-chen Chos-kyi 'byung-gnas (1699–1774); he followed the same route in the years 1723 and 1748 and refers to the journey of the Sixth Zhwa-dmar-pa. For a résumé of the account of the Eighth Si-tu Paṇ-chen, see Lewis & Jamspal (1988:194f. and 205f.).

9 For a mention of sKye-ba lung in a land grant document dating to 1730, see Clarke & Manandhar (1988:114 and 118f.). The Kungsang Dorje Lama mentioned in it is Kun-bzang Nyi-zla rdo-rje, as learned from the biography of gTer-dbon Nyi-ma seng-ge (1687–1738), who had likewise stayed in sKye-ba lung: see 'Phrin-las bdud-'joms: *Gu ru sū rya seng ge'i rnam thar mdor bsdus*, fol.11a.

(*spyan ras gzigs kyi bzlas lung*) and counselled the native inhabitants to perform beneficial acts, that is, to give up the killing of animals and so forth.

A somewhat longer passage of the *Bal yul du bgrod pa'i lam yig*, is devoted to the time spent in the village of Sa-'go li-ti. As its name, "Chief of the Locality" (*sa 'go = rdzong dpon*), suggests, an administrative figure who was tasked with certain official duties was stationed there; and indeed the text reads "the tax collector of the king of Nepal resides here" (*bal po'i rgyal po'i dpya phral* (= *khral*) *bsdu ba po yang der gnas pa*). The Sixth Zhwa-dmar-pa was overwhelmed with gifts, and a little later "the king of Li-ti" is singled out among the donators: "he is said to be of the same family as the king of Nepal" (*bal po'i rgyal po dang rigs gcig go zhes grags pa'i li ti rgyal po*).[10]

The trip went on further through Thang-skams, Yang-la-koṭ and Sebṭa; the latter place is more precisely identified as being situated in the territory of the Mang-kar. Adhering to the rule that "it is dangerous for Tibetans to walk through rice fields in the midday heat" (*nyi ma'i gung la sā lu'i zhing nang du song na bod kyi mi rnams kyi lus la nad bskyed do*), the Sixth Zhwa-dmar-pa continued his trek through the country of the Mang-kar and reached Sing-kar bha-dra, and shortly thereafter Si-pa. Next, the place called sDe-phur is lauded not only for its fertile fields and cool forests; there, it is said "in the middle of the territory, the leisurely river that comes down from Yol-mo gangs-rwa flows" (*yul gyi dbus su yol mo gangs rwa nas 'bab pa'i chu klung dal ba 'bab pa*). This was the spot where the Sixth Zhwa-dmar-pa traversed the Indravati Khola, which "in the summer (i.e. during the monsoon) has to be crossed by boat" (*dbyar gyi dus su ni grus bgrod par bya dgos*); the Indravati Khola arises from the confluence of the Melemchi Khola and the Yangri Khola, whose headwaters are in the territory of Helambu.

In his description of the beauty of the region that he wandered through the following day on his way to the pass called Bla-ma spyan-'dren, the Sixth Zhwa-dmar-pa employs a poetic image that suggests literary antecedents: "The lands are like a wiped golden basin".[11] The phrase "middle of the territory" (*yul gyi dbus*) adds force to the assumption that textual

---

10 Concerning the location of Li-ti (= Li-khri / Sindūra (?); in present-day speech Listi), see Clarke & Manandhar (1988:119): "... Listi, which is on the eastern flank of Bhairabkund on the Bhote Kosi." To my knowledge, only the king of Sankhu (on the edge of the Kathmandu Valley) has previously been described as a sovereign ruler who controlled the trade route; see Zanen (1986:140). For the role of local chieftains on the border between Nepal and Tibet in the 19th century, see Steinmann (1991:467–485).

11 *Bal yul du bgrod pa'i lam yig* (as in note 3), fol. 17a/1: *ljongs rnams gser gyi gzhong pa phyis pa bzhin*; cf. ibid, fol. 36a/2–3: "In the guide to the sacred site Yol-mo it is stated: 'In the middle of the territory are meadows that are like golden basins. There one finds a royal palace'." (*yol mo gnas yig tu yul gyi dbus spang gser gyi gzhong pa lta bu yod do / der rgyal po'i pho brang thob*). This is Gangs-yul, the area below rGod-tshang gling along the upper reaches of Melemchi Khola. Cf. the text *Yol mo gangs kyi ra ba'i gnad* (= *gnas*) *yig*, p. 521.4: *sa'i dbus ni rin po che'i gzhong pa 'dra ba yod / der rgyal po'i gling gdab dgos*.

sources lay behind the description of the idealized qualities of the landscape along the Indravati Khola.

For this reason I shall not follow that led the Sixth Zhwa-dmar-pa from Bla-ma spyan-'dren via Sang-ku, Viṣṇu's shrine Caṃgu Nārāyaṇa and the *stūpa* of Bodhnāth to Kathmandu proper but instead focus on the return trip. This took the dignitary of the bKa'-brgyud-pa school, after his successfully completed mission to the Kathmandu Valley, directly to Helambu; having been accompanied by King Lakṣminarasiṃha, Prince Pratāpamalla (reign: 1641–1674) and a large retinue to the *stūpa* of Bodhnāth, the Sixth Zhwa-dmar-pa on the following day set off back to Bla-ma spyan-'dren.

By way of the "land of the Mang-kar, where the river from Yol-mo gangs flows" (*yol mo gangs kyis* (= *kyi*) *chu rgyun 'bab pa'i mang kar gyi yul*), he slowly made his way to dPal-tshogs, the "inner part of the sacred site of Yol-mo" (*yol mo gangs rwa'i gnas khog*).[12] Besides the customary discussions with the local inhabitants, it may be noted that in dPal-tshogs the Sixth "Zhwa-dmar-pa performed the crown ceremony of his incarnation lineage" (*zhwa dmar kyi cod paṇ yang bgos*). After passage through the previously mentioned territory of Gangs-yul, the next station was rGod-tshang gling, the former abode of rGod-tshang ras-chen (1482–1559), a disciple of gTsang-smyon He-ru-ka (1452–1507).[13]

The site of rGod-tshang gling served as his base for an inspection tour of one of the places associated with Padmasambhava, called Yang-dag mchog-gi sgrub-phug. I shall not go into the details of this tour, beyond mentioning the fact that the Sixth Zhwa-dmar-pa again made extensive use of the *gnas yig* literature and that his destination was the mountain Yang-ri; in earlier times there was a temple on it that had been built by one Grub-thob rGyal-mtshan.[14]

---

[12] Here again *Bal yul du bgrod pa'i lam yig* (as in note 3) is cited, fol. 34b/3–4: *gnas yig tu lho phyogs na spang dang nags 'dres pa'i mtshams na jo bo spyan ras gzigs kyi lha khang dang so so skyes po'i grong gi sa*; cf. the *gnas yig* cited in note 11, pp. 521.5–522.1: *lho phyogs na spang dang nags 'dres pa'i ri gdong gcig yod / de'i dbus su 'phags pa spyan ras gzigs kyi lha khang dang / skye bo yongs kyi gnas thob*. The second half of the district name Sindhu Palchok doubtless derives from the toponym dPal-tshogs; Sindhu refers in my opinion to a tributary of the Indravati called Sindhu Khola.

[13] This rGod-tshang ras-chen is rGod-tshang ras-pa sNa-tshogs rang-grol, the author of a biography of gTsang-smyon He-ru-ka; see Smith (1969a:6). Two other of his works are accessible to me: *rJe btsun ras chung rdo rje grags pa'i rnam thar rnam mkhyen thar lam gsal ba'i me long*, 293 fols., and *bCom ldan 'das dpal 'khor lo sdom pa'i spyi bshad theg mchog bdud rtsi'i dga' ston ye shes chen po'i sman mchog*, 127 fols.

[14] *Bal yul du bgrod pa'i lam yig* (as in note 3), fol. 35b/2–37b/5. In this same connection, I have been able to identify a citation in a second *gnas yig*: *Yol mo gangs kyi ra ba'i lung byang snying gi ṭika*, p. 552.1–2. The biography of Grub-thob rGyal-mtshan is mentioned in the biography of gTer-dbon Nyi-ma seng-ge (as in note 9), fol. 18a. According to this source, a still earlier figure, one Grub-chen dPal-ldan rgyal-mtshan, had already constructed a temple on the mountain Yang-ri; he was a direct disciple of Rig-'dzin rGod-ldem 'phru-can (1337–1406).

Having returned to rGod-tshang gling, he was invited to the monastery Dzo-'dril dgon; this site had already been visited by such individual representatives of the lineage of the Yol-mo-ba sprul-skus as sNgags-'chang Śākya bzang-po, Nam-mkha' brgya-byin and bsTan-'dzin nor-bu (1598–1644), and the Sixth Zhwa-dmar-pa provides an etymology of the monastery's name: "in order to seek a site for a monastery [in Yol-mo] from his location in Mang-yul Ri-bo dpal-'bar, sNgags-'chang Śākya bzang-po flung a three-cornered *rdo gtor* [in that direction]; since it was a *gtor ma* weapon that revealed the truth, or else soil that had been rolled into a clump of *dzo* (?), thus [the present-day site] is called Dzo-'dril dgon".[15]

Another site that is described in details is the Mi-la-ras-pa cave sTag-phug seng-ge rdzong, which in earlier times had been a "tiger den" (*stag gi tshang*). The subsequent stops were Nags-thang, gTan-bu, dGung-sbrang and rTag-lam 'phrang; the Sixth Zhwa-dmar-pa left Helambu behind him. Having re-crossed the Indravati, he found himself in a "village of the sNye-shang" (*snye shang gi grong khyer*) called Tha-na-ni. A series of other names occurs, such as Shi-ta-bhū, Singhā-ra-bā-sa and Dar-kha-rgyal, and then at Yang-la-koṭ and Thang-skams it was back to the trade route, which took Chos-kyi dbang-phyug on to La-phyi.[16]

3. The Ethnographic Account

In the same way as the just completed summary of the Sixth Zhwa-dmar-pa's two-way trip provides but a cursory reading of the text, so too a summary of the concluding parts of the *Bal yul du bgrod pa'i lam yig* can give only a rough picture of the meticulous descriptions in the original. The diary-like portrayal of the sojourn in the Kathmandu Valley (fols. 18a/4–34a/2) together with the area orientation that follows upon the actual account of the trip contains a true goldmine of historical detail, allowing us to share the view that an educated man of religion from the 17th-century Tibet had of the flourishing culture of the Malla period.

As far as the area orientation is concerned, I shall merely point out several key aspects: the topographical location of the valley (surrounded by a chain of glaciers), bodies of water, flora and fauna, architecture, the beauty of women and their adornments, widely encountered songs, perfumery and woven goods. Remarks follow on the country's tax system, the morals

15 *Bal yul du bgrod pa'i lam yig* (as in note 3), fol. 38a/2–3: *sngags 'chang śākya bzang pos mang yul ri bo dpal dbar nas dgon gnas brtags pa'i phyir / rdo gtor zur gsum 'phangs nas bden pa bdar ba'i gtor zor ram dzo gang du 'dril ba'i sa yin pas dzo 'dril dgon zhes bya ba* ... For the Yol-mo-ba sprul-sku lineage and its activities in the Kathmandu Valley and in Helambu, see Ehrhard (2007:25–49) and chapter nine in the present volume. The meaning of the term *dzo* is unclear to me.

16 The present text was also used as a source for the biography of the Sixth Zhwa-dmar-pa, see, for example, Eighth Si-tu Paṇ-chen Chos-kyi 'byung-gnas and 'Be-lo Tshe-dbang kun-khyab: *sGrub brgyud karma kaṃ tshang brgyud pa rin po che'i rnam par thar pa rab 'byams nor bu zla ba chu shel gyi 'phreng ba*, vol. 2, p. 297.4: *bal yul du phebs pa'i lam yig*. For a résumé of the trip, see ibid, pp. 292.5–297.1.

of the people and the role of the king. Also mentioned are donations of gold equivalent to the donor's weight and the deluded practices of suttee and blood sacrifice.

The Brahmins are singled out among the country's religious specialists (a distinction being made between native Brahmins and those from India), and their privileged access to knowledge is stressed. Those who have declared their faith in the Buddhist teaching are primarily craftsmen, in particular "goldsmiths" *(gser mgar ba)*; despite the many old *vihāra*s and *stūpa*s, however, the current acceptance of Buddhism left much to be desired. The closing description of believers in the Kathmandu Valley runs: "They are of such a disposition as to be easily led" (*bkri sla ba'i rigs can*). Finally, following upon a few personal remarks on the individual phases of the journey, there comes that part of the text that I have termed a compressed ethnography. The Sixth Zhwa-dmar-pa here distinguishes the group of the Mang-kar from the sNye-shang, describes their homeland, and in the end offers a few last words on the characteristics of a territory that had the unjustified reputation of being a breeding ground of diseases.

In the following I shall merely present, in translation, the first part of the description of the Mang-kar and the sNye-shang people.

> "The so-called Mang-kar, which are under the sovereignty of the king of Nepal;[17] [they are] of Indian origin [and,] thanks to their riches in the fields in the hills surrounding Nepal, such as rice and sugarcane, as well as buffaloes and oxen etc., there are very many living [there]. Among them are the so-called *kha-sing*; they drink no beer etc. and are counted among the Brahmins.
>
> In short, these Mang-kar generally possess a certain amount of dexterity, such as the art of courage in battle etc. Since their sense of devotion is somewhat developed, most of them, when seeing a *Bla ma*, circumambulate him three times and bow down before him, and in some cases perform the gesture of giving rice and sugar, milk and butter, fruits and flowers etc.
>
> If there is some special need, such as individuals or relatives among them displaying bodily ailments, lacking riches or offspring, or livestock has fallen ill,

---

17 In Tibetan texts of the 17th century one finds, alongside *mang-kar* and *mang-gar*, the spelling *ma-gar*, see bsTan-'dzin nor-bu: *Rang gi rtogs pa brjod pa rdo rje sgra ma'i brgyud mangs*, vol. 1, p. 117.1. The journey of this disciple of the Sixth Zhwa-dmar-pa occurred in the years between 1614 and 1617, taking the young incarnation to the court of the Malla king Śivasiṃha (who ruled in Kathmandu from 1578 to 1619 and in Patan from 1598 to 1619). He followed the same route as his teacher and, like him too, visited Helambu; see ibid, *la stod / gnya' nang / rong shar gyi ljongs brgyud*. It is interesting that he mentions seeing on his return to Tibet from Kathmandu via sKyid-grong the "rTa-mangs of the eastern and western gorges" (*rong shar nub kyi rta mangs*), ibid, p. 121.6, about whom there is nothing in the travelogue of the Sixth Zhwa-dmar-pa.

Concerning the *Magar du sud*, who in the 12th century served the kings of the Kathmandu Valley as mercenaries, see de Sales (1991:26).

or damage has been done to the fields, [then they ask] that this [misfortune] be removed. And even of there is no special need, they say: "Since you are an excellent *Bla ma*, give your blessing for this." And the act of uttering the auspicious words, those which are appropriate, brings them joy and makes them content. They obviously do not harbour the least hope of receiving something in return etc.

The so-called sNye-shang, who derive from Tibetan stock, [also live] in the mountains of Nepal:[18] They have riches in the form of wheat, millet, oxen, poultry, pigs etc. along with numerous forms of conduct that have been kept alive by past dealings. They also understand the Tibetan language.

It is [generally] feelings of joy that they have towards Tibetans, and are well disposed towards them; their faithful truth in Tibetan *Bla ma*s is truly great, they call them *Me-me Rin-po-che*. Almost like a downpour of rain is how they strew about fragments of flowers and fruits; frequently they bow down, touch [a *Bla ma*'s] feet and offer to him whatever is within reach. Day and night they perform circumambulations, prostrations and prayers without cease. They utter extraordinary prayers for well-being in this and, most important, for well-being in the next life; they [likewise] make confession [of sins] in a proper manner.

In short, it almost appears as if they do not know the proper limits of placing bodies and riches at the service of the teaching. Now in these days they have [also] become habituated to positive acts leading to good [ends], such as the sparing of life [of captured animals], the renouncing of hunting etc.

[Such persons] as [preach] the *Maṇi* [*Mantra*] etc. [i.e.] respectable persons who have an attitude of [wanting to] help others, [in that they harbour] the thought, "Whatever bond with the holy is entered into, such as [the Mantra of the] Six Syllables etc., may it be of benefits for others"—when such persons go there [and are also] of a good spiritual disposition, then that is obviously very fine.

---

18 In the biography of Byang-chub brtson-'grus (1817–1856), an interesting figure of the 19th century who counted Khrong-sa dpon-slob 'Jigs-med rnam-rgyal (1825–1881), the father of the first king of Bhutan, among his disciples, I found the following etymology: "It is said that the name sNye-shang came about because it is a settlement that in earlier times was taken possession of by people of sNye-mo and Shangs in gTsang. Above it [is located] what has become famous under the name 'glacier-fringed Yol-mo [in] Nepal'"; see *rDo rje 'dzin pa chen po 'phrin las mnga' khyab mchog gi rdo rje'am byang chub brtson 'grus kyi rtogs pa brjod pa ngo mtshar nor bu'i snying po*, fol. 42a/6: *de yang sngar gyi dus gtsang snye mo dang shangs pa rnams kyis bzung pa'i grong yin pas snye shangs zhes ming du chags pa yin gsungs / de'i phu bal yul yol mo gangs kyi ra ba zhes yongs su grags pa.*

That Helambu lies in the upper part of the territories settled by the sNye-shang is confirmed in *Bal yul du bgrod pa'i lam yig* (as in note 3), fol. 48a/1: *lhag par yol mo gangs ra sogs / snye shang gi gnas kyi phu sa gad mtho ba dag tu ni*. Cf. the episode that occurred between Mi-la-ras-pa and the king of Bhaktapur in "a place of the sNye-shang" (*snye shang gnas shig*) north-east of Bhaktapur, ibid, fols. 28a/1–4 & 31a/4–b/3.

> [Such persons,] though, as fail to have [this] attitude of perfecting themselves and being of benefit to others, and who are only after riches—these deceivers will [merely] turn believers' heads. The danger that they [only] pile up causes leading to their own bad rebirth is obviously extremely great."

Bal yul du bgrod pa'i lam yig, fols. 45b/4–47a/2
bal po'i rgyal po rnams kyi mnga' 'og tu mang kar zhes bya ba'i / rgya gar gyi skye bo'i rigs rgyud (= brgyud) bal yul gyi 'khor yug gi ri sul gyi ljongs rnams su 'bras dang bur shing dang / ma he dang ba lang la sogs pa'i longs spyod la brten nas gnas (46a) pa'i skye bo rab tu mang po yod la / de dag gi nag tshan kha sing yang zer ba / chang sogs mi 'thung zhing bram ze'i phyogs su bslan pa zhig kyang yod de / mdor na mang kar gyi skye bo de rnams ni / phal cher g.yul du dpa' ba sgyu rtsal sogs cung zad byang ba yin la / dad pa'i 'du shes kyang cung che bas phal cher gyi (= gyis) bla ma mthong na / bskor ba gsum dang phyag byas / 'bras dang bur shing dang / 'o ma dang / mar dang / shing tog dang / me tog sogs sbyin pa'i rnam pa cung zad byed / rang rang dang nye du'i lus la nad yod pa'am nor dang bu la sogs pas dbul ba'am / phyugs la nad dang zhing la gnod pa byung ba sogs / dmigs bsal yod na de dag gi zhi ba dang / dmigs bsal med kyang khyed cag bla ma bzang por 'dug pas de la shis brjod gyis zer zhing / bde legs kyi tshig ji ltar 'os pa tsam brjod kyang dga' zhing mgu bar byed / sbyin pa'i lan sogs la re ba cung zad kyang mi byed par 'dug go / bal yul (46b) gyi ri brag rnams su bod kyi mi rigs las chad pa'i snye shang zhes bya ba'i skye bo / gro dang / khre dang / ba lang dang / bya phag la sogs pa'i nor dang / sngon kyi las kyis 'tsho ba chos shin tu mang ba yod pa rnams ni bod skad kyang shes / bod pa'i mi rigs la dga' tshor sred pa byed / bod kyi bla ma la ni shin tu yang dad mos che ste me me rin po cher zer zhing / me tog dang 'bras sil ma char bab pa tsam gtor / phyag mang du 'tshal / zhabs la gtugs (= gtug) cing dngos po ci yod 'bul / nyin mtshan khor yug du bskor phyag smon lam byed / tshe 'di dang lhag par phyi ma'i don du smon lam khyad par can 'debs / bshags pa tshul bzhin byed / mdor na lus longs spyod chos phyogs su bskol ba (= bkol ba) la chog mi shes pa tsam snang ste / da re kyang tshe thar dang rngon spong ba sogs dge ba la 'god pa'i legs byas de dag gi nang du ches shin tu mang ba byung / yig drug la sogs pa'i dge ba'i 'brel pa gang rung gzhan la phan thogs na snyam pa'i phan sems can gyi btsun pa ma ṇi ba sogs (47a) kyis rigs yin kyang der phyin na legs par snang ngo / 'on kyang rang nyid la yon tan dang gzhan la phan sems med cing nor don du gnyer ba'i zog po dag gis dad can de dag mgo bskor te / rang nyid ngan song sgrub pa'i rgyu bsogs (= bsog) pa'i nyen yang shin tu che ba zhig kyang snang ngo //

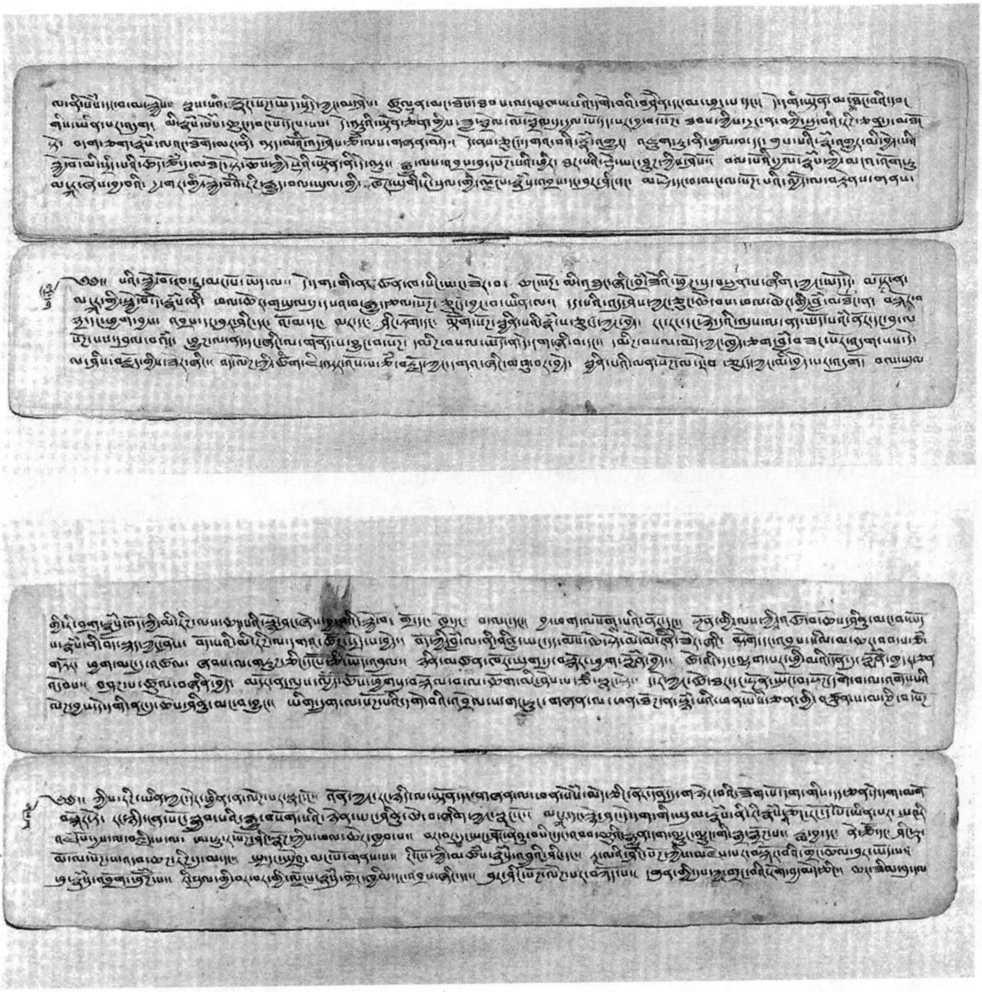

Facsimile of the Tibetan Manuscript, fols. 45b4–47a/2

"The Story of how Bla-ma Karma Chos-bzang came to Yol-mo": A Family Document from Nepal

It was the *Thu'u bkwan grub mtha'*, the masterpiece of Blo-bzang Chos-kyi nyi-ma (1737–1802) from dGon-lung monastery in Amdo, which provided me with a first introduction into the philosophical doctrines of the bKa'-brgyud-pa school of Tibetan Buddhism. This happened during the classes of dGe-bshes dGe-'dun blo-gros (1924–1979) at Hamburg University and I still remember the charged atmosphere when "Rinpoche" laid out his intricate explanations before the small band of dedicated students. Shortly after the untimely death of this remarkable teacher, I met for the first time Musashi Tachikawa, a Humboldt Research Fellow at the institute and – like the rest of us – attracted to the subtleties of Madhyamaka philosophy and everything its manifold Tibetan traditions had to offer.

After I moved to Nepal in 1988 to work on the Nepal-German Manuscript Preservation Project (NGMPP) the contact was renewed, and Musashi Tachikawa joined more or less regularly the lunch table at the Nepal Research Centre (NRC), always enthusiastic about his latest research activities. These included iconographical studies of Dharmadhātu and Vajradhātu maṇḍalas, the documentation of the Mother goddesses in the Kathmandu Valley, and the establishment of the Buddhist section at the National Museum of Nepal in Chauni. We also met at the National Archives of Nepal in Ramshah Path, where he was busy with a project to reprint important manuscripts from Asian countries. During one of these visits he brought along his Japanese translation of the chapter on the bKa'-brgyud-pa school in the *Thu'u bkwan grub mtha'*, and I was happy to see that my notes from the Hamburg classes had been of use for a fuller understanding of the text.[1]

As a contribution to the felicitation volume of Musashi Tachikawa I would like to present a Tibetan-language document which throws some light on the spread of the bKa'-brgyud-pa school in an area of Nepal that once served the great yogin Mi-la-ras-pa as a place for his spiritual retreats. It is a token of gratitude for common interests shared, and accompanied by heart-felt wishes for many more years of fruitful work.

---

1 See Tachikawa (1987). In addition to the annotated translation of the chapter on the bKa'-brgyud-pa school, the publication includes a facsimile of the relevant section from the Zhol edition of the works of Blo-bzang Chos-kyi nyi-ma, different charts of transmission lineages of the Shangs-pa and Mar-pa traditions, and a hand list of the main bKa'-brgyud-pa works published in India. For the joint research between Tibetan and Japanese scholars conducted at The Toyo Bunko, which resulted in the publication of annotated Japanese translations of several chapters of the *Thu'u bkwan grub mtha'*, see Fukuda (1999:11).

1. THE DOCUMENT

During an exploration tour of the NGMPP in the spring of 1989 to Yol-mo, a Bla-ma from Kshaden offered his help and guided the team to his family monastery in the southern part of the region. There he produced the collection of his religious books, and also a document which he held in great esteem, relating as it did the story of how his family line had settled in Yol-mo. The name of the Bla-ma was Karma Ras-chung, and this name still kept alive the memory of the fact that the first of his line had arrived from the monastery of Ras-chung phug in Central Tibet to the Himalayan borderlands.[2]

The document was filmed by the NGMPP under reel no. E 2332/4 (= running-no. E 43183), its size being 44.5x59 cm; it is written in *dbu can* and has twenty-seven lines. Corrections to the text are either written over crossed-out passages or marked by boxes (in two cases). The composite structure of the document cannot be immediately recognized, but upon closer inspection, it is clearly seen to fall into two parts. The first part (= lines 1–17) relates the story of how Bla-ma Karma Chos-bzang came to Yol-mo and provides a genealogy of his descendants, especially the branch of his son dKar-rgyud [bstan-pa'i rgyal-mtshan], who was himself the progenitor of seven sons, all of whom eventually moved to different areas in or around Yol-mo and settled there. The genealogy continues down to the fourth generation after dKar-rgyud [bstan-pa'i rgyal-mtshan] but refers to only those members of the family line of Karma Chos-bzang who stayed behind in the monastery of rGod-tshang gling. This was the monastery in Yol-mo where Bla-ma Karma Chos-bzang had settled after his final journey from Ras-chung phug.

The second part (= lines 17–27) gives a short description of the renovation of rGod-tshang gling executed by Bla-ma Karma Chos-bzang in a "bird year" (*bya lo*). On the occasion of the consecration ceremony for this renovation the local donors supporting the Bla-ma drew up a written contract which entitled Karma Chos-bzang to own the land around the monastery. The original version of this part of the document must have contained the thumb prints of the Bla-ma and the different donors as a sign of their approval of the agreement. That we have a later copy before us can also be seen from the fact that the name of a copyist is given. As he can be identified as one of the sons of dKar-rgyud [bstan-pa'i

2 The Bla-ma from Kshaden also acted as an informant for a Tibetan-Newari lexicon which may have originated in the Yol-mo area; see Cüppers (1992:416). The published version of this lexicon contains a photograph of Karma Ras-chung in front of his family monastery; see Cüppers, Tamot, Pierce (1996:238). For information on Ras-chung phug, located on a spur of the ridge separating the Yar-klungs and the 'Phyongs-rgyas valleys, see Ferrari (1958:51 & 127, note 265). This was the place where gTsang-smyon Heruka (1452–1507), the well-known promoter of the hagiographical traditions of Mi-la-ras-pa (1028–1111) and his teacher Mar-pa (1012–1097), passed away; gTsang-smyon Heruka was regarded as an incarnation of Mi-la-ras-pa's disciple Ras-chung-pa rDo-rje grags-pa (1083–1161). For a photograph of the monastery of Ras-chung phug (taken by H. Richardson), see chapter fourteen of the present volume (plate 1).

rgyal-mtshan], the original copy of the written contract – set down by Karma Chos-bzang himself – was obviously still available during the time of the Bla-ma's grandsons.

Those members of the family line who resided in the monastery of rGod-tshang gling eventually put together the two parts of the document, namely the arrival story-cum-genealogy and the land transfer, at the time of a descendant called dGra-'dul seng-ge. In the following I shall first provide some historical details concerning rGod-tshang gling in order to arrive at the corresponding western date of the original land grant. On the basis of the transmission history of the bKa'-brgyud-pa teachings associated with the monastery, I want then, secondly, to present a time frame within which the two parts of the document where joined by the descendants of Bla-ma Karma Chos-bzang. It seems that the need to do so arose around the time when the Śāha dynasty was making its presence felt in the region of Yol-mo.

2. THE MONASTERY OF RGOD-TSHANG GLING

The importance of the monastery called "Island of the Vulture's Nest" has already been noted by earlier research, a total of eighteen temples in Yol-mo having been traced back to rGod-tshang gling. It has also been noted that of the seven sons of dKar-rgyud [bstan-pa'i rgyal-mtshan] those who did not remain in the monastery were responsible for the founding of these temples; the family line of Bla-ma Karma Chos-bzang thus became the major "lama lineage" of the region. The documentary source of these details is a Tibetan religious history of Yol-mo composed by one Karma 'Phrin-las dbang-po, who is none other than the eldest of the seven sons and the one who took over rGod-tshang gling from his father dKar-rgyud [bstan-pa'i rgyal-mtshan].[3]

---

[3] For the evidence that rGod-tshang gling is the "oldest Sermo Lama temple" in Yol-mo, see Clarke (1980:19–21). The conditions in Yol-mo under which "*dgon pa* (literally 'solitary place', also retreat/ monastery/religious centre) ... became *lha khang* (temple)" has been described Clarke (1983:24). A facsimile of the documentary source for the history of rGod-tshang gling was published in Clarke (1980:26–27). Unfortunately Karma Chos-bzang's name was completely overlooked in the evaluation of this literary source, as was dKar-rgyud bstan-pa'i rgyal-mtshan's (his full name appears in this document). Karma Blo-bzang is recorded instead as the father of the seven sons. This misidentification resulted from a superficial reading of the document, which is structured around different "prophecies" (*lung bstan*) associated with the site; see Helambu Document 2, fol. 1a/3–5 (*pho brang chen po rgod tshang gling phyogs de ru / rgyal bas zhabs lcags (= bcags) lo rgyus zur tsam rjod (= brjod) / thub pas lung stan (= bstan) gu ru'i zhabs kyi (= kyis) lcags (= bcags) / ... / mar par (= mar pas) lung stan (= bstan) mi las (= mi la'i) zhabs kyi (= kyis) lcags (= bcags) / ... / tsang (= gtsang) smyon lung bstan rgod tshangs (= tshang) ra can (= ras chen) zhabs [kyis] lcags (= bcags) / ... / grub mchog lung bstan karma chos bzang zhabs kyi (= kyis) lcags (= bcags) / ... / mkhas grub chen po karma blo bzang gis / lung bstan ... / bka' (= dkar) rgyud stan pa'i (= bstan pa'i) rgyal mtshan zhabs kyi (= kyis) lcags (= bcags)*). The last statement suggests that Karma Blo-bzang, the "great scholar and siddha", was involved in installing dKar-rgyud bstan-pa'i rgyal-mtshan in rGod-tshang gling. For the person of [rNgog-ston] Karma Blo-bzang, see note 9.

Once we leave the written sources of the local historiography and try to place the oldest bKa'-brgyud-pa monastery in Yol-mo in a wider context, it soon becomes clear that rGod-tshang gling derives its name from its founder, rGod-tshang ras-chen or rGod-tshang ras-pa sNa-tshogs rang-grol (1482–1559), one of the two more famous disciples of gTsang-smyon Heruka. The other disciple is lHa-btsun Rin-chen rnam-rgyal (1473–1557). Both left biographies of their master, and in composing such hagiographical literature thus followed in his footsteps. Although there exists a biographical tradition of the latter disciple, we are still not very well informed about the life of rGod-tshang ras-pa: the only commonly agreed point is that he kept up Ras-chung phug after the death of gTsang-smyon Heruka and propagated there the spiritual teachings associated with Ras-chung-pa rDo-rje grags-pa (he is known to have composed a biography of Ras-chung-pa as well and to have made available printed versions of the so-called *Ras chung snyan brgyud*).

But there has survived a biography of a disciple of both rGod-tshang ras-pa and lHa-btsun Rin-chen rnam-rgyal which gives us a view of rGod-tshang gling at a time when the founder of the site was still alive. The name of the disciple is Byams-pa phun-tshogs (1503–1581), a native of the sKyid-grong area in Mang-yul Gung-thang. During a journey from this area to the Nepal Valley he was present at the ceremony concluding the building of the first temple at the site founded by his teacher:

> Myself, at the age of fifty-four years, in the autumn of the dragon-year (= 1556), when I went via Yol-mo for a circumambulation of Nepal, [the land of] moisture, and came to [the valley of] Glang-'phrang, my host mTsho-skyes and others requested empowerments from me, and there was established a complete, pure union [between teacher and disciples], accompanied by marvellous services.
>
> When I arrived then at rGod-tshang gling in Yol-mo, I thought: "This old Bla-ma of mine – after he came here he acted extensively for the benefit of others!", and in that very moment of recalling the Bla-ma many tears gushed forth. When there arose ever more memories of Chos-rje rGod-tshang-pa, in a state where my mind was overwhelmed by sorrow, [I saw] in a dream the master perform prodigiously, in a very majestic manner, adorned by the eight paraphernalia of [an ascetic living in] burial grounds. Afterwards he intoned spiritual songs in great number, and there came forth the following words:
>
> "When the mind is without movement and artifice – this is the Prātimokṣa [vow].
> When the mind of benefiting [others] is uninterrupted – [this] is the Bodhisattva [vow].
> When the grasping of [individual] characteristics is purified – [this] is the Mantra[yāna vow].
> Everything else is senseless behaviour: *Oṃ Āḥ Hūṃ*!"

> At that time I set up the guidance [for my spiritual practice] of the [*Phyag chen*] *yi ge bzhi pa* and the [*Na ro*] *chos drug* at rGod-tshang gling. For about one and a half months I made [the results] to come forth. On one occasion, in the *bla brang* of rGod-tshang gling, I remembered again and again the course of the life of the lord [rGod-tshang ras-pa], and there was [even] stronger belief in [his] profound introduction [to the nature of the mind].
>
> Once during that period Bla-ma Kun-dga'-ba is said to have produced [a manuscript copy of] the extensive [version of the *Prajñāpāramitā*] in 100.000 verses and erected a temple, [but] he passed away without having completed these [things]. After his son and the donors tied up the ends of this [affair], I myself was called for the consecration, and they performed [acts of] congratulation and so forth. At that time *gaṇacakra*s, offering substances and so forth, [all] marvellous [and] in accordance with the local customs, were forthcoming from the inhabitants of Yol-mo.[4]

At the time of the visit of Byams-pa phun-tshogs in the middle of the 16th century rGod-tshang gling had just been transformed from a simple "residence" (*bla brang*) of rGod-tshang ras-pa to a temple supervised by a caretaker and his family, and supported financially by local donors. When we look at the report of a later visitor to the site, we can see that the name of its founder was still embedded in people's memories, even though rGod-tshang gling itself was now referred to in more purely monastic terms. The following passage is

---

4 See Byams-pa phun-tshogs: *mKhas grub chen po byams pa phun tshogs kyi rnam thar*, fol. 83a/3–b/2 (*nged kyis kyang rang lo lnga bcud* (= *bcu*) *bzhi pa'i 'brug lo'i ston ser bal yul skor ba la yol mo rgyud* (= *brgyud*) *te 'gro ba'i* (= *'gro bas*) *glang'brang du sleb tshe gnas po mtsho skyes sogs kyi* (= *kyis*) *dbang zhus shing bsnyen bskur phun sum tshogs pa dang bcas rnams dkar gyi 'grel pa* (= *'brel pa*) *bzhag nas / yol mo'i rgod tshang gling du sleb dus / nged kyi bla ma sgres po* (= *bgres po*) *des 'dir phebs nas gzhan don rgya cher mdzad yod bsam bla ma dran pa'i mod la mchin mang po shor // rig pa skyo chad de ba'i ngang la chos rje rgod tshang pa yang yang dran pa byung bas / rmi lam du rje nyid dur khrod kyis* (= *kyi*) *chas brgyad kyi* (= *kyis*) *brgyan pa'i rnam pa can shin tu gzi brjid che bar mdzad nas / mgur mang po cig gsung ba'i rjes la / sems la g.yo sgyu med na so thar yin / phan sems rgyun chad med na byang sems yin / mtshan ma'i 'dzin pa dag na sngags sdom yin / gzhan rnams bcal* (= *chal*) *le bcol* (= *chol*) *le oṃ āh hūṃ zhes gsung byung ngo / des dus rgod tshang gling du yi ge bzhi pa dang chos drug gi 'khrid btsugs / zla ba phyed gnyis tsam la thon par byas / de'i skabs cig rgod tshang gling gi bla brang du rje'i rnam thar yang yang dran zhing / zab mo'i ngo sprod la yid shar du ches so // de'i tshe skabs cig du* (= *tu*) *bla* [83b] *ma kun dga' bas / 'bum rgyas pa dang lha khang bzhengs 'dug pas de rnams ma tshar ba la khang* (= *khong*) *rang grongs / de'i 'jug* (= *mjug*) *rnams sras po dang yon bdag rnams kyis bsdus nas rab gnas la nged bos nas bkra shis mnga' gsol sogs rgya cher byas / de'i tshe yol mo ba rnams kyis tshogs 'khor dang 'bul cha sogs yul lugs dang mthun pa phun sum tshogs pa byung*). For the valley called "Bull's Passage" (*glang 'phrang*), the etymology of this toponym, and its status as a "hidden valley" (*sbas yul*), see Ehrhard (1997b:345f.) and chapter sixteen in the present volume. This valley is located to the north of Yol-mo, and it is worth noting that in the 16th century Tibetan travellers passed through both areas on their way from Mang-yul Gung-thang to the Nepal Valley.

from a travel account by the Sixth Zhwa-dmar-pa Chos-kyi dbang-phyug (1584–1630), who felt an urge to see the different sacred sites of Yol-mo after returning from a journey to the Nepal Valley; this occurred in the final weeks of his life:

> The next day, when I went on continuously in a slow way, I arrived at what is called rGod-tshang gling, [the place where] rGod-tshang ras-chen had resided, the disciple of the noble gTsang-smyon [Heruka], a site where there had originally been established a *saṃgha* community with eight members. As I had been forgetful of the memorial services on the twenty-eighth day of the month before, being too busy with the way, I [now] performed the *maṇḍala* ritual of the five gods of *Śrī Cakrasaṃvara*, restoring the broken [commitment], and stayed for the night [there].[5]

At this point I want to return to the "family document" from Yol-mo and its story of the two journeys of Karma Chos-bzang. The narrative starts with the Bla-ma's initial arrival with a group of seven other monks, who were obviously under his supervision. The local headmen asked him to settle in Yol-mo, but he declined their request for the time being and returned to Ras-chung phug in Central Tibet; there he stayed for three years in the company of his teacher Zhabs-drung Grub-mchog dbang-po (1563–1618). Only after receiving the latter's permission to settle permanently in Yol-mo did he return for a second time and accept the offer of the local donors. When the narrative of Bla-ma Karma Chos-bzang's activities in Yol-mo is taken up again in the second part of the document, it is mentioned that he had renovated the monastery of rGod-tshang gling when performing religious services for the three cities of the Nepal valley. These services for the Malla rulers seem to have been the main reason why the land around rGod-tshang gling was offered to Bla-ma Karma Chos-bzang as "religious endowment" (*birtā*). This kind of land assignment in Nepal was by royal authority, and traditionally limited to Brahmins. As we have seen, the date of the renovation and the written title to the land was a "bird year".

---

5 See Chos-kyi dbang-phyug: *Bal yul bgrod pa'i lam yig nor bu'i spel ma'i 'phreng ba*, fol. 35a/5–b/2 (*de'i phyi nyin dal gyis song ba* [35b] *las / rgod tshang gling zhes bya ba / gtsang smyon pa'i slob ma / rgod tshang ras chen gyis bzhugs shing / dge 'dun gyi sde brgyad grwa zhig thog mar 'dzugs par mdzad par gnas su slebs te / zla ba snga ma'i nyi shu brgyad kyi dus mchod lam gyi brel bas g.yel te chad pa kha gso ba'i dpal 'khor lo sdom pa lha lnga'i dkyil chog rgyas pa shig bgyis shing zhag tu gnas so*). The monastery of rGod-tshang gling served as the base for the Sixth Zhwa-dmar-pa's visits to the sacred sites of Yol-mo associated with Padmasambhava and Mi-la-ras-pa. The place of Padmasambhava is called Yang-dag mchog-gi sgrub-phug and the site where the great yogin stayed during his spiritual practice, sTag-phug seng-ge rdzong; this latter toponym reminded pilgrims of the fact that the place had in earlier times been a "tiger den" (*stag gi tshang*). For an overview of the tour of Chos-kyi dbang-phyug in Yol-mo and the relevant passages of his travelogue, see Ehrhard (1997a:131f.) and chapter seventeen in the present volume.

If we take the "*saṃgha* community with eight members"—the original monastic community at rGod-tshang gling according to the Sixth Zhwa-dmar-pa—to be the group of eight monks who had moved from Ras-chung phug to Yol-mo at the behest of Zhabs-drung Grub-mchog dbang-po, and take into account the return trip of Bla-ma Karma Chos-bzang to Central Tibet, his three-year-stay in Ras-chung phug, and the final journey to rGod-tshang gling, then the renovation of the monastery and the "religious endowment" must have fallen in the period between the death of Zhabs-drung Grub-mchog dbang-po and the visit of Chos-kyi dbang-phyug to Yol-mo. As a corresponding western date for the "bird year" I would thus propose 1621 A.D.

3. THE TRANSMISSION OF THE PHYAG CHEN YI GE BZHI PA AND THE RAS CHUNG SNYAN BRGYUD

When Byams-pa phun-tshogs visited the site of rGod-tshang gling his spiritual practice centred around a combination of a Mahāmudrā teaching called the "Four-lettered One" (*yi ge bzhi pa*) and the "Six Doctrines" (*chos drug*) according to the system of the Indian Mahāsiddha Nāḍapāda also known as Nāropa (956–1040). This combination shows that the disciple of rGod-tshang ras-chen and lHa-btsun Rin-chen rnam-rgyal practiced teachings of the Dwags-po bKa'-brgyud-pa, namely the instructions transmitted through sGam-po-pa bSod-nams rin-chen (1079–1153). If we consult the biographies of gTsang-smyon Heruka written by rGod-tshang ras-chen and lHa-btsun Rin-chen rnam-rgyal, we can see that this particular combination of teachings also formed the central spiritual practice of the "Madman from gTsang" who received them from his own guru, Sha-ra Rab-'byams-pa Sangs-rgyas seng-ge (1427–1470), at the mere age of seventeen years in the region of Dwags-po in south-eastern Tibet.[6]

6 The transmission of the teachings of the Dwags-po bKa'-brgyud-pa from Sha-ra Rab-'byams-pa to his young disciple in the year 1469 took place at Zur-mkhar, the residence of Zur-mkhar-ba mNyam-nyid rdo-rje (1439–1475). For the descriptions of the following period of spiritual practice, see rGod-tshang ras-pa sNa-tshog rang-grol: *gTsang smyon he ru ka phyogs thams cad las rnam par rgyal ba'i rnam thar rdo rje theg pa'i gsal byed nyi ma'i snying po*, p. 22.2–4 (*phyag rgya chen po yi ge bzhi pa'i dmar khrid khyad chos kyi ngo sprod dang bcas pa gsan pas / mnyam bzhag gi stogs* (= *rtogs pa*) *mngar* (= *sngar*) *zhal mjal dus su ngo 'phrod pas las na 'phar rgyu mi 'dug kyang rjes thob la bogs dang brtsal* (= *rtsal*) *bsam gyis mi khyab pa thon / ... / de nas dpal na ro pa'i chos drug gi khrid yig rje mi las zin bris su mdzad pa'i steng nas dmar khrid du skyangs pas* (= *bskyangs pas*) */ zhag bco lnga tsam song ba'i tshe ...*); compare lHa-btsun Rin-chen rnam-rgyal: *Grub thob gtsang smyon pa'i rnam thar dad pa'i spu slong g. yo ba*, p. 11.7 (*da nas 'khrid kyi mgo btsugs nas / lta ba phyag rgya chen po yi ge bzhi pa / thabs lam na ro chos drug la zla ba gsum gyi bar du nyams khrid mdzad do*). A commentary on the Mahāmudrā teaching by lHa-btsun Rin-chen rnam-rgyal is available; see *rGyud kyi dgongs pa gtsor sngon pa phyag rgya chen po yi ge bzhi pa'i 'grel bshad gnyug ma'i gter mdzod*. For the definition of the Dwags-po bKa'-brgyud-pa as those adherents of the school who practice the *Phyag chen* and *Na ro chos drug* teachings passing through sGam-po-pa, see Smith (2001:40).

As there exists a biography of Sha-ra Rab-'byams-pa, we can trace back this transmission to his "main teacher" (*rtsa ba'i bla ma*), one Ngag-dbang grags-pa (1418–1496), who was the twelfth abbot of the sTag-lung monastery to the north of lHa-sa. Of the lineages of the *Phyag chen yi ge bzhi pa* which he conferred upon Sha-ra Rab-'byams-pa, two had passed through sGam-po-pa's disciple Phag-mo gru-pa rDo-rje rgyal-po (1110–1170) (here it should be noted that the twelfth abbot of sTag-lung was actually regarded by his contemporaries as the reincarnation of Phag-mo gru-pa rDo-rje rgyal-po). At their final meeting he particularly requested his disciple to spread the "oral lineage of the *Cakrasaṃvara* [Cycle]" (*bde mchog snyan brgyud*), the chief teaching of which is the so-called "oral lineage of Ras-chung[-pa]" (*ras chung snyan brgyud*), a specific tradition of the six doctrines of Nāropa fostered by Ras-chung-pa rDo-rje grags-pa. This task was later carried out mainly by gTsang-smyon Heruka, who compiled the twelve-volume *sNyan brgyud* collection and composed important textbooks for the further propagation of this specific tradition. The adherents of this tradition were known as the Ras-chung bKa'-brgyud-pa.[7]

A good overview of the transmission of the *Phyag chen yi ge bzhi pa* and the *Ras chung snyan brgyud* is provided by a work of Kaḥ-tog rig-'dzin Tshe-dbang nor-bu (1698–1755), who received these teachings in the region of Nub-ris, a Himalayan region to the south-west of Mang-yul Gung-thang, in the year 1729. According to this text the next person in the lineage after Byams-pa phun-tshogs (referred to by his alternative name gNas Rab-'byams-pa Blo-gros rab-yangs) was Grub-mchog dbang-po, the "incarnation from Ras-chung [phug]" (*ras chung sprul sku*). If one consults the biography of Byams-pa phun-tshogs, one finds indeed references to two visits of Grub-mchog dbang-po to sKyid-grong in order to receive the teachings of the *Phyag chen [yi ge bzhi pa]* and the *[Ras chung] snyan brgyud*. The young novice is identified as the reincarnation of rGod-tshang ras-chen,

7 The biography of the guru of gTsang-smyon Heruka bears the title *mKhas grub sha ra rab 'byams pa sangs rgyas seng ge'i rnam thar mthong ba don ldan ngo mtshar nor bu'i phreng ba thar 'dod yid 'phrog blo gsal mgul brgyan*, written by one Zla-ba rgyal-mtshan. According to the printing colophon, the block print was executed by Byams-pa phun-tshogs at his residence in Mang-yul Gung-thang in the year 1559; see ibid, pp. 500.6–501.4. In the same year, shortly after returning from his journey to Yol-mo and the Nepal Valley, he also printed the biography of Ras-chung-pa composed by his teacher rGod-tshang ras-chen; for the printing colophon, see Bacot (1954:292). The descriptions of the transmission of teachings from the sTag-lung abbot to Sha-ra Rab-'byams-pa can be found ibid, p. 461.2–4 (*khyad par phyag rgya chen po yi ge bzhi pa rgam po pa (= sgam po pa) nas dus gsum pa la brgyud pa dang / phag mo gru pa nas sgyer sgom zhig pa la brgyud pa dang / phag mo gru pa nas rnal 'byor gyi dbang phyug gling ras pa la brgyud pa'i lugs rnams nyams khrid du gsan ...*), and p. 479.4–5 (*bka' brgyud kyi chos bskor thams cad yongs su rdzogs par gnang / khyad par du bde mchog snyan brgyud 'di dar rgyas su spel cig gsung ngo*). For the circumstances surrounding the fact that Sha-ra Rab-'byams-pa and gTsang-smyon Heruka belonged to the Ras-chung bKa'-brgyud-pa, a subsect of the bKa'-brgyud-pa school that has now completely disappeared as a separate entity, see Smith (2001:61).

and his journeys from Ras-chung phug to the south-western border area were undertaken at the express wish of the Fifth Zhwa-dmar-pa dKon-mchog yan-lag (1525–1583).[8]

The next two persons who passed on the teachings after Grub-mchog dbang-po were rNgog-ston Karma Blo-bzang (16th/17th century) and rGyal-dbang seng-ge (born 1628). We are quite well informed about the life of the first figure, who had been a student at Ras-chung phug of both Grub-mchog dbang-po and the Sixth Zhwa-dmar-pa Chos-kyi dbang-phyug. Upon the request of the latter teacher he became the resident priest of Brag-dkar rta-so, the famous Mi-la-ras-pa site in Mang-yul Gung-thang. This position had also been held by Byams-pa phun-tshogs for some time, and this might have contributed to Karma Blo-bzang's status of being the reincarnation of the lineage-holder from the sKyid-grong area. Karma Blo-bzang travelled extensively in the Himalayan valleys of Mustang, Dolpo and Manang, renovating old structures of the bKa'-brgyud-pa school and erecting new buildings. He paid two visits to the region of Yol-mo and the monastery of rGod-tshang gling; during the first visit he renovated the monastery, while regarding the second stay, the name of his main disciple in the region is given as Karma Gu-ru (the eldest son of Bla-ma Karma Chos-bzang). These journeys can be placed in the middle of the 17th century, after the visit of the Sixth Zhwa-dmar-pa and around the time when the family estate of rGod-tshang gling had been handed over by Karma Gu-ru to his brother dKar-rgyud [bstan-pa'i rgyal-mtshan].[9]

---

8 The history of the transmission of the *Phyag chen yi ge bzhi pa* and the *Ras chung snyan brgyud* as it was received by Kaḥ-thog rig-'dzin is contained in Tshe-dbang nor-bu: *lHa rje mnyam med zla 'od gzhon nu'i bka' brygud phyag chen gdams pa ji tsam nod pa'i rtogs brjod legs bshad rin chen 'byung khungs*, pp. 214.1–215.4 & 215.4–216.5. The descriptions of the two meetings between Grub-mchog dbang-po and Byams-pa phun-tshogs can be found in the latter's biography (as in note 4), fol. 91b/3–4 (*de dus rje rin po che rgod tshang ras chen gyis* (= *gyi*) *sprul pa'i sku skyes grub mchog dbang po la / zhwa dmar cod paṇ 'dzin pa lnga pa dkon mchog yan lag gis chos zhu dgos rnams zhu ba la skyid grong gnas su song gsung ba'i lung bstan nas / rgod tshang sprul sku 'dir phebs phyag chen snyan rgyud* (= *brgyud*) *dgongs 'dus sogs kyi chos yongs su rdzogs pa 'bul ba dang bcas thugs dgongs rdzogs par bsgrubs*), and fol. 92a/1–2 (*yang ras chung phug nas sprul sku rin po che dpon slob rnams kyi dogs gcod zhal gdams / ma song ma rnams kyis bka' lung yongs su rdzogs pa dang bsnyen bkur zhabs tog phul tu phyin bas dges bar mdzad nas / slar yang dbus gtsang du phebs song* ...). Grub-mchog dbang-po set down in written form the teachings which he had received from Byams-pa phun-tshogs; see *Bla ma dam pa'i gsung rgyun gyi rim pa mthong dga'i nor bu'i phreng ba 'dod kun 'byung*.

9 A sketch of the life of rNgog-ston Karma Blo-bzang, based on his autobiography, is given in Ehrhard (2001:101–106) and chapter fourteen in the present volume. Brag-dkar bSam-gling, the main monastery of the bKa'-brgyud-pa school in sNye-shang (present-day Manang), was established by Karma Blo-bzang in the year 1664. It is interesting to see that this Bla ma from Ras-chung phug was not only propagating the teachings of the *Ras chung snyan brgyud*, but also "treasure works" (*gter ma*) of the rNying-ma-pa master Rig-'dzin 'Ja'-tshon snying-po (1585–1656). His disciple Karma Gu-ru was equally eager to receive transmissions of rNying-ma-pa teachings and travelled for that purpose to Mang-yul Gung-thang; there he obtained from the rNying-ma-pa master O-rgyan dpal-bzang (1617–1677) treasure works of Rig-'dzin bDud-'dul rdo-rje (1615–1672). See *Rigs brgya dbang po 'dren mchog slob dpon dpal bzang po'i*

Among the disciples of rNgog-ston Karma Blo-bzang, rGyal-dbang seng-ge is especially noted for having received the full transmission of the *Ras chung snyan brgyud*. Although a full-scale biography of him is not available, we know at least that he came from the region of Nub-ris; his place of origin there was called Zwa-phug Brag-dmar chos-gling, which he had inherited from his father, Bya-btang 'Od-zer rgya-mtsho (1574–1661), a practitioner of bKa'-brgyud-pa teachings of local fame.[10] The disciple of rGyal-dbang seng-ge who kept the site of Zwa-phug after the death of his teacher transmitted the *Phyag chen yi ge bzhi pa* and the *Ras chung snyan rgyud* teachings to Kaḥ-thog rig-'dzin in 1729; it seems that the transmission had become already quite rare by that time.

As a final comment on the "family document" from Yol-mo it should now be pointed out that a reincarnation of rGyal-dbang seng-ge appeared and that he was born in rGod-tshang gling as the son of Karma 'Phrin-las dbang-po, the keeper of the family estate after dKar-rgyud [bstan-pa'i rgyal-mtshan]. While this person is referred to in the document as "grandfather" or "forefather" Gar-dbang don-grub, in other literary sources he is called sPrul-sku Gar-dbang don-grub, the "reembodiment" (*sku'i skye ba*) of rGyal-dbang seng-ge from Zwa-phug. I may also mention in this regard the autobiographies of three teachers from the region of Kutang, to the south of Nub-ris, who all travelled to Yol-mo to receive teachings from sPrul-sku Gar-dbang don-grub at the monastery of rGod-tshang gling. The names of these teachers are Padma don-grub (1668–1744), Padma dBang-'dus (born 1697) and Padma lhun-grub (born 1708). The first of these visits occurred in the 1730s, a period marked by the founding of further rNying-ma-pa religious institutions in Yol-mo. To the adherents of this school of Tibetan Buddhism the area is known as "Yol-mo, [which is] enclosed by glaciers" (*yol mo gangs r[w]a*).[11]

---

rnam par thar pa dad pa'i spu long g.yo byed mthong bas yid 'phrog ngo mtshar 'phreng ba'i gtam rmad du byung ba, fol. 291a/2–4 (*de nas slar rang gi sgrub* [*gnas*] *u rgyan chos gling bzhugs dus su yol mo gangs ra nas bla ma karma gu ru dpon slob 'ga' 'byung ba la sprul sku snying thig dbang lung yongs su rdzogs su phul*). O-rgyan dpal-bzang had met rNgog-ston Karma Blo-bzang on several occasions and had founded the monastery of sKu-tshab gter-lnga in southern Mustang in the year 1668; see Ehrhard (1993c) and chapter thirteen in the present volume.

10 A biography of Bya-btang 'Od-zer has survived, which gives the year 1637 as the date of his moving to the site Zwa-phug Brag-dmar chos-gling; see rGyal-dbang seng-ge: *Bya btang 'od zer rgya mtsho'i rnam thar nges don rgya mtsho'i snying po*, fols. 40b/4ff. This text was composed by his son in the year 1665. His full name is given in the colophon as ['Chi-med] rGyal-dbang [phun-tshogs bstan-'dzin] seng-ge [bzang-po]; see ibid, fol. 59a/4. The autobiography of the rNying-ma-pa master O-rgyan dpal-bzang mentions an encounter with rGyal-dbang seng-ge; see the text (as in note 9), fol. 314a/2–3 (*de mtshams su zwa phug tu bla ma rgyal seng ge'i spyan 'dren zhus chos 'brel tsam phul bas gtang rag gis kyang mnyes par mdzad do*). For the transmission of the treasure cycles of Rig-'dzin 'Ja'-tshon snying-po from rGyal-dbang seng-ge to O-rgyan bstan-'dzin (1657–1737), a disciple of O-rgyan dpal-bzang, see Ehrhard (1998:4) and chapter twenty in the present volume.

11 The three travel accounts are available in *Autobiographies of Three Spiritual Masters of Kutang* (1979). For the visit of Padma don-grub, see ibid, p. 105.1–2 (*gnas yol mo gang* (= *gangs*) *ra la sprul sku*

One cousin of Me-me Gar-dbang don-grub was Karma rNam-mkhyen, and it was during the time of the latter's grandson that the written documents of the family monastery were put together in the form in which they are available to us now. The time frame for this final codification can safely be stated to be at the turn from the 18th to the 19th century. This was the period when old *birtā* land grants were being re-examined—and new ones given—by the rulers of the Śāha dynasty, and one such case involved a member of the "lama lineage" which traced back its history to the arrival of Bla-ma Karma Chos-bzang in Yol-mo.[12] The investigation into the original land transfer (or the issue of a new title) must have triggered the need to authenticate the circumstances of the bestowal of the original "religious endowment" to the ancestor, and so to set down the genealogy of his successors.

---

gar dbang don grub la rta 'phags (= phag) yid bzhin nor bu'i lung thob / 'ja' mtshon (= tshon) snying po gter ma yin / dag po (= dwags po) mthar (= thar) rgya (= rgyan) gi lung thob). The autobiography of Padma dBang-'dus devotes a whole chapter to the extended stay in Yol-mo and different meetings with sPrul-sku Gar-dbang don-grub. This master from Kutang used rGod-tshang gling as the starting and end point for a journey to the Nepal Valley; see ibid, pp. 313.1–345.2 (chapter title: *yol mo gangs ral (= ra) bal po'i dur khrod dang la phyi chu bar gsum gyis (= gyi) skor ro*). For the visit of Padma lhun-grub, see ibid, pp. 729.5–730.1 (*sprul sku karma gar dbang don grub kyi drung du / bde mchog mkha' gro (= 'gro) snyan brgyud kyi lung / sngo ba 'gyur gcig ma'i lung / bka' 'gyur ro mchog (= cog) kyi (= gi) lung / bsdom (= sdom) gsum kyi (= gyi) lung dang / dkon mchog spyi 'dus kyi tshe sgrub lcags kyi ri bo che'i dbang thog (= thob)*). A temple on the side of the mountain g.Yang-ri-ma and the monastery Padma'i-chos-gling were founded in Yol-mo by the rNying-ma-pa teacher gTer-dbon Nyi-ma seng-ge (1687–1738); for these activities in the years 1723 and 1727, see Ehrhard (2007) and chapter nine in the present volume.

12 A land grant for Lhakhang Gyang, a village temple in one of the most beautiful parts of the whole region, was given by Gīrvāṇa Yuddha Vikrama Śāha (1789–1816) to one of the descendants of Bla-ma Karma Chos-bzang. This land grant was later officialized by means of a copperplate in the year 1823. For the details of this copperplate, see Clarke (1980:20f. & 33); a description of this temple and its natural surroundings can be found in Jest (1981:81–83). Raṇa Bahādura Śāha (1777–1805), the father of Gīrvāṇa Yuddha Vikrama Śāha, had banished his first wife Rājarājeśvarī also called Bijyālakṣmī, to Yol-mo in 1804. Her sad journey home after the murder of her husband became the topic of a Newari poem, one of the most popular in the Nepal Valley; see Lienhard (1992b:98f.). It is possible that the land grant to Lhakhang Gyang was connected with the exile of Gīrvāṇa Yuddha Vikrama Śāha's stepmother to Yol-mo. As early as 1787 Raṇa Bahādura Śāha had already begun to examine *birtā* land grants in order to ascertain who held land, how much was held, and who had granted it. For the troublesome period of the rule of Raṇa Bahādura Śāha, which also included the Nepal-Tibet war from 1788 to 1792, see, for example, Stiller (1993:33–45).

[TRANSLATION]

[I]

I prostrate before and take refuge in the Three Jewels (i.e. Buddha, Dharma, Saṃgha), the infallible objects of refuge!

Now, first, the story of how Bla-ma Karma Chos-bzang came to [the region of] Yol-mo. The Bla-ma to whom the donors of Yol-mo gangs-rwa adhered is from Ras-chung phug [in] upper [Tibet]. Although it is a place far away, yet, for the benefit of both the dead and the living, the Bla-ma was invited to come [from there to Yol-mo]. And so, eight masters and disciples, including Bla-ma Karma Chos-bzang, the chant-leader Karma Thub-bstan and the head of discipline Karma dGe-legs, arrived in Yol-mo and stayed [there].

What would be of benefit for the donors having been addressed, the donors, headed by the elders of the land of Yol-mo, put a question in the following way: "Precious Bla-ma, since the teacher to whom the donors of the sacred site Yol-mo adhere, has come [to live] in a far-away place, please consider to remaining [here] continuously! And take a wife as well!"

Then [Karma Chos-bzang] spoke: "I am a pure monk, but if you, my donors, say such a thing, I will ask my main teacher successively about all the causes of the happiness of the sponsors, and then I will only return if the Bla-ma gives his consent."

And after installing the chant-leader Karma Thub-bstan in Yol-mo as the representative of the Bla-ma, he went to Ras-chung phug [in] upper [Tibet]. When he had been there three years, Zhabs-drung Grub-mchog dbang-po said [to him]: "Karma Chos-bzang, as your family line and [your work of] benefiting beings is in Yol-mo, I allow you to take a wife!"

After [the Bla-ma] gave this prophecy, [Karma Chos-bzang] returned to Yol-mo and married the nun I-pi Yi-dam and also [I-pi] Khrib-tse, the daughter of the elder brother of I-pi Yi-dam. The bone [i.e. paternal line] of the two "grandmothers" [was] Zhang-mo. To I-pi Yi-dam were born the sons Me-me Karma Gu-ru and Me-me dBang-chen; to I-pi Khrib-tse were born Me-me dKar-rgyud and Me-me Ngag-dbang. Then Karma Gu-ru spoke: "I am the eldest among us four! I am of a spiritual lineage where worldly deeds have been abandoned!" And [adding]: "Among you [younger] three kinsmen, you, brother dKar-rgyud, are the eldest", he bestowed upon him the family estate and the ownership of the monastery [rGod-tshang gling].

Then Me-me dKar-rgyud took [as wives] the nun Zhing-skyong-ma and I-pi Chos-legs, and seven sons were born [to him]. The eldest son, Me-me 'Phrin-las dbang-po, requested that a payment be given [to him in the form of] the ownership of the monastery of rGod-tshang gling. Me-me Don-grub rgyal-po stayed in sKyel-sdong, Me-me Thar-pa rgyal-po stayed in Bod-thang, Me-me Kun-dga' rgyal-po stayed in Gu-ru phug, Me-me mThong-ba rgyal-po stayed in Shab-ru, Me-me Chos rgyal-mtshan stayed in Shab-ru [as well], [and] Me-me Blo-gros dpal-bzang remained in rGod-tshang gling.

The son of Me-me 'Phrin-las dbang-po was Me-me Gar-dbang don-grub, the son of Blo-gros dpal-bzang [was] Karma rNam-mkhyen, [the latter's] son [was] 'Gyur-med rdo-rje, [and his] son [was] dGra-'dul seng-ge.

[II]
I prostrate before the Bla-ma, the Yi-dam and the beautiful mKha' 'gro [ma], who are accompanied by the entourage of an ocean of oath-bound guardians of the pronouncement [of the Buddha], [namely] the male and female Dharma protectors!

Please pay attention! I, Bla-ma Karma Chos-bzang, I completed the renovation of the monastery of rGod-tshang gling, at the time when I was safeguarding from hail the three islands of Yam-bu (= Kathmandu), Ko-khom (= Bhaktapur) [and] Ye-rang (= Patan), on the fifteenth day of the tenth Hor month of the bird-year; afterwards, for the purpose of offering congratulations for the consecration [of the renovated structure], the households of the donors of the three districts of Yol-mo and the male and female donors in their entirety [all] arrived for the consecration. At that time, after the elders held a discussion, [they said]: "The donors of Yol-mo gangs-rwa and the Bla-ma [Karma Chos-bzang], [these] two, have to put down hundred *taṃ[ka]* [each], [together with] a binding document that the donors will not abandon the Bla-ma, [and] a written contract that the Bla-ma will not abandon the donors."

After the elders held a talk [once more], [they said]: "This rice field, a *bhir-ta* (= *birtā*) for a durable lineage, we will offer to Me-me Karma Chos-bzang!"

And thus [followed] the hand signs (i.e. thumbprints) of Bla-ma [Karma Chos-bzang], the elders [and] the chief estates of the east: at the beginning the thumbprint of Bla-ma Karma Chos-bzang, below it the print of the elder Tshe-dbang grub-pa, below it the print of the elder Ri-skyabs, below it the print of the elder Bha-bu, below it the print of the elder Tsakka, below it the print of the elder dGos bsam-'phel, below it the print of the elder Nang-ga, below it the print of the elder lHa-sems, below it the print of the elder Nag-grub, below it the print of the elder Nang-ga thugs-rje, below it the print of the elder Nas-po, below it the print of the elder dGos-'joms, below it the print of [the elders of] the three chief estates of the three districts [of Yol-mo].

The copyist was Bla-ma sNgags-ram-pa Don-grub rgyal-po [of sKyel-sdong]. The dharma field for a durable lineage is a maṇḍalaic territory [the size] of a small cloth.

May it be virtuous!

[Tibetan text]

[I] -

// skyabs gnas bslu ba med pa dkon mchog gsum la phyag 'tshal zhing skyabs su mchi'o //

de yang dang po bla ma karma chos bzang yol mo la [2] *phebs pa'i lo rgyus ni / gnas yol mo gangs rwa'i sbyin bdag rnams kyi brten pa'i bla ma ni / stod ras chung phug yin / sa thag ring na yang gshin gson* [3] *gnyis kyi don la / bla ma drags phyin pa la / bla ma karma chos bzang / u (= dbu) mdzad karma thub bstan / chos khrims pa karma dge legs dang bca pa'i /* [4] *dpon slob brgyad yol mo la phebs nas bzhugs / sbyin bdag gi don gang yin pa rnams zhu tshar ba dang / yol mo yul gyi rgan po'i gtso mdzad pa'i sbyin bdag rnams* [5] *kyis 'di ltar zhus / bla ma rin po che / gnas yol mos (= mo'i) sbyin bdag rnams kyi brten pa'i bla ma / sa thag ring po 'dug pas / 'di ru brtan chag (= phyag) bzhugs* [6] *par thugs rjes gzigs pa dang / khyim thab gcig yang bzhes pa mdzod zhus pas / nga ni gtsang btsun zhig yin pas 'on kyang khyed sbyin bdag rnams kyi (= kyis) 'di 'dra* [7] *gsungs na / nga yi rtsa ba'i bla ma la / sbyin bdag rnams kyi skyid sdug gi rgyu mtshan thams cad rim par zhus nas / bla ma dgongs pa mi bkrol na mi yong gsungs* [8] *nas / yol mo la u (= dbu) mdzad karma thub bstan bla ma'i sku tshab la bzhugs nas / stod ras chung phug la phebs te lo gsum bzhugs nas zhabs drung grub* [9] *mchog dbang pos zhal nas / karma chos bzang khyod kyis (= kyi) mi brgyud dang 'gro don yolmo la yod pas / khyod rang khyim thab byed chog gsungs te lung bstan* [10] *gnang nas yol mo la phebs nas / i pi yi dam btsun mo dang i pi yi dam jo'i bu mo khrib tse yang tshun ma (= chung ma) bzhes / i pi gnyis kyi rus pa zhang mo / i pi yi dam* [11] *la / sras po me me karma gu ru dang me me dbang chen 'khrungs / i pi khrib tse la / me me dkar rgyud dang me me ngag dbang 'khrungs / de nas me me karma gu ru'i zhal nas /* [12] *'o rang bzhi'i nang nas nga che ba yin te / nga ni bya btang rgyu (= rgyud) yin gsungs nas / nu'o khyed spun gsum gyi nang nas / nu'o dkar rgyud khyed che ba yin pas /* [13] *rgyal gzhi (= gzhis) dang dgon pa'i mnga' thang gnang nas / me me dkar rgyud kyi (= kyis) btsun mo zhing skyong ma / i pi chos legs bzhes nas sras po bdun 'khrungs /* [14] *sras che ba me me 'phrin las dbang po rgod tshang gling dgon pa mnga' thang gnang phog zhu / me me don grub rgyal po skyel sdong la bzhugs / me me thar pa* [15] *rgyal po bod thang la bzhugs / me me kun dga' rgyal po gu ru phug la bzhugs / me me mthong ba rgyal po shab ru la bzhugs /* [16] *me me chos rgyal mtshan shab ru la bzhugs / me me blo gros dpal bzang rgod tshang gling la bzhugs / me me 'phrin las dbang pos (= po'i) sras po me me gar dbang don grub yin /* [17] *blo gros dpal bzang gi sras / karma rnam mkhyen gyi sras 'gyur med rdo rje yi sras po / dgra 'dul seng ge yin no /*

[II]

bla ma yi dam dpa' mkha' 'gro [18] *chos skyong bsrung ma bka' bsrung dang dam can rgya mtsho 'khor dang bcas pa rnams la phyag 'tshal lo //*

dgongs su gsol / nga bla ma karma chos bzang gis yam bu [19] *ko ba (= ko khom) ye rang gling gsum gyi ser bsrung mdzad dus rgod tshang gling gi dgon pa zhig gso la mdzad tshar nas bya lo'i hor zla bcu pa'i tshes bco lnga la rab gnas* [20] *bkra shis mnga' gsol mdzad pa'i don la yol mo'i yul sde gsum gyi sbyin bdag mi tshar (= tshang) dang sbyin bdag pho mo thams cad rab gnas la byon pa'i dus su* [21] *rgan pa rnams kyi (= kyis) bka' gros zhig mdzad nas yol mo gangs rwa'i sbyin bdag dang bla ma gnyis ni sbyin bdag gis bla ma skyur sa med pa'i gaṃ (= gan) rgya / bla mas sbyin bdag* [22] *skyur sa med pa'i ga (= gan) rgya taṃ brgya brgya bzhag pa yin / de nas rgan pa rnams kyi (= kyis) bka' gros gnang nas bla ma la mdung (= gdung) brtan pa'i bhir ta 'bras zhing de me me karma chos* [23] *bzang la 'phul ba yin pas / de nas bla ma dang rgan pa dang sha ra (= shar) dbu gzhi (= gzhis) rnams kyi phyag gi rtags / thog mar bla ma karma chos bzang gi phyag rtags* [24] *de 'og rgan pa tshe dbang grub pa'i rtags / de 'og rgan pa ri skyabs kyi rtags / de 'og rgan pa bha bu'i rtags / de 'og rgan pa tsakka'i rtags / de 'og* [25] *rgan pa dgongs bsam 'phel gyi rtags / de 'og rgan pa nang ga'i rtags / de 'og lha sems kyi rtags / de 'og rgan pa nas grub kyi rtags / de 'og* [26] *rgan pa nang thugs rje'i rtags / de 'og rgan pa nas po'i rtags / de 'og rgan pa dgos 'joms kyi rtags / de 'og yul sde gsum gyi dbu gzhi (= gzhis)* [27] *gsum gyi rtags /*

yi ge pa bla ma sngags ram pa don grub rgyal po yin lags / mdung (= gdung) brtan pa'i chos zhing yug chung gi maṇḍal sde yin no //

// dge'o //

[illegible]

VII.

Buddhist Teachers from Dolpo

Two Further Lamas of Dolpo: Ngag-dbang rnam-rgyal (born 1628) and rNam-grol bzang-po (born 1504)

In the 1980s and 1990s second editions of two books by D.L. Snellgrove were published, both dealing with the Tibetan-speaking regions of Nepal, particularly Dolpo. I think it worthwhile to begin by quoting two remarks in each of the prefaces to the new editions, inasmuch as they reflect the current state of research on written materials from these regions and their chronological identification. With reference to biographies of a locally renowned 17th-century lama and his disciples who succeeded him in the lineage (discovered in Kutang by M. Aris) Snellgrove stated: "... these represent a small part of the large amount of Tibetan local literature available in these areas, and demonstrate how much there remains to be brought into the light of the day before any Nepalese history of the northern parts of the country can ever be started." Then in the second preface, Snellgrove remarks concerning the dating of the Dolpo biographies: "The dates of the first three of these four Dolpo Lamas have been moved on by sixty years, viz. into the next sixty years cycle."[1] Snellgrove was mainly concerned with four lamas of the same tradition (i.e. the Ngor-pa sub-sect of the Sa-skya-pa school) and their activities in the two main valleys of Dolpo, and his last remark on chronology has significant repercussions, for now the dates of all three lamas fall in the 16th century: bSod-nams blo-gros (1516–1581), Chos-skyabs dpal-bzang (1536–1625) and dPal-ldan blo-gros (1527–1596). Only the last of the four, bSod-nams dbang-phyug (1660–1731), is a later representative of that lineage, of the 17th/18th century.

In the following I should like to present information on two further masters from the above succession of Dolpo lamas. Both had been identified by Snellgrove, but for various reasons were not included in his book: Ngag-dbang rnam-rgyal and rNam-grol bzang-po.[2]

---

1 Snellgrove (1961a=1989:xix); id. (1967=1992:preface to the second edition). The changes in the dates by one sixty-year cycle were put forward by Jackson (1978:218, note 86); id (1984:143, note 67). For the Kutang biographies, see Aris (1979a).

2 See Snellgrove (1967=1992:11): "As far as I know, there are no other biographies of lamas of this succession. That of *Merit Intellect*'s teacher, *Good Deliverance* (= rNam-grol bzang-po), might have been included, but it is concerned almost entirely with a list of works studied and meditations practised, and so

The main emphasis of this investigation is on the transmission of teachings as they are contained in a "biography" (*rnam thar*) and in a "record of teachings received" (*thob yig*). Thereby it should once again become clear that "spiritual genealogies" can provide data of historical worth, especially at the time when we are just beginning to sort out the influences of different schools of Tibetan Buddhism in a specific geographical area. Here I hope to trace such lineages through the period extending from the 15th to the 18th centuries in Dolpo, and in the process reveal some of the wealth of Tibetan local literature from the northern parts of Nepal that has been brought to light in recent years.

1. The *thob yig* of Ngag-dbang rnam-rgyal

The record of teachings received by Ngag-dbang rnam-rgyal was filmed by the NGMPP in 1984 in Syang (South Mustang), and it consists of records written down by Ngag-dbang rnam-rgyal himself. It covers the most important stations of his life, and extends from 1630 up to 1679. There is no colophon in the text, and only a short introduction, which states: "How I requested the kind instructions from the unparalleled, high and noble guides – if this has to some extent been set down as a list, it is such ..." There immediately follows his record of the encounter with the first teacher at the age of three. By retracing the different meetings with his teachers and the places where they occurred, it should be possible for us to sketch a rough picture of the lines of transmission Ngag-dbang rnam-rgyal became a part of.

Ngag-dbang rnam-rgyal's first teacher was named sPrul-sku bsTan-'dzin nor-bu, and he conferred an "empowerment of Amitāyus, the Buddha of Long Life" (*tshe dpag med dbang*), on his disciple at the "great meeting ground" (*'du gnas chen po*) mNga'-ris Khyung-rdzong dkar-po. Thus, in the year 1630, we find Ngag-dbang rnam-rgyal in Mang-yul Gung-thang, in particular in its capital, rDzong-dkar, where the young boy encountered the Third Yol-mo-ba sprul-sku bsTan-'dzin nor-bu (1598–1644).[3]

---

contains little information of general local interest. There are "Collected Spiritual Songs" (*mgur 'bum*) of Lama Ngag-dbang rnam-rgyal of gNam-gung ..." The last-mentioned work was filmed by the Nepal-German Manuscript Preservation Project (NGMPP) on two occasions: *Bya bral ngag dbang rnam rgyal gyi rang gi nyams len dran so'i (= bso'i) nyams dbyangs 'brel med kyis 'chal gtam 'ga' re yod ang*, 209 fols., reel no. L 62/4; and 197 fols., reel no. L 411/3.

3 For the quotation, see Ngag-dbang rnam-rgyal: *sPrang bhan (= ban) ngag dbang rnam rgyal bdag gi zab chos kyi thob yig dgos 'dod kun 'byung*, fol. 1b/3–4: *... bdag gi (= gis) 'tshung (= mtshungs) bral gyi 'dren mchog dam pa rnams las+bka' drin gyi gdams pa zhus pa'i tshul du cung zad tho ru bkod na 'di lta ste*. The founding of the palace bKra-shis Khyung-rdzong dkar-po under the Gung-thang king 'Bum-lde mgon (1253–1280) is mentioned, along with its alternative name, mNga'-ris rDzong-dkar, in Tshe-dbang nor-bu: *Bod rje lha btsad po'i gdung rabs mnga' ris smad gung thang du ji ltar byung ba'i tshul deb gter dwangs shel 'phrul gyi me long*, p. 102. For the Third Yol-mo-ba sprul-sku and his role in the Byang-gter tradition, see Ehrhard (2007) and chapter nine in the present volume.

A second empowerment of Amitāyus was received by an unidentified teacher at the age of four at Gung-thang rDo-rje brag. The next data pertain to Ngag-dbang rnam-rgyal's "homeland" (*rang phyogs*), where he studied under the teacher Chos-skyong dpal-bzang; the place is called "site of spiritual practice, glorious mTha'-dkar". There he also received from his teacher, in 1635, the reading of the "biography and spiritual songs" (*rnam mgur*).[4] Three years later Ngag-dbang rnam-rgyal was at another site, this one founded in the 16th century in northern Dolpo, namely Hrab. There he received various empowerments and readings from a certain 'Jam-dbyangs dPal-ldan bzang-po. From the last of the biographies translated by Snellgrove, we know that dPal-ldan bzang-po was still active in Hrab in the year 1670.[5]

Concerning his next two teachers we only know their names, but not their place of residence. The first one was dKa'-chen rDo-rje mgon-po. Ngag-dbang rnam-rgyal heard him recite the biographies of gTer-ston Guru Chos-dbang (1212–1270) and rJe Kun-dga' grol-mchog (1507–1566), among others. At the age of fifteen, in the year 1643, he happened to meet a yogin of the bKa'-brgyud-pa school whose name was Ras-chen Blo-'phel dpal-bzang. Extensive mention is made here of his receiving of the cycle *sNyan brgyud yid bzhin nor bu*, i.e. the so-called *Ras chung snyan brgyud*, while a cycle of the teachings of Padmasambhava, the *rDo rje phag mo zab khrid*, was also received. The latter is a "reconcealed treasure" (*yang gter*), having been recovered a second time by bsTan-gnyis gling-pa, who is also known as Padma Tshe-dbang rgyal-po (1480–1535).[6]

It was during this period that the "high and noble guide" dPal-ldan don-grub acquainted Ngag-dbang rnam-rgyal with the tradition that is of particular interest for us here. This

---

4 Ngag-dbang rnam-rgyal (as in note 3), fol. 2a/2–2b/1. The place referred to as sGrub-gnas dPal-gyi mtha'-dkar was founded by bSod-nams blo-gros, who was also responsible for the foundation of dMar-sgom; see Snellgrove (1967=1992:11). It is tempting to identify Chos-skyong dpal-bzang with Chos-skyabs dpal-bzang, the disciple and biographer of bSod-nams blo-gros, but the dates available suggest that the latter had already died by 1625. The person in question must thus be another representative of the line of succession.

5 Ngag-dbang rnam-rgyal (as in note 3), fols. 2b/1–3a/1. Concerning the foundation of Hrab by dPal-ldan blo-gros, the second disciple of bSod-nams blo-gros, see Snellgrove (1967=1992:11). For the studies of bSod-nams dbang-phyug under dPal-ldan bzang-po in 1670, see ibid, p. 241. A third teacher in Hrab is dPal-ldan rdo-rje. His works were filmed by the NGMPP: *Bla ma dam pa dpal ldan rdo rje'i rnam thar rags bsdus*, 119 fols., reel no. L 416/2, and *mKhas grub chen po dpal ldan rdo rje'i mgur 'bum reg (= rags) bsdus cig*, 118 fols., reel no. L 416/3.

6 Ngag-dbang rnam-rgyal (as in note 3), fols. 3a/1–5b/3. Regarding the transmission of the teachings of the bKa'-brgyud-pa, it should be mentioned that biographies of the great masters of the school were given as a "fortifying teaching" (*rgyab chos*) after the receiving of the actual "instruction" (*khrid*): *de'i rgyab chos su rje btsun mi la ras pa'i rnam thar 'gur (= mgur) 'bum lung ... de rnams kyi rgyab chos su dpal bzhad pa rdo rje yab sras kyi mgur rgyas pa / rgyal ba rgod tshang pa'i rnam thar rtsa ga ris ma / rje btsun gtsang pa he ru ka'i rnam thar rnams kyi lung rnams thob ...* This usage reminds us of how the concept of "fortifying teaching" is employed in the *gter ma* literature; see Ehrhard (1993a:34, note 9) and chapter ten in the present volume.

tradition is called "the system that has long existed, [that] of Chos-skyabs dpal-bzang, father and sons, the Dharmarājas of glorious dMar-sgom." Obviously Ngag-dbang rnam-rgyal was studying under the abbot of dMar-sgom at the time, and the expression "Chos-skyabs dpal-bzang, father and sons" refers to the lineage to which he was linked by his teacher, dPal-ldan don-grub. With a view towards improving our knowledge of the lineage, I shall now go into the details of the succession of four of the transmissions that run through dPal-ldan don-grub. Certain relations within the lineage will be highlighted, thereby allowing us a glimpse into the history of *gter ma* traditions in Dolpo and Mustang.

a. The Treasure Works of Nyang-ral Nyi-ma'i 'od-zer (1124–1192)

Ngag-dbang rnam-rgyal received the readings for the "empowerment" (*dbang*), the "sādhanas" (*sgrub thabs*) and the "sequence of ritual acts" (*las byang*) of the cycles *Guru che mchog dmar po* and *dPal mgon phyag bzhi pa.*[7]

The line of transmission—as much of it as it is of concern for our present purposes—can be presented in the following form:

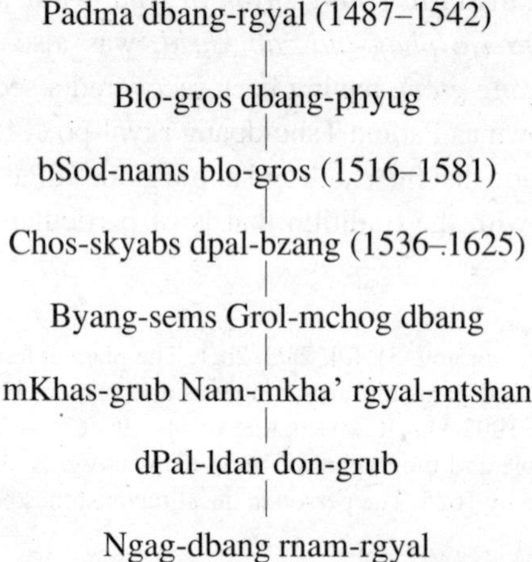

The main point of interest is that the founder of dMar-sgom and the disciples following him stand in the line of succession of mNga'-ris Paṇ-chen Padma dbang-rgyal, a renowned scholar and adept of the rNying-ma-pa school. The latter was born in Ma-thang in northern

7 For the different transmissions under the heading *dPal dmar sgom chos kyi rgyal po chos skyabs dpal bzang yab sras kyi ring lugs*, see Ngag-dbang rnam-rgyal (as in note 3), fols. 5b/3–8b/1. The text of the four in question is given in the appendices. The following teachings were also handed down by dPal-ldan don-grub: *Ma gcig rgyal thang lugs, Yang dag bcod (= gcod) kyi skor khros ma nag mo, Tshe dpag med grub rgyal ma (= mo), 'Jam dpal nāga rakṣa, Phyag rdor 'byung po 'dul byed, rGyal ba yang dgon pa'i bar do 'phrang grol* and *'Pho ba 'jug tshugs ma*; ibid, fols. 7a/6–8b/1.

Mustang, and counted among his teachers the First Yol-mo-ba sprul-sku Śākya bzang-po (15th/16th cent.) and Glo-bo mkhan-chen bSod-nams lhun-grub (1456–1532). As there is a passage that documents the kind of transmission that connected the first three members of our list, I shall give it in full:

> Then my precious Lama said: "Now you have become master of the secret spells of my rNying-ma cycles. Now you are not acting pusillanimously. The incomparable Padma dbang-rgyal said to me: 'When I give you this initiation, by holding to it you will obtain the supreme as well as the ordinary types of accomplishment in this very life.' Even as he said, I have given it to you. By holding to it you will gain the supreme and the ordinary types of accomplishment and there will be great benefit for many living beings." Thus I received the consecrations and textual initiations in full.[8]

b. The Treasure Works of dNgos-grub rgyal-mtshan (1337–1406)

There are two different treasure work cycles that were handed over by dPal-ldan don-grub to Ngag-dbang rnam-rgyal; their rediscovery is attributed to dNgos-grub rgyal-mtshan, also known as rGod-ldem 'phru-can: *Phyi sgrub 'gro ba kun grol* and *gSang sgrub guru sngon po*.[9] As their line of transmission differs to some extent, I shall treat them separately. The members of the lineage will be listed here only up to the first two teachers of dMar-sgom:

---

8 For the text of the first line of transmission, see Appendix A. Biographical data on mNga'-ris Paṇ-chen Padma dbang-rgyal and his activities in maintaining the continuity of the Byang-gter tradition are found in Boord (1993:28f.). The relationship that Padma dbang-rgyal and his younger brother Legs-ldan bDud-'joms rdo-rje (born 1512) enjoyed with their teachers Śākya bzang-po and Glo-bo mkhan-chen is sketched in Ehrhard (2007) and chapter nine in the present volume. The best source for the life of Padma dbang-rgyal is still rDo-rje brag Rig-'dzin Padma 'phrin-las: *'Dus pa mdo dbang gi bla ma brgyud pa'i rnam thar ngo mtshar dad pa'i phreng ba*, pp. 304–335. For the quote, see Snellgrove (1967=1992:98). The "precious Lama" is Blo-gros dbang-phyug; the Tibetan text can be found in Chos-skyabs dpal-bzang: *mKhas grub chen po bsod nams blo gros kyi nam par thar pa mthong ba don ldan dad pa'i gsal 'debs*, pp. 69.1–70.1.

9 For the text of the next two lines of transmission, see Appendix B. A résumé of the activities of dNgos-grub rgyal-mtshan, especially his rediscovery of hidden treasures, is provided by Boord (1993:22–28); for the two cycles under consideration, see, in particular, p. 26. Together with the *Nang sgrub rig 'dzin gdung sgrub* they form the "outer, inner and secret" *sādhana*s of the Byang-gter, ibid, p. 31. There are some problems with the dates of the progenitor of the Byang-gter tradition. I base the dates proposed on the text of Brag-dkar rta-so sprul-sku Chos-kyi dbang-phyug (1775–1837): *Byang gter thugs sgrub yang tig gces sgron gyi khrid yig gi bla ma brgyud pa'i lo rgyus rnam thar kha bskong nyung gsal du bkod pa*; according to this source dNgos-grub rgyal-mtshan was born in *me mo glang* (= 1337), the birth of his son rNam-rgyal mgon-po occurred during his sixty-first year (= 1397), and he died at the beginning of his seventieth year (= 1406).

dNgos-grub rgyal-mtshan (1337–1406)

Sangs-rgyas bstan-pa

Sangs-rgyas byams-bzang

Chos-rgyal bsod-nams (1442–1509)

Śākya bzang-po

Padma dbang-rgyal (1487–1542)

Blo-gros 'od-zer

Shes-rab rgyal-mtshan

bSod-nams blo-gros (1516–1581)

Chos-skyabs dpal-bzang (1536–1625)

As previously mentioned, mNga'-ris Paṇ-chen Padma dbang-rgyal counted among his teachers the First Yol-mo-ba sprul-sku Śākya bzang-po. With the help of our list we can now identify the previous teacher in that line of transmission: Chos-rgyal bsod-nams. He is worth mentioning for two reasons. First, he was a native of the Mustang region, his birthplace being called Glo-bo rGyam-dpal, and his father was a local lord, dPon-chen lHa-grub 'bum by name. He travelled extensively, visiting India and China, and in the Kathmandu Valley he met, in 1464, the famous Paṇḍita Vanaratna (1384–1468).

Secondly, his person is of some importance for the line of teachers at dMar-sgom, as its founder, bSod-nams blo-gros, considered himself to be the reincarnation of Chos-rgyal bsod-nams.[10] We can thus see that the influence of the Northern Treasurers was quite strong in Dolpo and Mustang in the 15th and the 16th centuries.

Let us now take a look at the second line:

dNgos-grub rgyal-mtshan (1337–1406)

rNam-rgyal mgon-po (born 1397)

[10] See Anonymous: *Rig 'dzin chos rgyal bsod nams gyi rnam thar* for a short biography of Chos-rgyal bsod-nams. As the introductory folio mentions the region of rDzar as the seat of his family line, we can identify him more exactly as a native of the Muktināth Valley. For the status of bSod-nams blo-gros as his incarnation, see Snellgrove (1967=1992:83) and the Tibetan text in Chos-skyabs dpal-bzang (as in note 8), pp. 10.5–11.3. A full account of the life of Chos-rgyal bsod-nams is to be found in id.: *mKhas grub bsod nams blo gros kyi gsang ba'i rnam thar*, pp. 174.3–180.4 (based on the subject's own records).

bSod-nams bzang-po
|
dPal-ldan rgyal-mtshan
|
rGyal-mtshan bum-pa
|
Bya-btang bSam-rgyal
|
dPal-ldan seng-ge
|
dKon-mchog [chos-]skyabs
|
Padma dbang-rgyal (1487–1542)
|
Blo-gros dbang-phyug
|
bSod-nams blo-gros (1516–1581)
|
Chos-skyabs dpal-bzang (1536–1625)

Thus a certain dKon-mchog [chos-]skyabs enters the picture as another teacher of mNga'-ris Paṇ-chen Padma dbang-rgyal, and I think it reasonable to identify him with the translator dKon-mchog chos-skyabs. Although not directly connected with the transmission of the *gter ma* teachings in the biography of Padma dbang-rgyal, he was, we know, responsible for transmitting the teachings of the Vajrāvalī to his student in the year 1523:

> At the age of thirty-seven he practised contemplation in dGe-lung in lower Glo-bo; at the time when he studied completely the empowerment of Vajrāvalī from Lo-chen dKon-mchog chos-skyabs, who was prophesied by the Ḍākiṇīs as an incarnation of Abhayākaragupta ...[11]

11 *See* Padma 'phrin-las (as in note 8), p. 391.5f.: *dgung lo so bdun pa la glo bo smad dge lung du thugs dam mdzad / slob dpon abhyakāra'i* (= *abhayākara'i*) *skye bar mkha' 'gros lung bstan te / lo chen dkon cog* (= *mchog*) *chos skyabs las rdo rje 'phreng ba'i dbang rdzogs par gsan dus* ... For *Vajrāvalī*, *Jyotirmañjarī* and *Niṣpannayogāvalī* as a unit, called "three cycles" (*skor gsum*) in Tibetan tradition, see Bühnemann and Tachikawa (1991:xvi): "According to Abhayākaragupta, the Vajrāvalī, a practical guide to all the preliminary rites preceding the initiation into the *maṇḍala*, is the main text while the NSP (= *Niṣpannayogāvalī*), which deals with *maṇḍalas* in detail, and the Jyotirmañjarī, which deals with the *homa* ritual exclusively, are supplementary." dKon-mchog chos-skyabs also assumed the function of *ācārya* (*slob dpon*) during the full ordination of Padma dbang-rgyal as monk; op. cit., p. 315.4.

c. The Treasure Works of Guru Chos-dbang (1212–1270)

The last two treasure cycles that Ngag-dbang rnam-rgyal received together with those of Nyang-ral Nyi-ma'i 'od-zer and dNgos-grub rgyal-mtshan are part of the rediscoveries of the early treasure revealer Guru Chos-dbang. They are called *Thugs rje chen po yang snying 'dus pa* and *'Khor ba dong sprugs*. As their titles suggest, both cycles are concerned with the spiritual practice of Mahākāruṇika, i.e. Avalokiteśvara.

Here is an overview of the final line of transmission:

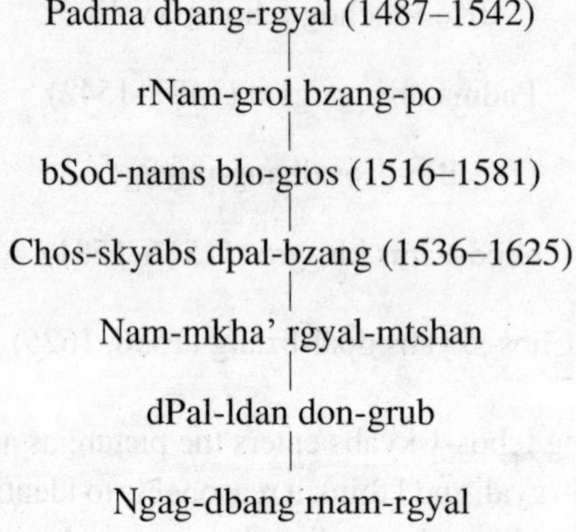

Along with Blo-gros dbang-phyug, we now have in the lama rNam-grol bzang-po a second disciple of mNga'-ris Paṇ-chen Padma dbang-rgyal who gave teachings to the first master of dMar-sgom. Since rNam-grol bzang-po will be the subject of the second part of the present paper, I shall here merely quote another passage, which shows how bSod-nams blo-gros came into contact with rNam-grol bzang-po:

> Then because of precious *Intellect Might*'s passing from sorrow, I had not received *Lord of Great Compassion, Stirrer of the Pit of Existence* or *Universal Saviour of Sentient Beings* and other doctrines. So I thought: "Would it be suitable to go and find a lama who could bestow upon me these religious cycles of the *Lord of Great Compassion*? In this later part of my life perhaps I should resolve everything into the *maṇi* prayer and just stay quiet?" Then one night my lama appeared to me in a dream and said: "Your personal deity is the *Stirrer of the Pit of Existence*. You will obtain this in the direction of the sunrise."[12]

---

12 For the text of the last line of transmission, see Appendix C. The cycles *Thugs rje chen po yang snying 'dus pa* and *'Khor ba gdong sprugs* are two of the eighteen major treasure discoveries attributed to Guru Chos-dbang; see Gyatso (1994:283, note 2). For the quote, see Snellgrove (1967=1992:99f.), and the Tibetan text in Chos-skyabs dpal-bzang (as in note 8), pp. 76.3–77.2. After this passage there follows a description of the empowerment for the cycle *Khor ba gdong sprugs* by rNam-grol bzang-po.

These few observations on the tradition of dMar-sgom should have made it clear that there is a strong presence of different *gter ma* cycles and their teachings in Dolpo and Mustang. It is also obvious now that the specific lineage of sMar-sgom goes back to the early treasure discoverers of the 12th to 14th centuries, the unifying figure for the different transmissions in the 15th and 16th centuries being mNga'-ris Paṇ-chen Padma dbang-rgyal.

We shall now continue to retrace the further contacts of Ngag-dbang rnam-rgyal and thereby come to a second phase of the spread of *gter ma* teachings. At the beginning of his twenty-ninth year, Ngag-dbang rnam-rgyal stayed in a place that is famous because of the former presence of the great yogin Mi-la-ras-pa (1040–1123): the "great sacred site White Rock, Horse Tooth" (*gnas chen brag dkar rta so*). There, to the north-west of sKyid-grong (again in Mang-yul Gung-thang), he met the teacher Karma Chos-'phel (died 1671) and received several transmissions from him that are peculiar to the system of the Karma Kaṃ-tshang, a subsect of the bKa'-brgyud-pa school. Two hierarchs of that sect that are mentioned in the lineage are the Sixth Zhwa-dmar-pa Chos-kyi dbang-phyug (1584–1630) and the Tenth Karma-pa Chos-dbyings rdo-rje (1604–1674).

Three years later, in 1660, Ngag-dbang rnam-rgyal studied under a second teacher of Brag-dkar rta-so, to whom he attached special importance, as can be seen from the epithet "Lineage Master for many of my lifetimes" (*bdag gi tshe rabs du ma'i rigs bdag*). The name of this teacher is Chos-rje Karma Blo-bzang, a person whose role as "resident" (*gnas 'dzin pa*) of Brag-dkar rta-so and propagator of the teachings of the bKa'-brgyud-pa and rNying-ma-pa in the Tibet-Nepal borderlands has still to be documented.[13] To provide an idea of his activities in the region of present concern, the following short passage may be quoted:

> After coming to Glo-bo, he inspected the holy site of Crystal-Mountain Dragon-Roar in Dol-po. In [the place] called gNam-gung he founded a monastery and established a retreat community, [thereby] acting greatly for the benefit of beings. Also the king of Jumla bowed down to him in devotion.[14]

---

[13] Ngag-dbang rnam-rgyal (as in note 3), fols. 8b/1–10a/5 and 10a/5–18a/6, lists the teachings received from Karma Chos-'phel and Karma Blo-bzang. For biographical information on the two teachers (Karma Chos-'phel being the successor of Karma Blo-bzang), see the chronicle of Brag-dkar rta-so sprul-sku Chos-kyi dbang-phyug: *Grub pa'i gnas chen brag dkar rta so'i gnas dang gdan rabs bla ma brgyud pa'i lo rgyus mdo tsam brjod pa mos ldan dad pa'i gdung sel drang srong dga' ba'i dal gtam*, fols. 30a/5–34a/2, and fols. 34a/2–35b/1. Further details on the life of Karma Blo-bzang can be found in Ehrhard (2001) and chapter fourteen in the present volume. It should be mentioned that Karma Blo-bzang took up the post at the instigation of Karma bsTan-skyong dbang-po, the gTsang sde-srid (reign 1620–1642). One work of Karma Blo-bzang's is available: *bKa' brgyud bstan pa lha gsangs (= bsangs) bkra shis char 'bebs snyan pa'i sgra dbyangs yid 'phrog rab mdzes*, 58 fols., NGMPP reel no. L 275/8, and 20 fols., reel no. L 405/3.

[14] Chos-kyi dbang-phyug (as in note 13), fol. 32a/5f.: *glo bor byon nas dol po shel gyi ri bo 'brug sgra'i gnas gzigs mdzad / gnam gung zhes par dgon pa btab cing sgrub sde btsugs 'gro don rgya cher mdzad*

In investigating the diffusion of *gter ma* cycles, their topicality and popularity, one should note the fact that Ngag-dbang rnam-rgyal received the following works from Karma Blo-bzang: *Yang zab dkon mchog spyi 'dus, Thugs rje chen po ngan song rang grol, Tshe dpag med gnam lcags rdo rje dngos grub kun 'dus, rTa phag yid bzhin nor bu* etc. These are all treasure works discovered by Rig-'dzin 'Ja'-tshon snying-po (1585–1656) and thus belong to a tradition that was newly established in the 17th century. The proximity of transmission is obvious from the succession of teachers: Rig-'dzin 'Ja'-tshon snying-po → Rig-'dzin dByings-rig dpal-'bar → rGyal-dbang Karma Blo-bzang.

Ngag-dbang rnam-rgyal returned on two more occasions to Brag-dkar rta-so. Particular mention is made of his study of the *Ras chung snyan brgyud*. The names of two other teachers turn up during this period: Zhabs-drung Khams-pa dKon-mchog lhun-grub and Zhabs-drung dPag-bsam ye-shes (1598–1667). It is sufficient to mention that the former belonged to the Sa-skya-pa school, and the latter to the 'Brug-pa subsect of the bKa'-brgyud-pa.[15]

It seems that the main studies of Ngag-dbang rnam-rgyal were finished with his continuous visits to Brag-dkar rta-so, and he eventually took up residence at gNam-gung. Nevertheless, the teachings of the rNying-ma-pa school also made their presence felt in the latter part of his life, all in the form of freshly revealed treasure works. At the age of forty-nine, in the year 1677, he came to receive the full transmission of the cycle *Dam chos sprul sku snying thig*. These teachings are attributed to Rig-'dzin bDud-'dul rdo-rje (1615–1672), a disciple of the above-mentioned Rig-'dzin 'Ja'-tshon snying-po. The teacher under whom Ngag-dbang rnam-rgyal studied the cycle was O-rgyan dpal-bzang (1617–1677), a native of southern Mustang.[16]

---

cing 'dzum lang rgyal pos kyang gus pas btud. For a modern-day description of pilgrimage around Crystal-Mountain Dragon-Roar, see Jest (1985). This was also one of the places where mNga'-ris Pan-chen Padma dbang-rgyal followed his spiritual practice; see rDo-rje brag Rig-'dzin Padma 'phrin-las (as in note 8), p. 316.2. The foundation of a monastery in gNam-gung thus predates the establishment of Shel dgon-pa by bsTan-'dzin ras-pa (1644/46–1723), another master attracted to Shel-gyi ri-bo 'brug-sgra. The manuscript of the works of bsTan-'dzin ras-pa mentioned by Snellgrove (1961a=1989:155) was filmed by the NGMPP, reel nos. L 409/8–L 410/10. For the printing history of the works, see bsTan-'dzin ras-pa: *rJe btsun bstan 'dzin ras pa de nyid kyi gsang ba'i rnam thar sa khyis phan gyis / mgur ma'i kha 'phros gnas ngo bzung tshul dkar chags dang bcas chos tshan lnga.*

[15] Khams-pa sKon-mchog lhun-grub is the "Khams Lama *Jewel Self-Created*" in Snellgrove (1967=1992:239f.); he was the one who set bSod-nams dbang-phyug, the last of the four lamas whose biographies were translated by Snellgrove, on his spiritual path. For dPag-bsam ye-shes, who was ordained by the Fifth 'Brug-chen dPag-bsam dbang-po (1593–1641) and who had his residence in the vicinity of Ri-bo dpal-'bar in Mang-yul Gung-thang, see Chos-kyi dbang-phyug: *dPal ldan gzhung 'brug bka' brgyud gser 'phreng gi bla ma brgyud pa'i rnam thar dang phyag rgya chen po'i spyi don ngo mtshar snyan gi sgra dbyangs*, fols. 52a/3–53a/4, and Bod mkhas-pa Mi-pham dge-legs rnam-par rgyal-ba (born 1618): *rJe btsun grub pa'i dbang phyug dam pa dpag bsam ye shes zhabs kyi rnam par thar pa mchog gi spyod yul rgya mtsho'i snying po*, 67 fols., NGMPP, reel no. L 13/5.

[16] For a rough sketch of the life of O-rgyan dpal-bzang, born in dGa'-rab rdzong, near present-day Thini,

Both the teachings of Rig-'dzin 'Ja'-tshon snying-po and of Rig-'dzin bDud-'dul rdo-rje originated in the far south-eastern provinces of Tibet, in sPo-bo and Kong-po. Through O-rgyan dpal-bzang, Ngag-dbang rnam-rgyal received another transmission that had made its appearance in the eastern part of Tibet: the *gNam chos thugs kyi gter kha snyan brgyud* of gTer-ston Mi-'gyur rdo-rje (1645–1667). The immediate distribution of these *gter ma* cycles to the south-western borderlands, such as Dolpo and Mustang, can partly be explained by the activities of charismatic figures like Karma Blo-bzang and O-rgyan dpal-bzang, but I think it is also reasonable to argue for the existence of certain "spiritual centres," i.e. geographical areas that were characterized by such special qualities as the former presence of Padmasambhava or Mi-la-ras-pa, and that were connected by a communications network of sorts in spite of the great distances. One of the spiritual centres in the south-west of Tibet was certainly the territory of Mang-yul Gung-thang with its district town sKyid-grong. As we shall see in the case of the last teacher of Ngag-dbang rnam-rgyal, it was in this territory and its periphery that a series of treasure cycles was discovered in the 17th century as well.

The name of this teacher is mNga'-ris gter-ston Gar-dbang rdo-rje (1640–1685), and Ngag-dbang rnam-rgyal met this treasure discoverer, who was twelve years his junior, in the year 1679. The first cycle he received was the *rDor sems thugs kyi me long*, a "reconcealed treasure" (*yang gter*) originally discovered by Rig-'dzin rGod-ldem 'phru-can. Gar-dbang rdo-rje is considered the reincarnation of this early *gter ston*, and the place where the treasure reemerged was the "hidden valley" (*sbas yul*) sKyid-mo lung. Along with the *Padma'i snyan brgyud yang gsang bla med*, two other cycles are described in detail: *Thugs rje chen po rtsa gsum snying thig* and *rDo rje phur pa spu gri reg gcod*. The sites of these treasure discoveries, like those in sKyid-mo lung to the north-east of sKyid-grong, are again located in Mang-yul Gung-thang; they are called Mang-yul 'Phags-pa'i khrus-khang and Mang-yul La-'debs stod-kyi gangs zhur-mo respectively.[17]

---

see Ehrhard (1993c) and chapter thirteen in the present volume; in the year 1668 he founded the monastery sKu-tshab gter-lnga. The biography of O-rgyan dpal-bzang was filmed by the NGMPP: O-rgyan dpal-bzang: *Rigs brgya dbang po 'dren mchog slob dpon dpal bzang po'i rnam par thar pa dad pa'i spu long g.yo byed mthong bas yid 'phrug ngo mtshar 'phreng ba'i gtam rmad du byung ba*, 309 fols. (incomplete), reel no. L 83/1. See Ngag-dbang rnam-rgyal (as in note 3), fols. 19a/1–25b/2 for a complete list of the teachings transmitted by O-rgyan dpal-bzang.

17 The list of teachings received from Gar-dbang rdo-rje is contained in Ngag-dbang rnam-rgyal (as in note 3), fols. 26a/3–31a/5. The preceding section (fols. 25b/2–26b/3) gives the transmissions received from a certain rJe-drung Ngag-dbang Zil-gnon rdo-rje at Grub-pa'i gnas-chen Ling-nga brag-dmar, another sacred spot associated with Mi-la-ras-pa. Zil-gnon rdo-rje was the first "master of the teachings" (*chos bdag*) of the treasures of Gar-dbang rdo-rje. The "bathing house of Ārya" (*'phags pa'i khrus khang*) refers to a section of the 'Phags-pa lha-khang, the temple of the sacred Avalokiteśvara statue in sKyid-grong; the area of La-'debs is located to the south of sKyid-grong. For another discovery of Gar-dbang rdo-rje in Byams-pa sprin-gyi lha-khang, the old *yang-'dul* temple of sKyid-grong, see Ehrhard (1993a:81,

With the works of mNga'-ris gter-ston Gar-dbang rdo-rje, which Ngag-dbang rnam-rgyal received from the treasure discoverer himself, the "record of teachings received" comes to an end. The name of dNgos-grub rgyal-mtshan, also known as Rig-'dzin rGod-ldem 'phru-can, and the treasures associated with him come up again in connection with Gar-dbang rdo-rje, and this is yet another indication of the vitality of the Byang-gter tradition in border regions like Dolpo. It would be worthwhile to identify the further spread of these *gter ma* teachings in that area,[18] but for the time being it should be enough to recognize two distinct phases in the diffusion of the *gter ma* teachings: an earlier one in the 15th and 16th centuries, and a later one in the 17th and 18th centuries.

2. THE *RNAM THAR* OF RNAM-GROL BZANG-PO

As the biography provides information on the location of rNam-grol bzang-po's birthplace and its broader topographical and political features, let us begin with a full quotation of the relevant passage:

> South-east of the king of the white glacier [mountains], Ti-se, and lake Ma-pham, swollen [with water]; under the domain of the king's great palace, the capital sMon-thang;
> at the neck of the sKu-la glacier, a place where siddhas have successively arrived;
> in a town which supports the monastery of Gr[w]a-lung;
> where provisions—whatever one wishes for—arise;
> where attendants and excellent riches spontaneously appear;
> [in that] place, [with] the valley of Ban-tshang in its middle—a protrusion [thereof], what is called Ne-lung—he was born.[19]

---

note 5) and chapter ten in the present volume.

[18] Another interesting figure, who was active in Tarap and Dolpo in the 17th and 18th centuries, is O-rgyan bstan-'dzin (1657–1737); for his spiritual songs, see O-rgyan bstan-'dzin: *rNal 'byor gyi dbang phyug o rgyan bstan 'dzin zhes bya ba'i ri khrod kyi nyams dbyangs*. A short biography of him has thrice been filmed by the NGMPP: O-rgyan bstan-'dzin: *sPrang rgan o rgyan bstan 'dzin pa'i rnam thar bsdus pa*, 133 fols. (incomplete), reel no. L 187/3; 157 fols., reel no. L 206/3; 95 fols., reel no. L 220/4. Like Ngag-dbang rnam-rgyal, he studied in Hrab and met Karma Blo-bzang and O-rgyan dpal-bzang. Like him, too, he received the treasure works of Gar-dbang rdo-rje from the *gter ston* himself. For the further spread of this tradition in Mugu (Mu-gum), see *Chos med bla gzugs gang shar rang sgrol (= grol) bdag gis chos kyi thob yig yid kyi mun bsel (= sel)*, 69 fols., NGMPP reel no. D 111/29. A full description of the life of O-rgyan bstan-'dzin can be found in Ehrhard (1998) and chapter twenty of the present volume.

[19] bSod-nams blo-gros: *mKhas grub chen po rnam grol bzang po'i rnam thar dad pa'i spu long g.yo byed ngo mtshar can*, pp. 17.4–18.2: *gangs dkar gyi rgyal po ti se dang / ma spangs (= pham) mtsho mo mer ba'i shar lho / rgyal po'i brang chen po rgyal sa smon thang gi chab 'og / sku la gang kyi mgul sgrub (= grub) thob rim par byon pa'i sgrub gnas gra lung dgon pa'i spyod yul gyi grong khyer / 'thun (= mthun) rkyen*

We can thus say that Ban-tshang, the easternmost valley of Dolpo, was at the beginning of the 16th century under the control of the kings of Mustang, while Gr[w]a-lung was obviously a site visited regularly by Buddhist yogins even before that time. rNam-grol bzang-po was not only born in the vicinity of Gr[w]a-lung, but the latter also happened to be his main residence during the later years of his life. This at least is the impression we get from the biography of his disciple bSod-nams blo-gros, who called his teacher the "lord of religion of Gr[w]a-lung".

Among the ancestors of rNam-grol bzang-po there was a sculptor and painter by the name of Kun-dga' 'bum, who was active, for example, in the execution of paintings and woodwork at the temples of Byams-pa lha-khang and Thub-chen lha-khang in Glo-bo smon-thang. These data from the biography tally with the fact that the temples date from the second quarter of the 15th century. A second relative is also mentioned for his qualities as a painter, but he travelled to gTsang province of Central Tibet as well and became a fine teacher at the monastery of Thub-bstan gSer-mdog-can, an institution established by Paṇ-chen Śākya mchog-ldan (1428–1507), who visited Mustang in the years 1472–1474.

After his first studies, and having received the novitiate vows from a certain mKhas-pa dPal-ldan bzang-po, rNam-grol bzang-po went to stay for some time in a monastery in northern Mustang. Although the biography mentions only the name bSam-grub gling and provides no further information, we know from another source that it was the very same bSam-grub gling (and around the same time) that mNga'-ris Paṇ-chen Padma dbang-rgyal was fully ordained. This took place in the presence of Glo-bo mkhan-chen bSod-nams lhun-grub.[20]

For rNam-grol bzang-po it was, nevertheless, not Mustang where he continued his further studies, but rather at Thub-bstan gSer-mdog-can in gTsang, the monastery previously frequented by his ancestors. There he took the vows of a fully ordained monk, along with the Bodhisattva vows. The lineage stands out as that of Ngor-chen Kun-dga' bzang-po (1382–1456) and Paṇ-chen Śākya mchog-ldan. The lineage of the "Madhyamaka tradition" (*dbu ma lugs*) of the Bodhisattva vows goes back to Kun-spangs Chos-kyi nyi-ma (1449–1524), and that of the "Yogācāra" (*sems tsam lugs*) back to Blo-gros bzang-po, both of whom were his teachers at Thub-bstan gSer-mdog-can.

'dod dgu 'byung ba / 'khor dang longs spyod phun sum tshogs pa lhun grub du 'byung ba'i gnas ban tshang lung pa'i dbus / 'bur du dod pa ne lung zhes bya bar sku 'khrungs so. An earlier teacher, who was also born in Ban-tshang, was the famous Jo-nang-pa Dol-po-pa Shes-rab rgyal-mtshan (1292–1361).

[20] For the family of rNam-grol bzang-po and his life up to his eighteenth year, see bSod-nams blo-gros (as in note 19), pp. 18.2–22.3. The ordination of Padma dbang-rgyal in bSam-grub gling in 1511 is mentioned in Padma 'phrin las (as in note 8), p. 315.1. A further reference to bSam-grub gling as the residence of Glo-bo mkhan-chen can be found in Jackson (1984:136); it is also said to be the place of his death (oral communication from D. P. Jackson).

rNam-grol bzang-po's studies of the mantras of the old and the new schools are not described in any great detail. We learn only that he studied under a large number of teachers and was able to keep all his commitments intact. The next three chapters of the biography are ordered according to the principles of "exhaustive investigation" (*mtha' dpyad pa*) through "hearing" (*thos pa*) and "reflecting on" (*bsam pa*) the Buddhist teaching, and finally its "practice as a spiritual experience" (*bsgom pa nyams len gyi tshul*). It is especially in the final two chapters that we are provided more information about rNam-grol bzang-po's teachers. The chapter on "hearing" lists only a summary of his studies in Prajñāpāramitā, Pramāṇa, Vinaya and Madhyamaka, and then describes his first teaching experiences in dPal-ldan Sa-skya and dPal-'khor bDe-chen in Upper Nyang (i.e. Gyantse).[21]

The first person mentioned in the chapter on "reflecting" is the "madman of Central Tibet" (*dbus smyon*), Kun-dga' bzang-po (1458–1532). rNam-grol bzang-po classified the teachings he received from this teacher under the headings "cycle of the way of release" (*grol lam gyi skor*) and "cycle of the way of method" (*thabs lam gyi skor*). The first group comprises such Mahāmudrā teachings as the *Phyag rgya chen po lhan cig skyes sbyor* and the *Phyag rgya chen po yi ge bzhi pa*; the second group consists of such teachings as the "six doctrines" (*chos drug*) of the 'Ba'-ra-ba bKa'-brgyud-pa, the *Ras chung snyan brgyud* and instructions of "inner heat" (*gtum mo*). The actual practice of these transmissions follows roughly the same order as listed before.[22]

The following two teachers are connected again with the monastery of Thub-bstan gSer-mdog-can. The first one we know of only under the name Sems-dpa' chen-po. rNam-grol bzang-po received the *sādhana*s of the Sa-skya-pa school from him. "Instructions for the practice of Mahākāruṇika" (*Thugs rje chen po'i dmar khrid*) are mentioned alongside works of Ngor-chen Kun-dga' bzang-po. Judging by the number of teachings received and the details of the different accounts, rNam-grol bzang-po's most important teacher for the transmissions of the Sa-skya-pa school was Kun-spangs Chos-kyi nyi-ma. A separate study

---

21 See bSod-nams blo-gros (as in note 19), pp. 22.3–29.3 for the further education of rNam-grol bzang-po and his studies at Thub-bstan gSer-mdog-can. Perhaps it should be mentioned that the second monastery of the Sa-skya-pa school which attracted students from the Mustang and Dolpo regions was rTa-nag Thub-bstan rnam-rgyal, founded by Go-rams-pa bSod-nams seng-ge (1425–1489). It was the training ground for both O-rgyan dpal-bzang (see note 16) and O-rgyan bstan-'dzin (see note 18). The third possibility was, of course, the monastery of Ngor E-waṃ Chos-ldan, founded in 1429 by Ngor-chen Kun-dga' bzang-po. It was in the latter that bSod-nams blo-gros began his training under the tenth abbot, dKon-mchog lhun-grub (1497–1557); see Snellgrove (1967=1992:86f.).

22 An account of the contact with dBus-smyon Kun-dga' bzang-po and the list of teachings can be found in bSod-nams blo-gros (as in note 19), pp. 29.3–34.3. The name of this teacher comes up when rNam-grol bzang-po instructs his disciple bSod-nams blo-gros in the "six doctrines"; see Snellgrove (1967=1992:102), and the Tibetan text in Chos-skyabs dpal-bzang (as in note 8), pp. 86.2–89.1. For a biography of dBus-smyon, see Ngag-dbang grags-pa: *rJe btsun kun dga' bzang po'i rnam par thar pa ris med dad pa'i spu long g.yo byed*. In it a visit to Thub-bstan gSer-mdog-can and a meeting with Paṇ-chen Śākya mchog-ldan are recorded; ibid, fol. 79a/1–b/1 & fol. 105a/3–b/1.

would be required to identify and analyze the various cycles that were imparted to the student from Dolpo by his master. We merely mention the fact that the list starts with the following two items: "Sixty teachings from the [Lam 'bras] 'Yellow Book'" (*po ti ser mo nas byung ba'i chos sna drug bcu*) and "Thirty-two teachings from the [Lam 'bras] 'Red Book'" (*po ti dmar po nas byung ba'i yi ge sna sum bcu rtsa gnyis*).

This brings us to the next teacher in the chapter on "reflecting": rJe-btsun dam-pa Kun-dga' grol-mchog (1507–1566). The teachings received from this master, who was a native of northern Mustang and eventually became the head of Jo-nang monastery, commence with a similar statement: *glegs bam nang bzhugs chos sna drug bcu*. Here again, it is impossible to deal with all the different teachings that were received. Let me simply state that the list ends with the cycles of s*Byor drug* (as transmitted by Dol-po-pa Shes-rab rgyal-mtshan), the *U rgyan bsnyen sgrub*, a set of teachings originating from Grub-chen O-rgyan-pa (1230–1309) and, again, the *Ras chung snyan brgyud*.[23] An interesting reference is to be found afterwards: Kun-dga' grol-mchog turned the wheel of the Dharma extensively in Bar-bong. The latter is the valley of Bar-rong to the south of Dolpo, through which there was a route connecting the Muktināth Valley and Jumla.

The chapter ends with two further teachers, and it is possible to identify at least one of them. He bears the epithet sTod-yul dam-pa, "the noble one from Upper [Tibet]". As the list of teachings contains the cycles *Thugs sgrub sngon po*, *'Gro ba kun grol* and *'Khor ba gdong sprugs,* the person in question must be mNga'-ris Paṇ-chen Padma dbang-rgyal, the rNying-ma-pa teacher of rNam-grol bzang-po. Finally, one Drin-can 'phags-pa is mentioned. Among other things, he gave Mahāmudrā teachings (*Phyag rgya chen po lnga ldan*) according to the system of the Tshal-pa bKa'-brgyud-pa.[24]

The application of the teachings to spiritual experience is the subject of the next chapter of the biography. In it rNam-grol bzang-po relates visions and other episodes that are signs of his accomplishments in the cycles he was initiated into. The distinction is made between the "cycle of the new secret mantras" (*gsang sngags gsar ma'i skor*) and the

---

23 For Sems-dpa' chen-po and Kun-spangs Chos-kyi nyi-ma, and the teachings transmitted by them, see bSod-nams blo-gros (as in note 19), pp. 34.3–35.2 and pp. 35.2–42.5; the section on Kun-dga' grol-mchog follows directly, ibid, pp. 42.5–49.5. I have described in a separate paper Kun-dga' grol-mchog's contacts with Indian yogins of the Naṭeśvarī branch at the holy site of Muktināth; see Ehrhard (1993b:24f.) and chapter twelve in the present volume. A short biography of Kun-dga' grol-mchog was filmed by the NGMPP under reel no. L 121/4: *rJe rtsun (= btsun) 'jam pa'i (= dpal) dbyangs kun dga' grol 'chog (= mchog) rnam thar ngo 'tshar (= mtshar)*, 26 fols.

24 See bSod-nams blo-gros (as in note 19), pp. 49.5–52.1 and p. 52.1–4 for the last two teachers. It should be pointed out that the teachings of the bKa'-brgyud-pa school received by rNam-grol bzang-po are specified on two occasions as being those of the 'Ba'-ra-ba and the Tshal-pa subsects. In this case, too, I would argue the need to consider the existence of the "spiritual centre" Mang-yul Gung-thang to be at least partly responsible for the continuation of these "minor traditions" up to the 16th century. One stronghold of the 'Ba'-ra-ba was, for example, Grwa-phu chos-gling near sKyid-grong, while rTa-sga dgon in Nub-ris had a strong impact on the presence of the Tshal-pa in western Tibet.

"cycle of the old secret mantras" (*gsang sngags rnying ma'i skor*). The first part is relatively short. Mention is made of the teachings he mastered in their full scope, and then two visions are taken special note of: those of Hevajra and of Cakrasaṃvara. In addition, several *yi dam*s (Vajrayoginī and others) appeared in his dreams.

The second part, in contrast gives detailed information on several episodes in the life of rNam-grol bzang-po that were directly connected with his spiritual practice of the teachings of Padmasambhava. It is now that the treasure works of Rig-'dzin rGod-ldem 'phru-can make their influence felt again—the *Thugs sgrub rnam gsum*, the "outer, inner and secret" *sādhana*s of the Byang-gter tradition. The signs indicating the successful practice of these teachings are given in the words of mNga'-ris Paṇ-chen Padma dbang-rgyal, whom rNam-grol bzang-po looked upon as being no different from Padmasambhava himself. This teacher also gave a prophecy to his disciple on how hindrances during the practice would be dissolved immediately.[25]

The life of rNam-grol bzang-po as represented in the transmission of the teachings he received in his early years, and in their practice later on, thus documents the presence of different schools of Tibetan Buddhism in Dolpo (and Mustang): the bKa'-brgyud-pa, the Sa-skya-pa, the Jo-nang-pa and the rNying-ma-pa. It is a good example of "the eclecticism that flourished in the Nepalese borderlands during the 15th and 16th centuries."[26] The influence rNam-grol bzang-po had on the tradition of dMar-sgom can be judged by the fact that his disciple bSod-nams blo-gros studied under him for twenty-five years. To trace the different traditions that shaped this teacher-disciple relationship would entail investigating the biographies translated by Snellgrove once again in more detail.[27]

---

25 The chapter *bsgom pa nyams len gyi tshul* covers pp. 53.1–86.3 in bSod-nams blo-gros (as in note 19). Here I have given only a brief résumé of the contents up to p. 68.5 (spiritual songs, of course, are not included). There follows a section in which bSod-nams blo-gros asks his teacher to identify his previous incarnations. Two are revealed: rNam-grol bzang-po was Bla-chen rGyal-ba bzang-po, a disciple of 'Ba'-ra-ba rGyal-mtshan dpal-bzang-po (1310–1391), in one previous lifetime, and after that he came back as Chos-kyi rgyal-mtshan, a student of Padma gling-pa (1450–1521).

26 See Jackson (1984:19), quoting E. G. Smith; and the continuation: "... that the religious developments in Dolpo in that period should be understood 'within the broader picture of the trends that were also predominant in the richer Mustang and throughout south-western Tibet'."

27 The biography of rNam-grol bzang-po (as in note 19) was concluded by bSod-nams blo-gros in the year 1573; for the period of studies under rNam-grol bzang-po, see ibid, p. 100.5 (*lo nyi shu rtsa lnga'i bar du zhabs kyi pad mo sten pa ...*). A slightly shorter period is given in Chos-skyabs dpal-bzang (as in note 8), p. 90.1f. (*dam pa de nyid rang lo sum bcu rtsa gsum pa la zhal mjal nas / lnga bcu rtsa lnga'i bar du bsten ...*); compare Snellgrove (1967=1992:103). His translation—"I first met this holy lama when he was 33 years old, and I stayed with him until he was 55"—must be corrected; bSod-nams blo-gros studied with rNam-grol bzang-po from his own thirty-third year up to his fifty-fifth year (i.e. 1548–1570). The not overly enthusiastic reception of the *Four Lamas of Dolpo* (by the general public) is reflected by Skorupski (1990): "... but the reasons for its uniqueness appear also to be the reasons for its being the least known of his writings." Its not being used as a reference work for matters dealing with the presence of the Byang-gter tradition in Nepal is exemplified in Boord (1993:33); the same applies to Samuel (1993:323–325).

Appendices

sPrang bhan (= ban) ngag dbang rnam rgyal bdag gi zab chos kyi thob yig dgos 'dod kun 'byung

A: fols. 5b/3–6a/5:

de msthams 'dren mchog dam pa dpal ldan don 'grub (= grub) kyi zhabs drung nas // dpal dmar sgom chos kyi rgyal po chos skyabs dpal bzang yab sras kyi ring lugs // myang nyi ma 'od zer kyi gter ma // gu ru che mchog drag po dmar po dang // dpal mgon phyag bzhi pa gnyis kyi dbang grub (= sgrub) thabs las byang dang bcas pa'i lung rnams legs par thob pa'i brgyud pa ni / chos sku snang ba mtha' yas // longs sku thugs rje chen po // sprul sku padma 'byung gnas // mkha' 'gro ye shes mtsho rgyal // mnga' bdag khri srong lde btsan // mnga' bdag sangs rgyas sras chung // zur ston rin chen rgyal mtshan // stogs (= rtogs) ldan chos nyid rang grol // bla ma sangs rgyas lhun dbang // sprul sku kun dga' bkra shis // mkhas grub rgyal sras chos rje // sngags 'chang legs pa dpal bzang // sprul sku myang ston chos dbang // mkhas grub rin chen dpal bzang // 'dren mchog 'jam dbyangs dpal bzang // mkhas btsun tshul khrims dpal bzang // mnyam med padma dbang rgyal // 'phags pa blo gros dbang phyug // yongs 'dzin bsod nams blo gros // 'dren mchog chos skyabs dpal bzang // byang sems grol mchog dbang // mkhas btsun nam mkha' rgyal mtshan // 'tshungs (= mtshungs) med dpal ldan don 'grub (= grub) // des bdag ngag dbang rnam rgyal la'o //

B: fols. 6a/5–b3, and 6b/3–7a/2

yang rig pa 'dzin pa dngos grub rgyal mtshan gyi gter ma // phyi grub (= sgrub) 'gro ba kun grol (= sgrol) zhal cig phyag bzhi pa'i dbang grub (= sgrub) thabs rnams legs par thob pa'i rgyud (= brgyud) pa ni // snang ba mtha' yas tshe dpag med mgon // spyan ras gzigs // padma 'byung // sku mchog rnam lnga // dngos grub rgyal mtshan // sangs rgyas bstan pa // sangs rgyas byams bzang // chos rgyal bsod nams // śākya bzang po // padma dbang rgyal // blo gros 'od zer // shes rab rgyal mtshan // bsod nams blo gros // chos skyabs dpal bzang // nam mkha' rgyal mtshan // rtsa ba'i bla ma dpal ldan don 'grub (= grub) // des bdag ngag dbang rnam rgyal la'o //

yang rigs (= rig) 'dzin dngos grub rgyal mtshan gyi gsang grub (= sgrub) gu ru sngon po'i dbang grub (= sgrub) thabs las byang dang bcas pa legs par thob pa'i rgyud (= brgyud) pa ni // chos sku kun bzang // rdo rje sems dpa'i (= dpa') // dga' rab rdo rje // śrī sing ha // padma 'byung gnas // ye shes mtsho rgyal // dngos grub rgyal mtshan // rnam rgyal mgon po // bsod nams bzang po // dpal ldan rgyal mtshan // rgyal mtshan bum pa // bya btang bsam rgyal // dpa ldan seng ge // dkon mchog skyabs // padma dbang rgyal // blo gros dbang phyug // bsod nams blo gros // chos skyabs dpal bzang // nam mkha' rgyal mtshan // rtsa ba'i bla ma dpal ldan don 'grub (= grub) // des bdag ngag dbang rnam rgyal la'o //

C: fols. 7a/2–6

yang gu ru chos dbang gi gter kha'i thugs rje chen po yang snying 'dus pa'i skor // 'khor ba gdong krugs (= sprugs) kyi dbang grub (= sgrub) thabs dang bcas pa legs par thob pa'i rgyud (= brgyud) pa ni // snang ba mtha' yas // thugs rje chen po // padma 'byung gnas // khri srong lde btsan // gu ru chos dbang // padma dbang chen // chos kyi rgyal mtshan // sangs rgyas kun grol // chos kyi rdo rje // don yod rgyal po // nor bu 'dzin pa // gshes (= bshes) gnyen nor bu // chos kyi gshes (= bshes) gnyen // nor bu bsam 'phel // śākya bzang po // padma dbang rgyal // rnam grol bzang po // bsod nams blo gros // chos skyabs dpal bzang // nam mkha' rgyal mtshan // rtsa ba'i bla ma dpal ldan don grub // des bdag la'o //

Sa-'dul dgon-pa:
A Temple at the Crossroads of Jumla, Dolpo and Mustang

The last three of his fourteen Himalayan expeditions brought Giuseppe Tucci (1894–1984) to Nepal and its north-western districts. The expedition in the year 1954 retraced the route from Pokhara to the northern part of Mustang—which Tucci had already covered in 1952—and took him afterwards to the region of Jumla. There he discovered the genealogical records of the Malla kings, once the rulers over a territory covering both the western parts of Nepal and the Tibetan regions of Purang and Guge.

On his way to Jumla, Tucci passed through the southern fringes of Dolpo and came across several religious edifices, about which he noted the following:

> Before reaching Pale one sees to the left of the Tarāpkhola the *bSam 'dul dgon pa* (on the map Chhandul Gompa): other small shrines are in the valley of the Bārbung kholā: *bDe c'en dpal ri* and *'Bri gung dgon pa.*[1]

Concerning the first site this information can be supplemented by the description of a fellow traveller, David Snellgrove, who paid a visit to the area two years later, i.e. in 1956:

> Sandul Monastery (SI: Chhandul Gömpa) is about five miles beyond Tārakot and stands at the junction of the Beri and the stream that descends from Tarap. Thus one has to cross the Bheri to reach the temple; the tracks lead down by crazy steps through the rocks to a tree-trunk bridge which spans a deep and narrow gorge. All the rocks are incised with the spell OṂ MAṆI PADME HŪṂ and one feels as though one were to enter some hidden idyllic valley, of which Tibetans love to tell, where men and animals live in peace and harmony.[2]

---

1 See Tucci (1956:37, note 1) and the attached map (see plate 1). This publication contains the results of Tucci's expeditions of 1952 and 1954. A popular version of the discovery of the historical records of the Malla kingdom is Tucci (1962). For an overview of the genealogy of the royal house—its last and most powerful ruler being Pṛthvīmalla (reign 1338–1358)—and remarks on Tucci's reconstruction of the origins of the Mallas, compare Sharma (1972:17–20 and 40f.). See also Klimburg-Salter (1991) for the different research expeditions of Tucci in the Himalayan regions.

2 Snellgrove (1961a=1989:39). A description of the temple itself can be found ibid, p. 40: "There are

The general state of decay and abandonment of temples and sanctuaries in the region of Tichurong around the upper course of the Bheri River, which bears the name Barbung near to its source north of the Dhaulāgiri, was some years later reconfirmed by the observations of Corneille Jest. But in the case of Sa-'dul dgon-pa (and the 'Bri-gung dgon-pa, lying further south-west, high above the Bheri), there were also signs that Buddhist traditions were being revitalized and religious shrines were being kept intact. These activities resulted from the enthusiasm of one Bla-ma in particular: the so-called Shangs Rin-po-che (died 1958).[3] Later the temple fell again into disrepair, and today only the inner sanctum at the rear side of the building reminds the visitor of earlier times when this site attracted pilgrims and religious dignitaries who were on their way to Jumla, Dolpo, Mustang and the regions beyond (see picture I).

As the history of the spread of Tibetan Buddhism in Tichurong / Barbung is still little documented and as this area lies halfway between the political and cultural centres of Jumla and Mustang, being traversed by one of the old Himalayan trade routes, I think it worthwhile to present here some recently discovered materials on Sa-'dul dgon-pa. The main historical guidelines are provided by the collection of spiritual songs of O-rgyan bstan-'dzin (1657–1737), which are structured around the principle events of his life. It was this teacher of the rNying-ma-pa school who brought Sa-'dul dgon-pa to new glory at the turn of the 17th and 18th centuries, and his name is still remembered among the people of Dolpo as one of their spiritual forefathers.

1. EDUCATION AND TRAVELS OF O-RGYAN BSTAN-'DZIN

The main teacher of O-rgyan bstan-'dzin and the one who ordained him and gave him his religious name was O-rgyan dpal-bzang (1617–1677), a native of southern Mustang and founder of the monastery sKu-tshab gter-lnga near present-day Thini. His ordination took place in the year 1668, and the location where the teacher and his disciple came together

---

traces of older building in some carved wooden beams, which display more expert craftsmanship, and one can see the stone foundations of other buildings behind the present temple, indicating that this site must once have been of far greater importance ... It is apparent that this temple receives little or no support nowadays."

3 See Jest (1971:75): "Ce qu'il faut souligner toute fois avec Snellgrove, c'est l'aspect d'abandon que l'on remarque dans les temples et les sanctuaires, aspect qui s'est encore accentué ces dernières années; le lama de Shang a bien essayé de redonner vie à la religion bouddhique en 1954–55 ...". Cf. Jest (1975:308): "Shang Rinpoche a séjourné cinq mois à Tichurong en 1951, les onzième et douzième mois à *sa-'dul dgon-pa*, les premier, deuxième et troisième à *'bri-guṅ*. Il a fait remettre en état les deux temples, redresser les chörten en ruines, recrépir et décorer les constructions élevées par le roi de Jumla. Le lama de Shang avait prédit qu'il construirait ou reconstruirait quatorze temples. Les deux derniers sont ceux de *sa-'dul* et de *'bri-guṅ*." On the rebuilding of Sa-'dul dgon-pa and 'Bri-gung dgon-pa by Shangs Rin-po-che and his travels in Mustang, Nyi-shang and sNar, cf. also Snellgrove (1961a=1989:37, 39f. and passim). The mummified corpse of the Bla-ma is still kept in northern Dolpo, as narrated by Jest (1985:140–147).

was called Kun-bzang brag. This name refers to a spot near sKag[-rdzong], the settlement next to Sa-'dul dgon-pa in the eastern direction.[4]

Following the advice of his teacher, O-rgyan bstan-'dzin proceeded at the age of seventeen to Central Tibet and took up his studies at the Sa-skya-pa monastery rTa-nag Thub-bstan rnam-rgyal. After visits to lHa-sa and bSam-yas, his return trip led him via Ding-ri and sNya-lam to the Kathmandu Valley and also to sKyid-grong and its holy mountain Ri-bo dpal-'bar. From the masters he met in the region of sKyid-grong, I would like to mention at least a certain rGyal-dbang seng-ge (born 1628); from him O-rgyan bstan-'dzin received the teachings of the treasure cycles of Rig-'dzin 'Ja'-tshon snying-po (1585–1656).[5]

Returning to his homeland—during his travels O-rgyan bstan-'dzin was once called "the man from the region of Dolpo"—he continued his studies under two further teachers. The first one was Bla-ma Thub-bstan dbang-po and the second, Bla-ma dPal-ldan rdo-rje. It is known from their respective biographies that Thub-bstan dbang-po was a follower of the 'Brug-pa bKa'-brgyud-pa school who had received teachings from the Fifth 'Brug-chen dPag-bsam dbang-po (1593–1641), and that dPal-ldan rdo-rje was a Sa-skya-pa master affiliated with the monastery of Hrab in northern Dolpo.[6]

---

4 For general information concerning O-rgyan dpal-bzang and the founding of the monastery of sKu-tshab gter-lnga, see Snellgrove (1979:79–81). The ordination of O-rgyan bstan-'dzin occurred on O-rgyan dpal-bzang's journey to the area of Barbung preceding the actual foundation of sKu-tshab gter-lnga in 1668; compare the data in Ehrhard (1993c) and chapter thirteen in the present volume. A second disciple of O-rgyan dpal-bzang who had received his religious name in Kun-bzang brag was Kun-bzang klong-yangs (1644–1699). A scion of the ruling family of sKag[-rdzong] in Barbung—not to be confused with Kagbeni, at the confluence of the Kāli Gaṇḍakī and Muktināth rivers—he eventually became the successor of O-rgyan dpal-bzang at sKu-tshab gter-lnga. For a description of this teacher's visit to sKag[-rdzong] and the spot Kun-bzang brag, see his autobiography: *rTogs brjod mu tig gi mchun bu (= chun po) zhes pa'i gtam*, fols. 16b/6–17b/3. A manuscript from sKag[-rdzong] was purchased by Tucci; see id. (1956:15).

5 For presenting the main events in the life of O-rgyan bstan-'dzin, I follow O-rgyan bstan-'dzin: *rNal 'byor gyi dbang phyug o rgyan bstan 'dzin zhes bya ba'i ri khrod kyi nyams dbyangs*, 227 fols., n.p., n.d.; for the period up to the stay in the area of sKyid-grong, see ibid, pp. 7.3–13.5. The text O-rgyan bstan-'dzin: *sPrang rgan o rgyan bstan 'dzin pa'i rnam thar bsdus pa*, 133 fols. (incomplete), NGMPP reel no. L187/3; 157 fols., reel no. L 206/3; 95 fols., reel no. L 220/4 was written by the author in his seventieth year upon the request of his disciples to produce a condensed version of the first work; cf. ibid, pp. 5.3–19.4 for the journey just mentioned.

The teacher rGyal-dbang seng-ge was one of the main disciples of Karma Blo-bzang, "resident" (*gnas 'dzin pa*) of the religious site Brag-dkar rta-so to the north-east of sKyid-grong. He was also in contact with O-rgyan dpal-bzang and Kun-bzang klong-yangs; see *Rigs brgya dbang po 'dren mchog slob dpon dpal bzang po'i rnam par thar pa*, fol. 314a/2–3, and the text mentioned in note 4, fol. 39b/2–4. In the year 1665 rGyal-dbang seng-ge wrote the biography of his father 'Od-zer rgya-mtsho (1574–1661): *Bya btang 'od zer rgya mtsho'i rnam thar*.

6 For Thub-bstan dbang-po, see *Bla ma rin po che sbas pa'i rnal 'byor pa chen po thub bstan dbang po'i rnams (= rnam) thar ngo tshar (= mtshar) smad (= rmad) 'byung (= byung)*, 31 fols. (incomplete),

Having completed this training in his twenty-fourth year (1681), O-rgyan bstan-'dzin pondered the question whether he should continue the studies of "the *Tantra*s of the system of the new [translations]" (*gsar ma lugs kyi rgyud*) and proceed a second time to Central Tibet, or stick to "the teaching of the old [translations]" (*rnying ma lugs kyi chos*) in the way he was instructed before. At that time a vision of Ye-shes mtsho-rgyal occurred to him and the divine lady uttered the following words: "You, son, are you not a priest of U-rgyan Padma[sambhava]? If you want the siddhis, [why] don't you go to request the teaching from Rig-'dzin Gar-dbang rdo-rje?" After more visionary experiences, and in the end asking his teacher dPal-ldan rdo-rje for leave, O-rgyan bstan-'dzin set out again for the region of sKyid-grong. After barely escaping death on a high pass because of heavy snowfall for three days, he finally reached the place called mNyam in the region of sKu-thang; and there, at "the Site of the Guru's (= Padmasambhava's) Spiritual Practices" (*gu ru'i sgrub gnas*), in a cave bearing the name Shel-phug, he met Rig-'dzin Gar-dbang rdo-rje (1640–1685) in person. The main teachings he received from the "treasure-discoverer" (*gter ston*) concerned the treasure-work *Zab tig chos dbyings rang gsal*, and there has survived a commentary which O-rgyan bstan-'dzin composed at a later time to a part of this cycle.[7]

Following the admonitions of the so-called mNga'-ris gter-ston to live in "solitary places (which are) hermitages" (*ri khrod dben gnas*) for progress in his spiritual discipline, O-rgyan bstan-'dzin afterwards devoted his time fully to the teachings of the newly discovered treasure-cycle. The next major event in his life was the death of Thub-bstan dbang-po in his twenty-ninth year, i.e. in 1686. With the aim of getting manufactured a proper "receptacle for the relics" (*gdung rten*) of his deceased teacher, O-rgyan bstan-'dzin directed his steps towards the valley of Kathmandu and brought back a magnificent statue of Padmasambhava. He was able to erect a temple for housing the image on the spot where

---

NGMPP reel no. L 123/2. Concerning the founding of a monastic settlement in Hrab by dPal-ldan blo-gros (1527–1596), see Snellgrove (1967:11). A further teacher associated with this site by the name of dPal-ldan bzang-po is known as well; see ibid, p. 241. For the writings of dPal-ldan rdo-rje, see the texts mentioned in Ehrhard (1996a, note 5) and chapter nineteen in the present volume. This period in the life of O-rgyan bstan-'dzin can be found in *Nyams dbyangs* (as in note 5), pp. 13.5–20.1.

[7] See *Nyams dbyangs* (as in note 5), p. 20.4, for the quote (*bu khyod u rgyan padma'i btsun pa ma yin nam / dngos grub 'dod na rig 'dzin gar dbang rdo rje la chos zhu ru mi 'gro'am*), and ibid, pp. 23.4–26.4, for the detailed account of his stay with the treasure-discoverer. It should be mentioned that O-rgyan dpal-bzang had visited Rig-'dzin Gar-dbang rdo-rje as well in the cave Shel-phug north of the Manaslu region with the aim of inspecting some of the findings of the treasure-discoverer; see Ehrhard (1993c) and chapter thirteen in the present volume.

Another teacher from Dolpo who had studied directly under Rig-'dzin Gar-dbang rdo-rje—in the year 1679—was Ngag-dbang rnam-rgyal (born 1628) from gNam-gung; on him and the teachings received, see Ehrhard (1996a) and chapter nineteen in the present volume. The commentary written by O-rgyan bstan-'dzin bears the title *bKa' rdzogs pa chen po zab tig chos dbyings rang gsal las phyag rgya chen po gnyug ma gcer mthong gi khrid*.

Thub-bstan dbang-po had had his living-quarters; this temple he called bDe-chen rDzong-gi lha-khang, and it served him as residence for the years to come. This temple is known still today under the name bDe-chen dpal-ri and is located to the south-east of Sa-'dul dgon-pa in the village Tangchen/Tachen, on the opposite side of the Bheri River.[8]

Finally, O-rgyan bstan-'dzin received teachings from Kun-bzang klong-yangs, the successor of O-rgyan dpal-bzang at sKu-tshab gter-lnga and his senior by thirteen years. Besides the reading of the biography of their common teacher, special mention is made of the treasure-cycles of Rig-'dzin gTer-bdag gling-pa (1646–1714). Just shortly before this encounter, in 1688, Kun-bzang klong-yangs had stayed in the presence of this treasure-discoverer at sMin-grol gling in Central Tibet. He had been well received there and had spent a period of altogether eight months at sMin-grol gling.[9]

2. RESTORATIONS OF SA-'DUL DGON-PA AND THEIR SPONSORS

With the year 1690 we come finally to the temple that is the subject of the present investigation. Obviously the building and the sacred items housed there were already at that time not well-kept:

See plate 2

---

8 See *Nyams dbyangs* (as in note 5), pp. 34.3–35.2, for the death of Thub-bstan dbang-po and the construction of the temple. In *O rgyan bstan 'dzin rnam thar* (as in note 5), p. 21.5–6, these events are condensed to three lines: *gdung brten (= rten) bzhengs ru (= bzheng du) bal du phyin / o rgyan sku nang gdung rnams bzhugs / da lta de (= bde) chen dpal rir bzhugs*. The biography of Thub-bstan dbang-po provides the information that this teacher was born in gTang-byon, on the borderline between Tibet and the gorges (*bod rong gnyis kyi so (= sa) mtshams*).

The epithet "temple of the fortress" (*rdzong gi lha khang*) suggests that the religious services held there were connected with the ruling family of sKag[-rdzong]. I suppose that the toponyms sTeng-shog / bTang-shog are alternative spellings for gTang-byon and thus refer to the same locality. The first spelling can be found in the biography of O-rgyan dpal-bzang and refers there to the spot from where the people came who attended the teachings during his stay in sKag[-rdzong]; see the text *Rigs brgya dbang po 'dren mchog slob dpon dpal bzang po'i rnam par thar pa*, fols. 315b/6–316a/1 (*... steng shog lung gang gi gra (= grwa) rigs thams cad 'dus nas*). According to the biography of Kun-bzang klong-yangs it was from bTang-shog that Karma Blo-bzang, the "resident" of Brag-dkar rta-so, was invited to sKag[-rdzong]; see the text (as in note 4), fol. 10a/6–b/1 (*rims (= rim) can btang shog lung bar spyan 'dren zhus khyad par bdag gis (= gi) pha dang a khu tshos skag rdzong du spyan 'dren zhu dus*). Karma Blo-bzang was the founder of gNam-gung in northern Dolpo; see Ehrhard (1993c, note 10) and chapter thirteen in the present volume.

9 For the studies with Kun-bzang klong-yangs, see *Nyams dbyangs* (as in note 5), pp. 38.1–42.3; cf. *O rgyan bstan 'dzin rnam thar* (as in note 5), pp. 22.1–3. In the biography of Kun-bzang klong-yangs (as in note 4), fols. 66a/4–67a/5, the study period is described in still greater detail; it was resumed in Kun-bzang brag near sKag[-rdzong] during conditions of extreme winter cold. For the visit of Kun-bzang klong-yangs to the monastery of sMin-grol gling and his studies with Rig-'dzin gTer-bdag gling-pa, see ibid, fols. 57b/3–65b/1. These data for the year 1688 are confirmed by the biography of the treasure-discoverer; see *gTer chen chos kyi rgyal po'i rnam thar dad pa'i shing rta*, pp. 314.6; 315.6 and 316.6. He is referred to there under the name Glo-bo bla-ma Kun-bzang klong-yangs or Glo-bo-pa Kun-bzang klong-yangs.

> Now, at the time of my thirty-fourth year, the *Bhūpala*, the ruler, the king of Jumla, Bhi-ri-sras [by name], as he had issued the strong request to renovate the *vihāra* of Sa-'dul, I restored the three inner sanctums and erected representations (i.e. statues) of Mahāmuni, O-rgyan Rin-po-che (i.e. Buddha Śākyamuni and Padmasambhava), and others. What amounted to a *zho* [of silver] from the king [of Jumla] himself, what amounted to a *zho* [of silver] from the ruler of Mustang, bSam-grub dpal-'bar [by name], and furthermore, what all the monastic community and commoners had brought together—great things [like] horses and yaks, and small things [like] white-wash (?)—when it [all] had been brought together and offered, the receptacles were set up [by me].[10]

A closer look should now be taken at the sponsors who are highlighted in this quotation. The identification of the king of Jumla poses some problems, as the name Bhi-ri-sras is a transliteration of a vernacular and can be interpreted in different ways (and thus made to apply to different historical persons). Given the fact that Tib. *sras* is the phonetic rendering of Nep. *śāhi*—as attested in a Tibetan document dated before the conquest of Jumla by Gorkha in the year 1789—we could hypothetically identify Bhi-ri-sras as one of the fourteen Śāhi or two Śāha kings of the Kallala dynasty of Jumla, who ruled the kingdom during the period from the 15th to 18th centuries.[11]

---

[10] *Nyams dbyangs* (as in note 5), p. 42.3–5: *yang rang lo so bzhi pa'i dus su / sa skyong mi'i dbang po 'dzum lang rgyal po bhi ri sras kyis / sa 'dul gyi gtsug lag khang gi zhig bsos* (= *gsos*) *byed dgos pa'i bka' nan ches pa'i btabs* (= *btab*) *kyis / gtsang khang gsum gyi zhig bsos* (= *gsos*) *dang / thub chen dang / o rgyan rin po che'i sku tshab sogs bzhengs pas / rgyal po rang gi zho gang / blo bo* (= *glo bo*) *sde pa bsam 'grub dpal 'bar gyi zho gang / gzhan yang skya ser kun gyi 'brel par / che ba rta dang g.yag / chung ba dkar cig* (= *rtsi*?) *gnyis kun gyi 'brel par phul nas rten bzhengs pas.* The funds for gilding the statues came from a man called gTang-byon-pa Yon-bdag bKra-shis phun-tshogs; see ibid, p. 43.3–6. He had also been the sponsor for the construction of the bDe-chen rDzong-gi lha-khang (see note 8).

[11] For the history of the Kallala dynasty which followed the royal house of the Mallas, see Pandey (1970) and (1971); the numbering of eleven kings whose names end with the suffix *rāj*, followed by the names of the fourteen Śāhi and the two Śāha kings can be found in Pandey (1970:45). The Tibetan document—a treatise between Jumla and Mustang—was edited and translated by Schuh (1994:69–78). We find there the names Big-ram-sras (= Vikramaśāhi) and Bir-bā-dhur-sras (= Vīrabahādurśāhi). The treatise opens by referring to the person of Balirāja, the founder of the Kallala dynasty (reign 1404–1445); see Schuh (1994:73).

It might be useful to point out that this name was used by Tibetan scholars generically to designate the ruler of this dynasty up to the 18th century. See Chos-kyi dbang-phyug: *dPal rig 'dzin chen po rdo rje tshe dbang nor bu'i zhabs kyi rnam par thar pa'i cha shas brjod pa ngo mtshar dad pa'i rol mtsho*, pp. 155.2–3: "... [this region,] which is part of India, [was ruled] in former times [by] the king of Ya-tshe (i.e. the Malla dynasty), and in his place, now, [by the ruler] called Balirāja. He puts faith in the philosophical teachings of the Tīrthikas and has brought twenty petty kingdoms under his rule. [This region] is known as Jumla ..." (*rgya gar yul gyi cha / sngon tshe ya tshe rgyal po'i shul / da lta bā* (= *ba*) *li rā tsa zhes / phyi rol grub mtha' la mos shing / rgyal phran nyi shur dbang bsgyur ba / 'dzum lang grags pa*).

The names Vikramaśāhi and Vīrabahādurśāhi might have served as possible candidates for the person of the Tibetan rendering Bhi-ri-sras, but their regnal years were 1602–1621 and 1635–1665 respectively, and thus they lived too early. A third candidate would be Vīrabhadraśāhi, but his reign (1665–1676) does not match the year of the renovation of Sa-'dul dgon-pa either. Nevertheless, an interesting detail of his kingship is that he ruled the country from Kakakot and Tibrikot. The first toponym I take to be identical with Tib. sKag-rdzong, the place in the vicinity of Sa-'dul dgon-pa which had provided residence for the teachers of the rNying-ma-pa and bKa'-brgyud-pa schools.[12]

If we turn now to the oral traditions of local kings in Tichurong, it is the person of Vīrabhadraśāhi—and especially his son—that are still remembered up to the present day. The name of this son is Vikram[a]śāh[i/a], and I take him to be the person who called for the renovation of Sa-'dul dgon-pa in the year 1690. This Vikramśāh (*Bhi-ri-sras*) can easily be confused with his predecessor of the same name (and this fact might have contributed to his local fame), but it is not only the name of Vikramśāh that still lives on in the region; a statue of the king also keeps his memory alive. This statue is kept in the inner sanctum of Sa-'dul dgon-pa and is a visible proof of the royal patronage of the site (see plate 3).[13]

The mention of a ruler of Mustang by the name of bSam-grub dpal-'bar comes as no surprise in the present context. We know from different sources that this ruler was very active in providing financial assistance to the Buddhist religion, and there exists a separate work describing his renovation of the Byams-pa lha-khang in Glo-bo smon-thang, the capital of Mustang, in the year 1663. That the temple at the crossroads of Jumla, Dolpo and Mustang was sponsored both by Vikramśāh and bSam-grub dpal-'bar can by implication be interpreted as a visible sign of the political (and cultural) dependence that tied Mustang to Jumla in the 17th and 18th centuries. This dependence must be taken into account when

---

12 Information concerning the rulers Vikramaśāhi, Vīrabahādurśāhi and Vīrabhadraśāhi is given by Pandey (1971:42–44 and 45f.). Compare also the following statement on the "castles" from which they wielded their rule: "... between A.D. 1599 and 1719, we find about ten kings of the dynasty who had ruled the Jumla valley from its various castles (*kots*). Either due to revolution or division of the property (state) ... each prince of the family had received a town along with the hills and the villages of its neighbourhood." (note: "The towns of late-medieval period in Western Nepal would not have been bigger than a modern village of the region."); ibid, pp. 42 and 58.

13 For the local traditions of Tichurong concerning king Vikram[a]śāh[i/a], see Fisher (1987:30): "... Bhadri Sah, who was in turn the father (by his Magar wife) of Vikram Sah, ... who is the only named historical figure generally remembered in Tichurong today. According to local legend, Vikram Sah ... was born in Yelakot ... below the Tichurong village of Gompa." On Yelakot/Yalakot as the old customs house before it was shifted downstream to Dunaih, see Fürer-Haimendorf (1975:208). Compare also Jest (1971:75): "Le seul personnage historique connu des Tichurong-pa est Bikram Saha ṭhakurī, roi de Jumla, qui a été le bienfaiteur des temples des *'bri-guṅ* et de *sa-'dul dgon-pa* où on conserve sa statue".

we deal with the history of religious structures in an area that is something of a border region between these two kingdoms.[14]

Concerning the actual renovation work, the fact is perhaps worth mentioning that felled trees were brought down from rTa-rong, i.e. the gorge of the Tarap Khola, by raft, but were in the end carried away by turbulent waters. About a thousand loads of wood had therefore to be transported to the "Plain of Sa-'dul" (*sa 'dul gyi thang*) by human labour. This should be sufficiently revealing of the first stage of restoring Sa-'dul dgon-pa, which obviously was initiated by royal orders.

The next years in the life of O-rgyan bstan-'dzin saw him mainly active at his residence in bTang-byon, the bDe-chen rDzong-gi lha-khang, and it was again the procuring of a further statue for this temple that made a second trip to the Kathmandu Valley necessary. There he paid a visit to the Svayambhūnāth Stūpa, ordered a statue of the future Buddha Maitreya from the artist Abhadeva in Patan, paid his respects to the Bodhnāth Stūpa, and held a *gaṇacakra*-feast at the top of the mountain Ri-bo 'big-byed, i.e. Jāmācok.[15]

At the age of forty-three, in the year 1700, O-rgyan bstan-'dzin assumed the task of a further renovation of Sa-'dul dgon-pa, this time not under official orders, it seems, but on his own. The three inner sanctums are mentioned again, along with the statues of Buddha Śākyamuni and Padmasambhava, and the difficulties of working at the spot because of an avalanche. In a spiritual song following the description of the different repair works, the "benefits of the sacred site" (*gnas kyi phan yon*) are praised by O-rgyan bstan-'dzin; he labelled this song an "inventory" (*dkar chag*) of the place. We can observe in it the process by which Sa-'dul dgon-pa and its wider surroundings are transformed into an idealized landscape and accorded at the same time the status of a "hidden land" (*sbas yul*). In the

---

14 In Jackson (1984:150) we find the following characteristic of bSam-grub dpal-'bar: "Everywhere, both within [Lo] and without, he sponsored the making of inconceivably many sacred images, books, and *stūpas*. Because he worshipped the [Three] Jewels with offerings, reverently served the monastic assembly, and was energetic in his meditations, he truly lived up to the name religious king." The text on the renovation of the Byams-pa lha-khang bears the title *rGyal ba'i rgyal tshab byams mgon gtso 'khor gsum gyi sku bsnyen la gzungs bzhugs kyi dkar chags dngos grub kun 'byung*, 22 fols., NGMPP reel no. L 143/2; for a first study of this text, cf. Gurung (1986).

The political dependency of Mustang upon Jumla in the 17th and 18th centuries has been dealt with by Schuh (1994:68–85). According to the material presented there, the sovereignty of Jumla over Mustang was firmly established by at least the reign of Vīrabahādurśāhi (i.e. the 1630s) and lasted around one hundred and fifty years.

15 For the mentioned detail of the renovation of 1690, see *Nyams dbyangs* (as in note 5), pp. 43.5–44.1: *yang shing chad pas rta rong nas chu log rgyugs pas / rta rong lung pa'i shing thams cad chu rud kyi* (= *kyis*) *khyer yongs pas / sa 'dul gyi thang la shing khur stong len rgyu byung ngo*. The visit to the Kathmandu Valley can be found in ibid, pp. 102.2–107.5. On the way back O-rgyan bstan-'dzin spent some time in "'Od-gsal sgang, the residence of my own teacher" (*rang gi bla ma'i gdan sa 'od gsal sgang*); this refers to the site of sKu-tshab gter-lnga in southern Mustang. There he came upon the two statues of Padmasambhava which were kept in "both the upper and lower monasteries" (*dgon pa yas mas gnyis*) and had been "the sacred objects" (*nang rten*) of Kun-bzang klong-yangs. Mention is also made of the

context of different schemes and names for classifying the area at the confluence of the Tarap Khola and the Bheri Khola, the fact emerges that the temple was originally founded by a certain Chos-rje Dar-pa, a siddha of the bKa'-brgyud-pa school.[16] The list of patrons opens with the names of the ruler of Mustang and the king of Jumla—followed by the local benefactors and their villages—and we can thus interpret also this second restoration of the temple as a visible sign of a specific political constellation in which Mustang was one of the petty states dominated by Jumla.

3. Later years and the visit of Kaḥ-thog rig-'dzin

It was again at his residence, the bDe-chen rDzong-gi lha-khang, that O-rgyan bstan-'dzin instructed his growing circle of disciples in the first years of the 18th century, using treasure-cycles like *Zab tig chos dbyings rang gsal* as the basic texts. On one occasion he made the noteworthy remark that the teachings of the "Great Perfection" (*rdzogs chen*) had in earlier times not reached the region of Dolpo. But this gets us ahead of the course of actual events. First we have to take note of the pilgrimage to the area of Mount Kailāśa and Lake Manosarowar in 1704 which was performed in the company of a group of his disciples. This intended "circumambulation of the snow mountain" (*gangs skor*) led O-rgyan bstan-'dzin first to the royal court of Jumla, where he received financial support from the kings of Jumla, including Mahārāja Vikramśāh (*Bhi-ri-sras*); such wording suggests that the power at the court was shared among different rulers at the time. Crossing the region of 'Om-lo lung—present-day Humla—he reached the sacred mountain and stayed at different places in the area, among them the famous cave known as rDzu-'phrul phug. His return took him via another route to the region of Sle-mi—present-day Limi—to the north-west of Dolpo, and there he paid a visit to a sacred mountain of some local renown, the so-called Shel-mo gangs.[17]

---

hermitage bearing the name Zom-bu ri in Sum-'bag; this toponym refers to present day Thini. For the stay of O-rgyan bstan-'dzin in sKu-tshab gter-lnga in the year 1699, see ibid, pp. 107.5–113.3.

[16] The renovation work in the year 1700 is described in *Nyams dbyangs* (as in note 5), pp. 125.5–134.4; for the difficulties to reach the spot, see ibid, p. 125.5 (*chu thags zhig thang la brtsugs pas dka' las shin tu che ba byung*). The text of the inventory can be found in ibid, pp. 126.4–129.4. The area in question is classified into an outer, inner and secret sacred site bearing the respective names Sa-'dul dgon-pa, O-rgyan byang-chub phan and Thar-pa rtse. This scheme is extended into a fivefold classification (*sku gnas / gsung gnas / thugs gnas / yon tan gnas / phrin las gnas*) by adding the names—and places—sTag-gyi rgyal-mtshan and rTa-gru dben-gnas.

Chos-rje Dar-pa is identified as a siddha who came from the Kailāśa area to the valley of Tichurong; he sacralized the site of Sa-'dul dgon-pa by depositing soil and stones from holy places in India, Nepal and Tibet. According to Jest (1971:75) and (1975:309), a certain Bla-ma Zla-ba seng-ge for the first time erected a temple on that spot; this statement is not confirmed by the present sources. For the "hidden valley" as a concept of religious space in southern Mustang, see Ehrhard (2001) and chapter thirteen in the present volume); cf. also Orofino (1991).

[17] For the remark on Dolpo, see *Nyams dbyangs* (as in note 5), p. 166.2 (*sprang po'i bsam pa la chos*

Passing Ting-kyu in upper Dolpo, O-rgyan bstan-'dzin then visited, for the first time, the valley of rTa-rab in the southern part of Dolpo—this at the invitation of the teachers and patrons from Me-skyems dgon-pa. The name of this monastery shows up several times more in his autobiographical works covering the years to come, and it was especially from it that the local tradition of the teachings of Padmasambhava spread further in that area.[18]

Nevertheless O-rgyan bstan-'dzin also continued his religious activities in Tichurong after having returned there. Eventually he gave way to urgent requests to become the "overseer" (*zhal bdag*) of 'Bri-gung dgon-pa, the temple on the lower course of the Bheri Khola above Yalakot. The fact that Vikramśāh, the local king in the line of Jumla rulers, had a special connection with 'Bri-gung dgon-pa is obvious from the two designations of the temple: it bears the name "the Jumla king's most excellent island of liberation" (*'dzum lang rgyal po'i thar pa gling mchog*) and—more prosaic—"monastery of king Bir" (*bir rgyal dgon pa*). It should also be remembered that according to the local tradition Vikramśāh was born in the village of Yalakot. O-rgyan bstan-'dzin thus attended to that religious edifice as well and finished his work with a proper act of consecration.

During the account of this period, the name bsTan-'dzin ras-pa (1644/46–1723) is mentioned, and we come to know that an exchange of letters took place between O-rgyan bstan-'dzin and this yogin of the 'Brug-pa bKa'-brgyud-pa school, who was a native of the Muktināth valley and the founder of Shel dgon-pa in upper Dolpo. This latter region was the destination of the next journey of O-rgyan bstan-'dzin. He met bsTan-'dzin ras-pa personally in Shel dgon-pa and performed afterwards the pilgrimage around the sacred mountain of Shel-gyi ri-bo ['brug-sgra], from which the monastery derived its name. Before the leg of the journey through the western part of upper Dolpo, the eastern part was traversed, and its inhabitants received public initiations from the priest. Two places are

---

rdzogs pa chen po 'di lngar (= *sngar*) *dol phyogs su ma dar ba yin te*). The description of the pilgrimage to the Kailāśa area can be found in ibid, pp. 178.3–198.1, containing the short data on the royal court of Jumla, ibid, p. 181.1–2 (*rgyal chen bhi ri sras sogs 'dzum lang rgyal po thams cad kyis mthun rkyen mdzad*).

Concerning the mountain Shel-mo gangs there exists a guidebook by a certain Padma dngos-grub: *gNas chen shel mo gangs gi dkar chags mthong ba rang grol*. For the contact of Zhabs-dkar Tshogs-drug rang-grol (1781–1851) with the people from this area of Limi and the sacred mountain, cf. Ricard (1994:308 and 321–328).

[18] The local historical tradition concerning rituals and religious beliefs of the rNying-ma-pa school in rTa-rab is described by Jest (1975:305): "Le rituel actuel et la forme donnée aux pratiques religieuses à Tarap sont l'oeuvre de lama *u-rgyan bstan-'jin*: originaire de la vallée de la Barbung, il a été surnommé *sta-bru u-rgyan bstan-'jin* parce qu'il a longtemps séjourné en méditation l'ermitage de *sta-bru* au Sud de Lang. Il appartenait à l'ordre des *rjogs-chen-pa*." For the relocation of Me-skyems dgon-pa to the valley of rTa-rab under Pha-rgod rTogs-ldan rgyal-po, see ibid, p. 308. This must have happened in the 17th century as O-rgyan bstan-'dzin mentions rTogs-ldan rgyal-po as one of his early teachers; *Nyams dbyangs* (as in note 5), p. 36.4. The biography and spiritual songs of Pha-rgod rTogs-ldan rgyal-po were microfilmed by the NGMPP during an expedition to Dolpo in the summer of 1995.

especially noted by O-rgyan bstan-'dzin, who devoted some spiritual songs to them: gNas-mchog Gra-lung and dMar-sgom. These are sites where teachers of the Ngor-pa subsect of the Sa-skya-pa school had been active from the 16th century onwards.[19]

Without going into more details of O-rgyan bstan-'dzin's further travels to Me-skyems dgon-pa in the valley of rTa-rab and to the villages in upper Dolpo—including a further meeting with bsTan-'dzin ras-pa—I want finally to direct attention again to the temple of Sa-'dul dgon-pa and its wider surroundings. According to the available written sources, it seems that from his sixtieth year onwards O-rgyan bstan-'dzin frequented sites to the north of Sa-'dul dgon-pa, near the village of Glang, as places conducive to the pursuit of his spiritual endeavours. One of these sites was called "Horse Ferry" (*rta gru*), and it is in connection with this toponym that the person of O-rgyan bstan-'dzin remained alive in the memory of generations of priests following his tradition. Another one was known to the local people by the name "Sun-Cave, the hermitage of the land of Glang" (*glang yul gyi ri khrod nyi ma phug*); this location served at the same time as residence for A-ni Chos-skyid, a female disciple of O-rgyan bstan-'dzin, remembered as well in southern Dolpo down to the present day.[20]

---

19 The activities in 'Bri-gung dgon-pa are related in *Nyams dbyangs* (as in note 5), pp. 239.2–260.3. The term "overseer" (*zhal bdag*) is also used for O-rgyan bstan-'dzin on the occasion of the second renovation of Sa-'dul dgon-pa; ibid, p. 126.3. For information on bsTan-'dzin ras-pa, his birthplace in the Muktināth valley, and his [re-]opening of the hidden valley sKyid-mo lung in the area of sKu-thang, see Ehrhard (1993b:25f.), (2001, note 14) and chapters twelve and thirteen in the present volume; cf. Schuh (1995:42–44) for a translation of the genealogy of bsTan-'dzin ras-pa's family.

Concerning the lineage of the masters of dMar-sgom, which was founded by bSod-nams blo-gros (1516–1581), and the site of Gra-lung, the residence of rNam-grol bzang-po (born 1504), the teacher of bSod-nams blo-gros, see Ehrhard (1996a) and chapter nineteen in the present volume. The biographies translated by Snellgrove (1967) deal with four representatives of this tradition. For a modern-day description of the pilgrimage around Shel-gyi ri-bo, see Jest (1985). A guidebook is also available: *gNas mchog shel gyi ri bo 'brug sgra'i dkar chags mthong ba don ldan dad pa'i skya rengs*, 18 fols., NGMPP reel no. E 2756/15.

20 For an ethnographic account of the village of Glang, see Jest (1975:70). A short résumé of the life of A-ni Chos-skyid can be found ibid, pp. 306f. (note: "A Tarap, il n'existe pas de copie de la biographie de la religieuse. Les religieux de Tarap dansent sur le thème de la vie de méditation de *a-ni chos-skyid* (danse appelée chos-bro), lors des cérémonies du onzième mois à Nimaphug (à Doro) et à Mekyem." In the meantime a copy of this biography has been located in Tarap: *mKha' 'gro ma o rgyan chos skyid gyi rnam thar bsdus pa*, 51 fols., NGMPP reel no. L 401/3. For a detailed study of the life of O-rgyan chos-skyid based on this manuscript, see Schaeffer (2004).

The following statement is made by O-rgyan bstan-'dzin in praise of the spiritual qualities of rTa-gru: "This sacred site—it is my hidden land ... The door to the sacred site [is] Sa-'dul, a place for giving [offerings]. The inner part of the sacred site [is] rTa-gru, a place of pristine awareness." See *Nyams dbyangs* (as in note 5), pp. 364.3–5: *gnas 'di ni nga yi sbas yul yin / ... / gnas sgo ni sa 'dul sbyin pa'i gnas / gnas nang ni rta gru ye shes gnas*, and *O rgyan bstan 'dzin rnam thar* (as in note 5), pp. 44.6–45.4 (with a different reading of the last line: *gnas nang ni lta (= rta) gru ting 'dzin gnas*).

A final example of the importance Sa-'dul dgon-pa achieved in the 18th century as a temple where religious discourses were given and as an entry point to hidden sites lying beyond can be found in the biography of Kaḥ-thog rig-'dzin Tshe-dbang nor-bu (1698–1755). As his stay in Sa-'dul dgon-pa in the year 1730 was followed by a personal encounter with O-rgyan bstan-'dzin in rTa-gru, I shall present this episode from the perspective of both persons in an appendix.[21] With this teacher from the region of Kaḥ-thog in Eastern Tibet, we have reached also the last formative element in the spiritual life of O-rgyan bstan-'dzin: although by four decades his junior, he counted Rig-'dzin Tshe-dbang nor-bu as one of his three main teachers (the other two being O-rgyan dpal-bzang and Rig-'dzin Gar-dbang rdo-rje).

After bringing a further renovation project to a successful end—this time at sKag-rdzong, in the vicinity of his old residence—and a last journey to his disciples in northern Dolpo, O-rgyan bstan-'dzin died seven years later in rTa-gru, the inner part of the hidden land he had created around the "Plain of Sa-'dul".

---

[21] On the itinerary of Rig-'dzin Tshe-dbang nor-bu before he reached Sa-'dul dgon-pa and his visits to the court of the king of Mustang and to Muktināth, see Ehrhard (1993b) and chapter twelve in the present volume. For his stay in Sa-'dul dgon-pa, the following data are provided by Chos-kyi dbang-phyug: *rNam thar* (as in note 11), p. 147.2–3: "What is called Sa-'dul, the naturally arisen cemetery, this most excellent great sacred site which was blessed by the Tathāgatī Vajravārāhī—for several days he stayed there and made extensive offerings [in the form] of sacrificial cakes for the Gaṇacakra ... All the commoners and the monastic community of that region bowed down to him in reverence ..." (*sa 'dul zhes rang byung gi dur khrod bcom ldan 'das ma rdo rje phag mo'i (= mos) byin gyis rlabs pa'i gnas mchog cher zhag shas bzhugs shing tshogs gtor gyi mchod pa rgya cher mdzad / ... yul de'i ser skya kun gyi (= gyis) gus par btud* ...).

At that time Rig-'dzin Tshe-dbang nor-bu also settled a military clash between "two petty states of the southern region" (*mon gyi rgyal khag gnyis*); see ibid, p. 147.5. This can only refer to Jumla and Parbat. For the next year, 1731, the autobiographical text of O-rgyan bstan-'dzin notes a war in which the states of Jumla, Parbat and Mustang were involved, costing many soldiers their lives; see *Nyams dbyangs* (as in note 5), pp. 445.5–446.5.

APPENDIX

The following two excerpts are taken (a.) from *Nyams dbyangs* (as in note 5), pp. 423.4–425.1 (the identical passage in *rNam thar* (as in note 5), pp. 53.6–56.3 is based on that) (= I), and (b.) *rNam thar* (as in note 11), pp. 148.1–6 (= II). Concerning the second work it should be noted that the author used as one of his sources for the life-story of Kaḥ-thog rig-'dzin Tshe-dbang nor-bu the autobiographical account *Ma bcos pa'i zog po sngags rig 'dzin pa tshe dbang nor bu rang nyid spyad rab chu klung las thig pa tsam kyu ru lugs su smos pa snyims pa'i chu skyes*. This work is written in verses and covers the main events up to the year 1730; it was set down upon the special request of O-rgyan bstan-'dzin at the time of the meeting between the two masters. See the colophon: "Earlier, in the presence of Guru [Padmasambhava], [there was one] who was called g.Yu-sgra snying[-po], [now] his incarnation, O-rgyan bstan-'dzin by name, this Vajrācarya himself, he made continued strong exhortations, and in response to them, on the tenth day of the black moon in the iron-horse year (= the third Tibetan month of 1730), [I] Tshe-dbang nor-bu, the Vidyādhara who is known as Kaḥ-thog-pa, spoke." Ibid, p. 611.5–6 (*sngon tshe gu ru'i spyan snga ru // g.yu sgra snying zhes rnam sprul ni // o rgyan bstan 'dzin zhes bya ba // rdo rje slob dpon de nyid kyis // yang yang nan gyis bskul ngor // lcags kyi nag zla'i tshes bcu la // kaḥ thog par grags pa rig pa 'dzin // tshe dbang nor bu de yi smras*).

[I]

When [I] the old beggar was seventy-four, he who was the final rebirth of Nam-mkha' snying-po, from the region of Khams in the east, the one with the name Great Vidyādhara from Kaḥ-thog, wandered about in India and Tibet in search of the holy Dharma. In the presence of many teachers with the three good qualities, he had abandoned the partiality of philosophical tenets, [and now] for his part he would ask for many instructions for [spiritual] ripening and liberation (i.e. initiations and teachings) from the nine yānas, the four classes of *Tantra*s and so on; on the other hand, upon many teachers and many [members of the] Saṃgha he would confer initiations and teachings [in return]. In every kingdom's realm he granted initiations for the multitude (i.e. the general public).

Having arrived then in the regions of Mustang and Dolpo, and having taken up residence at the great sacred site of Sa-'dul, he conferred [spiritual] ripening and liberation upon all Tibetans and inhabitants of the gorges. To the old man from the great sacred site of rTa-gru he presented letters again and again, saying that he was in need of treasure-teachings, like *Zab tig [chos dbyings rang gsal]* and so on. Then the old beggar, O-rgyan-pa, said: "To you, the great teacher who has conferred initiations upon all the Indians and Tibetans, I am not about to give [further] initiations and teachings." Nevertheless, he sent requests again and again.

After that, in a spurt of energy, he went straightway to the great sacred site rTa-gru; [and] in [our] mutual encounters, many compliments and sermons were pronounced [by him]. To him, I gave the five volumes of the profound treasures of the treasure-discoverer Gar-dbang [rdo-rje], and further, [treasure-cycles] like the *sPrul sku snying thig*: [all] the initiations, teachings and guidances of the Great Perfection etc. Upon me, he conferred the complete initiations and readings of the [treasure cycle *Klong gsal*] *mkha' 'gro snying thig*.[22] Similes of the most excellent and pure harmony [between us]: [we were] no different [from each other] than the sun from the sun, and [we] mixed [together] like milk in milk. In this way the prayer was made [by us] to meet again in a pure realm for all the lives of [future] rebirths.

sprang rgan bdun don bzhi'i dus / shar phyogs khams kyi sa phyogs nas / nam mkha'i snying po'i skyes mtha' zhig / ka (= kah) thog rigs (= rig) 'dzin chen po zhes / sdam (= dam) chos 'tshol phyir rgya bod nyul / bla ma bzang gsum mang po la / sgrub (= grub) mtha'i phyogs ris spangs nas ni / tshur la theg pa rim dgu dang / rgyud sde bzhi la sogs pa yis (= yi) / smin grol gdam pa (= gdams pa) mang po zhus / phar la bla ma mang po dang / dge 'dun mang la dbang lung snang (= gnang) / rgyal khams kun la khrom dbang bskur / de nas glo dol phyogs su phebs / gnas chen sa 'dul sdan (= gdan) bzhugs nas / bod rong kun la smin grol snang (= gnang) / gnas chen lta (= rta) gru'i rgad po la / zab tig la sogs ster (= gter) chos rnams / dgos zhes bka' shog yang yang gnang / de nas sprang rgan o rgyan pas / rgya bod kun la dbang bkur (= bskur) ba'i bla ma chen po khyed nyid la / dbang lung 'bul ma mi yong byas / de bzhin zhu yig yang yang phul / de nas shugs 'byung spyad pa yis / gnas chen lta (= rta) grur thal 'byung phebs / mjal 'khrad (= 'phrad) 'brel (= 'bel) gtam mang po mdzad / phar la gter ston gar dbang gi / zab gter po ti lnga po dang / gzhan yang sprul sku snying thig sogs / rdzogs chen dbang lung 'khrid sogs 'phul / tshur la mkha' 'gro snying thig gi / dbang lung yongs su rdzogs pa gnang / thugs snang dag pa mchog gis (= gi) dpe / nyi ma nyi ma dbyer med dang / 'o ma 'o ma 'dres pa ltar / skye ba tshe rabs thams cad du / dag pa'i zhing du mjal smon btab.

---

[22] The *sPrul sku snying thig* is a cycle of treasure-teachings unearthed by Rig-'dzin bDud-'dul rdo-rje (1615–1672) of Khams. On the contacts between O-rgyan dpal-bzang—the first teacher of O-rgyan bstan-'dzin—and this treasure-discoverer, and the spread of his teachings in southern Mustang, see Snellgrove (1979:79–81), Ehrhard (2001) and chapter thirteen in the present volume. On the *Klong gsal mkha' 'gro snying thig* cf. the following note.

[II]
At the age of thirty-three years, in the iron-dog [year] called *Sādhāraṇa* (= 1730), [Kaḥ-thog rig-'dzin] arrived in rTa-gru, a part of the country of the south. There the one who was prophesied by the Mahācārya [Padmasambhava] as an incarnation of g.Yu-sgra snying-po, and who was a direct disciple of the treasure-discoverer Gar-dbang rdo-rje snying-po, [i.e.] his Dharma son, the most excellent among the siddhas, O-rgyan bstan-'dzin [by name], because of his wish for a meeting, was issued an invitation, and thus [Kaḥ-thog rig-'dzin] arrived in rTa-glang.

[There] he listened to the initiations, guidance and teachings—[these] three in their entirety—of what had come forth as a treasure of Gar-dbang [rdo-rje] snying-po: *Zab tig chos dbyings rang gsal*, *Thugs rje chen po rtsa gsum snying thig*, *rDo rje phur pa spu gri reg gcod*, [and to the cycle called] *Thugs rje chen po 'gro ba kun grol* or *Nyon mongs rang grol* [of the tradition] of the "Northern Treasures"; and further, to the expounding of guidance for [the spiritual practice of] the rainbow body of [the system of] the honourable [sTag-sham] Nus-ldan [rdo-rje] (born 1655). On the other hand, he gave the initiations, guidance and readings of what had come forth as a treasure of Padma bDe-chen gling-pa (1663–1713), [the cycle] *Klong gsal mkha' 'gro snying thig*. And he appointed [O-rgyan bstan-'dzin] with his own breath as master [of this teaching] of the *sNying thig* [tradition].[23]

Again from Sa-'dul [Kaḥ-thog rig-'dzin] arrived by way of the rTa gorge at [the place called] 'Bum-pa, the great sacred site of the teacher from O-rgyan (= Padmasambhava) in lower rTa-rab, and stayed there for a while. From the dimension of the unmovable yoga of profound meaning, he made fall upon all striving disciples whatever stream [was necessary] for the way to complete liberation.[24]

dgung lo so gsum par thun mong te lcags kyi lor mon yul gyi cha rta grur byon / der slob dpon chen po'i (= pos) g.yu sgra snying po'i sprul par lung gis zin cing / gter ston gar dbang rdo rje'i snying po'i dngos slob chos sras dam pa grub mchog o rgyan bstan 'dzin nas mjal bzhed pas gdan 'dren byung ba bzhin rta glar (= glang) phebs / gar dbang snying po'i gter byon zab tig chos dbyings rang

[23] For information on the treasure-discoverer Padma bDe-chen gling-pa, who was one of the teachers of Kaḥ-thog rig-'dzin, and the unearthing of the cycle *Klong gsal mkha' 'gro snying*, see Ehrhard (1993b:87, note 17) and chapter ten in the present volume.

[24] The place where Kaḥ-thog rig-'dzin stayed in lower Tarap is known today under the name Ri-bo 'bum-pa. On the legends which associate the site with Padmasambhava, see Jest (1975:43 and 298). There is also a guidebook available: no title, 10 fols., NGMPP reel no. L 415/3. It can be dated to the 18th/19th centuries.

gsal dang / thugs rje chen po rtsa gsum snying thig / rdo rje phur pa spu gri reg gcod / byang gter thugs rje chen po 'gro ba kun grol lam / nyon mongs rang grol gyi dbang khrid lung gsum tshang ba / nus ldan zhabs kyi 'ja' sku'i khrid bka' yang gsan / phar la padma bde chen gling pa'i gter byon klong gsal mkha' 'gro snying thig gi dbang khrid lung bcas stsal zhing snying thig gi bdag por dbugs byung mnga' gsol bar mdzad / slar yang sa 'dul nas rta rong rgyud (= brgyud) de rta rab smad o rgyan gu ru'i gnas chen 'bum par byon te re zhig bzhugs / zab don gyi rnal 'byor g.yo ba med pa'i ngang nas gdul bya don gnyer can dag la rnam grol lam gyi chu bo'i rgyun ci yang 'beb par mdzad do.

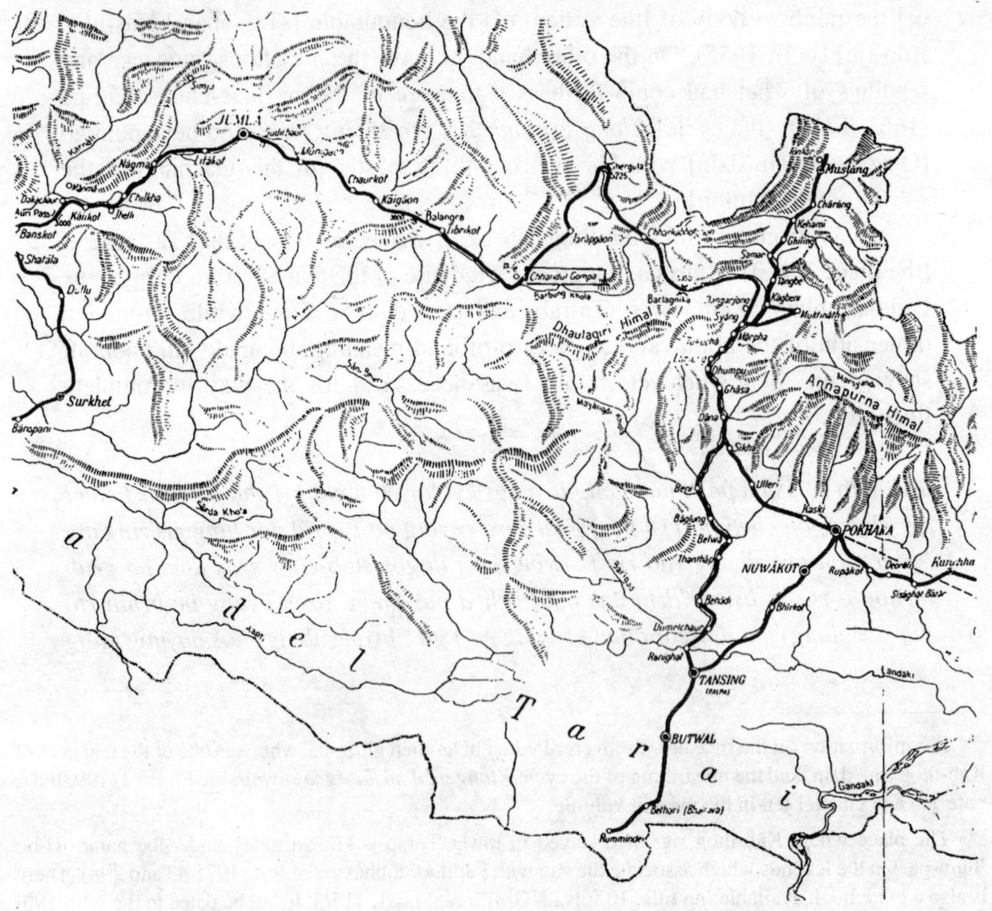

Plate 1: Map from Tucci (1956)

Plate 2: Photo taken by Ehrhard 1992

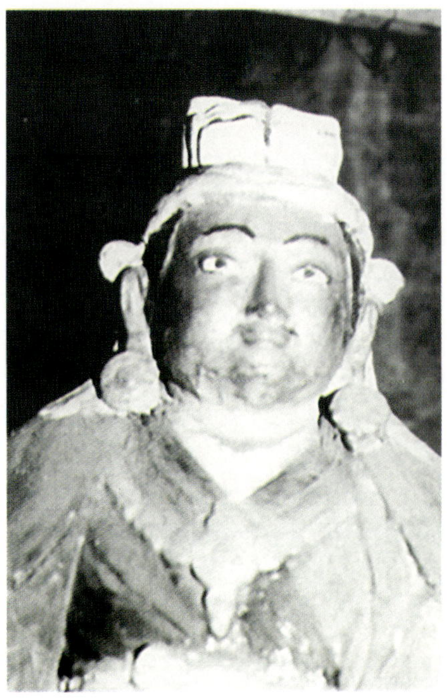

Plate 3: Photo taken by Ehrhard 1992

VIII.

Himalayan Treasure Discoverers

The Role of "Treasure Discoverers" and Their Writings in the Search for Himalayan Sacred Lands

... Et il revient
Mystérieux, traçant comme en des livres ses caractères d'or
Prendre possession et pouvoir sur son véritable domaine ...
Victor Segalen, *Thibet*

The second expedition undertaken by Jacques Bacot (1877–1965) through large tracts of the southern part of the province of Khams from May 1909 to March 1910 has without question had an influence on our notion of "hidden valleys" or "paradisiacal sites" in Tibet. As we learn in the foreword to Bacot's travel report, the actual destination of this expedition was the old kingdom of Poyul (*sPo-yul*) or Pomi (*sPo-smad*), whose territory Bacot approached during his first trip to East Tibet in 1907. The second trip may not have led him to the desired region either, but during the long months in the company of Tibetan nomads he was seized by the yearning for a new destination: Népémakö (*gNas Padma-bkod*) (**plate**), the place of refuge and hope for thousands of Tibetan families that wanted to ensure their own safety at the time, in the face of armed attacks by the Chinese.

It is, above all, the sense of unattainability that lends the territories of sPo-yul and gNas Padma-bkod their particular status in Bacot's travel report. A literary reworking and expansion of Bacot's approach to the white areas on the map—to the border of the promised paradise—are found in the output of the poet and ethnographer Victor Segalen (1878–1919). The whole of Tibet, in its unattainability, acquired for the latter a heightened inner reality, something on the order of a spiritual promise.[1]

To judge by the official pronouncements of the Tibetan Government-in-exile and the Western press, it is nowadays no longer possible to speak of a completely sealed-off geographical space where the huge volumes of the Brahmaputra's waters squeeze their

[1] See Bacot (1912:1–12) for a summary of the second expedition, as well as the new foreword by Blondeau (1988:VI); a description of Népémakö in exemplification of Tibetan beliefs related to *sbas yul* has been provided also by Large-Blondeau (1960:238f.). Concerning Segalen and his last major poem "Thibet", see, among others, Bevan (1987:123f.) and White (1987:208–221). A first involvement with the discourse that the Western European engaged in on the "sacred landscape" and religion of Tibet may be found in Bishop (1987) and (1993).

way through narrow gorges and finally issue out into the tropical forests of India. Indeed, territories like Kong-po, situated south-west of sPo-yul and north-west of gNas Padma-bkod, have already attracted the interest of modern day researchers, and maps and photos are available to the interested tourist.[2] Nevertheless, the sacred site called Lotus Splendour continues to harbour its secrets. (see. Plate 1)

In the following I should merely like to bring together some information that may shed light on the importance of gNas Padma-bkod had for the adherents of the rNying-ma-pa school from the 17th to the 20th centuries. These investigations allow one to characterize in more concrete terms and thereby to understand better important aspects of Tibetan religion and local politics. This preliminary collection of material is also intended to provide an impression of the attitude taken by the "treasure discoverers" (*gter ston*) and their disciples towards an untamed wilderness, one which awoke anxieties and terrors but also held out the prospect of spiritual satisfaction. Could the Tibetans' fantasies about the paradisiacal sites to their south have been a sort of reverse mirror image of the yearnings certain Europeans had for the mystical north?

The Three Awareness-Holders of the Hidden Land

In his history of the rNying-ma-pa school, bDud-'joms Rin-po-che (1904–1987) cites for the 14th sixty-year cycle (1807–1867) the names of three persons who he treats as contemporaries, terming them "three emanational awareness-holders, who opened the secret land of Pemakö as a place of pilgrimage." The three masters in question are Chos-gling Gar-dbang 'Chi-med rdo-rje (born 1763), sGam-po-pa O-rgyan 'Gro-'dul gling-pa (born 1757) and Rig-'dzin rDo-rje thogs-med (1746–1797).[3]

2 Concerning the massive deforestation in south-eastern Tibet, see Department of Information and International Relations, Central Tibetan Administration (1992:49): "In the Kongpo and Rawo Tamo areas of U-Tsang neighbouring the great bend in the Tsangpo as it turns into India, a concentration of over 20,000 Chinese army personnel and Tibetan prisoners are reported to be involved in felling dense old-growth forests of spruce, fir, cedar and broad-leaved species." Referring to this source of information, *Der Spiegel*, "Das geschundene Dach der Welt", no. 21 (1993:126), speaks of a regional ecological drama. For a research trip to Kong-po, see Karmay (1992), which contain references to the trips made by M. Brauen and C. Ramble. On the geographical location of gNas Padma-bkod, see Dudjom Rinpoche (1991) vol. II, map 8; for photos of the mountains rGya-la dpal-ri (7,151 m) and gNam-lcags 'bar-ba (7,651 m), ibid, vol. I, nos. 83 and 84. The documentation of several journeys to gNas Padma-bkod and the search for its sacred sites is available in Baker (2004).

3 Dudjom Rinpoche (1991, vol. I, p. 957; vol. II, p. 97): "Rik-dzin Dorje Thome is probably to be identified with Bacot's 'grand lama nommé Song-gye Tho-me'." A possible source of this identification is Kun-bzang Nges-don klong-yangs: *Bod du byung ba'i gsang sngags snga 'gyur gyi bstan 'dzin skye mchog rim byon gyi rnam thar nor bu'i do shel*, p. 348.5–6: "these three arrived at the same time [in gNas Padma-bkod]. As their aim was pure, they are known as the three awareness-holders who had power on the 'hidden land' (... *'di gsum dus mnyam byon zhing / thugs nang (= snang) gtsang bas sbas yul dbang ba'i rig 'dzin rnams (= rnam) gsum zhes su grags so*)." bDud-'joms Rin-po-che was born in gNas Padma-

Let me briefly describe here these three persons in reverse order. Rig-'dzin rDo-rje thogs-med is also called Brag-gsum gter-ston rDo-rje thogs-med after the site Brag-gsum mtsho in Kong-po; it was there that he found his first treasure works and opened a "hidden valley". Only after he met up with sGam-po-pa O-rgyan 'Gro-'dul gling-pa, however, did he bring to light any further treasure works; particular stress is laid on the discovery of an "introduction list" (*kha byang*) in the sPo-bo mDung-chu'i lha-khang. He founded a hermitage called Byang-gling btsan-phyug in gNas Padma-bkod, where he died at the age of fifty-one. The most important "masters of his teaching" (*chos bdag*) were sGam-po-pa O-rgyan 'Gro-'dul gling-pa and Chos-gling Gar-dbang 'Chi-med rdo-rje. Both Brag-gsum gter-ston and sGam-po-pa O-rgyan 'Gro-'dul gling-pa received support, during their activities in sPo-bo and gNas Padma-bkod, from Nyi-ma rgyal-po, the then "ruler" (*sde pa*) of the line of kings of sPo-smad.[4] Concerning sGam-po-pa O-rgyan 'Gro-'dul gling-pa, we know, furthermore, that he met another treasure discoverer in his younger years, namely Kong-po brug-thang gter-chen, also known as Kun-bzang bDe-chen rgyal-po (born 1736). In addition to opening the site gNas Padma-bkod—in the centre of which he had a new temple and new statues erected and discovered treasure works—sGam-po-pa O-rgyan 'Gro-'dul gling-pa is mentioned in the written sources above all in connection with the renovation of sPo-bo mDung-chu'i lha-khang. His son, rGyal-sras bDe-chen gling-pa, was the incarnation of the just mentioned Kun-bzang bDe-chen rgyal-po.[5]

---

bkod and descended from the family line of the ruler Kaḥ-gnam sde-pa from sPo-smad; ibid. vol. I, p. 972. His predecessor, bDud-'joms gling-pa (1835–1903) was in the process of opening the gate of the site of gNas Padma-bkod, in the company of numerous disciples and donors, when death overtook him, see Tshogs-khang sprul-skuTshe-dbang: *Mkhas grub rgya mtsho'i gtsug rgyan padma bde ba'i rgyal po'i rnam thar ngo mtshar mchog ldan*, pp. 13.5–14.2 and Baker (2004:306).

4 For the history of the Kaḥ-gnam sde-pa, see *sPo bo lo rgyus*, pp. 9–27 and passim. The person of Nyi-ma rgyal-po is dealt on pp. 19–21, where it is said that the strength and power of the line increased during this period (*'di'i dus su stobs dang mnga' thang ches cher 'phel*). Further, it is noted that the connection of priest and donor with Chos-rje sGam-po arose under his reign (*chos rje sgam po dang mchod yon sbyin bdag gi 'brel ba chags pa*). The person in question is sGam-po-pa O-rgyan 'Gro-'dul gling-pa, who was raised as the incarnation of sGam-po-pa (1079–1153) and who fulfilled the duties incumbent upon the representative of Dwags-la sgam-po. For a rather superficial assemblage of information on the history of the Kaḥ-gnam sde-pa cf. Rgya-mtsho Don-grub (1989). A more detailed treatment of the subject is contained in Schwieger (2002).

5 For brief biographies of Brag-gsum gter-ston and O-rgyan 'Gro-'dul gling-pa, see Kun-bzang Nges-don klong-yangs (as in note 3), pp. 339.5–349.1 and sTag-sgang mkhas-mchog Ngag-dbang blo-gros: *Bstan pa'i snying po gsang chen snga 'gyur nges don zab mo'i chos kyi 'byung ba gsal bar byed pa'i legs bshad mkhas pa dga' byed ngo mtshar gtam gyi rol mtsho*, pp. 589–590 and 738–742. It should be stressed that in the latter work sPo-bo mDung-chu'i lha-khang is characterized as "[one] of the temples erected by Dharmarāja Srong-btsan sgam-po that tame the borders (*chos kyi rgyal po srong btsan sgam pos bzhengs pa'i mtha' 'dul gyi gtsug lag khang spo bo mdung chu'i lha khang*)." It is, however, not a *mtha' 'dul* but a *yang 'dul* temple; see note 8. For a list of the monasteries founded by the two above-mentioned persons, see Waddell (1899=1991:278). Compare Sardar-Afkhami (1996:7-11) for the

Chos-gling Gar-dbang 'Chi-med rdo-rje likewise met Kun-bzang bDe-chen rgyal-po during his younger years, and when he was no more than twenty-three years old he raised treasure works in gNas Padma-bkod. Only after twelve years had elapsed—that is, in 1798—did he pass these cycles to a "master of his teachings", namely sGam-po-pa O-rgyan 'Gro-'dul gling-pa. In 1806, together with the latter, he opened the centre of gNas Padma-bkod as well as other sites, raising further treasure works there, erected *stūpas* etc.; it is said of him: "he took under his wing, through the four types of activities [of the tantric master], [a whole] assemblage of inhabitants of Klo and Mon" (*klo mon gyi 'gro pa rnams bsdu ba rnam pa bzhi'i 'phrin las kyis rjes su 'dzin par mdzad ...*).[6]

These few observations show that at the end of the 18th and beginning of the 19th century the paradisiacal site gNas Padma-bkod was already exerting a strong attraction among adherents of the rNying-ma-pa school, though it was obviously not large groups of liberation-seekers that approached the "hidden valley" but rather "treasure discoverers" and their disciples. Some of the masters belonged to bKa'-brgyud-pa school and enjoyed the support of the local rulers of sPo-smad.

Treasure Discoverers Active in the 17th to 18th Centuries

In order to gain a more complete picture of the treasure discoverers active at gNas Padma-bkod, we need to shift our attention now to a different and somewhat earlier group of masters linked to the site, beginning with Rig-'dzin Chos-rje gling-pa (1682–1725).

Like sGam-po-pa O-rgyan 'Gro-'dul gling-pa, Rig-'dzin Chos-rje gling-pa also received his education as an incarnation of the bKa'-brgyud-pa school: he was the reincarnation of one Zhabs-drung 'Chi-med dbang-po, the representative of Ras-chung phug in the valley of Yar-klungs. The years in which he fulfilled these duties were from 1687 to 1706.[7] Subsequently he moved to Tsa-ri, one of Tibet's oldest sacred sites, likewise

adventures of O-rgyan 'Gro-'dul gling-pa in gNas Padma-bkod.

6 For a short biography of Chos-gling Gar-dbang 'Chi-med rdo-rje, see sTag-sgang mkhas-mchog Ngag-dbang blo-gros, (as in note 5), pp. 590–592; his name derives, in my opinion, from his treasure work *Zab chos 'chi med thugs thig*. An additional name is Kun-bzang 'od-zer O-rgyan Gar-dbang bstan-pa'i nyi-ma. He is the one, among the various incarnations of Rig-'dzin Chos-rje gling-pa (1682–1725), to have been born in gNas Padma-bkod. See Kun-bzang Nges-don klong-yangs (as in note 3), p. 325.5–6. Rig-'dzin 'Jigs-med gling-pa (1729/30–1798) is likewise regarded as an incarnation of Rig-'dzin Chos-rje gling-pa (on the links of 'Jigs-med gling-pa with the students of Chos-rje gling-pa, see the chart in Goodman (1993:137).

7 A short biography of Rig-'dzin Chos-rje gling-pa is found in Kun-bzang Nges-don klong-yangs (as in note 3), pp. 321.3–327.6 and in sTag-sgang mkhas-mchog Ngag-dbang blo-gros, (as in note 5), pp. 412–415. The incarnation lineage of the representative of Ras-chung phug begins with rGod-tshang ras-chen sNa-tshogs rang-grol (1482–1559), a disciple of gTsang-smyon He-ru-ka (1452–1507). Following him came Zhabs-drung Grub-mchog dbang-po (1563–1618), and following the latter, Zhabs-drung 'Chi-med dbang-po. For further biographical data on Chos-rje gling-pa, see also Goodman (1993:198f.).

located in the south-east, on the border with India. From there he went to Kong-po and sPo-bo, where he discovered numerous treasure works. A fact worth noting is that these finds occurred both in the Bu-chu gser-gyi lha-khang, the *mtha' 'dul* temple located in Kong-po, and in the previously mentioned sPo-bo mDung-chu'i lha-khang. According to the tradition of the rNying-ma-pa school, the latter was the *yang 'dul* temple called Tshang-pa rlung-gnon. The exact identification of this temple and the determination of its geographical location have continued to present a problem for scholars.[8]

In sPo-bo, he further met up with the treasure discoverer sTag-sham Nus-ldan rdo-rje (born 1655) and was recognized by the latter as the master of his teaching. Following further trips to Central Tibet where, among others, he met lHa-bzang Khan (regnal period 1705–1717), he was drawn back a second time to Kong-po. Apparently under the impression that the rNying-ma-pa school was being persecuted by the Dzungars, he decided at this point to visit the site gNas Padma-bkod; he reached the "hidden valley" by way of sPo-bo without any problem and was welcomed by the "protector of the territory" (*zhing skyong*). On the way back, though, he suffered a serious rheumatic complaint and died shortly thereafter on the "border between Glo and sPo-bo" (*glo dang spo bo sa mtshams*). The following citation provides an impression of Rig-'dzin Chos-rje gling-pa's trip through gNas Padma-bkod:

> Having prepared clarifications of the sacred site and route descriptions etc., he put down [in writing] all of his visions. He also preached the teaching to the people of Glo, who were like animals, and thus laid the foundations for their predisposition towards it. The inhabitants of Glo themselves offered him their trust and services, according to the customs of their country.[9]

8 See Aris (1979b:23f.): "Unfortunately the temple of Rlung-gnon is too near the centre to fit convincingly into this group ... Until further evidence comes to light we shall have to accept Klong-rdol's location, the only one which seriously upsets the symmetry and logic of the scheme as a whole." See also the map, ibid, p. 16. In the summer of 1993, a manuscript of a *gter ma* cycle of Rig-'dzin Chos-rje gling-pa came into my hands; it bears the title *sPu (= sPo) bo 'dung (= mdung) chu tshangs pa rlung gnon mi tra'i (= maitri'i) lha khang nas spyan drangs pa'i gnod sbyin dzam bha la dmar po'i chos skor* and comprises hundred folios. One of the text, titled *Kha byang lo rgyus*, provides a further name of the temple: *khams gyi spo bo gdung (= mdung) chu yis (= yi) / rnam snang byams pa'i lha khang*. See also note 15.

9 sTag-sgang mkhas-mchog Ngag-dbang blo-gros, (as in note 5), p. 415: *gnas kyi gsal cha dang lam yig sogs mdzad nas gzigs snang thams cad gtan la btab / glo mi dud 'gro 'gra ba de rnams la'ang bka' chos bstsal nas chos kyi bag chags 'jog par mdzad / glo rnams kyis kyang dad gus dang zhabs tog yul lugs dang bstun pa'i bsnyen bkur btabs*. The spelling Glo is unusual; normally the border regions in south-eastern Tibet are called Klo-yul, and the inhabitants Klo-pa. Concerning the subdivision of the tribes of the Abor Mountains in Klo-dkar-po, Klo-nag-po and Klo-bkra-pa, see Wylie (1962:178).

None of the "route descriptions" (*lam yig*) by Rig-'dzin Chos-rje gling-pa of gNas Padma-bkod has, as far as I know, come to light. By way of compensation, though, an extensive text of a contemporary of his who likewise undertook a trip to gNas Padma-bkod has been preserved, that person being Sle-lung bZhad-pa'i rdo-rje (born 1697). I shall deal with this work only to the extent that it provides further insight into the treasure discoverers who were associated with the sacred site. It may first be noted, however, that there is a direct connection between Rig-'dzin Chos-rje gling-pa and Sle-lung bZhad-pa'i rdo-rje, his junior by fifteen years: from Kong-po the former had a prophecy delivered to the latter which identified him as the reincarnation of 'Ol-kha rJe-drung-pa.[10] The text of *gNas mchog padmo bkod du bgrod pa'i lam yig dga' byed bden gtam* comprises fifty-three folios and describes the adventures of Sle-lung bZhad-pa'i rdo-rje in gNas Padma-bkod in 1729; it offers a good starting point for further studies on the sacred site, particularly by virtue of the fact that a total of two volumes of the thirteen-volume collection of Sle-lung bZhad-pa'i rdo-rje's works are filled with texts belonging to the genres *lam yig* and *gnas yig*.[11]

The following passage may provide us with an idea of how the identification of particular spiritual qualities of the landscape came about:

> Not only are the footpaths in the gorges difficult to traverse, precisely such [sites] as De'u Rin-chen spungs-pa, the centre of the Dharmacakra in the heart [of the deity], and Brag-dkar bKra-shis rdzong, the centre of the Nirmāṇacakra in the navel, cannot be reached from this point; one would even emerge from a crevice in the mountain. [For] the mountain gNam-lcags 'bar-ba exists as a principal place of its own to the west of these sites. That this [i.e. the present location] is the border between the Dharmacakra in the heart [of the deity] and the Saṃbhogacakra in his throat, did not [formerly] exist as a widespread [notion], but since it has become fully clear at this point in time, now that I have brought into mutual agreement the [pertinent] sections from [the cycle] *rTa mgrin gongs*

10 Biographical data on Sle-lung bZhad-pa'i rdo-rje are also contained in Kun-bzang Nges-don klong-yangs (as in note 3), pp. 314.1–319.1 and sTag-sgang mkhas-mchog Ngag-dbang blo-gros, (as in note 5), pp. 632–635. The source for the prophecy is Sle-lung bZhad-pa'i rdo-rje: *Rigs pa 'dzin pa blo bzang 'phrin las kyi rtogs pa brjod pa skal bzang dga' ston*, p. 12.1–4. Further, Sle-lung bZhad-pa'i rdo-rje was a "master of the teaching" of the treasure teachings *gSang ba ye shes chos skor* of Rig-'dzin Chos-rje gling-pa; a similar relationship associates him with the teachings of the cycle *mKha' 'gro ma gsang ba ye shes*, which derive from gTer-bdag gling-pa (1646–1714).

11 Along with "route descriptions" and "place descriptions", there are also various "histories" (*lo rgyus*), which deal with such things as an encounter with Pho-lha-ba bSod-nams stobs-rgyas in 1730 (*Mi dbang bsod nams stobs rgyas rnam grol gling du byon pa'i lo rgyus*, 41 fols.) or a visit to the reconstructed monastery complex of sMin-grol gling in 1732 (*sMin grol gling du bskyod pa'i lo rgyus*, 15 fols.). Jackson (1987a:78) mentions a separate catalogue of the total of thirty-five texts; up to now this has not become available to me.

> *'dus*, which has appeared as a treasure work of Rig-'dzin Nus-ldan rdo-rje—that is, the compiled fragments containing place and route descriptions for Padma-bkod—I made this known to my travelling companion [with the words] "[It is] such and such."[12]

As the expressions *snying ga chos 'khor*, *lte ba sprul 'khor* and *mgrin pa longs spyod* (*'khor*) testify, Sle-lung bZhad-pa'i rdo-rje in describing the landscape based himself on a system of various *cakra*s that are lined up vertically along the main artery: in the throat, in the heart, and in the navel. R.A. Stein has already referred to the process by which a sacred site is realized both in the body of the yogin and in that of the deity, the individual parts of which correspond to various topographical features. He has further provided an analysis of gNas Padma-bkod as a site that was consecrated above all to a particular form of the deity *Vajravārāhī*: this site bears the name "*Vajravārāhī*, Tamer of the Nāgas" (*rdo rje phag mo klu 'dul ma*).[13]

What fails to come out clearly from Stein's analysis is the fact that there are a number of parallel schemata that have been used for representing the territory around the two mountains of Kong-po and sPo-bo, and also the impassable wilderness of gNas Padma-bkod, as a spiritual reality. Two of the schemata are called "Large Hidden Site Lotus Splendour" (*sbas gnas chen po padma bkod*) and "Hidden Site with the Five Cakras" (*sbas*

---

[12] Sle-lung bZhad-pa'i rdo-rje: *gNnas mchog padmo bkod du bgrod pa'i lam yig dga' byed bden gtam*, pp. 467.6–468.3: *rong gi lam 'phrang bgrod dka' bas ma gtogs / snying kha (= ga) chos 'khor gyi lte ba de'u rin chen spungs pa dang lte ba sprul 'khor gyi lte ba brag dkar bkra shis rdzong sogs kyang 'di nas ri sgo tsam las yong thebs mi 'dug / ri bo gnam lcags 'bar ba gnas de dag gi nub mthil po rang du 'dug / sngar yongs su grags par snying ga chos 'khor dang mgrin pa longs spyod kyi sa mtshams 'di yin mi 'dug kyang rig 'dzin nus ldan rdo rje'i gter byon rta mgrin dgongs 'dus kyi nang tshan padmo bkod kyi gnas yig dang lam yig dum bu khrigs bsdebs gung bsgrigs dus shin tu gsal bar snang bas zla grogs rnams la 'di dang 'di'o zhes ngo sprad.* As is apparent from the context in the cited passage, Sle-lung bZhad-pa'i rdo-rje entered the inner part of the "hidden valley" by way of gNam-lcags 'bar-ba and Padma shel-ri. Before he did so, he received a written message from the court of the Kaḥ-gnam sde-pa, in which it was stated: "This Padma-bkod belongs solely to the people of Kaḥ-gnam; it is not a place that the inhabitants of dBus and gTsang may enter (*padmo bkod 'di kaḥ gnam pa kho na dbang pa las dbus gtsang gi mi yong sa min* ...)", ibid, p. 467.1.

[13] See Stein (1988:40f.), for a sequential review of the parts of the deity's body, from one *cakra* to the next along the main artery (this review is carried out in the context of a description of Tsa-ri). For an analysis of gNas Padma-bkod and the projection of the body of the deity *Vajravārāhī* onto this geographical reality, see ibid, pp. 43–48. Stein chiefly drew on the text *O rgyan chen po padma 'byung gnas kyi ma 'ong lung bstan snyigs ma'i sems can la sbas yul padma bkod kyi gnas yig,* 36 folios (*texte mal établi*). This is the same manuscript that found its way to France in the hands of J. Bacot, and the one used by [Large-] Blondeau for her description of the pilgrimage route to gNas Padma-bkod; see [Large-]Blondeau (1960:238–240 plus accompanying map). Stein supplemented this source with data from the cycle *rTsa gsum yi dam dgongs 'dus* of sTag-sham Nus-ldan rdo-rje (19 vols.). Dehradun, 1971–1972.

gnas 'khor lo lnga ldan). I present these schemata, as found in one particular text, in the Appendix (Fig. 182).

TWO STILL EARLIER FORERUNNERS

An interesting feature of the quote from Sle-lung bZhad-pa'i rdo-rje is that certain sacred places lay in the centre of the various *cakra*s of the deity, and that the identification of these places—that is, their exact topographical location—was not always unequivocal. Evidently this identification was made by the leaders of the groups that penetrated into the extolled territory by consulting already existing writings and text collections. In the case of Sle-lung bZhad-pa'i rdo-rje, these are the works of sTag-sham Nus-ldan rdo-rje. We have already seen that Rig-'dzin Chos-rje gling-pa met this treasure discoverer, and that it was principally in the territory of sPo-bo that his teachings are said to have spread. He is also known as dGa'-ba-lung gTer-ston, since he was the one who opened the site of sPo-bo dGa'-ba-lung and brought to light there the cycle *Yi dam dgongs 'dus rta mchog rol pa*. This cycle contains detailed information about the sacred site of gNas Padma-bkod, including the distinction between "the outer twelve territories" (*phyi gling bcu gnyis*), "the inner forty ravines" (*nang sul bzhi bcu*) and "the sixteen secret territories" (*gsang gling bcu drug*).[14]

There is still another pair of treasure discoverers—and their connection with the "hidden land" must now be profiled in order to have a fuller understanding of the activities of the representatives of the rNying-ma-pa in the 17th century in south-eastern Tibet, namely bDud-'dul rdo-rje and 'Ja'-tshon snying-po. sTag-sham Nus-ldan rdo-rje was a "disciple of the treasure teachings" (*gter slob*) of the first master, Rig-'dzin bDud-'dul rdo-rje (1615–1672). Even though born in the vicinity of the royal court of sDe-dge, Rig-'dzin bDud-'dul rdo-rje felt drawn to the provinces of Central Tibet and to Kong-po. His first treasure discovery, however, was made only after he met another such discoverer, namely Rig-'dzin 'Ja'-tshon snying-po (1585–1656); the latter gave him the following instructions: "You should go to sPo-bo and devote yourself to the previously established practice; and at that point a prophecy will come to you, and you will have the opportune fortune [to find] a profound treasure work." And Rig-'dzin bDud-'dul rdo-rje did indeed, from that time on,

---

14 See *sPo bo lo rgyus*, p. 144; this information is taken from the text *gNas mchog dga' ba tshal gyi lo rgyus snying po mdor bsdus* (dGa'-ba-tshal is another name for dGa'-ba-lung). For a brief description of the monastery founded by sTag-sham Nus-ldan rdo-rje in dGa'-ba-lung and an account of the incarnations that succeeded him, see the text *rDo dung dgon pa'am dga' ba lung dgon gyi lo rgyus mdor bsdus*; ibid, pp. 110–114. An unusual feature of the history of this incarnation lineage, which was supported by the rulers of Kaḥ-gnam, is the distinction made between one sTag-sham O-rgyan bSam-gtan gling-pa and his incarnation sTag-sham Nus-ldan rdo-rje. Up to now the assumption has been that there was only one person with the name Nus-ldan rdo-rje bSam-gtan gling-pa; see the short biographies in Kun-bzang Nges-don klong-yangs (as in note 3), pp. 301.6–302.6 and sTag-sgang mkhas-mchog Ngag-dbang blo-gros, (as in note 5), pp. 574f.

uncover numerous treasure works and opened hidden lands. The following quotation provides one such example:

> Right after that, when a route description for the sacred site Padma-bkod from the sPo-bo mDung-chu'i lha-khang came to life in his hands, he took Rigs-ldan gNas-mtsho as his companion and proceeded with a large retinue of disciples to Padma-bkod. [There] he prepared a clarification of a temporary gate to the sacred site.[15]

But also Rig-'dzin 'Ja'-tshon snying-po, who was born in Kong-po and uncovered treasure works in, among other places, the *mtha' 'dul* temple Bu-chu gser-gyi lha-khang, brought to light texts associated with the "hidden land" gNas Padma-bkod. In the "realization cave" (*sgrub phug*) in Kong-'phrang, 'Ja'-tshon snying-po uncovered the cycle *rDo rje khro lod rtsal gyi sgrub skor*, together with a route description and prophecies for gNas Padma-bkod. We can judge the later spread of the cycle from the fact that a commentary of it by rTse-le[gs] sNa-tshogs rang-grol (1605–1677), another disciple of Rig-'dzin 'Ja'-tshon snying-po, has been preserved.[16]

CONCLUDING REMARKS

The 17th century was thus the particular period in which the sacred site of gNas Padma-bkod was systematically visited by treasure discoverers of the rNying-ma-pa school. It was during this same period that those writings which served as aids for later liberation-seekers in identifying the places visited by Padmasambhava were produced. As for the representation of gNas Padma-bkod as the body of Vajravārāhī Klu-'dul-ma, other traditions may also have exercised their influence. One need only consider, for example, the presence of the

---

[15] sTag-sgang mkhas-mchog Ngag-dbang blo-gros, (as in note 5), p. 569: *de nas spo bo mdong (= mdung) chu'i lha khang nas padma bkod kyi gnas kyi lam yig phyag tu son pa bzhin rigs ldan gnas mtsho zhes pa gzung (= gzungs) mar bzhes nas grwa 'khor mang po dang bcas padma bkod du phebs nas / gnas sgo rags rim zhig gsal cha mdzad*. For the above quotation, see ibid, p. 567: *khyod rang spo bor song la rtse gcig tu sgrub pa la 'bungs shig dang / de'i dus su khyos la lung bstan 'ong zhing zab gter gyi skal ba zhig yod do* and the version in Kun-bzang Nges-don klong-yangs (as in note 3), p. 299.5–6. A text concerning the *yang 'dul* temple had been preserved in *sPo bo lo rgyus*, pp. 118–124: *sPo bo'i mdung chu mkhar lha khang tshangs pa rlung gnon gtsug lag khang gi dkar chag*.

[16] For the treasure discoveries of 'Ja'-tshon snying-po, see, among other works, sTag-sgang mkhas-mchog Ngag-dbang blo-gros, (as in note 5), p. 444, and for the *Padma bkod kyi lam yig*, the passage in Kun-bzang Nges-don klong-yangs (as in note 3), p. 237.1. In rTse-le[gs] sNa-tshogs rang-grol: *sBas yul gyi lam yig padma dkar po las gsungs pa'i gu ru rdo rje khro lod kyi dbang chen*, pp. 243.6–244.6, the author provides the information that the treasures at Kong-'phrang were concealed with the purpose of removing obstacles during trips to such sites as sBas-pa'i gnas Padma-bkod. Concerning rTse-le[gs] sNa-tshogs rang-grol, who was born on the border between Dwags-po and Kong-po, see Blondeau (1987:126f.).

bKa'-brgyud-pa school in Tsa-ri from the 12th century on and the realization of the divine state by yogins there.

One additional thing I should like to point out here is the significance that the temples dating to the early royal period had for the treasure discoverers in the extreme south of Tibet, and for their search for the hidden paradises. As we have seen in the case of mDung-chu'i lha-khang in sPo-bo, both Rig-'dzin bDud-'dul rdo-rje and Rig-'dzin Chos-rje gling-pa, as well as Rig-'dzin rDo-rje thogs-med, uncovered treasure works in the *yang 'dul* temple in south-eastern Tibet before they set off for gNas Padma-bkod. I would see this circumstance as implying that contact with the site that was erected by Srong-btsan sgam-po and consecrated by Padmasambhava endowed the treasure discoverers with a power that enabled them to tame the wilderness lying beyond the border and to find the symbols of the Buddhist teaching in these inaccessible regions. We can observe this process in the 17th century not only in sPo-bo but also in south-western Tibet, in Mang-yul; there existed another *yang 'dul* temple, Byams-sprin lha-khang, which contained a hoard of old treasure teachings and was the starting point for trips to the "hidden valleys" in the south.[17] The status of the treasure discoverers, legitimized by their contact with the old temples and relics, confirmed their roles as "rulers" over the newly opened territories.

In order to round out, finally, the picture of the treasure discoverers associated with sPo-bo and gNas Padma-bkod, here is a summary list transmitted by the tradition:

> In Padma-bkod: gTer-ston Chos-rje gling-pa, rDo-rje thogs-med, rGyal-sras bDe-chen gling-pa; these three are known as the three awareness holders of the "hidden land". In the upper [part of] sPo-bo, bDud-'dul rdo-rje; below, gNam-lcags rdo-rje; in the middle, sTag-sham rdo-rje—the three who have attained [the state] of the vajra. So they are called.[18]

---

[17] See Ehrhard (1993a:81) and chapter ten in the present volume for Byams-sprin lha-khang and the treasure discoverers Rig-'dzin Gar-dbang rdo-rje (1640–1685) and Rig-'dzin Nyi-ma grags-pa (1647–1710). Concerning other masters of the rNying-ma-pa school who were active in the 16th and 17th centuries in Mang-yul and at the court of the kings of Gung-thang, and the openings of "hidden valleys", such as present-day Langthang, see Ehrhard (1997b) and chapter sixteen in the present volume.

[18] *sPo bo lo rgyus*, p. 210: *padma bkod du / gter ston chos rje gling pa / rdo rje thogs med / rgyal sras bde chen gling gsum la / sbas yul rig 'dzin rnam gsum du grags / spo bo stod la bdud 'dul rdo rje / smad la gnam lcags rdo rje / bar la stag sham rdo rje ste / rdo rje thob pa'i mi gsum zhes*. For a short biography of gNam-lcags rdo-rje rTsa-gsum gling-pa, see Kun-bzang Nges-don klong-yangs (as in note 3), pp. 335.2–336.5. Two of his disciples are sKyid-grong Thugs-mchog rdo-rje (the main teacher of 'Jigs-med gling-pa) and Rwa-ston sTobs-ldan rdo-rje; for biographical data on these two persons, see Goodman (1993:199–201). The reincarnation of the latter is the previously mentioned Kun-bzang bDe-chen rgyal-po (born 1736), the Kong-po brug-thang gter-chen; the latter's incarnation, in turn, is rGyal-sras bDe-chen gling-pa. For the activities of rGyal-sras bDe-chen gling-pa in gNas Padma-bkod, see Kun-bzang Nges-don klong-yangs: *Rig 'dzin rdo rje gsang ba rtsal gyi rtogs pa brjod pa sgra dbyangs lha mo'i gling bu*,

APPENDIX:

Two Representations of the "Hidden Site"
(Source: *Spo bo chos 'byung in Lo rgyus, pp. 200–201*)

sBas gnas chen po Padma bkod dbu rGya-la dpal-ri	
phyag gyas *(rdo-rje 'dzin-pa)* *Kong-po yul*	phyag gyon (sbal-pa 'dzin-pa) sPo-bo yul
nu-ma gyas *Ri-bo gNam-lcags 'bar-ba*	nu-ma gyon 'Dzum-chen Gangs-ri gnas
zhabs gyas *Ho-ga rta-ngam ma-nu'i gnas*	zhabs gyon gTum-skul shel dang 'ba'-ro gnas

Figure 1: Representation of the "hidden site" sBas-gnas chen-po Padma-bkod.

sBas gnas 'khor lo lnga ldan	
spyi-bo	bde-chen 'khor-lo rGya-la dpal-ri
mgrin-pa	longs-spyod kyi 'khor-lo mGon-po gnas Drag-po sgrub-phug
snying-ga	chos-kyi 'khor-lo Bod lung-pa
lte-ba	sprul-pa'i 'khor-lo Rin-spungs
gsangs-gnas	bde-skyong 'khor-lo Kṣipa gyu-rdzong

Figure 2: Representation of the "hidden site" sBas-gnas 'khor-lo lnga-ldan.

pp. 363.6–384.4 (the years 1842 to 1845).

Plate 1: Taken from Baker (2004)
View into gNos Padma-bkod from above mGon-po gnas

Political and Ritual Aspects of the Search for Himalayan Sacred Lands

INTRODUCTION

The 17th century was the particular period in which sacred sites like gNas Padma-bkod, in the south-eastern border region of Tibet, were systematically visited by treasure discoverers of the rNying-ma-pa school. The temples dating to the early royal period had a special significance for the treasure discoverers active at this time here in the extreme south of Tibet and also for their search for the hidden paradises.[1] Parallel to this phenomenon were the efforts to revive, by way of foundations or renovations of old structures, the "places of realization" (*sgrub gnas*) in areas that were once the southern border of the old Tibetan kingdom. In this context, a number of sites were chosen that possessed special qualities because the spiritual presence of Padmasambhava or the early yogins of the bKa'-brgyud-pa school.

An important scheme for classifying the sacred sites associated with Padmasambhava—sites prophesied by the master as spots for the spiritual exercises of his future disciples—consists of five so-called "solitary places" (*dben gnas*). One of these sites, in lHo-brag mKhar-chu, in the border region between Tibet and Bhutan, is termed "the solitary place of [Padmasambhava's] heart" (*thugs kyi dben gnas*). It is of significant interest that a monastery with the name of dGa'-ldan bDud-'joms gling was also founded in lHo-brag mKhar-chu under the predominantly dGe-lugs-pa regime established by the Fifth Dalai Bla-ma Blo-bzang rgya-mtsho (1617–1682) and the sDe-srid Sangs-rgyas rgya-mtsho (1653–1705).[2]

1 For the different "treasure discoverers" (*gter ston*) active in gNas Padma-bkod from the 17th to the 18th centuries, see Ehrhard (1994) and chapter twenty-one in the present volume. In a further article I have tried to show that the "hidden valley" (*sbas yul*) as a concept of religious space can be found in the same period in Glo-bo smad, i.e. in southern Mustang, on the local and regional level; see Ehrhard (1993c) and chapter thirteen in the present volume. It is interesting to note that the influence of treasure discoverers like Rig-'dzin bDud-'dul rdo-rje (1615–1672) is traceable in both the south-eastern and south-western border regions.

2 For the "five solitary places", see, for example, O-rgyan gling-pa: *O rgyan gu ru padma 'byung gnas kyi skye rabs rnam par thar pa rgyas par bkod pa padma bka'i thang yig*, chapter 95 (*ma 'ongs sgrub gnas bstan pa'i le'u*), p. 589.3–7: *sku yi dben gnas bsgrags kyi yang rdzong yin : gsung gi dben gnas bsam yas mchims phu ste : thugs kyi dben gnas lho brag mkhar chu yin : yon tan dben gnas yar klungs shel gyi brag*

By giving some details concerning the political and ritual aspects that accompanied the travels of Tibetan priests and yogins into border areas like lHo-brag mKhar-chu the following observations should make first of all clear that these journeys must be seen as an immediate response towards the religious and political situation that characterized Tibet at the beginning of the 18th century. This was a time when Tibet was involved in the power-struggle between the Dzungars and the Qing Dynasty, and when the border areas in the south had not only to be controlled by military and ritual means but offered protection and were places for spiritual revitalization. By implication I hope thus to show why the importance of these places was not restricted to the 17th century but continued up into the 18th century.

THE LIFE OF GRUB-THOB BLO-BZANG LHA-MCHOG

As a kind of introduction I would like to present some material concerning different sites in lHo-brag and the person of Grub-thob Blo-bzang lHa-mchog (1672–1747) from lHo-brag Gro-bo lung, based on his autobiography. There are two reasons for focusing on him: first, his name is directly connected with the monastery of dGa'-ldan bDud-'joms gling in mKhar-chu, and second, his religious activities included the opening and identifying of hidden valleys in the region of lHo-brag. This point is highlighted by Kaḥ-thog Si-tu Chos-kyi rgya-mtsho (1880–1925), who paid a visit to the sacred sites of lHo-brag mKhar-chu in the year 1919 and reported:

> The bhikṣu lHa-mchog, a disciple of Rig-'dzin Pad-'phrin (= rDo-rje brag Rig-'dzin Padma 'phrin-las (1640–1718)) [and] prophesied by 'Ol-kha rJe-drung (= Sle-lung bZhad-pa'i rdo-rje (born 1697)), [he] was an opener of the doors to a few minor solitary places and to sacred sites like Seng-ge ri and the hidden valley Long-mo lha-steng.[3]

: *'phrin las dben gnas mon kha seng ge rdzong* :. Cf. Dowman (1988:288–290) and Ricard (1994:272f.) for a description of this scheme, which is sometimes enlarged by a group of three further sites. In Ferrari (1958:56f.) one finds a list of the different sacred sites in lHo-brag mKhar-chu as described by 'Jam-dbyangs mKhyen-brtse dbang-po (1820–1892). It should be noted that near lHo-brag mKhar-chu is the location of the lHo-brag Khom-mthing lha-khang, one of the *mtha' 'dul* temples of Srong-btsan sgam-po. The foundation of the monastery dGa'-ldan bDud-'joms gling is mentioned in Ngag-dbang Blo-bzang rgya-mtsho: *Za hor gyi ban de ngag dbang blo bzang rgya mtsho'i 'di snang 'khrul pa'i rol rtsed rtogs brjod kyi tshul du bkod pa du kū la'i gos bzang las glegs bam gnyis pa,* vol. 3, pp. 417.15ff., and in Sangs-rgyas rgya-mtsho: *dPal mnyam med ri bo dga' ldan pa'i bstan pa zhwa ser cod pan 'chang ba'i ring lugs chos thams cad kyi rtsa ba gsal bar byed pa bai ḍū rya gser po'i me long*, p. 400.13–19 (the year of foundation was 1682). The ritual texts of this monastery were published under the title *Mkhar chu bdud 'joms gling gi 'don cha'i skor*, 1015 pp., Delhi: Konchog Lhadrepa, 1994. Several works of the Fifth Dalai Bla-ma are also contained in this collection.

3 Chos-kyi rgya-mtsho: *Si tu chos kyi rgya mtsho gangs ljongs dbus gtsang gnas bskor lam yig [nor bu*

Blo-bzang lHa-mchog began his religious career in the year 1679, when he received his name on the basis of a written document from the hand of the Fifth Dalai Bla-ma. The place where this occurred was also linked to the person of the spiritual and secular ruler of Tibet at that time; it was the monastery dGa'-ldan Don-gnyis gling, located in lHo-brag as well, and founded by the Fifth Dalai Bla-ma—in person—thirty years earlier in 1649.[4]

The main teacher of Blo-bzang lHa-mchog for the next years was a certain Ngag-dbang nor-bu, who also supervised his first retreat. In a detailed passage of the autobiography we find that Ngag-dbang nor-bu had been nominated by the Fifth Dalai Bla-ma and sDe-srid Sangs-rgyas rgya-mtsho to perform certain rituals in dGa'-ldan bDud-'joms gling. The reason for this lay in his ability to bring under control a certain demon called an "Indian demon who brings ruin to the land of Tibet" (*bod yul 'phung byed kyi rgya 'dre*), an "Indian demon of the border" (*mtha'i rgya 'dre zhig*), or simply a "demon of the border" (*mtha' 'dre*). Different journeys followed, and one brought the young novice also to lHa-sa, where he received his final ordination as a monk in the year 1696. This ceremony was supervised by dGe-slong 'Jam-dbyangs grags-pa in the Potala palace.[5]

---

zla shel gyi me long], p.309.4–5: (*... dge slong lha mchog ces rig 'dzin pad 'phrin slob ma / 'ol ka* (= *kha*) *rje drung pas lung bstan / ban* (= *dben*) *pa'i gnas phra na* (= *phran*) *re zung* (= *gzung*) *dang / seng ge ri / sbas yul long mo lha steng zer ba sogs gnas sgo 'phye mkhan zhig go*. Further remarks by Chos-kyi rgya-mtsho justify the conclusion that there existed a "line of incarnations" (*sku phreng*) of Grub-thob Blo-bzang lHa-mchog; they were known under the name bDud-'joms gling-pa'i sprul-sku.

4 Concerning the foundation of dGa'-ldan Don-gnyis gling in lHo-brag rDo-bo rdzong, see Ngag-dbang Blo-bzang rgya-mtsho (as in note 2), vol. 1, pp. 300.19–301.3, and Sangs-rgyas rgya-mtsho (as in note 2), pp. 397.24–398.4. Compare also Ishihama (1993:49). According to Grub-thob Blo-bzang lHa-mchog: *Lho brag gro bo lung grub thob blo bzang lha mchog rin po che'i rnam thar*, p. 16.1, this monastery was one of the "thirteen islands, [that are] the convents of donor and preceptor" (*mchod yon gyi grwa tshang gling bcu gsum*) of the government of the Fifth Dalai Bla-ma and sDe-srid Sangs-rgyas rgya-mtsho. This holds also true for the monastery dGa'-ldan bDud-'joms gling; see the list of the "thirteen colleges of teaching" (*chos grwa bcu gsum*) in Sangs-rgyas rgya-mtsho (as in note 2), pp. 396.14–400.19. The patron refers in this case to Gu-śri bsTan-'dzin chos-rgyal (1582–1655) and his successors. See the remark by Sum-pa mkhan-po (1704–1787) translated in Ho-chin Yang (1969:39).

5 The motives for nominating Ngag-dbang nor-bu for duties in dGa'-ldan bDud-'joms gling are described in Grub-thob Blo-bzang lHa-mchog (as in note 4), pp. 25.3–26.5. He is mentioned under the name Byang-gling bla-zur Ngag-dbang nor-bu in Sangs-rgyas rgya-mtsho (as in note 2), p. 400.14–15. This name links him to the rNying-ma-pa monastery gSang-sngags Byang-chub gling, founded by the Fifth Dalai Bla-ma in 1651 (just before his journey to the Manchu court); see Karmay (1991:344). gSang-sngags Byang-chub gling in Chu-shur is also counted as one of the thirteen *mchod yon gyi grwa tshang gling*; see the list in Sangs-rgyas rgya-mtsho (as in note 2), pp. 399.20–400.2.

Basic biographical information on the person of 'Jam-dbyangs grags-pa is provided by Karmay (1988a:16): "... a very learned monk and in his capacity as private secretary would often act as a scribe ... the Dalai Lama stated that this monk was an adept of the rDzogs-chen philosophy. He took an active part, with the Regent, in building the Red Palace of the Potala, the tomb of the Dalai Lama, and in establishing the commemoration day of the latter's death." See also the Appendix.

In 1703 Blo-bzang lHa-mchog visited lHa-sa a second time. At that time a change had taken place at the top of the Tibetan government which the monk from lHo-brag described with the following words:

> Then rGyal-dbang Tshangs-dbyangs rgya-mtsho (1683–1706) put on the costume clothing of the Dharmarāja Srong-btsan [sgam-po]; the eldest son of Mi-dbang Sangs-rgyas rgya-mtsho was installed and lifted to the throne, [which he occupied] together with King lHa-bzang (1658–1717) ...[6]

The unstable political situation which was created by this constellation, and which finally resulted in the end of the Qośot rule over Tibet and the invasion of the Dzungars in 1717, are generally known.[7] In the life of Blo-bzang lHa-mchog, this period was dominated by his meetings with rDo-rje brag Rig-'dzin Padma 'phrin-las and the spiritual practices he received from this master. Although rDo-rje brag suffered from attacks by king lHa-bzang, Blo-bzang lHa-mchog nevertheless visited there twice during this period. Between these visits he spent over five years in retreat in lHo-brag.

It was in lHo-brag that the news reached him of the death of rDo-rje brag Rig-'dzin, who had been killed by Dzungar soldiers in the year 1718. Knowledge of the decline of the teachings of the rNying-ma-pa school and the great sadness at the death of his teacher prompted Blo-bzang lHa-mchog soon afterwards to move to "a hidden sacred site" (*sbas gnas*). In the night following his decision, he conceived the idea to direct his steps to a sacred site named Seng-ge ri ("Lion Mountain"). Two factors motivated him: first, certain written documents had extolled this spot, including a "certificate of prophecies" (*lung byang*), and second, rGyal-dbang Lo ras-pa (1187–1250), an early master of the 'Brug-pa bKa'-brgyud-pa school, had already stayed for an extended period at the "Lion Mountain" and thus sanctified it.[8]

---

6 Grub-thob Blo-bzang lHa-mchog (as in note 4), p. 29.5–6: *de nas rgyal dbang tshangs dbyangs rgya mtsho chos rgyal srong btsan gyi chas bzhes / mi dbang sangs rgyas rgya mtsho'i sras bgres pa khri bkod dang / rgyal po lha bzang bcas kyi khri 'degs su* ... For these events, see Petech (1988:209f.). See ibid, p. 204 for references to the Sixth Dalai Bla-ma's renouncing his monastic vows and adopting the way of life of a temporal ruler. A description of the outer appearance and character of Tshangs-dbyangs rgya-mtsho can be found in the autobiography of Sle-lung bZhad-pa'i rdo-rje: *Rig pa 'dzin pa blo bzang 'phrin las kyi rtogs pa brjod pa skal bzang dga' ston*, pp. 65.5–66.6, and 79.3–80.6; he met the Sixth Dalai Bla-ma and his companions in the years 1702/03. The activities of the Fifth Dalai Bla-ma as a reincarnation of Srong-btsan sgam-po are described in Ishihama (1993:53f.).

7 See for example Petech (1972:32–50) and Dabringhaus (1994:37f. and 48–50). Compare the corresponding chapters in the biography of the ruler Mi-dbang bSod-nams stobs-rgyas, who was at the centre of the Tibetan resistance against the Dzungars; Tshe-ring dbang-rgyal: *Dpal mi'i dbang po'i rtogs par brjod pa ['jig rten kun tu dga' ba'i gtam]*, pp. 258.4–299.10 (*sog po jun gar gi dmag dpung bod du yong ba'i skor dang / rgyal po lha bzang pham nyes byung ba'i skor*).

8 The arrivals of Lo ras-pa dBang-phyug brtson-'grus in lHo-brag and his stay in Seng-ge ri is described,

I shall not go into the details of the journey that brought Blo-bzang lHa-mchog to the paradisiacal site. In the end he reached the "realization cave" (*sgrub phug*) and the "residence" (*gdan sa*) of rGyal-dbang Lo ras-pa and erected nearby a first provisional shelter. The autobiography of Blo-bzang lHa-mchog provides long descriptions of the natural beauty of the spot, including the varieties of bird songs and the manifold flowers and herbs. Accordingly Blo-bzang lHa-mchog called the place "Flower Island" (*me tog gling*).

The sacred site of Seng-ge ri, which was first identified as such by one of the early yogins of the bKa'-brgyud-pa school in the 13th century, in the early 18th century also attracted the attention and visits of other masters. For instance, the autobiography of Sle-lung bZhad-pa'i rdo-rje from 'Ol-kha states that he, too, visited sBas-yul Seng-ge ri in the year 1722 and met in the "inner part of the sacred site" (*gnas nang*) Blo-bzang lHa-mchog. Together they celebrated a *gaṇacakra*, and Sle-lung bZhad-pa'i rdo-rje was also impressed by the natural qualities of the place. A dream Sle-lung bZhad-pa'i rdo-rje had at the time had long-ranging effects for the spiritual bond between the two yogins. In the dream, he received a prophecy that a further hidden valley should be opened to the north-east of Seng-ge ri. According to the corresponding information in the biography of Blo-bzang lHa-mchog, this area was called sBas-gnas 'Or-mo lha-sa, and both source agree that in this area was located the palace of Yam-shud dmar-po, king of the *bTsan* demons.[9]

The prophecy that the hidden sacred site 'Or-mo lha-sa should be opened was obviously linked with the person of Blo-bzang lHa-mchog, but a few years had to pass before it came true. In the meantime, the civil war of 1727/28 had been brought to an end by Mi-dbang bSod-nams stobs-rgyas (1689–1747), and the Seventh Dalai Bla-ma bsKal-bzang rgya-mtsho (1708–1757) was installed, even if without any legal backing and while still in exile. A piece of good news for Blo-bzang lHa-mchog was that the rebirth of his teacher, bsKal-bzang Padma dbang-phyug (born 1720), had been officially enthroned in

for example, in Padma dkar-po: *Chos 'byung [bstan pa'i padma rgyas pa'i nyin byed]*, pp. 439.17–440.5, and in the biography written by rGod-tshang ras-pa: *Chos rje lo ras pa'i rnam par thar pa bdud rtsi'i phreng ba*, pp. 108.11ff. His activities in lHo-brag included the renovation of the mKhar-chu'i lha-khang, i.e. the lHo-brag Khom-mthing lha-khang (see note 2). rGyal-dbang Lo ras-pa is the founder of the lower 'Brug-pa school (*smad 'brug*).

9 Concerning Sle-lung bZhad-pa'i rdo-rje, his preceding incarnations, and his status as the rebirth of lHo-brag grub-chen Nam-mkha' rgyal-mtshan (1326–1401), see the data given in Ehrhard (1994:236, note 10) and chapter twenty-one in the present volume. His visit to Seng-ge ri is described in Sle-lung bZhad-pa'i rdo-rje (as in note 6), pp. 648.3–650.2. At the time he was on his way to Thig-phyi in lHo-brag, the former residence of lHo-brag grub-chen Nam-mkha' rgyal-mtshan. For the meeting of Tsong-kha-pa Blo-bzang grags-pa (1357–1419) with lHo-brag grub-chen in Thig-phyi in the year 1395, see Ehrhard (1992:50–52) and chapter three in the present volume. Shortly before Sle-lung bZhad-pa'i rdo-rje's arrival, another person came up with the information that in the year 1723 several entrances to the sacred site mKhan-pa ljongs should be opened; ibid, p. 651.1. This name refers to a mountain valley in Bhutan just south of the Tibetan border.

rDo-rje brag. This message was received by him with great joy, "like a peacock hearing the [rolling] sound of thunder" (*rma bya 'brug sgra thos pa bzhin*).

Soon afterwards, in the year 1733, the time was ripe to follow the instructions of Sle-lung bZhad-pa'i rdo-rje and to open the hidden site of 'Or-mo lha-sa. The autobiography gives a detailed description of the journey and of how Blo-bzang lHa-mchog identified different parts of the sacred landscape. As mentioned in the prophecy, he came upon the palace of Yam-shud dmar-po.

The next year Blo-bzang lHa-mchog was again in the company of Sle-lung bZhad-pa'i rdo-rje, and the subject of the opening of the sacred sites came up for discussion. During this time Blo-bzang lHa-mchog received a written document that recounted the events of the years 1722 up to 1733. At the farewell ceremony Sle-lung bZhad-pa'i rdo-rje spoke the following words to his guest: "What is of use to others, (i.e.) turns them towards the dharma, mainly the seizing, protecting and spreading of hidden sacred sites, you should do as much as you can!" Nearly identical words were spoken at a third and final meeting between the two masters; this happened a few years later at the time when the renovation of the temple of Thig-phyi in lHo-brag was brought to a successful end.[10]

The years 1734 and 1735 saw Blo-bzang lHa-mchog again in rDo-rje brag, where he met the young rDo-rje brag Rig-'dzin and offered him the teachings of the rDzogs-chen cycle *Thugs rje chen po 'khor ba dbyings sgrol*. His last years were spent in the region of Seng-ge ri and 'Or-mo lha-sa, and he also erected a temple at the latter spot. Shortly before his death he wrote down the monastic rules for his successors at the two sacred sites in lHo-brag.[11]

---

[10] The written document of Sle-lung bZhad-pa'i rdo-rje for Blo-bzang lHa-mchog can be found in Grub-thob Blo-bzang lHa-mchog (as in note 4), pp. 110.5–113.6 (*gsang lung them byang*). The second meeting took place in sPyan-g.yas, the home of the wife of Sle-lung bZhad-pa'i rdo-rje; for the valley of sPyan-g.yas, in the south of 'Phyongs-rgyas, see Ferrari (1958:53). For the quotation, see Sle-lung bZhad-pa'i rdo-rje (as in note 6), p. 123.3–4: *sbas gnas kyi 'dzin skyong spel gsum gtso bor gyur pa'i gzhan phan chos la bsgyur gang thub byed gos*. Cf. the words at the third meeting: *lhag tu sbas gnas kyi 'dzin skyong dang gzhan phan chos la bsgyur gang thub sogs sngar ltar byas phyin de rang gi yong 'dug*; ibid, p. 168.1.

[11] The transmission of the rDzogs-chen cycle *Thugs rje chen po 'khor ba dbyings sgrol* is mentioned also by bsKal-bzang Padma dbang-phyug: *Lha rigs kyi btsun pa bskal bzang padma'i ming can rang nyid kyi rtogs par brjod pa 'jam gnyen ut pa la gzhad pa'i dga' tshal [gzhon nu bun du'i yid 'phrog]*; pp. 159.3 and 187.2–188.1. The "monastic rules" (*bca' yig*) were written down in the year 1746 and are contained in Grub-thob Blo-bzang lHa-mchog (as in note 4), pp. 179.3–191.3. A ritual work dedicated to the protectors of 'Or-mo lha-sa (written by Sle-lung bZhad-pa'i rdo-rje) is contained in *mKhar chu bdud 'joms gling gi 'don cha'i skor* (as in note 2), pp. 611–615: *sBas gnas 'or mo lha sa'i gnas bsrung gi gsol mchod*.

POLITICAL AND RITUAL ASPECTS

The presence of Sle-lung bZhad-pa'i rdo-rje in the southern areas of Kong-po and lHo-brag and his persistent interest in the search for hidden valleys and their popularization should be interpreted against the background of his relationship with the "ruler" (*mi dbang*) bSod-nams stobs-rgyas from Pho-lha. An investigation of their relationship will help us understand better the religious and political practices that accompanied the search for paradisiacal sites in the south of Tibet.[12]

The first meeting between the twenty-eight-year-old priest and the thirty-seven-year-old, war-tested politician occurred, according to the available sources, in the year 1726. The place was rNam-grol gling, the residence of Sle-lung bZhad-pa'i rdo-rje in 'Ol-kha. At that time bSod-nams stobs-rgyas was on his way to the hot springs of 'Ol-kha stag-rtse and visited also the statue of Maitreya at rDzing-phyi, which had been renovated by Tsong-kha-pa Blo-bzang grags-pa. Although this journey of the ruler has been described by previous studies, the contact between Sle-lung bZhad-pa'i rdo-rje and bSod-nams stobs-rgyas has been altogether neglected; attention was focused exclusively on rJe-btsun Mi-'gyur dpal-gyi sgron-ma (1699–1769), the daughter of Rig-'dzin gTer-bdag gling-pa (1646–1714), and on the fact that the ruler received teachings of the rNying-ma-pa school from her.[13]

To put these contacts in a wider context, it must be pointed out that the rNying-ma-pa school suffered two phases of suppression at the beginning of the 18th century: in the years 1717 to 1720, during the invasion of the Dzungars, and in 1726 under the Manchu ruler Yung-chen. The later attack against the "teachings of the Old Translations" (*snga 'gyur gyi chos lugs*) were openly proclaimed by the emperor in the form of an edict which had been issued at the instigation of the Tibetan minister Khang-chen-nas (died 1727). Directly after the proclamation of the edict, bSod-nams stobs-rgyas reacted strongly against the accusation of heresy against the rNying-ma-pas.[14] This occurred shortly before bSod-nams stobs-

---

12 For a short résumé of Sle-lung bZhad-pa'i rdo-rje's journey to gNas Padma-bkod in the year 1729 and his connection with Rig-'dzin Chos-rje gling-pa (1682–1725), see Ehrhard (1994) and chapter twenty-one in the present volume. The following observations should also contribute some material towards an understanding of the religious situation in Tibet at a time when the Manchu dynasty asserted hegemony over Tibet. For the ambivalence on the part of the early Qing emperors towards Tibetan Buddhism, see Hevia (1993).

13 For the valley of Sle-lung, the residence rNam-grol gling, and the rDzing-phyi to the east thereof, see Wylie (1962:91) [the unidentified 'Ol-kha rJe-drung refers to the incarnation line of Sle-lung bZhad-pa'i rdo-rje]. The journey of bSod-nams stobs-rgyas to 'Ol-kha stag-rtse and the meeting with rJe-btsun Mi-'gyur dpal-gyi sgron-ma was previously dealt with by Petech (1972:109f.) and, based on that study, by Dhondup (1984:88).

14 An account of the persecutions of the rNying-ma-pa school at the beginning of the 18th century—also based on Petech (1972)—can be found in Martin (1990:5f.); compare Mayer (1992:183). The questions raised by Martin and Mayer concerning the "specific measures Khang-chen-nas brought against the

rgyas left for 'Ol-kha stag-rtse. Concerning his meeting with rJe-btsun Mi-'gyur dpal-gyi sgron-ma, the biography of the ruler reports only that the local people did not provide any offering or service to the daughter of Rig-'dzin gTer-bdag gling-pa, being afraid of the recently proclaimed edict that "no respect should be shown towards the followers of the old mantras" (*gsang sngags rnying ma'i srol 'dzin pa dag la bsnyen bskur mi bya'o*).

In spite of this, bSod-nams stobs-rgyas received her "in the traditional way" (*gna' bo'i srol ji lta ba bzhin tu*) and offered her his "battle horse" (*g.yul du 'jug pa'i bzhon pa*). From rJe-btsun Mi-'gyur dpal-gyi sgron-ma he obtained various initiations in return, including the cycle *Zab chos rig 'dzin thugs thig*, a treasure work of Rig-'dzin gTer-bdag gling-pa.[15]

A far longer passage in the biography of bSod-nams stobs-rgyas—immediately following the one just described—describes a meeting with a second person in the same year, 1726: none other than Sle-lung bZhad-pa'i rdo-rje. The ruler also received from this teacher various initiations and teachings, among which I shall mention only the "spiritual authorization" (*rjes su gnang ba*) for the deity sKrag-med nyi-shar. After the transmission of these teachings, Sle-lung bZhad-pa'i rdo-rje uttered a list of advice for the politician's serious consideration. They started with the characterization of Khang-chen-nas as an emanation of the deity sKrag-med nyi-shar and an assertion of his merits because of that status. But the power of these merits would soon be exhausted, as the minister was at the time "wounding the doctrine of the Great Secret's essence" (*da ni gsang chen snying po'i bstan pa la rma byin par byed*).

---

rNying-ma-pa sect" and "the reason for these foreign attacks on the rNying-ma-pas" could be answered by referring to the wording of the edict of 1726. We find there the explicit prohibition of ritual acts like "magic rites for subjugating the foe" (*drag las mnan pa*), "burning rites" (*bsreg pa*), or "hurling of weapon[-like] ritual offerings" (*gtor zor 'phang pa*); see the text in Tshe-ring dbang-rgyal: *Dpal mi'i dbang po'i rtogs pa brjod pa 'jig rten kun tu dga' ba'i gtam*, p. 482.15–17. These ritual acts are also known as *mnan sreg 'phang gsum*; for the textual basis of the three activities, see Boord (1993:197–206).

[15] Tshe-ring dbang-rgyal (as in note 14), pp. 494.20–495.14. This was obviously not the first contact between the lady from sMin-grol gling and bSod-nams stobs-rgyas, see Khyung-po ras-pa: *Rje btsun mi 'gyur dpal gyi sgron ma'i rnam thar [dad pa'i gdung sel]*, pp. 102.4ff. (*de skabs pho lha tha'i ji 'gyur med bsod nams stobs rgyas bka' blon gyi las stabs kyi dbang che zhing mi phyed pa'i dad gdung drag pos rje nyid la legs gsol gyi 'bul ba ...*). This meeting took place in the year 1719 and was followed in 1720 by the proposal of bSod-nams stobs-rgyas that the rJe-btsun-ma should move to Kong-po and by further contacts; see ibid, p. 104.5ff. It should be mentioned that rJe-btsun Mi-'gyur dpal-gyi sgron-ma in the year 1718 had escaped the Dzungar armies and had found refuge in the hidden land 'Bras-mo ljongs, present-day Sikkim; she had been welcomed there by the king, 'Gyur-med rnam-rgyal (regnal years 1701–1733), and by dPa'-bo 'Jigs-med rdo-rje (born 1682), the second incarnation of lHa-btsun Nam-mkha' 'jigs-med (1597–1653). See the account of these events in Bstan-pa'i sgron-me: *Gsang chen rnying ma'i 'dus sde 'og min o rgyan smin grol gling nges pa don gyi dga' ba'i tshal chen po'i dkar chag rang bzhin bden brjod ngo mtshar shel gyi adarśa*, pp. 6.20–7.13.

For bSod-nams stobs-rgyas himself, Sle-lung bZhad-pa'i rdo-rje came forward with some advice that obviously must be seen as relating to his strong reaction against the edict of the Manchu ruler Yung-chen. The tradition of the dGe-lugs-pa was thereby characterized as something the ruler could place confidence in (*zhwa ser cod pan 'chang ba'i rings lugs 'di ni yid brton rung ba'o*), the reason for this being the purity and continuity of the teachings of Padmasambhava, Atiśa and Tsong-kha-pa. What we witness here, is in my opinion, the effort on the part of the priest from rNam-grol gling to add some critical perspective to the standpoint of bSod-nams stobs-rgyas with the aim of dissolving the polarization between the dGe-lugs-pas and the rNying-ma-pas schools.[16]

Two years later, in 1728, Sle-lung bZhad-pa'i rdo-rje acted as a mediator between the Seventh Dalai Bla-ma bsKal-bzang rgya-mtsho and bSod-nams stobs-rgyas, who had just successfully ended the civil war. As Sle-lung bZhad-pa'i rdo-rje stated:

> The earth-monkey year (= 1728), a truly bad time for dBus and gTsang: I arrived in lHa-sa when the troops of gTsang had [just] reached Central Tibet. As the opening provided by [this] lucky coincidence suited [the purpose of] the ruler bSod-nams stobs-rgyas, I managed to pacify the disturbances between dBus and gTsang. Having performed a great wave of service for the excellent system of patron and priest and for the Highest Sovereign (i.e. the Dalai Bla-ma), I returned back.[17]

---

[16] For the meeting between bSod-nams stobs-rgyas and Sle-lung bZhad-pa'i rdo-rje, see Tshe-ring dbang-rgyal (as in note 14), pp. 495.15–499.5. This passage had been dealt with in some details, as the advice has up to now been ascribed to the daughter of gTer-bdag gling-pa (and thus the position of bSod-nams stobs-rgyas misrepresented); see Petech (1972:110): "She prophesied the ruin of Khang-chen-nas because of his persecution of the rNying-ma-pa, and tried to induce Pho-lha-nas to join her sect; of course he refused and reasserted his dGe-lugs-pa faith." See also Dhondup (1984:88). The role of Sle-lung bZhad-pa'i rdo-rje as mediator should be seen against the background of his role as reincarnation of lHo-brag grub-chen Nam-mkha' rgyal-mtshan and keeper of the visionary teachings of this master; cf. Sle-lung bZhad-pa'i rdo-rje (as in note 6), p. 618.5ff. In Ehrhard (1992:56) and chapter three in the present volume the integrative capacity of the teachings of lHo-brag grub-chen in 18th-century Tibet is already mentioned.

[17] See bZhad-pa'i rdo-rje: *Gnas thor bu rnams gyi lo rgyus ltad mo'i grong khyer*, p. 336.4–5 (*sa sprel lo dbus gtsang gi dus log chen mo'i gtsang dpung dbus su 'byor dus lha sar phyin / mi dbang bsod nams stobs rgyas dang rten 'brel gyi sgo 'grig ste dbus gtsang gi 'khrug pa zhi bar byas / gong sa mchog dang yon mchod lugs legs kyi zhabs 'debs (= 'degs) rlabs che ba bsgrubs nas phyir log ...*). Compare also the statement in Kun-bzang Nges-don klong-yangs: *Bod du byung ba'i gsang sngags snga 'gyur gyi bstan 'dzin skyes mchog rim byon gyi rnam thar [nor bu'i do shal]*, p. 315.1–2: "By furthering in a proper way the agreeable resolution between the Seventh Sovereign bsKal-bzang rgya-mtsho and the ruler, the *dharmarāja*, he averted the disagreeable conditions for them." (*gong sa bdun pa bskal bzang rgya mtsho dang mi dbang chos rgyal thugs mthun mthsams sbyor legs spel gyis sku'i gal rkyen bzlog*); see also Schwieger (1985:LXIV–LXV). For the relationship between the *yon bdag* ruler and the *mchod gnas* lama (*bla ma*) as the ideal foundation of Tibetan political theory, see Seyfort Ruegg (1991:448–451).

Here we have reached a point where we can look back on the journey of Sle-lung bZhad-pa'i rdo-rje to gNas Padma-bkod. This undertaking had occurred in the year 1729, shortly after bSod-nams stobs-rgyas came to power. In the relevant "description of the route" (*lam yig*) to the paradisiacal site are contained some clues as to Sle-lung bZhad-pa'i rdo-rje's motives for going at this particular time to the wilderness of south-eastern Tibet:

> The earth-male-monkey year (= 1728): as a means to turn aside the border armies in the iron-male-dog year (= 1730) I had to pass on towards the supreme sacred site gNas Padma-bkod. And as subsidiary conditions for these [undertakings] there was the necessity to execute countless sequences of auspicious ceremonies, such as feasts and fire offerings at the places of realization of the Guru (i.e. Padmasambhava) in the paradise grove of Kong-yul, offerings for Ge-sar at the solitary places touched by Ge-sar's feet, [and] atonement rituals for the great demon-protector in the places of [the deity] sKrag-med nyi-shar such as Brag-gsum mTsho-mo-che.[18]

This statement can be interpreted to mean that Sle-lung bZhad-pa'i rdo-rje began his journey with the goal of producing some stability in the southern border regions for the newly established government of bSod-nams stobs-rgyas. This was an urgent necessity because Central Tibet was still endangered by the attacks of the Dzungars and the problems with Bhutan were also acute. As it turned out, bSod-nams stobs-rgyas mastered all these difficulties successfully.[19]

---

[18] For the journey of Sle-lung bZhad-pa'i rdo-rje to gNas Padma-bkod in the year 1729 and the text Sle-lung bZhad-pa'i rdo-rje: *Gnas mchog padmo bkod du bgrod pa'i lam yig [dga' byed bden gtam]*, see Ehrhard (1994) and chapter twenty-one in the present volume; the quote is in the text, pp. 392.6–393.2 (*sa pho spre'u lo lcags pho khyi'i mtha' dmag bzlog pa'i thabs su gnas mchog padmo bkod du ngas kyis bskyod dgos pa dang / de dag gi cha rkyen du kong yul ljon pa'i tshal gyi gu ru'i sgrub gnas rnams su tshogs dang me mchod / ge sar gyi zhabs kyis bcags pa'i dben gnas rnams su ge sar gyi mchod pa / brag gsum mtsho mo che sogs skrag med nyi shar gyi gnas rnams su bdud mgon chen po'i gsol mchod sogs rim gro rten 'brel gyi rim pa mtha' yas pa byed dgos pa dang*). According to mDo-mkhar Zhabs-drung Tshe-ring dbang-rgyal (as in note 7), p. 496.9, the deity sKrag-med nyi-shar is a "protector" (*srung ma*) of the cycle *Gsang bdag snyan brgyud*. This is the name for the teachings of lHo-brag grub-chen; see Sle-lung bZhad-pa'i rdo-rje (as in note 6), p. 622.5 (*gzhan yang gsang bdag snyan brgyud kyi nang du / gshin rje tshe bdag dang sngags srung ma'i chos skor sogs yi dam lhas dngos su gsungs 'dug pa*).

[19] See Petech (1972:161): "The foreign policy of P'o-lha-nas scored a great success in this period"; and Dhondup (1984:97f.): "In his foreign policy Miwang Pholanay was able to secure suzerainty over Bhutan by following a similar policy of supporting all the Bhutanese factions as the Manchu did in Tibet ... Through the contacts in Ladakh, he succeeded in keeping a close watch on the movements of the Dzungars."

BUDDHIST MYTHS

Concerning the religious and political practices connected with the search for hidden valleys, it should be mentioned again that in the case of Sle-lung bZhad-pa'i rdo-rje the destinations were sites that only a few years earlier had been identified by persons like sTag-sham Nus-ldan rdo-rje (born 1655) and Rig-'dzin Chos-rje gling-pa (1682–1725). While these treasure discoverers first opened the sacred sites, i.e. tamed the wilderness through their rituals and became masters of the territory, their successors were able to share their footing by following the same routes and repeating the rituals of their masters at the previously established locations.

That this control over a certain territory was indeed transferred from a treasure finder to his disciple can be shown nicely in the case of gNas Padma-bkod. Rwa-ston sTobs-ldan rdo-rje (17th/18th centuries), a disciple of gNam-lcags rdo-rje rTsa-gsum gling-pa (17th century) and also of a certain Chos-gling bDe-ba'i rdo-rje (17th century), received from this latter teacher the order to open a particular site and write down a "clarification of the sacred site" (*gnas kyi gsal cha*). The words uttered on that occasion were: "Because you are the master [of this site] (*bdag po khyod yin pas* ...)."[20] We shall see now that during his journey in the year 1729 Sle-lung bZhad-pa'i rdo-rje obtained also rights on certain territories.

As mentioned in several passages of his works, this authorization came directly from the *ḍākiṇīs* on the form of so-called "introductory certificates" (*them[s] byang*) for the sacred sites to be opened. These places bear the name lHo-gling, Nub-gling and Byang-gling, and their topography is defined in relation to a "sacred mountain" (*gnas ri*) with the name "Heap of Jewels", i.e. Rin-chen spungs-pa.[21] The exact location of this mountain and surrounding places is material to the next meeting between Sle-lung bZhad-pa'i rdo-rje

---

20 For information on gNam-lcags rdo-rje rTsa-gsum gling-pa and Rwa-ston sTobs-ldan rdo-rje, see Ehrhard (1994:238, note 18) and chapter twenty-one in the present volume. Compare Ricard (1994:XXVIII, note 41) and the chart, ibid, p. 570. This information is based on sTag-sgang mkhas-mchog Ngag-dbang blo-gros, *Bstan pa'i snying po gsang chen snga 'gyur nges don zab mo'i chos kyi 'byung ba gsal bar byed pa'i legs bshad mkhas pa dga' byed ngo mtshar gtam gyi rol mtsho*, pp. 581.21–582.19; for the journey to gNas Padma-bkod, see ibid, p. 582.3–8. In the later part of his life Rwa-ston sTobs-ldan rdo-rje served as a "field of offering" (*mchod gnas*) for the ruler bSod-nams stobs-rgyas.

21 For this authorisation, see bZhad-pa'i rdo-rje: *lTal* (= *ltad*) *chung mkha' 'gro'i dga' chal* (= *tshal*) *gyi gnas sgo gsar du phye ba'i lam yig bden pa'i zungs ldan* in "Collected Works", vol. 9, p. 205.3–5 (*sa mo bya'i lo* (= 1729) *padmo bkod nas phyir 'khor dus kong yul ljon pa'i tshal las 'or shod kyi cha gnas lung du zhag phab pa'i tshe na ye shes kyi mkha' 'gros lung bstan pa'i gnas kyi thems byang du ma zhig thob par / lhun po rdza'i lho gling gsal dwangs ri bo che / nub gling zangs ri phu'i gnas / byang gling g.yu sgron ma'i bla mtsho rnams kyi thems byang* ...; compare also the text bZhad-pa'i rdo-rje: *Yid bzhin gyi nor bu ratna tā re'i lo rgyus mthong na kun dga'*, p. 275.2–4 (*zhi ba zhes pa sa mo bya'i lo (= 1729) gnas mchog chen po padmo bkod du bdag gis bskyod nas lha gcig nyi ma gzhon nu gdan drangs / 'or shod kyi cha las chims yul gnas lung zhes pa'i mdar slebs pa'i tshe na / ye shes kyi a ki 'dzom pa skyid dang mjal te ri bo rin chen phung ba'i lho nub byang gsum gyi gling gi thems byang rgyas par stsal*).

and bSod-nams stobs-rgyas, which took place in the year 1730, again in the residence of rNam-grol gling.

At that time one of the sacred sites which had been prophesied on the way back from Kong-po had already been opened; it was the so-called lHo-gling, now known under the name gNas-mchog gSal-dwangs ri-bo-che. As Sle-lung bZhad-pa'i rdo-rje was quickly back in rNam-grol gling, we must conclude that the mountain Rin-chen spungs-pa and surrounding places are located in the surroundings of his residence, i.e. in 'Ol-kha. Confirmation of this can be found, in fact, in a text dedicated to the meeting in rNam-grol gling in the year 1730. It is further documented in this work that on that occasion Sle-lung bZhad-pa'i rdo-rje climbed together with the ruler to the peak of the sacred mountain and made known to him the different sites he was authorized: "We climbed the peak of the sacred mountain; from my side, I offered [Mi-dbang bSod-nams stobs-rgyas] a rough identification of the layout of the sacred sites to the south and north of the mountain Rin-chen spungs-pa."[22]

Having just considered the transfer of control over a certain territory from one person to another, we can now see how a journey to a sacred site in the southern border areas can also result in the authority to idealize and spiritualize the landscape to which the traveler returned. The authorization was not restricted to Sle-lung bZhad-pa'i rdo-rje: in the same way the ruler Mi-dbang bSod-nams stobs-rgyas acquired a new status as an emanation of Yam-shud dmar-po, king of the *bTsan* demons. Although Sle-lung bZhad-pa'i rdo-rje makes the remark that this status was already known to him at their first meeting in the year 1726, it was only now, after his becoming the head of a new government and the first successes in his foreign policy that bSod-nams stobs-rgyas himself learned of it.

The importance of this new spiritual identity of the ruler is seen in the fact that the quotations from literary sources which Sle-lung bZhad-pa'i rdo-rje brought forward in this respect were included in the biography of bSod-nams stobs-rgyas, written three years afterwards, i.e. in 1733. These were, first, a passage from the cycle *gZigs snang gsang ba rgya can ma* of the Fifth Dalai Bla-ma, and second, a quotation from the writings of Chos-rje gling-pa.[23]

---

22 See the text bZhad-pa'i rdo-rje: *Mi dbang bsod nams stogs rgyas rnam grol gling du byon pa'i lo rgyus ngo mtshar 'bum snang* in "Collected Works", vol. 9, p. 327.1–2 (*gnas ri'i rtser phebs / bdag nas ri bo rin chen spungs pa lho byang gi gnas bkod rnams rags rim ngo sprod du phul*). In this text we find also the localization of the sacred mountain Rin-chen spungs-pa; ibid, p. 282.1–2 (... *'ol dga'i yul gru srid pa'i lha gnyan ger mtsho'i pho brang lhun po rdza'am ri bo rin chen spungs pa zhes yongs su grags pa* ...) For the opening of the site gNas-mchog gSal-dwangs ri-bo-che, i.e. lHo-gling, see bZhad-pa'i rdo-rje: *Yid bzhin gyi nor bu ratna tā re'i lo rgyus mthong na kun dga'* (as in note 21); this text was composed by Sle-lung bZhad-pa'i rdo-rje at the request of bSod-nams stobs-rgyas.

23 For the quotation from the cycle *gZigs snang gsang ba rgya can ma* that qualifies bSod-nams stobs-rgyas as an emanation of Yam-shud dmar-po, see bZhad-pa'i rdo-rje (as the first text in note 22), p.

CONCLUDING REMARKS

With these details I conclude my observations concerning the relationship between the ruler and the preceptor. It should have become clear that Sle-lung bZhad-pa'i rdo-rje played an hitherto unnoticed role in the development of bSod-nams stobs-rgyas from minister and warlord to the ruler of Tibet who provided his country with a certain degree of political stability up to his death in the year 1747. Further proof of the importance of this teachers for the undertakings of bSod-nams stobs-rgyas is the fact that the catalogue of the so-called *sNar thang bka' 'gyur* (sponsored by bSod-nams stobs-rgyas in the years 1730/31) came from the pen of Sle-lung bZhad-pa'i rdo-rje.[24]

Concerning the ongoing research on hidden valleys in Tibetan cultural areas, I might point out that, aside from questions of political history and religious geography, the different aspects of "Buddhist myths", i.e. the forms of symbolic representation, the ritual activities and spiritual practices that were part of the journeys into the untamed wilderness, are a field worthy of study.

As we saw in the case of Blo-bzang lHa-mchog, the *dharmapāla* Yam-shud dmar-po had his residence in the innermost recesses of the newly opened site in lHo-brag, and Sle-lung bZhad-pa'i rdo-rje went to gNas Padma-bkod to bring offerings to the deity sKrag-med nyi-shar. These protectors of the Buddhist teaching, their myths and connected rituals came alive in the persons of bSod-nams stobs-rgyas and Khang-chen-nas, two politicians during a particular difficult time for Tibet. And it is not a great surprise that this time of military attacks from outside and inner political conflicts should have coincided with a period when the paradisiacal sites in the south were promising not only refuge but also

---

282.4ff. Compare also Tshe-ring dbang-rgyal (as in note 7), pp. 79.4–80.10. In both cases the quotation is interpreted in the opposition between Khang-chen-nas (an emanation of the deity sKrag-med nyi-shar) and bSod-nams stobs-rgyas. The quotation from the writings of Chos-rje gling-pa can also be found in both sources and is ascribed to the text *Ātsarya sa le'i zhus len*, (p. 287.1ff. and pp. 80.10–82.18). But in a further work of bZhad-pa'i rdo-rje: *Lha gcig rdo rje skyabs byed kyi 'khrungs khang du dam can rgya mtsho'i bsti gnas gsar du bskrun pa'i deb ther rin po che 'phreng ba*, pp. 475.2ff., the quotation is ascribed to the text *rTsa gsum dril sgrub kyi lung bstan*. For Tibetan beliefs concerning the *dharmapāla* Yam-shud dmar-po, see Nebesky-Wojkowitz (1956:168–170). The myth of Yam-shud dmar-po (a younger brother of Buddha Śākyamuni who after creating initial disturbances was obliged as a protector of the teaching) is narrated in bZhad-pa'i rdo-rje: *Dam can bstan srung rgya mtsho'i rnam par thar pa cha shas tsam brjod pa [sngon med legs bshad]*, vol. II, p. 67.19–25.

24 This is the text *rGyal ba'i bka' 'gyur ro cog gi gsung pa rin po che srid gsum rgyan gcig rdzu 'phrul shing rta'i dkar chag ngo mtshar bkod pa rgya mtsho'i lde mig*, 127 fols. (missing from the "Collected Works"). It is mentioned in Zhabs-drung Tshe-ring dbang-rgyal (as in note 7), p. 82.19–20 and 746.1–2. For further information on this blockprint, see Jackson (1987a:93). The text has attracted the interest of concerned researchers; see Eimer (1994:310). bSod-nams stobs-rgyas and his sister Padma Chos-'dzoms were also active in propagating the tradition of the *rNying ma rgyud 'bum*; see Ehrhard (1997c) and chapter twenty-four in the present volume.

spiritual transformation. It is this very quality that makes up sacred sites according to Sle-lung bZhad-pa'i rdo-rje:

> Nowadays when one travels to these sacred mountains on naturally [experiences] resplendent terror and [at the same time] is at ease, and in one's stream of consciousness a new spiritual experience of the conception-free [unity of] bliss and emptiness flames up. [There are] the peculiar noises of the assemblage of the mothers, *ḍākiṇī*s, and non-humans, deep sighs are uttered, the sounds of songs, dances and instruments come forth, and the spontaneous sound of the secret *mantra*s rolls on; a sweet-smelling fragrance spreads round about, and so forth. The occurrence of these things in the shared experiences of different people is by itself enough to make [these places] an object to trust in![25]

[25] See bZhad-pa'i rdo-rje: *gNas chen zangs mdog dpal ri'i cha shas las 'phros pa'i gnas ri lo rgyus a ki dgyes pa'i glu dbyangs*, pp. 155.5–156.1 (*deng sang gi dus su gnas ri de dag tu bgrod pa na rang bzhin gyis 'jigs zil che ba dang / bag phebs pa dang / shes rgyud la sngar med pa'i bde stong rnam par mi rtogs pa'i nyams 'bar ba dang / ma mo mkha' 'gro dang / mi ma yin pa'i tshogs rnams kyi thug choms* (= *chom*) *dang / 'khun bu 'debs pa / glu gar dang rol mo'i sgra sgrog pa / gsang sngags kyi rang sgra ldir ba dang / dri zhim pa'i ngad 'thul ba sogs kyang kun gyi mthun snang du 'byung bar 'dug pa 'di kho nas kyang yid ches pa'i gnas su rigs mod*). The context of this passage provides further material for the origin of the sacred sites and the myth of Heruka (Maheśvara/Rudra); cf. Davidson (1991:229, note 6) with reference to the discussion of this myth by Sle-lung bZhad-pa'i rdo-rje: *Dam can bstan srung rgya mtsho'i rnam par thar pa cha shas tsam brjod pa sngon med legs bshad* (as in note 23), vol. I, pp. 1–103. For the inclusion of the ritual text *rGyal po rtse mdos* (otherwise unavailable) in the same collection, see Karmay (1991:343). The myth of Gaṇeśa (*tshogs bdag*) as narrated in this collection is referred to in Krishan (1992:65ff.).

APPENDIX

The Missing Summaries of the Cycle *gZigs snang gsang ba rgya can ma*

A unique source for research into the political and religious life of 17th-century Tibet and the field of Buddhist myth and ritual is the collection of manuscripts edited by S.G. Karmay under the title *Secret Visions of the Fifth Dalai Lama.* In the discussion of the works relating to the tradition of the cycle *gZigs snang gsang ba rgya can ma* the following statement is made: "There are no texts which contain summaries of the last five sections of the *rGya can.* These sections are devoted to the record of visions that occurred from 1674 to 1680 and the first few months of 1681", Karmay (1988a:18).

A further manuscript of the cycle was filmed by the Nepal-German Manuscript Preservation Project (NGMPP) in 1987: *gZigs snang gsang ba rgya can ma*, 578 fols., reel no. E 2134/2–E 2135/1; see Ehrhard (1993a:78f.) and chapter ten in the present volume; compare also Karmay (2002:22). A close inspection revealed the missing summaries in this collection. They are to be found in a text called *rGya can gyi 'khrul snang rnga chen ma shar bar gyi bkod pa zhing khams rgya mtsho'i yid 'phrog*, 64 fols. Here an overview of the five sections and the respective years of the summarized visions:

1. *Pad dkar rgya can*	fols.	2a/1–11b/2	1674–1675
2. *gDugs dkar rgya can*	fols.	11b/2–19b/6	1676
3. *Chos gdung g.yas 'khyil rgya can*	fols.	19b/6–33a/6	1676–1677
4. *gSer nya'i rgya can*	fols.	33a/6–49b/2	1678–1679
5. *rGyal mtshan rgya can*	fols.	49a/2–63a/5	1680–1681

According to the colophon the text was written in 1685 by 'Jam-dbyangs grags-pa, a monk who took active part in editing texts, especially in Fifth Dalai Bla-ma's later works. It was this time that thangkas depicting the visions of the Fifth Dalai Bla-ma were painted on the orders of sDe-srid Sangs-rgyas rgya-mtsho. The colophon reads (fol. 64a/6–b/6):

> The sequence of the visions of the sealed volume which manifested [in the period] from the wood-tiger [year] (= 1674) up to the [time when] the water-dog [year] (= 1682) had not yet appeared: when the artist 'Jam-dbyangs rin-chen drew the preliminary sketches [for the thangkas] to be set up by the ruler Sangs-rgyas rgya-mtsho—who came [to this world] as a master over the width of heaven and earth pursuant to the intent of the prince Mu-ne btsan-po—the full understanding [of the composition of the text] came forth mainly. [This work] was completed on the dMar-po ri,the palace of Ārya Lokeśvara, by the editor, the one who compiled it, the respectable Vidyādhara 'Jam-dbyangs grags-pa, on the tenth day

of the monkey month of the year *khro bo*, also called *khrodha* (= 1685), [i.e. the day] when one cries out for him who is called rDo-rje thogs-med rtsal, the old Mantrika from Za-hor, or Gang-shar rang-grol (i.e. the Fifth Dalai Bla-ma), at the special time when *vīra*s, *ḍākiṇī*s come together like clouds; and it was put to paper by Blo-bzang dbang-po, one whose technical skills attain [all] limits. May it be auspicious for all!

(*ces shing stag nas chu khyi ma shar bar byung ba'i rgya can gyi 'khrul snang rnams kyi bkod pa gnam sa'i khyon la mnga' bsgyur bar lha sras mu ne btsan po nyid bsam pas bzhin byon pa mi bdag sangs rgyas rgya mtshos bzheng ba'i sngon 'gro shog khrar lha ris pa 'jam dbyangs rin chen gyis 'dri* (= *'bri*) *dus mngon rtogs gtso bor gton* (= *bton*) *te / za hor gyi sngags rgan rdo rje thogs med rtsal lam gang shar rang grol du 'bod pas* (= *pa'i*) *khro rdha zhes pa khro bo'i lo sprel zla'i tshes bcur dpa' bo mkha' 'gro sprin bzhin du 'du ba'i dus khyad par can la 'phags pa 'jig rten dbang phyug gi gzhal med khang dmar po rir sbyar ba'i yi ge pa ni rigs 'dzin gyi btsun pa 'jam dbyangs grags pas bgyis shing shog thog tu mthar rgyas rig byed pa blo bzang dbang pos phab pa sarva mangale* (sic!) *bhavantu*).

Kaḥ-thog-pa bSod-nams rgyal-mtshan (1466–1540) and His Activities in Sikkim and Bhutan

[1]

The establishment of the monastery of Kaḥ-thog in Eastern Tibet in the year 1159 marked an important step in the consolidation of the rNying-ma-pa school of Tibetan Buddhism. Its founder, Kaḥ-dam-pa bDe-gshegs (1122–1192), occupies a prominent place in the transmission known as the "Spoken Teachings" (*bka' ma*). This specific teaching tradition was further spread by a number of abbots, known collectively as the "Succession of Teachers [Consisting of] Thirteen [Persons]" (*bla rabs bcu gsum*). According to one way of counting, the list begins with sPyan-snga bSod-nams 'bum[-pa] (born 1222) and ends with mKhas-grub Ye-shes rgyal-mtshan (1395–1458); the two immediate successors of Kaḥ-dam-pa bDe-gshegs, gTsang-ston rDo-rje rgyal-mtshan (1126–1216) and Byams-pa 'bum[-pa] (1179–1252), are not included in this particular list of successive regents of the glorious Kaḥ-thog monastery.[1]

In the historiographical literature of the rNying-ma-pa school the period of the next series of abbots—called the "Succession of Attendants [Consisting of] Thirteen [Persons]" (*drung rabs bcu gsum*)—is characterized by an increasing influence of the tradition of the "Treasure Teachings" (*gter ma*), which led to a slight diminishing of the importance of the Spoken Teachings tradition. This event is linked to the journey of Drung Nam-mkha' seng-ge, the first in this list of abbots, to the region of lHo-brag, where he became the "master of the teachings" (*chos bdag*) of the treasure-cycles of Rig-'dzin Ratna gling-pa (1403–1478). This particular phase of new spiritual developments within the teaching lineages of Kaḥ-thog in the 15th century was also the period when the exponent who would later create a sub-school known as the lHo-mon Kaḥ-thog-pa or Mon-lugs Kaḥ-thog-pa received his training.[2]

---

1 See Sangs-rgyas rdo-rje (born 1913): *dPal rgyal ba ka thog pa'i gdan rabs brgyud 'dzin dang bcas pa'i byung ba brjod pa rin po che'i phreng ba lta bu'i gtam*, fols. 31a/5–37a/4. The author states that this way of counting follows the *mTshan bsdoms gsol 'debs* of the teachers of Kaḥ-thog composed by Kaḥ-thog Si-tu Chos-kyi rgya-mtsho (1880–1925); ibid, fol. 31b/1–2. The same authority is acknowledged by mKhan-chen 'Jam-dbyangs rgyal-mtshan (born 1929): *gSang chen bstan pa'i chu 'go rgyal ba kaḥ thog pa'i lo rgyus mdor bsdus brjod pa 'chi med lha'i rnga sgra ngo mtshar rna ba'i dga' ston*, p. 54.3–5.

2 For the change in doctrinal emphasis from the Spoken Teachings to Treasure Teachings within the teaching lineages of Kaḥ-thog in the 15th century, see Ehrhard (1990a:88, note 20). For the counting of

A first assessment of the history of this sub-school in Bhutan was provided by the late Michael Aris. He opened his sketch of the rNying-ma-pa in Bhutan with a treatment of the lHo-mon Kaḥ-thog-pa, whom he called "[t]he first rNying-ma-pa to arrive in a formal sense". According to the historical sources available to him, it was one of the abbots of the above-mentioned first group of regents of Kaḥ-thog, a certain dBu-'od Ye-shes 'bum[-pa], who in the 13th century made his way to Bhutan on his way to Sikkim and founded in sPa-gro sTag-tshang the monastery of O-rgyan rtse-mo; the location of this old residence of the Kaḥ-thog-pa tradition was immediately above the main shrine of sTag-tshang. It is further stated that this master had two disciples, namely bSod-nams rgyal-mtshan and the latter's son rNam-grol bzang-po, who both settled at sTag-tshang in the sPa-gro valley.[3]

It was further noted by Aris that there exists a biography of bSod-nams rgyal-mtshan by a certain rNam-grol bzang-po, and also an autobiography, but he was obviously not in a position to consult these works. As we now have access to the biographical tradition of this teacher from Kaḥ-thog closely connected with the religious history of Sikkim and Bhutan, I want to readdress the issue of the arrival of the lHo-mon Kaḥ-thog-pa in the Himalayan valleys, and in particular at the famous Padmasambhava shrine near sPa-gro. This will be done in two steps: clarifying the identity of Ye-shes 'bum[-pa] from the Kaḥ-thog monastery, and giving an overview of the life of bSod-nams rgyal-mtshan, with special reference to his activities in Sikkim and Bhutan.

[2]

If one consults the biographical account of dBu-'od Ye-shes 'bum[-pa] in modern works dealing with the monastery of Kaḥ-thog and its different successions of abbots, one learns that this master had a great number of disciples from dBus and gTsang in Central Tibet, but there is no record of travels to either Sikkim or Bhutan. What is remembered about this particular regent is his rapport with the Sa-skya-pa scion 'Phags-pa Blo-gros rgyal-mtshan (1235–1280), who is said to have visited the rNying-ma-pa monastery in Khams on his way back from the Yüan court and to have received on that occasion the *sGyu 'phrul zhi khro* initiation from dBu-'od Ye-shes 'bum[-pa].[4]

Nam-mkha' seng-ge as the Second Drung and the difficulties of dating him, see Eimer (2002:331).

3 See Aris (1979b:153f.). There are two different sets of dates for dBu-'od Ye-shes 'bum[-pa], the third member of the *bla rabs bcu gsum* according to the enumeration advocated by Kaḥ-thog Si-tu Chos-kyi rgya-mtsho. As documented by Eimer (2002:327f. & 330), these dates are either 1254–1327 or 1242–1315. For the lHo-mon Kaḥ-thog-pa in Bhutan, compare also Aris (1994:23): "The Kathogpa school of eastern Tibet operated from within the Nyingmapa and established an early branch in Bhutan".

4 For biographical data on dBu-'od Ye-shes 'bum[-pa], see Sangs-rgyas rdo-rje (as in note 1), fol. 32a/1–b/3, and 'Jam-dbyangs rgyal-mtshan (as in note 1), pp. 42.20–44.12. Compare: lHa Tshe-ring: *mKha spyod 'bras mo ljongs kyi gtsug nor sprul pa'i rnal 'byor mched bzhi brgyud 'dzin dang bcas pa'i byung ba brjod pa blo gsar gzhon nu'i dga' ston.*, pp. 20.10–22.16, for an evaluation of the different

A journey to Central Tibet and to the "Rice Country" (*'bras mo ljongs*)—the name of modern-day Sikkim as known to the followers of Padmasambhava—is recorded in the case of still another master from Kaḥ-thog bearing the name Ye-shes 'bum-pa. This person is known as the "teacher from bZhag" (*bzhag bla*), a region in the Nyag-rong province of Khams, and his name turns up in the list of the "Succession of Scholars" (*mkhan rabs*) of Kaḥ-thog. One of the modern histories of the monastery provides the following account:

> He who is called Ye-shes 'bum-pa, the teacher from bZhag [in] Nyag-rong, a disciple of Jñānaketu, the one who is [both] learned and realized—this master of an ocean of the qualities of being learned, venerable [and] realized—in order to revive the stream of the doctrine in the regions of dBus [and] gTsang, and in order to search for the sacred site of the hidden valley "Rice Country", proceeded to the regions of dBus [and] gTsang. In the end, after accruing marvellous benefit for the doctrine and the beings, he passed away at the place of his spiritual practice in gTsang.[5]

The person referred to by the Sanskrit name "Jñānaketu" is the previously mentioned [mKhas-grub] Ye-shes rgyal-mtshan, the last member of the *bla rabs bcu gsum* of Kaḥ-thog. Both master and disciple thus belong to that phase in the history of Kaḥ-thog when the influence of the Treasure Teachings was increasing, the cultural practice of the search for hidden valleys in the Himalayan border regions by rNying-ma-pa masters from Eastern Tibet being least partly attributable to the change in the doctrinal emphasis within the teaching tradition. At the same time, the transmission of the Spoken Teachings was restructured and new commentaries were written. This becomes especially clear from a transmission represented by mKhas-grub Ye-shes rgyal-mtshan and bZhag-bla Ye-shes 'bum-pa. In the historiographical literature of the rNying-ma-pa school, this transmission is noted for having promulgated the *sGyu 'phrul drwa ba* and the *mDo dgongs pa 'dus*

---

historical sources concerning the person of dBu-'od Ye-shes 'bum[-pa], and the conclusion that this region of Kaḥ-thog could not have reached Sikkim. It is also noted that the misidentification of dBu-'od Ye-shes 'bum[-pa] and bZhag-bla Ye-shes 'bum-pa is responsible for the view that one of the early abbots of Kaḥ-thog was already travelling to the south; see ibid, p. 22.1–4.

5 See Sangs-rgyas rdo-rje (as in note 1), fol. 44a/1–4 (... *mkhas grub jñānaketu'i slob ma nyag rong bzhag bla ye shes 'bum pa zhes mkhas btsun grub pa'i yon tan rgya mtsho'i mnga' bdag de nyid dbus gtsang phyogs su bstan rgyun gso ba dang / sbas yul 'bras mo ljongs kyi gnas 'tshol phyir dbus gtsang phyogs su phebs te bstan 'gro'i don rmad du byung ba mdzad nas mthar gtsang gi sgrub gnas su sku gshegs*). The characterization of bZhag-bla Ye-shes 'bum-pa by 'Jam-dbyangs rgyal-mtshan (as in note 1), p. 73.13–20, contains nearly the same wording, but it leaves out the search for the "hidden valley" (*sbas yul*), while adding more information on the localities in gTsang: "At the end of his life he revived the doctrine in [places] like Zur 'Ug-pa lung and gSang-sngags gling" (*sku tshe'i mthar zur 'ug pa lung dang gsang sngags gling sogs kyi bstan pa nyams so gnang*).

pa—the main *Tantra*s of respectively Mahāyoga and Anuyoga—as a unified system, and it was this particular tradition which was continued by lHo-mon Kaḥ-thog-pa bSod-nams rgyal-mtshan and his disciple rNam-grol bzang-po.[6]

Having identified bZhag-bla Ye-shes 'bum-pa instead of dBu-'od Ye-shes 'bum[-pa] as the first scholar of Kaḥ-thog who directed his steps to the Himalayan border regions, we are able to date the arrival of the lHo-mon Kaḥ-thog-pa to Sikkim and Bhutan to the end of the 15th century. The initial spread of this sub-school can now be described on the basis of the biographical tradition of Kaḥ-thog-pa bSod-nams rgyal-mtshan.

[3]

The autobiography bears the title "Rosary of Stainless Wish-fulfilling Jewels" (*dri med yid bzhin nor bu'i phreng ba*) and was completed by bSod-nams rgyal-mtshan in sPa-gro sTag-tshang O-rgyan rtse-mo in the year 1539. Added to it is a work by his disciple rNam-grol [Ye-shes] bzang-po which covers the final events of his teacher's life; this text must have been composed in the year 1541, since it mentions an "ox year" (*glang lo*) for the consecration of the reliquary shrine of bSod-nams rgyal-mtshan. The place of composition of the latter work is given as "the upper part of dGe-rgyas 'Jag-ma lung, below the great glacier mDzod-lnga stag-rtse, the western gate of the glorious Rice Country".[7] This seems to suggest that the first representatives of the lHo-mon Kaḥ-thog-pa had their residences in both Sikkim and Bhutan, and became influential in these regions at about the same time.

In the following I will make use only of the autobiography, which is divided into three chapters, dealing respectively with prophecies concerning the person of bSod-nams rgyal-mtshan, with the teachers he relied upon during his spiritual training, and with the salvational means he had recourse to both for himself and for others. The second and third chapters are subdivided into five and eleven subsections respectively.

The initial part of the first chapter quotes from the *dGongs 'dus lung bstan bka' rgya ma*, that is, from "the cycle of the sealed pronouncements of prophecies for the future" (*ma*

---

6 The lineage of this transmission starts with Kaḥ-dam-pa bDe-gshegs, gTsang-ston rDo-rje rgyal-mtshan and Byams-pa 'bum[-pa], but includes only the second and the thirteenth members of the *bla rabs bcu gsum*, namely sPyan-snga Nam-mkha' rdo-rje (born 1223) and mKhas-grub Ye-shes rgyal-mtshan; see Dudjom Jikdrel Yeshe Dorje (1991:699). Among the new commentaries of the Spoken Teaching tradition during that period, mention must be made of Ye-shes rgyal-mtshan's exposition of the *Theg pa spyi bcings* of Kaḥ-dam-pa bDe-gshegs; see *Theg pa spyi bcings rtsa 'grel*, pp. 34–417. For the writings of Kaḥ-dam-pa bDe-gshegs and the commentary of Ye-shes rgyal-mtshan, see Dalton (2002:109–129).

7 See the dbu med text in *Shar kaḥ thog pa bsod names rgyal mtshan dpal bzang po'i rnam par thar pa*, p. 40.2–3 (*dpal 'bras mo bshongs (= gshongs) kyi nub sgo gangs chen mdzod lnga stag rtse'i zhol / dge rgyas 'jag ma lung gi phu*). The name "Great Glacier mDzod-lnga stag-rtse" for the Kangchenjunga range is already attested in the writings of Rig-'dzin rGod-ldem 'phru-can (1337–1406), one of the earliest and most prolific writers of literature concerning hidden valleys; see his *sBas yul 'bras mo ljongs kyi gnas yig bsdus pa*, p. 374.5. For the different gates leading to Sikkim as a hidden sanctuary, see note 10.

'ongs lung bstan bka' rgya ma'i skor) of the *Bla ma dgongs pa 'dus pa*, a treasure-cycle of Rig-'dzin Sangs-rgyas gling-pa (1340–1396). The works of this treasure-discoverer, along with ones of mNga'-bdag Nyang-ral [Nyi-ma'i 'od-zer] (1124–1192), Guru Chos[-kyi] dbang[-phyug] (1212–1270) and especially Rig-'dzin Ratna gling-pa, are listed at the beginning of the second chapter as those religious traditions which dominated the studies of bSod-nams rgyal-mtshan up to the age of seventeen years. The names of his teachers during that period include Kun-dga' 'bum[-pa], Brag-mgo rDo-rje dpal, dGe-'dun blo-gros and a certain La-rgyab Shes-rab dpal who transmitted the teachings of Klong-chen rab-'byams-pa (1308–1364) to the young student. But the first and most important teacher was his own uncle, whom he accompanied up to lHa-sa when the latter embarked on a journey to the regions of dBus and gTsang. This uncle is called in the autobiography mKhas-grub Ye-shes 'bum[-pa], and he is none other than bZhag-bla Ye-shes 'bum-pa from Nyag-rong province in Khams.[8]

For the next three years bSod-nams rgyal-mtshan stayed in the "land of the gorges" (*rong yul*) where he was advised by two further teachers how to follow the life of a yogin and practise austerities. It was only after this experience, at the age of twenty years, that he entered the monastery of Kaḥ-thog and took up his studies with the Great Ācārya Nam-mkha' dpal. This teacher imparted to him the classic works of the Spoken Teachings tradition and its exegetical literature, such as the *Theg pa spyi bcings* of Kaḥ-dam-pa bDe-gshegs; it is noted in the autobiography that this exposition was in the tradition of mKhas-grub Ye-shes rgyal-mtshan. In addition, Nam-mkha' dpal instructed his disciple in the different Indian and Tibetan commentaries on the *sGyu 'phrul drwa ba*, the authority of the Ācārya being based on the fact that he had penned an important commentary on this *Tantra*. This course of study having been mastered over a period of seven years, there followed further studies under a number of teachers, all associated with Kaḥ-thog monastery; among these we find the First Drung Nam-mkha' seng-ge and the Third Drung rGyal-mtshan rdo-rje.[9]

8 See the dbu-med text of the autobiography (as in note 7), pp. 45.6–57.3, for the studies up to the age of seventeen years. Only after his return from lHa-sa did bSod-nams rgyal-mtshan attend upon other teachers than his uncle. His own birthplace is given as the "land of gZhag (sic) of Nyag-rong [in] Khams" (... *mdo khams nyag rong gzhag gi yul*); see ibid, p. 47.3–4. This description has already been noted as an early reference to the "toponym" (*sa ming*) "Nyag-rong"; see Tashi Tsering (1993:103).

9 For the seven year study period with the Great Ācārya Nam-mkha' dpal, see the autobiography (as in note 7), pp. 60.2–65.5. The list of further teachers begins with the First Drung Nam-mkha' seng-ge and the Third Drung rGyal-mtshan rdo-rje; see ibid, pp. 65.5–72.2. A short biographical sketch of Nam-mkha' dpal can be found in the Kaḥ-thog history written by 'Jam-dbyangs rgyal-mtshan (as in note 1), p. 72.4–20. The title of the commentary of the *sGyu 'phrul drwa ba* is given there as *gSang snying ṭīkka dngul dkar me long* and is considered to be in the same class with the commentaries of Rong-zom Chos-kyi bzang-po (11th century), Klong-chen rab-'byams-pa and g.Yung-ston rDo-rje dpal (1285–1364). A biographical note on Nam-mkha' seng-ge, pointing out his role as a disciple of Rig-'dzin Ratna gling-pa, is contained ibid, pp. 66.10–67.13. Bya-bral Rin-po-ç̣he's work (as in note 1), fol. 42a/1, remarks that the

[4]
At the age of twenty-seven years, during a visit to the monastery of bZhag-yul dGon-gsar in his home region, bSod-nams rgyal-mtshan saw in a dream his uncle bZhag-bla Ye-shes 'bum-pa who urged him to come to Central Tibet and, more especially, to join him in opening dPal-gyi 'bras-mo gshongs, that is, Sikkim. He left soon afterwards for dBus and gTsang, the autobiography giving as the date for this departure the tenth Tibetan month of the year 1493.

Without going into the details of the journey, the autobiography relates next the meeting with the uncle at his residence, called Theg-chen chos-sdings, at the "northern gate" (*byang sgo*) of the hidden valley known as Rice Land. There follows an interesting account of the difficult process of finding the proper entry point into the sanctuary, with no success being met at the "eastern gate" (*shar sgo*) and the "southern gate" (*lho sgo*). It is also stated that bSod-nams rgyal-mtshan took up this search in place of his uncle bZhag-bla Ye-shes 'bum-pa, who had supplied him with the necessary guidebooks. The mission finally went to the "western gate" (*nub sgo*) and there came upon a site called dGe-rgyas 'Jag-ma lung; having passed through the "inner gate" (*nang sgo*), which bears the name g.Ya'-ma sTag-ri, the small group under the leadership of bSod-nams rgyal-mtshan arrived in the inner region of the sanctuary, said to be like a realm of the gods.[10]

The remaining two sections of the chapter, dealing with the teachers of bSod-nams rgyal-mtshan, describe activities after the death of bZhag-bla Ye-shes 'bum-pa, beginning

---

First Drung came from the same family as the first member of the *bla rabs bcu gsum*.

10 This subsection of the second main chapter has the title "Account of the Opening of the Gate to the Hidden Valley, [which is] a Sacred Site" (*sbas yul gnas sgo phyed pa'i rnam thar*); see the autobiography (as in note 7), pp. 72.2–82.5. The conception of "gates to the sacred site" (*gnas sgo*) in the four cardinal directions leading to the centre of a hidden land conceived as a *maṇḍala* is known from further cases; see, for example, the "four large gates" (*sgo chen po bzhi*) topographically located around the valley of Glang-'phrang—present-day Langtang—in Ehrhard (1997b:342–344) and chapter sixteen in the present volume. An elaborate description of the four entry points to the hidden valley of Sikkim can be found in *sBas yul 'bras mo ljongs kyi gnas yig phan yon dang bcas pa ngo mtshar gter mdzod* (block print), fols. 19a/6–28b/2 & 42b/5–44b/4. This work is the scriptural basis for the observations by Brauen-Dolma (1985:248f.) that the gates should be approached depending on the time of the year (in autumn from the east, in winter from the south, in spring from the west, and in summer from the north). The text in question is a compilation of different prophecies, consisting for the greater part of a long quotation from the ones of Rig-'dzin Sangs-rgyas gling-pa (1340–1396); see the relevant section in *Bla ma dgongs pa 'dus pa las / ma 'ongs lung bstan bka' rgya ma'i skor*, pp. 404.2–448.3 (= *sBas yul 'bras mo ljongs kyi gnas yig phan yon dang bcas pa ngo mtshar gter mdzod*, fols. 3a/5–56b/3). It should be noted that Rig-'dzin Sangs-rgyas gling-pa pays no attention to the western gate. A description of the entry through this gate can be found in the writings of Rig-'dzin rGod-ldem 'phru-can; see his *gNas 'bras mo 'dzongs* (= *gshongs*) *gi lam yig* (manuscript), fols. 3bff.; this text also mentions an inner gate with the name g.Ya-ma sTag-rtse (sic). For the observation that the text *sPyi'i them byang* of Rig-'dzin rGod-ldem 'phru-can—a work dealing with hidden valleys in general—contains numerous references to dPal-gyi 'bras-mo gshongs, compare Childs (1999:131, note 13).

with the funeral ceremonies on his behalf. The passing away of his first and most important teacher postponed for the time being a fuller engagement in the Himalayan valleys, and he discarded the idea of settling permanently in the inner part of the hidden valley just opened by him.

Travelling instead to lHa-sa and to bSam-yas in order to make offerings for bZhag-bla Ye-shes 'bum-pa, bSod-nams rgyal-mtshan came across the Seventh Karma-pa Chos-grags rgya-mtsho (1454–1506) in the Yar-klungs valley, and while still in the valley, at the site of Chu-mig dGon-gsar, he received teachings from a certain Grags-pa 'od-zer. As this master was a member of the family of Rig-'dzin Ratna gling-pa, bSod-nams rgyal-mtshan was able to receive those cycles of the treasure-discoverer's teachings which he had not obtained before. The next two teachers mentioned in the autobiography also imparted teaching traditions of the rNying-ma-pa school to him. In gTsang dMus-ston chen-po Kun-bzang dpal gave the "reading authorization" (*lung*) of the "Collected *Tantra*s of the Old [School]" (*rnying ma rgyud 'bum*), a detailed list of the contents of the thirty-five volumes being contained in the autobiography; from the same teacher he also received the *bKa' brgyad bde gshegs 'dus pa* cycle of mNga'-bdag Nyang-ral [Nyi-ma'i 'od-zer]. Finally, in La-stod lHo, bSod-nams rgyal-mtshan received the treasure-cycles of Rig-'dzin rGod-ldem 'phru-can from a teacher called Chos-rje sTon-chen Grags-pa rgyal-mtshan; this master also transmitted to him the treasure-cycles of Rig-'dzin Shes-rab me-'bar (1267–1326), a treasure-discoverer who had been active in the sPa-gro valley in Bhutan.[11]

[5]

After a three-year period from 1502 to 1505, devoted exclusively to the spiritual practice of these different teaching traditions at a site known as [Theg-chen] chos-sdings Yang-dben rDo-thang—obviously located in the vicinity of the former residence of his uncle bZhag-bla Ye-shes 'bum-pa—bSod-nams rgyal-mtshan pondered the idea of returning to his home region in Khams and to the monastery of Kaḥ-thog. At that time repeated invitations arrived at his hermitage in northern Sikkim from sPa-gro sTag-tshang, having been sent by a person named Bla-ma Ngang-brgyud rgyal-ba. He finally took up the

[11] For the last two subsections of the second chapter, see the autobiography (as in note 7), pp. 82.5–105.5. The list of the contents of the *rNying ma rgyud 'bum* collection in thirty-five volumes can be found ibid, pp. 92.2–98.6; this is a kind of provisional list, an extended version of which is said to be contained in the "list of teachings received" (*thob yig*) of bSod-nams rgyal-mtshan (up to now unavailable). The teacher dMus-ston chen-po Kun-bzang dpal is also known under the name Gling-chen Kun-bzang dpal, derived from his residence in gTsang, "the monastery of Gling-bu [in] Nyang-stod" (*nyang stod gling bu dgon pa*). This is known from the autobiography of the treasure-discoverer 'Gro-'dul Las-'phro gling-pa (1488–1553) who stayed for a period of one year with the master Kun-bzang dpal; see *Rig 'dzin chen po gter bton (= ston) las 'phro gling pa'i dus gsum gyi skye brgyud dang rnam par thar pa che long tsam zhig bkod pa me tog 'phreng mdzes*, pp. 387.1–391.1.

invitation. The autobiography records a request made by the Bhutanese disciple when his guest arrived for the first time at the celebrated Padmasambhava shrine of sTag-tshang:

> The regions of dBus-gtsang, mDo-khams, [and] especially [the monastery of] Kaḥ-thog—they are pure lands, [and] the Dharma will always spread [there]. [Here, in] our Land of the Mon, a barbarous border country, the Dharma has not been diffused: the beings who are foolish [and benighted] like animals—take care of them with [your] great affection! [And] especially at the pilgrimage site of the Great One from Oḍḍiyāna, at [this cave known as] "Tiger Den, Where Lions' Thoughts Are Accomplished", erect to completion a place for spiritual practice – [this] we request [you]![12]

The teacher from Kaḥ-thog provides the detailed story of the circumstances of the establishment of this site, to which he later gave the name "Tiger Den, the Peak of Oḍ iyāna" (*sTag-tshang O-rgyan rtse-mo*). A translation and edition of this part of the autobiography, which closes the second subsection of chapter three and covers the years 1507 to 1508, will be given on a later occasion. There remain nine subsections, dealing with the spiritual achievements of bSod-nams rgyal-mtshan and his further travels and teaching activities. I select three of them in order to sketch a rough picture of this part of his life-story.

The first one bears the title "An Account of How [the People of] Mon in the South Became Established in the Dharma" (*lho mon chos la bkod pa'i rnam thar*). At the beginning one finds the interesting statement of bSod-nams rgyal-mtshan that he was a recipient of all the Spoken Teachings of the rNying-ma-pa school and, although not a treasure-discoverer himself, had also obtained most of the Treasure Teachings available in his time. It was the transmission of the collection of *Tantra*s from both these teaching traditions which he gave to his disciples at the start of his effort to spread these lineages in Bhutan:

12 See the autobiography (as in note 7), pp. 114.6–115.2 (*dbus gtsang mdo khams khyad par bka'* (sic) *thog phyogs / dag pa'i zhing yin bstan pa nam yang dar / bdag cag mon yul mtha' khab chos mi dar / dud 'gro lta bu'i blun rmongs sems can la / brtse ba chen pos rjes su bzung ba* (= *gzung ba*) *dang / khyad par o rgyan chen po'i gnas chen ste / stag tshang seng ge bsam grub 'di nyid du / bsgrub* (= *sgrub*) *sde cig kyang rab tu 'dzugs par zhu*). For the gDung family of Ngang and their genealogy, see Aris (1979b:138f.); a person named rGyal-ba is listed in the accompanying table; see ibid, p. 136. At the beginning of the 16th century sTag-tshang was the most important pilgrimage site associated with Padmasambhava in the sPa-gro and Had valleys. See, for example, the biography of the 'Brug-pa bKa'-brgyud-pa yogin Grags-pa mtha'-yas (1469–1531), who paid visits to these sites after the death of his teacher lHa-btsun Kun-dga' chos-kyi rgya-mtsho (1432–1505). He, too, referred to sTag-tshang under the name of the Seng-ge bsam-'grub cave; see *rNal 'byor gyi dbang phyug grags pa mtha' yas dpal bzang po'i rnam thar mgur 'bum ngo mtshar nor bu'i phreng ba*, pp. 190.4–194.2.

> In the beginning, at [sPa-gro] sTag-tshang, the meeting ground of the Ḍākinīs, headed by dBang-phyug rgyal-mtshan, the sky-yogin, and by the teacher Ngang-brgyud rgyal[-ba] and so forth—for an assembly of about five hundred [persons] with the proper karma—I performed in their totality [the transmission of] the Collected *Tantra*s of the Old [School]. On these auspicious occasions, there were downpours of flowers, and marvellous signs and countless blessings appeared.[13]

After these initial transmissions in the western part of the country, bSod-nams rgyal-mtshan accepted an invitation from a certain rGyal-mtshan ye-shes, affiliated to a monastery called Kun-bzang gling. This is one of the monasteries founded by the great Klong-chen rab-'byams-pa in Bhutan, and is located in the sKur-stod valley. As the teacher from Kaḥ-thog travelled afterwards through the region of sNas-lung, where another of Klong-chen rab-'byams-pa's foundations can be found, one may surmise that he visited on this journey the sites associated with the famous codifier of the rDzogs-chen doctrine; and in fact, besides transmitting the cycles of the Spoken Teachings collectively called *sGyu 'phrul zhi khro phur gsum*, he also gave empowerments and instructions of the *sNying thig* cycles of Klong-chen rab-'byams-pa.

Another invitation having arrived from the valley of Bum-thang from a person named Tshe-dbang rgyal-po, bSod-nams rgyal-mtshan gave once again teachings including the *sGyu 'phrul zhi khro phur gsum*. On that occasion he encountered Rig-'dzin Padma gling-pa, who had just established his temple of gTam-zhing in Bum-thang. Further travels seem to have been mostly undertaken in the western valleys of Thim-phu and sPa-gro. For example, he was active in Glang-ma lung and in lCags-zam Thog-kha; these two places, located in Thim-phu and sPa-gro respectively, are known to have been residences of the gNas-rnying-pa, a school of Tibetan Buddhism which was firmly established in western Bhutan at the time.

But it was, of course, at O-rgyan rtse-mo that bSod-nams rgyal-mtshan chiefly propagated his teaching traditions, including the *bKa' brgyad bde gshegs 'dus pa*, the *Bla ma dgongs pa 'dus pa*, the "Southern Treasures" (*lho gter*) and the "Northern Treasures" (*byang gter*). At the same place, for the spiritual practice at sPa-gro sTag-tshang, he gave

---

[13] See the autobiography (as in note 7), pp. 132.6–133.3 (*thog mar stag tshang mkha' 'gro 'dus sa ru / nam mkha' rnal 'byor dbang phyug rgyal mtshan dang / bla ma ngang brgyud rgyal sogs gtso byas pa'i / las ldan lnga brgya tsam gcig 'tshogs pa la / rnying ma'i rgyud 'bum yongs su rdzogs par byas / dus bzang rnams su me tog char babs shing / ngo mtshar ltas dang byin rlabs dpag med byung*). This seems to be the first reference to the transmission of the *rNying ma rgyud 'bum* in Bhutan; surprisingly, it was a transmission from gTsang and not from Kaḥ-thog monastery. In the following period the main source for the diffusion of this collection of *Tantra*s was lHo-brag lHa-lung, the main seat of the teaching tradition of Rig-'dzin Padma gling-pa (1450–1521). For the importance of the Third Pad-gling gsung-sprul Tshul-khrims rdo-rje (1598–1669) in this process, see Ehrhard (1997c:256, note 8) and chapter twenty-four in the present volume.

a second time the transmission of the *Tantra*s of the Old School, on this particular occasion for people both from Mon-yul and from Tibet. Among the group of about one hundred disciples a Tibetan lady of noble origin is mentioned who offered the teacher a thirty-five-volume set of the *rNying ma rgyud 'bum*. The autobiography suggests that although there existed at that time diverse reading authorizations of this collection, the complete one as maintained by the master from Kaḥ-thog was quite rare.[14]

[6]
The subsection titled "An Extensive Account of Teachings [and] Initiations [which are] of Benefit for the Disciples of the Regions of dBus [and] gTsang" (*dbus gtsang phyogs kyi gdul bya la / chos dbang 'gro don rgyas pa'i rnam thar*) describes first travels to Bar-'brog in La-stod, to 'Bring-mtshams, and to mGo-yul. In the latter area bSod-nams rgyal-mtshan gave public discourses to a great number of people, headed by the "princess" (*dpon sa*) bDag-mo'i drung. He also revisited eastern gTsang, where his teacher Chos-rje Gling-chen, that is, Kun-bzang dpal from the monastery of Gling-bu, had since passed away. On that occasion he gave the complete initiations and instructions of the *bKa' brgyad bde gshegs 'dus pa* cycle in sPos-khang lHa-steng in Nyang-smad.

Concerning his travels in dBus, the autobiography states that they began in the year 1528—at the age of sixty-two—when he was invited by a teacher known as dKar-chen Kun-dga' grags-pa to the bSam-yas *vihāra*. There he was called upon to consecrate a colossal statue of the Precious Guru Padmasambhava. The project of erecting such a huge icon had been initiated for the "expulsion of armed forces" (*dmag bzlog*), a danger that was quite real at the time in Central Tibet. After the consecration from a throne in front of the bSam-yas pillar, he imparted teachings and initiations, and among the disciples are mentioned lHo-brag [rDo-rje gdan-pa] Chos-rje lHa-ro-ba and [bSam-yas] gDan-sa[-pa] Rab-'byams-pa dGe-ba'i blo-gros, both representatives of the teaching lineage of the master dKar-chen Kun-dga' grags-pa.[15]

---

14 The travels in the eastern and western valleys are related in the autobiography (as in note 7), pp. 133.3–142.2. For the eight monasteries founded by Klong-chen rab-'byams-pa in Bhutan, see Aris (1979b:315, note 19); compare Ehrhard (1992:54–56) and chapter three in the present volume, for that part of his family line descending from Bum-thang Thar-pa-gling. For a description of the erection of gTam-zhing based on the biography of Rig-'dzin Padma gling-pa, see Aris (1988:33–37); the consecration of the temple took place in the year 1505. The history of the gNas-rnying-pa in Bhutan and their residences in Glang-ma lung and lCags-zam Thog-kha is also treated by Aris (1979b:191–195 & 322, note 131). Concerning the second transmission of the *rNying ma rgyud 'bum* at O-rgyan rtse-mo, see the autobiography (as in note 7), pp. 142.3–143.6. The name of the Tibetan lady is given as rGyang-rtse dPon-sa bDag-mo drung and bDag-mo'i drung; she was thus a member of the ruling house of present-day Gyantse in gTsang. For the reading authorization of the *rNying ma rgyud 'bum*, see ibid, p. 143.1–2: (*ding sang gsang sngags rnying ma'i rgyud 'bum lung / skor le than thun yod pa mang 'dug kyang / yongs rdzogs bdag tsam min pa dkon pa 'dra*).

15 For the travels in gTsang and the events in bSam-yas, see the autobiography (as in note 7), pp. 144.1–

Having visited the different sacred sites in the surroundings of the bSam-yas *vihāra*, including 'Ching-phu (sic) and Brag-dmar g.Ya-ma lung, the teacher from Kaḥ-thog proceeded on to lHa-sa, where his local patron was a person called bKor gNyer-dpon or bKor-bdag rGyal-po. After giving teachings in lHa-sa sKyid-shod, he returned via La-stod to his residence in the sPa-gro valley of Bhutan, and there stayed in retreat for a longer period. bSod-nams rgyal-mtshan's last journey to gTsang took place in the year 1532, when he visited the court of the rGyang-rtse rulers. In front of an assembly of seven hundred people he imparted teachings and initiations from the traditions of the Spoken Teachings and the Treasure Teachings, including the cycle *Zab chos zhi khro dgongs pa rang grol* of Rig-'dzin Karma gling-pa (14th century).[16]

As a kind of overview of the disciples who continued his teaching tradition bSod-nams rgyal-mtshan lists about a dozen names in the subsection called "An Account of the Assembling of the Great [Spiritual] Sons who Transmitted the Dharma" (*chos brgyud bu chen 'dus pa'i rnam thar*). The enumeration starts with dKar-chen Kun-dga' grags-pa and includes both lHa-ro Chos-rje—now qualified as being a member of the family of Guru Chos[-kyi] dbang[-phyug] —and Rab-'byams-pa dGe-ba'i blo-gros, namely the respective representatives of dKar-chen Kun-dga' grags-pa's teaching lineage from lHo-brag and

---

156.1. dKar-chen Kun-dga' grags-pa is known to have been a lineage-holder of the treasure-cycles of Sangs-rgyas gling-pa and of Dri-med Kun-dga' (born 1347). For his position in the lineage of Dri-med Kun-dga' and the epithet "whitely [dressed] one" (*dkar po ba*), see the historiographical work of sTag-sgang mkhas-mchog Ngag-dbang blo-gros: *bsTan pa'i snying po gsang chen snga 'gyur nges don zab mo'i chos kyi 'byung ba gsal bar byed pa'i legs bshad mkhas pa dga' byed ngo mtshar gtam gyi rol mtsho*, pp. 466.9–467.3. In order to spread the teachings of Sangs-rgyas gling-pa, this master kept up four "residences" (*gdan sa*). They were known as Dwags-po dGongs-'dus gling (in the east), lHo-brag rDo-rje gdan (in the south), gTsang-gi zab-bu gling [= zab-phu lung] (in the west), and bSam-yas Ri-bo-rtse (in the north); see Karma Mi-'gyur dBang-gi rgyal-po (17 century): *gTer bton (= ston) brgya rtsa'i mtshan sdom gsol 'debs chos rgyal bkra shis stobs rgyal gyi mdzad pa'i 'grel pa lo rgyus gter bton (= ston) chos 'byung*, pp. 126.4–127.3. According to this passage dKar-chen Kun-dga' grags-pa was famous for renovating shrines and temples, among them the cave known as Nyi-zla [kha-sbyor] phug in sPa-gro sTag-tshang. For the erection of the colossal statue of Padmasambhava in lHo-brag by the treasure-discoverer mChog-ldan mgon-po (1497–1531), a disciple of dKar-chen Kun-dga' grags-pa, and the dangers of armed forces in Central Tibet during this particular period, see Ehrhard (2000a:35–37).

[16] The second part of the journey to dBus and the last visit to gTsang can be found in the autobiography (as in note 7), pp. 156.1–162.5. The period between these two travels was devoted to the composition of the main literary work known to exist from the pen of bSod-nams rgyal-mtshan. It bears the title *bKa' thams cad gsal bar ston pa byed pa / bstan pa thams cad kyi spyi 'grel / theg pa thams cad kyi shan 'byed / man ngag thams cad kyi dgongs don / sems kyi chos nyid mngon du rtogs pa'i me long / nyi 'od gsal ba*; see the Kaḥ-thog histories of Sangs-rgyas rdo-rje (as in note 1), fol. 44b/3–6, and of 'Jam-dbyangs rgyal-mtshan (as in note 1), pp. 74.17–75.2. The work was published, under the title *Theg pa thams cad kyi shan 'byed nyi 'od rab gsal*, in two parts (the year of composition was *lcags pho stag* = 1530). Like mKhas-grub Ye-shes rgyal-mtshan's exposition of the *Theg pa spyi bcings*, this work should be classified among the new commentaries of the Spoken Teachings tradition; see note 6.

bSam-yas. Two of the disciples were at the same time bSod-nams rgyal-mtshan's own teachers: dMus-ston chen-po Kun-bzang dpal from gTsang and Chos-rje sTon-chen Grags-pa rgyal-mtshan from La-stod lHo. The noble Tibetan lady dPon-sa'i bdag-mo drung is now identified as an "emanation of [Ye-shes] mTsho-rgyal" (*mtsho rgyal sprul pa*), the Tibetan consort of Padmasambhava. The list also contains the name g.Yang-lung [Chos-rje] Kun-dga' legs-pa'i 'byung-gnas; this person is always mentioned as being in the company of the female patron of bSod-nams rgyal-mtshan in the different episodes noted above.

One also finds in the list the name of Chos-rje Grags-pa rgyal-mtshan, one of the sons of Rig-'dzin Padma gling-pa; he was that offspring of the great treasure-discoverer from Bhutan who had inherited the temple of gTam-zhing in the valley of Bum-thang. Another disciple of the teacher of Kaḥ-thog was Rig-'dzin bsTan-gnyis gling-pa (1480–1535), whose alternative name is given in the autobiography as the "treasure-discoverer [from] Chu-bzang" (*chu bzang gter ston*).[17] The list closes with the names of two brothers, simply referred to as the "ones from mNga'-ris" (*mnga' ris pa*). This designation refers to mNga'-ris Paṇ-chen Padma dbang-rgyal (1487–1542) and to mNga'-ris rig-'dzin Legs-ldan bDud-'joms rdo-rje (born 1512). If one consults their biographies from a later historical tradition, one finds references to meetings of these teachers from Western Tibet with both the founder of the lHo-mon Kaḥ-thog-pa and with rNam-grol bzang-po, his immediate successor.[18]

---

17 For the subsection dealing with the different disciples, see the autobiography (as in note 7), pp. 175.4–180.3. Rig-'dzin bsTan-gnyis gling-pa was affiliated to the 'Brug-pa bKa'-brgyud-pa monastery of Chu-bzang and had met Rig-'dzin Padma gling-pa at the latter's temple gTam-zhing in the years 1519 and 1520. He returned to Bhutan in the year 1532 and raised treasure-works in two caves at the sacred site of sPa-gro sTag-tshang. These places are called Nyi-zla [kha-sbyor] phug and Seng-ge bsam-'grub phug; see his autobiography *Rigs* (sic) *'dzin bstan gnyis gling pa'i rnam thar las / rnal lam lung bstan gyi skor*, pp. 94.2–95.1; at the latter cave Rig-'dzin bsTan-gnyis gling-pa rediscovered teachings originally found there—and then hidden again—by Gu-ru Tshe-brtan rgyal-mtshan, an early treasure-discoverer active in Bhutan; see Ehrhard (1997b:341 & 350, note 12) and chapter sixteen in the present volume. After these findings, a meeting of the master from Chu-bzang with Chos-rje Kaḥ-thog-pa bSod-nams rgyal-mtshan is recorded in the text. Another disciple of Rig-'dzin Padma gling-pa who had retrieved treasure-cycles from sPa-gro sTag-tshang was the previously mentioned 'Gro-'dul Las-'phro gling-pa. He remained afterwards for one year in the company of bSod-nams rgyal-mtshan at O-rgyan rtse-mo, listening to his exposition of the lineages of the Spoken Teachings and Treasure Teachings; see the autobiography of 'Gro-'dul Las-'phro gling-pa (as in note 11), pp. 384.3–387.1.

18 See the biography of mNga'-ris Paṇ-chen Padma dbang-rgyal written by Padma 'phrin-las: *'Dus pa mdo dbang gi bla ma brgyud pa'i rnam thar ngo mtshar dad pa'i phreng ba*, p. 323.2 (*kaḥ thog pa chos rje bsod nams rgyal mtshan sogs bshes gnyen mang po dang chos skyes 'bul res mdzad*); this meeting with bSod-nams rgyal-mtshan occurred in 1529 during the latter's sojourn at the bSam-yas *vihāra*. mNga'-ris rig-'dzin Legs-ldan bdud-'joms rdo-rje was regarded as an incarnation of Rig-'dzin rGod-ldem 'phru-can and, like his predecessor, undertook to open dPal-gyi 'bras-mo gshongs. This happened after the death of his elder brother in the year 1542; for a meeting with rNam-grol bzang-po at the former residence of bZhag-bla Ye-shes 'bum-pa at [Theg-chen] chos-sdings, located at the northern gate of the hidden valley,

[7]
The final advice offered by bSod-nams rgyal-mtshan before he passed away at O-rgyan rtse-mo called for his disciples to follow their spiritual practice at such sacred sites in Tibet as Zab-phu lung and 'Ching-phu (sic) in the vicinity of the bSam-yas *vihāra*. But first and foremost they were urged to stay at the "great hidden valley" (*sbas yul chen po*) called dPal-gyi 'bras-mo gshongs and at sPa-gro sTag-tshang; and in the latter case at a site called Nyi-zla dmar-mo, which obviously refers to the previously mentioned Nyi-zla [kha-sbyor] phug. If one consults, in addition to the autobiography, the account by rNam-grol [Ye-shes] bzang-po, it becomes clear that in 1539 the master from Kaḥ-thog had a dream of the country known as Rice Land, and that this particular vision resulted in his handing over to his disciple a written scroll describing the entry through the western gate.[19]

Although the literary sources are quite reticent about the activities of the following representatives of the lHo-mon Kaḥ-thog-pa in Sikkim and Bhutan, it is known at least that in the middle of the 17th century the western gate was entered once more by a teacher from Eastern Tibet in order to gain access to dPal-gyi 'bras-mo gshongs, and that this time the journey resulted in the permanent presence of this sub-school of the rNying-ma-pa in the hidden valley of Sikkim. Such a settlement process had already occurred in Bhutan at the beginning of the 16th century, and one may attribute this to the fact that the memory of Padmasambhava and the expectation that his prophecies would be fulfilled were very much alive at the sacred shrine in the sPa-gro valley during that particular period.

---

see ibid, p. 371.6 (*slar yang 'bras gshongs phyogs su phebs te spa gro stag tshang nas rin po che kaḥ thog pa rnam grol bzang po drang lung chos sdings su phebs dang mjal*). mNga'-ris rig-'dzin also stayed for some time in sPa-gro sTag-tshang and obtained there an "introduction certificate" (*kha byang*) for a treasure-cycle which he later retrieved from the bSam-yas *vihāra*. See Padma 'phrin-las: *'Khor ba dbyings sgrol gyi khrid yig sbas don gsal ba lam bzang snying po*, p. 475.1–2 (*spa gro stag tshang du bzhugs dus o rgyan chen pos zhal bstan cing kha byang yang rnyed pa la brten nas bsam yas nas zab gter spyan drangs shing dben gnas bsam yas mchims phu legs par thugs snyans su bstan*).

[19] For the section of the final advice dealing with the sacred sites, see the autobiography (as in note 7), pp. 220.3–221.4. The dream of the year 1539 is to be found ibid, pp. 15.3–16.5. Concerning the "Four Great Yogins" (*rnal 'byor bzhi*) or the "Four Great Yogins [Who Are] Brothers" (*rnal 'byor mched bzhi*) associated with the definitive opening of dPal-gyi 'bras-mo gshongs—including Phun-tshogs rnam-rgyal (1604–1670), the first Buddhist ruler of Sikkim—, see the work of Sangs-rgyas rdo-rje (as in note 1), fols. 133b/4–135a/2. Additional information on Kaḥ-thog-pa Kun-tu bzang-po, who at that time entered through the western gate and founded in Sikkim a "site for a monastic community" (*dge 'dun gyi sde*), is contained in the work of lHa Tshe-ring (as in note 8), pp. 231.17–232.16.

IX

Manuscript and Block Print Traditions

Recently Discovered Manuscripts of the rNying ma rgyud 'bum from Nepal

I. Introduction

In the course of the growing body of research focusing on the history and transmission of the Tibetan Buddhist canon (*bKa' 'gyur* and *bsTan 'gyur*), the topic of the "*Tantra*s of the Early Translation Period" (*rnying rgyud*) has come up occasionally, and by now also three standard editions of the *rNying ma rgyud 'bum*, the "Collected *Tantra*s of the Early Translation Period", have been identified. Nevertheless I think what Anne-Marie Blondeau has stated is still valid:

> Il est vrai que, contrairement aux deux grandes collections canoniques du *bKa' 'gyur* et du *bsTan 'gyur*, l'histoire de la formation du canon rNying-ma-pa est mal connue et n'a pas été étudiée.[1]

---

[1] Blondeau (1991/92:86). Basic information on the different editions of the *rNying ma rgyud 'bum* are given, for example, in Ehrhard (1990a:88f.). For the exclusion and later reintroduction of the three volumes *rNying rgyud* in the *sDe dge bka' 'gyur*, see Imaeda (1981:234–236). Concerning the inclusion of the *rNying rgyud*, especially in the *bKa' 'gyur* of O-rgyan gling in Tawang (with a list of sixty extra titles), see Jampa Samten (1992:396–400). Jampa Samten also presented the following brief history of the *rNying ma rgyud 'bum*: "gTer-ston Ratna gling-pa (1403–1478) compiled the most comprehensive edition of the *rNying ma rgyud 'bum* at Lhun-grub pho-brang. Following that, Gong-ra Lo-chen gZhan-phan rdo-rje (1654–1714) with great effort collected the *rNying rgyud* and had three copies of the *rNying ma rgyud 'bum* written out, of which two copies were sent to Khams and Kong-po to serve as the basis for the *rNying ma rgyud 'bum* collections there. The sMin-gling edition of 1685, written out by the gTer-bdag gling-pa 'Gyur-med rdo-rje (1646–1714), the Padma 'od-gling edition of 1772 written out by the Kun-mkhyen 'Jigs-med gling-pa (1729/30–1798), and the xylographic edition of sDe-dge commissioned by the sGa-rje Tshe-dbang lha-mo, the queen of sDe-dge, in 1794–1798 are the most authentic and standardized editions of the *rNying ma rgyud 'bum*"; ibid, p. 397.

The dates of Gong-ra Lo-chen gZhan-phan rdo-rje should be corrected to 1594–1654; for basic biographical data, see Dudjom Rinpoche, vol. 1 (1991:723f.), and sTag-sgang mKhas-mchog Ngag-dbang blo-gros: *bsTan pa'i snying po gsang chen snga 'gyur nges don zab mo'i chos kyi byung ba gsal bar byed pa'i legs bshad mkhas pa dga' byed ngo mtshar gtam gyi rol mtsho*, p. 666.7–16. After the latter's death the Fifth Dalai Bla-ma Ngag-dbang Blo-bzang rgya-mtsho (1617–1682) nominated sMan-lung-pa Blo-mchog rdo-rje (1607–1671) as resident of the monastery gTsang Gong-ra; ibid, pp. 666.17–667.9. This teacher was responsible for transmitting the reading of the *rNying ma rgyud 'bum* to the Fifth Dalai Bla-ma.

It is not the purpose of the present paper to outline the complete history of the different editions of the *rNying ma rgyud 'bum* produced in Tibet from the 14th century onwards. Relevant studies are in progress[2], and we should soon be able to distinguish the relationship between the editions available and also learn more about the persons and circumstances that were responsible for their production. At present one promising approach is to focus on a specific, local tradition and document the way on which such a scriptural transmission was constituted and under what conditions the actual manuscripts were produced. Given that a xylograph of the *rNying ma rgyud 'bum* was commissioned only at the end of the 18th century,[3] this approach should be appropriate for the subject matter.

II. The discovery of the manuscripts

In 1979 I was taken on the staff of the Nepal-German Manuscript Preservation Project (NGMPP) and under the supervision of Michael Hahn was asked to catalogue some three hundred and forty microfilm reels which contained the Tibetan texts in the National Archives, Kathmandu. On these reels I discovered eight volumes of texts which I described at that time as "*rñyiṅ ma rgyud 'bum*, handwritten in silver."[4] Ten years later, in 1989, I managed to obtain permission from the Nepalese authorities to enter the repository of the National Archives and to check on the spot the Tibetan texts stored there on metal racks.

---

2 An overview of the different versions of the *rNying ma rgyud 'bum* and their history—including the unpublished notes collected by Dan Martin "A chronologically arranged list of prints and manuscripts (both available and unavailable) of the Rnying-ma Rgyud -'bum, based mainly on narrative historical sources"—can be found in Mayer (1996:223–242). See also Cantwell & Mayer (2006:4–141) for a catalogue of the sGang-steng manuscript from Bhutan and Cantwell & Mayer (2007:65–78) for the codicology of two *Tantras* as contained in the different *rNying ma rgyud 'bum* editions.

3 One copy of the xylographic edition is available to researchers in the Tucci Tibetan Fund in Rome; see Orofino (2002:211–223). Another copy is in the possession of the National Archives, Ramshah Path (transferred there from the National Museum, Chauni). The set consists of twenty-five volumes plus the inventory by 'Gyur-med Tshe-dbang mchog-grub (1761–1829). For a short sketch of the editorial history of this sDe-dge xylograph, see Smith (1970a:9); a list of contents can be found in *Bod ljongs zhib 'jug* (1984), no. 1, pp. 81–93.

Concerning the use of block printing for the *bKa' 'gyur* and *bsTan 'gyur*, compare the remark by Skilling (1991:138): "It was not until the first half of the eighteenth century, the age of classical xylograph *Kanjurs* and *Tanjurs*, that block printing became a practicable alternative to writing."

4 See Ehrhard (1980:245f.). The mistaken impression that the introductory folios of these volumes, written in golden letters, were in silver was due to the fact that I had only access to the positive copies of the microfilms. This collection of Tibetan works was microfilmed by the NGMPP in 1973/74 (reel nos. A 635–836 and B 543–682). The existence of the collection was first noted by Kaschewsky (1969:310-319). For the geographical area from which the set of the *rNying ma rgyud 'bum* originated, see Smith (1973:4): "... the Lug-lha manuscript originally from Khumbu in Nepal, volumes of which are in the National Archives in Kathmandu." Michael T. Much made this bibliographical reference accessible (Sigle *dkar chag gsum*, T–428–Sd 2/13, Library of the Institut für Tibetologie und Buddhismuskunde der Universität Wien).

Under the muddle of books, covered in dusty cloth, I was able to locate thirty-two volumes of an almost complete set of the *rNying ma rgyud 'bum*. Some of the books were nearly eaten up by worms and I had to discuss with my two Tibetan assistants the ethical and spiritual implications of either killing the worms, and thereby saving the books, or letting the worms complete their jobs, and thereby giving the Buddha's word over to destruction.

The most interesting discovery in this collection was in two of the last volumes: they contained rDzogs-chen Tantras that are not included in the *rNying ma rgyud 'bum* from dGon-pa byang in gTing-skyes, edited in 1975 by Dil-mgo mKhyen-brtse Rin-po-che.[5] The only hint about the origin of this collection was a seal on some of the volumes which indicated that the Tibetan books had once belonged to the private library of "Śrī Mahārāja Bhimsamṣer Jangbahadur Raṇa." This refers to Bhimsamser who assumed the prime ministership of Nepal in 1929 and retained it up to his death in 1932.

In the meantime I made contacts with local lamas of the regions of Kuthang and Nubri in the Gorkha district of Nepal (near the Manaslu peak), and in 1992 led a first expedition of the NGMPP to Ros (Samagaon). My surprise was great when I discovered there a complete manuscript set of the *rNying ma rgyud 'bum* in thirty-seven volumes. Immediately checking the last volumes, I found they were the same as the two volumes in the collection of the National Archives. Slob-dpon 'Gyur-med, the keeper of the books, also came forward with two inventories, both written by Brag-dkar rta-so sprul-sku Chos-kyi dbang-phyug (1775–1837). A first perusal of these inventories made it clear that the manuscript set was written out on behalf of this teacher from Brag-dkar rta-so at the beginning of the 19th century.[6]

---

5 For a list of the texts contained in vol. 35 (*ci*) and 36 (*chi*) of the *rNying ma rgyud 'bum* from the National Archives, see Appendix I. The contents of the thirty-three-volume edition from 1975 is described by Dil-mgo mKhyen-brtse Rin-po-che in *Rig pa 'dzin pa'i sde snod rdo rje theg pa snga 'gyur rgyud 'bum rin po che'i chos kyi bzhugs byang ratna'i do shal*, fols. 1b/2–16b/1. In a second, untitled text which accompanied the edition, Dil-mgo mKhyen-brtse Rin-po-che provides the information that "the original copies were the old books of dGon-pa byang, the residence of the supreme incarnation of Yol-mo Rig-'dzin bsTan-'dzin nor-bu" (*... ma phyi yol mo rig 'dzin bstan 'dzin nor bu'i mchog sprul gyi gdan sa dgon pa byang gi phyag dpe rnying pa ...*), fol. 2a/5.

An overview of the different members of the incarnation line of the Yol-mo-ba sprul-skus and their activities in the area of Mang-yul Gung-thang is given in Ehrhard (2007) and chapter nine in the present volume. A second line of incarnations emerged in the 18th century in the area of gTing-skyes, where Rig-'dzin Chos-'phel (1773–1836) chose dGon-pa byang as his place of residence; see mTha'-bral rdo-rje: *mTshungs med dpal mgon bla ma dam pa gting skyes dgon pa byang gi mchog gi sprul gyi 'khrungs rabs bcu'i rnam par thar pa mdo tsam brjod pa*. A catalogue for this edition was compiled by Kaneko (1982).

6 The existence in Slob-dpon 'Gyur-med's monastery of "... the entire records of Brag-dkar rta-so, a famous monastery in Kyirong belonging to the Bar-'brug tradition ..." was already signalled by Aris (1975:80). The volumes of the *rNying ma rgyud 'bum* went unnoticed at that time. For a study of the life and major writings of Chos-kyi dbang-phyug, the incarnation of Brag-dkar gdan-sa-pa Ye-shes chos-grags (1705–1772), see Ehrhard (2004a:89–124); some of his works are mentioned in the following notes.

With the help of the text describing how this specific set of the *rNying ma rgyud 'bum* was produced, it is possible to trace the history of this tradition from the Tibetan-Nepalese borderlands. The work also contains information about the origin of the manuscripts kept in the National Archives. In the following pages I would like to present an annotated translation of two excerpts from the relevant inventory.

III. A TRADITION FROM MANG-YUL SKYID-GRONG

[This is] how here in Mang-yul sKyid-grong the stream of reading transmissions and the stream of the books of the Collected *Tantra*s of the Early Translation Period appeared: When Nyang-ston mNga'-bdag Rig-'dzin rgya-mtsho, the personal disciple of the great treasure[-discoverer] of sMin-grol gling, father and sons, produced in Shel-dkar the blocks of the entire translated pronouncements of the Jina for the political head of Tibet, the ruler Mi-dbang Pho-lha-ba bSod-nams stobs-rgyas (1689–1747)[7]: through the pure intention of that noble spiritual friend, who was begged by the ruler to correct and supervise [the block printing], an appeal was made to the compassion of the great ruler, and thereby Ngag-dbang lHun-grub grags-pa from lHo-brag lHa-lung, who was holding the teaching tradition of the great treasure[-discoverer] Padma gling-pa, was regarded as a worthy vajrācārya whose teachings should be listened to and ordered to come to mNga'-ris stod accompanied by provisions.[8] Accordingly this noble spiritual

---

The two inventories for the *rNying ma rgyud 'bum* bear the titles:

rNying ma rgyud 'bum gyi glegs bam nang gi chos tshan bzhugs byang dkar chag dpe rdzi bsam 'phel nor bu'i 'phreng ba, 26 fols.

sNga 'gyur gsang chen rnying ma rgyud 'bum gyi glegs bam yongs rdzogs gzheng tshul dkar chag tu bkod pa rdzogs ldan snang ba gsar ba'i dga' ston, 14 fols. (= *dKar chag*).

The Tibetan text of the two excerpts translated from the second work is given in Appendix II[a] & II[b].

7 The printing of the so-called *sNar thang bka' 'gyur* by Mi-dbang bSod-nams stobs-rgyas in the years 1730–1732 is described by Petech (1972:160f.), and, based on that, by Harrison (1992:80f.); the Tibetan source is Tshe-ring dbang-rgyal (1697–1763): *dPal mi'i dbang po'i rtogs pa brjod pa 'jig rten kun tu dga' ba'i gtam*, pp. 739.11–748.17. The person responsible for the printing is several times mentioned under the name Rig-pa 'dzin-pa chen-po mNga'-bdag brag-pa; he can now be identified as Nyang-ston mNga'-bdag Rig-'dzin rgya-mtsho, a disciple of Rig-'dzin gTer-bdag gling-pa (1646–1714). For the special role of this print in the transmission of the *bKa' 'gyur* and existing inventories, see Eimer (1994:309f.) and passim. The author of the most comprehensive *dkar chag* is Sle-lung bZhad-pa'i rdo-rje (born 1697); for this priest's relationship with the ruler bSod-nams stobs-rgyas, see Ehrhard (1996b) and chapter twenty-two in the present volume. In the years 1741–1742, a manuscript copy of the *bsTan 'gyur* was written out on the orders of bSod-nams stobs-rgyas; see Skilling (1991:138f.).

8 The history of the "succession of residents" (*gdan rabs*) of lHo-brag lHa-lung, the main seat of the tradition of Rig-'dzin Padma gling-pa (1450–1521) in Tibet, can be found in sTag-sgang mKhas-mchog Ngag-dbang blo-gros, Gu-ru bKra-shis (as in note 1), pp. 653.4–664.4. The monastery was famous for its

friend reached, with a special purpose, dPal-mo chos-sding in La-stod, the [former] residence of Bo-dong Kun-mkhyen 'Jigs-med grags-pa.[9] The disciples who listened to the teaching on that occasion included the incarnation of Kham[s]-lung-pa gSang-sngags bstan-'dzin[10]; the *Mantradhara* [of the family] Grwa 'Dzam-gling, Shes-rab 'byung-gnas[11]; the *Mantradhara* [of the family] mDo-

---

two incarnation lines, the Pad-gling gsung-sprul and the Pad-gling thugs-sras. Since 1959 the seat of this tradition has been relocated in the monastery of gTam-zhing in Bhutan; see Imaeda and Pommaret (1987:19, 26f. & passim). The Third Pad-gling gsung-sprul Tshul-khrims rdo-rje (1598–1669), listened to a reading of the *rNying ma rgyud 'bum* at the family seat of gTer-ston Ratna gling-pa and also prepared a complete set of this collection; see sTag-sgang mKhas-mchog Ngag-dbang blo-gros, Gu-ru bKra-shis (as in note 1), p. 655.17–26. Both Gong-ra Lo-chen gZhan-phan rdo-rje and sMan-lung-pa Blo-mchog rdo-rje (see note 1) were given readings of the *rNying ma rgyud 'bum* by this teacher. The Fourth Pad-gling gsung-sprul Ngag-dbang Kun-bzang rdo-rje (1680–1723), produced an edition of the *rNying ma rgyud 'bum* in forty-six volumes when he had taken refuge from the Dsungar troops in the "hidden lands" (*sbas yul*) in the south; ibid, p. 660.2–14. The manuscript of the *rNying ma rgyud 'bum* from the monastery of mTshams-brag in Bhutan (in forty-six volumes), published 1982 in Thimphu, is said to come from a transmission received through Pad-gling gsung-sprul Tshul-khrims rdo-rje or one of the Pad-gling thugs-sras in the 17th century. For the general importance of these two incarnation lines in the transmission of the *rNying ma rgyud 'bum*, see Dudjom Rinpoche, vol. I (1991:734f.).

For the division of the territory of mNga'-ris skor-gsum into a western part (here called mNga'-ris stod) and an eastern part (mNga'-ris smad, with Mang-yul Gung-thang being the easternmost extension), see Petech (1990:52f.).

9 The text *Chos ldan sa skyong 'bur pa mi rje'i gdung rabs lo rgyus dri med baiḍūrya'i phreng ba*, fols. 13/3–17a/2, provides an overview of the history of the Bo-dong-pa school in the area of sPong-rong in Gung-thang; Kun-mkhyen 'Jigs-med grags-pa alias Phyogs-las rnam-rgyal (1375–1451) was the founder of the monastery of dPal-mo chos-sding; at that time there were four convents: gSang-sngags bDe-chen gling, sGrub-sde bSam-gtan gling, bShad-pa Chos-'khor gling and Dung-sgra mThon-smon gling. For the activities of Kun-mkhyen 'Jigs-med grags-pa and his predecessors in Shel-dkar, see Ngag-dbang Chos-'phel *La stod shel dkar chos sde dpal gyi sde chen po dga' ldan legs bshad gling gi lo rgyus dran pa'i gdung dbyangs*, p. 17f.

10 The incarnation line of the Kham[s]-lung-pa is connected with the monastery Nub-dgon in gTsang La-stod; see sTag-sgang mKhas-mchog Ngag-dbang blo-gros, (as in note 1), pp. 665.13–666.3. The predecessor of gSang-sngags bstan-'dzin was Kham[s]-lung-pa Rig-'dzin dBang-gi rgyal-po (1657–1731); two biographical works on him have been filmed by the NGMPP: *Bya bral khros med padma rig 'dzin dbang gi rgyal po'am ming gzhan nam mkha' rnam rgyal thog (= theg) mchog 'di ro (= ru) 'gyes (= dgyes) pa'i sde zhes pa bdag gi stogs (= rtogs) spyod (= brjod) mdor bstan*, 37 fols., reel no. L 5/18, and *dPal ldan bla ma kham lung pa chen po padma rig 'dzin dbang rgyal gyi rnam thar nyung ngu dad pa'i sa bon,* 9 fols., reel no. L 5/19. The author of the second work is Ngag-dbang ye-shes; concerning him, see note 11. For dNgos-grub phug, the residence of that incarnation in the sKyid-grong area, see note 16.

11 The family 'Dzam-gling (or 'Jam-gling) from the area of Grwa, northwest of sKyid-grong, is associated with the monastery of Grwa-phu chos-gling. This site of the 'Ba'-ra-ba bKa'-brgyud-pa was frequented, among others, by mKhas-dbang Sangs-rgyas rdo-rje (1569–1645). Shes-rab 'byung-gnas is the youngest of three brothers; the names of the other two are Ngag-dbang ye-shes (1700–1760) and Ngag-dbang Chos-grags rgya-mtsho. Shes-rab 'byung-gnas was the person responsible for the compilation

chen, 'Gyur-med rnam-rgyal.[12] To just nine teachers he offered the entire reading of the Collected *Tantras*.

At the end, the Vajradhara from lHo-brag spoke the following words: "The best among you, the disciples who listened to the teaching, should produce the entire volumes [of the collection] and should be able to increase the reading transmission to others. Even though they do not cause [the books] to be produced, they should by all means make sure they transmit [the reading transmission at least] one time." Thus were his orders.

Now, [regarding] the entire stream of the books of the Collected *Tantras*, that one has sought out as original exemplars [for copying]: the incarnation gSang-sngags bstan-'dzin, he commissioned the making of one set and offered it to [the monastery of] Thub-bstan rDo-rje brag.

The *Mantradhara* [of the family] 'Dzam-gling, Shes-rab 'byung-gnas, although not able to increase the stream of the reading transmission, with the help of sponsors from Grwa A-ya had made an entire [set of the] Collected *Tantras*; and this is the one which is kept nowadays in the A-ya'i lha-khang in the upper part of Grwa-yul in sKyid-grong.[13]

Kun-bzang 'Gyur-med lhun-grub [of the family] rDo-dmar (died 1767), using the above as the original commissioned an entire [set of the] Collected *Tantras* which was kept in Glang-'phrang, the so-called Hidden Valley Heavenly Gate of Half-Moon Form, in the solitary monastery of mNgon-dga' bSam-gtan gling. [Based on the same original] the lord of sPo[ng]-rong, Nam-mkha' dpal-bzang, had made an entire [set of the] Collected *Tantras*, which was kept in dPal-mo chos-sding.[14]

---

of the "Collected Works" (*bka' 'bum*) of Kaḥ-thog rig-'dzin Tshe-dbang nor-bu. For the activities of the three brothers, see *rJe btsun bla ma dam pa sman bsgom chos kyi rje kun dga' dpal ldan zhabs kyi rnam par thar pa dad pa'i pad tshal rgyas byed ngo mtshar nyin mor byed pa'i snang ba*, fol. 8b/1ff.

12 The tradition of the mDo-chen bKa'-brgyud-pa is described in a separate text: *dPal ldan gur rigs mdo chen brgyud pa'i lo rgyus nyung ngu'i ngag gi brjod pa padma rā ga'i phreng ba*, 22 fols. Mention of this tradition is made in Ehrhard (2007:44, note 53) and chapter nine in the present volume. 'Gyur-med rnam-rgyal was one of the sons of mDo-chen-pa rGyal-sras seng-ge (died 1752). Concerning the reading of the *rNying ma rgyud 'bum*, the text provides the following information: *dpal mo chos sding du lho brag pa ... ngag dbang lhun grub grags pa las snga 'gyur rgyud 'bum rin po che'i lung yongs rdzogs dang / rje 'ba' ra ba ngag dbang ye shes las 'dus pa mdo dbang chen mo tshang bar gsan*; ibid, 15a/6–b/2. For a complete translation of the text, see Ehrhard (2008:55–95).

13 For the A-ya'i lha-khang in Grwa-yul and a photograph of its ruins, see Ramble (2007:708f.). The A-ya temple is the highest of four ruined temples with the so-called 'Dzam-gling lha-khang close to it. This latter name obviously refers to the former monastery of Grwa-phu chos-gling; see note 11.

14 The family of the name rDo-dmar goes back to rDo-dmar-ba Mi-'gyur rdo-rje (born 1675). The latter chose as his residence the valley of Glang-'phrang (modern day Langtang in Nepal) and wrote a polemic

From the the vidyādhara [of the family] mDo-chen, 'Gyur-med rnam-rgyal, the entire reading of the Collected *Tantra*s was conferred upon his son, mDo-chen-pa Tshe-dbang 'Chi-med mgon-po (1755–1807); and together with a supplement of a few previously scattered volumes, the master, the honourable mDo-chen-pa ['Chi-med] mgon-po, accompanied by the master of dPal-sding, 'Gyur-med 'Phrin-las bstan-'dzin, uncle and nephew, later, in the wood-tiger year (= 1794), produced an entire [set of the] Collected *Tantra*s, which is kept today in the upper and lower residence in La-lde[bs].[15]

Through the pure intention of that female Bodhisattva, who stayed in dKar-ye dNgos-grub mtsho-gling, the reverend nun Padma Chos-'dzoms, sister of Mi-dbang Pho-lha-ba bSod-nams stobs-rgyas, Kham[s]-lung-pa [Padma] gSang-sngags bstan-'dzin was invited [to come] from dNgos-grub phug to bKar-ye.[16]

---

concerning the identification of this site as gNam-sgo zla-gam; see Ehrhard (1997b) and chapter sixteen in the present volume. Mi-'gyur rdo-rje had five offsprings: one daughter and four sons; one of them was Kun-bzang 'Gyur-med lhun-grub. For a description of Glang-'phrang in the year 1758 and a mention of Kun-bzang 'Gyur-med lhun-grub, see mDo-chen-pa Tshe-dbang 'Chi-med mgon-po: *Rig 'dzin chen po karma bdud 'joms kyi rnam par thar pa gsal bar byes pa'i nyin byed ngo mtshar snang ba'i gter mdzod*, p. 96.5ff.; the circumstances concerning his death can be found ibid, p. 130.6ff.

A short biographical note on Nam-mkha' dpal-bzang, the lord of sPong-rong, is contained in the chronicle of that family (as in note 9), fols. 9b/4–10b/5; his main teacher was Kaḥ-thog rig-'dzin Tshe-dbang nor-bu. According to this source, the production of an edition of the *rNying ma rgyud 'bum* was ordered by Nam-mkha' 'gyur-med, the son of Nam-mkha' dpal-bzang; ibid, fol. 11a/4: *snga 'gyur rnying ma rgyud 'bum sogs gzheng bar mdzad pa chos sding bka' 'gyur lha khang bzhugs.*

15 For the transmission of the reading of the *rNying ma rgyud 'bum* from 'Gyur-med rnam-rgyal to his son, mDo-chen-pa Tshe-dbang 'Chi-med mgon-po, see the latter's autobiography, *Gur gyi sngags ban tshe dbang 'chi med mgon po'i rang tshul chu 'babs su brjod pa lhung snyan pa'i chu sgra*, p. 27.2–5. The original volumes were borrowed from the temple of A-ya in Grwa; this edition was thus based upon the one produced by Shes-rab 'byung-gnas. A description of the copying of the *rNying ma rgyud 'bum* in 1794 can be found ibid, p. 101.1ff.; this passage mentions as well that the "original copy" (*ma dpe*) was the one from Grwa.

Biographical data on 'Gyur-med 'Phrin-las bstan-'dzin, who is also one of the members of the mDo-chen family, are contained in the family's chronicle (as in note 12), fols. 17a/6–18a/2. Special importance is attached to his renovation of the temple of dPal-ldan sding in La-lde[bs], south of sKyid-grong. This site was founded in the 13th century by a certain Chos-rje sTon-pa; see ibid, fols. 6b/5–7a/1.

16 For the location of dKar-ye in the vicinity of Mang-yul Ri-bo dpal-'bar and the presence of masters of the Byang-gter tradition there from the 16th century onwards, see Ehrhard (2007:44, note 51) and chapter nine in the present volume. A separate text dealing with this site is available: *dKar ye dngos grub mtsho gling gi gnas bshad lo rgyus ngang pa'i rgyal po'i mgrin glu*. It is mentioned there that the sister of Mi-dbang bSod-nams stobs-rgyas chose dKar-ye as a place of refuge because of the Dsungar attacks in Central Tibet. She went in the company of her teacher Grub-dbang O-rgyan bstan-'phel; ibid, fol. 2b/4. The latter was a disciple of Rig-'dzin gTer-bdag gling-pa and also "priest" (*dbu bla*) of Mi-dbang bSod-nams stobs-rgyas; he is mentioned under the name of Shangs-pa ras-chen in the biography of the ruler (as in note 7), pp. 549.7 and 564.17–18.

A description is available as well for the sacred site dNgos-grub phug: *dGon gnas mchog dngos grub*

After the reverend nun had provided the religious endowment and had urged Chos-dbyings khyab-brdal, the resident of the sacred site [dKar-ye], and also a great number of younger descendants of families from the tradition of the Old Ones to listen to the teaching, the incarnation of Kham[s]-lung-pa gNyags-ston, gSang-sngags bstan-'dzin [by name], bestowed the reading transmission of the entire Collected *Tantra*s [upon them].

On that occasion the reverend nun provided the gratification also for the two brothers, [i.e.] my teacher, the master of mGon-gnang, the honourable Rig-'dzin 'Phrin-las bdud-'joms (1726–1789), who had reached the age of seventeen years, together with his younger brother 'Gyur-med bstan-'dzin (1731–1776), and except for six volumes they heard the complete reading transmission of the Collected *Tantra*s.[17]

When I was seven years old, in the iron-ox year (= 1781), after from Ri-bo dpal-'bar O-rgyan 'Gro-'dul dbang-gi rgyal-po of [the family of] rDo-dmar had provided the religious endowment for about nine of us younger descendants, the master, the great vidyādhara of mGon-gnang, brought from Glang-'phrang all volumes of the Collected *Tantra*s and in a side valley of Brag-dkar rta-so, at the hidden sacred site called mChod-rten nag-po, I obtained what was granted, [i.e.] the reading transmission of about twenty volumes of [the collection], and the [reading transmission for the] remaining [volumes] at the monastery of Ri-bo dpal-'bar.

As the master, the honourable teacher, had earlier in dKar-ye not heard [the complete reading] from the incarnation [Kham[s]-lung-pa] gSang-sngags bstan-'dzin, as the reading of six volumes of the Collected *Tantra*s had already been given beforehand, he invited [later] the *Mantradhara* [of the family] mDo-chen,

---

kun 'byung gling gi lo rgyus gnas bshad nyung 'dus su bkod pa. This place served as residence for Kham[s]-lung-pa Rig-'dzin dBang-gi rgyal-po, and it was there that Kaḥ-thog rig-'dzin Tshe-dbang nor-bu left the mortal plane in 1755.

17 The main events in the life of Rig-'dzin 'Phrin-las bdud-'joms are sketched in Ehrhard (2007) and chapter nine in the present volume; the epithet "Master from mGon-gnang" goes back to his stay at the site of mGon-gnang in Mang-yul sKyid-grong. For the transmission of the *rNying ma rgyud 'bum* in the year 1742 in dKar-ye, see mDo-chen-pa Tshe-dbang 'Chi-med mgon-po (as in note 14), p. 32.2–5; the fact is also highlighted that only twenty-five volumes were received on that occasion (*glegs bam drug tsam gnang grub 'dug kyang de 'phros pu sti nyer lnga tsam gyi bka' lung nod pa'i skal bzang thob*). For a short biography of 'Gyur-med bstan-'dzin, see *gTer dbon rig 'dzin brgyud pa'i gdung rabs lo rgyus tshangs pa'i do shal*, fols. 14b/4–15b/1. There the information is provided that in dKar-ye the younger brother was invited by a son of Mi-dbang bSod-nams stobs-rgyas to the newly established monastery of Glang-chu in sKyid-grong. This Mi-dbang Gung sKu-zhabs is the elder son 'Gyur-med Tshe-brtan (died 1750); see *'Phags mchog thugs rje chen po rang byung wa ti bzang po'i rnam par thar pa ngo mtshar rmad du byung ba'i gtam dad pa'i nyin byed phyogs brgyar 'dren pa'i rta ljangs*, fol. 30b/2, and Ehrhard (2004a:266).

'Gyur-med rnam-rgyal, to Brag-dkar [rta-so]. At his side, when he heard the supplementary reading, I also obtained it completely.[18] (Appendix II/a)

This part of the inventory did not provide us yet with any clues about the production of the two sets of the *rNying ma rgyud 'bum* now accessible on microfilm, but we have at least a rough picture of the history of this particular tradition. It is remarkable, first of all, that the tradition was initiated and further propagated by Pho-lha-ba Mi-dbang bSod-nams stobs-rgyas and his sister Padma Chos-'dzoms. Secondly, the number of manuscripts sets produced and the regions covered by their distribution (to the north and south of Mang-yul sKyid-grong) show that in the 18th century this part of southern Tibet was not only offering protection to the rNying-ma-pa school at a difficult time but also served as a kind of catchment area for revitalizing their scriptural transmissions.

An important figure for the further spread of the teachings was obviously Rig-'dzin 'Phrin-las bdud-'joms, the master of mGon-gnang. In his last will, he asked his disciples to manufacture again a complete set of the *rNying ma rgyud 'bum*. Brag-dkar rta-so sprul-sku Chos-kyi dbang-phyug and his elder brother 'Phrin-las dbang-phyug (1772–1812) took this will to heart and supervised work on a further edition.[19] This would still not be the last one produced in Mang-yul sKyid-grong. Reading on in the inventory, we finally come to the record of how the manuscript set from Brag-dkar rta-so was produced.

---

18 The invitation to mDo-chen-pa 'Gyur-med rnam-rgyal to come from La-lde[bs] to Brag-dkar rta-so is also mentioned by mDo-chen-pa Tshe-dbang 'Chi-med mgon-po (as in note 14), p. 171.3, and id. (as in note 15), p. 57.2–4. At this occasion Tshe-dbang 'Chi-med mgon-po was present in person. Shortly afterwards he wrote down a *rGyud 'bum thob yig*; see ibid, p. 56.4–5. This text forms the basis of a corresponding chapter in the "List of Teachings Received" by Brag-dkar rta-so sprul-sku Chos-kyi dbang-phyug; see *Zab rgyas chos tshul rgya mtsho las rang skal du ji ltar thob pa'i yi ge rnam grol bdud rtsi'i bum bzang*, fol. 254a/2–3.

19 The importance of Rig-'dzin 'Phrin-las bdud-'joms as an author of rNying-ma-pa literature has already been indicated by Boord (1993:10–12). He, however, failed to identify the religious role of this teacher in the area here under consideration. For data on the edition of the *rNying ma rgyud 'bum* produced by the two brothers in the years 1789 to 1791—exactly the period when the two attacks by the Gorkha forces on Tibet took place—see dKar chag, fol. 9b/2–5 (*rje bla ma rig 'dzin mgon nang pa (= gnang pa) chen po de nyid nas rgyud 'bum yongs rdzogs zhig gzhengs gnang ba'i thugs bzhed nan gtan yod kyang ma 'grub par rjes su mdzad pa tha ma bstan skabs bka' chems su / rnying rgyud yongs rdzogs zhig dang / padma bka' thang shel brag ma'i par zhig gzheng thub pa bgyis zhes bka' phebs pa ltar / bdag cag rjes 'jug tha shal rnams nas rnying ma rgyud 'bum yongs rdzogs kyi phyi mo grwa a ya pa nas g.yar po bgyis pa'i yongs rdzogs gzheng ba ding sang yol mo dgon glang ra rgyag sa'am pad ma'i chos gling du bzhugs.* The temple of Glang-ra rgyag-sa in Yol-mo (and this edition of the *rNying ma rgyud 'bum* went up in flames in the year 1833. It was later reconstructed; see *Bya bral ba chos kyi dbang phyug gi rang 'tshang lhug par brjod pa 'khrul snang sgyu ma'i rol rtsed*, fol. 238a/1ff.

IV. WRITING OUT THE *RNYING MA RGYUD 'BUM*

Here now an account of the way this precious [collection of] Collected *Tantras* was newly produced: In the iron-horse year called *pramoda* (= 1810) it came to my ears that in sBra-chen [in the region of] sKyid-sbug there was located an entire [set of the] Collected *Tantras* commissioned by the honourable uncle sKyid-sbug-pa. I sent an invitation, such that they should be given on loan, and actually received the complete set of books. The original books of this [set] could be seen to have been copied from ones invited [earlier] from [the monastery] Theg-mchog gling in gTsang,[20] and it happened that [the texts mentioned in] the inventory for the production of the Collected *Tantras* of this very same [set] and the order [of the individual texts] were in slight disagreement.

Nevertheless, on the basis of this [collection], I gave the reading of all volumes of the Collected *Tantras* to more that ten [persons], including the teacher Chos-rgyal from rGya-yul in sKu-thang, the teachers, father and son, from Nyi-lhod in Tsum, the brothers Phun-tshogs, [my] nephews, from Byams-sprin [in sKyid-grong], the great meditator Karma bstan-'dzin from the monastery of dGa'-ldan in Tsum. [This I did] in mChod-rten nag-po, from the Dharma seat where earlier the teacher, this powerful vidyādhara (= 'Phrin-las bdud-'joms), had granted the reading of the Collected *Tantras*. And if one adds the three readings [of the whole collection] afterwards by all the many [persons] who were able to read, the entire volumes were read out [all in all] four times; then they were sent back to sKyid-sbug.

On that occasion the idea arose to produce a new [set of the] precious Collected *Tantras*. The paper was manufactured in Yol-mo, and starting on the 13th day of the 4th month of the water-bird year (= 1813) the entire volumes of the original copies of the Collected *Tantras* were brought from Glang-[']phrang, a request having been made to the teacher of [the family of] rDo-dmar, sKal-bzang lags, to lend them.

I assembled [persons] I came up with myself, [i.e.] a proper constellation of those in the province of sKyid-grong who had amassed the good qualities of being in the ranks of well-versed scribes. At the beginning there came forth no

20 The monastery of Theg-mchog gling in gTsang is mentioned in the biography of lHa-chen Bres-gshongs-pa (1602–1677); for the episode and the location (a small side valley between Drongtse and Nesar), see Dudjom Rinpoche, vol. 1 (1991:718), and vol. 2 (1991:478). This master received the transmission of the "*Sūtra* Which Gathers [All Intentions]" (*'dus pa'i mdo*) on two occasions: from Gong-ra Lo-chen gZhan-phan rdo-rje and from a certain Nam-mkha' 'brug-sgra, who is also known as Rong-pa rDzogs-chen-pa; this latter transmission took place in gTsang Theg-mchog gling. lHa-chen Bres-gshongs-pa in turn gave these teachings to sMan-lung-pa Blo-mchog rdo-rje, concerning whom, see notes 1 & 8.

more than ten scribes. Nevertheless, later, as restrictions were gradually lifted, a circle of fifteen people came forth, and finally a number of exactly twenty-nine. To each person there was [then] distributed one volume [of the original manuscript set], one reed pen of superior quality, whose ink was mixed with the bodily relics of the elder brother, the highest amongst the scholars, the noble one, and with the [powder of crushed] precious stones, [and] a paper bundle, whose unevennesses had been smoothed, together with rough paper.

Some of the well-versed scribes of good qualities wrote two volumes each; the slack periods of some [others, however,] prolonged [the work]. The quality of the letters being extremely bad and unclear, etc., because of awkward signs and superficial understanding, it turned out that the proper quality of some of the volumes did not come forth; as someone with an arrogant attitude did [thus] not show up at all, I urged them, one after the other, from the depth [of my heart], and so for about one month the chief scribes and the workers came together in a great number un Brag-dkar [rta-so] itself, where most of the provisions were laid up.

Some corrected the letters, some fashioned and polished the wood for the book covers, some sewed the silk [slips] for the front [of the books], the covering cloths, and the ribbons, some produced the buckles [for the ribbons], some drew the portraits of the gods [and applied] the varnish and paint, and some applied the golden letters on the cover pages and so forth. Like the mirage of a miraculous play, it had been started all at the same time, and on the 14th day of the great 4th month of the wood-dog [year] (= 1814) it was completed well and duly. (Appendix II/b)

The manuscript set of the *rNying ma rgyud 'bum* thus produced in the years 1813/1814 was later kept in Brag-dkar rta-so, and is today in the safe hands of Slob-dpon 'Gyur-med. What about the set which was discovered in the National Archives and which obviously belonged to the same tradition? In the inventory we find a reference to the production of a further manuscript set at that time: it was made by a disciple of Brag-dkar rta-so sprul-sku who is said to have belonged to the Nyang clan of gZhung in Rong-shar, and thus a member of the family responsible for the founding and upkeep of the main temple of Junbesi in Solu-Khumbu.[21]

---

[21] See *dKar chag*, fol. 11b/3–4: "When I told my own disciple-son, the teacher of the Nyang clan from gZhung in Rong-shar, O-rgyan 'Phrin-las bstan-'dzin [by name], which materials should be prepared at the outset and how financial help, which has to be induced, should be brought about, he was able to produce an entire [set of the] Collected *Tantra*s not long afterwards ..." (*rang gi slob bu rong shar gzhung gi nyang rigs bla ma o rgyan 'phrin las bstan 'dzin la thog ma'i rgyu sbyar zhing bskul ba'i mthun 'gyur byas par rgyud 'bum yongs rdzogs mi ring bar gzheng thub pas ...*).

The presence of the teaching lineage of Brag-dkar rta-so sprul-sku Chos-kyi dbang-phyug in the area

One can only speculate how this final product of the tradition of the *rNying ma rgyud 'bum* from Mang-yul sKyid-grong reached the private library of Bhimsaṃser in Kathmandu. We can at least identify one person who might have been involved in the transaction of the books, namely Sangs-rgyas bla-ma (1856–1939), another member of the Nyang clan; he renovated the gZhung temple in Junbesi in 1914 and completed the building of the monastery in sPyi-dbang in Phaphlu during the time when Bhimsaṃser was prime minister of Nepal.[22]

V. CONCLUSION

Approaching the subject of the history and transmission of the *rNying ma rgyud 'bum* by focusing on a specific, local tradition can thus provide insight into some of the issues that were crucial for the formation of this scriptural canon in general. Surely one thing is clear: Further research has to take into account questions concerning patronage and financing of different manuscripts sets; and the main patrons as well as the localities or religious institutions where the texts were copied must first of all be identified and put in a proper historical and geographical context. For the tradition as a whole, one of the best places to start would be with bZang-po dpal of the Zur family, who already at the beginning of the 14th century was responsible for a first edition of the *rNying ma rgyud 'bum*; financial and material support for this project was received from the Yüan emperor Buyantu (regnal years 1311–1320).[23] Once the origin and affiliation of different editions, and their prototypes, has been set up in a chronological perspective, the distribution of individual *Tantra*s and their text-critical evaluation should be able to supplement and sharpen the picture.

---

of Solu-Khumbu is described by Sangs-rgyas bstan-'dzin (1924–1990) in *Shar pa'i chos 'byung sngon med tshangs pa'i dbyu gu*, p. 80.3ff. and id. *Shar khum bu'i phyogs su snga 'gyur rnying ma'i chos brgyud bye brag pa rim par thob pa'i thob yig*, passim (the only name being similar to O-rgyan['Phrin-las] bstan-'dzin is Rig-'dzin O-rgyan [gSang-sngags] bstan-'dzin). For data on further persons in the 18th/19th century from the Nyang clan of gZhung connected with Brag-dkar rta-so sprul-sku and his teacher Rig-'dzin 'Phrin-las bdud-'joms, see Ehrhard (1993a:87–93) and chapter ten in the present volume.

22 On Sangs-rgyas bla-ma, his renovation of the main temple in Junbesi, and the founding of sPyi-dbang dgon-pa, see Sangs-rgyas bstan-'dzin (as in note 21, first text), pp. 57.2 & 74.4–80.3. Compare Ortner (1989:138–146) and id. (1990:83 & 86), especially for the protection of Sangs-rgyas bla-ma by the Raṇa family. The dates of the founding of sPyi-dbang dgon-pa differ between the two authors.

23 For the activities of Zur bZang-po dpal at the court of the emperor Buyantu, see Pema Tsering (1978:525 & 538), and Dudjom Rinpoche, vol. 1 (1991:669). Zur bZang-po dpal had established there a college for tantric studies and was responsible for the production of printed versions of the *Guhyagarbhatantra* and other texts (twenty-eight in all). These prints can thus be called *Hor par ma*; on further prints made at the court of the emperor Buyantu, see v.d. Kuijp (1993:282). The material support for Zur bZang-po dpal sent back to his family seat in 'Ug-pa/bya lung in gTsang was used for an edition of the *rNying ma rgyud 'bum*, which was called by later authors such as 'Jigs-med gling-pa, "[a] provisional [set of the] Collected *Tantras*" (*rgyud 'bum rags rim*).

APPENDIX I

Texts of vols. 35 (ci) and 36 (chi) of the *rNying ma rgyud 'bum* (= NGB) from the National Archives, Kathmandu, together with a concordance of identical texts from the *Vai ro rgyud 'bum* (= VGB), 8 vols. (Leh: S.W. Tashigangpa, 1971). The relationship between these two collections of *Tantra*s of the early translation period as regards contents has still to be worked out. A first attempt to classify the latter collection is cited in Germano (1994:237 & 266). According to Kapstein, the *Vai ro rgyud 'bum* represents a middle-to-late-12th-century redaction of the "Mind Series" (*sems sde*) lineages of the Zur family; see Kapstein (2008:276–288). With the additional thirty-six titles presented now, this hypothesis needs further corroboration.

NGB, VOL. CI, 385 FOLS.; NGMPP REEL NO. AT 23/2–24/1:

[1] *rDzogs pa chen po bar do gsang ba'i rgyud*, 5 chapters, fols. 1b–6b; VGB, vol. 4:68–72

[2] *Bar do gsang ba'i phyi ma'i rgyud*, 2 chapters, fols. 6b–7b; VGB, vol. 4:72–74

[3] *rDzogs pa chen po byang chub kyi sems rin po che spung pa man ngag gi rgyud*, 14 chapters, fols. 8a–14b; VGB, vol. 4:74–86

[4] *Rin po che snang byed kyi rgyud*, 17 chapters, fols. 14b–31b

[5] *Rin po che snang byed kyi rgyud*, 5 chapters, fols. 31b–36a

[6] *Rin po che rgyas pa chen po'i mdo*, 8 chapters, fols. 36a–46b

[7] *Ye shes rin po che 'bar ba*, 11 chapters, fols. 46b–59a

[8] *Byang chub kyi sems rin po che'i rgyud rgyas pa chen po'i mdo*, 51 chapters, fols. 59a–140a

[9] *Rin po che sgron ma zhes bya ba'i rgyud*, 12 chapters, fols. 140a–153a

[10] *Sems phyogs chen po'i mdzod / thig le gsang skor gyi mdzod kyi rtsa rgyud*, fols. 153a–155a

[11] *Sangs rgyas thams cad kyi dgongs pa / ma bcos ji bzhin pa'i don / ye shes kyi mar me chen po'i rgyud*, 11 chapters, fols. 155a–166a

[12] *Rin po che nyi zla brtsegs pa'i rgyud*, 15 chapters, fols. 166a–175b; VGB, vol. 5:247–268

[13] *Byang chub sems kyi man ngag / rin po che sgron ma 'bar ba'i rgyud*, 53 chapters, fols. 175b–209a

[14] *Byang chub sems dpa' yid skyob pa*, 18 chapters, fols. 209a–232b; VGB, vol. 7:287–340

[15] *Ye shes 'khor lo gsang ba snying po don* gyi rgyud, 14 chapters, fols. 232b–241a; VGB, vol. 6:43–59

[16] *sKu gsum ye shes lnga ldan gyi rgyud / 'jam dpal ye shes rgyan gyi dgongs pa*, 10 chapters, fols. 241a–245b

[17] *lHa 'dre gnyis med kyi rgyud*, 32 chapters, fols. 245b–286b; VGB, vol. 7:1–95

[18] *rDzogs pa chen po sku gsum ye shes lnga'i don bshad pa nyi zla kha sbyor seng ge sgra yi dgongs pa bshad pa'i rgyud,* 92 chapters, fols. 286b–363a

[19] *Nor bu rin po che'i rgyud*, 10 chapters, fols. 363a–366b; VGB, vol. 6:35–41

[20] *Nor bu rin po che 'od 'bar ba'i rgyud*, 12 chapters, fols. 366b–369b; VGB, vol. 6:163–169

[21] *Nor bu dri ma med pa'i rgyud*, 3 chapters, fols. 369b–372b; VGB, vol. 6:171–177

[22] *rDo rje rnal 'byor ma'i rgyud / mkha' gro ma 'dre skad*, 10 chapters, fols. 372b–377b; VGB, vol. 6:179–191

[23] *sKu gsum ja log skal pa 'od ldan gyi rgyud*, 24 chapters, fols. 377b–387b; VGB, vol. 6:193–213

NGB, vol. chi, 299 fols., NGMPP reel no. AT 24/2 (= B 662/3):

[1] *rDzogs pa chen po sku gsum ja log gi rgyud*, 12 chapters, fols. 1b–5b; VGB, vol. 6:235–240

[2] *Ye shes 'khor lo gting rdzogs chen po'i rgyud*, 23 chapters, fols. 5b–15b; VGB, vol. 6:241–263

[3] *Thig le gsang ba yang gter rgyud*, 11 chapters, fols. 15b–20a; VGB, vol. 6:265–276

[4] *gSang ba yang gter gyi rgyud*, 10 chapters, fols. 20a–26a; VGB, vol. 6:277–291

[5] *Ye shes zang thal gyi rgyud*, 21 chapters, fols. 26a–37b; VGB, vol. 6:293–317

[6] *Thig le spros pa gcod pa'i rgyud gsang ba yang gter*, 10 chapters, fols. 37b–41b; VGB, vol. 6:113–123

[7] *Thig le 'dus pa'i rgyud*, 10 chapters, fols. 41b–44b; VGB, vol. 6:423–430

[8] *A ti rdzogs pa chen po'i rgyud*, 9 chapters, fols. 44b–48b; VGB, vol. 6:525–535

[9] *A ti gcod kyi rgyud*, 11 chapters, fols. 48b–52b; VGB, vol. 6:537–547

[10] *rDo rje mkha' 'gro ma'i 'dres rgyud*, 51 chapters, fols. 52b–78b

[11] *'Phags pa 'jam dpal lta ba thod rgal chen po'i rgyud*, 10 chapters, fols. 78b–83b

[12] *Phyag na rdo rje drag po lta stangs ye shes thog 'bebs kyi rgyud*, 11 chapters, fols. 83b–88b

[13] *'Phags pa mi g.yo ba 'khor ba rang grol gyi rgyud*, 13 chapters, fols. 88b–92a

[14] *dBang bskur bla ma rin po che'i rgyud*, 5 chapters, fols. 92a–100b; VGB, vol. 6:329–347

[15] *lHa mo 'od zer can gyi rgyud*, 3 chapters, fols. 100b–104b; VGB, vol. 6:349–357

[16] *gSang ba yang gter sku gsum gyi rgyud*, 6 chapters, fols. 104b–106b; VGB, vol. 6:107–112

[17] *Thig le gsang ba yang gter*, 9 chapters, fols. 106b–112b; VGB, vol. 6:371–384

[18] *Thig le nyag gcig rgyud*, 12 chapters, fols. 112b–116a; VGB, vol. 6:416–423

[19] *Thig le 'dus pa phyi ma'i rgyud*, 16 chapters, fols. 116a–121a; VGB, vol. 6:430–441

[20] *Thig le 'dus pa'i rgyud phyi ma'i phyi ma*, 15 chapters, fols. 121a–125b; VGB, vol. 6:441–449

[21] - no title fols. 125b–131a

[22] *rTsod pa'i sgra'i 'khor lo'i rgyud*, 4 chapters, fols. 131a–133b; VGB, vol. 6:549–555

[23] *'Phags pa 'jam dpal gyi rgyud bzhi'i don gsal bar byed pa'i rgyud*, 6 chapters, fols. 133b–135b; VGB, vol. 2:114–118

[24] *Nam mkha' nyi zla'i rgyal po mu med mtha' yas kyi rgyud*, 27 chapters, fols. 135b–157a

[25] *Rin po che bdud rtsi bcud thig rigs drug g.yang sa gcod pa'i rgyud*, 8 chapters, fols. 157a–163b

[26] *Rin po che gser gyi nyi mas ma rig gti mug ka dag ye shes sangs rgyas rgyud*, 21 chapters, fols. 163b–174a

[27] *Rin po che bye ma reg gcod kyi klong sde'i spros pa gcod pa*, fols. 174a–177a

[28] *Rin chen spu gri 'bar ba sems sde'i spros pa gcod pa*, fols. 177a–181a

[29] *Chu gri 'bar bas dbang sde spros pa gcod pa*, fols. 181a–189a

[30] *Rin po che gzod chen 'bar bas chos sde'i spros pa gcod pa*, fols. 189a–198a

[31] *Rin po che ral gri 'bar bas rgyud sde spros pa gcod pa*, fols. 198a–200a

[32] *Rin po che mig sel zhes bya ba'i rgyud*, 24 chapters, fols. 200a–207b

[33] *Sangs rgyas thams cad kyi bstan pa bu gcig pa'i rgyud,* fols. 207b–224a

[34] *Man ngag snying gi dgongs pa rgyal ba'i bka' zhes bya ba'i rgyud*, 8 chapters, fols. 224a–235a

[35] *De bzhin gshegs pa thams cad sdus pa khu byug rtsa ba'i rgyud*, fols. 235a–239a

[36] *gSang ba yang khol gyi rgyud*, 7 chapters, fols. 239a–240a

[37] *gSang ba rgya mtsho'i rgyud dam pa'i dam pa / rnal 'byor kyi rnal 'byor / gsang ba thams cad kyi tig ka rgyud kyi rgyal po*, fols. 240a–249b

[38] *Nam mkha' rnam par dag thig le skur gsal gyi rgyud*, 13 chapters, fols. 249b-256a

[39] *Sangs rgyas thams cad sku gsung thugs kyi snying po bstan pa'i rgyud*, fols. 256a–262b

[40] *Sangs rgyas thams cad sku gsung thugs gsang ba chen po'i rgyud*, 6 chapters, fols. 262b–269a

[41] *bsTan pa thams cad kyi snying po sems can thams cad la sangs rgyas rang chas chen por bzhugs pa'I rgyud*, 7 chapters, fols. 269b–280b

[42] - same title as [41], 7 chapters, fols. 280b–285b

[43] *rGyal ba'i rdo rje sems dpa'i dgongs pa / bstan pa thams cad kyi bu gcig pa*, 7 chapters, fols. 285b–298b

APPENDIX II

[a] *dKar chag*, fols. 7b/6–9b/2:
mang yul skyid grong 'dir rnying ma rgyud 'bum gyi lung rgyun dang dpe rgyun ji ltar byung tshul ni / bod kyi srid skyong mi dbang pho lha ba bsod nams stobs rgyas [8a] *la smin gling gter chen yab sras kyi zhal slob myang ston mnga' bdag rig 'dzin rgya mtsho zhes shel dkar du rgyal ba'i bka' 'gyur yongs rdzogs kyi gsung par gzheng (= bzheng) skabs mi dbangs chen pos zhus dag dang do dam par bkas bsnyags pa'i bshes gnyen dam pa de nyid kyi thugs bskyed rnam par dag pas mi dbang chen po'i thugs rje bskul te lho brag lha lung pa gter chen padma gling pa'i chos brgyud 'dzin pa ngag dbang lhun grub grags pa zhes pa 'chad nyan gyi rdo rje slob dpon du 'os par dgongs nas bdag rkyen dang bcas / mnga' ris stod du byon par mngags pa ltar dge ba'i bshes gnyen dam pa des bo dong kun mkhyen grags pa'i gdan sa la stod dpal mo chos sding du ched gtad kyis byon / de skabs chos snyan slob ma ni / kham lung pa sku skyes gsang sngags bstan 'dzin / grwa 'dzam gling pa sngags 'chang shes rab 'byung gnas / mdo chen pa sngags 'chang 'gyur med rnam rgyal sogs bla ma dgu tsam la rgyud 'bum gyi lcags lung yongs su rdzogs par gnang /*

mthar lho brag pa rdo rje 'dzin pa de nyid kyi bka' las / khyed rang chos snyan slob ma rnams nas / rab rnams kyi (= kyis) glegs bam yongs rdzogs gzheng (= bzheng) shing / gzhan la lung 'chad spel thub pa / de ltar gzheng pa (= bzheng pa) ma 'grub kyang tshar re cis kyang 'chad spel thub pa byed dgos zhes bka' phebs zhing /

rgyud 'bum gyi dpe rgyun yongs rdzogs kyang phyi mor rtsal ba (= brtsal ba) la / sku skye gsang sngags [8b] *bstan 'dzin tshar gcig gzheng bar (= bzheng bar) mdzad pa thub bstan rdo rje brag tu 'bul bar mdzad / 'dzam gling pa sngags 'chang shes rab 'byung gnas kyi (= kyis) lung rgyun spel ma thub kyang grwa a ya pa sogs sbyin bdag rnams dang mthun mong gis rgyud 'bum yongs rdzogs gzheng pa (= bzheng pa) ding sang skyid grong grwa yul gyi stod du a ya'i lha khang du bzhugs pa 'di yin / de la phyi mo byas pa'i rdo dmar ba kun bzang 'gyur med lhun grub kyis rgyud 'bum yongs rdzogs bzheng bar mdzad pa sbas yul gnam sgo zla gam zhes glang phrang (= 'phrang) gi dben dgon mngon dga' bsam gtan gling du bzhugs pa dang / spo (= spong) rong rje dpon nam mkha' dpal bzang gis rgyud 'bum yongs rdzogs gzheng bar (= bzheng bar) mdzad pa dpal mo chos sding du bzhugs / mdo chen pa'i rig 'dzin 'gyur med rnam rgyal nas rigs sras rje mdo chen pa tshe dbang 'chi med mgon po la rgyud 'bum gyi ljags lung rdzogs par gnang zhing sngar po ti thor bu 'ga' zhig yod pa rnams kyi kha bskongs bcas phyis su shing stag lor rje mdo chen pa mgon po'i zhabs dang / dpal sding pa rje 'gyur med 'phrin las bstan 'dzin khu dbon lhan rgyas nas brgyud (= rgyud) 'bum yongs rdzogs bzhengs par mdzad pa ding sang lan rde'i bla brang gong 'og du bzhugs so //*

mi dbang pho lha ba bsod nam (= *nams*) *stobs rgyas kyi lcam mo dkar ye dngos grub mtsho gling du bzhugs pa'i rje btsun ma padma chos 'dzoms zhes byang chub sems ma de* [9a] *nyid kyi thugs bskyed rnam par dge bas dngos grub phug nas kham lung pa padma gsang sngags bstan 'dzin nyid dkar yer spyan drangs / rje btsun ma de nyid kyis chos kyi gzhi gzung nas gnas de'i gdan sa ba chos dbyings khyab brdal ba dang / gzhan yang rnying lugs kyi bla dbon du ma zhig la chos nyan par bskul te kham lung pa gnyags ston sku skye gsang sngags bstan 'dzin nas rgyud 'bum yongs rdzogs kyi ljags lung rtsal* (= *stsal*) *// de skabs bdag gi bla ma rje mgon nang pa* (= *gnang pa*) *rig 'dzin 'phrin las bdud 'joms zhabs dgung lo bcu bdun bzhes pa gcung 'gyur med bstan 'dzin bcas sku mched gnyis la'ang rje btsun ma nyid kyis bdag skyen* (= *rkyen*) *mdzad te rgyud 'bum gyi ljags lung po ti drug ma gtogs rdzogs par gsan /*

rje rig 'dzin mgon nang pa (= *gnang pa*) *chen po de nyid kyis kho bo cag rang lo bdun pa lcags glang lor ri bo dpal 'bar nas rdo dmar ba o rgyan 'gro 'dul dbang gi rgyal pos chos kyi gzhi gzung bar mdzad nas bdag cag bla dbon dgu tsam la glang phrang* (= *'phrang*) *nas rgyud 'bum glegs bam yongs rdzogs gdan drangs te brag dkar rta so'i ri bsul* (= *sul*) *sbas gnas mchod rten nag po zhes par po ti nyi shu tsam gyi ljags lung dang / de'i 'phros ri bo dpal 'bar dgon du rtsal ba* (= *stsal ba*) *nos zhing /*

sngar gong du rje bla ma dam pa [9b] *de nyid kyis dkar yer sku skyes* (= *skye*) *gsang sngags bstan 'dzin las rgyud 'bum pu sti drug gi lung sngon du gnang grub pas ma gsan pas mdo chen pa sngags 'chang 'gyur med rnam rgyal nyid brag dkar du gdan drangs te ljags lung gi kha skongs gsan par mdzad pa'i mur bdag cag gis kyang legs par nos so //*

[b] *dKar chag*, fols. 10a/1–11a/4:
skabs 'dir rgyud 'bum rin po che 'di nyid gsar du ji ltar gzheng tshul brjod pa ni / rab smyos ces pa lcags rta lor skyid sbug sbra chen du sku zhang skyid sbug pas gzheng pa'i rnying ma rgyud 'bum yongs rdzogs bzhugs yod tshul thos pa g.yar po gtong dgos tshul gyi gdan 'dren du gtang bar po ti tshang ma 'byor kyang de'i phyi mo gtsang theg mchog gling nas spyan drangs pa'i zhal shus pa yin 'dug pas 'di kha'i rgyud 'bum gyi bzhugs tshul dkar chag dang go rim cung zad mi mthun par snang yang de'i thog nas sku thang rgya yul bla ma chos rgyal / tsum nyi lhod bla ma yab sras / byams sprin dbon po phun tshogs mched / tsum dga' ldan dgon nas bsgom chen karma bstan 'dzin sogs bcu phrag lhag par mchod rten nag por snga sor rje bla ma rig pa 'dzin dbang de nyid kyis rgyud 'bum ljags lung rtsal ba'i (= *stsal ba'i*) *chos khri'i steng nas rgyud 'bum glegs bam yongs rdzogs kyi bklags lung bgyis shing / rjes su bklogs mkhan mang po'i tshar gsum bklog pa bcas sdom par po ti yong rdzogs tshar bzhi bklags nas skyid sbug tu skyel bar btang /*

skabs der rgyud 'bum rin [10b] *po che zhig gsar du bzheng pa'i blo skyes te yol mo nas shog bu sgrub ching chu bya lo sa ga zla ba'i tshes bcu gsum nas dbu brtsam (= brtsams) glang phrang (= 'phrang) nas rdo dmar ba bla ma skal bzang lags la rgyud 'bum gyi phyi mo glegs bam yongs rdzogs g.yar po zhus pa gdan drangs / skyid grong khul gyi yig mkhan legs gras spus bsdus pa'i 'gad gtsang zhig rang gzheng rtsis byas par / thog mar yig mkhan bcu tsam las ma byung kyang / de rjes rim par dog tshang (= 'tshang) gis bco lnga skor dang / mthar mi grang nyer dgu tsam byung ba mi rer po ti re dang snag tsha la gcen mkhas mchog dam pa de nyid kyi sku gdung dang / rin po che bsres pa / rgyu snyug re / tshal brtul ma shog bam re / bri gzhi shog bu bcas so sor bkye / yig mkhan spus legs pa 'ga' zhig gis pu ti gnyis re bris / kha cig gi le lo'i dus 'gyang dang / yig spus shin tu zhel zhing rod rtags rtog rtsing gis ma dag pa sogs glegs bam kha shas spus gtsang ba zhig byung ma song bas blo yid kheng pa zhig gtan nas ma byung kyang gting bskul rim par gtang bas phal cher tshags su chug pa'i brag dkar rang du zla gcig tsam dpon yig pa dang / las byed mang du bsags te / la las yi ge las zhu dag / la las glegs shing gi shing gzo (= bzo) dang 'gras (= 'gres) rgyag pa / kha gcig gdong dar dang zhal khebs* [11a] *glegs bam thag tshem pa (= 'tshem pa) kha cig glegs chab bco ba / la la lha ris dang rtsi tshon / 'ga' zhig dbu shog gi gser yig 'bri ba sogs sgyu ma'i mig 'phrul lta bu dus gcig tu brtsams par shing khyi sa ga chen po'i tshe bcu bzhi tshun la legs par grub /*

The Transmission of the *dMar khrid Tshem bu lugs* and the *Maṇi bka' 'bum*

1. Introduction

'Gos Lo-tsā-ba gZhon-nu dpal (1392–1481) in his Blue Annals gives a good overview of the various traditions of the Avalokiteśvara teachings that developed as independent traditions in Tibet with the start of the second spread of Buddhism in the 11th century. Among these doctrinal systems, which are termed the "Cycle[s] of Mahākāruṇika" (*thugs rje chen po'i skor*), those of the bhikṣunī Lakṣmīṅ[karā], Byang[-chub] sems[-dpa'] Zla-ba rgyal-mtshan and the siddha gNyan Tshem-bu-pa may be highlighted. The latter's tradition also bears the name "System of Tshem-bu[-pa], a Direct Instruction [on the Practice of Mahākāruṇika]" (*dmar khrid tshem bu lugs*).[1]

Together with the tradition of sKyer-sgang-pa, a representative of the school of the Shangs-pa bKa'-brgyud-pa, this group of Avalokiteśvara teachings was also familiar in the 16th century under the name "Four Families of Direct Instruction [on the Practice of Mahākāruṇika]" (*dmar khrid rigs bzhi*). This is clear from the collection of the "[More than] One Hundred Instructions" (*khrid brgya*), compiled by Jo-nang Kun-dga' grol-mchog (1507–1566). These direct instructions are teachings about the practice of Mahākāruṇika that were imparted in a vision to each of the founders of the individual traditions; these teachings thus fall under the category of "pure vision" (*dag snang*).[2]

In the following, I would like to direct my attention to the system of Tshem-bu-pa, with the aim of providing an initial overview of the circle of persons who transmitted this teaching in the period from the 12th to the 16th centuries. The second step will be to look into a further tradition of teaching concerning the practice of Mahākāruṇika that enjoyed great popularity in Tibet: that of the *Maṇi bka' 'bum* or *rGyal po bka' 'bum*. The present investigation may be seen as a contribution to the textual history of the "Hundred Thousand

---

[1] On the *Thugs rje chen po'i skor*, see gZhon-nu dpal: *Deb ther sngon po*, pp. 1173.1–1215.7, and on the *dMar khrid tshem bu lugs kyi skabs*, ibid, pp. 1213.12–1215.7; cf. Roerich (1949=1976:1006–1044 & 1043f.).

[2] A biography of sKyer-sgang-pa is likewise contained in gZhon-nu dpal (as in note 1), pp. 863.13–867.8; cf. Roerich (1949=1976:737–741). The *dMar khrid rigs bzhi* in Jo-nang Kun-dga' grol-mchog's compilation is found in *Zab khrid brgya dang brgyad kyi yi ge*, pp. 186.2–190.5; on this collection, see the information in Kapstein (1996:280ff.). For the classification of the *dMar-khrid* tradition as a "visionary system of meditation", see Gyatso (1992:99).

Proclamations of the Maṇi [Mantra]" (*maṇi bka' 'bum*) otherwise known as the "Hundred Thousand Proclamations of King [Srong-btsan sgam-po]" (*rgyal po bka' 'bum*), a collection of works that has aroused the interest of generations of Western scholars.[3]

2. THE SYSTEM OF TSHEM-BU-PA

According to the account in the history of 'Gos Lo-tsā-ba—completed 1476—, the siddha Tshem-bu-pa received the teachings for the practice of Avalokiteśvara in a direct vision from the Ḍākiṇī bDag-med-ma (*nairātmya*) and passed them on to six disciples. The siddha pursued his activities principally in Central Tibet, in the region of g.Yas-ru. One Byang-chub 'od, who bore the surname sPyi-bo lhas-pa, is mentioned as the most important of his disciples. He in turn maintained close contact with two of "the five great masters of the Sa-skya[-pa school]" (*sa skya gong ma lnga*), having been a disciple of Grags-pa rgyal-mtshan (1147–1216) and having taught and taken part in the ordination of Sa-skya Paṇḍita Kun-dga' rgyal-mtshan (1182–1251). From the siddha Tshem-bu-pa he received two works in which the Avalokiteśvara teachings were fixed in writing: *Phyi theg pa lam rim spungs kyi don khrid* and *Nang gsang sngags kyi dmar khrid*.[4]

Of the next two transmitters of the teachings, the only thing known is that they held the post of *mkhan-po* in the monasteries of sTag-bde brag-dmar and Phyi-'brum dgon-gsar respectively. The second of the two transmitted the Avalokiteśvara teachings to one Zhang Kun-spangs-pa. The consequence of this was that these teachings spread in all directions and had a great effect: for it was during the time of this teacher that the system of Tshem-bu-pa numbered among the "four great instructions [for the practice of Mahākāruṇika] among the Jo-nang-pas" (*jo nang pa'i khrid chen bzhi*); and its "method of instruction" (*'khrid lugs*) coincided with the teachings of Mahāmudrā (*phyag chen*) and with the first step in the practices of the Ṣaḍaṅga Yoga of the Kālacakra teachings. It is thus obvious that Zhang Kun-spangs-pa was a representative of the Jo-nang-pa school. Indeed, he was none other than Kun-spangs[-pa] Thugs-rje brtson-'grus (1243–1313), the founder of the monastery Jo[-mo] nang in gTsang province.[5]

---

3 Among the investigations on the *Maṇi bka' 'bum* there may be mentioned Blondeau (1984) and Kapstein (1992); on the significance of this tradition for the cultural memory of Tibetans, see Dreyfus (1994) & (1995). Both Sørensen (1994:13) and van der Kuijp (1996:48) point out the desirability of producing a text-critical edition of this heterogeneous collection.

4 On sPyi-bo lhas-pa, see the remarks by Jackson (1987b:27). The two works, as far as I know, have not been preserved. They belong to the genre of "instructional writings" (*khrid yig*), which are defined as "practical manuals explicating particular systems of meditation, yoga and ritual"; see Kapstein (1996:276).

5 For a brief biography of Kun-spangs-pa, see gZhon-nu dpal (as in note 1), pp. 904.17–905.17; cf. Roerich (1949=1976:771–77). Further texts are described by van der Kuijp (1994:190–193). Kun-spangs-pa's contribution to the codification of the Ṣaḍaṅga Yoga is given due recognition by Stearns (1996:147–

The *Blue Annals* offer no further details on the history of these Avalokiteśvara teachings. For an overview of the persons that were responsible for the spread of the teachings from the 14th century on, one must turn to a text from the pen of bTsun-pa Chos-legs (1437–1521). This younger contemporary of 'Gos Lo-tsā-ba wrote an "instructional text" (*khrid yig*) on the system of Tshem-bu-pa in 1509 and, as is common in this genre, prefaced the actual instructions with a detailed "history of the lineage of teachers" (*bla ma brgyud pa'i lo rgyus*).

According to this text, Kun-spangs[-pa] Thugs-rje brtson-'grus was succeeded by a master who likewise was active in the construction of Jo[-mo] nang. His name is Chos-rje Sher-'bum, and his short biography contains detailed information on the toils he underwent during the construction of the monastery; furthermore, he was the author of numerous writings of the Jo-nang-pa school. Among the "textbooks" (*yig cha*) concerning Avalokiteśvara teachings we also find a work on the system of Tshem-bu-pa by him.[6] From Chos-rje Sher-'bum the teachings passed on to a teacher of the late bKa'-gdams-pa school, namely rGyal-sras Thogs-med[bzang-po] (1295–1369). In the present context it may merely be pointed out that the name of this master is intimately connected with the transmission of various cycles of the practice of Mahākāruṇika, such as that of the "fasting meditation" (*smyung gnas*); in this case, too, he figures within the tradition of Chos-rje Sher-'bum.[7]

With the appearance of those persons who, according to the text of bTsun-pa Chos-legs, proceeded to transmit the system of Tshem-bu-pa after rGyal-sras Thogs-med, the geographical centre of gravity in the spread of the teachings shifts from Central to

149); on the individual steps of the Ṣaḍaṅga Yoga, see Orofino (1996:129–139). The *jo nang pa'i khrid chen bzhi* are the previously mentioned *dmar khrid rigs bzhi*.

6 For a biography of Chos-rje Sher-'bum, see bTsun-pa Chos-legs: *Thugs rje chen po'i dmar khrid don tshan lnga pa*, fols. 3b/5–6b/6; his role as a disciple of Thugs-rje brtson-'grus has been referred to by Stearns (1999:182, note 44). The work of Chos-rje Sher-'bum served as a basis for Kun-dga' grol-mchog's summary of the system of Tshem-bu-pa; see *Zab khrid brgya dang brgyad kyi yi ge*, p. 188.2 (*čhos rje shes (= sher) 'bum pa'i khrid yig las btus so*), and *Khrid brgya'i spyi chings rnam par spel ba*, p. 57.7 (*khrid so gnyis pa tshem bu lugs rin po che sher 'bum pa'i khrid yig steng nas myang khrid lhag par smin pa*). Along with the "Great Instructional Text" (*khrid yig chen mo*) of Bla-ma dam-pa bSod-nams rgyal-mtshan (1312–1375), Kun-dga' grol-mchog also used the instructional works of Byang-chub sems-dpa' rGyal-ba ye-shes and rTogs-ldan mKha'-spyod dbang-po, i.e. the second Zhwa-dmar-pa (1350-1405); ibid, pp. 57.7–58.3.

7 See bTsun-pa Chos-legs (as in note 6), fols. 6b/6–7a/3, for the person of rGyal-sras Thogs-med. For a detailed treatment the biography titled *bDud rtsi thig pa* is referred to; a sketch of the life of rGyal-sras Thogs-med based on that biography is given by Jackson (1984:74, note 37). On the place of Chos-rje Sher-'bum and rGyal-sras Thogs-med within the tradition of the practice of the Ekādaśamukha-Avalokiteśvara, see 'Od-dpag rdo-rje: *Thugs rje chen po bcu gcig pa'i bla ma brgyud pa'i rnam thar nor bu'i phreng ba*, pp. 113.2–175.5. On the status of rGyal-sras Thogs-med as an incarnation of Byang[-chub] sems[-dpa'] Zla-ba rgyal-mtshan, see Smith (1970b:11).

Southwestern Tibet. Coming to occupy the focus of attention, are various teachers associated with the monastery of Shel-dkar chos-sde in La-stod lHo – representatives of the Bo-dong-pa school, in other words. Thus, following rGyal-sras Thogs-med, it is Lo-chen Byang-chub rtse-mo (1315–1392) and dKa'-bzhi-pa Nam-mkha' 'od-zer (died 1401) who are named as the next two persons in the tradition. From the chronicle of Shel-dkar chos-sde, written in the 18th century, it is known that the translator Byang-chub rtse-mo and his disciple Nam-mkha' 'od-zer number as the second and twelfth holders respectively of the early monastery's abbatial seat. Concerning Nam-mkha' 'od-zer himself, it may be added here that he was a member of the family of rulers of sPong-rong in Byang; this family produced other abbots for the monastery of Shel-dkar.[8]

After mKhan-chen dPal-ldan grub, a disciple of Nam-mkha' 'od-zer born in La-stod lHo, we come to three persons in this tradition of the Avalokiteśvara teachings who need to be noted more carefully, since they are important for the later account. The first one mentioned is one bDag-nyid chen-po bZang-po rgyal-mtshan, whose brother was a "trading lord" (*tshong dpon*) in the fortress of Shel-dkar. bZang-po rgyal-mtshan for his part performed the duties of a *slob-dpon* in one of the colleges of Shel-dkar chos-sde; his college bore the name gNas-'og grwa-tshang and was one of the twenty-one colleges into which the monastery (founded in 1385) was divided. As the short biography notes in detail, he listened at this time to numerous teachings that came from India, such as those of the Ṣaḍaṅga Yoga, and devoted himself in particular to the study of the *Maṇi bka' 'bum*, a work of Srong-btsan sgam-po, the "king who was an incarnation [of Mahākāruṇika]" (*sprul pa'i rgyal po*).

A connection between the teachings of Avalokiteśvara and those of the *Kālacakratantra* can be seen in the spiritual practice of bZang-po rgyal-mtshan: "Outwardly he practiced [the deity] Mahākāruṇika" (*phyi ltar thugs rje chen po la thugs dam mdzad*), and "inwardly he made the Ṣaḍaṅga [Yoga] the focus of his practice" (*nang du sbyor ba yan lag drug la thugs dam gyi 'thil (= mthil) mdzad*).[9]

---

8 See bTsun-pa Chos-legs (as in note 6), fols. 7a/3–12b/2 for biographies of Lo-chen Byang-chub rtse-mo and Nam-mkha' 'od-zer; cf. Wangdu & Diemberger (1996:70–72, 87). A short biography of Nam-mkha' 'od-zer on the basis of the "family chronicle" (*gdung rabs*) of the princes of sPong-rong is found in Chos-kyi dbang-phyug: *Chos ldan sa skyongs 'bur pa mi rje'i gdung rab (= rabs) lo rgyus dri med baiḍūrya'i 'phreng ba*, fol. 6a/3–b/2. If the entire text is combed through, then the tenth, thirteenth and eighteenth early abbots are also seen to have come from this family; on them, see Wangdu & Diemberger (1996: 86–90).

9 For the biography of bZang-po rgyal-mtshan, see bTsun-pa Chos-legs (as in note 6), fols. 13a/5–14a/2. The date of the founding of Shel-dkar chos-sde under lHo-bdag Chos-kyi rin-chen (died 1402) may be found in Wangdu & Diemberger (1996:73) and Jackson (1996:101). The gNas-'og grwa-tshang owed its existence to sDe-pa gNas-'og-pa, a local chieftain, who was ruling in the region to the southwest of Shel-dkar; cf. Wangdu & Diemberger (1996:57).

The next two persons likewise followed the teachings of the Bo-dong-pa school, and during their studies stayed at the gNas-'og grwa-tshang of Shel-dkar monastery; at the beginning of the 15th century this college was known for catering primarily to monks from West Tibet (*mnga' ris pa'i grwa rgyun 'bab sa*). The first one was called mKhas-grub chen-po dPal-ldan sangs-rgyas (1391–1455) and hailed from Gro-shod, a region in West Tibet that at the time fell within the domain of the kings of mNga'-ris Gung-thang. Following initial studies at the monastery of Chos-lung in Byang – and at rDzong-dkar chos-sde in Gung-thang – dPal-ldan sangs-rgyas met, at Shel-dkar chos-sde, his principal teacher, bDag-nyid chen-po bZang-po rgyal-mtshan. Along with teachings on the practice of Mahākāruṇika according to the system of Tshem-bu-pa and the *Maṇi bka' 'bum*, he received from him the teachings of the Ṣaḍaṅga Yoga (*kong rang gi thugs dam gyi 'thil (= mthil) dus 'khor sbyor drug / maṇi bka' 'bum / khyad par khrid zab mo 'di la sogs pa chos mang du gsan*). Once bDag-nyid chen-po bZang-po rgyal-mtshan had retired from his duties as *slob-dpon* of the college of gNas-'og, his disciple took over his official responsibilities. During this time, the Bo-dong Paṇ-chen 'Jigs-med grags-pa (1375–1451) numbered among the teachers of dPal-ldan sangs-rgyas.

In response to an invitation from King Khri lHa-dbang rgyal-mtshan (1404–1464), dPal-ldan sangs-rgyas spent his later years in mNga'-ris Gung-thang, and was also active at Chos-sdings and more particularly the monastery mNgon-dga'.[10] Several years after the death of dPal-ldan sangs-rgyas, his "Complete Works" (*bka' 'bum*) were compiled in nine volumes and brought out as manuscripts.[11]

The second teacher's name was bSam-grub dpal (died 1498), and his homeland was in the "heartland" (*rtsa ba'i yul*) of the kings of mNga'-ris Gung-thang, more precisely identified as Ko-ron in the area of Ku-thang Nub-ris. He took the upāsaka vows under mKhas-grub chen-po dPal-ldan sangs-rgyas in mNgon-dga' monastery, and shortly thereafter resumed

10 The first monastery of the Bo-dong-pa school in Gung-thang was in existence as early as 1394; on the founding of rDzong-dkar chos-sde, see Wangdu & Diemberger (1996:74) and Jackson (1996:101). The foundation story of mNgon-dga' is found in Tshe-dbang nor-bu: *Dwangs shel 'phrul gyi me long*, p. 127.3–19; these events are dealt with there in the section on King Khri rNam-rgyal lde (1422–1502), who counted dPal-ldan sangs-rgyas among his teachers. According to Chos-kyi dbang-phyug (as in note 8), fol. 16b/2–3, [mNga'-ris Nya-ma] mNgon-dga' was originally brought into being by rDzong-dkar bla-chen Chos-dpal bzang-po (1371–1439); in the following years it served as a domicile for dPal-ldan sangs-rgyas and his nephew dPal-ldan seng-ge (1414–1498).

11 For the short biography of dPal-ldan sangs-rgyas, see bTsun-pa Chos-legs (as in note 6), fols. 14b/2–18a/3. Not a single volume of the "Complete Works" has to my knowledge survived. The writing out of the manuscripts in the years 1474–1475 is described by 'Jigs-med bzang-po & dBang-phyug dpal-ldan: *dPal ldan bla ma dam pa chos legs mtshan can gyi rnam thar*, fols. 58a/6–59a/2; the financing of this edition was assumed by King Khri rNam-rgyal lde. A tenth volume contained a biography of dPal-ldan sangs-rgyas written by dPal-ldan dar (1424–1510) along with two biographies of Bo-dong Paṇ-chen 'Jigs-med grags-pa (*yar 'brog ma dang ngag dbang ma gnyis*); for these two biographies, see Diemberger et al. (1997:13–15).

his studies in the gNas-'og grwa-tshang in Shel-dkar chos-sde; there his teacher was dBang-phyug dpal-ldan, and he also met Bo-dong Paṇ-chen 'Jigs-med grags-pa.

Concerning the later years of bSam-grub dpal, we know that he spent them in his native region, where the "hermitage" (*dben gnas*) of 'Tsho-rkyen was located. In the monastery of mNgon-dga' – like Chos-sdings, located in the south-western region of rDzong-dkar – he gathered, later in life, a large circle of disciples; among them was King Khri rNam-rgyal lde (1422–1502) of Gung-thang.[12]

3. bTSUN-PA CHOS-LEGS AND HIS DISCIPLES

Since a detailed biography exists of bTsun-pa Chos-legs, the disciple of bSam-grub dpal who penned the instructional text on the system of Tshem-bu-pa, we shall turn now to bTsun-pa Chos-legs and his efforts to spread the Avalokiteśvara teachings. In 1472 bTsun-pa Chos-legs visited bSam-grub dpal in the monastery of rTa-sga – a site of the Tshal-pa bKa'-brgyud-pa that at the time was under the Bo-dong-pa school – and asked the teacher for an initiation into the Mahākāruṇika cycle *Thugs rje chen po 'gro 'dul*. The latter is a "treasure-work" (*gter ma*) of mNga'-bdag Nyang-ral Nyi-ma'i 'od-zer (1124–1192) that had been handed down together with the *Maṇi bka' 'bum*. This tradition is explicitly highlighted as being among the various teachings that bTsun-pa Chos-legs received from his teacher (*rgyal po srong btsan sgam po'i bka' 'bum dbang dang bcas pa*).[13]

At the age of forty-eight, in the year 1485, bTsun-pa Chos-legs for the first time himself transmitted the teachings on the practice of Mahākāruṇika according to the system of Tshem-bu-pa: as the successor to bSam-grub dpal in the monastery of rTa-sga. The years between this first public teaching and the composition of his instructional text contain still other events that shed light on how the Avalokiteśvara teachings were kept alive in mNga'-ris Gung-thang. For example, there is one report of a monk from Nyi[-ma] phug in "Upper Mustang" (*glo bo stod*) who found his way to the master of the Bo-dong-pa school in 'Tsho-rkyen and asked him for the teachings of the *Maṇi bka' 'bum*. Upon this request bTsun-pa Chos-legs spoke the following words: "If one has not realized the mind [in its true nature], then one does not understand the 'Hundred Thousand Pronouncements of the

---

12 For a short biography of bSam-grub dpal, see bTsun-pa Chos-legs (as in note 6), fols. 18a/3–23a/3. The hermitage of 'Tsho-rkyen later also served bTsun-pa Chos-legs as a retreat site; see the description of his first arrival in 1478 by way of Ku-thang Nub-ris and rTa-sga monastery in 'Jigs-med bzang-po dBang-phyug dpal-ldan (as in note 11), fols. 63a/3ff.

13 The biography of bTsun-pa Chos-legs has previously been drawn on by Vitali (1997:1023ff.) for an account of the history of the nomad territory of Byang and mNga'-ris. On the founding of rTa-sga, the most important community of the Tshal-pa bKa'-brgyud-pa in West Tibet, in the years between 1195 and 1200, see Vitali (1996:394). [Nub-ris] rTa-sga dgon is described, as a site of the Bo-dong-pa school, by Chos-kyi dbang-phyug (as in note 8), fol. 16b/4–5. For bTsun-pa Chos-legs study there, see 'Jigs-med bzang-po & dBang-phyug dpal-ldan (as in note 11), fol. 57b/3 and 66b/2.

King [Srong-btsan sgam-po]'" (*sems ngo ma 'phrod na rgyal po'i bka' 'bum mi go zer ba*). After conferring the initiation of the *Thugs rje chen po 'gro 'dul*, bTsun-pa Chos-legs administered a brief instruction on the practice of the Mahākāruṇika according to the system of Tshem-bu-pa, which was supplemented in turn by a "reading-authorization" (*lung*) of the *Maṇi bka' 'bum*. The monk from Mustang ended by promising to recite the collection of works a hundred times in a loud voice (*kong gis kyang bka' 'bum brgya tshar zhig sgrog pa'i dam bca' phul te*).

When in 1508, shortly before the instructional text was put to paper, bTsun-pa Chos-legs presented the teachings of the *Thugs rje chen po dmar khrid* a further time at the court of rDzong-dkar, the *Maṇi bka' 'bum* collection was logically termed the "supportive teaching" (*rgyab chos*) of the system of Tshem-bu-pa. If a further episode in the instruction of the Avalokiteśvara teachings in rDzong-dkar is considered, then a picture emerges according to which the combination of the "system of Tshem-bu-pa" (*tshem bu lugs*) together with the "treasure teachings" (*gter chos*) of the *Thugs rje chen po 'gro 'dul* and the *Maṇi bka' 'bum* characterize the transmission of the Avalokiteśvara teachings in mNga'-ris Gung-thang.[14]

Not only was bTsun-pa Chos-legs responsible for putting the teachings of the siddha Tshem-bu-pa into fixed written form, he also produced manuscripts of the *Maṇi bka' 'bum*. The biography reports that he wrote a copy in 1486 for the well-being of his mother (*de dus ma'i don du maṇi bka' 'bum zhig kyang bzhengs*), and when in 1518 the "textbooks" composed by him were arranged into individual "volumes" (*glegs bam*), another copy was prepared (*rgyal po bsrong btsan sgam po'i bka' 'bum zhig kyang bsgrubs*). It was only after the death of bTsun-pa Chos-legs that the means became available to produce a block print of the collection of texts, the cost being defrayed by King Khri Kun-dga' rnam-rgyal lde (died 1524) and his family. This edition is thus visible testimony to the esteem that the master of the Bo-dong-pa school enjoyed at the court of mNga'-ris Gung-thang as the teacher of Khri Kun-dga' rnam-rgyal lde.[15]

Another disciple of bTsun-pa Chos-legs directly involved in the production of the block print bore the name mNyam-med Chos-dbang rgyal-mtshan (1484–1549). Since

---

14 The three examples of the Avalokiteśvara teachings transmitted by bTsun-pa Chos-legs are found in 'Jigs-med bzang-po dBang-phyug dpal-ldan (as in note 11), fols. 97a/6–b/3, 100a/1–3 and 107b/5–6. For the various works of the cycle *Thugs rje chen po 'gro 'dul* according to the *Rin chen gter mdzod*, compiled by Kong-sprul Blo-gros mtha'-yas (1813–1899), see Schwieger (1995:nos. 808–811).

15 On the manuscripts of the *Maṇi bka' 'bum*, see 'Jigs-med bzang-po & dBang-phyug dpal-ldan (as in note 11), fols. 72b/2 and 111b/5. The 1521 print was part of the "memorial ceremonies" (*dgongs rdzogs*) of the royal family that followed upon the death of bTsun-pa Chos-legs; see ibid, fol. 138b/2–4 (*de'i dbyar chos rgyal khu dbon rnams kyis / nyid kyi dgongs pa rdzogs thabs la sku'i rten du zhal skyin sku tsha dang mnyam pa / gsung gi rten du chos rgyal srong btsan bsgam po'i bka' 'bum gyi par / thugs kyi rten du gdung thal dang / gdung khang gi rdul rdzas sogs las rgyu byas pa'i rnam rgyal mchod rten gser shog sogs bzang rtsi phun sum tshogs pas brgyan pa sgrub par mdzad de*).

various writings of his have become available, it is possible to add further details about this block print from the year 1521. For example, we learn that the edition, together with the "print colophon" (*spar byang*) was completed in the eleventh month, and that in the following year King Khri Kun-dga' rnam-rgyal lde gave the reading-authorization of the *Maṇi bka' 'bum* to Chos-dbang rgyal-mtshan. The occasion for this was the printing of another text, a "hymn" (*bstod pa*) to the lineage of the kings of mNga'-ris Gung-thang. Further, a document written by Chos-dbang rgyal-mtshan has been preserved that makes it clear that another member of the royal family sent a copy of the freshly produced *Maṇi bka' 'bum* to the Mustang court as a present for Glo-bo mkhan-chen bSod-nams lhun-grub (1456–1532).[16]

4. THE TRANSMISSION OF THE *MAṆI BKA' 'BUM*

Among the collection of Tibetan texts in the National Archives in Kathmandu is found an edition of the *Maṇi bka' 'bum* in two volumes (327 and 319 fols., NGMPP reel nos. AT 167/4 and AT 167/5–168/1), assignable to the tradition of works from mNga'-ris Gung-thang. This edition bears no separate print colophon, but a look at the "catalogue" (*dkar chag*) is enough to identify the text as a 16th-century block print from the region in question. This catalogue is titled *Bla ma brgyud pa'i gsol 'debs lo rgyus dkar chags* (12 fols.), and is of interest for the question of how the teachings of the Mahākāruṇika were transmitted because at the beginning and at the end of the actual *Maṇi bka' 'bum dkar chags* (fols. 5b/1–12a/2) two section were added that contain the names of the teachers that transmitted this cycle.

In contrast to the older part of the *Maṇi bka' 'bum dkar chags* which describes the contents and structure of the collection of works, these two sections were written at the time the collection was being printed in mNga'-ris Gung-thang. The first section can be subdivided into three "supplicatory prayers" (*gsol 'debs*) (fols. 1b/1–3b/6, 3b/6–5a/1, 5a/1–6), the last of which contains the "lineage of direct transmission" (*nye brgyud*) of the teachings of Srong-btsan sgam-po. All of these prayers end with an invocation of the teachers with whom we have become acquainted with as the representatives of the Bo-dong-pa school in La-stod lHo and Gung-thang: bDag-nyid chen-po bZang-po rgyal-

16 On the printing, see Chos-dbang rgyal-mtshan: *Rin po che nor bu'i phreng ba*, fol. 51a/5–b/1 (*maṇi bka' 'bum / las tshogs cha lag dang bcas pa / spar phud la le bdun ma rnams kyi zhus dag / zhal bkod / spar rkos stobs che ba / spar byang gi gsung rtsom rnam dang / ... sbrul lo zla ba bcu gcig pa yan la rdzogs par mdzad*), and on the printing of the hymn and the reading-authorization, ibid, fol. 51b/5–6 (*chos rgyal mes dbon rnam gsum dang / gung thang rgyal brgyud kyi bstod pa rnams spar du bsgrubs pa'i zhal bkod / zhus dag do dam / spar byang gi gsung rtsom rnams mdzad / de'i skabs su gong ma chen po'i drung du / maṇi bka' 'bum lung yang gsan no*). The document written to Glo-bo mkhan-chen is found in Chos-dbang rgyal-mtshan: *Mgur 'bum*, fols. 28a/7–29b/6 (*glo bo smon thang du / chos rje bsod nams lhun grub la / gong ma khri bkra shis dpal 'bar gyi phul ba*).

mtshan, dPal-ldan sangs-rgyas, bSam-grub dpal and bTsun-pa Chos-legs. The second section is a prose résumé of the transmission, the last person listed being King Khri Kun-dga' rnam-rgyal lde:

> [From the] Dharmakāya Amitābha [to the] Saṃbhogakāya Avalokiteśvara, [from him to the] Nirmāṇakāya [b]Srong-btsan sgam-po, [from him to] Ācārya Padmasambhava. The latter [gave] Prince Khri [b]Srong lde-btsan what had been hidden [in the way of teachings] by the ancestor [b]Srong-btsan sgam-po under the right foot [of the statue] of Hayagrīva [in the chamber] along the northern side of the main temple of Ra-sa ['phrul-snang], in the side girders, and in the right thigh [of the statue] of the Yakṣa Nāga Kubera, [namely] the three main [sādhanas], the eight lesser [sādhanas], the one hundred and fifty-five upadeśas – whatever was there. With the words "I will show it [to you]!" [Padmasambhava] ascended magically into heaven along with the king, [Khri Srong lde-btsan]. The king, having seen all the treasures, acquired great confidence, and made the object of his spiritual practice the more than one thousand sādhanas of Mahākāruṇika, the instructions of the cycle *Gab pa mngon phyung*, the [stages of the] *bsKyed[-rim]* and the *rDzogs[-rim]* of the thousand Mahākāruṇika-Buddhas, and [the text on the] benefit of seeing the personal deity [of Srong-btsan sgam-po] and the testaments [formulated prior to] [b]Srong-btsan sgam-po's death.
>
> Following this, Grub-thob dNgos-grub brought to light the teachings of the cycle of sādhanas of the Mahākāruṇika from under the right foot of [the statue] of Hayagrīva and gave them to mNga'-bdag Nyang-ral [Nyi-ma'i 'od-zer], the rebirth of the son of the gods Khri [b]Srong lde-btsan. Nyang [Nyi-ma'i 'od-zer] for his part brought out from under the foot of [the statue] of Hayagrīva in the chapel of Mahākāruṇika the [more than] one hundred and fifty upadseśas and gave them to La-stod-pa Mi-bskyod rdo-rje. The latter gave [the teachings] to rJe-btsun Śākya bzang-po, who, having performed numerous repairs on the embankment around Ra-sa ['phrul-snang], obtained a prophecy and uncovered the cycle *Gab pa mngon phyung* and [the works of the] *Sūtra* cycle from the Yakṣa house of [the 'Phrul-snang temple]; he [in turn] gave all cycles of the teaching of the king who was an incarnation [of Mahākāruṇika] to the precious teacher lHa-rje dGe[-ba] 'bum.[17]

[17] After Grub-thob dNgos-grub and mNga'-bdag Nyang, rJe-btsun Śākya bzang-po is the third treasure-discoverer who uncovered the works of the *Maṇi bka' 'bum* in the temple of Ra-sa 'phrul-snang in the 12th and 13th centuries; on his discoveries and the question of his identity (he is also given the name Śākya-'od), see Kapstein (1992:82), Blondeau (1994:32) and Sørensen (1994:17 & 586). If the observations of Macdonald (1971:184–185) hold, then it was [La-stod-pa] Mi-bskyod rdo-rje who bore the name Śākya-'od; cf. gZhon-nu dpal (as in note 1), p. 196.1–2, and Roerich (1949=1976:155).

> This latter gave them to lCam-mo Ye-shes mchog; she to Grub-thob Chu-sgom-pa; he to mTha'-bzhi Bya-bral-ba; he to 'Jam-dbyangs bSod-nams seng-ge; he to Bla-ma bKra-shis rgyal-mtshan; he to Blo-gros rgyal-mtshan, [a rebirth of rJe-btsun Śākya bzang-po] who was responsible for the embankment around Ra-sa ['phrul-snang]; he to 'Phags-mchog Nor-bu bzang-po; he to Chos-rje bZang-po rgyal-mtshan; he to mKhas-grub dPal-ldan sangs-rgyas; he to the respected teacher bSam-grub dpal; he to mKhas-grub dam-pa Chos-legs mtshan-can; he to the ruler, the Dharmarāja, Khri Kun-dga' rnam-rgyal lde. (see Appendix I)

One special feature of the edition of the *Maṇi bka' 'bum* from mNga'-ris Gung-thang is the presence of illustrations of the persons who transmitted these teachings – from the treasure-discoverer Grub-thob dNgos-grub to mKhas-grub dPal-ldan sangs-rgyas. Some of these illustrations have been reproduced below (see Appendix II). Also worth noting is the fact that the tradition represented by these block prints contains neither the *Ārya-Karaṇḍavyūha-nāma-mahāyānasūtra* nor the *'Phags pa byang chub sems dpa' spyan ras gzigs dbang phyug phyag stong spyan stong dang ldan pa thogs pa mi mnga' ba'i thugs rje chen po'i sems rgya cher yongs su rdzogs pa zhes bya ba'i gzungs*, which are the two main works of the cult of the Bodhisattva Avalokiteśvara in India and China. Their absence supports the hypothesis that the so-called "Punakha edition" of Bhutan directly descends from the tradition of mNga'-ris Gung-thang.[18]

5. CONCLUSION

For detailed information about the line of teachers of the *dMar-khrid Tshem-bu lugs*, it is the instructional work of bTsun-pa Chos-legs that has proved to be most helpful. In the case of the transmission of the *Maṇi bka' 'bum*, on the other hand, only the two additional sections of the catalogue are of any use for obtaining insight into the history of this *gter ma* cycle. The question thus arises whether such instructional works also exist for the practice of Mahākāruṇika according to the system of Srong-btsan sgam-po.

Among the "[More than] One Hundred Instructions" compiled by Jo-nang Kun-dga' grol-mchog there is found an instruction corresponding to the *rGyal po bka' 'bum*. A work

---

[18] Among studies on the two works of the cult of the Bodhisattva Avalokiteśvara, see especially Mette (1996) & (1997) and Reis-Habito (1994). The dependence of the "Punakha edition" upon an edition from the region of Gung-thang has already been noted by Kapstein (1992:164); cf. also Sørensen (1994:642). The fact that the majority of editions from the 17th century do not contain these two works bears witness to the wide extent of this text tradition; see Ngag-dbang Blo-bzang rgya-mtsho: *Gang gā'i chu rgyun*, vol. 3, p. 133.1–2 (*da lta mdo skor ni lo rgyus chen mo [/] za ma tog bkod pa'i gzungs / phyag stong spyan stong gi gzungs dang gsum la ngos 'dzin yang phyi ma gnyis glegs bam khrod du mi 'dug*). It should be noted that both works are here termed *dhāraṇīs*; on the etymology and function of *dhāraṇīs*, see for example Strickmann (1996:65–68).

of lHa-rje dGe-ba 'bum is cited as the written source. We may thus assume that the first instructional work was written immediately after the recovery of the teachings by the three treasure-discoverers. The work of lHa-rje dGe-ba 'bum has yet to surface; the same applies to the instructional work of Gangs-ri-ba Shes-rab rgyal-mtshan, a disciple of mNga'-ris Paṇ-chen Padma dbang-rgyal (1487–1542). We know of this work through the "record of teachings received" (*gsan yig*) of the Fifth Dalai Bla-ma, which preserves the different lineages of initiations and instructions of the *Maṇi bka' 'bum*. In the lineages recorded by the Fifth Dalai Bla-ma, it is again the representatives of the Bo-dong-pa school, such as bDag-nyid chen-po bZang-po rgyal-mtshan, mKhas-grub dPal-ldan sangs-rgyas and his nephew dPal-ldan seng-ge to whom the transmission of the *Maṇi bka' 'bum* is traced.[19]

The continuation of that tradition by mNga'-ris Paṇ-chen Padma dbang-rgyal and Gangs-ri-ba Shes-rab rgyal-mtshan, at least, is accessible in the writings of Rig-'dzin Chos-kyi grags-pa (1597–1659). This master of the 'Bri-gung-pa school composed two supplements to the instructional works of Gangs-ri-ba Shes-rab rgyal-mtshan, together with a short introduction into the history of the practice of Mahākāruṇika according to the system of Srong-btsan sgam-po.[20]

19 On the work of lHa-rje dGe-ba 'bum, see Kun-dga' grol-mchog: *Zab khrid brgya dang brgyad kyi yi ge*, p. 351.1 (*lha rje dge 'bum gyi khrid yig las btus so*). The writings of Shes-rab rgyal-mtshan are named by the Fifth Dalai Bla-ma in the sections *smin byed kyi dbang* and *grol byed kyi khrid*; see Ngag-dbang Blo-bzang rgya-mtsho (as in note 18), vol. 3, p. 131.6–132.3. Cf. ibid, p. 151.3–6 (*rje phyogs las rnam rgyal gyi dbang chog gi steng nas thob pa'i dbang gi rgyud pa*), and p. 152.3 (*nyams khrid dang de'i yi ge rgyal sras shes rab rgyal mtshan gyis mdzad pa'i lung gi brgyud pa*).

20 The two supplements were also incorporated by 'Jam-mgon Blo-gros mtha'-yas into the *Rin chen gter mdzod*; see the information on the works of Shes-rab rgyal-mtshan and these supplements in Schwieger (1995:nos. 802–803. The historical introduction of Rig-'dzin Chos-kyi grags-pa bears the title *Chos rgyal srong btsan sgam po'i bka 'bum gyi las tshogs phreng ba skor gsum gyi lo rgyus mdor bstan pa* and is contained in the booklet "Bri gung bka' brgyud", vol. 2 (*rgyal lugs thugs rje chen po'i khrid yig*), Dehra Dun, 1996, pp. 1–23.

APPENDIX I

The following section is contained in *Bla ma brgyud pa'i gsol 'debs lo rgyus dkar chags* (= *Maṇi bka' 'bum*, vol. Ka), NGMPP reel no. AT 167/4, fol. 12a/2–b/5; it bears the title "succession of the transmission of these teachings" (*chos skor 'di rnams kyi brgyud pa rim pa*).

> *chos sku snang ba mtha' yas / longs sku spyan ras gzigs dbang / sprul sku bsrong btsan sgam po / slob dpon padma 'byung gnas / 'dis rgyal sras khri bsrong lde btsan la / nyid kyi mes po bsrong btsan sgam pos / ra sa'i dbu rtse byang ngos kyi rta mgrin gyi zhabs 'og dang / gdung khol dang gnod sbyin na ga ku pe ra'i brla g.yas pa la / thugs rje chen po'i sgrub thabs rtsa gsum / phran brgyad / zhal gdams brgya dang lnga bcu rtsa lnga sbas nas yod / bstan gyis gsungs nas rdzu 'phrul gyis rgyal po dang lhan gcig nam mkha' la byon nas / lha sa'i gter thams cad gzigs pas / thugs yid ches nas / thugs rje chen po stong rtsa'i sgrub thabs dang / gab pa mngon phyung gi zhal gdams / thugs rje chen po sangs rgyas stong rtsa'i bskyed (= skyed) rdzogs / thugs dam mthong ba'i (= 'thong ba'i) phan yon / bsrong btsan 'da' kha'i bka' chems rnams la thugs dam du mdzad /*
>
> *de'i rjes su grub thob dngos grub kyis thugs rje chen po'i sgrub skor gyi chos rnams / rta mgrin gyi zhabs 'og nas phyung nas / lha sras khri bsrong lde btsan gyi skye ba mnga' bdag nyang la gnang / nyang gis kyang zhal gdams brgya dang lnga bcu po thugs rje chen po'i lha khang gi rta mgrin gyi zhabs 'og nas bton nas / la stod pa mi bskyod (= skyod) rdo rje la gnang / des rje btsun śākya bzang po la gnang / des ra sa'i chu rags dang zhig gsos mang po mdzad pas lung bstan thob nas gnod sbyin khang pa nas gab pa mngon phyung gi bskor rnams dang / mdo bskor rnams bton nas / sprul pa'i rgyal po'i chos bskor thams cad bla ma rin po che lha rje dge 'bum la gnang / des lcam mo ye shes mchog la / des grub thob chu sgom pa la / de mtha' bzhi bya bral ba la / des 'jam dbyangs bsod nams seng ge la / des bla ma bkra shis rgyal mtshan la / des ra sa'i chu rags pa blo gros rgyal mtshan la / des 'phags mchog nor bu bzang po la / des chos rje bzang po rgyal mtshan la / des mkhas grub dpal ldan sangs rgyas la / des yongs 'dzin dam pa bsam grub dpal la / des mkhas grub dam pa chos legs mtshan can la / des gong ma chos kyi rgyal po khri kun dga' rnam rgyal lde la gnang ngo //*

Appendix II

The edition of the *Maṇi bka' 'bum* in the National Archives in Kathmandu contains a total of eighteen illustrations which are partly damaged. Here are representations of the early masters of the transmission of the cycle up to lHa-rje dGe-ba 'bum and the "sister" Ye-shes mchog (nos. 1–6). The final illustrations are those of the two Bo-dong-pa teachers who spread the teachings in La-stod lHo and Mang-yul Gung-thang (nos. 7–8):

1. Slob-dpon Grub-thob dNgos-grub
(vol. Ka, fol. 220a, left side)

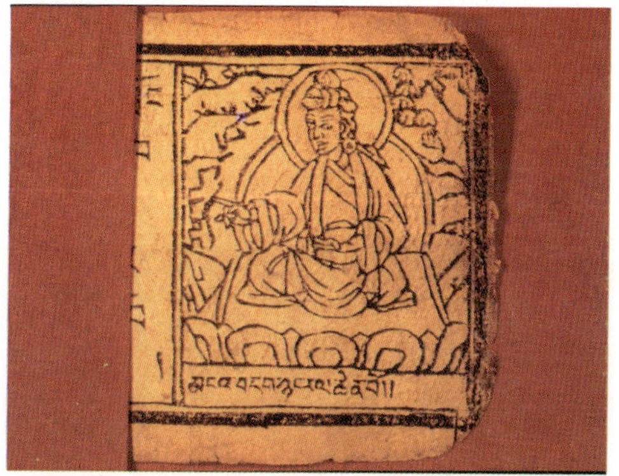

2. mNga'-bdag Nyang Ral-pa can
(vol. Ka, fol. 220a, right side)

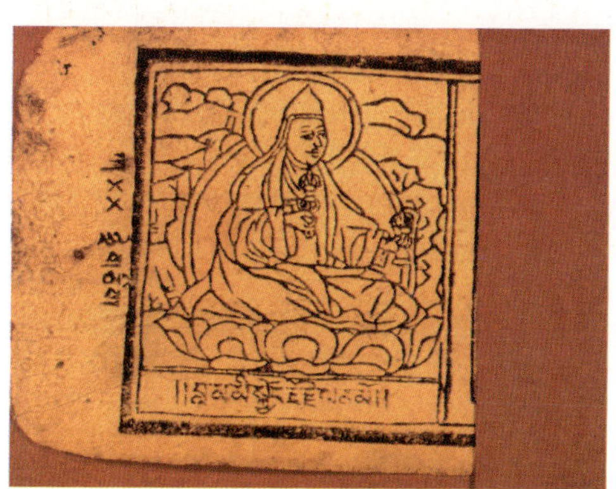

3. Bla-ma Mi-bskyod rdo-rje
(vol. Ka, fol. 221a, left side)

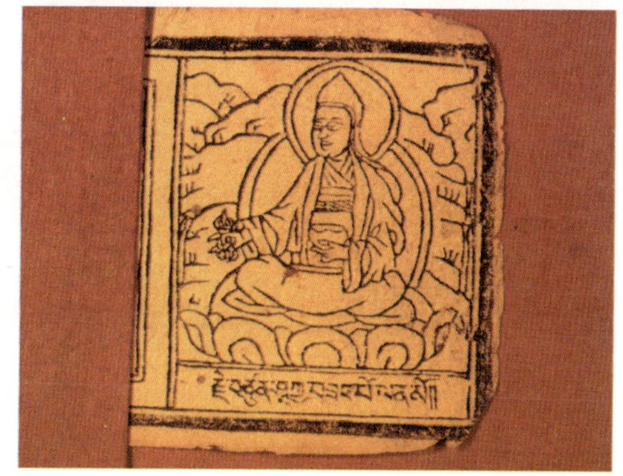

4. rJe-btsun Śākya bzang-po
(vol. Ka, fol. 221a, right side)

5. Bla-ma lHa-rje dGe-ba 'bum
(vol. Ka, fol. 326b, left side)

6. lCam-mo Ye-shes mchog
(vol. Ka, fol. 326b, right side)

7. Chos-rje bZang-po rgyal-mtshan
(vol. Kha, fol. 319a, left side)

8. mKhas-grub dPal-ldan sangs-rgyas
(vol. Kha, fol. 319a, right side)

The Transmission of the *Thig le bcu drug* and the *bKa' gdams glegs bam*

I. Introduction

While working on literary sources dealing with the self-originated Avalokiteśvara statues, and especially the legends concerning the Ārya Wa-ti bzang-po from Mang-yul sKyid-grong, I came across a passage in the collection of texts called "The Book of the bKa'-gdams[-pa Tradition]" (*bka' gdams glegs bam*) referring to three of these statues and identifying them with three famous bKa'-gdams-pa masters of the 11th and 12th centuries. Like the statues Ārya Wa-ti bzang-po, Ārya 'Ja'-ma-li and Ārya 'Bu-khang, they are called "Three Brothers" (*sku mched gsum*), and this label stands for Po-to-ba (1027/31–1105), Phu-chung-ba (1031–1109) and sPyan-snga-pa (1038–1103), the three well-known disciples of 'Brom-ston rGyal-ba'i 'byung-gnas (1005–1064) who transmitted the teachings of Atiśa Dīpaṃkaraśrījñāna (982–1054) in Tibet.

A closer look at this passage shows that the identification of Avalokiteśvara icons with bKa'-gdams-pa masters is part of a longer discussion concerning the incarnation status of the disciples of 'Brom-ston rGyal-ba'i 'byung-gnas. It turns out that they are also regarded as embodiments of the "Protectors of the Three [Tantric] Families" (*rigs gsum mgon po*): Phu-chung-ba being an emanation of Avalokiteśvara, Po-to-ba of Mañjuśrī, and sPyan-snga-pa of Vajrapāṇi. As we find the whole discussion at the end of the biography of Atiśa known as *rNam thar rgyas pa yongs grags*,[1] the impression is one of following a strategy to unify the three important transmitters of bKa'-gdams-pa teachings at a time when the tradition as such had spread already from mNga'-ris skor-gsum in the west up to the domain of the king of Tsong-kha in the east.

The problem of the author of the biography of Atiśa was that he used the scheme of the three Avalokiteśvara brothers to legitimate the status of the disciples of 'Brom-ston rGyal-ba'i 'byung-gnas as incarnations of the protectors of the three tantric families. He

---

[1] See *Jo bo rje dpal ldan a ti sha'i rnam thar bka' gdams pha chos*, pp. 223.20–226.1; this biography of Atiśa, written by mChims Nam-mkha' grags (1210–1285), the seventh abbot of dPal sNar-thang, is found in all accessible editions of the *bKa' gdams glegs bam*. *Jo bo rje dpal ldan a ti sha'i rnam thar bka' gdams pha chos* is a modern edition of its first part based on the sDe-dge xylograph produced by Si-tu Paṇ-chen Chos-kyi 'byung-gnas (1700–1774); if not otherwise mentioned I quote from this edition in the following.

seemed to have had his own doubts about this strategy, since he states that the "scriptural source" (*khungs*) for this kind of identification does not come from the bKa'-gdams-pa tradition itself. By the 15th century, however, such doubts were no longer entertained and as a literary source for the episode which brings together Po-to-ba, Phu-chung-ba and sPyan-snga-pa as the "Three Brothers Ārya [Avalokiteśvara]" (*'phags pa sku mched gsum*), another text from the biographical tradition was brought forward; it bears the title *Jo bo rje'i rnam thar lam yig*. Unfortunately this work, an apocryphal text considered to be a composition of 'Brom-ston rGyal-ba'i 'byung-gnas himself, does not contain any reference to either the self-originated Avalokiteśvara statues nor to the three bKa'-gdams-pa masters. The reason for taking this text as the source for the identification of these two triads was obviously its mention of the Svayambhūcaitya in Nepal as an important stopover during Atiśa's journey to Tibet.[2] According to the passage in the *rNam thar rgyas pa yongs grags*, it was precisely at this sacred site in Nepal where the spiritual identities of Po-to-ba, Phu-chung-ba and sPyan-snga-pa were revealed by "non-humans" (*mi ma yin*) to a yogin who had joined their company in circumambulating the caitya.

Having reaped these marginal results from consulting the works of the *bKa' gdams glegs bam* for which it is famous—i.e. the different texts concerning the biographical tradition of Atiśa—I decided to take a closer look at the collection as a whole and try to find out if there were more hints of Avalokiteśvara teachings, of how they were transmitted, and of the geographical areas where this took place. It was only then that I discovered the importance of the spiritual practice of the cycle of the "Sixteen Spheres" (*thig le bcu drug*) for the way the collection of texts made its appearance and how it was handed down in the generations following the three brothers.

II. The "Archaic Version" of the *bKa' gdams glegs bam*

In one of the historiographical works of the bKa'-gdams-pa tradition written in the 15th century we find a good overview of the *bKa' gdams glegs bam* based on the classification of its content into different "scriptural sections" (*dpe tshan*). The collection as a whole consists of fifty-four of these sections, which are divided first into four "preparatory teachings" (*sbyor ba'i chos*) and into the remaining sections, which make up the "main part of the book" (*glegs bam dngos gzhi*). It is explicitly stated that the first four sections should not be confounded with the main part.

---

2 The reference to the *Jo bo rje'i rnam thar lam yig* as the literary source for the identification between icons and masters is contained in bSod-nams lha'i dbang-po: *bKa' gdams rin po che'i chos 'byung rnam thar nyin mor byed pa'i 'od stong*, pp. 319.8–320.4; this work was composed in the year 1484. The text of Ngag-dbang Kun-dga' bsod-nams grags-pa: *dGe ba'i bshes gnyen bka' gdams pa rnams kyi dam pa'i chos 'byung ba'i tshul legs par bshad pa ngo mtshar rgya mtsho*, written in 1634, is for the greater part a verbatim copy of the earlier work; for the same reference, see ibid, pp. 118.18–119.12. Atiśa's stay at the Svayambhūcaitya according to the *Jo bo rje'i rnam thar lam yig* is treated by Decleer (1996:40).

The four preparatory teachings turn out to be two works attributed to 'Brom-ston rGyal-ba'i 'byung-gnas, with the titles *'Brom chos kyi rgyal po nyid kyis logs su nan gyi gtad pa'i bka' rgya* and *Rang rgyud skul ma 'debs pa dad pa'i ljon shing*. The first work is also known under the short title "The Book's Sealed Command" (*glegs bam kyi bka' rgya*) and should, according to its colophon, be read both prior to and after the promulgation of the actual book. The second work, too, consists for the most part of verses to be recited by the religious practitioner following this specific teaching of the bKa'-gdams-pas.

Although they do not actually belong to the main part of the *bKa' gdams glegs bam*, the two remaining works are characterized as being of "great importance for the preparatory [teachings] and the main part [of the book], [these] two" (*sbyor dngos gnyis kar gal che*). The first one bears the alternative titles *gLegs bam gyi chos 'byung* or *lHa chos bdun ldan gyi bla ma brgyud pa rnams kyi rnam thar*, both titles suggesting that this text will shed light on the individual teachers who transmitted the *bKa' gdams glegs bam*. The second work is devoted to the "doctrine of the sixteen spheres" (*thig le bcu drug bstan pa*) and more specifically to the "practice [of these teachings] as a spiritual experience" (*nyams len*). As different iconographical forms of Avalokiteśvara are described in this text, it is obviously the best literary source concerning the actual spiritual practices relating to the Great Compassionate One in the book of the bKa'-gdams-pa tradition.

The classification of the collection into different scriptural sections ends with a fifth work which should not be included in the main part. It is the text *rGyal ba yab sras kyi bkod pa phun sum tshogs pa'i gter* (or *Thugs dam jo bo yab sras kyi bkod pa phun sum tshogs pa'i gter*), and the historiographical work of the 15th century again gives a reason for this fact. It is stated that "because [the text] appears as something that was later made by the one from sNar-thang, it is perceived as a condensed version, and thus this [work] should not be confounded with the main part."[3] Indeed, at the end of the text we find a note that it was set down in writing at dPal sNar-thang, the "place of seclusion of [all] the scholars and siddhas" (*mkhas grub kyi dben gnas*). Although a date for the composition is given, i.e. a "male water-tiger year" (*chu pho stag gi lo*), there is no author's name stated.

The colophons of these two works, which stand out as quite important for the transmission history of the *bKa' gdams glegs bam* and its Avalokiteśvara teachings, in both cases give dPal sNar-thang as the place of composition, and in the *gLegs bam gyi chos 'byung* again we find a male water-tiger year as the date when the text was written down.

---

3 The whole classification of the contents of the *bKa' gdams glegs bam* into different scriptural sections can be found in Lo-dgon sPyan-snga-pa bSod-nams lha'i dbang-po (as in note 2), pp. 379.8–380.8; cf. A-mes zhabs Ngag-dbang Kun-dga' bsod-nams grags-pa (as in note 2), pp. 178.8–179.7. The just cited quotation closes this classification (*... phyis snar thang pas byas par snang bas / don bsdu lta bur snang la / 'di dang dngos gzhi la mi the'o*). It was H. Eimer who first pointed out this classificatory scheme in the work of bSod-nams lha'i dbang-po, characterizing it at the time as a "still more archaic form of the *bKa' gdams glegs bam*"; see Eimer (1984:45 & 47, note 11).

All things considered, the evidence seems quite strong that the two works came from the pen of the same man, who composed them in the same year in the monastery of dPal sNar-thang in gTsang province. This evidence is supported in the form of a rhetorical question by another historiographical work of the bKa'-gdams-pa tradition from the 15th century;[4] we are introduced thus to mKhan-chen Nyi-ma rgyal-mtshan (1225–1305), the ninth abbot of dPal sNar-thang:

> Now, the ninth upādhyāya of sNar-thang, mKhan-chen Nyi-ma rgyal-mtshan, listened to these teachings in their entirety and lived them as a spiritual experience. Afterwards, on the eighth day of the third Tibetan month of the male water-tiger year (= 1302) he produced the śastra *Thugs dam rgyal ba yab sras kyi bkod pa phun sum tshogs pa* and the [accompanying] paintings.
>
> Then on the thirtieth day of the twelfth Tibetan month of the same year, he wrote down the great history of the [doctrine of the] *lHa chos* [*bdun ldan*] as it came forth from the words of Bla-ma 'Brom[-ston Kumāramati] (born 1271); and as one says that also the instruction text for living the Sixteen Spheres as a spiritual experience called *Lag len zung 'jug nyi zla'i thig le* was composed in sNar-thang [at that time]: isn't this just [the same] upādhyāya [who composed the other two works]?
>
> It is certain that the *[bKa' gdams] glegs bam* originated in sNar-thang as well, it having been set down in writing [by mKhan-chen Nyi-ma rgyal-mtshan as] what was lodged in the mind of 'Brom-ston Kumāra[mati].[5]

The ninth abbot of dPal sNar-thang is thus the person who wrote down the three mentioned introductory works in the year 1302—each seemingly quite important for an understanding of the *bKa' gdams glegs bam* in its formative phase. As the quotation suggests further,

---

4 This text was composed in 1494, i.e. ten years after the historiographical work of bSod-nams lha'i dbang-po. The author, Las-chen Kun-dga' rgyal-mtshan, associated with the monastery of rTse-thang in the Yarlung valley, had been a direct disciple of bSod-nams lha'i dbang-po and we find a biographical sketch of his teacher in the same work; see ibid, vol. 1, pp. 622.2–624.6; cf. also van der Kuijp (1987a:125, note 6).

5 See Kun-dga' rgyal-mtshan: *bKa' gdams kyi rnam par thar pa bka' gdams chos 'byung gsal ba'i sgron me*, vol. 2, p. 248.1–6 (*de la snar thang mkhan po dgu pa mkhan chen nyi ma rgyal mtshan gyis / chos 'di dag ma lus par gsan te thugs nyams su bzhes shas chu pho stag gi lo nam thongs kyi zla ba'i tshes brgyad la thugs dam rgyal ba yab sras kyi bkod pa phun sum tshogs pa'i bstan bcos dang / ras bris de bzhengs / de nas lo de'i rgyal zla ba'i sum cu'i tshes la bla ma 'brom gyi gsung las byung ba ltar lha chos kyi lo rgyus chen mo de mdzad / thig le bcu drug nyams su blang ba'i 'khrid yig lag len zung 'jug nyi zla'i thig le zhes bya ba de yang snar thang du mdzad zer ba snang bas / mkhan po 'di nyid yin nam snyam mo / snar thang du glegs bam mched pa yang / 'brom ston ku ma ra nyid kyi thugs la bzhugs pa yi ger bkod par nges so*).

mKhan-chen Nyi-ma rgyal-mtshan was also involved in bringing the larger work into some kind of definite form by recording the words of his teacher 'Brom Kumāramati. But before coming to this decisive event in the process of codification, I shall give an overview of the sections of the main part as they are presented in the later historiographical literature.

With five of the fifty-four sections having been bracketed out—the two works attributed to 'Brom-ston rGyal-ba'i 'byung-gnas and the three works of mKhan-chen Nyi-ma rgyal-mtshan—there remain forty-nine sections in that part of the *bKa' gdams glegs bam* conceived as the central core of the book. They are divided into the twenty-six sections of the so-called "Teachings for the Father" (*pha chos*) and the twenty-two sections of the "Teachings for the Sons" (*bu chos*); to this is added an "Additional Chapter" (*kha skong gi le'u*), containing prophecies etc.

We are quite well informed about the twenty-two sections of the *bKa' gdams bu chos*, which consist of the "Twenty Teachings for rNgog [Legs-pa'i shes-rab]" (*rngog chos nyi shu*) and the "Two Teachings for Khu-ston brtson-'grus" (*khu chos gnyis*). They have already been described as examples of Buddhist narrative literature dealing with the former lives of 'Brom-ston rGyal-ba'i 'byung-gnas, the narrator being Atiśa himself, who was staying on the mountain lHa-ri snying-po in Yer-pa. These narratives, which are said to have been requested from Atiśa by rNgog Legs-pa'i shes-rab (11th century) and by Khu-ston brtson-'grus (1011–1075) themselves, contain not only a great amount of Buddhist dogmatic doctrine, but also numerous teachings concerning political morals of Buddhist rulers. They are thus of special importance for an analysis of the formation of political and religious ideologies in Tibet in the 13th and 14th centuries.[6]

The twenty-six sections of the *bKa' gdams pha chos* are for the greater part related to a work by Atiśa with the title *Byang chub sems dpa' nor bu'i phreng ba* (*Bodhisattvamaṇyāvali*) and its commentary in twenty-three chapters. The number of these chapters matches with the twenty-three sections of the "Teachings for the Father", the latter term referring to 'Brom-ston rGyal-ba'i 'byung-gnas as the person who requested the master for an explanation of these teachings. The commentary is thus an exchange of "questions and answers" (*zhus lan*) between Atiśa and his main Tibetan disciple. Bibliographical data on Atiśa's text and an overview of the different chapters of the commentary are already available, and I will only point out the relation of this text to another work of the famous Buddhist scholar from modern-day Bengal.[7]

---

6 For an overview of the *bKa' gdams bu chos*, see Schuh (1981a:1-23 (= nos. 1–3)). The same volume also contains an analysis of the four prayers contained in all printed versions of the *bKa' gdams glegs bam*, the last one providing details of the way the texts were compiled by mKhan-chen Nyi-ma rgyal-mtshan in dPal sNar-thang in the year 1302; cf. ibid, pp. 302–305 (= no. 352). The block print used for this description was the one from dGa'-ldan Phun-tshogs gling (17th century).

7 For an overview of the contents of the *Bodhisattvamaṇyāvali* and its commentary, see Meisezahl

An interesting statement in this respect was made by gTsug-lag phreng-ba (1504–1566), the second dPa'-bo sprul-sku, in his compendium on the religious history of Tibet:

> [The text] *Byang chub sems dpa' nor bu'i phreng ba,* [which is] the root [of the *bKa' gdams glegs bam*], is a condensed version of the words of Jo-bo [Atiśa] by 'Brom[-ston rGyal-ba'i 'byung-gnas]. And as this [text] and the letter to the king Neyapāla composed by Jo-bo [Atiśa] for the greater part made their appearance as one and the same [work], it is said that this king is of one mind-stream with 'Brom[-ston rGyal-ba'i 'byung-gnas].[8]

According to this quotation the text of the *Bodhisattvamanyāvali*[9] is typologically similar to an epistle addressed to King Neyapāla, a ruler of the late Pāla dynasty who was a contemporary of Atiśa. To identify this letter according to Tibetan classifications we need to look at a collection of works translated all by Atiśa and his different Tibetan collaborators, and known under the title "The Hundred-and-some Small Teachings of the Lord [Atiśa]" (*jo bo'i chos chung brgya rtsa*). This collection was transmitted as a separate teaching tradition, as we can see, for example, from the *gSan yig* of the Fifth Dalai Bla-ma. It contains both the *Byang chub sems dpa' nor bu'i phreng ba* and the letter to King Neyapāla, the latter work bearing the title *Dri ma med pa rin po che'i 'phrin yig* (*Vimalaratnalekha*) and forming the last item in the collection. The works of this collection are listed in the historiographical work of the bKa'-gdams-pa tradition used as the starting point for the present investigation, the letter to King Neyapāla, written as a privy advice, being classified under the literary genre of *nītiśāstra* (*lugs kyi bstan bcos*).[10]

(1990:448–450); the block print for this description was again the one from dGa'-ldan Phun-tshogs gling. The cover title for both works is *Jo bo yab sras kyi gsung bgros pha chos rin po che'i gter mdzod byang chub sems dpa' nor bu'i phreng ba rtsa 'grel sogs*; the commentary alone bears the title *Pha chos nyi shu rtsa drug las zhus lan gyi dngos gzhi nor bu'i phreng ba le'u nyi shu rtsa gsum pa.*

8 See gTsug-lag phreng-ba: *Chos 'byung mkhas pa'i dga' ston*, pp. 709.21–710.1 (*... rtsa ba byang chub sems dpa' nor bu'i phreng ba ni 'brom gyis jo bo'i gsung bsdus pa yin la 'di dang jo bos nirya (= neya) pa la (= pāla) la 'phrin yig mdzad pa phal cher gcig tu byung bas rgyal po de 'brom dang thugs rgyud gcig pa'o zhes ...*)

9 The Fifth Dalai Bla-ma Ngag-dbang Blo-bzang rgya-mtsho (1617–1682) identifies the text as a translation by Atiśa himself, and adds in a note that the identification of this work in the *bKa' gdams glegs bam* as a version orally transmitted by 'Brom-ston rGyal-ba'i 'byung-gnas is somewhat off the mark, contradicting as it does the generally accepted definitions of the "Teachings for the Father" and the "Teachings for the Sons"; see Ngag-dbang Blo-bzang rgya-mtsho *Zab pa dang rgya che ba'i dam pa'i chos kyi thob yig gangā'i chu rgyun,* vol. 1, p. 89.4–5 (*byang chub sems dpa' nor bu'i phreng ba jo bo nyid kyi rang bsgyur du mdzad pa [chos rje dpa' bo'i gsan yig na 'di bka' gdams kyi rtsa ba yin pas 'brom gyis gsungs pa'i phyogs mdzad pa ni cung zad ma dgongs par mngon te pha 'brom ston gyis zhus nas jo bos gsungs pa la pha chos dang bu khu rngog gnyis zhus nas gsungs par bu chos zhes grags pas so]*).

10 Cf. bSod-nams lha'i dbang-po (as in note 2), pp. 377.8–378.1, and Ngag-dbang Kun-dga' bsod-nams grags-pa (as in note 2), pp. 176.5–7.

It has been shown that this letter to the king of the Pāla dynasty was put down in writing by Atiśa around 1040 on his journey through Nepal and western Tibet, while the *Byang chub sems dpa' nor bu'i phreng ba* was composed at least three years later—which makes the *Dri ma med pa rin po che'i 'phrin yig* the literary model for the central text of the *bKa' gdams glegs bam*. We should particularly keep in mind the fact that gTsug-lag phreng-ba used the typological similarity between the two texts to construe a kind of spiritual identity between 'Brom-ston rGyal-ba'i 'byung-gnas and the Indian ruler; in this way the *bKa' gdams pha chos* was open to interpretation in the interest of political and religious ideologies.[11]

But what are the spiritual practices described in the commentary of the *Byang chub sems dpa' nor bu'i phreng ba*, the sections of which form, together with the root-text, the main teaching of the whole book? If we restrict ourselves to chapters two to five in the long dialogue between Atiśa and 'Brom-ston rGyal-ba'i 'byung-gnas, we are introduced to the "four gods" (*lha bzhi*), i.e. Buddha Śākyamuni, Avalokiteśvara, Acala and Tārā; among these the Great Compassionate One is called the "God whose [Religious] Share is Tibet" (*bod kyi lha skal*). These four divine beings are claimed by Atiśa to be his personal meditative deities (*nga yi lha nyid lha bzhi ste*). In chapter three the question concerning a "selection" (*'dam kha*) of the most effective teachings of the Buddhist doctrine leads to the importance of the "Three Baskets" (*sde snod gsum*), i.e. Vinaya, Sūtra and Abhidharma. One of the statements of Atiśa is that "this selection of the doctrine is the best" (*chos kyi 'dam kha de ni mchog go*). After a presentation in chapter four of the combination of the four gods and the Three Baskets as a teaching called "sevenfold divine doctrine" (*lha chos bdun ldan*), chapter five elaborates "how one enters into the main part [of the spiritual practice]" (*dngos gzhi la 'jug pa*) of this specific teaching.

The actual practice is then described as an emanation of the four divine beings, starting with Buddha Śākyamuni and leading consecutively to Tārā Avalokiteśvara and Acala in a process of mental creation. Upon the request of 'Brom-ston rGyal-ba'i 'byung-gnas, Atiśa clarifies that the actual iconographical forms of the individual meditation deities are in this case not so important, since this teaching is an "instruction for holding them in the mind" (*sems 'dzin pa'i man ngag*). The whole procedure of spiritual practice is called the "method of contemplating the divine doctrine" (*lha chos kyi bsgom lugs*).[12]

---

[11] For the *Jo bo'i chos chung brgya rtsa* as listed by the Fifth Dalai Bla-ma in his *Thob yig*, see the text (as in note 9), vol. 1, pp. 89.1–101.6, where a critical remark is once again made of Chos-rje dPa'-bo's position of regarding the two works as one, and the point insisted upon that the "texts" (*dpe*) and their "reading [authorization]" (*lung*) should be kept apart; see ibid, p. 100.3–5. A comparison of the *Vimalaratnalekha* and the different versions of the *Bodhisattvamaṇyāvali* in the *bKa' gdams glegs bam* and the bsTan 'gyur has shown that the version familiar to the bKa'-gdams-pa tradition cannot be considered the original one; see Eimer (1981:323ff.).

[12] See *Jo bo yab sras kyi gsung bgros pha chos rin po che'i gter mdzod byang chub sems dpa' nor bu'i phreng ba rtsa 'grel sogs*, pp. 27.2–71.3. This edition of the *bKa' gdams pha chos* is a manuscript version

Returning one last time to the classification of the *bKa' gdams glegs bam* into scriptural sections, one may note that the three missing sections—to reach the number twenty-six for the *bKa' gdams pha chos*—are called *bKa' rgya ma*, *Ma 'ongs lung bstan* and *rDo rje'i glu*.[13] The first work is again set on the mountain lHa-ri snying-po in Yer-pa, and it is said to have been delivered on the occasion when Atiśa "turned the wheel of the sevenfold divine doctrine" (*lha chos bdun ldan gyi 'khor lo bskor ba*). Given that at the beginning and at the end of this text a stanza from the *Byang chub sems dpa' nor bu'i phreng ba* is quoted which corresponds to chapter sixteen of the commentary, we can regard the text as a kind of sub-commentary to that particular chapter. The *rDo rje'i glu* section contains the final instructions of Atiśa to 'Brom-ston rGyal-ba'i 'byung-gnas—again in the form of questions and answers—and is dated to a "male wood-horse" (*shing pho rta*) year (= 1054); this is the generally accepted date for the year when Atiśa passed away. The section titled *Ma 'ongs lung bstan*, finally, is devoted to different prophecies, mentioning for example the three main disciples of 'Brom-ston rGyal-ba'i 'byung-gnas as incarnations of the protectors of the three tantric families. Concerning the foundations of monasteries of the bKa'-gdams-pa tradition, one such institution in the province gTsang is mentioned, obviously with reference to dPal sNar-thang, and we also hear of the future establishment of sTabs-ka'i dgon-pa.

III. THE TRANSMISSION OF THE *THIG LE BCU DRUG*

In the later historiographical works of the bKa'-gdams-pa tradition the three disciples of 'Brom-ston rGyal-ba'i 'byung-gnas, known as the "Three Brothers", are associated with three different teaching lineages. The lineage going back to sPyan-snga-pa is called *bKa' gdams ngag pa* in these works, while the one deriving from Po-to-ba bears the name *bKa' gdams gzhung pa*. The teachings of the *bKa' gdams glegs bam* are associated with the person of Phu-chung-ba, this tradition being classified in the works of the 15th century as a "secret teaching" (*gsang chos*).

That Phu-chung-ba occupies a special position within this group, which is sometimes enlarged by a fourth brother, Kham-pa lung-pa Śākya Yon-tan (1025–1115), is reflected in the earlier historical literature. Let me quote, for example, from the work of Myang-ral Nyi-ma'i 'od-zer (1124–1192) on the history of the Buddhist doctrine in Tibet:

---

of the lHa-sa block print dating from after 1940. The complete xylograph of this edition of the *bKa' gdams glegs bam* was reproduced in Sikkim in the years 1977 to 1990; compare *Ka dam Pha cho*, part three, pp. 629.4–666.3.

13 In all block print editions of the *bKa' gdams glegs bam* these three sections are grouped together with the two sections *Khu chos gnyis* and the "additional chapter" (*kha skong gi le'u*) of the *bKa' gdams bu chos*; they are then placed at the end of the whole book under the title *bKa' rgya / khu chos gnyis / lung bstan / rdor glu / kha skong rnams*. The manuscript version of the lHa-sa xylograph (as in note 12) presents these works immediately after the *Byang chub sems dpa' nor bu'i phreng ba* and its commentary.

> Among the [spiritual] sons of Jo-bo [Atiśa], the oldest [is] rGyal-ba'i 'byung-gnas, the teacher from the 'Brom [family]. His disciples [are] the precious "Three Brothers" and others. [Concerning] dGe-bshes Phu-chung-ba: not relying on disciples, [who are like] sons, he only performed his religious practice. From Po-to-ba and sPyan-snga Rin-chen, [these] two, [further] disciples, [who are like] sons, arose individually; they are known as the "followers of the authoritative scriptures" and the "followers of the instructions", [these] two.[14]

In order to assess the development of the teaching lineage associated with Phu-chung-ba, I want to return now to the text *Glegs bam gyi chos 'byung* of mKhan-chen Nyi-ma rgyal-mtshan, which we have already identified as the most promising literary source for information on the different teachers who transmitted the *bKa' gdams glegs bam*. Attention should be paid foremost to the circumstances under which the book made its appearance and how Avalokiteśvara teachings are described in it.

In the introductory verses the "precious lineage of the seven[fold] divine doctrine" (*lha chos bdun gyi brgyud pa rin po che*) is brought into a connection with the "seven precious beings" (*skyes bu rin chen bdun*), namely the following persons: 'Brom-ston rGyal-ba'i 'byung-gnas – rNgog Legs-pa'i shes-rab – mNga'-ris-pa Shes-rab rgyal-mtshan – Phu-chung-ba – Rin-chen rgyal-mtshan – Zhang-ston Dar-ma rgyal-mtshan – sTabs-ka-ba Byang-chub bzang-po. We can thus differentiate between an early transmission, up to Phu-chung-ba, and a later transmission, from him to a person whose name shows his connection with the already-mentioned sTabs-ka'i dgon-pa. These two transmissions I shall call the "legendary" one and the "local" one.

The early—or legendary—transmission centres on two persons: rNgog Legs-pa'i shes-rab, a personal disciple of Atiśa and founder of gSang-phu sNe'u-thog college, and Shes-rab rgyal-mtshan, a native of western Tibet, who is said to have also studied with the Indian master. Rather than go into the details of the extensive narrative of how the "*kalyāṇamitra* from gSang-phu [sNe'u-thog]" (*bshes gnyen gsang phu ba*) received this special teaching, I simply note that rNgog Legs-pa'i shes-rab set down the latter teaching for the first time in the form of a "book" (*glegs bam*). The transmission of the teaching to

---

14 See Nyi-ma'i 'od-zer: *Chos 'byung me tog snying po sbrang rtsi'i bcud*, p. 469.13–17 (*jo bo sras kyi thu bo 'brom ston pa rgyal ba'i 'byung gnas / de'i slob ma rin po che sku mched gsum la sogs so / dge bshes blo chung* {*phul chung*} (= *phu chung*) *pas slob bu ma bsten par sgrub pa kho na mdzad do /* {*po*} *to ba dang / spyan snga rin chen gnyis las / slob bu so sor byung ba la / bka' gdams gzhung pa dang / man ngag pa gnyis su grags so*). The same characterization of Phu-chung-ba can still be found in the 14th century; see Śākya Rin-chen sde: *Yar lung jo bo'i chos 'byung*, p. 98.5–10. For the change in the presentation of Phu-chung-ba as a holder of a specific teaching lineage in the 15th century—and the chapter devoted exclusively to him and the *bKa' gdams glegs bam*—, see Kun-dga' rgyal-mtshan (as in note 5), vol. 2, pp. 183.1–251.5. For the term *dge bshes* as a title of bKa'-gdams-pa teachers like 'Brom-ston rGyal-ba'i 'byung-gnas, see Tarab Tulku (2000:18).

mNga'-ris-pa Shes-rab rgyal-mtshan is described thus: "Now, the way the book was transmitted from his (i.e. rNgog Legs-pa'i shes-rab's) hand" (*da de'i phyag nas glegs bam ji ltar brgyud pa'i tshul*). In the account concerning mNga'-ris-pa Shes-rab rgyal-mtshan it is stated that rNgog Legs-pa'i shes-rab handed over to his disciple this "[miraculously] manifested book" (*sprul pa'i glegs bam*) and soon afterwards conferred upon him initiation into the maṇḍala of the Sixteen Spheres. The same account also gives details of the personal encounter between mNga'-ris-pa Shes-rab rgyal-mtshan and Phu-chung-ba during which the book was passed on to the disciple of 'Brom-ston rGyal-ba'i 'byung-gnas.[15]

The longest section in the text of mKhan-chen Nyi-ma rgyal-mtshan concerns events dealing with Phu-chung-ba's special status as transmitter of the sevenfold divine doctrine. The four meditative deities of Atiśa are several times referred to, and we find an interesting classification of the "four gods" in terms of whom they should be entrusted to. As this discussion of different "entrustments" (*bka' babs*) follows immediately upon an enquiry into the nature of Atiśa's teaching lineages of "authoritative scripture" and "instruction", and as Po-to-ba and sPyan-snga-pa figure quite prominently in this section, I would see the document as mainly being concerned with establishing a teaching lineage of Phu-chung-ba along its own lines. This can be dated around the 12th and 13th centuries, given that one comes upon the name of sKyer-sgang-pa (1154–1217) as one of the teachers who were entrusted with the spiritual practice of the Great Compassionate One. In this section Phu-chung-ba is credited with not differing from his teacher 'Brom-ston rGyal-ba'i 'byung-gnas (who at one point takes the form of the Ṣaḍakṣarī formula *Oṃ maṇi padme hūṃ*). Manifesting himself as Avalokiteśvara Khasarpaṇa, Phu-chung-ba delivers a prophecy concerning the next holder of the teaching lineage.[16]

---

[15] For rNgog Legs-pa'i shes-rab, see Nyi-ma rgyal-mtshan: *Zhus lan nor bu'i phreng ba lha chos bdun ldan gyi bla ma brgyud pa rnams kyi rnam thar* in *Jo bo rje dpal ldan a ti sha'i rnam thar bka' gdams pha chos*, pp. 314.14–336.20, and for mNga'-ris-pa Shes-rab rgyal-mtshan, ibid, pp. 336.21–352.9; the authorship of the second section is ascribed to Phu-chung-ba. In the historiographical work of bSod-nams lha'i dbang-po the transmission of the *bKa' gdams glegs bam* is treated, accordingly, in the context of the teaching lineages of rNgog Legs-pa'i shes-rab. These lineages are divided into one extending to his nephew rNgog Lo-tsā-ba Blo-ldan shes-rab (1059–1109) and another to mNga'-ris-pa Shes-rab rgyal-mtshan; see pa bSod-nams lha'i dbang-po (as in note 2), pp. 362.4–366.6 & 366.4–368.4, and Ngag-dbang Kun-dga' bsod-nams grags-pa (as in note 2), pp. 160.8–164.9 & 164.9–166.12.

[16] For the section on Phu-chung-ba, see Nyi-ma rgyal-mtshan (as in note 15), pp. 352.10–396.15 (supposedly written by Rin-chen rgyal-mtshan). The classification of the "four gods" according to whom they should be entrusted to can be found ibid, p. 360.1–20. This is the literary source for the treatment of the same subject in the historiographical works of the bKa'-gdams-pa tradition; see bSod-nams lha'i dbang-po (as in note 2), pp. 367.4–6, and Ngag-dbang Kun-dga' bsod-nams grags-pa (as in note 2), pp. 165.13–16 (*lha bzhi ni rab tu byung ba'i cha nas śākya thub pa / tshad med pa bzhi la dge sbyor byed pa'i cha nas thugs rje chen po / 'gro don byed pa'i cha nas rje btsun ma sgrol ma / gnyen po bsten pa'i cha nas mi g.yo ba*).

The disciple of Phu-chung-ba was born in the valley of Klungs-shod and in his young years met the bKa'-gdams-pa teacher sNe'u zur-pa (1042–1118). In his later life he studied many years under Zhang Ka-ma-pa (1057–1131) from the same tradition, and was ordained by the latter. The name he received on that occasion was Rin-chen rgyal-mtshan. The section treating his person represents a quite long interpolation on the "book [containing] the vast number of pronouncements of the Buddha in their entirety" (*sangs rgyas kyi bka' rab 'byams thams cad kyi glegs bam*), while also containing dialogues of the "Three Brothers" about this special scripture. At one point the latter is even taken out of a small wooden box and displayed before the eyes of the excited observers: "The [miraculously] manifested teaching" (*sprul pa'i chos*) is identified as the text *Zhus lan nor bu'i phreng ba*, i.e. *Byang chub sems dpa' nor bu'i 'phreng ba*, and called a "great treasure script" (*gter yig chen mo*). Rin-chen rgyal-mtshan, according to the narrative, is able to acquire this special book only after six months spent mastering the propitiation of Avalokiteśvara; only then does he meet Phu-chung-ba and obtain from him the initiation into the maṇḍala of the Sixteen Spheres. This happened at a site known as rTs[w]a sGyer-mo, its actual name being Phug-rings.[17]

Rin-chen rgyal-mtshan followed his spiritual practices not only at this site, but also travelled extensively, reaching western Tibet and Nepal. During a stay in Rwa-sgreng he met his future disciple Zhang-ston Dar-ma rgyal-mtshan. The latter had arrived there as a member of the entourage of Dar-ma grags (1103–1174), a master holding the teaching lineage of the bKa'-gdams gzhung-pa through Shar-ba-pa Yon-tan grags (1070–1141). Dar-ma grags is known to have been the founder of sTabs-ka'i dgon-pa in the Mal-gro valley, and it was at this monastery that Rin-chen rgyal-mtshan gave teachings to a great number of monks from dBus and gTsang shortly before the death of Dar-ma grags in the year 1174. Afterwards Zhang-ston Dar-ma rgyal-mtshan followed Rin-chen rgyal-mtshan to various sites, including Phug-rings, where he received the transmission of the *Byang chub sems dpa' nor bu'i phreng ba*. Among further episodes in the life of Zhang-ston Dar-ma rgyal-mtshan I highlight only his visit to the 'Phrul-snang temple in lHa-sa, where he paid reverence to the statue of the thousand-armed Avalokiteśvara. After the icon proceeded to manifest the forms of Avalokiteśvara with four and two arms, dialogues took place between Zhang-ston Dar-ma rgyal-mtshan and the Great Compassionate One, during which the former is identified as an incarnation of the king lHa bla-ma Ye-shes 'od

---

[17] This rough résumé of the life of Rin-chen rgyal-mtshan is again based on sNar-thang mkhan-chen Nyi-ma rgyal-mtshan (as in note 15); see ibid, pp. 396.16–438.9. The section is supposed to be in Rin-chen rgyal-mtshan's own words. For the interpolation of the episode concerning the "Three Brothers", their dialogues and the revealing of the book, see ibid, pp. 400.2–431.15. The number of pages is said to have been 672 (*drug brgya bdun cu rtsa gnyis shog bu'i tshad*).

(947–1024); it is prophesied that Byang-chub bzang-po, a person again born in the valley of Klungs-shod to the north of the Mal-gro valley, will be his disciple.[18]

With sTabs-ka-ba Byang-chub bzang-po we have reached the last member of what I have called above the later "local" transmission. He was born into the "'Brom family" (*'brom gyi mi brgyud*), and the place where he received the transmission of the book and the maṇḍala of the Sixteen Spheres from his teacher was again Phug-rings; this site is described by later authors as the "birthplace of the precious 'Brom[-ston rGyal-ba'i 'byung-gnas]" (*'brom rin po che'i khrungs yul*). After studying nine years with Zhang-ston Dar-ma rgyal-mtshan, and upon the death of his teacher, Byang-chub bzang-po went to sTabs-ka'i dgon-pa and pursued there his spiritual practice of the Great Compassionate One.

According to the colophon of the *gLegs bam gyi chos 'byung*, the introductory verses with the list of the "seven precious beings" mentioned above came from the pen of a certain Slob-dpon Nam-mkha' rin-chen, who is also known under the name sTabs-ka-ba Nam-mkha' rin-chen, having been the disciple of sTabs-ka-ba Byang-chub bzang-po. With him we enter now that phase in the transmission of the *bKa' gdams glegs bam* and its teachings when these were no longer restricted to a single person—we can thus speak of a broadened transmission.

The details of the life of sTabs-ka-ba Nam-mkha' rin-chen are said to have been written down by him personally. The first thing we note is that he too was born into the 'Brom family. After receiving the initiation into the maṇḍala of the Sixteen Spheres, he travelled with his teacher to different secluded spots—for example to the "Fortress of Nepal" (*bal po'i rdzong*) where a temple of Atiśa was located (due to the great heat they were only able to stay for a period of half a month there). For fifteen years, up to the age of forty-five, sTabs-ka-ba Nam-mkha' rin-chen remained in the company of his teacher; after that—like sTabs-ka-ba Byang-chub bzang-po—he moved to sTabs-ka'i dgon-pa and spent the rest of his days there. Among the highlighted activities was his continuously preaching to worthy disciples the "profound meanings of the precious book" (*glegs bam rin po che'i zab don rnams*). There are several dates given in the account of his life, enough to propose for sTabs-ka-ba Nam-mkha' rin-chen's lifetime the years 1214–1286.[19]

---

[18] See Nyi-ma rgyal-mtshan (as in note 15), pp. 438.10–456.15. The dialogues between the thousand-armed Avalokiteśvara and Zhang-ston Dar-ma rgyal-mtshan refer to the hiding of "treasure scripts" (*gter yig*) in pillars of the 'Phrul-snang temple. It should be remembered that the literary cycles of the Avalokiteśvara teachings of the rNying-ma-pa tradition made their appearance in the central temple of lHa-sa in the 12th and 13th centuries; see Ehrhard (2000b:207f. & 210, Appendix I) and chapter twenty-five in the present volume.

[19] For Byang-chub bzang-po, see sNar-thang mkhan-chen Nyi-ma rgyal-mtshan (as in note 15), pp. 456.18–471.15 and for Nam-mkha' rin-chen, pp. 471.16–488.16; both narratives are ascribed to sTabs-ka-ba Nam-mkha' rin-chen. The history of the transmission of the *bKa' gdams glegs bam* in later historiographical works is based on the text used by us here; compare the account in Kun-dga' rgyal-mtshan (as in note 5), vol. 2, pp. 192.3–242.5. The 15th-century author opens this chapter with a quotation

This leaves us with the final part of the text on the transmission of the "sevenfold divine doctrine", written by the ninth abbot of dPal sNar-thang and dealing with the life of his own teacher 'Brom Kumāramati. This master is another member of the family of 'Brom-ston rGyal-ba'i 'byung-gnas. At the age of seven he met sTabs-ka-ba Nam-mkha' rin-chen in sTabs-ka'i dgon-pa and received from him the reading authorization of the work *Byang chub sems dpa' nor bu'i phreng ba*, which he learned by heart at the age of fifteen (this date corresponds to the year 1285). Already before, in 1282, he had received first ordinations in dPal sNar-thang under mChims Nam-mkha' grags (1210–1285), the seventh abbot. After further studies he finally settled down in dPal sNar-thang in the year 1294, spreading the teaching lineage of his family tradition according to the wishes of his preceptor.

We may pause over the fact that 'Brom Kumāramati learned the whole scripture by heart; as stated above, it was mKhan-chen Nyi-ma rgyal-mtshan who set down in writing what his own teacher had kept stored in his mind. Later authors, such as Yongs-'dzin Ye-shes rgyal-mtshan (1713–1793), assert that it was the special kindness of 'Brom Kumāramati, sometimes regarded as an incarnation of his ancestor 'Brom-ston rGyal-ba'i 'byung-gnas, which made possible the appearance of the *bKa' gdams glegs bam* as a collection of texts. It was thus a specific oral transmission of the teachings which led to the first manuscript version in dPal sNar-thang in the year 1302. This change from an oral culture to one depending on manuscripts is signalled by the disappearance of the "[miraculously] manifested book" of rNgog Legs-pa'i shes-rab. One has the impression that this work, said to have been set down by its author in writing despite the reservations of 'Brom-ston rGyal-ba'i 'byung-gnas, takes on, in the long narratives of the early and later transmission, the function of a sacred authorization of this specific teaching lineage. It seems that up to the end of the 13th century this lineage had spread only among a limited group of persons: for the most part, the bKa'-gdams-pa monastery of sTabs-ka and members of the 'Brom family, the birthplace of 'Brom-ston rGyal-ba'i 'byung-gnas being a favourite spot for spiritual practices in the initial phase.[20] sTabs-ka-ba Nam-mkha' rin-chen, the

---

from sTabs-ka-ba Nam-mkha' rin-chen according to which the latter was the only holder of the transmission at his time; see ibid, p. 192.3–4 (*slob dpon nam rin gyi zhal nas / yongs su rdzogs pa gzhon nu rgyal mtshan ni / phal cher 'dzin pa tshul khrims 'bar du gda' / phyogs tsam gsal bar rin chen gsal ba yin / ding sang du na kho bo nyid du zad / byang chub bzang po'i thugs dgongs rdzogs gyur cig*). For this quotation and the interlinear commentary (identifying the persons in the first three lines as the "Three Brothers"), see Nyi-ma rgyal-mtshan (as in note 15), p. 302.11–15.

20 The residence of Phu-chung-ba in the 'Phan-yul region was also located in the immediate vicinity of one of the sites where Dar-ma grags, the founder of sTabs-ka'i dgon-pa had stayed. This at least is what the pilgrimage guide book written by Brag-dgon sprul-sku 'Jam-dbyangs bstan-pa rgya-mtsho (1824–1906) claims; see *dBus gtsang gi gnas bskor byed tshul rag bsdud tsam zhig brjod pa mi brjed dran pa'i gsal 'debs gzur gnas mkhas pa'i rna rgyan*, fol. 4a/2–3 (*de nas 'phan yul gyi yul (= yung) lnga zhes pa'i phur / phu chung ba'i gdan sa phu chung dang / stabs ka ba'i gdan sa khra phu zhes pa yod*).

master who finally started to make this lineage's teachings available to a greater public, is also regarded as the one responsible for the disappearance of the mysterious book, which he is said to have inserted into the sKu-'bum, the great caitya, at sTabs-ka'i dgon-pa.[21]

Although the maṇḍala of the Sixteen Spheres occupies a central position within this transmission, from rNgog Legs-pa'i shes-rab onwards, the text concerning the history of the *lHa chos bdun ldan* does not give any detailed information on the actual form of these spheres. We can only suggest that the four meditative deities of Atiśa formed the basis or substratum of this specific spiritual practice. As already noted above, we are dependent on the particular work of mKhan-chen Nyi-ma rgyal-mtshan belonging to the literary genre of "instruction text" (*khrid yig*). The actual process of the unfolding of the Sixteen Spheres is contained in the "main part" (*dngos gzhi*) of the text and we find in this scenario of manifesting and dissolving light-circles, next to divinities like Prajñāpāramitā also the Indian Buddhist masters Maitreyanātha and Nāgārjuna, whose teaching lineages play an important role in the bKa'-gdams-pa school. The central deity is the thousand-armed Avalokiteśvara, who figures as the first and the seventh *thig le*; the iconographical form of the Great Compassionate One with two arms is also represented two times, namely as the third and fourth *thig le*.

In order to gain a visual impression of the arrangement of the different spheres as a tradition idealizing Atiśa and 'Brom-ston rGyal-ba'i 'byung-gnas as divine beings, I present a scroll painting of the *Thig le bcu drug* in an appendix (see Plts. 1 & 2). This painting is based on the instruction text of mKhan-chen Nyi-ma rgyal-mtshan, the captions of the Sixteen Spheres corresponding exactly to this work. We can find a seventeenth *thig le* added to this set, showing the Fifth Dalai Bla-ma Ngag-dbang Blo-bzang rgya-mtsho. The painting thus belongs to the "close transmission" (*nye brgyud*) of this teaching lineage, which the Fifth Dalai Bla-ma had received in a vision of 'Brom-ston rGyal-ba'i 'byung-gnas in the year 1652. In that year the worldly and spiritual ruler of Tibet set out from 'Bras-spungs monastery on a journey to China and the first episode along the way described in the account of his visionary experiences concerns his encounter with 'Brom-ston rGyal-ba'i 'byung-gnas. This happened at rTs[w]a sGyer-mo (or Phug-rings), the birthplace of

---

21 For the life of 'Brom Kumāramati, see the final part of sNar-thang mkhan-chen Nyi-ma rgyal-mtshan (as in note 15), pp. 488.17–495.11. On the role of sTabs-ka-ba Nam-mkha' rin-chen in making the teachings public and the special role of 'Brom[-ston] Kumāramati as the one whose powers of memory tapped the "original [manuscript] copy" (*ma phyi*) of the *bKa' gdams glegs bam*, see Ye-shes rgyal-mtshan: *Lam rim bla ma brgyud pa'i rnam thar*, pp. 918.16–919.2. Like the other historiographical works, this text contains the episode on the insertion of the book into the sKu-'bum at sTabs-ka'i dgon-pa; see ibid, p. 910.24–25 (*bka' gdams sprul pa'i glegs bam chen mo ni slob dpon nam mkha' rin chen gyis stabs ka'i mchod rten gyi nang du bzhugs su gsol zhes 'byung ngo*). Concerning the traditional view that 'Brom-ston rGyal-ba'i 'byung-gnas had reservations about putting down the teachings into written form—something that had to wait for his reincarnation 'Brom[-ston] Kumāramati—; see Boussemart (1999:218f.).

Atiśa's most important disciple, and the site where the later or "local" transmission of the teachings of the *bKa' gdams glegs bam* had taken place.[22]

IV. THE OLDEST BLOCK PRINT OF THE *BKA' GDAMS GLEGS BAM*

The further transmission of Phu-chung-ba's teaching lineage after its codification in the form of a manuscript is quite well documented in the historiographical works of the 15th century. After mKhan-chen Nyi-ma rgyal-mtshan the following line of teachers is given in these works: Rin-chen byang-chub – Rigs-kyi bdag-po'i dpal – Byang-chub dpal – Bla-ma bSod-nams 'od-zer – mKhan-chen Sangs-rgyas bzang-po – Bya-bral-ba bSod-nams bzang-po – U-yug-pa Bla-ma dPal-'byor. The last person passed the tradition on to a certain Chos-rje Seng-ge rgyal-mtshan, who was for some time the abbot of sTag-tshang Chos-'khor sgang in gTsang province. About him we know that he saved the teachings centring on the text *Byang chub sems dpa' nor bu'i phreng ba* from being nearly extinguished. The merit gained in preserving the "lineage of the [sevenfold] divine doctrine" (*lha chos kyi brgyud*) earned Chos-rje Seng-ge rgyal-mtshan recognition for being a reincarnation of 'Brom-ston rGyal-ba'i 'byung-gnas. From him the tradition reached the "translator" (*skad gnyis smra ba*) Thugs-rje dpal (14th/15th century) and then rJe dGe-'dun grub (1391–1451), who later became known as the First Dalai Bla-ma.[23]

The *gSan yig* of the Fifth Dalai Bla-ma shows the transmission of the *bKa' gdams glegs bam* passing through the same lineage up until it branches off after Bya-bral-ba bSod-nams bzang-po. From there it goes on to one Bla-ma dPal-ldan-pa and then to Nam-mkha' 'od-zer, an otherwise unknown person who also bears the name sTag-tshang Chos-'khor-ba mKhan-chen. In either case we see that the monastery of sTag-tshang Chos-'khor

---

[22] The captions of the individual spheres as reproduced on the painting should be compared with *Nyams len snying gi thig le'i gsal byed zung 'jug nyi zla'i thig le* in *Jo bo rje dpal ldan a ti sha'i rnam thar bka' gdams pha chos*, pp. 533.4–555.20. Among the later works concerning the rituals related to the Sixteen Spheres and its maṇḍala I shall only refer to three works of Yongs-'dzin Ye-shes rgyal-mtshan: *bKa' gdams thig le bcu drug gi ngag 'don*, 28 fols., *bKa' gdams lha chos bdun ldan gyi man ngag*, 42 fols., and *bKa' gdams thig le bcu drug gi dkyil chog bka' gdams gsal byed*, 100 fols.; the first two works are contained in vol. da, and the third one in vol. tsa of his writings. For the visit of the Fifth Dalai Bla-ma to rTs[w]a sGyer-mo at the age of thirty-six years and his vision of 'Brom-ston rGyal-ba'i 'byung-gnas, see Karmay (1988a:34f.). Cf. *Ngag-dbang Blo-bzang rgya-mtsho: rGyal ba'i dbang po'i thams cad mkhyen cing gzigs pa chen po'i gsang ba'i rnam thar rgya can ma,* pp. 23.5–25.1.

[23] This is the line of transmission recorded by Las-chen Kun-dga' rgyal-mtshan, who had received it from rJe dGe-'dun grub; see rTse-thang Las-chen Kun-dga' rgyal-mtshan (as in note 5), vol. 2, pp. 248.6–250.4. Concerning Chos-rje Seng-ge rgyal-mtshan it is stated that in the later part of his life he held the seat of the monastery sTag-tshang Chos-'khor sgang; for the foundation of this monastery in gTsang by Lo-chen sKyabs-mchog dpal bzang-po, see ibid, p. 181.5. The same line of transmission up to rJe dGe-'dun grub can also be found in the historiographical work of Paṇ-chen bSod-nams grags-pa: *bKa' gdams gsar rnying gi chos 'byung yid kyi mdzes rgyan*", p. 35.1–2. Paṇ-chen bSod-nams grags-pa, the fifteenth throne-holder of dGa'-ldan, was a disciple of Las-chen Kun-dga' rgyal-mtshan.

sgang played an important role in keeping this special bKa'-gdams-pa teaching alive in the 15th century. After two further teachers this transmission is vouchsafed to gNyug-la Paṇ-chen Ngag-dbang grags-pa (1458–1515), another important link in the further spread of the *bKa' gdams glegs bam*.[24]

There exists a short biographical sketch of this master from gNyug-la or sMyug-la in the province of dBus, and it tells us that he not only "held the true system of the bKa'-gdams[-pa tradition]" (*bka' gdams kyi srol dngos 'dzin*), but was also regarded as a reincarnation of sPyan-snga-pa, one of the "Three Brothers". It is said that Ngag-dbang grags-pa had made the promise to give the teachings of the *bKa' gdams glegs bam* and the empowerment of the *Thig le bcu drug* every year, and that these teachings had been followed by auspicious signs—rains of flowers and so forth. We have at least one eyewitness account of this hagiographical episode, which shows the importance of gNyug-la Paṇ-chen for the popularization of this teaching lineage at the beginning of the 16th century.[25]

The residence of Ngag-dbang grags-pa in gNyug-la or sMyug-la was called g.Yul-rgyal rdzong. This is the same place in the province of dBus that brought forth the manuscript copy of the *bKa' gdams glegs bam* on the basis of which the first xylograph edition of the collection of texts was produced. A pair of brothers, known to be nephews of gNyug-la Paṇ-chen, provided the copy. Although this fact is known from earlier research, the date of the printing project was thought to be in the years 1478 and 1479. As the biography of the person behind the project is now available, we can correct the dates and shift them one sixty-year-cycle forward to the period between the years 1538 and 1539. I have dealt with this oldest block print of the *bKa' gdams glegs bam* elsewhere, and here

24 For the transmission of the *bKa' gdams glegs bam* in the record of teachings received by the Fifth Dalai Bla-ma; see the text (as in note 9), vol. 2, pp. 88.4–95.1. Further lineages include the one passing through bSod-nams lha'i dbang-po, who was also a teacher of gNyug-la Paṇ-chen Ngag-dbang grags-pa; see, for example, the two transmissions of the *bKa' gdams lha bzhi* in the chapter on the *Kriyātantra* in the same text of the Fifth Dalai Bla-ma, vol. 1, pp. 221.6–222.6, and pp. 222.6–226.2. Cf. also the lineages of the transmission of the *bKa' gdams lha bzhi* and the *Thig le bcu drug* as part of the collection of the "[More than] One Hundred Instructions" (*khrid brgya*) of Jo-nang Kun-dga' grol-mchog (1507–1566) in vol. 2, p. 283.1–3, and p. 284.1–4.

25 The biographical sketch of gNyug-la Paṇ-chen is contained in Chos-kyi 'byung-gnas & Be-lo Tshe-dbang kun-kyab: *sGrub brgyud karma ka tshang brgyud pa rin po che'i rnam par thar pa rab 'byams nor bu zla ba chu shel gyi phreng ba*, vol. 1, pp. 648.3–649.3; see especially p. 648.6–7 (*bka' gdams glegs bam kyang lo re la lan re gnang ba'i dam bca' mdzad*). The eyewitness account of this event can be found in the biography of the 'Ba'-ra-ba bKa'-brgyud-pa master Nam-mkha' rgyal-mtshan (1475–1530); see Kun-dga' dpal-'byor *dPal ldan bla ma dam pa sprul sku nam mkha' rgyal mtshan dpal bzang po'i rnam par thar pa / dgos 'dod kun 'byung nor bu'i 'phreng ba*, NGMPP reel no. L 18/14, fol. 18a/5–b/1 & fol. 19a/3–5 (... *zab chos bsam gyis mi khyab pa gsan / bka' gdams glegs bam gnang ba'i dus su / me tog gi char dang / dri bzang rgyun mi 'chad pa yong gin 'dug pas / dam 'di nyid mgon po spyan ras gzigs kyi sprul pa yin nges snyam nas / mi phyed dad pa thob / sge sbyor la bogs thon zhing / khyad par snying rje la bogs chen po byung gsung*).

merely reproduce a passage from the biography of the Bo-dong-pa scholar Chos-dbang rgyal-mtshan (1484–1549) describing the events immediately after the manuscript copy arrived from Central Tibet:

> The steward [Nam-mkha' dkon-mchog] and close friends brought the original copy of the *bKa' gdams [glegs bam]* from dBus [and] gTsang on the twenty-fifth day of the month of December [in the year 1537] after the Precious One (= Chos-dbang rgyal-mtshan) had taken up residence in [the palace of] rDzong-dkar. They arrived safely.
>
> As at that time the official Kun-spangs don-grub from g.Yul-rgyal rdzong offered [to Chos-dbang rgyal-mtshan] a silk scroll painting of the White Tārā, [the latter] was especially pleased, and consecrated it, [on which occasion] he said: "It has happened that Bhaṭṭārikā Tārā from among the four gods of the bKa'-gdams[-pa tradition] has arrived [in person]. It is an opportune favour [and] an auspicious sign that the printing of the *bKa' gdams glegs bam* will be completed [in time]." Wherever he went [later], he [always] carried this sacred object in his hands.[26]

The palace of rDzong-dkar in this quotation refers to the residence of the kings of Mang-yul Gung-thang. In the 16th century their domain offered good conditions for producing block print editions of what one might call "Buddhist Classics". A final point I want to make concerning the printing colophon of the *bKa' gdams glegs bam* is that we find, among the sponsors of the undertaking, representatives of the teaching lineage of the bKa'-gdams-pa tradition going back to Nag-tsho Lo-chen Tshul-khrims rgyal-ba (born 1011). This translator brought Atiśa from the Indian plains via Mang-yul Gung-thang to Tibet and stayed many years in the company of the master. Nag-tsho Lo-chen was a native of this kingdom bordering on Nepal, while another person contributing to the production of the printing blocks of the *bKa' gdams glegs bam* came from Yang-thog, the former residence of Tshul-khrims rgyal-ba.

---

26 See *mTshan ldan bla ma dam pa mnyam med chos dbang rgyal mtshan gyi rnam par thar pa / rin po che nor bu'i phreng ba*, fol. 90b/3–6 (*rgyal zla'i nyer lnga la / gsol dpon grogs mched kyis dbus gtsang nas / bka' gdams kyi phyi mo spyan drangs nas / rin po che pa* (sic) *rdzong dkar na bzhugs ring la nye zho med par 'khor re / de dus g.yul rgyal rdzong pa nang so kun spangs don grub gyis / rje btsun ma sgrol ma dkar mo'i gos thang gcig phul bas / lhag par dges shing rab gnas mdzad cing / bka' gdams lha bzhi'i ngang nas rje btsun ma sgrol ma phebs byung / thugs rje myur / bka' gdams glegs bam gyi spar 'grub pa'i rten 'brel yin gsung / sku de gang phebs su snoms phebs par mdzad do*). The first attempt to date this print was made by Schuh (1981b:353–355). For the four different print editions of the *bKa' gdams glegs bam* (not including the print from sDe-dge), see Eimer (1977:72–96). On the life of Chos-dbang rgyal-mtshan, see Ehrhard (2000a:23–50).

V. CONCLUSIONS

The change from a manuscript culture to block print culture in the transmission of the *Thig le bcu drug* and the *bKa' gdams glegs bam* occurred in a geographical area in which originated not only the writings concerning the biographical tradition of Atiśa, but also a particular lineage of his Avalokiteśvara teachings. In the later historiographical writings of the bKa'-gdams-pa tradition, this teaching lineage is known as the "Transmission of the Pronouncements of Nag-tsho [Lo-chen]" (*nag tsho'i bka' brgyud*). The origin of the biographical tradition—and the role played by Lag-sor-pa (or Phyag-sor-pa) in going to Yang-thog in Mang-yul Gung-thang in order to solicit from Tshul-khrims rgyal-ba the life-story of Atiśa—has already been dealt with in earlier research.[27] It should be added that the transmission of Mahākāruṇika-Ṣaḍakṣara teachings which Atiśa had received from his teacher Rāhulaguptavajra also ran through Nag-tsho Lo-chen and his disciple Lag-sor-pa, the special feature of this lineage being that all its members encountered the Great Compassionate One face to face.

After Lag-sor-pa the lineage was continued by Bya 'Dul-ba 'dzin-pa (1100–1174), also called dGe-bshes Zul-phu-ba, the author of the biography of Atiśa known as *rNam thar rgyas pa*. He in turn gave these special teachings to 'Phags-pa lCe-sgom-pa and mNga'-ris-pa Shes-rab rgyal-mtshan. 'Phags-pa lCe-sgom-pa has received some attention recently, so there is reason to come back to mNga'-ris-pa Shes-rab rgyal-mtshan, whom we have met already as a key figure in the early transmission of the *bKa' gdams glegs bam*, and as a teacher of Phu-chung-ba. We thus have a chronological problem with his being a contemporary of lCe-sgom-pa (ca. 1140/50–1220). As already pointed out, information disseminated concerning Phu-chung-ba can be seen as an attempt to construct an independent teaching lineage in the 12th and 13th centuries, and I would regard the inclusion of mNga'-ris-pa Shes-rab rgyal-mtshan in the early – or legendary – transmission of the book of the bKa'-gdams-pa tradition as part of this attempt. Both 'Phags-pa lCe-sgom-pa and mNga'-ris-pa Shes-rab rgyal-mtshan transmitted the instructions of the "Transmission of the Pronouncements of Nag-tsho [Lo-chen]" to the "mahāsiddha" (*grub thob chen po*) sKyer-sgang-pa, who had already played a role in the account of Phu-chung-ba's special status as transmitter of the sevenfold divine doctrine.[28]

---

27 For Lag-sor-pa as initiator of the biographical tradition of Atiśa, see Eimer (1982:41–51).

28 The transmission history of the *Nag tsho'i bka' brgyud* is again to be found in Kun-dga' rgyal-mtshan (as in note 5), vol. 2, pp. 390.4ff.; for the Mahākāruṇika-Ṣaḍakṣara lineage, see ibid, pp. 397.3ff. A treatment of 'Phags-pa lCe-sgom-pa was undertaken by Sørensen (1999); for the contacts of the siddha with sKyer-sgang-pa, see especially pp. 193f. The lineage of sKyer-sgang-pa was later absorbed into the Shangs-pa bKa'-brgyud-pa tradition and was known as one of the "Four Families of Direct Instruction [on the Practice of Mahākāruṇika]" (*dmar khrid rigs bzhi*); see Ehrhard (2000b:199) and chapter twenty-five in the present volume.

I come back now to the incarnation status of the bKa'-gdams-pa masters Po-to-ba, Phu-chung-ba and sPyan-snga-pa, and their identification respectively with the Avalokiteśvara icons Ārya Wa-ti bzang-po, Ārya 'Ja'-ma-li and Ārya 'Bu-khang. From the 12th century onwards the cult of these statues, like the one for the thousand-armed Avalokiteśvara in the 'Phrul-snang temple in lHa-sa, gradually became quite popular in south-western and Central Tibet. As the three statues of Padmapāṇi Lokeśvara were located either in Mang-yul Gung-thang or Nepal, they eventually became known to early members of the teaching lineage of Nag-tsho Lo-chen Tshul-khrims rgyal-ba, who transmitted the biographical tradition of Atiśa and a particular spiritual practice of the Great Compassionate One. Such identification of Avalokiteśvara icons with bKa'-gdams-pa masters, at a time when Phu-chung-ba's status was being raised to an incarnation of Avalokiteśvara, can only be explained in the context of an oral tradition.[29] It was probably spread by travellers who visited the three statues in Mang-yul Gung-thang and in Nepal, whence it found its way into the biographical writings of Atiśa, supplementing the role of the "Three Brothers" as embodiments of the protectors of the three tantric families known from the *Ma 'ongs lun bstan* section of the *bKa' gdams glegs bam*.

[29] The statue of the Ārya Wa-ti bzang-po, the so-called "Lord of [Mang-yul] sKyid-grong" (*skyid grong jo bo*), occupies a central position in prophecies concerning the spiritual identity of Byang-sems Zla-ba rgyal-mtshan (11/12th century). The latter transmitted Avalokiteśvara teachings of Bhikṣuṇī Lakṣmiṅ[karā] which passed through Atiśa as well; see Kun-dga' rgyal-mtshan (as in note 5), vol. 2, pp. 328.3–333.1. The teaching lineages of Byang-sems Zla-ba rgyal-mtshan and Bhikṣuṇī Lakṣmiṅ[karā] are counted as two doctrinal systems when subsumed under the "Four Families of Direct Instructions [on the Practice of Mahākāruṇika]".

APPENDIX

The scroll painting of the Sixteen Spheres reproduced here is from the volume *Bod kyi thang ka*, Peking: Rig-dngos dpe-skrun khang, 1984, no. 98. In the description on p. 173 of the volume it is said that the painting is located in the Potala palace. The caption of the seventeenth *thig le* reads *"Thams cad mkhyen pa ngag dbang blo bzang rgya mtsho la namaḥ"*. The central deity's caption has also this formula of veneration, while all other captions simply give the name of the *thig le* in question as found in the "instruction text" of mKhan-chen Nyi-ma rgyal-mtshan. The numbering of the spheres and the wording of the legends in the following list is according to this text:

1. *Phyi'i bkod pa bsam gyis mi khyab pa* (= Thousand-armed Avalokiteśvara)
2. *Mi mjed kyi bkod pa* (= Buddha Śākyamuni)
3. *Bod khams* (= Padmapāṇi Lokeśvara)
4. *gNas khang dang bris pa dkyil 'khor* (= Padmapāṇi Lokeśvara)
5. *Yum sher phyin* (= Prajñāpāramitā)
6. *De'i sras thub pa* (= Buddha Śākyamuni)
7. *De'i sras snying rje chen po* (= Thousand-armed Avalokiteśvara)
8. *De dag gi ye shes sgrol ma* (= Tārā)
9. *De nyid khros pa* (= Ugratārā)
10. *De rnams kyi rang bzhin mi g.yo ba* (= Acala)
11. *Thams cad kyi ngo bo a ti sha* (= Atiśa Dīpaṃkaraśrījñāna)
12. *rGyal ba'i 'byung gnas* (= 'Brom-ston)
13. *rGya chen spyod pa* (= Maitreyanātha)
14. *Zab mo lta ba* (= Nāgārjuna)
15. *Nyams len byin rlabs* (= Vajradhara)
16. *Byang chub chen po* (= Bodhicitta)

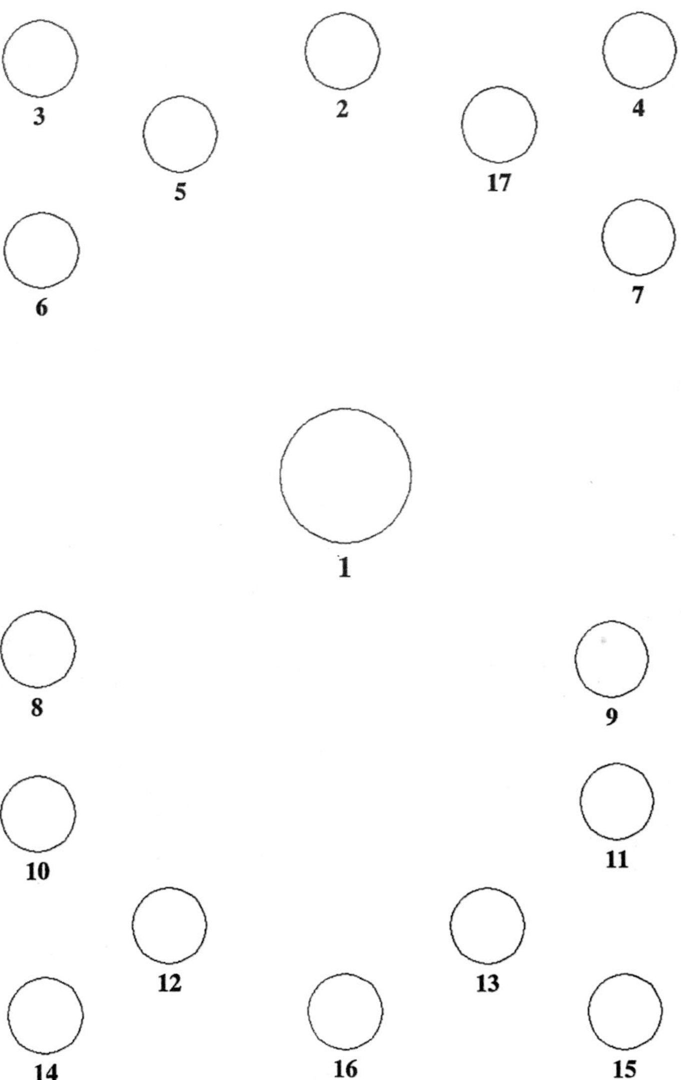

Plate 1

Plate 2

Original publication details

1. "Observations on Prāsaṅgika-Madhyamaka in the rÑiṅ-ma-pa school." In *Tibetan Studies: Proceedings of the 4th Seminar of the International Association for Tibetan Studies. Schloss Hohenkammer. Munich 1985* (= Studia Tibetica. Quellen und Studien zur tibetischen Lexikographie, 2). Munich 1988, pp. 139–147.

2. "Some Historical Delineations Concerning Madhyamala Philosophy in the rNying-ma-pa school." Unpublished. Paper presented at the Csoma de Kőrös Symposium, Sopron, Hungary, 2. September 1987.

3. "The 'Vision' of rDzogs-chen: A Text and its Histories." In *Tibetan Studies: Proceedings of the 5th Seminar of the International Association for Tibetan Studies. Narita 1989*, Vol. 1 (= Monograph Series of Naritasan Institute for Buddhist Studies, Occasional Papers, 2). Narita, 1992, pp. 47–57.

4. "A Renovation of Svayaṃbhūnāth-Stūpa in the 18th Century and Its History (According to Tibetan Sources)." *Ancient Nepal. Journal of the Department of Archaeology*, 114, 1989, pp. 1–9.

5. "Further Renovations of Svayaṃbhūnāth-Stūpa (from the 13th to the 17th Centuries)." *Ancient Nepal. Journal of the Department of Archaeology*, 123-125, 1991, pp. 10–20.

6. "Old and New Tibetan Sources Concerning Svayaṃbhūnāth." *Zentralasiatische Studien*, 36, 2007, pp. 105–130.

7. "The Stūpa of Bodhnāth: A Preliminary Analysis of the Written Sources." *Ancient Nepal. Journal of the Department of Archaeology*, 120, 1990, pp. 1–9.

8. "The Register of the Reliquary of Lord Raṅ-rig ras-pa." *Vienna Journal of South Asian Studies*, 46, 2002, pp. 146–167.

9. "A Forgotten Incarnation Lineage: The *Yol-mo-ba sPrul-skus* (16th to 18th Centuries)." In *The Pandita and the Siddha: Tibetan Studies in Honour of E. Gene Smith*. Dharamshala, 2007, pp. 25–49.

10. "Two Documents on Tibetan Ritual Literature and Spiritual Genealogy." *Journal of the Nepal Research Centre*, 9, 1993, pp. 77–100.

11. "A Monument of Sherpa Buddhism: The Enlightenment Stūpa in Junbesi." *The Tibet Journal*, 29:3 (= Special Issue: Tibetan Monuments), 2004, pp. 75–92.

12. "Tibetan Sources on Muktināth: Individual Reports and Normative Guides." *Ancient Nepal. Journal of the Department of Archaeology*, 134, 1993, pp. 23–39.

13. "Concepts of Religious Space in Southern Mustāṅ: The Foundation of the Monastery of sKu-tshab gter-lnga." In *Kāgbeni: Contributions to the Village's History and Geography* (= Giessener Geographische Schriften, 77). Giessen, 2001, pp. 235–246.

14. "Religious Geography and Literary Traditions: The Foundation of the Monastery Brag-dkar bSam-gling." *Journal of the Nepal Research Centre*, 12, 2001, pp. 101–114.

15. "Pilgrims in Search of Sacred Lands." In *Sacred Landscape of the Himalaya. Proceedings of an International Conference at Heidelberg 25-27 May 1998* (= Österreichische Akademie der Wissenschaften, Phil.-Hist. Klasse Denkschriften, 308 / Veröffentlichungen zur Sozialanthropologie, 4). Vienna, 2003, pp. 95–110.

16. "A 'Hidden Land' in the Tibetan-Nepalese Borderlands." In *Maṇḍala and Landscape* (= Emerging Perceptions in Buddhist Studies, 6). New Dehli, 1997, pp. 335–364.

17. "'The Lands Are like a Wiped Golden Basin': The Sixth Zhva-dmar-pa's Journey to Nepal and his Travelogue (1629/30)." In *Les Habitants du toit du Monde. Études recueillies en hommage à Alexander W. Macdonald* (= Recherches sur la Haute Asie, 12). Nanterre, 1997, pp. 125–138.

18. "'The Story of How *bla-ma* Karma Chos-bzang Came to Yol-mo': A Family Document from Nepal." In *Three Mountains and Seven Rivers. Prof. Musashi Tachikawa's Felicitation Volume.* Dehli, 2004, pp. 581–600 & 607.

19. "Two Further Lamas of Dolpo: Ngag-dbang rnam-rgyal (born 1628) and rNam-grol bzang-po (born 1504)." *Journal of the Nepal Research Centre*, 10, 1996, pp. 55–75.

20. "Sa-'dul dgon-pa: A Temple at the Crossroads of Jumla, Dolpo and Mustang." *Ancient Nepal. Journal of the Department of Archaeology*, 140, 1998, pp. 3–19.

21. "The Role of 'Treasure Discoverers' and their Writings in the Search for Himalayan Sacred Lands." *The Tibet Journal*, 19:3 (Special Issue: Powerful Places and Spaces in Tibetan Religious Culture), 1994, pp. 3–20.

22. "Political and Ritual Aspects of the Search for Himalayan Sacred Lands." *Studies in Central & East Asian Religions*, 9, 1996, pp. 37–53.

23. "Kaḥ thog pa bSod nams rgyal mtshan (1466–1540) and his activities in Sikkim and Bhutan." *Bulletin of Tibetology*, 39:2 (Special Issue: Contributions to Sikkimese History), 2003, pp. 9–26.

24. "Recently Discovered Manuscripts of the rNying ma rgyud 'bum from Nepal." In *Tibetan Studies: Proceedings of the 7th Seminar of the International Association for Tibetan Studies, Graz 1995*, vol. 1 (= Österreichische Akademie der Wissenschaften, Phil.-Hist. Klasse, Denkschriften, 256 / Beiträge zur Kultur- und Geistesgeschichte Asiens, 21). Vienna 1997, pp. 253–267.

25. "The Transmission of the *dMar-khrid Tshem-bu lugs* and the *Maṇi bka' 'bum*." In *Vividharatnakaraṇḍaka: Festgabe für Adelheid Mette* (= Indica et Tibetica, 37). Swisttal-Odendorf, 2000, pp. 199–215.

26. "The Transmission of the *Thig-le bcu-drug* and the *bKa' gdams glegs bam*." In *The Many Canons of Tibetan Buddhism* (= Brill's Tibetan Studies Library, 2:10). Leiden 2002, pp. 29–56.

Bibliography

TIBETAN TEXTS

Anonymous

gNas chen chu mig brgya rtsa'i dang cong zhi sku tshab gter lnga mu li rin chen gangs gu ru gsang phug sna ris jo bo sogs kyi dkar chags dngul dkar me long, 10 fols. (manuscript). In "*Rare Tibetan Texts from Nepal*: A collection of guides to holy places, lives of religious masters, and khrid yig by the famed Rdza Ro-phu Bla-ma." Dolanji: Tashi Dorje, pp. 61–80.

Bla ma rin po che sbas pa'i rnal 'byor pa chen po thub bstan dbang po'i rnams (= rnam) thar ngo tshar (= mtshar) smad (= rmad) 'byung (= byung), 31 fols. (incomplete manuscript). NGMPP reel no. L 123/2.

Rig 'dzin chos rgyal bsod nams gyi rnam thar, 8 fols. In "Collected Biographies and Prophecies of the Byaṅ gter Tradition." Gangtok: Sherab Gyaltsen, 1983, pp. 235–250.

Karma Blo-bzang (16th/17th cent.)

mKhas grub chen po karma blo bzang ba rnam thar mchod sprin rgya mtsho, 84 fols. (manuscript).

Karma Mi-'gyur dBang-gi rgyal-po, Zab-bu gDan-sa-pa (17th cent.)

gTer bton brgya rtsa'i mtshan sdom gsol 'debs chos rgyal bkra shis stobs rgyal gyi mdzad pa'i 'grel pa lo rgyus gter bton chos 'byung, 174 fols. Darjeeling: Taklung Tsetrul Rinpoche Pema Wangyal, 1978.

Kaḥ-dam-pa bDe-gshegs (1122–1192)

Theg pa spyi bcings rtsa 'grel, 417 pp. Chengdu: Si-khron mi-rigs dpe-skrun khang, 1997.

Kun-dga' grol-mchog, Jo-nang rje-btsun (1507–1566)

Khrid brgya'i spyi chings rnam par spel ba ngo mtshar chos kyi sgo mang, 10 fols. In "gDams ngag mdzod", vol. 18. Paro: Lama Ngodrup & Sherab Drimey, 1979, pp. 47–66.

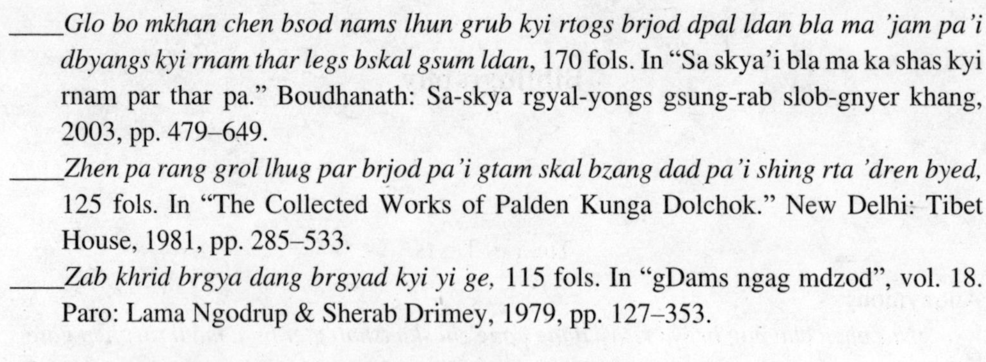
____*Glo bo mkhan chen bsod nams lhun grub kyi rtogs brjod dpal ldan bla ma 'jam pa'i dbyangs kyi rnam thar legs bskal gsum ldan*, 170 fols. In "Sa skya'i bla ma ka shas kyi rnam par thar pa." Boudhanath: Sa-skya rgyal-yongs gsung-rab slob-gnyer khang, 2003, pp. 479–649.

____*Zhen pa rang grol lhug par brjod pa'i gtam skal bzang dad pa'i shing rta 'dren byed*, 125 fols. In "The Collected Works of Palden Kunga Dolchok." New Delhi: Tibet House, 1981, pp. 285–533.

____*Zab khrid brgya dang brgyad kyi yi ge*, 115 fols. In "gDams ngag mdzod", vol. 18. Paro: Lama Ngodrup & Sherab Drimey, 1979, pp. 127–353.

Kun-dga' rgyal-mtshan, rTse-thang Las-chen (b. 1440)
bKa' gdams kyi rnam par thar pa bka' gdams chos 'byung gsal ba'i sgron me, 2 vols., 315 fols. & 315 fols. New Delhi: B. Jamyang Norbu, 1972.

Kun-dga' snying-po, Jo-nang Taranātha (1575–1635)
Grub chen bhuddhagupta'i rnam thar rje btsun nyid kyi zhal lung las gzhan su rang rtog gi dri mas ma sbags pa'i yi ge yang dag pa'o, 23 fols. In "The Collected Works of Jonang rJe-bstun Kun-dga' snying po", vol. 17. Leh: C. Namgyal & Tsewang Taru, 1985, pp. 531–75.

____*rGyal khams pa tā ra nā thas bdag nyid kyi rnam thar nges par brjod pa'i deb gter shin tu zhib mo bcos lhug par rtogs brjod*, 331 fols. In "ibid", vol. 1. Leh: C. Namgyal and Tsewang Taru, 1982, pp. 1–662.

Kun-dga' rdo-rje, Tshal-pa Si-tu (1309–1364)
Deb ther dmar po, 151 pp. Beijing: Mi-rigs dpe-skron-khang, 1981.

Kun-dga' dpal-'byor (15th/16th cent.)
dPal ldan bla ma dam pa sprul sku nam mkha' rgyal mtshan dpal bzang po'i rnam par thar pa dgos 'dod kun 'byung nor bu'i phreng ba, 48 fols. (blockprint). NGMPP reel-no. L 18/14.

Kun-bzang klong-yangs (1644–1696)
rTogs brjod mu tig gi mchun bu zhes pa'i gtam, 93 fols. (manuscript). NGMPP reel no. L 406/2.

Kun-bzang nges-don klong-yangs, Sixth Dog-sprul Rig-'dzin (b. 1814)
Bod du byung ba'i gsang sngags snga 'gyur gyi bstan 'dzin skyes mchog rim byon gyi rnam thar nor bu'i do shal, 186 fols. Dalhousie: Damchoe Sangpo, 1976.

____*Rig-'dzin rdo rje gsang ba rtsal gyi rtogs par brjod pa sgra dbyangs lha mo'i gling bu*, 189 fols. In "Lives of Lha-btsun Kun-dga'-chos-kyi-rgya-mtsho and Rdo-rje-gsaṅ-ba rtsal." Darjeeling: Kargyud Sungrab Nyamso Khang, 1974, pp. 199–577.

Kun-bzang chos-'phel (20th/21st cent.)

rNam grol rtsangs rdo dmar ba'i gdung rabs lo rgyus deb ther padma rāga'i do shal, 319 pp. Delhi: Dakney Tsan Domar Namdrolling, 1998.

Kun-bzang don-grub (18th cent.)

Gu ru pad ma'i rnam thar las thang yig ga'u ma'i dkar chags, 7 fols. In "Padma'i thang yig ga'u ma." Dalhousie: Damche Sangpo, 1981, pp. 1–13.

Kun-bzang dpal-ldan, mKhan-po (1872–1943)

Gangs ri'i ljongs kyi smra ba'i seng ge gcig pu 'jam mgon mi pham rgya mtsho'i rnam thar snying po bsdus pa dang gsung rab kyi dkar chag snga 'gyur bstan pa'i mdzes rgyan, 56 fols. In "Collected Writings of 'Jam-mgon 'Ju Mi-pham rgya-mtsho", vol. 7 (= Ngagyur Nyingmay Sungrab 66). Gangtok: Sonam Tobgay Kazi, 1976, pp. 621–731.

____*Nges shes rin po che'i sgron me'i tshig gi don gsal ba'i 'grel chung blo gros snang ba'i sgo 'byed*, 97 fols. (manuscript). Clement Town, U.P.: Nyingma Lama's College, n.d.

Klong-chen Rab-'byams-pa, Kun-mkhyen (1308–1364)

Chos dbyings rin po che'i mdzod kyi 'grel pa lung gi gter mdzod, 212 fols. (xylograph). Gangtok: Dodrupchen Rinpoche, n.d.

____*Theg pa chen po'i man ngag gi bstan bcos yid bzhin rin po che'i mdzod kyi 'grel pa padma dkar po*, 2 vols., 250 fols. & 196 fols. (xylographs). Gangtok: Dodrupchen Rinpoche, n.d.

____*Theg pa mtha' dag gi don gsal bar byed pa grub pa'i mtha' rin po che'i mdzod*, 206 fols. (xylograph). Gangtok: Dodrupchen Rinpoche, n.d.

____*rDzogs pa chen po sems nyid ngal gso'i 'grel pa shing rta chen po*, 2 vols., 309 fols. & 220 fols. (xylographs). Gangtok: Dodrupchen Rinpoche, 1973.

____*Zhus len bdud rtsi'i gser phreng*, 17 fols. In "Mkha' 'gro sNying thig", part 2 (= Snying thig ya bzhi, vol. 5). New Delhi: Trulku Tsewang Jamyang and L. Tashi, 1971, pp. 1–34.

____*Rin chen dbang gi phreng ba*, 52 fols. In "Mkha' 'gro sNying thig", part 1 (= Snying thig ya bzhi, vol. 4). New Delhi: Trulku Tsewang Jamyang and L. Tashi, 1971, pp. 121–226.

dKon-mchog rgyal-dbang (16th cent.)
mTshan ldan bla ma dam pa mnyam med chos dbang rgyal mtshan rnam par thar pa / rin po che nor bu'i phreng ba, 129 fols. (xylograph). NGMPP reel no. L 66/5 (= 389/13–390/1).

bsKal-bzang Padma dbang-phyug, Third rDo-rje brag Rig-'dzin (b. 1720)
Lha rigs kyi btsun pa bskal bzang padma'i ming can rang nyid kyi rtogs par brjod pa 'jam gnyen ut pa la gzhad pa'i dga' tshal gzhon nu bun du'i yid 'phrog, 185 fols. Leh: Pema Choden, 1973, pp. 1–370.

Khyung-po ras-pa (b. 1715)
rJe btsun mi 'gyur dpal gyi sgron ma'i rnam thar dad pa'i gdung sel, 119 fols. Thimphu: National Library of Bhutan, 1984.

mKhas-btsun bzang-po (1921–2009)
Bod du sgrub brgyad shing rta mched brgyad las snga 'gyur rnying ma'i bla ma brgyud pa'i rnam thar ngo mtshar rgya mtsho'i stod cha: Biographical Dictionary of Tibet and Tibetan Buddhism 3 (= The Rñiṅ-ma-pa Tradition 1). Dharamsala: Library of Tibetan Works and Archives, 1973.

____*Bod du sgrub brgyad shing rta mched brgyad las snga 'gyur rnying ma'i bla ma brgyud pa'i rnam thar ngo mtshar rgya mtsho'i smad cha:* Biographical Dictionary of Tibet and Tibetan Buddhism 4 (= The Rñiṅ-ma-pa Tradition 2). Dharamsala: Library of Tibetan Works and Archives, 1973.

____*Bod du sgrub brgyad shing rta mched brgyad las 'brug pa bka' brgyud kyi bla ma brgyud pa'i rnam thar:* Biographical Dictionary of Tibet and Tibetan Buddhism 8 (= The bKa'-brgyud-pa Tradition 2). Dharamsala: Library of Tibetan Works and Archives, 1981.

mKhyen-rab rgya-mtsho, 'Dul-'dzin (16th cent.)
Sangs rgyas gnyis pa'i chos 'byung dris lan nor bu'i phreng ba, 306 fols. (manuscipt). Gangtok: Dzongsar Chentse Labrang, 1981.

Gar-dbang rdo-rje, mNga'-ris gter-ston (1640–1685)
bKa' rdzogs pa chen po rdor sems thugs kyi me long las lo rgyus gsal byed sgron me, 5 fols. In "rDor sems thugs kyi me long and Thugs rje chen po rtsa gsum snying thig: Liturgico – contemplative practices and prophecies revealed by Gter-ston Gar-dbang-rdo-rje." Darjeeling: Chopal Lama, 1984, pp. 19–27.

____*Thugs rje chen po rtsa gsum sñiṅ thig*. "A Cycle of Buddhist practice focussing upon a form of Avalokiteśvara", 193 pp. Dalhousie: Damchoe Sangpo, 1985.

____*rDor sems thugs kyi me long*. In "rDor sems thugs kyi me long and Thugs rje chen po rtsa gsum snying thig: Liturgico – contemplative practices and prophecies revealed by Gter-ston Gar-dbang-rdo-rje", 94 pp. Darjeeling: Chopal Lama, 1984, pp. 1–196.

Gu-ru Tshe-brtan rgyal-mtshan (12th/13th cent.)

gNam sgo zla gam lam yig, 16 fols. (manuscript). NGMPP reel no. L 278/9.

____*sBas yul dkar po ljongs kyi gnas yig,* 6 fols. In "Tibetan Guide to Places of Pilgrimage: A Collection of Guidebooks (*gnas yig*) to Places of Pilgrimage in Tibet and China from the Library of Burmiok Athing T. D. Densapa." Dharamsala: Library of Tibetan Works and Archives, 1985, pp. 193–205.

____*sBas yul gnam sgo zla gam gyis (= gyi) gnas yig lam byang gsal ba'i me long,* 9 fols. (manuscript). NGMPP reel no. L 290/2.

____*sBas yul padma'i tshal gyi gnas yig kun tu gsal ba'i me long,* 20 fols. Gangtok: Bla-ma Zla-ba and Sherab Gyaltsen, 1983.

Grags-pa mtha'-yas (1469–1531)

rNal 'byor gyi dbang phyug grags pa mtha' yas dpal bzang po'i rnam thar mgur 'bum ngo mtshar nor bu'i phreng ba, 242 fols. Gangtok: Gonpo Tseten, 1977.

Grub-mchog dbang-po, Zhabs-drung (1563–1618)

Bla ma dam pa'i gsung rgyun gyi rim pa mthong dga'i nor bu'i phreng ba 'dod kun 'byung, 89 fols. (manuscript). NGMPP reel no. L 957/2.

Grub-thob Blo-bzang lHa-mchog (1672–1747)

Lho brag gro bo lung grub thob blo bzang lha mchog rin po che'i rnam thar, 98 fols., n.p., n.d.

dGe-'dun chos-'phel (1905–1951)

dBu ma'i zab gnad snying po dril ba'i legs bshad klu sgrub dgongs rgyan, 67 fols. (typeset edition). Gangtok: Sherab Gyaltsen, 1983.

'Gro-'dul las-'phro gling-pa (1488–1553)

Rig 'dzin chen po gter bton (= ston) las 'phro gling pa'i dus gsum gyi skye brgyud dang rnam par thar pa che long tsam zhig bkod pa me tog 'phreng mdzes, 325 fols. Gangtok & Delhi: Gonpo Tseten, 1979.

'Gyur-med Kun-bzang rnam-rgyal, Second Zhe-chen Rab-'byams-pa (b. 1710)

rGyal ba gnyis pa kun mkhyen ngag gi dbang po'i gsung rab las mdzod bdun ngal gso gsang ṭīka rnams rmad byung 'phrul gyi phyi chos ji ltar bsgrub pa'i tshul las brtsoms pa'i ngo mtshar gtam gyi gling bu skal bzang rna ba'i dga' ston, 79 fols. (manuscript). Gangtok: Dodrup Sangya Lama, 1976.

'Gyur-med Tshe-dbang mchog-grub, dGe-rtse Paṇḍita (1764–1824)

Nges don dbu ma chen po'i tshul rnam par nges pa'i gtam bde gshegs snying po'i rgyan, n.p., n.d.

____*bDe bar gshegs pa'i bstan pa thams cad kyi snying po rig pa 'dzin pa'i sde snod rdo rje theg pa snga 'gyur rgyud 'bum rin po che'i rtogs pa brjod pa lha'i rnga bo che lta bu'i gtam*, 2 vols. In "rNying ma rgyud 'bum", vols. 35–36. Thimphu: Lama Ngodrup, 1973–1975.

____*Slob dpon chen po padmas mdzad pa'i gsang sngags nang gi lam rim pa rgya cher 'grel pa sangs rgyas gnyis pa'i dgongs rgyan*, 456 fols. (= Smanrtsis Shesrig Spendzod 35). Leh: S.W. Tashigangpa, 1972, pp. 1–914.

rGod-ldem 'phru-can, Rig-'dzin (1337–1406)

gNas 'bras mo 'dzongs (= gshongs) gi lam yig, 13 fols. (manuscript). NGMPP reel no. L 278/8.

____*sBas yul spyi'i them byang*, 17 fols. In "Collected Biographies and Prophesies of the Byaṅ gter Tradition." Gangtok: Sherab Gyaltsen, 1983, pp. 463–95.

____*sBas yul 'bras mo ljongs kyi gnas yig bsdus pa*, 16 fols. In "Rare Texts of the dPal-spungs Tradition." Gangtok: Sherab Gyaltsen, 1981, pp. 357–90.

____*Yol mo gangs kyi ra ba'i gnad (= gnas) yig*, 5 fols. In "Collected Biographies and Prophecies of the Byaṅ gter Tradition." Gangtok: Sherab Gyaltsen, 1983, pp. 515–524.

____*Yol mo gangs kyi ra ba'i lung byang snying gi ṭika*, 10 fols. In "ibid", pp. 537–555.

rGyal-dbang seng-ge (b. 1628)

s*Prul sku rig 'dzin chen po gar dbang rdo rje snying po'i phyi'i rnam par thar pa nges don rgya mtsho*, 57 fols. (xylograph), n.p., n.d.

____*Bya btang 'od zer rgya mtsho'i rnam thar nges don rgya mtsho'i snying po*, 61 fols. (manuscript). NGMPP reel no. L 452/4.

rGod-tshang ras-pa (1189–1258)

Chos rje lo ras pa'i rnam par thar pa bdud rtsi'i phreng ba, 113 fols. Hsining: mTsho-sngon mi-rigs dpes-skrun khang, 1993

rGod-tshang ras-pa, sNa-tshog rang-grol (1482–1559)

rGyud kyi dgongs pa gtsor sngon pa phyag rgya chen po yi ge bzhi pa'i 'grel bshad gnyug ma'i gter mdzod, 87 fols. (xylograph), NGMPP reel no. L 956/8.

____*gTsang smyon he ru ka phyogs thams cad las rnam par rgyal ba'i rnam thar rdo rje theg pa'i gsal byed nyi ma'i snying po*, 146 fols. (xylograph). In "The Life of the Saint of Gtsaṅ" (= Śata-Piṭaka Series 79). New Delhi, 1969, pp. 1–292.

Ngag-dbang Kun-dga' bsod-nams grags-pa, A-mes zhabs (1597–1659)
dGe ba'i bshes gnyen bka' gdams pa rnams kyi dam pa'i chos 'byung ba'i tshul legs par bshad pa ngo mtshar rgya mtsho, 190 pp. Hsining: mTsho-sngon mi-rigs dpe-skrun khang, 1995.

Ngag-dbang grags-pa, sMyug-la Paṇ-chen (1458–1515)
rJe btsun kun dga' bzang po'i rnam par thar pa ris med dad pa'i spu long g.yo byed, 89 fols. In "bKa'-brgyud-pa Hagiographies", vol. 2. Tashigang: Khams-sprul Don-brgyud nyi-ma, 1971, pp. 383–560, and 112 fols., n.p., n.d.

Ngag-dbang chos-'phel (20th cent.)
La stod shel dkar chos sde dpal gyi sde chen po dga' ldan legs bshad gling gi lo rgyus dran pa'i gdung dbyangs, 74 fols. Delhi : Ngagwang Tobgye, 1985.

Ngag-dbang Chos-'phel rgya-mtsho, Lo-chen Dharma śrī (1654–1717)
sDom gsum rnam par n̄ges pa'i 'grel pa legs bshad ngo mtshar dpag bsam gyi snye ma, 317 fols. In "rNying ma bka' ma rgyas pa", vol. 37. Kalimpong: Dubjung Lama and Madha Nikunj, 1982–1983, pp. 39–671.

____*gTer chen chos kyi rgyal po'i rnam thar dad pa'i shing rta*, 177 fols. In "The Life of gTer-bdag gling-pa 'Gyur-med rdo-rje of sMin-grol gling", vol. 1. Paro: Lama Ngodrub and Sherab Drimey, 1982, pp. 1–354.

Ngag-dbang bstan-'dzin nor-bu, rDza-rong-phu bla-ma (1867–1940)
gCod yul nyon mongs zhi byed kyi bka' gter bla ma brgyud pa'i rnam mthar sbyin rlabs gter mtsho, 158 fols. (= Ngagyur Nyingmay Sungrab Series 21). Gangtok: Sonam T. Kazi.

____*Dus mthar chos smra ba'i ngag dbang bstan 'dzin nor bu'i rnam thar 'chi med bdud rtsi'i rol mtsho*, 497 fols. (xylograph), n.p., n.d.

____*sPyod yul nyon mongs zhi byed log 'dren zil gnon ltas ngan g.yang 'gug gi khrid gzhung ma rig mun sel,* 101 fols. In "Rare Tibetan Texts from Nepal: A collection of guides to holy places, lives of religious masters, and khrid yig by the famed Rdza Ro - phu Bla-ma." Dolanji: Tashi Dorje, 1976, pp. 375–577.

____*Rong phu rdza yi gangs kyi gnas yig dad pa'i gdong ldan dga' skyed dbyar gyi rnga sgra,* 14 fols. (xylograph), n.p., n.d.

Ngag-dbang rdo-rje, Nas-lung-pa (17th cent.)
Bal yul mchod rten 'phags pa shing kun dang de'i gnas gzhan rnams kyis (= kyi) dkar chag mdor bsdus, 8 fols. (xylograph). NGMPP reel no. E 816/12.

____*Bal yul 'phags pa shing kun dang de'i gnas gzhan rnams kyi dkar chag*, 10 fols. In Wylie (1970: 43–48) (Appendix B).

Ngag-dbang rnam-rgyal (b. 1628)
sPrang bhan (= ban) ngag dbang rnam rgyal bdag gi zab chos thob yig dgos 'dod kun 'byung, 31 fols. (manuscript). NGMPP reel no. L 63/1.

Ngag-dbang dpal-bzang, mKhan-po (1879–1941)
rDzogs pa chen po bla ma yang tig las gnyis ka'i yang yig nam mkha' klong chen gyi rnam par bshad pa nyi ma snang ba, 115 fols. (manuscript). In "Three Works on the Structure of Rdzogs-chen (Atiyoga) Practice by mKhan-po Ngag-dbang-dpal-bzang of Kaḥ-thog." New Delhi: B. Jamyang Norbu, 1972, pp. 215–441.
____*gZhi khregs chod skabs kyi zin bris bstan pa'i nyi ma'i zhal lung snan brgyud chu bo'i bcud 'dus*, 60 fols. (manuscript). In "Works on the practice of Mahāyoga, Anuyoga and Atiyoga according to the oral transmission of the sÑiṅ-thig Masters." Bylakuppe/ Paro: Pema Norbu & Dilgo Chentse, 1985, pp. 1–120.
____*'Od gsal rin chen snying po padma las 'brel rtsal gyi rtogs brjod ngo mtshar sgyu ma*, 147 fols. "The Autobiographical Reminiscences of Ngag-dbang-dpal-bzang, Late Abbot of Kaḥ-thog Monastery." (= Ngagyur Nyingmay Sungrab 1). Gangtok: Sonam T. Kazi, 1969, pp. 1–293.

Ngag-dbang Blo-gros grags-pa (1920–1975)
dPal ldan jo nang pa'i chos 'byung rgyal ba'i chos tshul gsal byed zla ba'i sgron me, 591 pp. Hsining: mTsho-sngon mi-rigs dpe-skrun khang, 1992.

Ngag-dbang Blo-bzang rgya-mtsho, Fifth Dalai Lama (1617–1682)
Gangs can yul gyi sa la dpyod pa'i tho ris kyi rgyal blon gtso bor brjod pa'i deb ther / rdzogs ldan gzhon nu dga' ston dpyid kyi rgyal mo'i glu dbyangs, 202 pp. Beijing: Mi-rigs dpe-skrun-khang, 1988.
____*rGyal ba'i dbang po thams cad mkhyen cing gzigs pa chen po'i gsang ba'i rnam thar rgya can ma:* "A Record of the Visionary Experiences of the Fifth Dalai Lama Ngag-dbang-blo-bzang-rgya-mtsho", 212 fols. (= Smanrtis Shesrig Spendzod 42). Leh: S. W. Tashigangpa, 1972, pp. 5–507.
____*Byang pa'i rig 'dzin chen po ngag gi dbang po'i rnam par thar pa ngo mtshar bkod pa'i rgya mtsho,* 64 fols. In "bKa' ma mdo dbang gi bla ma brgyud pa'i rnam thar" (= Smanrtsis Shesrig Spendzod 37). Leh: S. W. Tashigangpa, 1972, pp. 427–553.
____*Za hor gyi ban de ngag dbang blo bzang rgya mtsho'i 'di snang 'khrul pa'i rol rtsed rtogs brjod kyi tshul du bkod pa du kū la'i gos bzang pa*, 3 vols., 718 pp., 532 pp. & 454 pp. Hsining: Bod-ljongs mi-dmangs dpe-skrun khang, 1989–1991.
____*Zab pa dang rgya che ba'i dam pa'i chos kyi thob yig gang gā'i chu rgyun.* In "Collected Works (Gsung-'bum) of the Vth Dalai Lama, Ngag-dbang Blo-bzang rgya-mtsho", vols. 1–4. Gangtok: Sikkim Research Institute of Tibetology, 1991–1992.

____*Zur thams cad mkhyen pa chos dbyings rang grol gyi rnam thar theg mchog bstan pa'i shing rta,* 121 fols. (xylograph). In "Collected Works (Gsung-'bum) of the Vth Dalai Lama, Ngag-dbang Blo-bzang rgya-mtsho", vol. 9. Gangtok: Sikkim Research Institute of Tibetology, 1992, pp. 1–242.

Ngag-dbang bSod-nams rgyal-mtshan (19th cent.)

Lhar bcas 'gro ba'i mchod sdong jo bo sku mched gsum sngon byung gi gtam rabs brjod pa rin chen baiḍūrya sngon po'i pi vaṃ, 61 pp. Dharamsala: Bod-ljongs mnga'-ris rig-gzhung gces-skyong khang, 1988.

Chos-kyi rgya-mtsho, Kaḥ-thog Si-tu (1880–1925)

Si tu chos kyi rgya mtsho gangs ljongs dbus gtsang gnas slor lam yig nor bu zla shel gyi me long, 270 fols. (xylograph). Tashijong: Sungrab Nyamso Gyunphel Parkhang, 1972.

Chos-kyi dbang-phyug, Brag-dkar rta-so sPrul-sku (1775–1837)

dKar ye dngos grub mtsho gling gi gnas bshad lo rgyus ngang pa'i rgyal po'i mgrin glu, 5 fols. (manuscript). NGMPP reel-no. L 381/4.

____*Grub pa'i gnas chen brag dkar rta so'i gnas dang gdan rabs bla ma brgyud pa'i lo rgyus mdo tsam brjod pa mos ldan dad pa'i gdung sel drang srong dga' ba'i dal gtam*, 48 fols. (manuscript). NGMPP reel no. L 380/5–381/1.

____*dGon gnas mchog dngos grub kun 'byung gling gi lo rgyus gnas bshad nyung 'dus su bkod pa*, 5 fols. (manuscript). NGMPP reel no. L 381/4.

____*sNga 'gyur gsang chen rnying ma rgyud 'bum gyi glegs bam yongs rdzogs gzheng tshul dkar chag tu bkod pa rdzogs ldan snang ba gsar ba'i dga' ston*, 14 fols. (manuscript), n.p., n.d.

____*Chos ldan sa skyongs 'bur pa mi rje'i gdung rab (= rabs) lo rgyus dri med baiḍūrya'i 'phreng ba* (manuscript), 18 fols. (manuscript). NGMPP reel nos. L 380/5–L 381/1.

____*dPal ldan mgur rigs mdo chen brgyud pa'i lo rgyus tshangs pa'i do shal*, 19 fols.

____*dPal ldan gzhung 'brug pa bka' brgyud gser 'phreng gi bla ma brgyud pa'i rnam thar dang phyag rgya chen po'i spyi don ngo mtshar snyan gi sgra dbyangs*, 78 fols. (manuscript). NGMPP reel nos. L 380/5–L 381/1.

____*dPal ldan rig 'dzin kaḥ thog pa chen po tshe dbang nor bu'i zhabs kyi rnam thar mdor bsdus dad pa'i sa bon*, 8 fols. (manuscript). In "Collected Works of Kaḥ-thog Rig-'dzin chen-po Tshe-dbang nor-bu", vol. 1. Dalhousie: Damchoe Sangpo, 1976, pp. 377–91.

____*dPal rig 'dzin chen po rdo rje tshe dbang nor bu'i zhabs kyis rnam par thar pa'i cha shas brjod pa ngo mtshar dad pa'i rol mtsho*, 187 fols. (manuscript). In "Collected Works (Gsung-'bum) of Kaḥ-thog Tshe-dbang-nor-bu", vol. 1. Dalhousie: Damchoe Sangpo, 1976, pp. 1–376.

____*'Phags mchog thugs rje chen po rang byung wa ti bzang po'i rnam par thar pa ngo mtshar rmad du byung ba'i gtam dad pa'i nyin byed phyogs brgyar 'dren pa'i rta ljangs,* 56 fols. NGMPP reel nos. L380/5–381/1.

____*Bya bral ba chos kyi dbang phyug gi rang 'tshang lhug par brjod pa 'khrul snang sgyu ma'i rol rtsed,* 265 fols. (manuscript). NGMPP reel no. L 376/9–L 377/1.

____*Byang gter thugs sgrub yang tig gces sgron gyi khrid yig gi bla ma brgyud pa'i lo rgyus rnam thar kha bskong nyung gsal du bkod pa,* 8 fols. (manuscript). NGMPP reel no. L 380/5–L 381/1.

____*gTer dbon rig 'dzin brgyud pa'i gdung rabs lo rgyus tshangs pa'i do shal,* 18 fols. (manuscript). In "A history of the descendants of Gter-ston Bstan-gnyis gling-pa by Brag-dkar-rta-so sPrul-sku Mi-pham-chos-kyi dbang-phyug with other of the author's works." Delhi: Lama Dawa, 1982, pp. 1–36.

____*Zab rgyas chos tshul rgya mtsho las rang skal du ji ltar thob pa'i yi ge rnam grol bdud rtsi'i bum bzang,* 379 fols. (manuscript). NGMPP reel no. L 377/3.

Chos-kyi dbang-phyug, Sixth Zhwa-dmar-pa (1584–1630)

Bal yul du bgrod pa'i lam yig nor bu spel ma'i 'phreng ba, 48 fols. (manuscript). NGMPP reel no. L 387/3.

Chos-kyi 'byung-gnas, Eighth Si-tu Paṇ-chen (1699–1774)

Ta'i si tur 'bod pa karma bstan pa'i nyin byed kyi rang tshul dangs por brjod pa dri bral shel gyi me long, 371 fols. (xylograph) (= Śata-Piṭaka Series 77). New Delhi: Lokesh Chandra, 1968.

Chos-kyi 'byung-gnas, Eighth Si-tu Paṇ-chen (1699–1774) & **'Be-lo Tshe-dbang kun-khyab** (18th cent.)

sGrub brgyud karma kaṃ tshang brgyud pa rin po che'i rnam par thar pa rab 'byams nor bu zla ba chu shel gyi 'phreng ba, 2 vols., 341 fols. & 350 fols. New Delhi: D. Gyaltsan & Kesang Legshay, 1972.

Chos-skyabs dpal-bzang (1536–1625)

mKhas grub chen po bsod nams blo gros kyi nam par thar pa mthong ba don ldan dad pa'i gsal 'debs, 86 fols. (manuscript). Dalhousie/Delhi: Damchoe Sangpo, 1985, pp. 1–172.

____*mKhas grub bsod nams blo gros kyi gsang ba'i nam thar,* 16 fols. (manuscript). Dalhousie/Delhi: Damchoe Sangpo, 1985, pp. 173–203.

Chos-grags bzang-po (14th cent.)

Kun mkhyen dri med 'od zer gyi rnam thar mthong ba don ldan, 46 fols. In "Bima sNying thig", part 3 (= Snying thig ya bzhi, vol. 9). New Delhi: Trulku Tsewang Jamyang and L. Tashi, 1971, pp. 1–91.

Chos-dbang rgyal-mtshan (1484–1549)
mTshan ldan bla ma dam pa chos dbang rgyal mtshan gyi mgur 'bum, 241 fols. (manuscript). NGMPP reel nos. L 65/5–L 66/1.

____*mTshan ldan bla ma dam pa mnyam med chos dbang rgyal mtshan gyi rnam par thar pa / rin po che'i nor bu'i phreng ba*, 129 fols. (blockprint). NGMPP reel-nos. L 66/5 (= L 389/13–390/1).

'Jam-dbyangs rgyal-mtshan, mKhan-chen (b. 1929)
gSang chen bstan pa'i chu 'go rgyal ba kaḥ thog pa'i lo rgyus mdor bsdus brjod pa 'chi med lha'i rnga sgra ngo mtshar rna ba'i dga' ston, 240 pp. Chengdu: Si-khron mi-rigs dpe-skrun khang, 1996.

'Jam-dbyangs bstan-pa rgya-mtsho, Brag-dgon sprul-sku (1824–1906)
dBus gtsang gi gnas bskor byed tshul rag bsdud tsam zhig brjod pa mi brjed dran pa'i gsal 'debs gzur gnas mkhas pa'i rna rgyan, 44 fols. (manuscript). Dharamsala: Library of Tibetan Works and Archives, Acc. no. 11013.

'Jigs-bral Ye-shes rdo-rje, Second bDud-'joms Rin-po-che (1904–1987)
gSang sngags snga 'gyur rnying ma pa bstan pa'i rnam gzhag mdo tsam brjod pa legs bshad snang ba'i dga' ston, 232 fols. (xylograph). Kalimpong: Dudzom Rinpoche, 1967.

'Jigs-med grags-pa, Bo-dong Paṇ-chen (1375–1451)
rGyal rtse chos rgyal gyi rnam par thar pa dad pa'i lo thog dngos grub char 'beb, 379 fols. Hsining: Bod ljongs mi dmangs spe krun khang, 1987.

'Jigs-med gling-pa (1729–1791)
rDzogs pa chen po klong chen snying tig gi gdod ma'i mgon po'i lam gyi rim pa'i khrid yig ye shes bla ma, 83 fols. (manuscript). In "Klong chen snying thig", vol. 3. Paro: Lama Ngodrup, 1976, pp. 298–462.

'Jigs-med bzang-po (15th/16th cent.) & **dBang-phyug dpal-ldan** (15th/16th cent.)
dPal ldan bla ma dam pa chos legs mtshan can gyi rnam thar, 150 fols. (xylograph). NGMPP reel no. L 66/7-67/1.

Nyi-ma rgyal-mtshan, sNar-thang mkhan-chen (1225–1305)
Zhus lan nor bu'i phreng ba lha chos bdun ldan gyi bla ma brgyud pa rnams kyi rnam thar, 255 pp. In "Jo bo rje dpal ldan a ti sha'i rnam thar bka' gdams pha chos." Hsining: mTsho-sngon mi-rigs dpe-skrun khang, 1994, pp. 299–504.

Nyi-ma'i 'od-zer, mNga'-bdag Myang (1124–1192)

Chos 'byung me tog snying po sbrang rtsi' bcud, 544 pp. (= Gangs can rig mdzod 4). Lhasa: Bod-ljongs mi-dmangs dpe-skrun khang, 1988.

gTer-ston sprul-pa lha-btsun (?–?)

sBas yul padma'i tshal gyi lam byang, 4 fols. In "Collected Biographies and Prophesies of the Byang gter Tradition." Gangtok: Sherab Gyaltsen, 1983, pp. 507–13.

sTag-sgang mkhas-mchog Ngag-dbang blo-gros, Gu-ru bkra-shis (18th/19th cent.)

bsTan pa'i snying po gsang chen snga 'gyur nges don zab mo'i chos kyi 'byung ba gsal bar byed pa'i legs bshad mkhas pa dga' byed ngo mtshar gtam gyi rol mtsho, 5 vols. Delhi: Lama Ngodrup and Sherab Drimed, 1986, and 1076 pp. Hsining: mTsho-sngon mi-rigs par-khang, 1990.

bsTan-gnyis gling-pa, Rig-'dzin (1480–1535)

Rigs (sic) *'dzin bstan gnyis gling pa'i rnam thar las / rnal lam lung bstan gyi skor,* 83 fols. (manuscript). In "Collected songs of spiritual realisation and visionary writings of bsTan-gñis-gliṅ-pa Padma-tshe-dbaṅ-rgyal-po." Delhi: Dawa Lama, 1982, pp. 1–167.

bsTan-pa'i sgron-me (b. 1933)

Gsang chen rnying ma' i 'dus sde 'og min o rgyan smin grol gling nges pa don gyi dga' ba'i tshal chen po'i dkar chag rang bzhin bden brjod ngo mtshar shel gyi adarśa, 397 pp. Hsining: Zi-ling mi-rigs par-khang, 1992.

bsTan-'dzin Chos-kyi nyi-ma, Fourth Khams-sprul Rin-po-che (1734–1779)

Yul chen po nye ba'i tshandho ha bal po'i gnas kyi dkar chag gangs can rna ba'i bdud rtsi, 32 fols. *Kailash: A Journal of Himalayan Studies* 3:2, 1975, pp. 89–144.

bsTan-'dzin nyi-ma (19th cent.)

gNas chen mo le gangs dang gu ru gsang phug gi dkar chag kun snang gsal sgron, 16 fols. NGMPP reel-no. L 407/5.

bsTan 'dzin nor-bu, sKyabs-rje Brag-dkar-ba (1899–1959)

gDan rabs lo rgyus drang srong dga' ba'i dal gtam gyi kha skong, 33 fols. In "sKyabs rje brag dkar pa dkar brgyud bstan 'dzin nor bu'i gsung 'bum skor" (= Smanrtsis Shesrig Spendzod 142). New Delhi 1996, pp. 1–66.

bsTan-'dzin nor-bu, Third Yol-mo sprul-sku (1598–1644)

rTogs brjod mkhas pa'i rna rgyan, 19 fols. In "The Autobiography and Collected Writings (*gsung thor bu*) of the Third Rig-'dzin Yol-mo-ba sPrul-sku bstan-'dzin nor-bu", vol. 1. Dalhousie: Damchoe Sangpo, 1977, pp. 6–44.

____*Rang gi rtogs pa brjod pa rdo rje sgra ma'i brgyud (= rgyud) mangs,* 102 fols. In "ibid", pp. 63–267.

____*La phyi gnya' nang skor gyi lam yig*, 5 fols. In "Collected Writings of Yol-mo sprul-sku bsTan-'dzin nor-bu." Delhi, Lama Dawa, 1982, pp. 77-87.

bsTan-'dzin rnam-dag (b. 1926)

sNga rabs bod kyi byung ba brjod pa'i 'bel gtam lung gi snying po. Delhi: Paljor Publications, 1996.

____*Bod yul gnas kyi lam yig gsal ba'i dmig bu*, 57 pp., n.p., n.d.

bsTan-'dzin ras-pa (1644/46–1723)

rJe btsun bstan 'dzin ras pa de nyid kyi gsang ba'i rnam thar sa khyis phan gyis / mgur ma'i kha 'gros gnas ngo bzung tshul dkar chag dang bcas chos tshan lnga, 52 fols. (xylograph). NGMPP reel no. L 410/10.

____*rNal 'byor gyi dbang phyug bstan 'dzin ras pa'i rnam thar mdzad pa nyung ngu gcig*, 17 fols. (xylograph). NGMPP reel no. E 1791/12.

____*rNal 'byor gyi dbang phyug bstan-'dzin ras pa'i zhal gdams mgur du gsungs pa rnams*, 67 fols. (xylograph). NGMPP reel no. L 257/27.

mTha'-bral rdo-rje (20th cent.)

mTshungs med dpal mgon bla ma dam pa gting skyes dgon pa byang gi mchog gi sprul gyi 'khrungs rabs bcu'i rnam par thar pa mdo tsam brjod pa. Thimphu/Delhi: Kunzang Tobgyal & Mani Dorje, 1979.

Dil-mgo mKhyen-brtse Rin-po-che (1910–1991)

Rig pa 'dzin pa'i sde nod rdo rje theg pa snga 'gyur rgyud 'bum rin po che'i chos kyi bzhugs byang ratna'i do shal, 16 fols., n.p., n.d.

mDo-sngags bstan-pa'i nyi-ma, Bod-pa sPrul-sku (1898–1959)

Kun mkhyen bla ma'i zhal lung sangs rgyas lag 'chang, 14 fols. In "Collected Texts of the rNying-ma-pa rDzogs-chen tradition." Gangtok/Delhi: Pema Thinley, 1985, pp. 311–330.

____*lTa grub shan 'byed gnad kyi sgron me yi tshig don rnam bshad 'jam dbyangs dgongs rgyan*, 134 fols. (manuscript), n.p., n.d.

____*dBu ma bzhi brgya pa'i tshig don rnam par bshad pa klu dbang dgongs* rgyan, 134 fols. (xylograph) (= Treasures of the Mi-pham philosophical Tradition, vol. 1). Junbesi: Sherpa Lama Ngawang Topgay, 1978.

____*Sher phyin mngon par rtogs pa'i rgyan gyi tshig don rnam par bshad pa mi pham zhal lung*, 133 fols. (xylograph) (= Treasures of the Mi-pham philosophical Tradition, vol. 2). Junbesi: Sherpa Lama Ngawang Topgay, 1978.

rDo-rje dpal, g.Yung-ston-pa (1284–1365)

Lo rgyus rgyal ba g.yung gis mdzad pa, 9 fols. In "mKha' 'gro snying thig", part 2 (= Snying thig ya bzhi, vol. 5). New Delhi: Trulku Tsewang Jamyang & L. Tashi, 1971, pp. 405–22.

Nam-mkha' rgyal-mtshan, lHo-brag Grub-chen (1326–1401)

lHo brag grub chen bka' 'bum, 2 vols. "Collected Writings of lHo-brag Grub-chen Nam-mkha' rgyal-mtshan." New Delhi: Tshering Dargye, 1972, and "The Collected Works (Gsung-'bum) of lHo-brag Grub-chen Nam-mkha' rgyal-mtshan." Thimphu/ Delhi: Kunsang Tobgyel, 1985.

Nam-mkha' rdo-rje (1486–1553)

dPal ldan bla ma dam pa sprul sku nam mkha' rgyal mtshan dpal bzang po'i rnam par thar pa / dgos 'dod kun 'byung nor bu'i 'phreng ba, 148 fols. (xylograph). NGMPP reel no. L 18/14. Also in "Bka' brgyud gser 'phreng chen mo: The Biographies of Eminent Gurus in the Transmission Lineage of Teachings of the 'Ba'-ra Dkar-brgyud-pa Sect." Dehradun: Ngawang Gyaltsen and Ngawang Lungtok, 1970, vol. 2 (manuscript), pp. 394–521.

sNa-tshogs rang-grol, rTse-le[gs] (1605–1677)

Chos rje mi pham mgon pos dri ba snga phyi tha dad mdzad pa'i dri lan thor bu'i skor rnams phyogs gcig tu bsdebs, 201 fols. In "The Complete Works of rTse-le rGod-tshang-pa Padma-legs-grub", vol. 5. Gangtok: Mgon-potshe-brtan, 1979, pp. 1–405.

____*sBas yul lam yig padma dkar po las gsungs pa'i gu ru rdo rje khro lod kyi dbang chen,* 23 fols. In "The Complete Works of rTse-le rGod-tshang-pa Padma-legs-grub", vol. 6. Gangtok: Mgon-potshe-brtan, 1979, pp. 217–62.

____*Rig 'dzin chen po 'ja' tshon snying po sku tshe myug gi rnam thar mdor bsdus ngo mtshar snang byed,* 15 fols. In "The Complete Works of rTse-le rGod-tshang-pa Padma-legs-grub", vol. 1, Gangtok: Mgon-po-tshe-brtan, 1979, pp. 407–433.

Padma dkar-po, Fourth 'Brug-chen (1527–1592)

Chos 'byung bstan pa'i padma rgyas pa'i nyin byed (= Gangs can rigs mdzod 19), 464 pp. Lhasa: Bod-ljongs bod-yig dpe-rnying dpe-skrun khang, 1992.

Padma rnam-rgyal, Third Zhe-chen rgyal-tshab (1871–1926)
sNga 'gyur rdo rje theg pa gtso bor gyur pa'i sgrub brgyud shing rta brgyad kyi byung ba brjod pa'i gtam mdor bsdus legs bshad padma dkar po'i rdzing bu, 283 fols. (manuscript) (= Smanrtsis Shesrig Spendzod 10). Leh: S.W. Tashigangpa, 1971.

Padma 'phrin-las, Second rDo-rje brag Rig-'dzin (1640–1718)
'Khor ba dbyings sgrol gyi khrid yig sbas don gsal ba lam bzang snying po, 107 fols. In "Rituals of Rdo-rje-brag", vol. 2 (= Smanrtsis Shesrig Spendzod 66). Leh: S. W. Tashigangpa, 1973, pp 467–639.

____*'Dus pa'i mdo dbang gi bla ma brgyud pa'i rnam thar ngo mtshar dad pa'i phreng ba,* 213 fols. In "bKa' ma mdo dbang gi bla ma brgyud pa'i rnam thar" (= Smanrtsis Shesrig Spendzod 37). Leh: S. W. Tashigangpa, 1972, pp. 1–425.

Padma dbang-'dus (b. 1697)
mKha' mnyam 'gro ba'i rtsug (= gtsug) brgyan (= rgyan) pad ma dbang 'dus kyi rnam par thar pa gsal bar bkod pa la rmongs mun thib po sal (= sel) ba'i sgron me, 176 fols. In "Autobiographies of Three Spiritual Masters of Kutang." Thimphu: Kunsang Topgay & Mani Dorji, 1979, pp. 145–495.

dPal-ldan tshul-khrims (1904–1972)
Sangs rgyas g.yung drung bon gyi bstan pa'i byung ba brjod pa'i legs bshad skal pa bzang po'i mgrin rgyan rab gsal chu shel nor bu do shel, 521 pp. Lhasa: Bod ljongs mi dmangs dpe skrun khang, 1988.

'Phrin-las chos-'phel (?–?)
gNas chen shel gyi ri bo 'brug sgra'i dkar chag mthong ba don ldan dad pa'i skya rengs, 18 fols. (manuscript). NGMPP reel no. E 2756/15.

'Phrin-las bdud-'joms, Rig-'dzin mGon-gnang-pa (1726–1789)
Gu ru sū rya seng ge'i rnam thar mdor bsdus, 36 fols. (manuscript). NGMPP reel-no. E 2691/6.

Byang-chub brtson-'grus (1817–1856)
rDo rje 'dzin pa chen po 'phrin las mnga' khyab mchog gi rdo rje'am byang chub brtson 'grus rtogs pa brjod pa kyi go mtshar nor bu'i snying po, 172 fols. (xylograph). 2 vols., n.p., n.d.

Byams-pa phun-tshogs, gNas Rab-'byams-pa (1503–1581)
mKhas grub chen po byams pa phun tshogs kyi rnam thar ngo mtshar snang ba'i nyin byed yid bzhin nor bu dgos 'dod kun 'byung dad pa'i gsal 'debs, 93 fols. (xylograph). NGMPP reel no. L 783/3.

Blo-gros rgyal-mtshan, Sog-bzlog-pa (1552–1624)
Slob dpon sangs rgyas gnyis pa padma 'byung gnas kyi rnam pa thar pa yid kyi mun sel, 128 fols., n.p., n.d.

Blo-bzang grags-pa, Tsong-kha-pa (1357–1419)
dKa' gnad chen po brgyad kyi brjed byang, 16 fols. (xylograph). Zhol par-khang.
____*rJe btsun red mda' ba chen po la zhu yig*, 7 fols. In "The Tibetan Tripiṭaka. Tokyo/ Kyoto: Suzuki Research Foundation, 1955–1961", vol. 153, pp. 57.2.5–60.2.3.
____*Bla ma dbu ma pa la mdo khams su phul ba*, 3 fols. In "ibid", vol. 153, pp. 60.2.3–61.1.1.
____*lHo brag mkhan chen phyag rdor ba la zhu lan sman mchog bdud rtsi'i phreng ba*, 1 fol. In "ibid", vol. 153, pp. 61.1.1–61.4.2.

Blo-bzang 'phrin-las, Dar-han mKhan-sprul (19th cent.)
'Jam mgon chos kyi rgyal po tsong kha pa chen po'i rnam pa thar pa thub bstan mdzes pa'i rgyan gcig, 648 fols. Hsining: mTsho-sngon mi-rigs dpe-skrun-khang, 1981.

Blo-bzang tshul-khrims, Čaqar dGe-bshes (1740–1810)
rJe thams cad mkhyen pa tsong kha pa chen po'i rnam thar go sla bar brjod pa bde legs kun gyi 'byung gnas, 88 fols. In "The Collected Works (gSung-'bum) of Cha-har dGe-bshes Blo-bzang-Tshul-khrims." Reproduced from a set of xylographic prints from the Peking blocks. New Delhi: Chatring Jansar, 1971, vol. 2, pp. 7–183.

Ma-pham rdo-rje (1460–1530)
rNal 'byor gyi dbang phyug grags pa mtha' yas dpal bzang po'i rnam thar mgur 'bum ngo mtshar nor bu'i phreng ba, 242 fols. (manuscript). Gangtok: Gonpo Tseten, 1977.

Mi-'gyur rdo-rje, rDo-dmar Zhabs-drung (b. 1675)
gNam sgo zla gam gyi nges pa brjod pa sum rtse na dga' ma'i glu dbyangs, 5 fols. In "The Collected Works (gsung thor bu) of rDo-dmar Zhabs-drung Mi-'gyur rdo-rje." New Delhi: Ngagwang Tobgay, 1981, pp. 373–381.
____*gNam sgo zla gam gyi ngos 'dzin phan bde snying po*, 12 fols. In "ibid", pp. 355–371.

Mi-pham dGe-legs rnam-par rgyal-ba, Bod mkhas-pa (b. 1618)
rJe btsun grub pa'i dbang phyug dam pa dpag bsam ye shes zhabs kyi rnam par thar pa mchog gi spyod yul rgya mtsho'i snying po, 67 fols. (xylograph). NGMPP reel no. L 13/5.

Mi-pham rgya-mtsho, 'Jam-mgon (1846–1912)

Nges shes rin po che'i sgron me, 27 fols. In "Collected Writings of 'Ju Mi-pham rgya-mtsho", vol. 8 (= Ngagyur Nyingmay Sungrab 67). Gangtok: Sonam Tobgay Kazi, 1976, pp. 71–123.

____*lCang skya'i lta mgur gyi mchan 'grel*, 23 fols. In "Collected Writings of 'Ju Mi-pham rgya-mtsho", vol. 3 (= Ngagyur Nyingmay Sungrab 62). Gangtok: Sonam Tobgay Kazi, 1976, pp. 821–67.

____*Don rnam par nges pa shes rab ral gri*, 17 fols. In "Collected Writings of 'Ju Mi-pham rgya-mtsho", vol. 3 (= Ngagyur Nyingmay Sungrab 60). Gangtok: Sonam Tobgay Kazi, 1976, pp. 787–820.

____*Theg pa chen po rgyud bla ma'i bstan bcos kyi mchan 'grel mi pham zhal lung*, 106 fols. In "Collected Works of 'Ju Mi-pham rgya-mtsho", vol. 3 (= Ngagyur Nyingmay Sungrab 60). Gangtok: Sonam Tobgay Kazi, 1976, pp. 349–562.

____*bDe gshegs snying po'i stong thun seng ge'i nga ro*, 22 fols. In "ibid", pp. 563–608.

____*dBu ma rgyan gyi rnam bshad 'jam dbyangs bla ma dgyes pa'i zhal lung*, 208 fols. In "Collected Writings of 'Ju Mi-pham rgya-mtsho", vol. 12 (= Ngagyur Nyingmay Sungrab 71). Gangtok: Sonam Tobgay Kazi, 1976, pp. 1–416.

____*gZhan stong khas len seng ge'i nga ro*, 20 fols. In "Collected Writings of 'Ju Mi-pham rgya-mtsho", vol. 11 (= Ngagyur Nyingmay Sungrab 70). Gangtok: Sonam Tobgay Kazi, 1976, pp. 359–400.

____*Yid bzhin mdzod kyi grub mtha' bsdus pa*, 38 fols. In "Klong-chen Rab-'byams-pa: *Theg pa chen po'i man ngag gi bstan bcos yid bzhin rin po che'i mdzod kyi 'grel pa padma dkar po*", vol. 2. Gangtok: Dodrupchen Rinpoche, n.d., pp. 924–999.

____*Le'u bco brgyad pa'i tshig 'grel*, 7 fols. In "ibid", pp. 1176–89.

____*gSang 'grel phyogs bcu'i mun sel gyi spyi don 'od gsal snying po*, 258 fols. In "rNying ma bka' ma rgyas pa", vol. 27. Kalimpong: Dubjung Lama and Madhav Nikunj, 1982–1983, pp. 209–467.

Mi-pham phun-tshogs shes-rab, sTag-rtse sku-skye (1654–1715)

rJe btsun rdo rje 'chang dngos mi pham ngag dbang snyan grags dpal bzang po'i rnam par thar pa ngo mtshar rgya mtsho'i zlos gar, 126 fols. (xylograph). In "The Biography of the Second sDing-po-che Cog-gra Mi-pham-ngag-dbang-snyan-grags-dpal-bzang and Other Biographical Material Connected with the 'Brug-pa Dkar-brgyud-pa Tradition." Darjeeling: Chopal Lama, 1984, pp. 273–523.

____*Grub dbang rang rig zhabs kyi rnam thar la gsol ba 'debs pa*, 7 fols. (xylograph). NGMPP reel no. L 100/22.

____*Grub dbang rang rig ras pa'i sku bstod kyi 'grel bshad rdo rje gsung pa'i mdzes rgyan,* 11 fols. (xylograph). NGMPP reel no. L 100/24.

sMan-lha phun-tshogs, Dol-po mkhan-po (20th/21st cent.)

Nepāl nang pa'i gnas yig dngul dkar me long, 123 pp. Kathmandu, 1996.

gTsug-lag phreng-ba, Second dPa'-bo (1504–1566)

Chos 'byung mkhas pa'i dga' ston, 2 vols., 1527 pp. Beijing: Mi-rigs dpe-skrun-khang, 1986.

bTsun-pa Chos-legs (1437–1521)

Thugs rje chen po'i dmar khrid don tshan lnga pa, 123 fols. (xylograph). NGMPP reel no. L 263/4.

Tshe-dbang 'Chi-med mgon-po, mDo-chen-pa (1755–1807)

Gur gyi sngags ban tshe dbang 'chi med mgon po'i rang tshul chu babs su brjod pa lhung lhung snyan pa'i chu sgra, 80 fols. (manuscript). In "Collected Writings and Autobiographical Material of mDo-chen-pa Tshe-dbaṅ-'chi-med-mgon-po." Dalhousie: Damchoe Sangpo, 1979, pp. 11–163.

____*Rig 'dzin chen po karma bdud 'joms kyi rnam par thar pa gsal bar byed pa'i nyin byed ngo mtshar snang ba'i gter mdzod*, 133 fols. (manuscript). Delhi: Lama Dawa, 1982.

Tshe-dbang nor-bu, Kaḥ-thog Rig-'dzin (1698–1755)

bKa' tha ma don rnam par nges pa nges don snying po'i mdo dkar chag bsam 'phel nor bu'i phreng ba, 5 fols. In "Collected Works of Kaḥ-thog Rig-'dzin chen-po Tshe-dbang nor-bu", vol. 5. Damchoe Sangpo, 1976, pp. 517–525.

____*dPal rig pa 'dzin pa chen po tshe dbang nor bu'i gsung mgur zhal gdams kyi tshogs ji snyed pa,* 79 fols. In "The Collected Works of Kaḥ-thog Rig-'dzin chen-po Tshe-dbang nor-bu", vol. 2. Dalhousie: Damchoe Sangpo, 1976, pp. 1–153.

____ *dPal rig 'dzin chen po rdo rje tshe dbang nor bu'i zhabs kyi rnam par thar pa'i cha shas kyi brjod pa ngo mtshar dad pa'i rol mtsho*, 187 fols. In "ibid", vol. 1, pp. 1–376.

____*Bod rje lha btsad po'i gdung rabs mnga' ris smad gung thang du ji ltar byung ba'i tshul deb gter dwangs shel 'phrul gyi me long.* In "Bod kyi lo rgyus deb ther khag lnga" (= Gangs can rig mdzod 9). Lhasa: Bod ljongs bod yig dpe rnying dpe skrun khang, 1990, pp. 87–150.

____*Ma bcos pa'i zog po sngags rig 'dzin pa tshe dbang nor bu rang nyid spyad rab chu klung las thig pa tsam kyu ru lugs su smos pa snyims pa'i chu skyes*, 26 fols. In "The Collected Works of Kaḥ-thog Rig-'dzin chen-po Tshe-dbang nor-bu", vol. 1. Dalhousie: Damchoe Sangpo, 1976, pp. 561–612.

____*lHa rje mnyam med zla 'od gzhon nu'i bka' brygud phyag chen gdams pa ji tsam nod pa'i rtogs brjod legs bshad rin chen 'byung khungs.* In "The Collected Works of Kaḥ-thog Rig-'dzin chen-po Tshe-dbang nor-bu", vol. 2. Dalhousie: Damchoe Sangpo, 1976, pp. 155–243.

Tshe-ring dbang-rgyal, mDo-mkhar Zhabs-drung (1697–1763)
dPal mi'i dbang po'i rtogs par brjod pa 'jigs rten kun tu dga' ba'i gtam, 861 pp. Chengdu: Si-khron mi-rigs dpe-skrun khang, 1981.

Tshogs-khang sprul-sku Tshe-dbang (1928–1994)
Mkhas grub rgya mtsho'i gtsug rgyan padma bde ba'i rgyal po'i rnam thar ngo mtshar mchog ldan, 25 fols. (manuscript), n.p., n.d.

Tshogs-drug rang-grol, Zhabs-dkar-ba (1781–1851)
sNyigs dus 'gro ba yongs kyi skyabs mgon zhabs dkar rdo rje 'chang chen po'i rnam par thar pa rgyas par bshad pa skal bzang gdul bya thar 'dod rnams kyi re ba skong ba yid bzhin nor bu bsam 'phel dbang gi rgyal po, 485 fols. (xylograph). In "The Autobiography of Zhabs-dkar sNa-tshogs (sic!) rang-grol of A-mdo together with his O rgyan sprul pa'i glegs bam", 2 vols. Dolanji: Tsering Wangyel, 1975, and 1097 pp. 1–970. Hsining: mTsho sngon mi rigs dpe skrun khang, 1982.
____*bsTan 'gro yongs la phan pa'i o rgyan sprul pa'i glegs bam*, 106 fols. (xylograph). In "ibid", vol. 2, pp. 371–581.

gZhan-phan Chos-kyi snang-ba, mKhan-po gZhan-dga' (1871–1927)
mKhas par bya ba'i gnas drug bstan pa shes bya gsal ba'i me long, 38 fols. Bir/Delhi: Tsondü Senghe, 1985.

gZhan-phan mtha'-yas, rDzogs-chen rgyal-sras (b. 1800)
Zhe chen dbon sprul rin po che'i dri lan drang pa'i sa bon, 18 fols. In "Collected Works of rDzogs-chen rgyal-sras gZhan-phan mtha'-yas", vol. 1. Thimphu: Lama Ngodrup, 1984, pp. 524–43.
____*dPal yul dbon sprul rin po che'i dris len zla zhun snang ba*, 38 fols. In "ibid", vol. 2, pp. 271–309.

gZhon-nu dpal, 'Gos Lo-tsā-ba (1392–1481)
Deb ther sngon po, 2 vols., 1274 pp. Chengdu: Si-khron mi-rigs dpe-skrun khang, 1984.

bZhad-pa'i rdo-rje, Sle-lung rje-drung (b. 1697)
Dam can bstan srung rgya mtsho'i rnam par thar pa cha shas tsam brjod pa sngon med legs bshad, 2 vols., 311 pp. & 346 pp. Leh: T. S. Tashigang, 1979.
____*lTal (= ltad) chung mkha' 'gro'i dga' chal (= tshal) gyi gnas sgo gsar du phye ba'i lam yig bden pa'i zungs ldan,* 9 fols. (xylograph). In "The Collected Works (Gsuṅ 'bum) of Sle-luṅ Rje-druṅ Bźad-pa'i rdo-rje", vol. 9. (= Smanrtsis Shesrig Spendzod 123). Leh: T. Sonam and D. L. Tashigang, 1984, pp. 203–19.

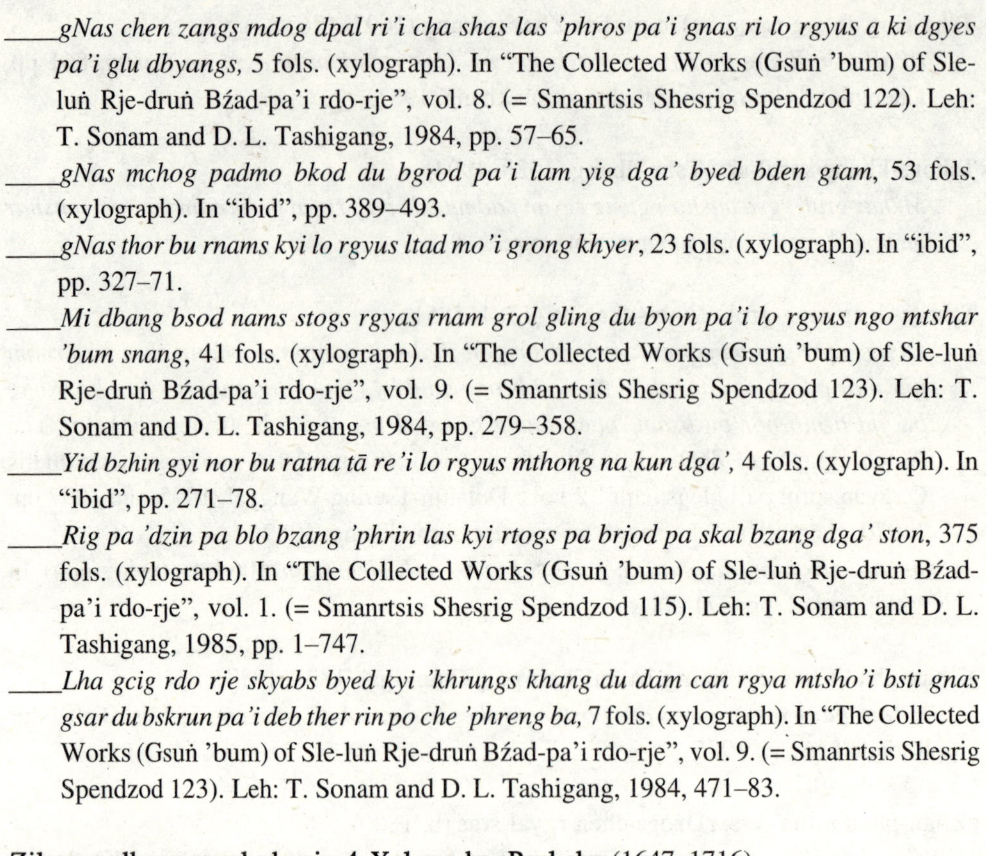

____*gNas chen zangs mdog dpal ri'i cha shas las 'phros pa'i gnas ri lo rgyus a ki dgyes pa'i glu dbyangs,* 5 fols. (xylograph). In "The Collected Works (Gsuṅ 'bum) of Sle-luṅ Rje-druṅ Bźad-pa'i rdo-rje", vol. 8. (= Smanrtsis Shesrig Spendzod 122). Leh: T. Sonam and D. L. Tashigang, 1984, pp. 57–65.

____*gNas mchog padmo bkod du bgrod pa'i lam yig dga' byed bden gtam*, 53 fols. (xylograph). In "ibid", pp. 389–493.

____*gNas thor bu rnams kyi lo rgyus ltad mo'i grong khyer*, 23 fols. (xylograph). In "ibid", pp. 327–71.

____*Mi dbang bsod nams stogs rgyas rnam grol gling du byon pa'i lo rgyus ngo mtshar 'bum snang*, 41 fols. (xylograph). In "The Collected Works (Gsuṅ 'bum) of Sle-luṅ Rje-druṅ Bźad-pa'i rdo-rje", vol. 9. (= Smanrtsis Shesrig Spendzod 123). Leh: T. Sonam and D. L. Tashigang, 1984, pp. 279–358.

____*Yid bzhin gyi nor bu ratna tā re'i lo rgyus mthong na kun dga'*, 4 fols. (xylograph). In "ibid", pp. 271–78.

____*Rig pa 'dzin pa blo bzang 'phrin las kyi rtogs pa brjod pa skal bzang dga' ston*, 375 fols. (xylograph). In "The Collected Works (Gsuṅ 'bum) of Sle-luṅ Rje-druṅ Bźad-pa'i rdo-rje", vol. 1. (= Smanrtsis Shesrig Spendzod 115). Leh: T. Sonam and D. L. Tashigang, 1985, pp. 1–747.

____*Lha gcig rdo rje skyabs byed kyi 'khrungs khang du dam can rgya mtsho'i bsti gnas gsar du bskrun pa'i deb ther rin po che 'phreng ba,* 7 fols. (xylograph). In "The Collected Works (Gsuṅ 'bum) of Sle-luṅ Rje-druṅ Bźad-pa'i rdo-rje", vol. 9. (= Smanrtsis Shesrig Spendzod 123). Leh: T. Sonam and D. L. Tashigang, 1984, 471–83.

Zil-gnon dbang-rgyal rdo-rje, 4. Yol-mo-ba sPrul-sku (1647–1716)

sPrul pa'i rig 'dzin chen po zil gnon dbang rgyal rdo rje'i phyi'i rnam thar ngo mtshar rmad byung rna ba'i bdud rtsi, 44 fols. In "The Autobiographical Reminiscences and Writings of the 17th Century Nyingmapa Visionary Rig 'dzin Zil-gnon dbang-rgyal rdo-rje." Gangtok & Delhi: Gonpo Tseten, 1977, pp. 1–87.

Zla-ba rgyal-mtshan (15th cent.)

mKhas grub sha ra rab 'byams pa sangs rgyas seng ge'i rnam thar mthong ba don ldan ngo mtshar nor bu'i phreng ba thar 'dod yid 'phrog blo gsal mgul brgyan (xylograph), 26 fols. In "Rare dKar-brgyud-pa Texts from Himachal Pradesh." New Delhi: Urgyan Dorje, 1976, pp. 451–501.

'Od-dpag rdo-rje (14th/15th cent.)

Thugs rje chen po bcu gcig pa'i bla ma brgyud pa'i rnam thar nor bu'i phreng ba, 114 fols. Delhi: Damchoe Sangpo, n.d.

'Od-gsal rgya-mtsho, Ri-bo-che sku-skye (16th cent.)
Rig 'dzin chen po gter ston las 'phro gling pa'i dus gsum gyi skye brgyud dang rnam par thar pa che long tsam zhig bkod pa me tog 'phreng mdzes, 314 fols. Gangtok: Gonpo Tseten, 1979.

Ye-shes rgyal-mtshan, Yongs-'dzin (1713–1793)
Lam rim bla ma brgyud pa'i rnam thar, 922 pp. Lhasa: Bod-ljongs mi-dmangs dpe-skrun khang, 1990.

Yon-tan rgya-mtsho, mDo-smad-pa (1932–2002)
Gyi na pa zhig gi blo'i sprin rum las 'ongs pa'i gdong lan lung dang rigs pa'i thog mda', 214 fols. New Delhi, 1979.

Yon-tan bzang-po, mKhan-po A-pad (b. 1927) et. al.
dKar chag mthong bas yid 'phrog chos mdzod bye ba'i lde mig. "A Bibliography of Sa-skya-pa Literature", 456 pp. New Delhi, 1987.

Rang-rig ras-pa (d. 1683)
rJe btsun khyab bdag chen po rang rig ras chen gyi gsung mgur dang zhal gdams 'du med bdud rtsi'i rlabs chen (= Smanrtsis Shesrig Spendzod 111). Leh: S. W. Tashigang, 1982.

Rin-chen rnam-rgyal, lHa-btsun (1473–1557)
Grub thob gtsang smyon pa'i nam thar dad pa'i spu slong g.yo ba, 65 fols. In "Bde mchog mkha' 'gro snyan rgyud (Ras chung snyan brgyud)", vol. 1. (= Smanrtsis Shesrig Spendzod 11). Leh: S. W. Tashigangpa, 1971, pp. 1–129.
____*rNam 'byor dbang phyug lha btsun chos kyi rgyal po'i rnam thar smad cha*, 32 fols. (xylograph). NGMPP reel no. E 2673/25.

Rong-zom Chos-kyi bzang-po (11th cent.)
lTa ba'i brjed byang chen mo, 30 fols. In "Selected Writings (Gsuṅ thor bu) of Roṅ-zom Chos-kyi bzaṅ-po" (= Smanrtis Shesrig Spendzod 73). Leh: S.W. Tashigangpa, 1974, pp. 187–246.
____*mDo sngags kyi grub mtha' mthun mi mthun mdor bsdus kyi bskyud byang*, 3 fols. In "Rong zom bka' 'bum." Thimphu: Kunsang Tobgay, 1976, pp. 439–44.
____*gSang sngags rdo rje theg pa'i tshul las snang ba lhar bsgrub pa*, 14 fols. In "Selected Writings (Gsuṅ thor bu) of Roṅ-zom Chos-kyi bzaṅ-po" (= Smanrtsis Shesrig Spendzod 73). Leh: S.W. Tashigangpa, 1974, pp. 125–50.

Sangs-rgyas gling-pa, Rig-'dzin (1340–1396)

Bla ma dgongs pa 'dus pa las / ma 'ongs lung bstan bka' rgya ma'i skor, 263 fols. (manuscript). In "The Collected Prophecies from the Bla ma Dgoṅs 'dus Revelation of Gter-chen Saṅs-rgyas-gliṅ-pa." Gangtok & Delhi: Sherab Gyaltsen, pp. 1–523.

Sangs-rgyas rdo-rje, Bya-bral Rin-po-che (b. 1913)

dPal rgyal ba kaḥ thog pa'i gdan rabs brgyud 'dzin dang bcas pa'i byung ba brjod pa rin po che'i phreng ba lta bu'i gtam, 143 fols. (manuscript), n.p., n.d.

____*gSol 'debs le'u bdun dang / 'ja' mtshon dkon spyi / zhi 'khro sogs sgrub thabs snying po rnams dang / gzhan yang chos spyod smon lam skor bcas kyi dkar chag mthong thos thar lam sgo byed,* 5 fols. (manuscript), n.p., 1985.

Śākya Rin-chen sde (14th cent.)

Yar lung jo bo'i chos 'byung, 186 pp. Lhasa: Bod-ljongs mi-dmangs dpe-skrun khang, 1988.

Sangs-rgyas rgya-mtsho, sDe-srid (1653–1705)

dPal mnyam med ri bo dga' ldan pa'i bstan pa zhwa ser cod pan 'chang ba'i ring lugs chos thams cad kyi rtsa ba gsal bar byed pa bai ḍū rya gser po'i me long, 523 pp. Beijing: Khrung-gi'i bod-kyi-shes-rig spe-skrun khang, 1989.

Sangs-rgyas rgyal-mtshan, gTsang-smyon He-ru-ka (1452–1507)

rJe btsun mi la ras pa'i rnam thar rgyas par phye ba mgur 'bum, 626 pp. In "rNal 'byor dbang phyug chen po mi la ras pa'i rnam mgur." Hsining: mTsho-sngon mi-rigs dpe-skrun khang, 1989, 196–812.

Sangs-rgyas bstan-'dzin, mKhan-po (1924–1990)

Ne shar lo rgyus jo glang gangs ,od. "Snowlight of Everest, A History of the Sherpas of Nepal", 178 pp. (= Nepal Research Centre Publications 18). Stuttgart, 1992.

____*Shar khum bu'i phyogs su snga 'gyur rnying ma'i chos brgyud bye brag pa rim par thob pa'i yig,* 13 fols. (manuscript). NGMPP, reel no. L 235/6.

____*Shar pa'i chos 'byung sngon med tshangs pa'i dbyu gu,* 55 fols. In "Documents pour l'étude de la religion et de l'organisation sociale des Sherpa", vol. 1. Junbesi/Paris-Nanterre, 1971.

Sangs-rgyas bzang-po (b. 1894)

mTsho skyes gsang gsum chos 'byung padma'i rgyal tshab, 25 fols. (xylograph), n.p., n.d.

____*Sangs rgyas bzang po'i rnam thar zhes bya ba'i me long,* 86 fols. (incomplete manuscript). NGMPP reel no. L 145/8.

bSod-nams grags-pa, Paṇ-chen (1478–1554)

bKa' gdams gsar rnying gi chos 'byung yid kyi mdzes rgyan, 103 fols. (manuscript). In "Two Histories of the bKa'-gdams-pa Tradition." Gangtok & Delhi: Gonpo Tseten, 1977, pp. 1–206.

bSod-nams rgyal-mtshan, Kaḥ-thog-pa (1466–1540)

bKa' thams cad gsal bar ston pa byed pa / bstan pa thams cad kyi spyi 'grel / theg pa thams cad kyi shan 'byed / man ngag thams cad kyi dgongs don / sems kyi chos nyid mngon du rtogs pa'i me long / nyi 'od gsal ba, 2 vols., 230 fols. & 181 fols. (manuscript). Delhi: Kunzang Tobgyal, 1979.

____*Shar kaḥ thog pa bsod nams rgyal mtshan dpal bzang po'i rnam par thar pa*, 77 fols. Gangtok: Dzongsar Jamyang Khyentsey Labrang, 1979.

bSod-nams dpal bzang-po (14th/15th cent.)

Dus gsum sangs rgyas thams cad kyi thugs kyi rten 'phags pa shing kun gyi dkar chag, 5 fols. In "Rare Tibetan Texts from Nepal: A collection of guides to holy places, lives of religious masters, and khrid yig by the famed Rdza Ro -phu Bla-ma." Dolanji: Tashi Dorji, 1976, pp. 81–90.

bSod-nams blo-gros (1516–1581)

mKhas grub chen po rnam grol bzang po'i rnam thar dad pa'i spu long g.yo byed ngo mtshar can, 53 fols. (manuscript). Dalhousie/Delhi: Damchoe Sangpo, 1985.

bSod-nams 'od-zer, mKhan-chen (13./14. cent.)

dPal ldan bla ma dam pa grub chen u rgyan pa'i rnam par thar pa byin rlabs kyi chu rgyun, 122 fols. (manuscript). Gangtok: Sherab Gyaltsen Lama, 1976.

bSod-nams lha'i dbang-po, Lo-dgon sPyan-snga-pa (1423–1496)

bKa' gdams rin po che'i chos 'byung rnam thar nyin mor byed pa'i 'od stong, 94 fols. In "Two histories of the bKa'-gdams-pa Tradition." Gangtok & Delhi: Gonpo Tseten, 1977, pp. 207–393.

bSod-nams lhun-grub, Glo-bo mkhan-chen (1456–1532)

Mi'i dbang po mgon po rgyal mtshan gyi dri lan padma'i snying po, 3 fols. In "The Collected Works of Glo-bo mkhan-chen bSod-nams lhun-grub", vol. 3. New Delhi: Ngagwang Topgay, 1977, pp. 15–20.

lHa-btsun 'Gyur-med, 'Jigs-bral bstan-'dzin dpa'-bo (19th/20th cent.)

sBas yul 'bras mo ljongs kyi gnas yig phan yon dang bcas pa ngo mtshar gter mdzod, 68 fols. (xylograph).

lHa Tshe-ring, mKhan-po (b. 1960)

mKha spyod 'bras mo ljongs kyi gtsug nor sprul pa'i rnal 'byor mched bzhi brgyud 'dzin dang bcas pa'i byung ba brjod pa blo gsar gzhon nu'i dga' ston. "A Saga of Sikkim's Supremely Revered Four Pioneer Nyingmapa Reincarnates and Their Torchbearers", 263 fols. Gangtok, 2002.

lHag-bsam bstan-pa'i rgyal-mtshan, mKhan-po (19th/20th cent.)

Don rnam par nges pa shes rab ral gri'i 'grel pa thub bstan yongs su rdzogs pa'i snang byed, 56 fols. Bylakuppe/Delhi: Pema Norbu Rin-po-che, 1984, pp. 1–111.

O-rgyan gling-pa (1329–1367)

O rgyan guru padma 'byung kyi skyes rabs rnam par thar pa rgyas par bkod pa gnas padma bka'i thang yig, 361 fols. Delhi: Sherab Gyaltsen Lama and Acharya Shedup Tendzin, 1985 and Chengdu: Si-khron mi-rigs dpe-skrun khang, 1988, 792 pp.

O-rgyan chos-'phel (b. 1755)

O rgyan chos 'phel gyi nyi tshe skye ba 'di'i rtogs brjod phyi yi rnam thar, 253 fols. (manuscript). NGMPP reel no. L 407/11.

O-rgyan dpal-bzang (1617–1677)

Rigs brgya dbang po 'dren mchog slob dpon dpal bzang po'i rnam par thar pa dad pa'i spu long g.yo byed mthong bas yid 'phrog ngo mtshar 'phreng ba'i gtam rmad du byung ba, 309 fols. (incomplete manuscript). NGMPP reel no. L83/1.

O-rgyan bstan-'dzin (1657–1737)

bKa' rdzogs pa chen po zab tig chos dbyings rang gsal las phyag rgya chen po gnyug ma gcer mthong gi khrid, 127 fols. (manuscript). Delhi: Lama Dawa, 1983.

____*rNal 'byor gyi dbang phyug o rgyan bstan 'dzin zhes bya ba'i ri khrod kyi nyams dbyangs*, 227 fols., n.p., n.d.

____*sPrang rgan o rgyan bstan 'dzin pa'i rnam thar bsdus pa*, 133 fols. (incomplete manuscript). 95 fols., n.p, n.d.

Different authors

A Collection of Records of Teachings and Initiations Received by Masters of the Gur-phu or mDo-chen Tradition of the Rnying-ma-pa, 605 pp. Dalhousie: Damchoe Sangpo, 1980.

Ka dam Pha cho, part 3. Gangtok: Sikkim Research Institute of Tibetology, 1980, pp. 611–895.

mKhar chu bdud 'joms gling gu 'don cha'i skor, 1015 pp. Delhi: Konchog Lhadrepa, 1994.

Jo bo rje dpal ldan a ti sha'i rnam thar bka' gdams pha chos, 900 pp. Hsining: mTsho-sngon mi-rigs dpe-skrun khang, 1994.

Jo bo yab sras kyi gsung bgros pha chos rin po che'i gter mdzod byang chub sems dpa' nor bu'i phreng ba rtsa 'grel sogs, 753 pp. Dharamsala: Tibetan Cultural Printing Press, 1992.

sPo bo lo rgyus, 214 pp. Xining: Bod-ljongs mi-dmangs dpe-skrun khang, 1988.

Bod rgya tshig mdzod chen mo, 3 vols. Beijing, 1985.

Maṇi bka' 'bum / rGyal po'i bka' 'bum, 2 vols., 327 & 319 fols. (xylograph). NGMPP reel nos. AT 167/4 & AT 167/5–168/1.

WESTERN SOURCES

Allen, N. J. (1997): "'And The Lake Drained Away': An Essay in Himalayan Comparative Mythology." In *Maṇḍala and Landscape* (= Emerging Perspectives in Buddhist Studies 5). New Delhi, pp. 435–51.

Ardussi, J. A. (1999): "Gyalse Tenzin Rabgye and the Founding of Taktsang Lhakhang." In *Bhutan: Journal of Bhutan Studies* 1:1, pp. 36–63.

Aris, M. (1975): "Report on the University of California Expedition to Kutang and Nubri in Northern Nepal in Autumn 1973." *Contributions to Nepalese Studies* 2:2, pp. 45–87.

____(1979a): *Introduction: Autobiographies of Three Spirituals Masters of Kutang*. Thimphu.

____(1979b): *Bhutan: The Early History of a Himalayan Kingdom*. Warminster.

____(1986): *Sources for the History of Bhutan* (= Wiener Studien zur Tibetologie und Buddhismuskunde 14). Vienna.

____(1988): "The Temple-Palace of gTam-zhing as Described by Its Founder." *Arts Asiatiques* 43, pp. 33–39.

____(1989): *Hidden Treasures and Seccret Lives: A Study of Pemalingpa (1450–1521) and the Sixth Dalai Lama (1683–1706)*. Shimla/Delhi.

____(1990): "Man and Nature in the Buddhist Himalayas." *Himalayan Environment and Culture*. Shimla/New Delhi, pp. 85–101.

____(1994): *The Raven Crown: The Origins of Buddhist Monarchy in Bhutan*. London.

Aufschnaiter, P. (1976): "Lands and Places of Milarepa." *East and West* 26 (New Series) 1–2, pp. 175–90.

Baker, I. (2004): *The Heart of the World: A Journey to the Last Secret Place*. London

Bacot, J. (1912): *Le Tibet Révolté. Vers Népémako, la terre promise des Tibétains*. Reprint (1988), Paris.

____(1951): "Titres et colophons d'ouvrages non canoniques tibétaines: textes et traduction." *Bulletin de l'École Française d'Extrême-Orient* 44, pp. 275–337.

Bellezza, J. V. (1997): *Divine Dyads: Ancient Civilization in Tibet*. Dharamsala.

Bentor, Y. (1996): *Consecration of Images and Stūpas in Indo-Tibetan tantric Buddhism* (= Brill's Indological Library 11). Leiden/New York/Cologne.

Berg, E. (1998): "The Sherpa Pilgrimage to Uomi Tsho in the Context of the Worship of the Protector Deities Ritual Practices: Ritual Practices, Local Meanings and This-Wordly Requests." *Himalayan Research Bulletin* 18:1, pp. 19–34.

____(2008): *The Sherpa Dumji Masked Dance Festival: An Ethnographic Description of the 'Great Liturgical Performance' as Celebrated Annually According to the Tradition of the Lamaserwa Clan in the Village Temple of Gonpa Zhung Solu*. Lumbini.

Bevan, D. G. (1987): "Forever Shangri-La? The Literary Image of Tibet." *Chö Yang: The Voice of Tibetan Religion and Culture* 1:3, pp. 123–25.

Bishop, P. (1989): *The Myth of Shangri-La: Tibet, Travel Writing and the Western Creation of Sacred Landscape*. London

____(1993): *Dreams of Power: Tibetan Buddhism and the Western Imagination*. London.

Blondeau, A. M. (1960): "Les Pèlerinages tibétains." In *Les Pèlerinages* (= Sources orientales 3). Paris, pp. 199–246.

____(1972): "Review of *Shar pa'i chos 'byung*." *Journal Asiatique* 260:3–4, pp. 404–7.

____(1982/83): "Religions tibétaines." In *Annuaire de l'École Pratique des Hautes Études, Ve Section, Sciences Religieuses* 41, pp. 123–31.

____(1984): "Le Découvreur du *Maṇi bka' 'bum* était-il Bon-po?" In *Tibetan Buddhist Studies* 1 (= Bibliotheca Orientalis Hungarica 29:1). Budapest, pp. 77–123.

____(1987): "Une polémique sur l' authenticité des Bka' thang au 17éme siècle." In *Silver on Lapis: Tibetan Literary Culture and History* (= The Tibet Society Twentieth Anniversary Celebration Volume). Bloomington, pp. 125–61.

____(1988): "La controverse soulevée par l'inclusion de rituels bon-po dans le Rin-chen gter-mjod: Note préliminaire." In *Tibetan Studies* (= Studia Tibetica: Quellen und Studien zur tibetischen Lexikographie 2). Munich, pp. 55–67.

____(1991/92): "Religions tibétaines." In *Annuaire de l'École Pratique des Hautes Études. Section des Sciences Religieuses* 100, pp. 85–89.

____(1994): "Bya-rung kha-shor, légende fondatrice du bouddhisme tibétain." In *Tibetan Studies* 1 (= The Institute for Comparative Research in Human Culture, Occasional Papers 1:1). Oslo, pp. 31–48.

Boord, M. J. (1993): *The Cult of the Deity Vajrakilaya.* (= Buddhica Britannica, Series Continua 4). Tring.

Boussemart, M. S. (1999): *Dromteunpa, l'humble yogi - ou le renouveau du bouddhisme au Tibet du XIème siecle*. Marzens.

Brauen-Dolma (1985): "Millenarianism in Tibetan Religion." In *Soundings in Tibetan Civilization*. New Delhi, pp. 245–56.

Broido, M. (1985): "Padma dkar-po on the Two Satyas." *The Journal of the International Association of Buddhist Studies* 8:2, pp. 7–39.

Brinkhaus, H. (1993): "The Textual History of the Different Versions of the Svayaṃbhūpurāṇa." In *Nepal, Past and Present: Proceedings of the France-German Conference Arc-et-Senans, June 1990.* New Delhi, pp. 63–71.

____(2001): "Śāntikara's Nāgasādhana in the Svayaṃbūpurāṇa." *Journal of the Nepal Research Centre* 12, pp. 17–38.

Brough, J. (1947): "Legends of Khotan and Nepal." *Bulletin of the School of Oriental and African Studies* 12:1, pp. 333–39.

Bühnemann, G. & Musashi, T. (1991): *Niṣpannayogāvalī: Two Sanskrit Manuscripts from Nepal* (= Bibliotheca Codicum Asiaticorum 5). Tokyo.

Buffetrille, K. (1989): "La restauration du monastère de Bsam-yas: Un exemple de continuité dans la relation chapelain-donateur au Tibet." *Journal Asiatique* 277:3–4, pp. 363–411.

____(1997): "Un guide de pèlerinage inédit d'un lama sherpa." In *Les habitants du toit du monde: Études recueillies en hommage à Alexandre W. Macdonald* (= Recherches sur la Haute Asie 12). Nanterre, pp. 441–59.

____(2000): *Pélerins, lamas et visionnaires. Sources orales et écrites sur les pélerinages tibétains* (= Wiener Studien zur Tibetologie und Buddhismuskunde 46). Vienna.

Bulnois, L. (1973): *Bibliographie du Nepal. Vol. 3 (Sciences naturelles), Tome 1 (Cartes du Nepal dans les bibliotheques de Paris et de Londres)*. Paris.

Cancik, H. (1985/86): "Rome as sacred landscape. Varro and the end of Republican Religion in Rome." *Visible Religion. Annual of Religious Iconography* 4–5, pp. 250–65.

Cantwell, C. & Mayer, R. (2006): "The sGang-steng rNying-ma'i rGyud-'bum Manuscript from Bhutan." *Revue d'Études tibétaines* 11, pp. 4–141.

____(2007): *The Kīlaya Nirvāṇa Tantra and the Vajra Wrath Tantra: Two texts from the Ancient Tantra Collection* (= Österreichische Akademie der Wissenschaften, Phil.-Hist. Klasse, Denkschriften 349 / Beiträge zur Kultur- und Geistesgeschichte Asiens 52). Vienna.

Cech, K. (1992): "A Religious geography of Tibet According to the Bon Tradition." In *Tibetan Studies* 2 (= Monograph Series, Occasional Papers 2). Narita, pp. 387–92.

Chaudhury, H. M. (1995): "Earthquakes in the Himalaya." In *The Himalaya: Aspects of Change: A Selection.* New Delhi, pp. 48–68.

Childs, G. H. (1993): "Journey to the Hidden Valley (sBas-yul) of Gnam-sgo zla-gam: Perspectives of the Tibetan Concept of Himalayan Refuges." Unpublished Master thesis. Indiana University.

____(1997). "A Note on the Tibetan Origin of the Sherpa Serwa Lineage." *Himalayan Research Bulletin* 17:2, pp. 23–25.

____(1999): "Refuge and Revitalization: Hidden Himalayan Sanctuaries (Sbas-yul) and the Preservation of Tibet's Imperial Lineage." In *Acta Orientalia* 60, pp. 126–58.

Clarke, G. E. (1980): "A Helambu History." *Journal of the Nepal Research Centre* 4, pp. 1–38.

____(1983): "The Great and Little Tradition in the Study of Yolmo." In *Contributions on Tibetan Language, History and Culture* 1 (= Wiener Studien zur Tibetologie und Buddhismuskunde 11). Vienna, pp. 21–37.

Clarke, G. E. & Manandhar, T. (1988): "A Malla Copper-Plate from Sindhu-Palchok." *Journal of the Nepal Research Centre* 8, pp. 105–39.

Cüppers, C. (1992): "Some Remarks on a Tibetan-Newari Lexicon cum Phrase Book." In *Tibetan Studies* 2 (= Monograph Series of the Naritasan Institute for Buddhist Studies, Occasional Papers 2). Narita, pp. 413–19.

____(1993): "Zhabs-dkar Bla-ma Tshogs-drug rang-grol's Visit to Nepal and his Contribution to the Decoration of the Bodhnāth Stūpa." In *Nepal, Past and Present: Proceedings of the Franco-German Conference Arc-et-Senans*, June 1990. Paris, pp. 151–58.

Cüppers, C. Tamot, K. & Pierce, Ph. (1996): *A Tibetan-Newari Lexicon cum Phrase Book* (= Nepalica 10). Bonn.

Dabringhaus, S. (1994): *Das Qing-Imperium als Vision und Wirklichkeit. Tibet in Laufbahn und Schriften des Song Yun (1752–1835)* (= Münchener Ostasiatische Studien 69). Stuttgart.

Dalton, J. P. (2002): "The Uses of the Dgongs pa 'dus pa'i mdo in the Development of the Rnying-ma School of Tibetan Buddhism." Unpublished Ph.D. thesis. University of Michigan.

Dargyay, E. K. (1977): "Tsong-kha-pa and his relation to Atiśa and Padmasambhava." In *Buddhist Thought and Asian Civilisation: Essays in Honour of Herbert V. Guenther on His Sixtieth Birthday.* Emeryville, pp. 16–26.

Davidson, R. M. (1991): "Reflexions on the Maheśvara Subjugation Myth: Indic Materials, Sa-skya-pa Apologetics, And the Birth of Heruka." *The Journal of the International Association of Buddhist Studies* 14:2, pp. 197–235.

Decleer, H. (2000): "Si tu Paṇ chen's Translation of the Svayaṃbhū Purāṇa and His Role in the Development of the Kathmandu Valley Pilgrimage Guide (*gnas yig*) Literature." *Lungta* 13, pp. 33–64.

Department of Information and International Relations, Central Tibetan Administration (1992): *Tibet: Environment and Development Issues*. Dharamsala.

Dhondup, K. (1984): *The Water Horse and Other Years: A History of 17th and 18th Century Tibet*. Dharamsala.

Diemberger, H. (1992): "Lovanga (Lo 'bangs pa?), Lama and Lhaven (Lha bon): Historical Background, Syncretism and Social Relevance of Religious Traditions among the Khumbo (East Nepal)." In *Tibetan Studies* 2 (= Monograph Series of the Naritasan Institute for Buddhist Studies, Occasional Papers 2). Narita, pp. 421–33.

Diemberger, H., Wangdu, P., Kornfeld, M., Jahoda, C. (1997): *Feast of Miracles. The Life and the Tradition of Bodong Chole Namgyal (1375/6–1451 A.D.) according to the Tibetan Texts "Feast of Miracles" and "The Lamp Illuminating the History of Bodong.* Clusone.

Dobremez, J. F. & Jest, C. (1976): *Manaslu: Hommes et Milieux des vallées du Népal Central*. Paris.

Dowman, K. (1973): *The Legend of the Great Stupa*. Berkeley.

____(1981): "A Buddhist Guide to the Power-Places of the Kathmandu Valley." *Kailash: A Journal of Himalayan Studies* 8:3–4, pp. 183–291.

____(1988): *The Power-Places of Central Tibet: The Pilgrim's Guide*. London & New York.

Dreyfus, G. (1994): "Proto-Nationalism in Tibet." In *Tibetan Studies* 1 (= The Institute for Comparative Research in Human Culture, Occasional Papers 1:1). Oslo, pp. 205–18.

____(1995): "Law, State, and Political Ideology in Tibet." *Journal of the International Association of Buddhist Studies* 18:1, pp. 117–38.

Dudjom Rinpoche (1991): *The Nyingma School of Tibetan Buddhism: Its Fundamentals and History*. Translated and edited by Gyurme Dorje and Matthew Kapstein. Boston.

Dhungel, R. (1988): "Svayambhu Sthita Syamarapa Lama Dasanko Tibbati Abhilekhanra Tyasako Nepali Anuvada." *Nepal Economist* 6 (May–June 1988), pp. 4–11.

Ehrhard, F.-K. (1980): "Tibetan Texts in the National Archives, Kathmandu." *Journal of the Nepal Research Centre* 4.

____(1989): "A Renovation of Svayaṃbhūnāth-Stupa in the 18th Century and its History (according to Tibetan sources)." *Ancient Nepal: Journal of the Department of Archaeology* 114, pp. 1–9.

____(1990a): *Flügelschläge des Garuḍa: Literar- und ideengeschichtliche Bemerkungen zu einer Liedersammlung des rDzogs-chen*. (= Tibetan and Indo-Tibetan Studies 3). Stuttgart.

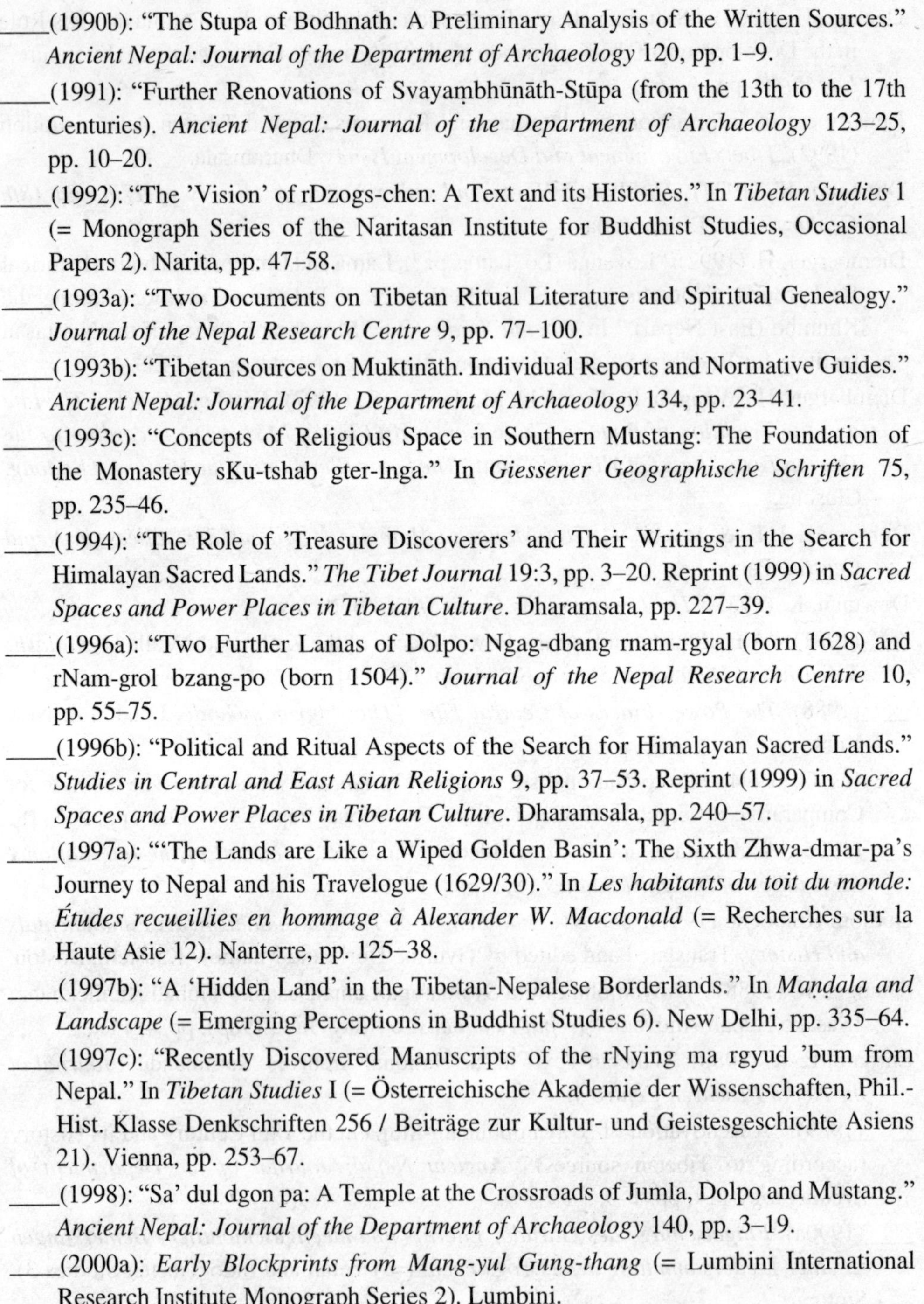

____(1990b): "The Stupa of Bodhnath: A Preliminary Analysis of the Written Sources." *Ancient Nepal: Journal of the Department of Archaeology* 120, pp. 1–9.

____(1991): "Further Renovations of Svayaṃbhūnāth-Stūpa (from the 13th to the 17th Centuries). *Ancient Nepal: Journal of the Department of Archaeology* 123–25, pp. 10–20.

____(1992): "The 'Vision' of rDzogs-chen: A Text and its Histories." In *Tibetan Studies* 1 (= Monograph Series of the Naritasan Institute for Buddhist Studies, Occasional Papers 2). Narita, pp. 47–58.

____(1993a): "Two Documents on Tibetan Ritual Literature and Spiritual Genealogy." *Journal of the Nepal Research Centre* 9, pp. 77–100.

____(1993b): "Tibetan Sources on Muktināth. Individual Reports and Normative Guides." *Ancient Nepal: Journal of the Department of Archaeology* 134, pp. 23–41.

____(1993c): "Concepts of Religious Space in Southern Mustang: The Foundation of the Monastery sKu-tshab gter-lnga." In *Giessener Geographische Schriften* 75, pp. 235–46.

____(1994): "The Role of 'Treasure Discoverers' and Their Writings in the Search for Himalayan Sacred Lands." *The Tibet Journal* 19:3, pp. 3–20. Reprint (1999) in *Sacred Spaces and Power Places in Tibetan Culture*. Dharamsala, pp. 227–39.

____(1996a): "Two Further Lamas of Dolpo: Ngag-dbang rnam-rgyal (born 1628) and rNam-grol bzang-po (born 1504)." *Journal of the Nepal Research Centre* 10, pp. 55–75.

____(1996b): "Political and Ritual Aspects of the Search for Himalayan Sacred Lands." *Studies in Central and East Asian Religions* 9, pp. 37–53. Reprint (1999) in *Sacred Spaces and Power Places in Tibetan Culture*. Dharamsala, pp. 240–57.

____(1997a): "'The Lands are Like a Wiped Golden Basin': The Sixth Zhwa-dmar-pa's Journey to Nepal and his Travelogue (1629/30)." In *Les habitants du toit du monde: Études recueillies en hommage à Alexander W. Macdonald* (= Recherches sur la Haute Asie 12). Nanterre, pp. 125–38.

____(1997b): "A 'Hidden Land' in the Tibetan-Nepalese Borderlands." In *Maṇḍala and Landscape* (= Emerging Perceptions in Buddhist Studies 6). New Delhi, pp. 335–64.

____(1997c): "Recently Discovered Manuscripts of the rNying ma rgyud 'bum from Nepal." In *Tibetan Studies* I (= Österreichische Akademie der Wissenschaften, Phil.-Hist. Klasse Denkschriften 256 / Beiträge zur Kultur- und Geistesgeschichte Asiens 21). Vienna, pp. 253–67.

____(1998): "Sa' dul dgon pa: A Temple at the Crossroads of Jumla, Dolpo and Mustang." *Ancient Nepal: Journal of the Department of Archaeology* 140, pp. 3–19.

____(2000a): *Early Blockprints from Mang-yul Gung-thang* (= Lumbini International Research Institute Monograph Series 2). Lumbini.

____(2000b): "The Transmission of the *dMar-khrid tshem-bu lugs* and the *Maṇi bka' 'bum.*" In *Vividharatnakaraṇḍaka*: *Festgabe für Adelheid Mette* (= Indica et Tibetica 37). Swisstal-Odendorf, pp. 199–215.

____(2001): "Religious Geography and Literary Traditions: The foundation of the Monastery Brag-dkar bsam-gling." *Journal of the Nepal Research Centre* 12, pp. 101–14.

____(2002a): "The Register of the Reliquary of Lord Rang-rig ras-pa." In *Wiener Zeitschrift für die Kunde Südasiens* 46, pp. 146–67.

____(2002b): *Life and Travels of Lo-chen bSod-nams rgya-mtsho* (= Lumbini International Research Institute Monograph Series 5). Lumbini.

____(2003): "Pilgrims in Search of Sacred Lands." In *Sacred Landscape of the Himalaya. Proceedings of an International Conference at Heidelberg 25–27 May 1998* (= Österreichische Akademie der Wissenschaften, Phil.-Hist. Klasse Denkschriften 308 / Veröffentlichungen zur Sozialanthropologie 4). Vienna, pp. 95–110.

____(2004a): *Die Statue und der Tempel des Ārya Va-ti bzang-po: Ein Beitrag zur Geschichte und Geographie des Tibetischen Buddhismus* (= Contributions to Tibetan Studies 2). Wiesbaden.

____(2004b): "Spiritual Relationships between Rulers and Preceptors: The Three Journeys of Vanaratna (1384–1468) to Tibet." In *Proceedings of the Conference on the Relationship between Religion and State (chos srid zung 'brel) in Traditional Tibet* (= Lumbini International Research Institute Proceeding Series 1). Lumbini, pp. 245–65.

____(2004c): "A Monument of Sherpa Buddhism: The Enlightenment Stūpa in Junbesi." *The Tibet Journal* 29:3 (= Special Issue: Tibetan Monuments), pp. 75–92.

____(2007): "A Forgotten Incarnation Lineage: The Yol-mo-ba sPrul-skus (16th to 18th Centuries)." In *The Paṇḍita and the Siddha: Tibetan Studies in Honour of E. Gene Smith.* Dharamsala, pp. 25–49.

____(2008): *A Rosary of Rubies: A Chronicle of the Gur-rigs mDo-chen Tradition from South-Western Tibet* (= Collectanea Himalayica: Studies in the History and Culture of the Himalayas and Tibet 2). Munich.

Ehrhard, F.-K., Pierce, P. & Cüppers, C. (1991): *Views of the Bodhnāth-Stūpa.* Kathmandu.

Eimer, H. (1977): *Berichte über das Leben des Atiśa (Dīpaṃkāraśrījñāna): Eine Untersuchung der Quellen* (= Asiatische Forschungen 51). Wiesbaden.

____(1981): "Die ursprüngliche Reihenfolge der Verszeilen in der Bodhisattvamaṇyāvalī." *Zentralasiatische Studien* 15, pp. 323–30.

____(1982): "The Development of the Biographical Tradition Concerning Atiśa (Dīpaṃkāraśrījñāna)." *The Journal of the Tibet Society* 2, pp. 41–51.

____(1984): "Zur Faksimile-Ausgabe eines alten Blockdruckes des Bka' gdams glegs bam." *Indo-Iranian Journal* 27, pp. 45–47.

____(1994): "Zur Problematik der Stellung des Narthang Druckes in der Überlieferung des Tibetischen Kanjur." *Zeitschrift der Deutschen Morgenländischen Gesellschaft,* Supplement 10. Stuttgart, pp. 307–12.

____(2002): "Daten von frühen Äbten und Lehrern des Klosters Kaḥ thog in Derge (Khams)." *Archiv orientální* 71:3, pp. 319–32.

Eimer, H. & P. Tsering, (1979): "Äbte und Lehrer von Kaḥ thog. Eine erste Übersicht zur Geschichte eines Rnying ma pa-Klosters in Derge/Khams." *Zentralasiatische Studien* 13, pp. 457–509.

____(1981): "A List of Abbots of Kaḥ thog Monastery according to handwritten Notes by the late Katog Ontrul." *The Journal of the Tibet Society* 2, pp. 11–14.

Ekvall, R. B. & Downs, J. F. (1987): *Tibetan Pilgrimage*. Tokyo.

Ellingson, T. (1992): "Himalayan Studies in 1991: An Editorial View." *Himalayan Research Bulletin* 12:1–2, pp. 4–5.

Emmerick, R. E. (1967): *Tibetan Texts Concerning Khotan* (= London Oriental Series 19). London.

Everding, K.-H. (1988): *Die Präexistenzen der lCang skya Qutuqtus. Untersuchungen zur Konstruktion und historischen Entwicklung einer lamaistischen Existenzlinie* (= Asiatische Forschungen 104). Wiesbaden.

Falk, M. (1943): *Nāma-Rūpa and Dharma-Rūpa*. Calcutta.

Ferrari, A. (1958): *Mk'yen brtse's Guide to the Holy Places of Central Tibet* (= Serie Orientale Roma 16). Rome.

Fisher, J. F. (1987): *Trans-Himalayan Traders. Economy, Society, and Culture in Northwest Nepal*. New Delhi.

Fontein, J. (1995): "Relics and Reliquaries, Texts and Artefacts." In *Function and Meaning in Buddhist Art* (= Gonda Indological Studies 3). Groningen, pp. 21–31.

Fukuda, Y. (1999): "Japanese Research on Tibetan Buddhism, 1984-98." In *Tibetan Studies in Japan* (= Asian Research Trends: A Humanities and Social Science Review 9). Tokyo, pp. 1–18.

von Fürer-Haimendorf, C. (1975): *Himalayan Traders. Life in Highland Nepal*. London. Reprint (1988), New Delhi.

Gebauer, H. D. (1983): *Caves of India and Nepal*. Schwäbisch Gmünd.

Germano, D. (1994): "Architecture and Absence in the Secret Tantric History of the Great Perfection (*rdzogs chen*)." In *Journal of the International Association of Buddhist Studies* 17:2, pp. 203–335.

Germano, D. and Gyatso, J. (2000): "Longchenpa and the possession of the Dakiṇīs." In *Tantra in Practice*. Princeton, pp. 239–65.

Geshe G. Lodrö (1974): *Geschichte der Kloster-Universität Drepung mit einem Abriss der Geistesgeschichte Tibets* (= Abhandlungen aus dem Gebiet der Auslandskunde 73, Reihe B, vol. 42). Wiesbaden.

Gettelman, N. M. (1982): "Letter of the First Westerner to Visit Bhutan-Tibet-Nepal." *Kailash: A Journal of Himalayan Studies* 9:1, pp. 97–110.

____(1990): "Karma bsTan-skyong dbang-po and the Jesuits." In *Reflections on Tibetan Culture: Essays in Memory of Turrell V. Wylie* (= Studies in Asian Thought and Culture 12). Lewiston/Queenston/Lampeter, pp. 269–77.

Goodman, S. D. (1981): "Mi-pham rgya-mtsho: An account of his Life, the Printing of his Works, and the Structure of his Treatise entitled mKhas-pa'i tshul-la 'jug-pa'i sgo." *Wind Horse* 1 (= Proceedings of the North American Tibetological Society). Berkeley, pp 58–78.

____(1993): "Rig-'dzin 'Jigs-med gling-pa and the Klong-chen sNying-thig." In *Tibetan Buddhism: Reason and Revelation* (= Bibliotheca Indo-Buddhica 124). Delhi, pp. 133–46 & 184–207.

Guenther, H. V. (1976): *Buddhist Philosophy in Theory and Practice*. Boulder/London.

Gurung, J. (1986): "Jyampā (vyams-pa) gumbāko karchyāgamā ullekhita tithimitiharū: blo (mustāṅ) rājyako etihāsika kālakrama-eka carcā." *Contributions to Nepalese Studies* 13:2, pp. 215–37.

Gutschow, N. (1997): *The Nepalese Chaitya: 1500 Years of Buddhist Votive Architecture in the Kathmandu Valley* (= Lumbini International Research Institute Monograph Series 1). Lumbini.

Gyatso, J. (1985): "The development of the *gCod* tradition." In *Soundings in Tibetan Civilisation*. New Delhi, pp. 74–98.

____(1992): "Genre, Authorship, and Transmission in Visionary Buddhism: The Literary Traditions of Thang-stong rGyal-po." In *Tibetan Buddhism: Reason and Revelation* (= Bibliotheca Indo-Buddhica 124). Delhi, pp. 95–106 & 170–75.

____(1994): "Guru Chos-dbang's *Gter 'byung chen mo*. An Early Survey of the Treasure Tradition and Its Strategies in Dicussing Bon Treasure." In *Tibetan Studies* 1 (= The Institute for Comparative Research in Human Culture, Occasional Papers 1:1). Oslo, pp. 275–87.

____(1998): *Apparitions of the Self: The Secret Autobiographies of a Tibetan Visionary*. Princeton.

Hamilton, F. B. (1819): *An Account of the Kingdom of Nepal*. Reprint (1986), New Delhi.

Harrison, P. (1992): "Meritorious activity or waste of time? Some Remarks in the Editing of Texts in the Tibetan Kanjur." In *Tibetan Studies* 1 (= Monograph Series of the Naritasan Institute for Buddhist Studies, Occasional Papers 2). Narita, pp. 77–93.

Hazod, G. (1991): "Die 'Herkunft' and die 'Ankunft' des tibetischen Königs. Zu den Momenten einer Ideologie der Souveränität in der Legende des 'Od lde spu rgyal." In *Tibetan History and Language: Studies Dedicated to Uray Géza on his Seventieth Birthday* (= Wiener Studien zur Tibetologie und Buddhismuskunde 26). Vienna, pp. 193–220.

Hevia, J. (1993): "Lamas, Emperors, and Rituals: Political Implications in Qing Imperial Ceremonies." *The Journal of the International Association of Buddhist Studies* 16:2, pp. 243–78.

Ho-Chin Yang (1969): *The Annals of Kokonor* (= Indiana University Publications, Uralic and Altaic Series 106). The Hague.

Hoffman, H. (1965): *Märchen aus Tibet.* Munich.

Hodgson, B. H. (1880): *Miscellaneous Essays relating to Indian Subjects*. London. Reprint (1992), New Delhi.

Hoheisel, K. & Rinschede, G. (1989): "Raumwirksamkeit von Religionen und Ideologien." *Praxis Geographie* 19:9, pp. 6–11.

Huber, T. (1989): "A Pilgrimage Guide to La-phyi: A Study of Sacred and Historical Geography in South-Western Tibet." Unpublished M.A. dissertation. University of Canterbury.

____(1990): "Where exactly are Cāritra, Devikoṭa and Himavat? A Sacred Geography Controversy and the Development of Tantric Buddhist Pilgrimage Sites in Tibet." *Kailash: A Journal of Himalayan Studies* 16:3–4, pp. 121–64.

____(1994): "Putting the *gnas* back into *gnas-skor*: Rethinking Tibetan Buddhist pilgrimage practice." *The Tibet Journal* 19:2, pp. 23–60. Reprint (1999) in *Sacred Spaces and Powerful Places in Tibetan Culture*. Dharamsala, pp. 77–104.

____(1997): "A Guide to the La-phyi *Maṇḍala*: History, Landscape and Ritual in South-Western Tibet." In *Maṇḍala and Landscape* (= Emerging Perceptions in Buddhist Studies 6). New Delhi, pp. 233–86.

____(2000): *The Guide to India: A Tibetan Account by Amdo Gendun Chöphel.* Dharamsala.

Huntington, J. C. (2002): "The Iconography of Svayambhu Mahachaitya: The Main Mandalas." *Orientations* 33:10, pp. 16–23.

Imaeda, Y. (1981): "Notes sur le Kanjur de Dergé." In *Tantric and Taoist Studies in Honour of R. A. Stein* I (= Mélanges Chinois et Bouddhiques 20), pp. 227–36.

Imaeda, Y. & Pommaret, F. (1987): "Le monastère de gTam-zhing (Tamshing) au Bhoutan Central." *Arts Asiatiques* 42, pp. 19–30.

Irwin, J. (1980): "The Axial Symbolism of the Early Stupa: An Exegesis." In *The Stupa, its Religious, Historical and Architectural Significance* (= Beiträge zur Südasienforschung 55). Wiesbaden, pp. 12–38.

Ishihama, Y. (1993): "On the Dissemination of the Belief in the Dalai Lama as a Manifestation of the Bodhisattva Avalokiteśvara." *Acta Asiatica: Bulletin of the Institute of Eastern Culture* 64, pp. 38–56.

Jackson, D. P. (1976): "The Early History of Lo (Mustang) and Ngari." *Contributions to Nepalese Studies* 4:1, pp. 39–56.

____(1978): "Notes on the History of Se-rib and Nearby Places in the Upper Kali Gandaki Valley." *Kailash: A Journal of Himalayan Studies* 6:3, pp. 195–227.

____(1984): *The Mollas of Mustang. Historical, Religious and Oratorical Traditions of the Nepalese-Tibetan Borderland.* Dharamsala.

____(1985): "Madhyamaka Studies among the early Sa-skya-pas." *The Tibet Journal* 10:2, pp. 20–34.

____(1987a): *The 'Miscellaneous Series' of Tibetan Texts in the Bihar Research Society, Patna: A Handlist* (= Tibetan and Indo-Tibetan Studies 2), Stuttgart.

____(1987b): *The Entrance Gate for the Wise: Sa-skya Paṇḍita on Indian and Tibetan Traditions of Pramāṇa and Philosophical Debate*, 2 vols. (= Wiener Studien zur Tibetologie und Buddhismuskunde 17:1–2. Vienna.

____(1996): *A History of Tibetan Painting: The Great Painters and Their Traditions* (= Österreichische Akademie der Wissenschaften, Phil.-Hist. Klasse, Denkschriften 242). Vienna.

____(1998): "A Reviver of Sa-skya-pa Scriptural Studies in 20th-Century Central Tibet." In *Les habitants du toit du monde. Études recueillies en hommage à Alexander W. Macdonald* (= Recherches sur la Haute Asie 12). Nanterre, pp. 139–53.

Jampa Samten (1992): "Notes on the bKa' 'gyur of O-rgyan-gling, the Family Temple of the Sixth Dalai Lama (1683–1706)." In *Tibetan Studies* 1 (= The Institute for Comparative Research in Human Culture, Occasional Papers 1:1). Oslo, pp. 393–402.

Jest, C. (1971): "Traditions et croyances religieuses des habitants de la vallée de Tichurong (Nord-Ouest du Népal)." *L'Ethnographie* 65, pp. 66–86.

____(1975): *Dolpo, Communautés de langue tibétaine du Népal.* Paris.

____(1981): *Monuments of Northern Nepal.* Paris.

____(1984/85): "Report on the Monuments of Northern Nepal: Monuments of Rasuwa District." *Ancient Nepal: Journal of the Department of Archaeology* 85, pp. 13–21.

____(1985): *La Turquoise de vie: Un pélerinage tibétain.* Paris.

Kaneko, E. (1982): *Ko Tantra Zenshû Kaidai Mokuroku* (*Descriptive Catalogue of the rNying ma rgyud 'bum*). Tokyo.

Kapstein, M. (1988): "Mi-pham's Theory of Interpretation." In *Buddhist Hermeneutics* (= Studies in East Asian Buddhism 6). Honolulu, pp. 149–74.

____(1988/89): "The Purificatory Gem and its Cleansing: A Late Tibetan Polemical Discussion of Apocryphal Texts." *History of Religions* 28:3, pp. 217–44.

____(1992): "Remarks on the *Maṇi bKa'-'bum* and the Cult of Avalokiteśvara in Tibet." In *Tibetan Buddhism: Reason and Revelation* (= Bibliotheca Indo-Buddhica 124). Delhi, pp. 79–93 & 163–69.

____(1996): "*gDams ngag: Tibetan Technologies of the Self.*" In *Tibetan Literature: Studies in Genre*. Ithaca, New York, pp. 275–89.

____(2009): "The Sun of the Heart and the Bai-ro-rgyud-'bum." In *Tibetan Studies in Honor of Samten Karmay*. Dharamsala, pp. 275–88.

Karmay, S. G. (1988a): *Secret Visions of the Fifth Dalai Lama: The Gold Manuscript in the Fournier Collection*. London.

____(1988b): *The Great Perfection: A Philosophical and Meditative Teaching of Tibetan Buddhism*. Leiden.

____(1990): "A propos d'un sceau en or offert par l'empereur Shunzi." In *Tibet: Civilisation et Société*. Paris, pp. 121–24. Reprint (1998) as "The Gold Seal: The Fifth Dalai Lama and Emperor Shun-chih." In *The Arrow and the Spindle: Studies in History, Myths, Rituals and Beliefs in Tibet*, vol. 1. Kathmandu, pp. 518–22.

____(1991): "L'Homme et le Boeuf: Le Rituel des *Glud* ('*rançon*')." *Journal Asiatique* 279:3–4, pp. 327–81. Reprint (1998) as "The Man and the Ox: A Ritual for offering the Glud." In *The Arrow and the Spindle*, vol. 1. Kathmandu, pp. 339–79.

____(1992): "A Pilgrimage to Kongpo Bon-ri." In *Tibetan Studies* 2 (= Monograph Series, Occasional Papers 2). Narita, pp. 527–39. Reprint (1998) in *The Arrow and the Spindle*, vol. 1. Kathmandu, pp. 211–29.

____(2000): "Dorje Lingpa and His Rediscovery of the 'Gold Needle'." *Bhutan: Journal of Bhutan Studies* 2:2, pp. 1–38. Reprint (2005) in *The Arrow and the Spindle*, vol. 2., Kathmandu, pp. 119–145.

____(2002): "The Rituals and their Origins in the Visionary Accounts of the Fifth Dalai Lama." In *Religion and Secular Culture in Tibet: Tibetan Studies 2* (= Brill's Tibetan Studies Library 2:2). Leiden/Boston/Cologne, pp. 21–40. Reprint (2005) in *The Arrow and the Spindle*, vol. 2., Kathmandu, pp. 73–94.

Kaschewsky, R. (1969): "Bericht über eine literarische und buddhologische Sammelarbeit in Nepal 1968/69 (mit Anhängen über Tibetica in Kathmandu und Gangtok)." *Zentralasiatische Studien* 3, pp. 310–19.

____(1971): *Das Leben des lamaistischen Heiligen Tsong-kha-pa Blo-bzang grags-pa (1357–1419),* part I (= Asiatische Forschungen 32:1). Wiesbaden.

____(1982): "Zu einigen tibetischen Pilgerplätzen in Nepal." *Zentralasiatische Studien* 16, pp. 427–442.

____(1994): "Muktinath: A Pilgrimage Place in the Himalayas." In *Pilgrimage in the Old and New World* (= Geographia Religionum 8). Berlin, pp. 139–68.

Kawamura, L. S. (1981a): "An Analysis of Mi-pham's *mKhas-'jug*." *Wind Horse* 1 (= Proceedings of the North American Tibetological Society). Berkeley, pp. 112–26.

____(1981b): "An Outline of Yāna-Kauśalya in Mi-pham's *mKhas-'jug*." *Indogakku Bukkôgaku Ronshû* 29:1, pp. 956–61.

____(1982): "An Analysis of Yāna-Kauśalya in Mi-pham's *mKhas-'jug*." *Bulletin of Buddhist Cultural Studies Ryûkoku University* 20, pp. 1–19.

____(1983): "The Akśayamatinirdeśasūtra and Mi-pham's *mKhas-'jug*." In *Contributions on Tibetan and Buddhist Religion and Philosophy* 2 (= Wiener Studien zur Tibetologie und Buddhismuskunde 11), pp. 131–45.

Keay, J. (2000). *The Great Arc: The Dramatic Tale of How India was Mapped and Everest was Named*. London.

Kirkpatrick, C. (1811): *An Account of the Kingdom of Nepal*. Reprint (1986), New Delhi.

Klimburg-Salter, D. E. (1991): "The Tucci Himalayan Archive." *East and West* 41:1–4, pp. 379–83.

Kohn, R. (1997): "The Ritual Preparation of a Tibetan Sand *Maṇḍala*." In *Maṇḍala and Landscape* (= Emerging Perceptions in Buddhist Studies 6). New Delhi, pp. 346–405.

Kölver, B. (1986): "Stages in the Evolution of a World Picture." *Numen: International Review for the History of Religion* 32:2, pp. 131–68.

____(1992): *Re-Building a Stūpa: Architectural Drawings of the Svayaṃbūnāth* (= Nepalica 5). Bonn.

____(2000): "The Size of the Stūpa." *Contributions to Nepalese Studies* 27:1, pp. 103–5.

Kramer, J. (2008): *A Nobel Abbot from Mustang: Life and Works of Glo bo Mkhan chen (1436–1532)* (= Wiener Studien zur Tibetologie und Buddhismuskunde 68). Vienna.

Krishan, Y (1992): "Ganeśa in Tibet." *The Tibet Journal* 17:2, pp. 65–71.

van der Kuijp, L. W. J. (1978): "Phya-pa chos-kyi seng-ge's impact on Tibetan Epistemological Theory." *Journal of Indian Philosophy* 5:4, pp. 355–69.

____(1983): *Contributions to the Development of Tibetan Buddhist Epistemology* (= Alt- und Neu-Indische Studien 26). Wiesbaden.

____(1987a): "The Monastery of Gsang-phu ne'u thog and its Abbatial Succession from ca. 1073 to 1250." *Berliner Indologische Studien* 3, 103–27.

____(1987b): "An Early Tibetan View of the Soteriology of Buddhist Epistemeology: The Case of 'Bri-gung 'Jig-rten mgon-po." *Journal of Indian Philosophy* 15:1, pp. 57–70.

____(1993): "Two Mongol Xylographs (*hor par ma*) of the Tibetan Text of Sa skya Paṇḍita's Work on Buddhist Logic and Epistemology." *Journal of the International Association of Buddhist Studies* 16:2, pp. 279–98.

____(1994): "Apropos of Some Recently Recovered Texts Belonging to the *Lam 'bras* Teachings of the Sa skya pa and Ko brag pa." *Journal of the International Association of Buddhist Studies* 17:2, pp. 175–201.

Kvaerne, P. (1998): "Khyung-sprul 'Jigs-med nam-mkha' rdo-rje (1897–1955): An early twentieth-century Tibetan pilgrim in India." In *Pilgrimage in Tibet*. Richmond, pp. 71–84.

Lauf, D. I. (1972): "Vorläufiger Bericht über die Geschichte und Kunst einiger lamaistischer Tempel in Bhutan." *Ethnologische Zeitschrift Zürich* 2, pp. 79–110.

Le Bon, G. (1981): *Voyages au Nepal* (= Itineriaria Asiatica 1). Reprint (1986), Bangkok.

Levi, S. (1905): *Le Népal: Etude historique d'un Royaume Hindou*, 2 vols. Reprint (1985/86), Paris.

Lewis T. T. and Jamspal L. (1988): "Newar and Tibetans in the Kathmandu Valley: Three New Translations from Tibetan Sources." *Journal of Asian and African Studies* 36, pp. 187–211.

Lienhard, S. (1992a): "Kṛṣṇaism in Nepal." In *Aspects of Nepalese Tradition* (= Nepal Research Centre Publication 19). Stuttgart, pp. 227–34.

____(1992b): *Songs of Nepal: An Anthology of Nevar Folksongs and Hymns.* Delhi.

Lindtner, C. (1981): "Atiśa's Introduction to the Two Truths." *Journal of Indian Philosophy* 9:2, pp. 161–214.

Lipman, K. (1981): "A Controversial Topic from Mi-pham's Analysis of Śāntarakṣita's Madhyamakālaṃkāra." *Wind Horse* 1 (= Proceedings of the North American Tibetological Society). Berkeley, pp. 40–57.

____(1992): "What is Buddhist Logic? Some Tibetan Developments of Pramāṇa Theory." In *Tibetan Buddhism: Reason and Revelation* (= Bibliotheca Indo-Buddhica 124). Delhi, pp. 25–44 & 151–52.

Lo Bue, E. (1985): "The Newar Artists of the Nepal Valley: An Historical Account of their Activities in Neighbouring Areas with Particular Reference to Tibet." *Oriental Art* 31:3, pp. 262–77.

____(1988): "Cultural Exchange and Social Interactions between Tibetans and Newars from the Seventh to the Twentieth Century." *International Folklore Review* 6, pp. 86–114.

Locke, J. K. (1980): *Karunamaya: The Cult of Avalokitesvara-Matsyendranath in the Valley of Nepal*. Kathmandu.

____(1985): *Buddhist Monasteries of Nepal*. Kathmandu.

Lopez, Donald S. (2006): *The madman's middle way: reflections on reality of the Tibetan monk Gendun Chopel*. Chicago & London.

Macdonald, A. (1970): "Le Dhānyakaṭaka de Man-luṅs Guru." *Bulletin de l'École Française d'Extrême-Orient* 57, pp. 169–213.

Macdonald, A. W. (1973a): "A Nepalese Copper Plate from the Time of Prithvinarayan Shah's Father." *Kailash: A Journal of Himalayan Studies* 1:1, pp. 6–7.

____(1973b): "The Lama and the General." *Kailash: A Journal of Himalayan Studies* 1:3, pp. 225–36. Reprint (1987) in *Essays on the Ethnology of Nepal and South Asia*, vol. 2, Kathmandu, pp. 1–10.

____(1975): "A Little Read Guide to the Holy Places of Nepal: Part I." *Kailash: A Journal of Himalayan Studies* 3:2, pp. 88–144.

____(1979): "A Tibetan Guide to some of the Holy Places of the Dhaulagiri-Muktināth Area of Nepal." In *Studies in Pali and Buddhism*. Delhi, pp. 243–53.

____(1980a): "The Writing of Buddhist History in the Sherpa Area of Nepal." In *History of Buddhism*. New Delhi, pp. 121–32. Reprint (1987) in *Essays on the Ethnology of Nepal and South Asia*, vol. 2,. Kathmandu, pp. 54–66.

____(1980b): "The Coming of Buddhism to the Sherpa Area of Nepal." *Acta Orientalia Hungaricae* 34, pp. 139–46. Reprint (1987) in *Essays on the Ethnology of Nepal and South Asia*, vol. 2,. Kathmandu, pp. 67–74.

____(1987): "Avant-propos." *L'Ethnographie* (= numéro spécial: *Rituels himalayens*) 83:100–1, pp. 5–13.

____(1989): "Note on the Language, Literature and Cultural Identity of the Tamang." *Kailash: A Journal of Himalayan Studies* 15:3–4, pp. 165–90.

____(1990): "Hindu-isation, Buddha-isation then Lama-isation or: What happened at La-phyi?" In *Indo-Tibetan Studies* (= Buddhica Britannica, Series Continua II). Tring, pp. 199-208.

Macdonald A. W. & Dvags-po Rin-po-che (1981): "Un guide peu lu des lieux-saints du Népal (II ème partie)." In *Tantric and Taoist Studies in Honour of R. A. Stein* 1 (= Melanges Chinois et Bouddhiques 20). Bruxelles, pp. 237–73. Reprint (1987) as "A Little Read Guide to the Holy Places of Nepal: Part II." In *Esssays on the Ethnology of Nepal and South Asia*, vol. 2, Kathmandu, pp. 100–34.

Macdonald, A. W. & **Stahl,** A. V. (1979): *Newar Art*. New Delhi.

Makidono, T. (2011): "An Entrance to the Practice Lineage as Exemplied in Kaḥ thog dGe rtse Mahāpaṇḍita's Commentary on Sa skya Paṇḍita's Sdom gsum rab 'bye." In *Revue d'Etudes Tibétaines* 22, pp. 215–42.

Malla, K. P. (1983): "The Limits of Surface Archeology" (book review). *Contributions to Nepalese Studies* 11:1, pp. 125–33.

Martin, D. (1990): "Bonpo Canons and Jesuit Canons: On Sectarian Factors Involved in the Ch'en-lung Emperor's Second Goldstream Expedition of 1771–1776. Based primarily on Tibetan sources." *The Tibet Journal* 15:2, pp. 3–28.

____(1994): "Pearls from Bones: Relics, Chortens, Tertons and the Sign of Saintly Death in Tibet." *Numen: International Review for the History of Religions* 41, pp. 273–324.

Mathes, K.-D. (1999): "The Sacred Crystal Mountain in Dolpo: Beliefs and Pure Visions of Himalayan Pilgrims and Yogis." *Journal of the Nepal Research Centre* 11, pp. 61–90.

____(2001): "The High Mountain Valley of Nar (Manang) in the 17th Century according to Two Tibetan Autobiographies." *Journal of the Nepal Research Centre* 12, pp. 167–94.

____(2008): *A Direct Path to the Buddha Within: Gö Lotsawa's Mahāmudrā Interpretation of the Ratnagotravibhāga*. Boston.

Matsumoto, S. (1982): "Mādhyamika Philosophy in Tibet: On the mtha' bral dbu ma'i lugs" (jap.). *Tôyo Gakujutsu Kenkyû* 21/22, pp. 161–78.

Mayer, A. L. (1990): "Die Gründunglegende Khotans." In *Buddhistische Erzählliteratur und Hagiographie in türkischer Überlieferung* (= Veröffentlichungen der Societas Uralo-Altaica 27). Wiesbaden, pp. 37–65.

Mayer, R. (1990): "Tibetan Phur-pas and Indian Kīlas." *The Tibet Journal* 15:1, pp. 3–41. Corrected version in *The Buddhist Forum* 2 (Seminar Papers 1988–1990). Delhi (1992), pp. 163–92.

____(1996): *A Scripture of the Ancient Tantra Collection: The Phur-pa bcu-gnyis.* Oxford.

Messerschmidt, D. A. (1989): "The Hindu Pilgrimage to Muktinath, Nepal. Part I. Natural and Supernatural Attributes of the Sacred Field." *Mountain Research and Development* 9:2, pp. 89–104. "Part II. Vaishnava Devotees and Status Reaffirmation." Ibid, pp. 105–18.

Mette, A. (1996): "Beschreibung eines Kultbildes im Gilgit-Manuskript des Kāraṇḍavyūha." *Berliner Indologische Studien* 9/10, pp. 217–23.

____(1997): *Die Gilgitfragmente des Kāraṇḍavyūha* (= Indica et Tibetica 29). Swisstal-Odendorf.

Mimaki, K. (1982): "Le commentaire de Mipham sur le Jñānasārasamuccaya." In *Indological and Buddhist Studies* (= Volume in Honor of Professor J. W. de Jong on his Sixtieth Birthday). Canberra, pp. 353–76.

Mumford, S. R. (1990): *Himalayan Dialogue. Tibetan Lamas and Gurung Shamans in Nepal*. Kathmandu.

Namkhai Norbu (1986): *The Crystal and the Way of Light: Sutra, Tantra and Dzogchen.* New York/London.

de Nebesky-Wojkowitz, R. (1956): *Oracles and Demons of Tibet: The Cult and Iconography of the Tibetan Protective Deities*. Reprint (1975), Graz.

Nimri-Aziz, B. (1978): *Tibetan Frontier Families: Reflections of Three Generations from D'ing ri*. New Delhi.

Oldfield, H. A. (1880): *Sketches from Nepal*, 2 vols. London. Reprint (1981), Delhi.

Oppitz, M. (1968): *Geschichte und Sozialordnung der Sherpa* (= Khumbu Himal 8 / Beiträge zur Sherpa-Forschung 6). Innsbruck.

____(1982): "lCags dpon sangs gyas dpal ,byor: rus yig (Text des 'Berichts von den Knochen') in der Originalfassung." In *Die Sherpa und ihre Nachbarn* (= Khumbu Himal 14 / Beiträge zur Sherpa-Forschung 6), pp. 285–95. Innsbruck.

Orofino, G. (1991): "The Tibetan Myth of the Hidden Valley in the Visionary Geography of Nepal." *East and West* 41:1–4, pp. 239–71.

____(1996): "On the *ṣaḍaṅgayoga* and the Realisation of Ultimate Gnosis in the Kālacakratantra." *East and West* 46:1–2, pp. 127–43.

____(2002): "I Centomila Tantra degli Antichi. L'edizione di sDe dge del rNying ma rgyud 'bum nel fondo Tucci dell Is.I.A.O." In *Facets of Tibetan Religious Tradition and Contacts with Neighbouring Cultural Areas* (= Orientalia Venetiana 12). Firenze, pp. 211–23.

Ortner, S. B. (1978): *Sherpas through their Rituals*. Cambridge.

____(1989): *High Religion: A Cultural and Political History of Sherpa Buddhism.* Princeton.

____(1990): "Patterns of History: Cultural Schemas in the Foundings of Sherpa Religious Institutions." In *Culture through Time: Anthropological Approaches*. Stanford, pp. 57–93.

Pal, P. (1991): *Art of the Himalayas: Treasures from Nepal and Tibet*. New York.

Pandey, R. N. (1970): "The Kallala Dynasty of the Jumla Valley." *Ancient Nepal: Journal of the Department of Archaeology* 12, pp. 45–52.

____(1971): "The History of the Kallala Dynasty." *Ancient Nepal: Journal of the Department of Archaeology* 15, pp. 39–61.

____(1971/72): "The Rise and Developement of the Baisi States." *Ancient Nepal: Journal of the Department of Archaeology* 16, pp. 54–59; 17, pp. 52–56; 18, pp. 50–64.

____(1996): "Buddhist Monuments of Western Nepal." *Journal of Nepalese Studies* 1:1, pp. 87–99.

Parfionovitch, Y. et al. (1992): *Tibetan Medical Paintings: Illustrations of the Blue Beryll Treatise of Sangye Gyamtsho* (1653–1705), 2 vols. London.

Pema Dorjee (1996): *Stupa and its Technology: A Tibeto-Buddhist Perspective*. New Delhi.

Pema Tsering (1978): "*rÑiṅ-ma-pa* Lamas am Yüan-Kaiserhof." In *Proceedings of the Csoma de Körös Symposium held at Matrafured, Hungary, 24-30 September 1976*. Budapest, pp. 511–17.

Petech, L. (1972): *China and Tibet in the Early XVIIIth Century: History of the Establishment of Chinese Protectorate in Tibet* (= Monographies du T'oung Pao 1). Leiden.

____(1984): *Medieval History of Nepal (ca. 750–1482)*. 2nd rev. ed. (= Serie Orientale Roma 54). Rome.

____(1988): *Selected Papers on Asian History* (= Serie Orientale Roma 60). Rome.

Pettit, J. W. (1999): *Mipham's Beacon of Certainty: Illuminating the Vision of Dzogchen, the Great Perfection.* Boston.

Pohle, P. (1993): "Geographical Research in the Cultural Landscape of Southern Mustang." *Ancient Nepal: Journal of the Department of Archaeology* 134, pp. 57–81.

Pommaret, F. (1990): *Bhutan Guidebook*. Hongkong/London.

____(1996): "On Local and Mountain Deities in Bhutan." In *Reflections of the Mountain: Essays on the History and Social Meaning of the Mountain Cult in Tibet and the*

Himalaya (= Österreichische Akademie der Wissenschaften, Phil.-Hist. Klasse 254 / Veröffentlichungen zur Sozialanthropologie 2). Vienna, pp. 39–56.

Prats, R. (1984): "Tshe-dbang nor-bu's Chronological Notes on the Early Transmission of the Bi ma Sñying thig." In *Tibetan and Buddhist Studies* 2 (= Bibliotheca Orientalis Hungarica 29:2). Budapest, pp. 197–210.

Puntsho, K. (2005): *Mipham's Dialectics and the Debates on Emptiness: To be, not to be or neither.* London/New York.

____(2007): "'Ju Mi pham rNam rgyal rGya mtsho: His Position in the Tibetan Religious Hierarchy and a Synoptic Survey of his Contributions." In *The Paṇḍita and the Siddha: Tibetan Studies in Honour of E. Gene Smith.* Dharamasala, pp. 191–209.

Rai, P. K. (1994): *Along the Kali Gandaki: The Ancient Salt Route in Western Nepal.* New Delhi.

Ramble, C. (1984): "The Lamas of Lubra: Tibetan Bonpo Householder Priests in Western Nepal." D. Phil. Thesis, University of Oxford.

____(1987): "The Muktinath Yartung: A Tibetan Harvest Festival in its Social and Historical Context." In *L'Ethnographie* (= numéro spécial: *Rituels himalayens*) 83:100–1, pp. 221–46.

____(1995): "Gaining ground: Representations of territory in Bon and Tibetan popular tradition." *The Tibet Journal* 20:1, pp. 83–124. Reprint (1999) as "The politics of sacred space in Bon and Tibetan popular tradition." In *Sacred Spaces and Power Places in Tibetan Culture*. Dharamsala, pp. 3–33.

____(1997): "Tibetan pride of place: Or, why Nepal's Bhotiyas are not an ethnic group." In *Nationalism and Ethnicity in a Hindu Kingdom* (= Studies in Anthropology and History 20). Amsterdam, pp. 379–413.

____(2007): "The Aya: Fragments of an unknown Tibetan Priesthood." In *Pramāṇakīrtiḥ: Papers Dedicated to Ernst Steinkellner on the Occasion of His 70th Birthday* 2 (= Wiener Studien zur Tibetologie und Buddhismuskunde 70:2). Vienna, pp. 683–720.

Ramble, C. & Vinding, M. (1987): "The Bem-Chag: Village Record and the Early History of Mustang District." *Kailash: A Journal of Himalayan Studies* 13:1–2. Kathmandu, pp. 5–47.

Regmi, D. R. (1965): *Medieval Nepal: Part A (Early Medieval Period, 750–1530 A.D.).* Calcutta.

Reinhard, J. (1978): "Khenbalung, the Hidden Valley." *Kailash: A Journal of Himalayan Studies* 6:1, pp. 5–35.

Reis-Habito, M. D. (1994): *Die Dhāraṇī des Großen Erbarmens des Bodhisattva Avalokiteś-vara mit tausend Händen und Augen* (= Monumenta Serica Monograph Series 27). Nettetal.

Rgya-mtsho Don-grub (1989): "An Account of the History of dPo-smad Ka-gnam sde-pa." *Tibet Studies: Journal of the Tibetan Academy of Social Science* 1, pp. 83–89.

Rhodes, N. G. (1989): "The Monetarisation of Nepal in the Seventeenth Century." *Kailash: A Journal of Himalayan Studies* 15:1–2, pp. 113–17.

Rhodes, N. G., Gabrisch, K. & Valdettaro, C. (1989): *The Coinage of Nepal from the Earliest Times until 1911* (= Royal Numismatic Society Special Publication 21). London.

Ricard, M. et al. (1994): *The Life of Shabkar: The Autobiography of a Tibetan Yogin*. Albany.

Ricca, F. & Lo Bue, E. (1993): *The Great Stupa of Gyantse: A Complete Tibetan Pantheon of the Fifteenth Century*. London.

Riccardi Jr., T. (1973): "Some Preliminary Remarks on a Newari Painting of Swayambhunaṭh." *Journal of the American Oriental Society* 93:3, pp. 334–40.

Richardson, H. E. (1967): "A Tibetan Antiquarian in the XVIIIth Century." In *Bulletin of Tibetology* 4:3, pp. 5–8. Reprint (1998) in *High Peaks, Pure Earth*. London, pp. 379–82.

Risley, H. G. (1894): "History of Sikkim and its Rulers." In *Gazeeter of Sikkim*. Calcutta. Reprint (1972), New Delhi (= Bibliotheca Himalayica I:8).

Roerich, G. N. (1949): *The Blue Annals*. Calcutta. Reprint (1979), Delhi.

Roloff, C. (2009): *Red mda' ba: Buddhist Yogi-Scholar of the Fourteenth Century: The Forgotten Reviver of Madhyamaka Philosophy in Tibet* (= Contributions to Tibetan Studies 7). Wiesbaden.

Rose, L. E. (1990): "Modern Sikkim in a Historical Perspective." In *Reflections on Tibetan Culture: Essays in Memory of Turrell V. Wylie* (= Studies in Asian Thought and Religion 12). Lewiston/Queenston/Lampeter, pp. 59–74.

von Rospatt, A. (1999): "On the Conception of the Stūpa in Vajrayāna Buddhism: The Example of the Svayambhūcaitya of Kathmandu." *Journal of the Nepal Research Centre* 11, pp. 121–47.

____(2001): "A Historical Overview of the Renovations of the Svayambhūcaitya at Kathmandu." *Journal of the Nepal Research Centre* 12, pp. 195–241.

____(2011): "The Past Renovations of Svayambhūcaitya." In *Light of the Valley: Renewing the Sacred Art and Traditions of Svayambhu*. Cazadero, pp. 157–206.

de Rossi Filibeck (1988): *Two Tibetan Guide Books to Ti-se and La-phyi* (= Monumenta Tibetica Historica I:4). Bonn.

de Sales, A. (1991): *Je suis né de vos jeux de tambour: La Religion chamanique des Magar du Nord* (= Recherches sur la Haute Asie 11). Nanterre.

Samuel, G. (1993): *Civilized Shamans: Buddhism in Tibetan Societies*. Washington.

Sardar-Afkhami, H. (1996): "An Account of Padma-Bkod: A Hidden Land in Southeastern Tibet." *Kailash: A Journal of Himalayan Studies* 18:3–4, pp. 1–22.

Sato, M. (1980): "Versuch einer Umschreibung des tibetischen Buddhismus vor Tsong kha pa." *Acta Orientalia Academiae Scientiarum Hungaricae* 34, pp. 209–17.

Schaeffer, K. R. (2004): *Himalayan Hermitess: The Life of a Buddhist Nun.* Oxford/ New York.

Schayer, S. (1921): "Vorarbeiten zur Geschichte der mahāyānistischen Erlösungslehren." In *Untersuchungen zur Geschichte des Buddhismus und verwandter Gebiete*, pp. 39–50. Reprint (1923) as *Mahāyāna Doctrines of Salvation*. London.

Schicklgruber, C. (1996): "Mountain High, Valley Deep: The *yul lha* of Dolpo." In *Reflections of the Mountain*, pp. 115–32. (= Österreichische Akademie der Wissenschaften, Phil.-Hist. Klasse, Denkschriften 254). Vienna.

Schubert, J. (1935): "Der tibetische Mahatmya des Wallfahrtsortes Triloknath." *Artibus Asiae* 5, pp. 76–78 & 127–36.

Schuh, D. (1973): *Tibetische Handschriften und Blockdrucke sowie Tonbandaufnahmen tibetischer Erzählungen* 5 (= Verzeichnis der orientalischen Handschriften in Deutschland 11:5). Wiesbaden.

____(1974): "Ein Rechtsbrief des 7. Dalai Lama für den tibetischen Residenten am Stūpa von Bodnāth." *Zentralasiatische Studien* 8, pp. 423–53.

____(1976): *Tibetische Handschriften und Blockdrucke* 6 (= Verzeichnis der orientalischen Handschriften in Deutschland 11:6). Wiesbaden.

____(1981a): *Tibetische Handschriften und Blockdrucke* 8 (= Verzeichnis der orientalischen Handschriften in Deutschland 11:8). Wiesbaden.

____(1981b): *Grundlagen tibetischer Siegelkunde. Eine Untersuchung über tibetische Siegelaufschriften in 'Phags-pa-Schrift* (= Monumenta Tibetica Historica 3:5). Sankt Augustin.

____(1981c): "Eine Herrscherurkunde des 5. Dalai Lama aus dem Jahre 1676." In *Grundlagen tibetischer Siegelkunde* (= Monumenta Tibetica Historica 3:5), pp. 309–15. Bonn.

____(1988): *Das Archiv des Klosters kKra-shis-bsam-gtan-gling von sKyid-grong*, 1. Teil (= Monumenta Tibetica Historica 3:6). Bonn.

____(1990): "The Political Organisation of Southern Mustang during the 17th and 18th Centuries." *Ancient Nepal: Journal of the Department of Archaeology* 119, pp. 1–5. Also published (1992) in *Aspects of Nepalese Traditions* (= Nepal Research Centre Publications 19). Stuttgart, pp. 235–45.

____(1992): *Untersuchungen zur Geschichte des südlichen Mustang*. 115 pp., unpublished manuscript.

____(1994): "Investigations in the History of the Muktinath Valley and Adjacent Areas, Part I." *Ancient Nepal: Journal of the Department of Archaeology* 137, pp. 9–91. Kathmandu.

____(1995): "Investigations in the History of the Muktinath Valley and Adjacent Areas, Part II." *Ancient Nepal: Journal of the Department of Archaeology* 138, pp. 5–54, Kathmandu.

Schwieger, P. (1985): *Die Werksammlungen Kun-tu bzang-po'i dgongs-pa zang-thal, Ka-dag rang-byung rang-shar und mKha'-'gro gsang-ba ye-shes-kyi rgyud* (= Verzeichnis der orientalischen Handschriften in Deutschland 11:9). Wiesbaden.

____(1988) [1989]: "Zur Rezeptionsgeschichte des gSol 'debs le'u bdun ma und des gSol 'debs bsam pa lhun grub ma." *Zentralasiatische Studien* 21, pp. 29–47.

____(1989): *Die ersten dGe-lugs-pa Hierarchen von Brag-g.yab (1572–1692)* (= Monumenta Tibetica Historica 2:3). Bonn.

____(1990): *Tibetische Handschriften und Blockdrucke* 10 *(Die mTshur-phu-Ausgabe der Sammlung Rin-chen gter-mdzod chen-mo, Bde. 1–14)* (= Verzeichnis der orientalischen Handschriften in Deutschland 11:10). Stuttgart.

____(1995): *Tibetische Handschriften und Blockdrucke* 11 *(Die mTshur-phu-Ausgabe der Sammlung Rin-chen gter-mdzod chen-mo, Bde. 15–34)* (= Verzeichnis der orientalischen Handschriften in Deutschland 11:11). Stuttgart.

____(1999): *Tibetische Handschriften und Blockdrucke* 12 *(Die mTshur-phu-Ausgabe der Sammlung Rin-chen gter-mdzod chen-mo, Bde. 34–40)* (= Verzeichnis der Orientalischen Handschriften in Deutschland 11:12). Stuttgart.

____(2002): "A Preliminary Historical Outline of the Royal Dynasty of sPo-bo." In *Tractata Tibetica et Mongolica: Festschrift für Klaus Sagaster zum 65. Geburtstag* (= Asiatische Forschungen 145). Wiesbaden, pp. 215–29.

Seeber, C. G. (1994): "Reflections on the Existence of Castles and Observation Towers in the Area under Investigation, the South Mustang." *Ancient Nepal: Journal of the Department of Archaeology* 136, pp. 81–87.

Seyfort Ruegg, D. (1963): "The Jo nang pas: A school of Buddhist Ontologists according to the Grub mtha' shel gyi me long." *Journal of the American Oriental Society* 83, pp. 73–91.

____(1969): *La Théorie du Tathāgatagarbha et du Gotra: Études sur la sotériologie et la gnoséologie du bouddhisme* (= Publications de l'École Française d'Extrême-Orient 70). Paris.

____(1973): *Le Traité du Tathāgatagarbha de Bu-ston rin chen grub* (= Publications de l'Ecole Française d'Extrême-Orient 88). Paris.

____(1980): "On the reception and early classifications of the dBu ma (Madhyamaka) in Tibet." In *Tibetan Studies in Honour of H. Richardson*. Warminster, pp. 277–79.

____(1982): "Towards a Chronology of the Madhyamaka School." In *Indological and Buddhist Studies* (= Volume in Honour of Professor J. W. de Jong on his Sixtieth Birthday). Canberra, pp. 505–30.

____(1983): "On the thesis and assertion in the Madhyamaka/dBu ma." In *Contributions on Tibetan and Buddhist Religion and Philosophy* 2 (= Wiener Studien zur Philologie und Buddhismuskunde 11). Vienna, pp. 205–41.

____(1988): "A Karma bKa' brgyud work on the lineages and traditions of the Indo-Tibetan dBu ma (Madhyamaka)." In *Orientalia Iosephi Tucci memoriae dicata* (= Serie Orientale Roma 64:3). Rome, pp. 1249–80.

____(1991): "mChod yon, yon mchod and mchod gnas/yon gnas: On the historiography and semantics of a Tibetan religio-social and religio-political concept." In *Tibetan History and Language: Studies dedicated to Uray Géza on his seventieth birthday.* (= Wiener Studien zur Tibetologie und Buddhismuskunde 26). Vienna, pp. 329–51.

Sharma, P. R. (1972): *Preliminary Study of the Art and Architecture of the Karnali Basin, West Nepal*. Paris.

Shrestha, T. B. (1984/85): *Parvatarājyako aitihāsika rūparekhā*. Kirtipur.

Skilling, P. (1991): "A Brief Guide to the Golden Tanjur." In *The Journal of the Siam Society* 79:2, pp. 138–46.

Skorupski, T. (1990): "The Life and Adventures of David Snellgrove." In *Indo-Tibetan Studies* (= Buddhica Britannica, Series Continua 2). Tring, pp. 1–21.

Slusser, M. S. (1982): *Nepal Mandala: A Cultural Study of the Kathmandu Valley*, 2 vols. Princeton.

Smith, E. G. (1968): "Introduction." In *The Autobiography and Diaries of Si-tu Paṇ-chen* (= Śata Piṭaka Series 77). New Delhi, pp. 5–23. Reprint (2001) in *Among Tibetan Texts*. Boston, pp. 87–98.

____(1969a): "Preface." In *The Life of the Saint of gTsaṅ* (= Śata Piṭaka Series 79). New Delhi, pp. 1–37. Reprint (2001) in *Among Tibetan Texts*. Boston, pp. 59–80.

____(1969b): "Introduction." In *Jam-mgon ju Mi-pham-rgya-mtsho. gZhan gyis brtsad pa'i lan mdor bsdus pa rigs lam rab gsal de nyid snang byed: An Answer to Blo-bzang-rab-gsal's Refutation of the Author's Sher le nor bu ke to ka and its Defense, the brGal lan nyin byed snang ba* (= Ngagyur Nyingmay Sungrab 5). Gangtok, pp. 1–11. Reprint (2001) in *Among Tibetan Texts*. Boston, pp. 227–33.

____(1970a): "Introduction." In *Kongtrul's Encyclopaedia of Indo-Tibetan Culture* (= Śata Piṭaka Series 80), pp. 1–87. New Delhi. Reprint (2001) in *Among Tibetan Texts*. Boston, pp. 235–72.

____(1970b): "Introduction." In *Bka' brgyud gser 'phreng: A Golden Rosary of Lives of Eminent Gurus* (= Smanrtsis Shesrig Spendzod 3). Leh, pp. 1–15. Reprint (2001) in Among Tibetan Texts. Boston, pp. 39–51.

____(1973): Unpublished handout from the XXIXème Congrès des Orientalistes, Paris.

____(2001): *Among Tibetan Texts: History & Literature of the Himalayan Plateau.* Boston.

Snellgrove, D. (1957): *Buddhist Himalaya.* Oxford.

____(1959): *The Hevajra Tantra*. A Critical Study, 2 vols. (= London Oriental Series 6). London.

____(1961a): *Himalayan Pilgrimage: A Study of Tibetan Religion by a Traveller through Western Nepal*. Oxford. Reprint (1989). Boston & Shaftesbury.

____(1961b): "Shrines and temples of Nepal." *Arts Asiatiques* 8:3, pp. 91–120.

____(1967): *Four Lamas of Dolpo*. Oxford. Reprint (1992), Kathmandu.

____(1979): "Places of Pilgrimage in Thag (Thakkhola)." *Kailash: A Journal of Himalayan Studies* 7:2, pp. 75–170.

Sørensen, P. K. (1994): *Tibetan Buddhist Historiography. The Mirror Illuminating the Royal Genealogies: An Annotated Translation of the XIVth Century Tibetan Chronicle rGyal-rabs gsal-ba'i me-long* (= Asiatische Forschungen 128). Wiesbaden.

____(1999): "The Prolific Ascetic lCe-sgom Shes-rab rdo-rje alias lCe-sgom zhig-po." *Journal of the Nepal Research Centre* 11, pp. 176–200.

van Spengen, W. (1987): "The Nyishangba of Manang: Geographical Perspectives on the Rise of a Nepalese Trading Community." *Kailash: A Journal of Himalayan Studies* 13:3–4, pp. 131–282.

Stearns, C. (1980): "The Life and Teachings of the Tibetan Saint Thang-stong rgyal-po." Unpublished Master Thesis, University of Washington.

____(1996): "The Life and Tibetan Legacy of the Indian *Mahāpaṇḍita* Vibhūticandra." *Journal of the International Association of Buddhist Studies* 19:1, pp. 127–71.

____(1999): *The Buddha from Dolpo: A Study of the Life and Thought of the Tibetan Master Dolpopa Sherab Gyaltsen*. Albany.

Stein R. A. (1961): *Une Chronique ancienne de bSam-yas* (= Publications de l'Institut des Hautes Études Chinoises, Textes et Documents I). Paris.

____(1966): "Nouveaux Documents Tibétains sur le Mi-ñag Si-hia." In *Mélanges de Sinologie offerts à Monsieur Paul Demieville*. Paris, pp. 281–89.

____(1987): *Le Monde en petit. Jardins en miniature et habitation dans la pensée religieuse d' Extrême-Orient*. Paris.

____(1988): *Grottes-Matrices et lieux saints de la déesse en Asie Orientale* (= Publications de l' École Française d' Extrême-Orient 151). Paris.

Steinmann, B. (1991): "The Political and Diplomatic Role of a Tibetan Chieftain (*'go ba*) on the Nepalese Frontier." In *Tibetan History and Language: Studies Dedicated to Uray Géza on His Seventieth Birthday* (= Wiener Studien zur Tibetologie und Buddhismuskunde 26). Vienna, pp. 467–85.

Stiller, L. S. (1993): *Nepal: Growth of a Nation*. Kathmandu.

Stoddard, H. (1985): *Le Mendiant de l' Amdo* (= Recherches sur la Haute-Asie 9). Nanterre.

Strickmann, M. (1996): *Mantras et mandarins : Le Bouddhisme tantrique en Chine*. Paris.

Sweet, M. J. (1979): "*Bodhicaryāvatāra* 9:2 as a Focus for Tibetan Interpretations of the Two Truths in the Prāsangika Mādhyamika." *Journal of the International Association of Buddhist Studies* 2, pp. 79–89.

Tarab Tulku (2000): *A Brief History of Tibetan Academic Degrees in Buddhist Philosophy* (= NIAS Reports 43). Copenhagen.

Tashi Tsering (1993): *An Historical Oration from Khams: The Ancient Recitations of Nyag rong by Aten Dogyaltshang* (= Tibetan Literature Series 1). New Delhi.

Thrangu Rinpoche (1978): *The Open Door to Emptiness*. Kathmandu.

Tillemans, T. (1983): "The 'neither one nor many' argument for *Śūnyatā* and its Tibetan Interpretations." In *Contributions on Tibetan and Buddhist Religion and Philosophy* 2 (= Wiener Studien zur Tibetologie und Buddhismuskunde 11:2), pp. 305–20.

Tucci, G. (1931): "The Sea and Land Travels of a Buddhist Sadhu in the Sixteenth Century." *The Indian Historical Quarterly* 7:4, pp. 683–702.

____(1940): *Travels of Tibetan Pilgrims in the Swat Valley*. Calcutta.

____(1953): *Tra Giungle e Pagode*. Rome. Reprint (1977) as *Journey to Mustang 1952* (= Bibliotheca Himalayica I:23). Kathmandu.

____(1956): *Preliminary Report on Two Scientific Expeditions in Nepal* (= Seria Orientale Roma 10 / Materials for the Study of Nepalese History and Culture I). Rome.

____(1958): *Minor Buddhist Texts* 2 (= Serie Orientale Roma 9:2). Rome.

____(1962): *Nepal: The Discovery of the Mallas*. London.

____(1971): *Deb t'er dmar po gsar ma: Tibetan Chronicles by bSod nams grags pa* (= Seria Orientale Roma 24). Rome.

Tulku Thondub (1984): *The Tantric Tradition of the Nyingmapa*. Marion.

Tachikawa, M. (1987): *A Study of the Grub mtha' of Tibetan Buddhism 5: On the Chapter of the bKa' brgyud pa of Thu'u bkwan's Grub mtha'* (= Studia Tibetica 13). Tokyo.

Uebach, H. (1979): "Notes on the Tibetan kinship term *dbon*." In *Tibetan Studies in Honour of Hugh Richardson*. Warminster, pp. 301–9.

____(1999): "On the thirty-seven holy places of the Bon-pos in the Tibetan Empire." In *Studia Tibetica et Mongolica (Festschrift Manfred Taube)* (= Indica et Tibetica 34). Swisttal-Odendorf, pp. 261–77.

Vajracharya, G. (1987): "An Interpretation of Two Similar Nepalese Paintings in the Light of Nepalese Cultural History." In *Heritage of the Kathmandu Valley* (= Nepalica 4). Sankt Augustin, pp. 31–42.

Vajracarya, D. & Malla, K. P. (1985): *The Gopālarājavaṃśāvalī* (= Nepal Research Centre Publications 9). Wiesbaden.

Verhagen, P. (2001): "Studies in Indo-Tibetan Buddhist Hermeneutics 1: Issues of Interpretation and Translation in the Minor Works of Si-tu Paṇ-chen Chos-kyi 'byung-gnas (1699?–1774)." *Journal of the International Association of Buddhist Studies* 24:1, pp. 61–88.

Viehbeck, M. (2012). "The Case of 'Ju Mi-pham (1846–1912) and dPa'-ris Rab-gsal (1840–1912): A study in Dgag lan Debate." Unpublished PhD thesis, University of Vienna.

Vinding, M. (1988): "A History of the Thak Khola Valley, Nepal." *Kailash: A Journal of Himalayan Studies* 14:3–4, pp. 167–211.

____(1998): *The Thakali: A Himalayan Ethnography.* London.

Vitali, R. (1990): *Early Temples of Central Tibet*. London.

____(1996): *The Kingdoms of Gu.ge Pu.hrang: According to mNga'.ris rgyal.rabs by Gu.ge mKhan.chen Ngag.dbang grags.pa*. New Delhi.

____(1997): "Nomads of Byang and mNga'-ris smad. A Historical Overview of Their Interaction in Gro-shod, 'Brong-pa, Glo-bo and Gung-thang from the 11th to the 15th Century." In *Tibetan Studies* 2 (= Österreichische Akademie der Wissenschaften, Phil.-Hist. Klasse, Denkschriften 256). Vienna, pp. 1023–36.

Wach, J. (1922): *Der Erlösungsgedanke und seine Deutung*. Leipzig.

Waddel, L. A. (1882): "Note on the Ma-gu-ta or Cha-rung ka-shor Stupa: A Celebrated Place of Lamaist Pilgrimage in Nepal." In *Proceedings of the Asiatic Society of Bengal,* pp. 186–89.

____(1899): *The Buddhism of Tibet or Lamaism: With its Mystic Cults, Symbolism and its Relation to Indian Buddhism*. London. Reprint (1991). Delhi.

Walleser, M. (1917): *Die Streitlosigkeit des Subhūti* (= Heidelberger Akademie der Wissenschaften, Phil.-Hist. Klasse 13).

Wangchuk, D. (2004): "The rNying-ma Interpretations of the Tathāgatagarbha Theory." In *Wiener Zeitschrift für die Kunde Südasiens* (*Vienna Journal of South Asian Studies*) 48, pp. 171–213.

____(2008): "Cross-Referential Evidence For Establishing A Relative Chronology of Klong chen pa's Works." In *Contributions to Tibetan Buddhist Literature. PIATS 2006. Proceedings of the Eleventh Seminar of the International Association for Tibetan Studies. Königswinter 2006* (= Beiträge zur Zentralasienforschung 14). Halle, pp. 195–244.

____(2009): "A Relativity Theory of the Purity and Validity of Perception in Indo-Tibetan Buddhism." In *Yogic Perception, Meditation and Altered States of Consciousness* (= Österreichische Akademie der Wissenschaften, Phil.-Hist. Klasse Sitzungsberichte 794 / Beiträge zur Kultur- und Geistesgeschichte Asiens 65). Vienna, pp. 215–39.

Wangdu, P. & Diemberger, H. (1996): *Shel Dkar Chos 'Byung: History of the "White Crystal": Religion and Politics of Southern La stod* (= Österreichische Akademie der Wissenschaften, Phil.-Hist. Klasse, Denkschriften 225). Vienna.

Wangmo, J. (2005) : *The Lawudo Lama: Stories of Reincarnation from the Mount Everest Region.* Somerville.

White, K. (1987): *L' esprit nomade*. Paris.

Wiesner, U. (1977): *Nepal: Königreich im Himalaya: Geschichte und Kultur im Kathmandu-Tal*. Schauenberg.

Wilhelm, F. & Panglung, L. (1979): *Tibetische Handschriften und Blockdrucke* 7 (= Verzeichnis der orientalischen Handschriften in Deutschland 11:9). Stuttgart.

Wright, D. (1877): *Nepal: History of the Country and People.* Cambridge. Reprint (1966), Calcutta.

Wylie, T. L. (1962): *The Geography of Tibet According to the 'Dzam-gling-rgyas-bshad* (= Serie Orientale Roma 25). Rome.

____(1970): *A Tibetan Religious Geography of Nepal* (= Serie Orientale Roma 42). Rome.

Yoshimizu, Ch. (1989): *Descriptive Catalogue of the Naritasan Institute Collection of Tibetan Works* 1. Naritasan.

Zanen, M. (1986): "The Godess Vajrayogini and the Kingdom of Sankhu (Nepal)." In *L'Espace du Temps II. Les Sanctuaires dans le Royaume* (= Collection Puruṣārtha 10), pp. 125–66.

Index

Abhayākaragupta, 319
Acala, 433, 446
Ācārya Nam-mkha' dpal, 383
Ādinātha, 111
Amitābha, 113, 168, 421
Amitāyus, 314f.
Aṃśuvarman, 78f., 82, 100f.
Ānanda, 78
Ang rdo-rje, 181
A-ni Chos-skyid, 341
Anuyoga, 168, 382
Arniko, 70
Ārya 'Bu-khang, 427, 445
Ārya 'Ja'-ma-li, 427, 445
Ārya Lokeśvara, 377
Ārya Wa-ti bzang-po, 57, 140, 231, 241, 245, 250f., 274, 427, 445
Āryadeva, 5, 7
Aṭaka, 40
Atiśa, 36, 213, 371, 427f., 431–36, 438, 440f., 443–46
Atiyoga, 167f.
Avalokiteśvara, 57, 111, 113, 168, 186–88, 211, 213, 231, 241, 245, 250f., 274, 286, 320, 323, 413–16, 418f., 421f., 427–29, 433, 435, 437f., 440, 444–46
Avalokiteśvara Khasarpaṇa, 436
Avataṃsakasūtra, 122
A-ya, 400f.
A-ya'i lha-khang, 400
A-yu. *See* Nyang-rigs O-rgyan bstan-'dzin

Balirāja, 336
Bal-yul, 77
Ban-tshang, 324f.
'Ba'-ra-ba bKa'-brgyud-pa, 326f., 399
Bar-bong, 230, 232, 234, 327
Bar-'brog, 388
Bar-'brug, 397
Bar-bung, 223
Bar-rong, 223, 327
bCa'-sne sgang, 286
bDag-chen rNam-rgyal grags-bzang, 68
bDag-med-ma, 414
bDag-mo'i drung, 388
bDe-chen dpal-ri, 335
bDe-chen rDzong-gi lha-khang, 335f., 338f.
bDe-chen steng, 286
bDe-grol, 125f.
bDe-mchog lhan-skyes, 212
bDe-skyid bsam-gling, 170, 181, 183f.
bDe-skyid bsam-grub, 207–9
bDe-skyid chos-gling, 182
bDud-'dul, 144
bDud-'dul rdo-rje, 13. Karma-pa, 59
bDud-'joms gling-pa, 353
bDud-'joms gling-pa'i sprul-sku, 365
Bhatgaon, 65
Bhaṭṭārikā Tārā, 443
Bhāvaviveka, 25
Bhikṣu Jñānasiddhi, 76
Bhikṣunī Lakṣmiṅ[karā], 445
Bhimsaṃser, 406
Bhi-ri-sras, 210, 336f.
Bhoṭīya, 97
Bhu-kaṃ, 79
Big-ram-sras, 336

Bijyālakṣmī, 304
Bir-ba-dhur, 'Dzum-lang rgyal-po, 210
Bir-bā-dhur-sras, 336
bKa'-brgyud 'Phrin-las shing-rta, 7. 'Brug-chen, 58f., 61
bKa'-brgyud-pa, 66, 121, 202, 213, 285, 294, 296f., 301–3, 315, 321f., 327f., 337, 339, 354, 363, 367
bKa'-gdams gzhung-pa, 437
bKa'-gdams-pa, 43f., 415, 427–30, 432, 434–37, 439, 442–44
bKar-ye, 401
bKor gNyer-dpon, 389
bKor-bdag rGyal-po, 389
bKra-shis chos-'phel, 248
bKra-shis khyi-'dren, 44
bKra-shis mthong-smon, 169f.
bKra-shis phun-tshogs, gTang-byon-pa Yon-bdag, 336
bKra-shis stobs-rgyal, Byang-bdag, 141, 160
Bla-chen rGyal-ba bzang-po, 328
Bla-ma bKra-shis rgyal-mtshan, 422
Bla-ma bSod-nams 'od-zer, 441
Bla-ma bTsan-po, 69, 71
Bla-ma dBu-ma-pa, 37
Bla-ma dPal-ldan rdo-rje, 333
Bla-ma dPal-ldan-pa, 441
Bla-ma Karma Chos-bzang, 294–96, 299f., 302, 304–6
Bla-ma Karma Gu-ru, 235
Bla-ma Kun-dga'-ba, 298
Bla-ma 'Phags-rtse, 182f.
Bla-ma rDo-rje bzang-po, 169
Bla-ma sNgags-ram-pa Don-grub rgyal-po, 306
Bla-ma spyan-'dren, 287f.
Bla-ma Thub-bstan dbang-po, 333
Bla-ma Zla-ba seng-ge, 339
Blo-bzang Chos-kyi nyi-ma, 294
Blo-bzang Chos-'phel, 106f., 110
Blo-bzang dbang-po, 378
Blo-bzang dPal-ldan ye-shes, 3. Paṇ-chen Bla-ma, 59
Blo-bzang grags-pa, rJe Tsong-kha-pa, 18, 36–46, 48, 367, 369, 371
Blo-bzang lHa-mchog, 365–68, 375
Blo-bzang rgya-mtsho, 133
Blo-gros bzang-po, 325
Blo-gros dbang-phyug, 316f., 319f.
Blo-gros dpal-bzang, 306
Blo-gros mtha'-yas, 'Jam-mgon Kong-sprul, 28, 419, 423
Blo-gros 'od-zer, 318
Blo-gros rab-yangs, gNas Rab-'byams-pa. *See* Byams-pa phun-tshogs, gNas Rab-'byams pa
Blo-gros rgyal-mtshan, 422
Blo-gros rgyal-mtshan, Sog bzlog-pa, 127
Bod lung-pa, 361
Bodhgayā, 68, 82, 181, 187
Bodhisattvamaṇyāvali, 431, 433
Bodhnāth, 57–59, 61, 63, 65–67, 72, 74, 82, 95–104, 106f., 109, 111, 114, 122–25, 130, 138–40, 142, 148, 159, 234, 241, 245, 265, 288, 338
Bo-dong-pa, 68, 399, 416–19, 423, 425, 443
Bod-pa sprul-sku, 49
Bod-thang, 305
Bon-po, 124, 214, 218, 220, 240, 246f.
Brag-dkar, 222, 230
Brag-dkar bKra-shis lding, 221
Brag-dkar bKra-shis rdzong, 356
Brag-dkar bSam-gling, 229, 231f., 235f., 302
Brag-dkar rta-so, 177, 184, 215, 222f., 229–31, 235–37, 245f., 248, 302, 321f., 333, 335, 397, 402f., 405
Brag-dmar g.Ya-ma lung, 389
Brag-gsum mtsho[-mo-che], 353, 372

Brag-mgo rDo-rje dpal, 383
'Bra-mon sgrong-pa, 110
'Bras-mo ljongs/gshongs, 221, 270, 272f., 370, 384, 390f.
'Bras-spungs, 104, 440
'Bri-bstim, 273
'Bri-gung dgon-pa, 332, 340f.
'Bri-gung ,Jig-rten mgon-po, 233
'Bri-gung Kun-dga' rin-chen, 100
'Bri-gung mthil, 45
'Bri-gung-pa bKa'-brgyud-pa, 127, 284, 423
'Bri-gung Rin-chen phun-tshogs, 127, 267
'Bring-mtshams, 388
Brin-gyi chu-dbar, 105
'Brom, 435, 438f.
'Brug-pa bKa'-brgyud-pa, 65, 72, 103f., 106–10, 136, 188, 213, 224, 236, 243, 250, 322, 333, 340, 366f., 386, 390
bSam-grub dpal, 417f., 421f.
bSam-grub dpal-'bar, 213, 243, 336–38
bSam-grub gling, 325
bSam-grub lde, 66
bSam-grub phug, 234
bSam-grub rtse, 132
bSam-gtan gling, 48, 142
bSam-sding, 135
bSam-yas, 96, 101, 124, 126f., 138, 219, 221, 244, 247, 333, 385, 388–91
bSam-yas Ri-bo-rtse, 389
bShad-pa Chos-'khor gling, 399
bShes-gnyen rnam-rgyal, lHa-mdong Lotsā-ba, 73
bsKal-bzang Padma dbang-phyug, 367
bsKal-bzang rgya-mtsho, 7. Dalai Bla-ma, 60, 367, 371
bSod-nams blo-gros, 232, 313, 315f., 318–20, 325f., 328, 341
bSod-nams bzang-po, 319
bSod-nams dbang-phyug, 135, 313, 315, 322
bSod-nams dpal bzang-po, 83
bSod-nams lha'i dbang-po, 429f., 436, 442
bSod-nams lhun-grub, Glo-bo mkhan-chen, 76, 81, 125, 202f., 317, 325, 420
bSod-nams rgyal-mtshan, Bla-ma dam-pa, 415
bSod-nams rgyal-mtshan, lHo-mon/Mon-lugs Kaḥ-thog-pa, 379f., 382–87, 390f.
bSod-nams rgyal-po, 232
bSod-nams rgya-mtsho, 74
bSod-nams stobs-rgyas, Mi-dbang Pho-lha-ba, 56–58, 60, 134, 356, 366f., 369–75, 398, 401–3
bSod-rgyal Rin-po-che, 244
bsTan-'dzin chos-dbang, mNga'-bdag Nyang-ral, 284
bsTan-'dzin Chos-dar, 170
bsTan-'dzin Chos-kyi blo-gros, 284
bsTan-'dzin Chos-kyi nyi-ma, 4. Khams-sprul, 60, 73, 100, 283
bsTan-'dzin nor-bu, 245
bsTan-'dzin nor-bu, Brag-dkar-ba, 215
bsTan-'dzin nor-bu, 3. Yol-mo-ba sprul-sku, 101–3, 114, 128–44, 146f., 149, 151, 160f., 222, 284, 314, 397
bsTan-'dzin phrin-las, 134
bsTan-'dzin ras-pa, 104, 205–7, 209, 224, 322, 340f.
bsTan-'dzin rdo-rje, 61, 160, 170, 177
bTang-byon, 338
bTang-shog, 335
bTsum, 123, 136, 141, 188
bTsun-pa Chos-legs, 230, 415, 418f., 421f.
Bu-chu gser-gyi lha-khang, 129, 355, 359
Buddha Maitreya, 338
Buddha Rāṣṭrapāla, 76

Buddha Śākyamuni, 76f., 78f., 81, 83, 113, 181f., 186, 190, 233, 245f., 336, 338, 375, 433, 446
Buṃga = Bungamati, 79
Buṃga Lokeśvara = Ārya Bhu-kaṃ 79
'Bum-lde mgon, 70, 314
'Bum-pa, 345
Bum-thang, 46–48, 387, 390
Bum-thang Thar-pa-gling, 388
Bu-ston Rin-chen grub, 185
Buyantu, 406
Bya 'Dul-ba 'dzin-pa, 444
Bya-bral bKra-shis 'byung-gnas, 45
Bya-bral-ba bSod-nams bzang-po, 441
Bya-btang bSam-rgyal, 319
Bya-btang 'Od-zer rgya-mtsho, 303, 333
Bya-rgod phung-po-ri, 148
Bya-rung kha-shor, 57, 64, 82, 95f., 98, 100f., 106, 108–14, 123, 125, 127, 130–32, 137f., 142, 145, 148f.
Byams-pa 'bum[-pa], 379, 382
Byams-pa lha-khang, 232, 325, 337f.
Byams-pa phun-tshogs, gNas Rab-'byams-pa, 74, 229f., 297f., 300–2
Byams-pa sprin-gyi lha-khang, 136, 143–46, 148, 162f., 241, 245, 261, 264, 323, 360, 404
Byams-pa'i dpal, Khro-phu Lo-tsā-ba, 82
Byang, 67, 232, 241, 246, 416–18
Byang Ngam-ring, 125f.
Byang-bdag Rigs-'dzin. *See* bKra-shis stobs-rgyal, Byang-bdag
Byang-chub brtson-'grus, 291
Byang-chub bzang-po, 438
Byang-chub dpal, 441
Byang-chub 'od, 414
Byang-chub rtse-mo, 416
Byang-chub sems-dpa' rGyal-ba ye-shes, 415
Byang-chub sems-dpa' Zla-ba rgyal-mtshan, 413, 415, 445
Byang-gling, 373
Byang-gling btsan-phyug, 353
Byang-gter, 123, 125f., 129, 132f., 137, 143f., 147f., 314, 317, 324, 328, 401
Byang-sems Grol-mchog dbang, 316
Byar-smad, 250, 274
Byar-smad Jo-bo, 245
bZang-po dpal, 406
bZang-po grags-pa, 134
bZang-po rdo-rje, sGam-po-pa sprul-sku, 140
bZang-po rgyal-mtshan, bDag-nyid chen-po, 416f., 421–23, 426
bZhag, 381
bZhag-yul dGon-gsar, 384

Cakrasaṃvara, 65, 82, 214, 299, 301, 328
Cakrasaṃvara-maṇḍala, 77f., 82
Cakrasaṃvaratantra, 202, 206, 210
Caṃgu Nārāyaṇa, 288
Candrakīrti, 7, 13, 20
'Cang, 139
Ca-thang, 147
Catuḥśataka, 31
'Chi-med mgon-po, mDo-chen-pa, 146, 148, 176, 401, 403
'Ching-phu, 389, 391
Chos-blon Padma Gung-btsan, 122, 124, 130, 134, 153
Chos-dbang, 111
Chos-dbang rgyal-mtshan, mNyam-med, 419f., 443
Chos-dbyings khyab-brdal, 402
Chos-dbyings rdo-rje, 10. Karma-pa, 136, 230f., 284, 321
Chos-dpal bzang-po, rDzong-dkar bla-chen, 417
Chos-'dzin, 141

Chos-gling bDe-ba'i rdo-rje, 373
Chos-gling Gar-dbang 'Chi-med rdo-rje, 352–54
Chos-grags rgya-mtsho, 114
Chos-grags rgya-mtsho, 7. Karma-pa, 385
Chos-grub rgya-mtsho, 10. Zhwa-dmar-pa, 59
Chos-kyi bstan-'dzin 'phrin-las, 101
Chos-kyi 'byung-gnas, 8. Si-tu Paṇ-chen, 28, 58f., 73f., 99f., 286, 427
Chos-kyi dbang-phyug, Brag-dkar rta-so sprul-sku, 57, 61, 72–74, 149, 162, 169, 177, 184, 230, 246, 274, 397, 403, 405f.
Chos-kyi dbang-phyug, Kun-mkhyen, 262
Chos-kyi dbang-phyug, 6. Zhwa-dmar-pa, 74, 111, 128, 131f., 136, 222, 229–31, 283–90, 299f., 302, 321
Chos-kyi don-grub, 8. Zhwa-dmar-pa, 235
Chos-kyi rgyal-mtshan, 328
Chos-kyi rgya-mtsho, 365
Chos-kyi sgron-me, 135
Chos-lung, 417
Chos-nyid rang-grol, 147
Chos-rgyal, 404
Chos-rgyal bsod-nams, 75, 318
Chos-rgyal dbang-po'i sde, Byang-bdag rigs-'dzin, 128, 132
Chos-rje Dar-pa, 339
Chos-rje dPa'-bo, 433
Chos-rje Gling-chen, 388
Chos-rje lHa-ro-ba, lHo-brag rDo-rje gdan-pa, 388
Chos-rje Seng-ge rgyal-mtshan, 441
Chos-rje sGam-po, 353
Chos-rje Sher-'bum, 415
Chos-rje sTon-pa, 401
Chos-sdings, 417f.
Chos-skyabs dpal-bzang-po, 83, 313, 315f., 318–20
Chos-skyong dpal-bzang, 315
Chu-bzang, 390
Chu-mig brgya-rtsa, 207–9, 212, 231
Chu-mig Byang-chub bdud-rtsi, 73
Chu-mig dGon-gsar, 385
Chu-mo, 268
Churi-Ghyang, 265
Chu-shur, 365
Co-pa, 110, 111

Dag-pa shel-ri, 245
Dar-kha-rgyal, 289
Dar-ma grags, 437, 439
Dar-rtse-mdo, 221
'Dar-thil, 286
dBang-phyug brtson-'grus, Lo ras-pa, 366f.
dBang-phyug dpal-ldan, 418
dBang-phyug rdo-rje, 9. Karma-pa, 128
dBang-phyug rgyal-mtshan. *See* dBang-phyug dpal-ldan
dBang-rgyal rdo-rje, 241–44
dBus, 69, 135, 138
dBus-gtsang, 386
dByangs-can grub-pa'i rdo-rje, 184f.
De-bum rā-dza, 204
De'u Rin-chen spungs-pa, 356
Devīkoṭa, 202
dGa'-ba-lung gTer-ston, 358
dGa'-bo ,Jogs-pa, 214
dGa'-ldan, 441
dGa'-ldan bDud-'joms gling, 363–65
dGa'-ldan Byams-pa gling, 132
dGa'-ldan Chos-'phel gling, 72, 104
dGa'-ldan Don-gnyis gling, 365
dGa'-ldan Pho-brang, 136
dGa'-ldan Phun-tshogs gling, 432
dGa'-rab rdo-rje, 175
dGa'-rab rdzong, 220, 225, 234, 322
dGa'-thang nub-ma, 127
dGe-bshes dGe-'dun blo-gros, 294

dGe-bshes rGyal-ba dpal-bzang, 44
dGe-bshes Zul-phu-ba, 444
dGe-dkar, 242, 244, 247–50
dGe-'dun blo-gros, 383
dGe-'dun Chos-'phel, 35
dGe-'dun grub, 1. Dalai Bla-ma, 441
dGe-'dun rgya-mtsho, 2. Dalai Bla-ma, 36
dGe-ldan-pa, 68
dGe-lugs-pa, 5, 7, 12, 26, 35f., 104, 121, 185, 244, 363, 371
dGe-lung, 319
dGe-rgyas 'Jag-ma lung, 382, 384
dGe-ri, 188
dGon-lung, 294
dGon-pa byang, 150, 397
dGon-pa gsar-ba, 215
dGon-pa Me-'byems, 232
dGon-pa sGang, 248f.
dGon-pa sGar, 242
dGos bsam-'phel, 306
dGos-'joms, 306
dGra-'dul seng-ge, 296, 306
dGung-sbrang, 289
Dharmapāla, 41, 185
Dharmarāja Viśvadeva, 76
Dhaulāgiri, 210–13, 218, 223, 247, 250f., 332
Dhvajabhadra, 38
Dil-mgo mKhyen-brtse Rin-po-che, 397
Ding-ri, 57, 264, 333
dKa'-chen rDo-rje mgon-po, 315
dKar-rgyud bstan-pa'i rgyal-mtshan, 295f., 302f.
dKar-ye dNgos-grub mtsho-gling, 140f., 147f., 401f.
dKon-mchog chos-skyabs, 319
dKon-mchog legs-pa, 68
dKon-mchog lhun-grub, 326
dKon-mchog yan-lag, 5. Zhwa-dmar-pa, 302
dMar-po ri, 377
dMar-sgom, 232f., 315–18, 320f., 328, 341
dNgos-grub mtsho-gling, 139
dNgos-grub phug, 399, 401
dNgos-grub rgyal-mtshan, 317f., 320, 324
dNgul-chu, 184
Dol, 139
Dol-po, 104, 201, 222–25, 230, 232–35, 321
Dol-po sKag, 223, 225
Don-grub chos-gling, 182f.
dPa'-bo 'Jigs-med rdo-rje, 370
dPag-bsam dbang-po, 5. 'Brug-chen, 322, 333
dPag-bsam ye-shes, 236, 322
dPal 'Bri-gung-pa chen-po Ratnalakṣmi. *See* 'Bri-gung Rin-chen phun-tshogs
dPal sNar-thang, 427, 429–31, 434, 439
dPal Ti-pha-phad, 220
dPal-'dar, 122
dPal-gyi rdo-rje, 138
dPal-'khor bDe-chen, 326
dPal-khud, 270
dPal-ldan blo-gros, 313, 315, 334
dPal-ldan bzang-po, 315, 334
dPal-ldan dar, 417
dPal-ldan don-grub, 233, 315–17, 320
dPal-ldan rdo-rje, 315, 333f.
dPal-ldan rgyal-mtshan, 319
dPal-ldan sangs-rgyas, 417, 421
dPal-ldan sding, 401
dPal-ldan seng-ge, 319, 417, 423
dPal-ldan zla-ba, 13
dPal-mo chos-sding, 399f.
dPal-mo dpal-thang, 427, 429–31, 434, 439
dPal-sding, 401
dPal-spungs, 6
dPal-thang, 264, 270, 271
dPal-tshogs, 288
dPon-chen Blo-gros, 44

dPon-chen lHa-grub ,bum, 318
dPon-chen Śākya bzang-po, 66f., 69f., 80
dPon-chen Seng-ge, 44
dPon-drung bDe-skyid bsam-grub, 207, 209
dPon-drung [khri-pa] Tshe-gnas rgyal-po, 207–9
dPon-drung khri-sde Ngag-dbang rnam-rgyal, 210
dPon-drung Khro-bo dar-po, 209
dPon-drung Khro-bo rgyal-mtshan, 232
dPon-drung Khro-bo rnam-rgyal, 231
dPon-drung Khro-bo tshe-dbang, 207
dPon-drung rin-po-che bSod-nams rgyal-po, 231
dPon-sa'i bdag-mo drung, 390
Drag-po sgrub-phug, 361
Drang-so dGa'-ldan, 141
Drang-so dGa'-ldan-pa, 141
Drang-so gTer-ston Śākya bzang-po. See Śākya bzang-po, 1. Yol-mo-ba sprul-sku
Drang-so sNgags-'chang Śākya bzang-po. *See* Śākya bzang-po, 1. Yol-mo-ba sprul-sku
Drang-so sprul-sku chen-po. *See* Śākya bzang-po, 1. Yol-mo-ba sprul-sku
'Dre-lung skyo-mo, 272f.
'Dren-mchog Chos-kyi dbang-phyug. *See* Chos-kyi dbang-phyug, Brag-dkar rta-so sprul-sku
'Dren-mchog Padma rgyal-po, 169
Dri-med Kun-dga', 389
Drin-can 'phags-pa, 327
Drung Nam-mkha' seng-ge, 380, 383
Drung rGyal-mtshan rdo-rje, 383
Dum-kham, 286
Dung-sgra mThon-smon gling, 399
Du-va-ri-ka, 110
Dwags-la sgam-po, 245, 353
Dwags-po, 265, 300, 359
Dwags-po bKa'-brgyud-pa, 300
Dwags-po dGongs-'dus gling, 389
'Dzam-gling, 399f.
'Dzam-gling lha-khang, 400
Dza-vi, 205
Dza-vi-ba Grub-chen Dzā-ha-bhi, 206
Dzo-'dril dgon, 289
'Dzum-chen Gangs-ri gnas, 361

Ekādaśamukha-Avalokiteśvara, 415

gaṇacakra, 78, 80, 133, 204, 298, 338, 367
Gaṇeśa, 65f., 79, 376
Gaṅgā, 189
Gangs Rin-po-che. *See* Ti-se (Kailāśa)
Gangs zhur-mo, 323
Gang-shar rang-grol, 378
Gangs-ri khang-sa, 185
Gangs-ri thod-dkar, 245
Gangs-yul, 287f.
Gar-dbang Chos-kyi dbang-phyug. *See* Chos-kyi dbang-phyug, 6. Zhwa-dmar-pa
Gar-dbang don-grub, 303
Gar-dbang rdo-rje, mNga'-ris gter-ston, 108, 144, 163, 165, 223f., 240, 261, 263f., 267, 273f., 323f., 334, 342, 344f., 360
Garuḍa, 35
[g]Cong-[g]zhi, 212f., 243f., 249f.
gCung Ri-bo-che, 131, 232
gDan-sa Thel, 75
Ge-sar, 372
Gīrvāṇa Yuddha Vikrama Śāha, 304
Glang, 341
Glang Dar-ma, 138
Glang-chu, 402
Glang-ma lung, 387f.

Glang-'phrang, 147, 176, 262–64, 269–75, 297, 400–2
Glang-ra rgyag-sa, 403
Gling-bu, 385, 388
Gling-chen Kun-bzang dpal. *See* Kun-bzang dpal, dMus-ston chen-po
Glo, 355
Glo-bo, 125, 220, 222, 230, 233, 319, 321
Glo-bo dGe-dkar, 247
Glo-bo rGyam-dpal, 318
Glo-bo smad, 363
Glo-bo smon-thang, 325, 337
gNam-gung, 222, 314, 321f., 334,
gNam-lcags 'bar-ba, 352, 356
gNam-lcags rdo-rje [rTsa-gsum gling-pa], 360, 373
gNam-sgo zla-gam, 262, 268–72, 274, 401
gNas Padma-bkod, 221, 351–60, 363, 369, 372f., 375
gNas-chen Devikoṭi, 105
gNas-mchog Gra-lung, 341
gNas-mchog gSal-dwangs ri-bo-che, 374
gNas 'og grwa-tshang, 416–18
gNas-rnying-pa, 387f.
gNubs Nam-mkha'i snying-po, 56
gNya'-lam, 222, 225, 285
gNya'-nang, 57, 231, 262–64, 271, 274
gNya'-nang khur-bu, 270
gNya'-nang rtsa-sgo, 262
gNya'-nang stod, 262
gNyan Tshem-bu-pa, 413
gNyug-la, 442
Goma, 76–78
Go-ma-sa-la-gan-dha, 73, 76–78, 81f.
Gopālarājavaṃśāvalī, 96, 99
Go-rams-pa bSod-nams seng-ge, 220, 326
Gorkhā, 58f.
Gośṛṅga, 77
Gośṛṅga-vyākaraṇa-sūtra, 76–78, 83
Govicandra Mahāvihāra, 74
Grags-pa blo-gros, 41
Grags-pa 'byung-gnas, 6. Phag-mo-gru sDe-srid, 75
Grags-pa mtha'-yas, 386
Grags-pa 'od-zer, 47f., 385
Grags-pa rgyal-mtshan, 47, 414
Grags-pa rgyal-mtshan, Chos-rje ston-pa, 385, 390
Grags-pa rgyal-mtshan, 5. Phag-mo-gru sDe-srid, 75, 82
'Gram, 284, 286
Gram-so/Drang-so [rdzong], 124f., 139
Gṛdhakūta, 81
Grod[-pa] phug, 231, 285
'Gro-'dul Las-'phro gling-pa, 385, 390
Grom-pa rGyang[s], 134
Gro-shod, 230, 417
Grub-chen dPal-ldan rgyal-mtshan, 288
Grub-dbang O-rgyan bstan-'phel, 401
Grub-dbang Padma nor-bu, 56
Grub-mchog dbang-po, 229f., 301f.
Grub-thob Blo-bzang lHa-mchog, 364f.
Grub-thob Chu-sgom-pa, 422
Grub-thob dNgos-grub, 421f., 425
Grub-thob rGyal-mtshan, 288
Grub-thob Seng-ge ye-shes, 233
'Grum-pa lha-khang, 212
Grwa, 399, 401
Grwa A-ya, 400
Gr[w]a-lung, 324f., 341
Grwa-phu chos-gling, 241, 327, 399f.
Grwa-yul, 400
gSang-phu sNe'u-thog, 10, 435
gSang-sngags bDe-chen gling, 399
gSang-sngags bstan-'dzin, Kham[s]-lung-pa, 148, 399–402
gSang-sngags Byang-chub gling, 365
gSang-sngags chos-dar, 177
gSang-sngags chos-gling, 232f.
gSang-sngags gling, 381

gSang-sngags rdo-rje, 266
gSer-ba Ye-shes rgyal-mtshan, 182f.
gSer-bzang ras-chen, 146
gSer-ldan-pa, 38
gSer-mdog-can, 325f.
gTam-zhing, 387f., 390, 399
gTan-bu, 289
gTang-byon, 335
gTer-dbon Nyi-ma seng-ge, 142–47, 286, 288, 304
gTing-skyes, 150, 397
gTsang, 57, 59, 68f., 104, 124, 128f., 132, 134–36, 138–40, 388
gTsang-gi zab-bu gling, 389
gTsang Gong-ra, 395
gTsang La-stod, 399
gTsang-nag-pa brTson-'grus seng-ge, 10
gTsang-po, 261
gTsang-rong, 264
gTsang-ston rDo-rje rgyal-mtshan, 379, 382
gTsang Theg-mchog gling, 404
gTsug-lag dga'-ba, 7. dPa'-bo, 58f., 61
gTsug-lag phreng-ba, 2. dPa'-bo, 78, 432f.
gTum-skul shel dang 'ba'-ro gnas, 361
Gu-ge, 66
Guhyagarbhatantra, 22, 31, 168, 406
Guhyapati, 40
Guhyeśvarī, 82
Gumvihāra, 99
Gung-thang, 66, 70, 125–27, 135, 143, 147, 203, 231, 266f., 275, 314, 360, 399, 417f., 420, 422
Gur, 222
Gu-ru bDe-ba, 72, 104
Guru Chos-dbang, gTer-ston, 142, 315, 320, 383, 389
Gu-ru gZhan-phan, 45
Gu-ru phug, 305
Guru Rin-po-che. *See* Padmasambhava
Guru Śākya rgyal-mtshan, 144
Gu-ru Tshe-brtan rgyal-mtshan, 267–69, 271f., 390
Gu-śri bsTan-'dzin chos-rgyal, 365
g.Ya-ma bKra-shis-'khyil, 35
g.Ya'-ma sTag-ri, 384
g.Ya-ma sTag-rtse, 384
Gyam-ring-po, 76
g.Yang-ri-ma, 145, 304
g.Yas-ru, 414
'Gyes-phug, 139
g.Yu-lding-ma, 182f., 191
g.Yul-rgyal rdzong, 442f.
'Gyur-med bstan-'dzin, 402
'Gyur-med mThu-stobs rnam-rgyal, Zhe-chen dbon-sprul, 28
'Gyur-med 'Phrin-las bstan-'dzin, 401
'Gyur-med rdo-rje, 306
'Gyur-med rdo-rje, gTer-bdag gling-pa, 148, 159, 161–63, 173, 176, 179, 186, 208, 335, 356, 369–71, 395, 398, 401
'Gyur-med rnam-rgyal, mDo-chen-pa, 58, 60, 370, 400f., 403
'Gyur-med Theg-mchog bstan-'dzin, 2. rDzogs-chen Padma Rig-'dzin, 17
'Gyur-med Tshe-brtan, 402
'Gyur-med Tshe-dbang mchog-grub, Kaḥ-thog dGe-rtse Paṇḍita, 19, 24–29, 396
g.Yu-sgra snying-po, 184, 343, 345
gZhad, 128
gZhag, 383
gZhan-dga', 244f.
gZhan-phan Chos-kyi snang-ba, 244
gZhan-phan rdo-rje, Gong-ra Lo-chen, 395, 399, 404
gZhis-ka-rtse, 285
gZhon-nu dpal, 'Gos Lo-tsā-ba, 69, 413–15
gZho-stod Ti-sgro, 45
gZhung, 405f.
gZims-'og Rin-po-che, 245

Had, 386
Hanuman, 81
Hayagrīva, 46f., 421
Hevajra, 328
Hevajratantra, 201–3, 205f., 242
Himālaya, 82
Ho-ga rta-ngam ma-nu'i gnas, 361
Hrab, 315, 324, 333f.
Hūṃkāra, 176

Indra, 77
I-pi Chos-legs, 305
I-pi Khrib-tse, 305
I-pi Yi-dam, 305

Jagajjyotirmalla, 284
Jalandhara, 65
Jāmācok/Jāmāvca, 81, 338
Jambudvīpa, 71, 76
'Jam-dbyangs bSod-nams seng-ge, 422
'Jam-dbyangs bstan-pa rgya-mtsho, Brag-dgon sprul-sku, 439
'Jam-dbyangs dPal-ldan bzang-po, 315
'Jam-dbyangs grags-pa, 173, 365, 377
'Jam-dbyangs Kha-che, 41
'Jam-dbyangs mKhyen-brtse dbang-po, 28, 364
'Jam-dbyangs rin-chen, 377
'Jam-dpal chos-lha, Lo-paṇ ras-chen, 183
'Jam-dpal rgya-mtsho, 39
Jaya Jagajjayamalla, 145
Jayabhimadeva, 70
Jayaprakāśamalla, 58–61
'Jigs-bral Ye-shes rdo-rje, bDud-'joms Rin-po-che, 24, 352
'Jigs-byed Nag-po, 102
'Jigs-med gling-pa, 14, 109, 354, 360, 395, 406
'Jigs-med grags-pa, Bo-dong Paṇ-chen/Bo-dong Kun-mkhyen. *See* Phyogs-las rnam-rgyal, Bo-dong Paṇ-chen/Bo-dong Kun-mkhyen
'Jigs-med Nam-mkha' rdo-rje, Khyung-sprul, 246f.
'Jigs-med rnam-rgyal, Khrong-sa dpon-slob, 291
Jñānaketu, 381
Jñānasārasamuccaya, 5, 13
Jñānasiddhi, 76f., 80
Jo-bo 'Jam-dpal rdo-rje, 244
'Jo-grub 'od-zer, 44
Jo[-mo] nang, 203, 327, 414f.
Jo-mo Tshe-ring-ma, 186
Jo-nang Tāranātha, 128, 131, 203
Jo-nang-pa, 20, 68, 128f., 207, 230, 328, 414f.
'Jo-sras dKon-mchog-skyabs, 44
Jyotirmañjarī, 319

Kāgbeni, 220, 225
Kaḥ-dam-pa bDe-gshegs, 379, 382f.
Kaḥ-gnam, 357f.
Kaḥ-gnam sde-pa, 353, 357
Kaḥ-thog, 11, 24, 27f., 31, 55f., 203, 342f., 379–83, 385–91
Kaḥ-thog Si-tu Chos-kyi rgya-mtsho, 364, 379f.
Kaḥ-thog-pa Kun-tu bzang-po, 391
Kakṣaka, 77
Kālacakra, 131, 414
Kālacakratantra, 68, 416
Kala-Siddhi, 44
Kāli Gaṇḍakī, 219, 221, 223, 249, 333
Kanakamuni, 77
Kaṇika, 106, 110
Kaṇṭha-sthāna, 42
Karma bDud-'joms. *See* 'Phrin-las bdud-'joms, mGon-gnang-pa
Karma/Kaṃ-tshang bKa'-brgyud-pa, 128, 229–31, 235

Karma Blo-bzang, rNgog-ston, 222f., 229–36, 296, 302f., 321–24, 333, 335
Karma bstan-'dzin, 404
Karma bsTan-skyong dbang-po, gTsang sde-srid, 129, 135f., 230, 284–86, 321
Karma chags-med, Rāga-asya, 185
Karma Chos-bzang, 295f., 299, 305
Karma Chos-'phel, 222, 321
Karma dBang-rgyal, 232
Karma dGe-legs, 305
Karma Don-grub, 170, 177, 183f.
Karma Gu-ru, 234, 302, 305
Karma Nges-don, Nyang-rigs bla-ma, 163, 169, 177, 183
Karma 'Phrin-las dbang-po, 296, 303
Karma Phun-tshogs rnam-rgyal, gTsang sde-srid, 132
Karma Ras-chung, 295
Karma rNam-mkhyen, 304, 306
Karma Thub-bstan, 305
Karma Thub-bstan snying-po rnam-par rgyal-ba, 131
Karmārapāṭaka, 202
Kāruṇyapāṭaka, 202
Kāśyapa, 65, 77, 79, 98, 101, 187
Kham[s]-lung-pa gNyags-ston, 402
Kham-pa lung-pa Śākya Yon-tan, 434
Khams, 55, 58f., 144, 183
Khams Mi-nyag, 67, 82
Khams-bu lung, 264
Khams-pa sKon-mchog lhun-grub, 322
Khang-chen-nas, 369–71, 375
Khasa, 97, 99
Kha-shwa, 100
Khasti, 98f.
'Khor-chags (Khojarnāth), 241
'Khor-lo sdom-pa. *See* Cakrasaṃvara
Khri bDud-'dul mgon-po, lde 267
Khri Kun-dga' rnam-rgyal lde, 422, 419–21
Khri lHa-dbang rgyal-mtshan, 135, 417
Khri rNam-rgyal lde, 66, 417f.
Khri Srong lde'u-btsan, 56, 124, 127, 168, 421
Khri-rgyal bSod-nams dbang-phyug lde, 126–28, 132, 135
Khri-rgyal 'Bum-lde mgon, 203
Khro-bo bsam-grub, 232
Khro-bo dpal-mgon, 243
Khro-bo rnam-rgyal, 232
Khro-bo skyabs-pa, 206
Khros[-ma] nag[-mo], 113
Khum-bu, 183
Khu-ston brtson-'grus, 431
Khyung Tshang-ba, 264
Khyung-rdzong dkar-po, 57, 314
Kiṃdol, 60, 81
Kiṃdol Vihāra, 58f., 71, 148
Klo-bkra-pa, 355
Klo-dkar-po, 355
Klo-nag-po, 355
Klong-chen rab-'byams-pa, 8–14, 17–21, 25f., 29–31, 45, 47f., 161, 188, 244f., 383, 387f.
Klong-rdol, 355
Klo-yul, 354f.
Klu-lnga, 129
Klu-mo dkar-mo, 183
Klungs-shod, 437f.
Ko-khom, 306
Kong-'phrang, 359
Kong-po, 128f., 164, 221, 323, 352f., 355–59, 361, 369f., 372, 374, 395
Kong-po brug-thang gter-chen, 353, 360
Kong-po lha-chu, 274
Ko-ron, 417
Kriyātantra, 442
Kṣipa gyu-rdzong, 361
Kubilai Khan, 68–70
Kumāra-Kārttikeya, 60

Kumāramati, 'Brom-ston, 430f., 439f.
Kun-bzang bDe-chen rgyal-po. *See* Kong-po brug-thang gter-chen
Kun-bzang brag, 333, 335
Kun-bzang dpal, dMus-ston chen-po, 385, 388, 390
Kun-bzang gling, 387
Kun-bzang 'Gyur-med lhun-grub, 400f.
Kun-bzang klong-yangs, Glo-bo bla-ma/ Glo-bo-pa, 207–10, 212, 223, 234, 248, 333, 335, 338
Kun-bzang mthong-grol rdo-rje, 1. 'Khrul-zhig, 184, 187
Kun-bzang Nges-don klong-yangs, 101
Kun-bzang Nyi-zla grags-pa, 125, 143, 266f.
Kun-bzang 'od-zer O-rgyan Gar-dbang bstan-pa'i nyi-ma, 354
Kun-bzang Rig-grol rdo-rje, 250
Kun-dga' 'bum, 325
Kun-dga' 'bum[-pa], 383
Kun-dga' bzang-po, dBus-smyon, 326
Kun-dga' bzang-po, Ngor-chen, 218, 325f.
Kun-dga' grags-pa, bSam-yas dkar-chen, 267, 389
Kun-dga' grol-mchog, Jo-nang rje-btsun, 128, 203f., 232, 234, 315, 327, 413, 415
Kun-dga' legs-pa, 7. Phag-mo-gru sDe-srid, 75
Kun-dga' legs-pa'i 'byung-gnas, 9. g.Yang-lung Chos-rje, 390
Kun-spangs Chos-kyi nyi-ma, 325–27
Kun-spangs don-grub, 443
Kun-spangs-pa Thugs-rje brtson-'grus, 414f.
Kun-tu bzang-po, 38
Kuśinagara, 95
Ku-thang Nub-ris, 417f.
Ku-thang rTsum, 222–24
Ku-ti, 285
Lag-sor-pa, 444
La-kha-gangs, 264
Lakṣminarasiṃha, 284f., 288
Lakṣmīṅ[karā], 413
La-ldebs, 141, 222, 241, 323, 401, 403
Lam 'bras, 327
La-phyi, 105, 202, 206, 248, 264, 273, 275, 284f., 289
La-phyi Chu-dbar, 136
La-rgyab Shes-rab dpal, 383
Las-'brel-rtsal, 47
Las-chen Kun-dga' rgyal-mtshan, 430, 441
Las-kyi rdo-rje, 40f.
La-stod, 141, 388f., 399
La-stod Byang, 68, 82, 125f., 131f., 147
La-stod lHo, 68, 82, 124, 136, 139, 183, 390, 416, 420, 425
La-stod rGyal-gyi śrī-ri, 105, 183, 214
lCags-zam Thog-kha, 387f.
lCam-mo Ye-shes mchog, 422, 426
lCang-lo-can. *See* Aṭaka
lCe-sgom-pa, 444
Legs-ldan bDud-'joms rdo-rje, mNga'-ris rig-'dzin, 122, 125–28, 132f., 147, 160, 317, 390f.
Legs-rtse, 221
lHa bla-ma Ye-shes 'od, 437
lHa-btsun Kun-dga' chos-kyi rgya-mtsho, 386
lHa-btsun Nam-mkha' 'jigs-med, 221, 270, 272f., 370
lHa-btsun Rin-chen rnam-rgyal, 61, 74, 177, 230, 275, 297, 300
lHa-bzang [Khan], 355, 366
lHa-chen Bres-gshongs-pa, 404
lHag-bsam[bstan-pa'i] rgyal-mtshan, 6, 22
lHa-gdong, 104, 107
lHa-lung, 138
lHa-lung dPal-gyi rdo-rje, 114, 138
lHa-mtsho srin-mtsho, 264, 270

lHa-ri snying-po, 431, 434
lHa-rje dGe[-ba] 'bum, 421, 423, 425f.
lHa-ro Chos-rje, 389
lHa-sa, 58f., 245, 301, 365f., 371, 383, 385, 389
lHa-sa sKyid-shod, 389
lHo, 67
lHo sPa-gro, 221
lHo-bdag Chos-kyi rin-chen, 416
lHo-brag, 37f., 43f., 48, 109, 127, 364–69, 375, 379, 389, 400
lHo-brag Gro-bo lung, 364
lHo-brag Khom-mthing lha-khang, 364, 367
lHo-brag lHa-lung, 387, 398
lHo-brag mKhar-chu, 363f.
lHo-brag rDo-bo rdzong, 365
lHo-brag rDo-rje gdan, 389
lHo-brag sMra-bo-lcog, 182
lHo-gling, 373f.
Lhun-grub brtsegs pa, 102
Lhun-grub pho-brang, 395
Lhun-grub steng, 6
Licchavi, 97–100
Li-khri, 287
Ling-nga brag-dmar, 323
Li-ti, 287
Li-yul, 76–78, 81, 182
Lo-chen bSod-nams rgya-mtsho, 75
Lo-chen Byang-chub rtse-mo, 416
Lo-chen Dharma-śrī, 28f.
Lo-chen 'Gyur-med bde-chen, 131
Lo-chen mChog-gi sprul-sku, 128
Lo-chen Ratnabhadra, 128, 149
Lo-chen sKyabs-mchog dpal bzang-po, 441
Long-mo lha-steng, 364
Lug-lha, 396
Lu-ma-dgo-dmar, 57
Ma-cig Rwa-ma, 135
Madhyamaka, 6–8, 10–15, 19–21, 24–27, 29–31, 35f., 38, 294
Madhyamakālaṃkāra, 5, 9, 13f.
Madhyamakaratnapradīpa, 25
Madhyamakāvatāra, 7, 20, 31
Ma-gcig Lab-sgron, 262
Ma-gu-ta, 95
Mahādeva, 111
Mahādeva-Gaṇeśa, 60
Mahākāla, 81, 149
Mahākāruṇika, 148, 168, 187f., 320, 326, 413–23, 444f.
Mahākāruṇika-Ṣaḍakṣara, 444
Mahāmudrā, 300, 326f, 414
Mahāmuni. *See* Buddha Śākyamuni
Mahāpaṇḍita Śāriputra, 66–69, 82f.
Mahāpaṇḍita Vanaratna, 68f., 74f., 79, 83, 318
Mahāyoga, 167f., 382
Maheśvara, 376
Maitreya, 232, 369
Maitreyanātha, 440, 446
Mal-gro, 437f.
Malla, 61, 98, 100, 111, 131f., 139, 148, 204, 230, 285, 289, 290, 299, 331, 336
Mānadeva, 96–100
Mandarava, 44
Mang-kar, 286–88, 290
Mang-yul, 122, 139, 162f., 215, 231, 241, 245f., 248, 250f., 261, 271f., 274f., 360
Mang-yul Gung-thang, 72f., 82, 125, 127, 132, 134f., 148, 183, 188, 215, 220f., 229f., 235, 297f., 301f., 314, 321–23, 327, 397, 399, 425, 443–45
Mang-yul Ri-bo dpal-'bar, 105, 122, 126, 134f., 137, 142f., 147, 221f., 272f., 289, 322, 333, 401f.
Mang-yul sKyid-grong, 139, 141f., 147, 149, 398, 402f., 406, 427, 445

Maṇi-Yoginī, 96
Mañjuśrī, 7, 65, 186, 241, 250, 427
Mañjuśrī-mūla-tantra, 76, 78, 83
Ma-pham (Manosarowar), 112, 214, 240, 324, 339
Māricī, 82
Mar-pa, 105, 122, 295
Mar-pa bKa'-brgyud-pa, 294
Mar-phag/Mārphā, 219
Mar-yul, 108
Ma-thang, 316
Maudgalyāyana, 81
Māyādevī, 81
mChims Nam-mkha' grags, 427, 439
mChod-rten nag-po, 402, 404
mDo[-bo]-che[n], 136, 138, 141, 143, 146, 148, 400–2
mDo-chen [bKa'-brgyud-pa], 148, 222, 400
mDo-khams, 221, 386
mDo-sngags bstan-pa'i nyi-ma, Bod-pa sprul-sku, 5, 7, 21, 23
mDung-chu'i lha-khang, 360
mDzod-lnga stag-rtse, 382
Me-me Blo-gros dpal-bzang, 305
Me-me Chos rgyal-mtshan, 305
Me-me dBang-chen, 305
Me-me dKar-rgyud, 305
Me-me Don-grub rgyal-po, 305
Me-me Gar-dbang don-grub, 304, 306
Me-me Karma Chos-bzang, 306
Me-me Karma Gu-ru, 305
Me-me Kun-dga' rgyal-po, 305
Me-me mThong-ba rgyal-po, 305
Me-me Ngag-dbang, 305
Me-me 'Phrin-las dbang-po, 305f.
Me-me Thar-pa rgyal-po, 305
Me-skyems dgon-pa, 340f.
Me-tog dpag-yas, 183, 191
mGar-phug, 244, 246, 248
mGar-phug sprul-sku, 246
mGon-gnang, 149, 402f.
mGon-po gnas, 361
mGon-po rgyal-mtshan, 202
mGo-yul, 388
mGrin-stan, 42
Mi-bskyod rdo-rje, La-stod-pa, 421, 425
Mi-'gyur dpal-gyi sgron-ma, 369f.
Mi-'gyur rdo-rje, gTer-ston, 323
Mi-la-ras-pa, 57, 72, 105, 122, 184, 230f., 245, 248, 262, 272f., 285, 289, 291, 294,f. 299, 302, 321, 323
Ming, 82
Mi-nyag, 82
Mi-pham dbang-po, 6. 'Brug-chen, 108
Mi-pham Ngag-dbang snyan-grags dpal-bzang, sDing-po-che Cog-gra, 213
Mi-pham phun-tshogs shes-rab, sTag-rtse sku-skye-ba, 65, 104, 213, 243
Mi-pham rgya-mtsho, 5–14, 18–23, 26f., 30f., 49, 167
Mi-pham yongs-'dus, 212f.
mKha'-spyod dbang-po, 2. Zhwa-dmar-pa, 415
mKhan-chen dPal-ldan grub, 416
mKhan-chen gZhan-dga', 219
mKhan-chen 'Jam-dbyangs rgyal-mtshan, 381
mKhan-chen Mon-gra-pa, 44
mKhan-chen mTsho-sna-pa, 44
mKhan-chen Nyi-ma rgyal-mtshan, 430f., 435f., 439–41, 446
mKhan-chen rGyal-sras bzang-po, 44
mKhan-chen Sangs-rgyas bzang-po, 441
mKhan-chen Seng-ge bzang-po, 44
mKhan-pa ljongs. *See* mKhan-pa lung
mKhan-pa lung, 259, 260f., 263–65, 267
mKhan-po Kun-bzang dpal-ldan, 6, 18
mKhan-po Ngag-dbang dpal-bzang, 11, 14, 31

mKhan-po Sangs-rgyas bstan-'dzin, 162, 166f., 175, 180, 183, 283, 406
mKhar-chu, 364
mKhar-chu'i lha-khang, 367
mKhas-dbang Sangs-rgyas rdo-rje, 399
mKhas-grub dam-pa Chos-legs mtshan-can, 422
mKhas-grub dPal-ldan sangs-rgyas, 417, 422f., 426
mKhas-grub Nam-mkha' rgyal-mtshan, 316
mKhas-mchog Padma legs-grub. *See* rTse-le[gs] sNa-tshogs rang-grol
mKhas-pa dPal-ldan bzang-po, 325
mNga'-ris, 275, 390, 418
mNga'-ris Gung-thang, 417–20, 422
mNga'-ris Jo-bo, 213
mNga'-ris rDzong-dkar, 314
mNga'-ris skor-gsum, 399, 427
mNga'-ris smad, 399
mNga'-ris stod, 399
mNgon-dga', 417f.
mNgon-dga' bSam-gtan gling, 400
mNyam, 334
Mon[-yul], 44, 48, 268, 354, 386, 388
mTha'-bzhi Bya-bral-ba, 422
mTha'-dkar, 315
mThu-stobs rdo-rje, 150
mTshams-brag, 399
mTsho padma, 246
mTsho-sgo, 125
mTsho-skyes, 297
mTsho-sna, 44
mTsho-sna-pa, 44
mTshur-phu, 59
Mu-gum, 324
Mu-khun can, 203
Mu-khun-kṣe-ṭa. *See* Mu-mu-ni-se-ṭa
Muktikṣetra, 203, 243
Muktināth, 104, 201, 203–12, 214f., 218, 220, 224f., 231f., 234, 240, 242–44, 246f., 249f., 318, 327, 333, 340–42
Mu-ku, 205
Mukuṭakṣetra. *See* Muktikṣetra
Mu-le, 211
Mu-mu-ni-se-ṭa, 201
Mu-ne btsan-po, 377
Munmuni, 202, 242
Mu-ṭa-ṣata. *See* Mu-mu-ni-se-ṭa
Myang, 131

Nāḍapāda. *See* Nāropa
Nāgārjuna, 7, 21, 25, 79–81, 83, 103, 440, 446
Nags-thang, 289
Nālandā, 110
Nalendra. *See* Nālandā
Nam-mkha' brgya-byin, 2. Yol-mo-ba sprul-sku, 127f., 130, 143, 154, 289
Nam-mkha' 'brug-sgra, 404
Nam-mkha' dkon-mchog, 443
Nam-mkha' dpal, 383
Nam-mkha' dpal-bzang, 400f.
Nam-mkha' 'gyur-med, 401
Nam-mkha' kun-bzang, 143f.
Nam-mkha' 'od-zer, 416, 441
Nam-mkha' rdo-rje, 45
Nam-mkha' rgyal-mtshan, 320
Nam-mkha' rgyal-mtshan, 'Ba'-ra-ba, 442
Nam-mkha' rgyal-mtshan, lHo-brag grub-chen, 36–46, 48, 367, 371f.
Nam-mkha' rin-chen, 438
Nam-mkha' seng-ge, 44
Nam-mkha' snying-po, 343
Namo Buddha, 245
Nar, 225
Nārāyaṇa, 96
Nāropa, 110, 300f.
Nas-lung, 103f.
Nas-lung Ngag-dbang rdo-rje, 72

Naṭeśvarī, 204, 327
Navakot, 65
Ne-lung, 324
Neyapāla, 432
Ngag-dbang Blo-bzang rgya-mtsho, 5. Dalai Bla-ma, 109, 114, 122, 129, 131–34, 136f., 139f., 142, 160, 173, 363–66, 374, 377f., 395, 423, 432f., 440–42
Ngag-dbang bsTan-'dzin nor-bu, rDza-sprul, 184f., 187, 189, 259–61
Ngag-dbang bu-khrid, 207
Ngag-dbang chos-grags, 220
Ngag-dbang Chos-grags rgya-mtsho, 399
Ngag-dbang Chos-kyi blo-gros, 2. 'Khrul-zhig, 181
Ngag-dbang grags-pa, 301
Ngag-dbang grags-pa, gNyug-la Paṇ-chen, 442
Ngag-dbang Kun-bzang rdo-rje, 4. Pad-gling gsung-sprul, 399
Ngag-dbang Kun-dga' lhun-grub, 240f.
Ngag-dbang lHun-grub grags-pa, 398
Ngag-dbang nor-bu, 365
Ngag-dbang Nor-bu bzang-po, sTeng-po-che bla-ma, 184, 187, 189
Ngag-dbang rdo-rje, 71, 103–7
Ngag-dbang rgyal-mtshan, 184, 191
Ngag-dbang rgya-mtsho, sTag-tshang ras-pa, 110
Ngag-dbang rnam-rgyal, 210, 233, 313–17, 320–24, 334
Ngag-dbang ye-shes, 399
Ngam-ring, 131f.
Ngam-shod, 173
Ngang, 386
Ngang-brgyud rgyal-ba, 385, 387
Ngor E-waṃ Chos-ldan, 326
Ngor-pa, 240f., 313, 341
Nirmāṇacakra, 356
Nispannayogāvalī, 319
Nor-'dzin dbang-mo, 135
Nor-bu bde-chen, mDo-bo che-ba, 141, 144, 147f., 222
Nor-bu lde, 66
Nu, 108
Nub-dgon, 399
Nub-gling, 373
Nub-ris, 201, 230f., 303, 327
Nus-ldan rdo-rje bSam-gtan gling-pa, 358
Nyag-rong, 381, 383
Nyang, 163, 169, 177, 181–84, 326, 405f.
Nyang-rigs O-rgyan bstan-'dzin, 191
Nyang-smad, 388
Nyang-stod, 385
Nye-shang, 225
Nyi-lhod, 404
Nyi-ma grags-pa, gTer-ston, 65f., 144f.
Nyi[-ma] phug, 418
Nyi-ma rgyal-po, 353
Nyi-ma seng-ge, 44, 144
Nyi-ma'i 'od-zer, mNga'-bdag Nyang-ral, 44, 108f., 127, 142, 182, 316, 320, 383, 385
Nyin-byed gling, 132f.
Nyi-shang, 332
Nyi-zla dmar-mo, 391
Nyi-zla [kha-sbyor] phug, 389–91
Nyi-zla grags-pa, 266f.

Oḍḍiyāna, 108–10, 176, 386
'Od-gsal Klong-yangs, 45
'Od-gsal sgang, 212, 224, 338
'Ol-kha, 39, 367, 369, 374
'Ol-kha rJe-drung[-pa]. *See* Sle-lung bZhad-pa'i rdo-rje
'Ol-kha stag-rtse, 39, 369f.
'Om-lo lung, 339
Ong bKra-shis rtse-mo, 209
O-rgyan bstan-'dzin, 223, 249, 303, 324, 326, 332–35, 338–45

O-rgyan byang-chub phan, 339
O-rgyan che-mchog, 244
O-rgyan chen-po. *See* Padmasambhava
O-rgyan chos-gling, 37
O-rgyan chos-'phel, 240–44, 246, 249f.
O-rgyan chos-skyid, 341
O-rgyan dpal-bzang, 144, 207f., 213, 219–25, 234, 248f., 302f., 322–24, 326, 332–35, 342, 344
O-rgyan gling, 110, 395
O-rgyan gling-pa, 268
O-rgyan 'Gro-'dul dbang-gi rgyal-po, 402
O-rgyan 'Gro-'dul gling-pa, 353
O-rgyan gSang-sngags bstan-'dzin, mDo-chen-pa, 148, 176
O-rgyan 'Jigs-med Chos-kyi dbang-po, rDza dpal-sprul, 28
O-rgyan['Phrin-las] bstan-'dzin, 405f.
O-rgyan Rin-po-che. *See* Padmasambhava
O-rgyan-pa Rin-chen dpal, 286, 327, 343
'Or-mo lha-sa, 367f.

Padma bDe-ba'i rgyal-po, 246
Padma bDe-chen gling-pa, 169, 345
Padma Chos-'dzoms, 375, 401, 403
Padma dBang-'dus, 212, 303f.
Padma dbang-rgyal, Kham-lung-pa. *See* dBang-gi rgyal-po, Kham[s]-lung-pa
Padma dbang-rgyal, mNga'-ris Paṇ-chen, 28, 125, 127, 316–22, 325, 327f., 390, 423
Padma don-grub, 303
Padma Las-'brel-rtsal, 43, 46f., 165
Padma lhun-grub, 303f.
Padma 'od-gling, 395
Padma 'phrin-las, 2. rDo-rje brag Rig-'dzin, 122, 127, 136, 148, 364, 366, 368
Padma rdo-rje, 112–14
Padma shel-ri, 357
Padma thar-phyin, 183
Padma Tshe-dbang rgyal-po. *See* Rig-'dzin bsTan-gnyis gling-pa
Padma'i-chos-gling, 144f., 304
Padma'i-tshal, 123, 262, 270
Padma-bkod, 223, 357, 359f.
Padma-las-'brel-rtsal, 165
Padmapāṇi Lokeśvara, 111, 241, 445f.
Padma-rnam-rgyal, 2. Zhe-chen rgyal-tshab, 47
Padmasambhava, 36f., 43–46, 49f., 83, 96, 102f., 107, 113, 122, 124, 126, 129, 134, 140, 145, 166–68, 176, 182, 186f., 207, 210–12, 214f., 218f., 221–24, 240, 242f., 245–47, 249f., 260, 262–64, 266f., 269, 271–73, 286, 288, 299, 315, 323, 328, 334, 336, 338, 340, 343, 345, 359f., 363, 371f., 380f., 386, 388–91, 421
Pāla, 432f.
Paṇ-chen bSod-nams grags-pa, 441
Paṇ-chen Śākya mchog-ldan, 325f.
Pārthivendramalla, 64f., 103, 111
Paśupatināth, 67, 82, 95, 99
Pha-drug Chos-bskor sgang, 140
Phag-mo gru, 136
Phag-mo gru-pa rDo-rje rgyal-po, 301
Phag-mo'i mngal-chu, 82
'Phags-mchog Nor-bu bzang-po, 422
'Phags-pa Blo-gros rgyal-mtshan, 68, 70, 380
'Phags-pa lCe-sgom-pa, 444
'Phags-pa lha, 66
'Phags-pa lha-khang, 323
'Phags-pa rang-byung, 82
'Phags-pa shing-kun, 64, 67, 82, 103. *See also* Svayambhūnāth
'Phan-yul, 439
'Phan-yul Nā-len-dra, 245
Pha-rgod rTogs-ldan rgyal-po, 340
Pho-lha, 56

Pho-lha-ba, 58
'Phrin-las bdud-'joms, mGon-gnang-pa, 57, 143–50, 162, 176, 184, 402f., 406
'Phrin-las chos-dbang, 245
'Phrin-las dbang-phyug, 403
Phu-chung-ba, 427f., 434–37, 439, 441, 444f.
Phug-mo-che, 159, 180
Phug-rings, 437f., 440
'Phung-chu, 125
Phun-tshogs chos-'phel, 222
Phun-tshogs rnam-rgyal, 221, 391
Phur-ba rdo-rje, 181
Phyag-rdor nor-bu, sGam-smyon, 103, 129, 131, 134, 137, 139f., 143, 149
Phyag-sor-pa, 444
Phya-pa Chos-kyi seng-ge, 10
Phyi-'brum dgon-gsar, 414
Phyogs-las rnam-rgyal, Bo-dong Paṇ-chen/Bo-dong Kun-mkhyen, 68, 135
'Phyongs-rgyas, 132, 221, 295, 368
Po-to-ba, 427f., 434–36, 445
Prāsaṅgika-Madhyamaka, 5–14, 18–20, 22f., 25, 27, 29f.
Pratāpamalla, 111, 139, 142, 288
Pṛthvīmalla, 331
Pṛthvīnārāyaṇa Śāha, 58–61
Puṇya Vajra, 95
Puṇyaśrībhadra, 83
Purang, 214

Qianlong, 73

Ra rDo-rje-grags, 262
Rab-brtan kun-bzang 'phags-pa, 69
Rab-'byams-pa dGe-ba'i blo-gros, 388f.
Rab-rgyal rtse-mo, 205–7
Rag-ma, 139, 142
Rāhulaguptavajra, 444
Rājarājeśvarī, 304
Ral-pa can, 425
Raṇa Bahādura Śāha, 304
Raṇajitmalla, 58
Rang-byung rdo-rje, 3. Karma-pa, 45, 46, 185, 189f.
Rang-grol rdo-rje, 104
Rang-rig, 108
Rang-rig ras-pa, 64–66, 72, 74, 79, 81, 103f., 106–14, 243
Ra-sa 'phrul-snang, 421f., 437f., 445
Ras-chen Blo-'phel dpal-bzang, 315
Ras-chung bKa'-brgyud-pa, 301
Ras-chung phug, 229, 235f., 295, 297, 299–302, 305, 354
Ras-chung-pa rDo-rje grags-pa, 295, 297, 301
Ras-dgon, 58
Ratna gling-pa, 162, 183, 187f., 383, 385, 395, 399
Ratnamalla, 61, 66
rDo-dmar, 400, 402, 404
rDo-dmar-ba Kun-bzang bsTan-pa'i rgyal-mtshan, 148
rDo-dmar-ba Mi-'gyur rdo-rje, 147, 259, 268–75, 400f.
rDo-rje brag, 136–38, 208, 244, 315, 366, 368, 400
rDo-rje bzang-po, 183
rDo-rje dpal, g.Yung-ston[-pa], 46, 383
rDo-rje gling-pa, 265
rDo-rje gro-lod, 134, 221
rDo-rje 'jigs-bral, 163, 169f., 183
rDo-rje nor-bu, 160, 170
rDo-rje rgyal-mtshan, 160, 170f., 177f.
rDo-rje thogs-med, Brag-gsum gter-ston. *See* Rig-'dzin rDo-rje thogs-med
rDo-rje thogs-med rtsal, 378
rDzar, 201, 206, 208–10, 214, 222, 224, 232, 243, 250, 318
rDza-rong phu, 181, 184, 187

rDzar-rdzong, 203
rDzing-phyi, 369
rDzogs-chen Padma Rig-'dzin, 263
rDzong, 205f., 208f., 222, 224, 232
rDzong rab-rgyal rtse, 208
rDzong-dkar, 70, 231, 314, 418f., 443
rDzong-dkar chos-sde, 417
rDzu-'phrul phug, 339
Red-mda'-ba gzhan-nu blo-gros, 36f.
rGa Lo-tsā-ba, 264
rGod-tshang gling, 231, 234, 287–89, 295–300, 302–6
rGod-tshang-pa mGon-po rdo-rje, 286, 297
rGya-la dpal-ri, 352, 361
rGyal gNam-phur, 220
rGyal-ba'i 'byung-gnas, 'Brom-ston, 427f., 431–36, 439f., 446
rGyal-dbang seng-ge, 235, 243f., 302f., 333
rGyal-gling, 138f.
rGyal-mtshan bum-pa, 319
rGyal-mtshan dpal-bzang-po, 'Ba'-ra-ba, 328
rGyal-mtshan ye-shes, 387
rGyal-rtse, 69, 389
rGyal-sras bDe-chen gling-pa, 353, 360
rGyal-sras seng-ge, mDo-chen-pa, 400
rGyal-sras Thogs-med[bzang-po], 415f.
rGyal-sras Zla-ba grags-pa, 47f.
rGyal-tshab Dar-ma rin-chen, 7
rGyang[s] Yon-po lung, 126, 134, 140
rGyang-rtse dPon-sa bDag-mo drung, 388
rGya-yul, 404
Ri-bo 'big-byed, 338
Ri-bo bkra-bzang, 126
Ri-bo 'bum-pa, 345
Ri-bo gNam-lcags 'bar-ba, 361
Ri-bo gru-'dzin, 128
Ri-bo-che, 131
Rig-'dzin bDud-'dul rdo-rje, 144, 169, 207, 221, 246, 248, 273, 302, 322f., 344, 358, 360, 363
Rig-'dzin bsTan-gnyis gling-pa, 354–56, 358, 360, 369, 373–75
Rig-'dzin Chos-kyi grags-pa, 423
Rig-'dzin Chos-'phel, 397
Rig-'dzin Chos-rje gling-pa, 354–56, 358, 360, 369, 373–75
Rig-'dzin dBang-gi rgyal-po, Kham[s]-lung-pa, 399, 402
Rig-'dzin dbang-po. *See* rDo-rje 'jigs-bral
Rig-'dzin dByings-rig dpal-'bar, 322
Rig-'dzin Gar-gyi dbang-phyug, 127
Rig-'dzin 'Gyur-med rdo-rje, Nyang-gdung bla-ma, 181, 184, 191
Rig-'dzin 'Ja'-tshon snying-po, 159–63, 165, 168f., 172, 232, 241, 273, 302f., 322f., 333, 358f.
Rig-'dzin Karma gling-pa, 389
Rig-'dzin Klong-gsal snying-po, 186f.
Rig-'dzin mChog-ldan mgon-po, 123, 147, 264–67, 389
Rig-'dzin Ngag-gi dbang-po, 132–34, 136, 138, 141, 160
Rig-'dzin Nus-ldan rdo-rje, 357
Rig-'dzin Nyi-ma grags-pa, 162, 263f., 360
Rig-'dzin Nyi-ma seng-ge, 162f., 176
Rig-'dzin Nyi-zla klong-gsal, 260–64, 270
Rig-'dzin O-rgyan [gSang-sngags] bstan-'dzin, 406
Rig-'dzin Padma 'phrin-las, 150
Rig-'dzin Padma rdo-rje, rDo-dmar-ba, 144, 147
Rig-'dzin 'Phrin-las dbang-phyug, 128f.
Rig-'dzin rDo-rje thogs-med, 352f., 360
Rig-'dzin rGod-ldem 'phru-can, 126, 134, 142f., 161, 259–61, 267f., 271f., 275, 288, 317, 323f., 328, 382, 384
Rig-'dzin rgya-mtsho, Nyang-ston mNga'-bdag, 398

Rig-'dzin Sangs-rgyas gling-pa, 383f.
Rig-'dzin Shes-rab me-'bar, 385
Rig-'dzin sTobs-ldan dbang-po, 138, 140–42, 222
Rig-pa 'dzin-pa chen-po mNga'-bdag brag-pa, 398
Rigs-ldan gNas-mtsho, 359
Rin-chen byang-chub, 441
Rin-chen rgyal-mtshan, 435–37
Rin-chen spungs-pa, 373f.
Ri-skyabs, 306
rJe Drang-so ba. *See* Śākya bzang-po, 1. Yol-mo-ba sprul-sku
rJe-drung Ngag-dbang Zil-gnon rdo-rje, 323
Rlung-gnon, 355
rMa-bya Byang-chub brtson-'grus, 10
rNam-grol bzang-po, 233, 313, 320, 324–28, 341, 380, 382, 390f.
rNam-grol gling, 369, 371, 374
rNam-rgyal grags-pa, 68
rNam-rgyal mgon-po, 317f.
rNgog Legs-pa'i shes-rab, 431, 435f., 439f.
rNgog Lo-tsā-ba Blo-ldan shes-rab, 436
rNying-ma-pa, 5f., 8–10, 13f., 18–20, 22–24, 26–28, 30f., 35–37, 43, 55f., 59, 65, 72, 100, 103, 109, 122, 126, 129, 132f., 136f., 140, 143f., 147, 159, 162, 164, 166, 182, 188, 207f., 210, 213f., 219f., 224, 240f., 244, 247, 249, 265f., 283, 302–4, 316, 321f., 327f. 332, 337, 340, 352, 354f., 358–60, 363, 365f., 369–71, 379–81, 385f., 391, 395, 403, 438
Rong-pa rDzogs-chen-pa, 404
Rong-shar, 405
Rong-zom Chos-kyi bzang-po, 9, 22, 24, 383
Ṛṣīśvara, 73, 245
rTag-lam 'phrang, 289
rTa-glang, 345
rTag-pa gnas-sa, 286
rTa-gru [dben-gnas], 339, 341–45
rTa-mangs, 290
rTa-nag Thub-bstan rnam-rgyal, 220, 326, 333
rTa-rab, 232f., 340f., 345
rTa-rong, 338
rTa-sga, 80, 418
rTa-sga dgon, 327, 418
rTogs-ldan rgyal-po, 340
rTs[w]a sGyer-mo, 437, 440f.
rTse-le[gs] dgon-pa, 265
rTse-le[gs] sNa-tshogs rang-grol, 161, 166, 265, 273, 359
rTse-thang, 41, 430
rTsib-ri, 104, 107
Ru-gnon, 134
Rwa-sgreng, 244, 250, 437
Rwa-ston sTobs-ldan rdo-rje, 360, 373

Sa-bzang Ma-ti Paṇ-chen, 27
Ṣaḍaṅga Yoga, 131, 414–17
Sa-dga', 57
Sa-dmar, 244
Sa-'dul, 336, 338, 341–43, 345
Sa-'dul dgon-pa, 249, 331–33, 335, 337–39, 341f.
Sa-'go li-ti, 287
Śākya bDud-'dul, 235
Śākya bzang-po, 1. Yol-mo-ba sprul-sku, 44, 66f., 70, 95, 98–102, 121–27, 130f., 134, 137–39, 142f., 147, 154, 161, 265–67, 289, 317f., 421f., 425
Śākyadevi, 44
Śākyamuni, 76–79, 81, 83, 113
Śākya-'od, 421
Sa-le-'od, 262
Samantabhadra, 80, 175, 186
Saṃvarodayatantra, 82
Sa-ngan, 56

Sang-ku, 288
Sangs-rgyas bla-ma, 247f., 406
Sangs-rgyas bstan-pa, 318
Sangs-rgyas byams-bzang, 318
Sangs-rgyas bzang-po, 219, 244–50
Sangs-rgyas gling-pa, 389
Sangs-rgyas rdo-rje, Bya-bral Rin-po-che, 161
Sangs-rgyas rgyal-mtshan, gTsang-smyon He-ru-ka, 61, 66f., 74, 79, 81, 105, 122f., 177, 183, 288, 295, 297, 299–301, 354
Sangs-rgyas rgya-mtsho, sDe-srid, 109, 363, 365f., 377
Sangs-rgyas seng-ge, Sha-ra Rab-'byams-pa, 300f.
Sangs-rgyas sgra-'od, 44
Sangs-sngags bstan-'dzin, 176
Śantapuri, 69, 73, 75, 78, 82
Śantaputri, 79, 81
Śāntarakṣita, 5, 124
Śāntikara, 73
Śāriputra, 78, 81
Sa-skya, 70, 125, 187, 326
Sa-skya Paṇḍita Kun-dga' rgyal-mtshan, 202, 414
Sa-skya-pa, 7, 25, 68, 70, 76, 202, 207, 218, 220, 240, 245, 248, 266f., 313, 322, 326, 328, 333, 341, 380, 414
Sa-sprin, 139
sBas-gnas 'Or-mo lha-sa, 367
sBas-pa'i gnas Padma-bkod, 359
sBas-yul mKhan-pa lung, 264
sBas-yul Seng-ge ri, 367
sBra-chen, 404
sDe-dge, 358, 395f.
sDe-pa gNas-'og-pa, 416
sDe-phur, 287
Sebṭa, 287
Seng-ge bsam-'grub, 267
Seng-ge bsam-'grub phug, 386, 390
Seng[-ge] gdong[-ma], 186
Seng-ge ras-pa. 109
Seng-ge ri, 364, 366–68
sGam-po-pa bSod-nams rin-chen, 300f., 353
sGam-po-pa O-rgyan 'Gro-'dul gling-pa, 352–54
sGam-smyon sprul-sku. *See* Phyag-rdor nor-bu, sGam-smyon
sGang-steng, 396
sGa-rje Tshe-dbang lha-mo, 395
sGo-mang, 104f.
sGrom-bu lha-khang, 212
sGrub-gnas dPal-gyi mtha'-dkar, 315
sGrub-pa chen-po sTag-rtse-ba. *See* Mi-pham phun-tshogs shes-rab, sTag-rtse sku-skye-ba
sGrub-sde bSam-gtan gling, 399
Shab-ru, 305
Shangs, 291
Shangs Rin-po-che, 332
Shangs-pa bKa'-brgyud-pa, 413, 444
Shangs-pa ras-chen. *See* Grub-dbang O-rgyan bstan-'phel
Shan-ta-spu-gri. *See* Śantaputri
Shar Khum-bu, 259
Shar-ba-pa Yon-tan grags, 437
Shel dgon-pa, 104, 224, 322, 340
Shel-dkar, 125, 136, 142, 285, 398f., 416f.
Shel-dkar chos-sde, 416–18
Shel-dkar rdzong, 136, 140
Shel-gyi ri-bo ['brug-sgra], 322, 340f.
Shel-mo gangs, 339f.
Shel-phug, 223, 334
Sher, 139
Sher[-pa] mkhan-po, 67, 82f.
Shes-rab 'byung-gnas, 399–401
Shes-rab rdo-rje, Smyung-gnas bla-ma, 188, 248

Shes-rab rgyal-mtshan, Dol-po-pa, 27, 318, 325, 327
Shes-rab rgyal-mtshan, Gangs-ri-ba, 423
Shes-rab rgyal-mtshan, mNga'-ris-pa, 435f., 444
Shing-skam, 286
Shi-ta-bhū, 289
Sho-rong, 182f.
Shud-phu, 37, 41, 43
Shud-phu (bu) dPal-gyi seng-ge, 37, 43
Shud-phu Mes-tshab [rgyal-po], 43f.
Shud-phu Mes-tshab dpal, 44
Shud-phu Zla-ba rgyal-mtshan, 44
Siddhinarasiṃha, 284f.
Singhā-ra-bā-sa, 289
Sing-kar bha-dra, 287
Si-pa, 287
Śivadeva, 99f.
Śivapurī, 96
Śivasiṃha, 131f., 290
sKag, 206, 209, 222–24, 232
sKag[-rdzong], 210, 333, 335, 337, 342
sKrag-med nyi-shar, 370, 372, 375
sKu-la, 324
sKur-stod, 387
sKu-thang, 334, 341, 404
sKu-tshab gter-lnga, 144, 207–10, 212f., 218f., 224f., 234, 248f., 303, 323, 332f., 335, 338f.
sKu-zhabs Klu-sgrub, 246
sKyar-skya [s]gang-pa, 206, 220, 231f.
sKye-ba lung, 222, 224, 286
sKyel-sdong, 305f.
sKyer-sgang-pa, 413, 436, 444
sKyid-grong, 56–58, 61, 126, 136, 139, 141, 162, 177, 188, 221–23, 225, 231, 241, 245, 250f., 261, 265f., 274, 290, 297, 301f., 321, 323, 327, 333f., 399–402, 404
sKyid-grong bSam-gtan gling, 104
sKyid-grong Thugs-mchog rdo-rje, 360
sKyid-mo lung, 123, 126, 223f., 261, 274, 323, 341
sKyid-sbug, 404
sKyid-sbug-pa, 404
Sle-lung, 369
Sle-lung bZhad-pa'i rdo-rje, 48, 356–58, 364, 367–76, 398
Sle-mi/Sli-mi, 230, 339
Slob-dpon 'Gyur-med, 397, 405
Slob-dpon 'Jo-yang, 44
Slob-dpon Nam-mkha' rin-chen, 438
Slob-dpon rDo-rje, 44
Slob-dpon sKal-ldan, 25
sMan-lung-pa Blo-mchog rdo-rje, 395, 399, 404
sMar-sgom, 321
sMin[-grol] gling, 28f., 181, 185–87, 189f., 208, 244, 335, 356, 370, 395, 398
sMon-thang, 241, 243f., 246, 248, 324
sMra-bo cog, 109
sMyug-la, 442
sNar, 234f., 332
sNa-ri, 211
sNa-ri Jo-bo, 210, 213, 251
sNar-thang, 429f.
sNas-lung, 387
sNa-tshogs rang-grol, rGod-tshang ras-chen, 288, 297–301, 354
sNe['u]-gdong, 75
sNe'u zur-pa, 437
sNgags-'chang Che-mchog rdo-rje, 143, 148, 162
sNgags-'chang Karma'i mtshan-can, 144
sNgags-'chang Nam-mkha' kun-bzang, 136, 143f.
sNgags-'chang Nam-mkha' seng-ge, 136, 141, 144, 148
sNgags-'chang rDo-rje bzang-po, 183
sNgags-'chang Tshe-ring, 211, 214

sNgo-ri, 262
sNya-lam, 333
sNyan-grags dpal bzang-po, 2. lCogs-grwa sprul-sku, 104
sNye-mo, 291
sNye-shang, 203, 222, 230–32, 234f., 289–91, 302
sNye-shang Brag-dkar, 222
Sog-sprul Gu-ru, 104
Som-po, 220, 222f.
sPa-gro sTag-tshang, 223, 267f., 380, 385–87, 389–91
sPa-gro sTag-tshang O-rgyan rtse-mo, 380, 382, 386–88, 390f.
sPang-sgang, 286
sPang-zhing, 188
sPo-bo, 323, 351–53, 355, 357f., 360f.
sPo-bo dGa'-ba lung, 358
sPo-bo mDung-chu'i lha-khang, 353, 355, 359
sPong-rong, 399–401, 416
sPos-khang lHa-steng, 388
sPo-smad, 351, 353f.
sPos-ri, 240, 241
sPra-bdun, 241, 246
sPrul-sku Gar-dbang don-grub, 303f.
sPyang-kyi spu med, 286
sPyan-gyas, 368
sPyan-snga bSod-nams 'bum[-pa], 379
sPyan-snga Nam-mkha' rdo-rje, 382
sPyan-snga[-pa] Rin-chen, 427f., 434–36, 442, 445
sPyi-bo lhas-pa, 414
sPyi-dbang, 406
sPyi-dbang dgon-pa, 406
Sras Zla-ba grags-pa, 46f.
Śrī Harṣa, 73
Śrī Jayajyotirmalladeva, 67, 82
Śrī Mahārāja Bhimsaṃser Jangbahadur Raṇa, 397
Śri Śivadeva, 99
Śrīsiṃha, 176
Srong-btsan sgam-po, 129, 134, 241f., 247, 353, 360, 364, 366, 414, 416, 419–23
sTabs-ka, 439
sTabs-ka'i dgon-pa, 434f., 437–40
sTabs-ka-ba Byang-chub bzang-po, 435, 438
sTabs-ka-ba Nam-mkha' rin-chen, 438–40
sTag-bde brag-dmar, 414
sTag-gyi rgyal-mtshan, 339
sTag-lung, 301
sTag-phug seng-ge rdzong, 289, 299
sTag-sham Nus-ldan rdo-rje, 345, 355, 358, 360, 373
sTag-sham O-rgyan bSam-gtan gling-pa, 358
sTag-tshang Chos-'khor sgang, 441f.
sTag-tshang Chos-'khor-ba mKhan-chen, 441
sTed, 215
sTeng-[b]shod lung, 232
sTeng-po-che dgon-pa [Theg-mchog gling], 170, 181, 184, 186f., 191
sTeng-shog/bTang-shog, 335
Sthaṃ Vihāra, 79
sTobs-ldan shugs-'chang rtsal. *See* bsTan-'dzin nor-bu, 3. Yol-mo-ba sprul-sku
sTod-yul dam-pa, 327
Śuddhodana, 81, 182
Sukhāvati, 40, 191
Sum-'bag, 339
Sum-po, 222
Suvarṇavarman, 77, 79, 81f.
Svātantrika-Madhyamaka, 12, 25
Svayambhūnāth, 55, 57–75, 77, 79, 81–83, 95f., 99, 103, 105–7, 123, 131, 148, 159, 188, 234, 241, 245, 284, 338, 428
Svayambhūpurāṇa, 59, 63, 73, 77, 81

Takṣaka, 77
Tārā, 186f., 433, 443, 446
Tathāgatagarbha, 22, 26, 30
Thags, 211, 233, 246–51
Tha-na-ni, 289
Thang-skams, 287, 289
Thang-stong rgyal-po, 131, 162
Thar-pa-gling, 46–48
Thar-pa rtse, 339
Theg-chen chos-sdings [Yang-dben rDo-thang], 384f., 390
Theg-mchog gling, 404
Thig-phyi, 37f., 44, 367f.
Thim-phu, 387
Thub-bstan chos-gling, 181
Thub-bstan dbang-po, 333–35
Thub-chen lha-khang, 325
Thugs-rje dpal, 441
Thugs-sras Nam-mkha' rgyal-mtshan, 125
Tichurong, 223, 332, 337, 339f.
Ting-kyu, 340
Ting-nge-'dzin bzang-po, Myang-ban, 168
Tīrthanātha, 205
Ti-se (Kailāśa), 66, 105, 202, 206, 214, 240, 242, 246, 324, 339, 340
Tsakka, 306
Tsa-mi Sangs-rgyas grags, 149
Tsang-rang, 243
Tsa-ri, 105, 108, 187, 202, 206, 245, 354, 357, 360
Tsa-ri Dag-pa shel-ri, 104
Tse-kur 'bab-chu, 64
Tshal-pa bKa'-brgyud-pa, 80, 230, 327, 418
Tshang-pa rlung-gnon, 355
Tshangs-dbyangs rgya-mtsho, 6. Dalai Bla-ma, 366
Tshe-brtan rgyal-mtshan, 267f.
Tshe-dbang bSod-nams rgyal-po, 143
Tshe-dbang grub-pa, 306
Tshe-dbang kun-khyab, 'Be-lo, 289
Tshe-dbang nor-bu, Kaḥ-thog rig-'dzin, 27f., 55–62, 65, 70, 74, 100, 129, 134f., 144, 146, 148, 162, 169, 176f., 201–3, 208, 212, 215, 242, 246, 248f., 266, 301–3, 339, 342f., 345, 400–2
Tshe-dbang rgyal-po, 387
Tshe-gnas rgyal-po, 208–10
Tshem-bu-pa, 413–15, 417–19
Tshe-rog, 246, 250
Tshogs-bsham, 286
Tshogs-drug rang-grol, Zhabs-dkar-ba, 27, 35–37, 40, 48, 95, 125, 149, 340
'Tsho-rkyen, 418
Tshug, 223
Tshul-khrims rdo-rje, 3. Pad-gling gsung-sprul, 387, 399
Tshul-khrims rgyal-ba, Nag-tsho Lo-tsā-ba, 443–45
Tsong-kha, 427
Tsum, 404
Tsu-ti, 265
Tukchā, 225

'Ug-pa/bya lung, 406
'Ug-po gling, 220
Ugratārā, 446
Upacchandoha, 73, 82
Uṣṇīṣavijayā, 186, 188
U-yug-pa Bla-ma dPal-'byor, 441

Vairocana, 176
Vaiśakhā, 190
Vaiśālī, 78
Vaiśravana, 40, 78, 81
Vajranātha, 206
Vajrapāṇi, 38, 40, 42–45, 188, 241, 427
Vajrasādhu, 274
Vajrāsana, 187, 190
Vajrasattva, 173–75, 178, 186

Vajrāvalī, 319
Vajravārāhī, 108f., 205f., 342, 357
Vajravārāhī Klu-'dul-ma, 359
Vajrayoginī, 96, 99, 328
Vasubandhu, 79
Vibhūticandra, 79
Vijaya Vīrya, 77
Vikram[a]śāh[i/a], 284, 336f., 339f.
Vikrant, 96
Vimalamitra, 176, 188
Vināyaka, 66, 81
Vindhya, 81
Vīrabahāduršāhi, 336–38
Vīrabhadraśāhi, 337
Viśṇu, 60
Viśvadeva, 76f.
Viśvakarman, 337

Yakṣa Nāga Kubera, 421
Yakṣamalla, 100
Yamarāja, 44
Yam-bu, 306
Yam-shud dmar-po, 367f., 374f.
Yang-dag mchog-gi sgrub-phug, 288, 299
Yang-la-koṭ, 287, 289
Yang-le-shod, 57
Yang-ri, 288
Yang-thog, 443f.
Yar-'brog, 135
Yar-'brog rJe btsun-ma, 135
Yar-[k]lung[s], 221, 229, 235, 295, 354, 385
Ya-tshe, 336
Ye-rang, 306
Yer-pa, 431, 434
Ye-shes 'bum-pa, bZhag-bla, 381, 383f., 390
Ye-shes 'bum[-pa], dBu-'od, 380f.
Ye-shes chos-grags, Brag-dkar gdan-sa-pa, 177, 397
Ye-shes dpal-'byor, Sum-pa mkhan-po, 365
Ye-shes mchog, 425
Ye-shes me-lha, 209
Ye-shes mtsho-rgyal, 44–46, 168, 176, 221, 334, 390
Ye-shes rgyal-mtshan, mKhas-grub, 379, 381–83, 389
Yogācāra, 26, 30, 325
Yol-mo, 102, 105, 121–23, 126, 132, 144–50, 188, 231, 234, 262, 265, 270f., 275, 287–89, 291, 294–306, 403f.
Yongs-'dzin Ye-shes rgyal-mtshan, 439
Yu-gu-li, 82
Yu-mo grub-chen Mi-bskyod rdo-rje, 28
Yung-chen, 369, 371

Zab-phu lung, 391
Za-hor, 132, 378
Zang-zang lha-brag, 261
Zhabs-drung 'Chi-med dbang-po, 354
Zhabs-drung dPag-bsam ye-shes, 322
Zhabs-drung dPal-ldan don-grub, 232
Zhabs-drung Grub-mchog dbang-po, 299f., 305, 354
Zhabs-drung Khams-pa dKon-mchog lhun-grub, 322
Zhang Ka-ma-pa, 437
Zhang Kun-spangs-pa, 414
Zhang-mo, 305
Zhang-ston Dar-ma rgyal-mtshan, 435, 437f.
Zhe-chen, 244
Zhi-ba'i blo-gros, ,Bri-gung sKyabs-mgon, 245
Zhig-po gling-pa. *See* Rig-'dzin Gar-gyi dbang-phyug
Zhing-skyong-ma, 305

Zil-gnon dbang-rgyal rdo-rje, 4. Yol-mo-ba sprul-sku, 102, 114, 125, 130, 135, 137–42, 144–48, 150–52, 155, 162, 176
Zil-gnon rdo-rje, 323
Zla-ba grags-pa, 48
Zla-ba nor-bu, 185
Zla-gam gnam-sgo, 263f., 270
Zom-bu ri, 339
Zur, 406f.
Zur bZang-po dpal, 406
Zur Chos-dbyings rang-grol, 129, 134, 136, 160
Zur 'Ug-pa lung, 381
Zur-mang, 244
Zur-mkhar, 300
Zur-mkhar-ba mNyam-nyid rdo-rje, 300
Zwa-phug, 303
Zwa-phug Brag-dmar chos-gling, 303